Contemporary Portfolio Theory
and
Risk Management

Contemporary Portfolio Theory
— and —
Risk Management

ALAN L. TUCKER
Temple University

KENT G. BECKER
Temple University

MICHAEL J. ISIMBABI
Morgan State University

JOSEPH P. OGDEN
SUNY-Buffalo

West Publishing Company
Minneapolis/St. Paul • New York • Los Angeles • San Francisco

EDITING AND PRODUCTION: *Graphic World Publishing Services*
ILLUSTRATIONS: *Graphic World, Inc.*
DESIGN: *Jeanne Wolfgeher*
COVER DESIGN: *Jeanne Wolfgeher*
COVER IMAGE: *Thomas Lochray/The Image Bank*

WEST'S COMMITMENT TO THE ENVIRONMENT

In 1906, West Publishing Company began recycling materials left over from the production of books. This began a tradition of efficient and responsible use of resources. Today, up to 95 percent of our legal books and 70 percent of our college and school texts are printed on recycled, acid-free stock. West also recycles nearly 22 million pounds of scrap paper annually—the equivalent of 181,717 trees. Since the 1960s, West has devised ways to capture and recycle waste inks, solvents, oils, and vapors created in the printing process. We also recycle plastics of all kinds, wood, glass, corrugated cardboard, and batteries, and have eliminated the use of Styrofoam book packaging. We at West are proud of the longevity and the scope of our commitment to the environment.

Production, Prepress, Printing and Binding by West Publishing Company.

TEXT IS PRINTED ON 10% POST CONSUMER RECYCLED PAPER — PRINTED WITH SOY INK

Library of Congress Cataloging-in-Publication Data

Contemporary portfolio theory and risk management / Alan L. Tucker . . . [et al.].
    p.   cm.
Includes index.
   ISBN 0-314-02822-6
   1. Portfolio management.   I. Tucker, Alan L.
HG4529.5.C66   1994
332.6—dc20
                                            93-41551
                                            CIP

To Emily   A.L.T.

To my mother Lois and the memory of my father Ivan.   K.G.B.

To my late parents, Joseph and Hannah, my wife Michelle, and my son
Michael Jr.   M.J.I.

To Vonda, Sara and Laura   J.P.O.

Contents in Brief

Contents

Preface

There are currently over 3,800 mutual funds in the United States. There is over \$1.6 trillion invested in these funds, and recent average growth in these funds has been about 16 percent per annum. While some of this growth stems from capital appreciation of the funds' existing assets, most has been through *de novo* investment. The pension fund universe in the U.S. is over \$3 trillion. The larger pension funds, such as those of AT&T, the California Public Employees Retirement System, the Rockefeller Foundation, and TIAA-CREF, often employ dozens of managers to oversee the funds' assets. Indeed, more than 80 percent of all corporate pension plans with assets greater than \$2 billion have more than 10 managers, and of all plans with assets greater than \$50 million, fewer than one-third have only one investment manager. Growth has also occurred in college endowments, trusts, and discretionary accounts, among others. With such vast markets it is no wonder that professional portfolio management has become an intensely competitive and analyzed industry.

The principal purpose of this book is to provide a comprehensive and contemporary introduction to the theory and practice of combining securities to form optimal portfolios. In addition, since there has been historically large volatility in the financial markets over the past fifteen years, this book is intended to provide a rigorous treatment of the management of the risk of a preexisting portfolio position. In the context of this book, risk management refers to the use of derivative securities and other techniques to modify portfolio composition and thus portfolio risk and expected return. Consequently, a careful reading of *Contemporary Portfolio Theory and Risk Man-*

agement should provide an analytic framework for constructing and managing optimal security portfolios.

The approach that we adopt with this book is a holistic one, which hopefully provides a proper balance between theory and practice. If the book solely emphasized one-period equilibrium models with homogeneous investor expectations and perfect markets, then the reader surely would not be prepared for employment in a world that only approximates these assumptions and in a field searching for inefficiencies that yield a few extra basis points of return. On the other hand, an approach that omitted a proper element of theory would be purely ad hoc, leaving the student confused and devoid of a systematic and analytic approach toward portfolio management. Indeed, in this case the book would amount to little more than something akin to Peter Lynch's "20 Golden Rules."

This book differentiates itself from other portfolio management texts in a number of ways. Foremost, an entire section is devoted to portfolio risk management. The modern portfolio manager must be cognizant of how to safeguard a portfolio through employment of futures, options, swaps, portfolio insurance, and other financial products and strategies. In addition, this book describes how these products and strategies are employed in more proactive asset allocation strategies. Second, this book offers a contemporary treatment of asset pricing and the efficient markets hypothesis, including recently developed multifactor pricing models and empirical evidence of market anomalies and systematic price movements that tend to refute the long-held belief that security prices follow a random walk. This material is addressed with an eye to its practical implications for portfolio management. Third, this book provides a modern treatment of the theory of the term structure of interest rates, bond pricing, and the management of bond funds. Finally, this book is devoted strictly to portfolio theory and risk management and does not offer coverage of investment topics such as earnings estimation and the evaluation of securities analysis. As a result, the size and cost of the book are less forbidding, and an instructor can cover the entire book in one semester. In addition, the chapters can be covered in a sequential fashion.

This book consists of an introductory chapter and five parts. Part 1 deals with the formation of optimal portfolios. Here we identify the properties of a portfolio of risky assets, given the properties of its component securities, describe what makes one portfolio preferred to another, and demonstrate how preferred portfolios are constructed. We also address expected utility maximization and the selection of a uniquely optimal portfolio and conclude with an analysis of portfolio management in an international setting. Part 2 examines the development and testing of asset pricing models and the efficient markets hypothesis. Part 3 provides treatment of interest rates, bond pricing, and bond fund management. Risk management and efficient asset reallocation are the subjects of Part 4, and Part 5 concludes the book with measures and evidence of the performance of professional money managers. Feature items throughout illustrate applications, research, innovations, successes, and failures and are designed to motivate the reader by demonstrating that the principles developed within, while seemingly abstract at times, are actually employed in the real world. Selected references and self-test problems and solutions are offered at the end of most chapters. Finally, extensive computer software is available and is described in the appendix. You are encouraged to employ the software to enhance the learning experience.

In developing this book we received invaluable help from a number of generous individuals. We thank the following reviewers for their instructive comments: Allen S. Anderson, University of Akron; S. G. Badrinath, Northeastern University; Charles J. Corrado, University of Missouri-Columbia; Joseph E. Finnerty, University of Illinois-Champaign-Urbana; Der-Ann Hsu, University of Wisconsin, Milwaukee; Steven V. Mann, University of South Carolina-Columbia; Linda J. Martin, Arizona State University-Tempe; Thomas V. Schwarz, Southern Illinois University-Carbondale. We also thank Ju Kim for his work in developing the software.

We hope that you enjoy this book and encourage you to write us expressing your comments and suggestions.

A.L.T.
K.G.B.
M.J.I.
J.P.O.

About the Authors

Alan L. Tucker, Ph.D., has authored or coauthored three textbooks and more than 25 articles appearing in such journals as the *Journal of Financial and Quantitative Analysis, Journal of Finance, Review of Economics and Statistics, Journal of Banking and Finance, Journal of International Money and Finance, Journal of Financial Research*, and *Journal of Portfolio Management*. He is the coeditor of the *Journal of Financial Engineering* and an associate editor of the *Global Finance Journal*. He is currently a director of the Southern Finance Association and is an associate with Marshall & Associates, a financial engineering and risk management consulting firm located in New York.

Kent G. Becker is an Assistant Professor of Finance at Temple University. He has published articles dealing with international capital markets and derivative securities in the *Journal of Finance, Financial Analysts Journal, Journal of Financial Research* and other journals. He earned a Ph.D. in Business Administration from the University of Illinois at Urbana.

Michael J. Isimbabi holds a Ph.D. in Finance from Temple University. His research concerns asset pricing, particularly multifactor models, and issues in international financial markets. He has published in the *Journal of Banking and Finance, Journal of International Money and Finance,* and other journals and periodicals. He has worked as a director of credit for Icon Limited, Nigeria, and possesses an extensive background in civil and electrical engineering.

Joseph P. Ogden is an Associate Professor of Finance at State University of New York-Buffalo. He has published numerous articles in publications such as *Journal of Finance* and *Journal of Financial and Quantitative Analysis*. He received a Ph.D. in finance from Purdue University.

CHAPTER *1*

Introduction

Pension funds, mutual funds, insurance companies, banks, thrifts, and other institutions are required by law to hold diversified portfolios of financial assets. The motivation for this legal constraint stems from a central tenet of contemporary portfolio theory, namely that portfolios of risky assets—even if constructed in a haphazard fashion—exhibit less return dispersion than does an isolated risky asset. Corporations may also be viewed as portfolios of assets, and most individuals own a portfolio of assets. *Portfolio theory* is principally concerned with the construction of optimal portfolios given the properties of each of the assets in the investor's opportunity set. Such construction may be more complicated than you first anticipate, given the vast number of possible assets, the various positions that can be assumed in each, and the differences among investors and their attitudes toward risk. In the context of this book, *risk management* refers to the use of derivative securities (futures and options in particular) and other techniques (such as swap arrangements and portfolio insurance) to modify portfolio composition and thus portfolio risk and expected return. The purpose of this book is to introduce you to the concepts, problems, and applications of contemporary portfolio theory and risk management. A careful reading of this book should provide you with an analytic framework for constructing and managing optimal portfolios. While we focus on portfolios of financial assets such as stocks and bonds, the principles developed herein are also applicable to real assets. Also, since the principles underlying portfolio theory have important implications for equilibrium asset pricing, part of this book is devoted to issues in asset pricing and capital market efficiency and their consequences for practical portfolio management.

This chapter serves as an introduction to the rest of the book. We begin by discussing the motivation for studying portfolio theory, following with a brief history of contemporary portfolio theory and risk management. We then provide a simple example of the theory of choice under certainty in order to introduce to you some of the important concepts and procedures involved in our subsequent analysis. We conclude with an outline of the remaining chapters and their flow. An appendix describes mutual funds and broad investment styles.

Motivation for Studying Portfolio Theory

The concepts of market efficiency and asset pricing are intimately related to the formation of portfolios and thus to the study of portfolio theory. While Part 2 of this book deals more rigorously with these concepts, assume for now that "market efficiency" simply means that asset prices are in equilibrium and that "asset pricing" relates expected security returns to a broad market index, such as the Standard and Poor's 500 (SP500). As will be demonstrated later, an important consequence of this assumption is that investors should be compensated only for systematic market risk and not that component of a security's risk that is unique to the security's issuer. To eliminate this nonsystematic risk, investors should hold an *index fund*, which is defined as a portfolio that is constructed to exactly replicate the broad market index (here the SP500). We will call such a strategy the *passive* approach: an asset allocation approach in which the proportions of wealth invested in each asset are identical to each asset's pro rata share in the market index. Many mutual funds subscribe to this approach (e.g., Vanguard's SP500 index fund). Indeed, by year-end 1991 more than $340 billion was invested in index funds by institutional investors (e.g., pensions). The existence of index funds can be clearly linked to the concept of market efficiency and to empirical evidence (discussed below) that tends to support the concept. In addition, their existence is linked to free riding on the work of other security analysts, who ensure that securities are fairly priced and that markets are indeed efficient. Because of their simple construction and management, index funds are often referred to as no-brainers by Wall Street investors. Appendix 1 describes index funds and other mutual funds in greater detail and more clearly defines the concept of passive (and active) management styles as employed in this book.

Now notice that an important and somewhat perverse implication for the study of portfolio theory follows from the above discussion; namely, if the concepts of market efficiency and asset pricing as defined above hold, and thus investors engage in the passive asset allocation approach, then there is really no *practical* need to study portfolio theory. Each investor should hold an index fund and in turn trade the riskless asset to achieve the desired risk level. That's it! So if you believe in market efficiency and related asset pricing theories (and many scholarly people do), then you may consider putting down this book, or better yet, returning it for a refund while it's still in good condition. Moreover, even if you believe that some asset prices are not in equilibrium but that you cannot systematically identify such assets, then you should again engage in the passive approach. Empirical evidence, including a classical study by Jensen (1968), generally finds that professional money managers have underperformed a broadly diversified market index (on a risk-adjusted basis) over a lengthy period of time. Indeed, a major company that evaluates management performance recently found that during the past 20 years the SP500 outperformed more than 80 percent of (nonindex) fund managers.

However, we do not encourage you to return this book just yet, and for more than just self-aggrandizing reasons. First, even if markets were efficient and asset pricing models correctly specified, portfolio theory could still be studied for aesthetic reasons. Second, there is a considerable and growing body of evidence that suggests that markets may be inefficient. For instance, several recent studies document persistent seasonalities (the January effect, the turn-of-the-month effect, the day-of-the-week effect, and others) in stock and other asset prices, implying that these prices do not move randomly over time. Another widely documented anomaly found that until very recently smaller firms exhibited greater risk-adjusted returns than larger firms (the small-firm effect), implying that extant asset pricing models may be misspecified. Evidence also suggests that investors tend to overreact to informational events (the overreaction hypothesis); for instance, recent empirical studies document that stocks that have performed poorly in the past (losers) subsequently tend to outperform past winners. Chapters 12 and 13 provide details about such market anomalies, which have yet to be proven spurious. The point being made here is that if capital markets are somewhat inefficient and/or pricing models are somewhat misspecified, then an investor may choose to engage in an active asset allocation strategy. An *active* approach can be defined as any deviation from a passive asset allocation approach, that is, as any deviation from replicating a broad market index. For instance, an investor may want to construct a portfolio that is tilted toward the stocks of smaller firms, given the existence of the small-firm effect. If an investor is going to engage in the active approach, then it is judicious to study the concepts and principles developed in this book. They will help the investor who engages in an active asset allocation strategy to form optimal portfolios from a given investment opportunity set (e.g., small firm stocks). Thus potential capital market inefficiency and model misspecification may provide, at least in part, the motivation for studying portfolio theory, especially from a normative perspective.

Another factor that motivates the study of portfolio theory arises from the increasing practice of overseas diversification. By analogy, if international capital markets are efficient and expected security returns are determined by some broad international index, then investors should hold an international index fund. However, the rationale for holding an index fund is much weaker internationally than domestically. There is very little evidence to suggest that an international model can adequately describe security returns. Chapters 8 and 12 review this evidence. Thus, in an international setting a passive asset allocation approach is not justifiable, at least on empirical grounds. This result provides another basis for active asset allocation and, potentially, the study of portfolio theory.

A BRIEF HISTORY OF CONTEMPORARY PORTFOLIO THEORY AND RISK MANAGEMENT

When studying any subject it helps to possess a familiarity with the subject's chronological development. This section provides a history of contemporary portfolio theory and risk management. The history is brief because the subject matter is only forty years old.

The history begins with the work of Harry Markowitz (1952), a recent recipient of the Nobel Prize in economics. In 1952 Markowitz demonstrated how to create a frontier of optimal (or "efficient") portfolios, each having the highest possible expected rate of return for a given level of risk—as measured by the standard deviation of portfolio returns. However, this technique was so computationally demanding (given the available technology) that practical application of his optimal allocation model was difficult.

In 1963, however, William Sharpe (also a recent Nobel laureate) developed a simplified version of his mentor's model, one that was less demanding with respect to computational effort. It was based on an approximating formula for portfolio return variance known as the single index model. This model, combined with technological advances, allowed contemporary portfolio theory to be readily applied in the real world. Today, Markowitz's model is widely used to allocate wealth across different types of assets, and Sharpe's model is widely used to allocate wealth within asset groups, especially common stock. Indeed, Markowitz himself currently employs these techniques to manage security portfolios as a director of the global portfolio research department of Daiwa Securities Trust Company.

Also in the early 1960s, financial economists began to investigate how Markowitz's model influenced the valuation of securities. The investigation focused on the impact of optimal portfolio formation within a frictionless marketplace. The result of the investigation became what is now known as the capital asset pricing model (CAPM), developed independently by William Sharpe (1964), Jan Mossin (1966), and John Lintner (1965). This model demonstrates that an asset's equilibrium return is a linear function of its systematic risk. Specifically, an asset's return is equal to the riskless rate of interest plus a risk premium that depends on the asset's covariance with a broadly diversified market portfolio. The CAPM is still widely used today despite a heated debate concerning its validity (Roll 1977). This debate has fostered alternative asset pricing paradigms, including the arbitrage pricing model (APM) and various multifactor approaches first introduced in the mid-1980s. In turn, asset pricing models have revolutionized the performance measurement of professional money managers by allowing performance to be assessed on a risk-adjusted basis.

In the mid-1960s Eugene Fama provided an elegant definition of security market efficiency: if information is rapidly and efficiently digested by market analysts, it is impossible to generate abnormal returns through any form of security analysis. Also, since informational events occur randomly, security prices should move randomly such that technical analysis is fruitless. Fama's insights led to several financial innovations, including stock index mutual funds, whose philosophy is to mimic a broad market index and to reduce the costs associated with more active portfolio management approaches. Index funds have proven to be popular in recent years, especially among U.S. pension fund managers. In 1987 about $130 billion of pension fund equities was held in index funds. In 1992 about $381 billion of pension equities (or about 38%) was held in such funds. Since Fama's argument hundreds of empirical investigations have focused on market efficiency and on the ability to detect abnormal profit opportunities. Overall, the evidence is very mixed. Recently, Fama (1991) has revised some of his earlier discussion and categorization relating to the efficient markets hypothesis, which is reviewed in Chapter 13.

With the late 1960s and early 1970s came the advent of market volatility not witnessed since the great crash of 1929 and the 1930s (Schwert 1989). Some evidence of this is provided in Figure 1.1, which shows how the U.S. price index, inflation rate, and dollar-yen exchange rate all became radically more volatile during this period. Volatility in these ("sticky") fundamental macroeconomic factors in turn caused increased volatility in ("less sticky") financial asset prices. In short, financial markets became riskier, with the 1980s exhibiting more volatility than any other post–World War II decade. Sources of this increased risk include important changes in monetary policy, the demise of fixed exchange rates that prevailed under the Bretton Woods agreement, and the OPEC oil price shocks of the period.

Financial engineers reacted to this increased risk by developing securities and strategies that helped investors manage risk better. In 1972 the Chicago Mercantile Exchange began to trade currency futures

FIGURE 1.1

Economic Volatility

Panel A. U.S. Price Index, 1800–1985 (1967 = 100)

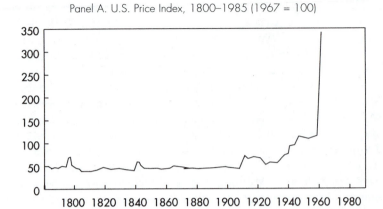

Panel B. Inflation (CPI, two-year moving average, percent change)

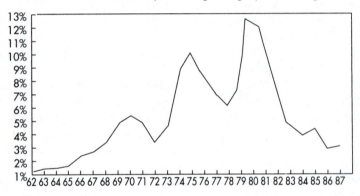

Panel C. Percent Change in U.S. Dollar - Japanese Yen Exchange Rate

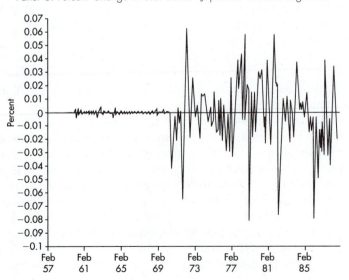

contracts. This event marked the first time that a financial futures contract was ever successfully traded. In 1975 the first interest rate futures appeared, and in 1983 the first stock index futures ("pinstripe pork bellies") appeared, encouraged by the work of Stephen Figlewski and Stanley Kon (1982). Options trading also exploded in the 1970s and 1980s. Stock index options, currency options, interest rate options, and futures options were all introduced. The valuation of options was facilitated by the work of Fisher Black and Myron Scholes (1973), who developed an option pricing model grounded in an elegant arbitrage argument that has been used in the development of other financial risk management techniques. These new financial products have also proven to be very popular for tactical asset reallocation practices (Part 4).

One of these techniques is portfolio insurance, developed by Hayne Leland (1980) and Mark Rubinstein (1985). This risk management strategy was very popular before the worldwide stock market crash of October 1987 and has recently begun to see renewed life. Also in the early 1980s, currency and interest rate swaps evolved as important risk management tools. These were followed by commodity swaps in 1987 and equity swaps, developed by financial engineers at Bankers Trust, in late 1989. Swaps, communications developments, and other financial and techno- logical innovations witnessed during the 1980s also led to increased international investment, principally through the establishment of inter- national mutual funds. Today, about $43 billion of U.S. pension fund equities is invested in foreign index mutual funds.

This brings us up to date on the history of portfolio theory and risk management. From Markowitz to today the management of security portfolios has been a dynamic and applied science motivated by the desire to help investors make their money work harder so that people's lives are enriched.

THE THEORY OF CHOICE: THE CERTAINTY CASE

Subsequent chapters will address a number of important concepts, including the investment opportunity set, indifference curves, expected utility maximization, market equilibrium, and others. This section briefly introduces these concepts, thereby providing a preview of the materials that follow. In addition, our purpose here is to introduce you to the two-step procedure used to solve any problem of economic choice. The first step is to determine the available investment options, or opportunity set. The second step is to specify how to choose among these available options. This choice commonly requires knowledge about the investor's utility function. We illustrate this two-step procedure in a simple setting, namely where all outcomes are known with certainty. However, the procedure can be applied to more complex problems whose outcomes are risky. Also, we will show how individual solutions to the problem of economic choice (i.e., investor equilibria) can be aggregated to determine equilibrium in the entire market.

Economic Choice Problem

Consider an investor who is scheduled to receive a guaranteed income of $25,000 in each of two periods, say, years. The only investment vehicle available is a government-insured one-year CD yielding 10 percent per annum. In addition, assume that the investor can borrow capital at 10 percent. The economic choice problem presented to the investor is how much to save (or consume) in each year.

Investor Opportunity Set

The first step to solving this problem is to determine the investor's opportunity set. One available option is to save nothing, consuming $25,000 in each year. This option is denoted by the point O_1(Option 1) in Figure 1.2. Another possibility is to save all first-period income and consume everything in the second period. Second-period consumption would be $52,500, or $25,000(1.10) + $25,000. This second option is labeled O_2 in Figure 1.2.[1] A third option (O_3 in Figure 1.2) is to consume everything in the first year by borrowing against second-year income. First-period consumption would be $47,727, or $25,000 + $25,000(1.10)^{-1}$.

FIGURE 1.2

The Investment Opportunity Set

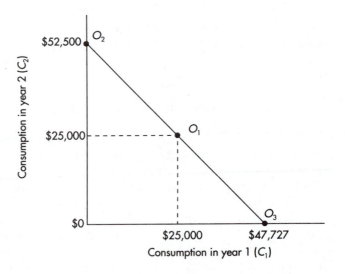

---

[1]For simplicity, we assume that the investor will not starve to death in the first period. Likewise, for our third option we assume that the investor will not starve to death in the second period.

Notice that points O_1, O_2, and O_3 lie along a straight line in Figure 1.2. In fact, every combination of two-period consumption available to the investor lies along this straight line. Hence, this line represents the investor's opportunity set. The equation of this line is

$$C_2 = \$52{,}500 - (1.10)C_1,$$

where C_2 and C_1 represent consumption in year 2 and year 1, respectively. The intercept is $52,500, following from zero consumption in year 1 (O_2). The slope is –1.10, reflecting the fact that each dollar of income consumed in the first year reduced second-year consumption by $1.10, since interest income was foregone.

Investor Utility

The second step required to solve the problem of economic choice under certainty is to choose among the vast number of combinations contained in the investor's opportunity set. This requires knowledge of his or her attitude toward current and future consumption, which can be represented graphically by indifference curves. A set of indifference curves (known as an indifference map) for a representative investor is shown in Figure 1.3. The name indifference curve derives from the fact that an investor is indifferent (utility-neutral) to any combination along the curve. For instance, for the first indifference curve, I_1, the investor is indifferent to the present and future consumption combinations A, B, and C. The convex shape of the indifference curves reflects the usual characteristics

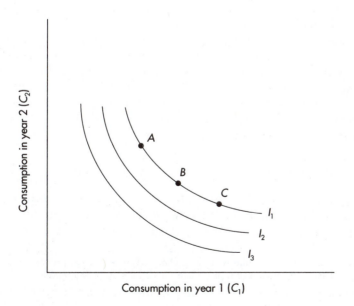

FIGURE 1.3

An Indifference Map for a Representative Investor

1 · *Introduction*

FIGURE 1.4

Invest or Equilibrium (O*)

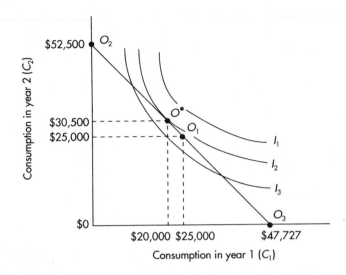

exhibited by rational economic agents, namely insatiability, diminishing marginal utility, and diminishing marginal substitutability.[2] For now, it is most important to recognize that higher (more northeasterly) indifference curves are associated with greater utility, since the investor can consume more in both years.

Investor Equilibrium

Armed with the knowledge of the investor's opportunity set and indifference map, we are ready to solve our problem, that is, determine investor equilibrium. By superimposing Figures 1.2 and 1.3 we determine the point at which the set of indifference curves is just tangential to the investment opportunity set. This point, labeled $O*$ in Figure 1.4, represents the optimal combination of consumption in years 1 and 2 for our investor. In other words, $O*$ represents investor equilibrium. Here the investor will consume $20,000 in year 1 and $30,500 in year 2. This combination will ensure that the investor attains the highest (most northeasterly) indifference curve that is in fact attainable given the available investment opportunities, thus optimizing utility.[3]

Market Equilibrium

Part 2 examines how the aggregation of individual investor equilibria leads to market equilibrium and the development of equilibrium asset pricing models. To preview this aggregation procedure, we'll now extend

---

[2] We assume that you are familiar with these characteristics through previous introductions to utility theory. A discussion of utility theory is contained in Chapter 7.

[3] If our problem involved risky outcomes, then we would determine investor equilibrium by optimizing expected utility.

our economic choice problem to determine equilibrium in the money market—that is, to determine an equilibrium rate of interest that clears the market.

At a 10 percent rate of interest, our investor was willing to lend $5,000, the difference between $25,000 in income and $20,000 in period 1 consumption. If we sum across all investors who wish to lend when the interest rate is 10 percent, we obtain one point on the supply curve prevailing in the money market. Reciprocally, summing across all investors who wish to borrow when rates are 10 percent yields one point on the demand curve. Now, as interest rates change, the amount of money that our investor is willing to lend also changes. Other investors will change the amount they lend or borrow too. Thus, by varying the interest rate, we should be able to generate complete money market supply and demand schedules. The equilibrium interest rate lies at their point of intersection. It is the rate that equates the amounts of money supplied for lending and demanded for borrowing. Since this market clearing rate is determined by each investor's choice problem, and since the solution of each of these problems depends on investor income and attitude toward consumption (tastes or preferences), we can conclude that equilibrium interest rates are ultimately determined by investors' incomes and tastes, at least in our simple setting.

THE THEORY OF CHOICE: THE UNCERTAINTY CASE— A PREVIEW

Our previous analysis assumed certainty, since the CD offered a fixed rate of return. In reality, however, assets exhibit uncertain returns. We know this because we observe different rates of interest contemporaneously in the economy. Without uncertainty, only one rate of interest (namely, the riskless rate) would prevail. If two or more different assets exhibiting *certain* outcomes paid different rates of interest, then arbitrage opportunities would be presented. Investors would borrow at the lower rate by selling (shorting) the lower-yielding asset and invest the proceeds in the higher-yielding asset. Proceeding to a logical conclusion, everyone would invest in the higher-yielding asset and no one would be willing to purchase the lower-yielding asset. Thus, only one interest rate would prevail if all investment outcomes were certain. Consequently, the fact that we observe different interest rates in the economy must indicate that not all investment outcomes are certain. Uncertainty affects market rates of interest, with riskier assets presumably exhibiting greater expected rates of return.

The remainder of this book is principally concerned with the economic theory of choice when investment outcomes are *uncertain*. While the same two-step procedure of generating the opportunity set and identifying investor preferences will apply, solving the problem will be much more complex because of the uncertainty. Also, unlike our previous graphical analysis, this will require the arithmetic of expected utility maximization or other selection criteria. Chapters 2 through 6 provide an analysis of the opportunity set under risk.

OUTLINE OF THE BOOK

The contents of this book proceed in a manner that parallels the historical development of portfolio theory and risk management. You are encouraged to read the chapters in a sequential fashion.

The book is divided into five parts. The first deals with the formation of optimal portfolios. In short, it principally concerns the theory developed by Markowitz and Sharpe. Part 1 is divided into four sections: Portfolio Formation (Chapters 2–4), A Simplified Approach to Portfolio Formation (Chapters 5 and 6), Optimal Portfolio Selection (Chapter 7), and The International Dimension (Chapter 8). Section 1 concerns identifying the properties of a portfolio of risky assets given the properties of its component assets, describing what makes one portfolio preferred to another, and demonstrating how preferred portfolios can be constructed. Thus Section 1 of Part 1 provides the basics about the theory of portfolio selection.

Section 2 of Part 1 is devoted to the simplification and practical implementation of the theory provided in the first section. Topics include the estimation of input data and the application of Sharpe's single index model.

Section 3 deals with the selection of the unique portfolio that maximizes an individual investor's expected utility. Expected utility maximization is the most widely recognized and theoretically sound criterion for choosing a unique portfolio from the efficient frontier.

Part 1 concludes with Section 4 (Chapter 8), which extends the principles of portfolio theory to an international setting. Allowing for overseas diversification expands the investment opportunity set—provided that world markets are not duplicative—thus leading to enhanced portfolio performance.

Part 2, Equilibrium Asset Pricing and Market Efficiency, contains three sections. Section 1 (Chapters 9–11) deals with models of equilibrium asset pricing. If investors behave as portfolio theory dictates they should, then their investment actions can be aggregated to determine asset prices. The pricing models examined are the CAPM, alternative forms of the CAPM, and the APM. Multifactor pricing models in the spirit of Chen, Roll, and Ross (1986) are also examined. Section 2 (Chapter 12) provides evidence of empirical tests of these models, and Section 3 (Chapter 13) provides a discussion of the efficient market hypothesis and related evidence. Implications of this evidence for portfolio formation are offered.

Part 3 of the book represents a slight digression from the historical chronology provided earlier. Chapters 14 and 15 deal with interest rates and bond fund management. Fixed-income securities present some special issues not presented by common stock, principally because bonds and bond prices are more complicated than their equity counterparts. Part 3 addresses these issues.

Part 4 picks up with risk management and financial engineering. Chapters 16 through 19 deal with futures, options, swaps, and portfolio insurance, respectively. Thus Part 4 is concerned with the derivative securities and techniques used to modify portfolio composition to insulate portfolio value from adverse changes in variables like interest rates and foreign exchange rates. In addition, Part 4 demonstrates how these recent innovations can be used in more proactive asset allocation strategies.

The book concludes with Part 5 (Chapter 20), which concerns the performance evaluation of professional money managers. There are several performance evaluation measures and a large body of empirical evidence to assess performance, especially that of mutual funds. We describe these measures and provide a summary of this body of empirical evidence in Part 5.

SUMMARY

Portfolio theory concerns the construction of optimal portfolios given the properties of the individual assets that make up the investment opportunity set. Risk management refers to the use of derivative securities and other techniques to efficiently modify portfolio composition. The purpose of this book is to introduce you to the concepts, problems, and applications of contemporary portfolio theory and risk management and to provide you with an analytic framework for constructing and managing optimal portfolios. The contents of this book proceed in a manner that generally parallels the chronological development of portfolio theory and risk management, beginning with the principles of Markowitz in the early 1950s and ending with the financial engineering techniques of the early 1990s. We turn next to Part 1, which concerns the theory of economic choice under uncertainty.

REFERENCES

Ariel, R. 1987. A monthly effect in stock returns. *Journal of Financial Economics* 18:161–174.

Balvers, R., T. Cosimano, and B. McDonald. 1990. Predicting stock returns in an efficient market. *Journal of Finance* 45:1109–1128.

Black, F., and M. Scholes. 1973. "The pricing of options and corporate liabilities." *Journal of Political Economy* 81:637–659.

Branch, B. 1977. A tax loss trading rule. *Journal of Business* 50:198–207.

Campbell, J. 1987. Stock returns and the term structure. *Journal of Financial Economics* 18:373–399.

Chen, N. 1991. Financial investment opportunities and the macroeconomy. *Journal of Finance* 46:529–554.

Chen, N., R. Roll, and S. Ross. 1986. Economic forces and the stock market. *Journal of Business* 59:386–403.

Chopra, N., J. Lakonishok, and J. Ritter. 1992. Measuring abnormal performance: do stocks overreact? *Journal of Financial Economics* 31: 235–268.

Cox, J., J. Ingersoll, and S. Ross. 1985. An intertemporal general equilibrium model of asset prices. *Econometrica* 53:363–384.

Cumby, R., and J. Glen. 1990. Evaluating the performance of international mutual funds. *Journal of Finance* 45:497–521.

DeBondt, W., and R. Thaler. 1985. Does the stock market overreact? *Journal of Finance* 40:793–805.

Evans, J., and S. Archer. 1968. Diversification and the reduction of dispersion. An Empirical Analysis. *Journal of Finance* 23:761–767.

Fama, E. 1965. The behavior of stock prices. *Journal of Business* 38:34–105.

Fama, E. 1970. Efficient capital markets: a review of theory and empirical work. *Journal of Finance* 25:383–417.

Fama, E. 1991. Efficient capital markets: II. *Journal of Finance* 46:1575–1617.

Fama, E., and K. French. 1988. Permanent and temporary components of stock prices. *Journal of Political Economy* 96:246–273.

Ferson, W., and C. Harvey. 1991. The variation of economic risk premiums. *Journal of Political Economy* 99:385–415.

Figlewski, S., and S. Kon. 1982. Portfolio management with stock index futures. *Financial Analysts Journal* 38:52–60.

Fisher, L. 1966. Some new stock market indexes. *Journal of Business* 39:191–225.

French, K. 1980. Stock returns and the weekend effect. *Journal of financial economics* 8:55–69.

Friedman, M. 1957. *A theory of the consumption function*. Princeton: Princeton University Press.

Gatto, M., R. Geske, R. Litzenberger, and H. Sosin. 1980. Mutual fund insurance. *Journal of Financial Economics* 8:283–317.

Hirshleifer, J. 1969. *Investment, interest, and capital*. Englewood Cliffs, NJ: Prentice-Hall.

Jensen, M. 1968. The performance of mutual funds in the period 1945–1964. *Journal of Finance* 23:389–415.

Keim, D. 1983. Size-related anomalies and stock return seasonality: further empirical evidence. *Journal of Financial Economics* 12:12–32.

Leland, H. 1980. Who should buy portfolio insurance? *Journal of Finance* 35:581–594.

Leland, H. 1985. Option pricing and replication with transaction costs. *Journal of Finance* 40:1283–1301.

Lintner, J. 1965. The valuation of risky assets and the selection of risky investments in stock portfolios and capital budgets. *Review of Economics and Statistics* 47:13–37.

Lo, A., and G. MacKinlay. 1988. Stock prices do not follow random walks. Evidence from a simple specification test. *Review of Financial Studies* 1:41–66.

Lucas, R. 1978. Asset prices in an exchange economy. *Econometrica* 46:1429–1445.

Markowitz, H. 1952. Portfolio selection. *Journal of Finance* 7:77–91.

Markowitz, H. 1959. *Portfolio selection. Efficient diversification of investments.* New York: John Wiley & Sons.

Modiglioni, F., and J. Pogue. 1974. An introduction to risk and return. *Financial Analysts Journal* 30:68–80.

Modiglioni, F., and J. Pogue. 1974. An introduction to risk and return. Part II. *Financial Analysts Journal* 30:69–86.

Mossin, J. 1966. Equilibrium in a capital market. *Econometrica* 34:768–783.

Roll, R. 1977. A critique of the asset pricing theory's tests. *Journal of Financial Economics* 4:129–176.

Roll, R., and S. Ross. 1980. An empirical investigation of the arbitrage pricing theory. *Journal of Finance* 35:1073–1103.

Ross, S. 1976. The arbitrage theory of capital asset pricing. *Journal of Economic Theory* 13:341–360.

Rubinstein, M. 1985. Alternative paths to portfolio insurance. *Financial Analysts Journal* 41:42–52.

Rubinstein, M., and H. Leland. 1981. Replicating options with positions in stock and cash. *Financial Analysts Journal* 37:63–71.

Schwert, G. September 1989. Why does stock market volatility change over time? *Journal of Finance* 44:1115–1153.

Sharpe, W. 1963. A simplified model of portfolio analysis. *Management Science* 277–293.

Sharpe, W. 1964. Capital asset prices. A theory of market equilibrium under conditions of risk. *Journal of Finance* 19:425–442.

Sharpe, W. 1967. Portfolio analysis. *Journal of financial and quantitative analysis* 2:76–84.

Sharpe, W. 1970. *Portfolio theory and capital markets.* New York: McGraw-Hill.

Solnik, B., and B. Noetzlin. 1982. Optimal international asset allocation. *Journal of Portfolio Management* 9:11–21.

Smith, C., C. Smithson, and D. Wilford. 1990. *Managing financial risk.* New York: Harper Business.

Tucker, A. 1991. *Financial futures, options, and swaps.* St. Paul: West Publishing.

Von Neumann, J., and O. Morgenstern. 1947. *Theory of games and economic behavior.* Princeton: Princeton University Press.

Wagner, W., and S. Lau. 1971. The effect of diversification on risk. *Financial Analysts Journal* 27:48–53.

Questions and Problems

1. Define the terms *portfolio theory* and *risk management.*

2. Discuss why you might or might not engage in the study of portfolio theory. Be sure to include descriptions of the passive and active asset allocation approaches.

3. Provide a time line displaying the chronological development of contemporary portfolio theory and risk management.

4. Describe the two-step procedure used to solve any problem of economic choice.

5. Define the following concepts: investment opportunity set; indifference curve; indifference map; utility maximization; investor equilibrium; market equilibrium.

6. Discuss the properties of insatiability, diminishing marginal utility, and diminishing marginal substitutability. Provide a representative utility function that exhibits these properties.

7. If investors were risk-neutral, only one interest rate would prevail in the economy. Explain why.

8. If investment outcomes were all certain, only one interest rate would prevail in the economy. Explain why.

9. Assume that you have income equal to $50,000 in each of two periods. Also, you can lend or borrow at 8 percent. What is the equation for your investment opportunity set?

10. Graph the linear opportunity set from problem 9. Superimposing a representative indifference map, identify investor equilibrium.

11. Assume that the lending rate remains unchanged at 8 percent but that the borrowing rate is now 12 percent. What is the maximum that you can consume in each period? Graph your new investment opportunity set. Explain why it is kinked.

Self-Test Problems

ST-1. Assume that an investor has income equal to $50,000 in each of two years and that the borrowing and lending rates of interest are both 5 percent. What is the equation for the investment opportunity set? Graph this set, superimpose a representative indifference map, and identify investor equilibrium.

ST-2. Now assume that the borrowing rate rises from 5 percent to 10 percent. Graph the new investment opportunity set and new equilibrium.

Solutions to Self-Test Problems

ST-1. If $C_1 = \$0$, then $C_2 = \$30,000 + \$30,000(1.05) = \$61,500$. If $C_2 = \$0$, then $C_1 = \$30,000 + \$30,000(1.05)^{-1} = \$58,571$. The slope is the negative of 1 plus the interest rate, or -1.05. So the equation of the opportunity set is

$$C_2 = \$61,500 - (1.05)C_1.$$

The opportunity set is given by the line $O_3O_1O_2$ in the following figure.

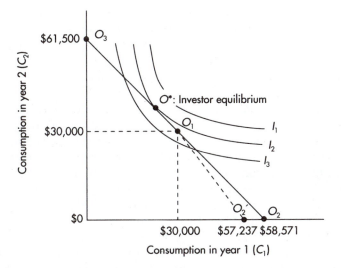

ST-2. If $C_1 = \$0$, then $C_2 = \$30,000 + \$30,000(1.05) = \$61,500$. If $C_2 = \$0$, then $C_1 = \$30,000 + \$30,000(1.10)^{-1} = \$57,273$. The new opportunity set is given by the line $O_3O_1O_2'$ in the above graph. The set kinks at O_1 (where no borrowing or lending occurs), since the borrowing rate has increased. The equilibrium is unaffected, though, since the investor originally loaned money in year 1.

A P P E N D I X

1

Mutual Funds

Investment companies (a.k.a. mutual funds) can be open-end or closed-end. An open-end fund has no limit as to the number of its shares outstanding; the number changes as new investments are made in the fund or as existing participants redeem their shares. In contrast, a closed-end fund has a fixed number of shares outstanding; therefore, its shares cannot be redeemed but must be traded like ordinary common stock. There are only about 250 closed-end funds in the United States today, and their shares are typically traded on the over-the-counter market, although some trade on the New York Stock Exchange (NYSE). On the other hand, there are well over 3,000 open-end funds in the United States, managed by companies like the Delaware Group, Fidelity, Merrill Lynch, Putnam, Shearson, and Vanguard. The term *mutual fund* in this book will generally refer to open-end funds, which are sold on the basis of their net asset value (NAV). An open-end fund's NAV is its assets less liabilities, divided by shares outstanding. In other words, NAV is the fund's book value per share. Closed-end fund share prices are determined in market trading, so NAV and market value per share are the same. A particularly bothersome empirical finding is that closed-end fund share prices are commonly below their true intrinsic values.

Load funds are mutual funds that charge an up-front participation fee, typically 6 percent to 8.5 percent, which is shared by the mutual fund's salesman and that salesman's investment firm. On the other hand, no-load funds have no sales charge, so their shares are bought and redeemed at NAV. Still, many no-load funds charge a redemption fee, often less than 1 percent, to cover their redemption expenses. In addition, some redemption fees may only be applied if shares are redeemed too soon, say within six months of purchase. Index funds often engage in this practice to reduce their need to hold idle cash positions. Holding cash frustrates the ability of the fund's manager to track the target index's performance closely. Hence, temporary redemption fees are used by index funds to reduce tracking error.

All funds have managers who oversee the fund's trading activities in light of the fund's objectives, which are discussed below. The manager receives a management fee, often a percentage of the fund's total assets. The typical percentage is 0.5 percent. Thus the manager who can perform successfully and attract more capital into the fund receives higher compensation. In addition, some managers may receive a partial fixed compensation, and index fund managers are typically compensated in part on how well they track the target index.

An investor must receive a fund prospectus before purchasing shares. The prospectus provides the usual information about the fund's objectives, management, past performance, and so on. You can call an investment firm to receive a prospectus, and these firms often advertise their funds in business periodicals and national and regional newspapers. At this writing the Securities and Exchange Commission (SEC) is deliberating whether or not to allow firms to provide more detailed advertisements that would in turn permit investors to purchase shares directly through newspaper coupons.

Mutual funds have different objectives to cater to different clienteles. A listing of fund objectives follows. The figures in parentheses represent the percentage of U.S. mutual funds that have the accompanying objective (1991):

Tax exempt (22%)
Income (17%)
Growth (16%)
Growth and income (9%)
Money market (11%)
International (4%)

Precious metals (2%)
Index and other (19%)

Tax-exempt funds typically invest in municipal securities that are free from federal, and often state and local, taxes. Income funds are tilted toward coupon bonds and dividend-paying common stocks. Growth funds aggressively seek capital appreciation and are generally riskier. Growth and income funds, mixtures of the other two, are often called balanced funds. Money market funds, which are very safe, invest in various money market instruments like Treasury bills and high-grade commercial paper. International funds invest in one or more countries overseas, and precious metals funds commonly invest in mining stocks and gold and silver. A fund that is restricted to a particular asset such as gold or to a particular sector such as utilities is often called a special-purpose fund.

Index funds exhibit low security turnover and fees and are designed to track a target index. Index funds that target a broad market index have a special role in this book, as they stand in for a passive asset allocation approach. Keep in mind that funds that track narrower indexes, known as sector funds, are *not* regarded as passively managed. Examples include funds that track a specific industry index such as the Dow-Jones utilities index or the like. While such funds have low security turnover and low fees, they do not offer the type of diversification offered by, say, the SP500 or NYSE composite index. Only funds targeting broad domestic market indexes are considered passive in the context of this book. In an international context funds that track broad market indexes, like the Morgan Stanley world index, are considered passive.

There are typically three signs of an actively managed fund. The first sign is a propensity to market time. For instance, bond fund managers are typically market timers, changing their interest rate exposures as their interest rate forecasts vary over time. The second sign is a propensity to engage in security analysis to identify mispriced securities. Funds that conduct such analyses commonly have greater fees and loads to finance their research. A third sign of active management is sector rotation, wherein a fund alters its exposure to various economic sectors (e.g., autos) based on sector forecasts. Thus all three signs of active management have a common origin: trading on forecasts. If a fund is well diversified and does not utilize forecasts for trading, then it will track a broad market index and will be considered passively managed in the context of this book.

Market timing and other forecast-based approaches can be very risky. For example, in the ten years ending December 1992, the SP500 rose 347%, including reinvested dividends. Those who missed the best four months of the decade, however, would have had their return cut to 191%. Missing the best six months would have shrunk the return to 147%. On the other hand, missing the SP500's six worst months, including October 1987, would have increased the return to 745%.

Portfolio Analysis

T HE ECONOMIC AGENT LIVING IN A WORLD OF PERFECT CERTAINTY FACES AN
easy task: to allocate wealth over time so as to maximize total
utility. With no risk the interest rate on the risk-free asset provides
the information necessary to evaluate the investment. However,
once the economic agent steps out of the simplified environment of
perfect certainty and into the real world, the task of selecting a
portfolio of financial assets becomes much more difficult; a quick
examination of the financial section of the *Wall Street Journal*
indicates that thousands of U.S. financial assets such as stocks,
corporate and municipal bonds, foreign currencies, agricultural
commodities, and options and futures on numerous assets are
available to investors. In addition, foreign securities are available
along with over-the-counter instruments such as swaps and
forward contracts. Another complicating factor is that these
securities have varying levels of risk. Thus it should be obvious that
a systematic method for selecting financial assets is necessary.

Part 1 of this book presents contemporary portfolio theory
concepts that allow economic agents to identify portfolios of
financial assets that maximize satisfaction for the investor. After
studying Part 1 you will understand the derivation of the optimal

portfolio of risky and risk-free assets for an economic agent. To accomplish this task we utilize the two-step procedure addressed in Chapter 1: (1) develop the relevant opportunity set and (2) combine the opportunity set with the preferences for the agent. The goal of Chapters 2 through 6 is to develop a representation of the opportunity set under uncertainty. Chapters 2 and 3 utilize the pioneering analysis of Harry Markowitz to develop measures of the expected portfolio return and risk. Once this is accomplished, a graphical depiction of the opportunity set can be derived. Chapter 4 discusses several analytical methods for approximating the opportunity set.

Chapters 5 and 6 discuss a set of assumptions developed by William Sharpe that simplify the task of deriving the opportunity set. Investor preferences are discussed in Chapter 7. By combining the investor opportunity set discussed in Chapters 2 through 6 with investor preferences (Chapter 7), we are able to identify the optimal portfolio of assets. Chapter 8 addresses international diversification. ∎

C H A P T E R · *2*

Opportunity Sets

Introduction

Chapter 1 examined the theory of choice under certainty, that is, when investment outcomes are known. A single payoff, the rate of return on the risk-free asset, provided all the information necessary to evaluate the investment. In reality, however, most investment outcomes are unknown or risky. The presence of risk considerably complicates the asset selection process because a single payoff will no longer describe the performance of the asset. Instead there is a set of possible asset payoffs. To summarize the possible asset returns, measures of the central tendency and dispersion, which is a proxy for risk, must be obtained.

Typically, however, securities are not held in isolation but instead as part of portfolios. Thus our ultimate interest concerns portfolio expected return and risk. This chapter discusses in detail the calculation of the expected return and the variance of a portfolio, stressing the interactive effects between its component securities. Using these summary measures to describe the portfolio, we provide a graphical depiction of the set of possible combinations of risk and return. Thus we provide a representation of the opportunity set under risk.

A basic understanding of algebra and calculus are the only prerequisites necessary for understanding the portfolio theory material presented in Sections 1 and 2. Knowledge of statistical material such as measures of central tendency, dispersion, and association is helpful; however, the discussion of statistical concepts and applications is largely self-contained.

Most of the important equations in the portfolio theory sections, such as the portfolio expected return and variance, are fully derived. Less mathematically inclined readers may prefer to skip the derivations in these chapters. However, an understanding of the derivation of these important measures provides for a richer comprehension of the material.

RETURNS

We begin our treatment of the opportunity set under risk by calculating returns for individual securities. We start with dollar returns.

Dollar Returns

The dollar return on an investment is the gain or loss in the value of the initial investment. The dollar return is split into two components. First, the income component consists of direct cash payments from the asset. Examples of cash payments include dividends from holding equity and interest payments from owning coupon bonds. The income component is generally stable. Firms try to increase dividends at a constant rate over time and interest payments on a bond typically are fixed.

The second component of the dollar return is the capital gain or loss, which is attributable to changes in the value of the asset relative to its original purchase price. Asset prices continually change as new information that affects the value of the asset arises. For example, if a firm unexpectedly receives a large government contract, expected profits will increase and the share price will increase, holding other information constant. If oil prices increase substantially, costs will increase for airline firms and expected profits will decrease, resulting in a reduction in the share price.

Analytically, the dollar return over a period is represented as

(2.1) $$dollar\ return = (D_1 + (P_1 - P_0))H$$

where D_1 is the total cash payments over the period, P_1 is the ending asset price, P_0 is the price paid for the asset, and H is the number of units held.

To illustrate the calculation of the dollar return, assume that 100 shares of XYZ Corporation are purchased for $100 per share and the firm plans to pay an annual dividend of $4 per share. One year later the stock price is $110. The realized capital gain is ($110 − $100) × 100 shares = $1,000, and the dividend is $4 × 100 shares = $400. Thus the dollar return is $1,000 + $400 = $1,400.

Percentage Returns

Is $1,400 a large gain? It depends on the initial investment. If the investment was $1 million, the gain relative to the investment is trivial, while the gain is spectacular if the initial outlay was $100. To account for the effect of the size of the initial outlay on investment performance, calculate returns as a percentage of the initial investment. The percentage return, r, is calculated by dividing the dollar return by the initial investment:[1]

(2.2)
$$r = \frac{D_1 + (P_1 - P_0)}{P_0}$$

Equation 2.2 can be rearranged to express the return in terms of the dividend yield and capital gain yield:

(2.3)
$$r = \frac{D_1}{P_0} + \frac{(P_1 - P_0)}{P_0}$$

The first right-hand term of equation 2.3 is the dividend yield, and the second right-hand term is the yield from the capital gain. In this example the dividend yield is $4/$100 = 4\% and the capital gain yield is $10/$100 = 10\% for a total (pretax) return of 14%.

Annualizing Percentage Returns

Suppose that another asset is purchased for $50 and sold four years later for $70. If no dividends were paid, the return (ignoring taxes) over the four-year period is ($70 − $50)/$50 = 40%. While it may initially appear that this asset outperformed the first security, such an inference would be bogus. To compare the performance of the stocks, returns must be converted to a common holding period. The common period can be daily, weekly, or monthly, but comparisons are usually made on an annual basis. No calculations are necessary for the first security because it was held for one year. For the second asset the growth rate is associated with a four-year appreciation of $20. The familiar formula $PV(1 + g)^n = FV$, where PV is the present value of an asset, FV is the future value, g is the growth rate, and n is the number of years, yields this calculation:

$$\$50(1 + g)^4 = \$70$$
$$g = (70/50)^{1/4} - 1 = 8.78\%$$

---

[1] The number of units of the asset held, H (shares in this example), cancels because it is present in the numerator and denominator.

The first investment provided superior performance (14%) because the annualized return for the second investment was only 8.78%. The same procedure can be used to annualize any holding period return.

Calculating Average Returns

Suppose that you are given yearly returns for a security for the past 50 years and you want a measure of central tendency. One possible measure is a simple arithmetic average, obtained by summing the 50 yearly returns and dividing by the number of years. However, extreme observations, particularly on the low side, can introduce problems when using this measure. For example, suppose that an investment generates returns of 50%, 100%, and –100% in each of three successive years. The average return method indicates that the investment performance is positive, yielding an average return of 16.67% per year: (50% + 100% – 100%) ÷ 3 = 16.67%. However, the end-of-period wealth is zero, since a –100% return was realized in the third period.

An alternative measure of central tendency is the geometric rate of return, which is the growth rate needed for the initial amount to grow to the ending value.[2] The geometric return is calculated by taking the tth root of the product of 1 plus the individual returns, or:

(2.4)
$$r_g = [(1 + r_1)(1 + r_2) \ldots (1 + r_t)]^{1/t} - 1$$

where r_g is the geometric return, r_1 through r_t are the respective returns and t is the terminal period. In this example the geometric return equals zero because the third-year return, r_3, is –100%.

To illustrate the calculation of a geometric return, assume that the following yearly returns were realized on a security investment:

YEAR	RETURN
1987	6%
1988	30
1989	25
1990	–15

The average return was $(0.06 + 0.30 + 0.25 - 0.15)/4 = 11.5\%$, while the geometric return was $[(1.06)(1.30)(1.25)(.85)]^{1/4} - 1 = 10\%$. The average return will always be greater than the geometric return because the latter takes compounding into consideration, assuming that the per-period returns are not constant.

---

[2]The continuously compounded rate of return for period t is the value of Φ_T such that $1 + R_t = e^{\Phi_T}$, where $e = 2.714 \ldots$ is the base of the natural logarithms and $1 + R_t$ is the end of period value of \$1 invested at period $t - 1$. Thus $\Phi_T = ln(1 + R_t)$. See Fama (1976) for a detailed discussion of the relationship between logarithmic and arithmetic returns.

Expected Returns and Risk

Before purchasing a risky asset, you should obtain an estimate of its expected rate of return over the relevant time frame. Also, since the actual return can be much different from the expected, an estimate of return dispersion should also be obtained. *Return dispersion* is a measure of the asset's risk or propensity to deviate from its expected value. Obtaining estimates of an individual asset's expected return and risk requires some knowledge about probability theory.

Basic Concepts of Probability Theory

The starting point of any discussion of probability theory is the random variable. A *random variable* is a rule that assigns a number to possible outcomes of a random experiment. Two important points are apparent. First, there is uncertainty about the outcome of the experiment, and second, the outcomes can be assigned numerical values. An example is the change in the gross domestic product for the next quarter. This is a random variable because there is uncertainty regarding the announced figure and a numerical value can be assigned to the announcement (+3% for example). Another example of a random variable is the return of the SP500 for the next month. This return is obviously uncertain, and it can be described in numerical terms.

A random variable may be either discrete or continuous. A discrete random variable can take on at most a countable number of values. Examples include the number of automobiles sold in the United States next month, the number of votes obtained by a candidate for office, and the number of students enrolled in a particular class. A continuous random variable can take on any value in an interval. Examples of continuous random variables include the amount of time to complete a project and the temperature tomorrow. It is impossible to list all possible values of a continuous random variable because there are an infinite number of possibilities.

Probability numbers provide measures of the likelihood of each possible outcome of a random variable. Probability numbers are measured on a scale from 0 to 1, with 0 probability implying that the outcome is impossible and a probability of 1 implying that the event is certain. The probabilities must satisfy two conditions. First, the probability cannot be negative, and second, the sum of the probabilities for all outcomes of a random variable must equal 1.

Once the outcomes of a random variable are determined and probabilities are assigned to each outcome, a probability distribution can be derived. A *probability distribution* is simply a graphical representation of the probabilities of all possible outcomes of a random variable.

Consider a coin that is tossed twice. The random variable is the number of heads obtained. The probability of obtaining 0 heads is .25, 1 head is .50,

FIGURE 2.1

Probability Distribution for Coin Toss: Number of Heads Obtained in Two Tosses

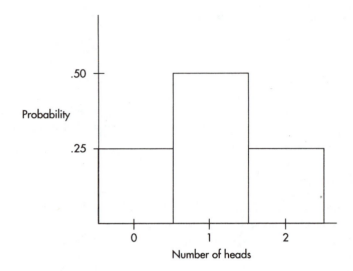

and two heads is .25. Figure 2.1 presents a probability distribution for this experiment. The possible outcomes are established (0,1,2) along with their associated probabilities (.25, .50, .25). Note that the probabilities sum to 1. (For a more interesting real world example of distributions, jump to Figure 2.4, which provides frequency distributions for financial asset returns.)

Population Expected Value

The probability distribution provides information about possible outcomes and their accompanying probabilities. While graphical inspection of the distribution can be useful, summary measures that quickly and accurately describe the distribution are desirable.

The first important summary measure is central tendency, which is a measure of the center of the distribution. This measure represents the expected value or average of the distribution. In other words, this measure gives the average value that will be obtained if the random experiment is repeated a large number of times.

To illustrate the concept of expected value, assume that a coin is flipped once. The participant of the game wins $100 if the result is heads and loses $50 if the coin comes up tails. If the coin is flipped a very large number of times, it is reasonable to anticipate that half of the trials will result in heads and the other half in tails. Suppose that the coin is tossed a million times. If 50% of the flips result in heads, the amount received is $50 million ($100 × .5 × 1 million) and the outflow is $25 million (−$50 × .5 × 1 million). The total payoff is $25 million ($50 million − $25 million), or $25 per toss.

An easier way to calculate the expected value is to weight the possible outcomes by their probabilities and sum over all of the occurrences. The expected value in this example is $100(.5) + −$50(.5), or $25 per toss. More formally, suppose that X is a discrete random variable and x is its possible outcomes. The expected value of the random variable $E(X)$ is

(2.5)
$$E(X) = \sum_{i=1}^{T} x_i p_i$$

where x_i is the outcome in state i and p_i is its corresponding probability of occurrence.

The expected return for asset k, $E(r_k)$, is

(2.6)
$$E(r_k) = \sum_{i=1}^{T} p_i r_{ki}$$

where r_{ki} is the ith possible outcome for the asset k return.

To illustrate the calculation of the expected return, suppose that you are considering the purchase of two securities. You access the following returns associated with the state of the economy and the probability associated with each state:

	PROB.	ASSET 1	ASSET 2
Recession	.25	−10%	−20%
Moderate growth	.50	10	15
Boom	.25	20	30

The expected or mean return is simply the sum of the products of the corresponding probabilities and returns. The expected return of asset one is $E(r_1) = .25(-10\%) + .50(10\%) + .25(20\%) = 7.5\%$. The expected return for asset two is $E(r_2) = .25(-20\%) + .50(15\%) + .25(30\%) = 10\%$. Asset two exhibits a greater expected return.

Population Variance

Because asset returns are uncertain over time, an important question is how likely it is that the return will be close to the expected value. To answer this question requires a measure of the dispersion of the distribution. One method of obtaining a measure of return dispersion is to examine the deviations from the mean: $r_1 - E(r), r_2 - E(r), \ldots, r_N - E(r)$, where $r_1, r_2, \ldots, r_N$ represent a population of numerical values with mean $E(r)$. It appears that the mean of the deviations is a reasonable measure of dispersion. However, the sum of the deviations will always equal zero; some of the deviations will be positive and some negative, and they will cancel. To illustrate, assume a population of three returns, r_1, r_2, r_3, with mean $E(r)$. The deviations from the mean are $r_1 - E(r), r_2 - E(r), r_3 - E(r)$. Arranging them produces $(r_1 + r_2 + r_3) - 3 E(r)$. The sum of the observations equals the mean times the number of observations: $3 E(r) - 3 E(r) = 0$.

Thus significance lies not in the sign of the deviations but in its magnitude. The deviations must be treated the same regardless of their sign. One way to accomplish this is to square the deviations: $[r_1 - E(r)]^2$, $[r_2 - E(r)]^2, \ldots, [r_N - E(r)]^2$. The average or expected value of these squared dispersions is called the *variance*.[3] The variance is represented by the Greek symbol sigma squared, σ^2. The variance for asset k is

(2.7)
$$\sigma_k{}^2 = \sum_{i=1}^{T} p_i (r_{ki} - E(r_i))^2.$$

The square root of the variance is called the *standard deviation* and is denoted by σ.

In this example the variance of asset one is

$$\sigma_1{}^2 = (-10 - 7.5)^2 \,.25 + (10 - 7.5)^2 \,.50 + (20 - 7.5)^2 \,.25 = 118.75, \text{ or } \sigma_1 = 10.9\%.$$

The variance of the second asset is

$$\sigma_2{}^2 = (-20 - 10)^2 \,.25 + (15 - 10)^2 \,.50 + (30 - 10)^2 \,.25 = 337.5, \text{ or } \sigma_2 = 18.37\%.$$

Variance as a Measure of Risk

The variance of returns (or standard deviation) is a common measure of asset risk in portfolio theory. The variance measures the spread of a return distribution and as such gives equal weight to positive and negative deviations from the mean. However, investors welcome positive deviations and suffer from negative dispersions; intuitively it would appear that a downside risk measure, which considers only negative return deviations, is a superior measure of risk. One alternative is to average only squared negative deviations while assigning a zero value to positive deviations. Despite its intuitive appeal, this measure (called the *semivariance*) is rarely used. The reason for the lack of interest in the semivariance is that return distributions are typically symmetric around the mean, implying that assets with a high semivariance will also have a high variance. Positive and negative return deviations are equally likely when the distribution is symmetric.

Figure 2.2 illustrates two symmetric return distributions with the same mean. The returns of asset 1 have a low variance because most of the observations are concentrated around the mean. In contrast, returns of

---

[3] An alternative measure of dispersion entails taking the absolute value of the deviations. The expected value of absolute deviations from the mean is called the *mean absolute deviation*. This measure is employed infrequently because problems arise when using this measure to make inferences about a population, based only on sample observations. See Newbold (1990) for more information on this measure.

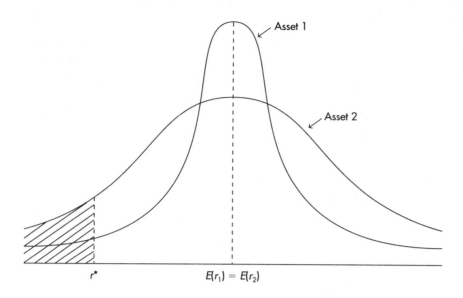

FIGURE 2.2

Return Distribution for High- and Low-Variance Assets

asset 2 are more uncertain, as the variance of returns is larger than for asset 1. Suppose that an investor defines a return below r^* as unacceptably low. Inspection of Figure 2.2 indicates that the probability of obtaining an extremely low return is greater for the high-variance asset. The area to the left of r^* is higher for asset 2, implying a greater likelihood of a very low return. Therefore, for return distributions that are symmetric, the variance will have the same ramification for the investment decision as a measure of downside risk. Thus, the return variance is an appropriate risk measure for most financial assets.

Sample Expected Return and Variance

With the population mean and variance measures, subjective probability was used to estimate the mean and standard deviation of possible returns. The investor generated relevant states (the condition of the economy in our example) and estimated the probability of each state and the asset return associated with each state.

Another method for estimating the expected value and variance of a security entails sampling previous returns. In reality the true probability distribution that is generating security returns is not observable. Consequently, it is necessary to sample previous returns and assume that the underlying distribution does not change over time.

Suppose that Figure 2.3 illustrates the continuous probability distribution for an asset's returns over the next year. The expected return is 10%. Because this distribution is not observable, returns must be sampled so the expected return and variance can be estimated.

FIGURE 2.3
Return Distribution
for an Asset with an
Expected Return
of 10%

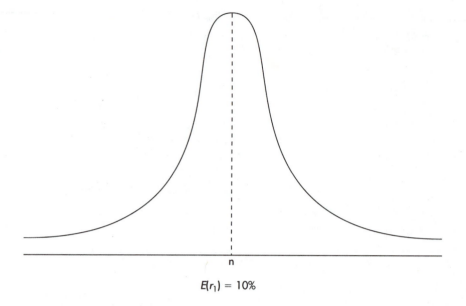

$E(r_1) = 10\%$

The sample mean for asset k is

(2.8)
$$E(r_k) = \frac{\displaystyle\sum_{i=1}^{N} r_{ki}}{N}$$

where N is the number of return observations. Suppose that returns for the past five years are 12%, –5%, 15%, 7%, 20%. The sample mean is $(12\% + -5\% + 15\% + 7\% + 20\%) \div 5 = 9.8\%$. Note that the sample mean is different from the population mean of 10%. Although the sample mean is an unbiased estimator of the population mean, errors can occur.[4] The sample size can be increased to provide more accurate estimates. However, assume that the underlying probability distribution is constant; increasing the sample size increases the probability that the distribution of returns has changed shape over the longer sample period. In general it is acceptable to increase the sample size as long as you believe that the distribution has not changed significantly. It would not be prudent to sample returns during a period in which the firm has changed its product line dramatically or participated in major acquisitions.

When calculating the sample variance, the sum of the squared deviations from the mean is divided by $N - 1$, using the sample mean as a proxy for the unobservable population mean. As compensation for using

---

[4] If a sample statistic has a sampling distribution with a mean equal to the population parameter, the statistic is said to be an *unbiased estimator* of the parameter.

a proxy measure, divide by $N-1$, yielding an unbiased estimate of the population variance.

(2.9)
$$\sigma_k^2 = \frac{\sum_{i=1}^{N} (r_{ki} - E(r_k))^2}{N-1}.$$

The sample variance in this example is

$$\sigma_k^2 = \frac{(12\% - 9.8\%)^2 + (-5\% - 9.8\%)^2 + (15\% - 9.8\%)^2 + (7\% - 9.8\%)^2 + (20\% - 9.8\%)^2}{5-1}$$

$$= 362.8/4 = 90.7 \text{ or}$$
$$\sigma_k = 9.52\%.$$

Risk and Return: A Historical Perspective

Exhibit 2.1 provides a historical perspective on average rates of return and risk for financial assets from 1926 through 1988. Small stocks produced the highest yearly average return, at 17.8%, with larger stocks delivering an average return of 12.1%. Predictably, investors in bonds and money market instruments realized a much lower return, 5.3% for corporate bonds and 3.6% for Treasury bills. While holders of stock enjoyed higher average returns, returns were highly variable. The standard deviation of small stocks was 35.6% per year and 20.9% for large stocks. The high return for small stocks was 142.9% and the low was −49.8%. Variability for bonds was much lower, with annual standard deviations of 8.4% and 3.3% for long-term corporate bonds and Treasury

EXHIBIT 2.1

Performance Statistics for Annual Returns 1926–1988

	Arithmetic Mean	Geometric Mean	Standard Deviation	High	Low
Large Stocks	12.1%	10.0%	20.9%	54.0% (1933)	−43.3% (1931)
Small Stocks	17.8	12.3	35.6	142.9 (1933)	−49.8 (1931)
Long-Term Corporate Bonds	5.3	5.0	8.4	43.8 (1982)	−8.1 (1969)
U.S. Treasury Bills	3.6	3.5	3.3	14.7 (1981)	0.0 (1940)
Inflation	3.2	3.1	4.8	18.2 (1946)	−10.3 (1932)

Source: Roger G. Ibbotson and Rex A. Sinquefield, *Stocks, Bonds, Bills, and Inflation: Historical Returns.* (The Financial Analysts Research Foundation, University of Virginia, 1984, updated in 1988.)

FIGURE 2.4

Return Distributions
for U.S. Financial
Assets

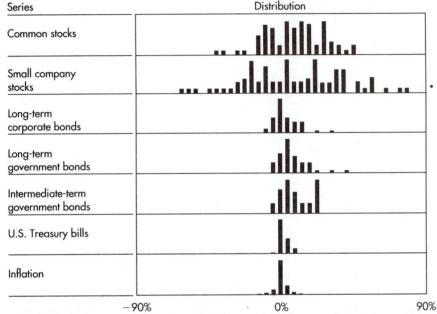

bills, respectively. The lowest return for corporate bonds was −8.1% and 0% for Treasury bills.

Figure 2.4 provides frequency distributions for the various financial assets. These distributions clearly demonstrate the risky nature of small stocks in contrast to corporate and government bonds.

Volatility is not constant. As an illustration of this, Exhibit 2.2 provides daily and monthly SP500 standard deviations for various decades. Volatility was great during the 1930s, as illustrated by the daily and monthly data. During the 1980s, volatility was high for the daily data but not the monthly returns.

CALCULATING EXPECTED RETURN AND RISK FOR A PORTFOLIO

We have developed a framework for calculating the expected return and risk of individual securities. However, investors typically hold a portfolio of assets. Thus the main concern to investors is not the performance of each individual security but the collective performance of the portfolio. In this section we address the expected return and risk of portfolios of assets. With this information probability distributions can be developed for the portfolio.

EXHIBIT 2.2

Daily and Monthly Volatility for Various Decades

Time	Daily Returns Standard Deviation	Monthly Returns Standard Deviation
1885–1889	0.3791%	3.8056%
1890–1899	0.9565	5.1294
1900–1909	0.8515	4.4310
1910–1919	0.7706	3.9642
1920–1929	1.0188	4.9566
1930–1939	1.9352	10.7456
1940–1949	0.8793	4.8097
1950–1959	0.6956	3.4041
1960–1969	0.6245	3.5095
1970–1979	0.8575	4.9535
1980–1989	1.1050	4.8458
ALL	1.0259	5.3566

Source: Charles P. Jones and Jack W. Wilson, "Is Stock Price Volatility Increasing?" *Financial Analysts Journal*, Nov.-Dec. 1989, 20-26.

Expected Return of a Portfolio

The expected return of a two-asset portfolio is given by

$$E(r_P) = E[w_1 r_1 + w_2 r_2], \tag{2.10}$$

where w_1 and w_2 are the percentages of the portfolio invested in securities 1 and 2, respectively. The sum of the asset weights equals one because of the following budget constraint:

$$(\text{\# units of } 1)(P_1) + (\text{\# units of } 2)(P_2) = \text{total portfolio value} \tag{2.11}$$

where P_1 and P_2 are the respective asset prices. The percentage of the portfolio that is invested in each security (the weights) is derived by dividing all terms of equation 2.11 by the total portfolio value. The weights sum to one.

Since the expected value of the sum of two random variables (returns in this case) is equal to the sum of the expected values of each random variable, equation 2.11 can be expressed as follows:

$$E(r_P) = E(w_1 r_1) + E(w_2 r_2) \tag{2.12}$$

Furthermore, the expected value of a constant times an expected value is the constant multiplied by the expected value. Therefore, since the weights represent constants, equation 2.12 can be simplified:

$$E(r_P) = w_1\, E(r_1) + w_2\, E(r_2). \tag{2.13}$$

Therefore, the expected return for a portfolio consisting of N assets is given by

(2.14) $$E(r_P) = w_1 \, E(r_1) + w_2 \, E(r_2) + \ldots + w_N \, E(r_N)$$

Thus, the expected return of a portfolio is simply a weighted average of the expected returns of the component securities. To illustrate the calculation of the expected return, assume that an investor holds a portfolio of two securities. The investor, with total wealth of $10,000, buys shares of security 1 for $7,000 and puts the remaining amount, $3,000, in asset 2. The investor expects asset 1 to produce a return of 18% over the next year and security 2 to produce a 12% return. Given this information, the expected portfolio return is[5]

$$\left[\frac{\$7,000}{\$10,000} \times 18\% \right] + \left[\frac{\$3,000}{\$10,000} \times 12\% \right] = 16.2\%.$$

Short Selling

In the previous example the two weights are positive because the investor purchased the assets in the hope of selling them at a higher price. This is a *long position*. However, it is possible for an investor to pursue the opposite strategy, borrowing shares from a broker, selling them at the prevailing market price, and buying the shares back later, hopefully at a lower price. Here the profit per share is the selling price minus the purchase price. This strategy is known as *short selling* or a *short position*. Short selling can be represented by a negative weight, $w_i < 0$.

Assume that a friend owns ten ounces of gold. You believe that the price of gold will decrease from its present level, say $400. To profit from this belief you borrow the ten ounces and sell the gold for $400 per ounce. You invest the money in other financial assets. Two months later, as anticipated, the price of gold has decreased to $380. You purchase ten ounces of gold at the prevailing market price, using funds from the initial sale, and return the gold to your friend. The profit on the short

---

[5] We can also calculate the expected return in dollar terms. The expected dollar return for asset 1 is $7,000 × 18% = $1260 and $3,000 × 12% = $360 for asset 2. The expected total dollar return for the portfolio is the sum of the individual investment returns, $1260 + $360 = $1620. The general formula for the dollar return for a two asset portfolio is

$$\text{dollar return} = (\$ \text{ in stock } 1)E(r_1) + (\$ \text{ in stock } 2)E(r_2)$$

The percentage return on the initial wealth, $10,000, can be obtained by dividing the dollar return by $10,000.

$$\frac{\$1,620}{\$10,000} = \left[\frac{\$7,000}{\$10,000} \times 18\% \right] + \left[\frac{\$3,000}{\$10,000} \times 12\% \right] = 16.2\%.$$

selling of the gold is $20 an ounce in addition to earnings on the interim investment.

While the minimum return for a long position is −100%, losses are unlimited for a short seller. If you buy gold for $400, the most that you can lose is $400 if the price decreases to zero. However, losses are unlimited for the short seller because the asset price can increase without limit. In this example, if the gold is shorted for $400 an ounce and the price increases to $1,000, the percentage return is ($400 − $1,000) ÷ $400 = −150% for the period.

In this simplified example the investor could invest the proceeds from the short sale in other financial assets. In reality, only large financial institutions can invest the proceeds. Small investors pursuing this strategy must set aside proceeds from the sale and post additional money as a margin.[6,7]

Let's return to the example in which the investor has $10,000 and the expected returns are 18% and 12% for securities 1 and 2, respectively. Suppose that the investor shorts $3,000 of asset 2. This leaves $13,000 for the purchase of security 1 ($10,000 initial capital plus $3,000 short sale proceeds). Thus, the weight of security 1 is $13,000 ÷ $10,000 = 1.30. Since the investor sells $3,000 of asset 2, the weight is −$3,000 ÷ $10,000 = −.30. The weights sum to 1, satisfying the budget constraint. The expected return of this portfolio is $E(r_p) = (1.30 \times 18\%) + (−.30 \times 12\%) = 19.8\%$.

To summarize, the expected return of a portfolio is a weighted average of the expected values of the component assets. A long position is represented by a positive weight and a short sale by a negative weight. The sum of the weights must equal one.

Variance of a Portfolio

At first glance calculating the variance of a portfolio seems easy: simply calculate a weighted average of the component security variances. However, this method is incorrect because it omits the interaction of the securities in the portfolio. As will be demonstrated in Chapter 3, one of the tenets of contemporary portfolio theory is that the risk of the portfolio is commonly less than the risk of any of the component assets, provided that they are not perfectly positively correlated.

---

[6] The margin that is required for retail equity investors is 50% of the total value of the transaction. For example, on a short sale of $10,000, $5,000 of the investor's money must be kept in the account in addition to the $10,000 from the sale. Whether the investor earns interest on the $15,000 depends on his or her relationship with the broker. Large retail investors can sometimes earn interest (usually at the broker's call rate), while small investors usually do not.

[7] Dividends declared to stockholders of record during the time of the short sale belong to the registered owner of the shares. Since the lender of the shares does not technically own shares, the borrower of the shares must pay an amount equal to the dividends to the original owner from his or her account.

THE FATHER OF PORTFOLIO THEORY

B efore the work of Harry Markowitz the field of investments focused on valuing individual securities, primarily through the use of balance sheets and income statements. Ad hoc accounting rules, many outlined in Benjamin Graham's and William Dodd's book *Security Analysis*, were designed to identify securities that were temporarily selling below or above intrinsic (book) value.

Markowitz changed the field's focus to an analysis of portfolios of assets in his 1952 paper "Portfolio Selection," published in the *Journal of Finance*. Rather than using accounting information, Markowitz employed a statistical approach to measure the risk and return of portfolios. The major result of this work is that a rational investor will diversify because a portfolio of assets will have less risk than any of the component securities, provided that the assets are less than perfectly positively correlated. His approach also allowed investors to calculate a series of efficient portfolios, each having the highest expected return for a given level of risk. (This will be discussed in Chapter 3.)

Markowitz is currently the Marvin Speiser Distinguished Professor of Finance and Economics at Baruch College, CUNY, and director of research for DAIWA Security Trust Company.

In addition to teaching, he helped develop computer languages at the RAND Corporation and IBM, worked with General Electric to solve manufacturing problems using computer simulations, and managed portfolios.

For his contributions to the field of finance, Markowitz won the 1990 Nobel Prize for economics. His Nobel Memorial Prize lecture, presented at the Royal Swedish Academy of Sciences in Stockholm in December 1990, appears in the June 1991 issue of the *Journal of Finance*.

Before deriving the variance of a portfolio, we will illustrate the risk reduction properties of diversification through a simple example.[8] Suppose that an island economy (i.e., closed) has only two industries, a resort and a local retailer of umbrellas. The resort suffers during a rainy year while the umbrella retailer thrives. The resort is very profitable during dry years while sales plummet for the umbrella firm. The probability is 50% for a rainy year and 50% for a dry year. Further, if the year is dry the resort stock price will increase by 60% while the umbrella retailer's stock price will suffer a decline of 30%. During a rainy year the returns are reversed, up 60% for the umbrella firm and down 30% for the resort.

		RETURNS	
	PROBABILITY	RESORT	UMBRELLA RETAILER
Rainy year	.50	−30%	60%
Dry year	.50	60	−30

---

[8] This example is from Malkiel (1990).

For a resort investor the expected return is $(.50 \times -30\%) + (.5 \times 60\%)$ $= 15\%$. The expected return for the umbrella company investor is the same. It should be obvious that the risks of investing in the stocks are substantial. A \$100 investment in resorts will suffer a loss of \$65.70 if three consecutive rainy years occur.[9] However, the risk is reduced substantially through diversification. Suppose that the investor buys \$50 of resort stock and \$50 of the umbrella stock. During a rainy year the profit on the umbrella firm is \$30 ($\$50 \times 1.60 - \$50$) and the loss on the resort stock is \$15 ($\$50 \times .70 - \$50$) for a total profit of \$15 and a total return of 15\%. The same result holds during a dry year.

The risk is great when the stocks are held in isolation. However, risk (return dispersion) is completely eliminated when the stocks are held as a portfolio consisting of 50\% of the resort stock and 50\% of the umbrella retailer. The elimination of risk is due to the fact that the firms respond differently to the weather, so the correlation between the returns is low. As long as the fortunes of firms are not highly correlated, diversification reduces risk.

Now assume that a tennis racket retailer opens on the island and sells shares to the public. Would an investment in this firm reduce risk? Probably not, because returns on the resort and the tennis racket retailer respond in a similar way to the weather. Rain will result in low sales for both the resort and racket firms. Similarly, an investment in a raincoat retailer would not reduce risk because of its high correlation with the umbrella firm.

In reality it is not possible to find companies that are perfectly negatively correlated. Stock prices generally respond to common factors such as interest rates, currency changes, and election results. Thus there is a positive correlation among the business fortunes of most firms. However, because this correlation is not perfect, diversification still reduces risk.

This example shows that the computation of the risk of a portfolio is more complicated than the computation of its expected return because the interaction among securities must be considered.

The *variance of a portfolio*, σ_P^2, is the expected value of the squared deviations of the returns for the portfolio from its mean return. The variance of a two-stock portfolio is given by equation 2.15, where $r_{1,i}$ is the return for security 1 in state i, $r_{2,i}$ is the return for asset 2 in state i with a corresponding probability of p_i, and $r_{P,i}$ is the return of the portfolio in state i.

(2.15) $\sigma_P^2 = E[r_{P,i} - E(r_P)]^2 = \sum_{i=1}^{N} p_i\{[w_1 r_{1,i} + w_2 r_{2,i}] - [w_1 E(r_1) + w_2 E(r_2)]\}^2.$

---

[9] The probability of three rainy years in a row is $(.5)^3 = .125$.

Grouping terms for the individual securities and factoring out the weights yields:

(2.16)
$$\sigma_P{}^2 = \sum_{i=1}^{N} p_i \Big(\{w_1[r_{1,i} - E(r_1)]\} + \{w_2[r_{2,i} - E(r_2)]\} \Big)^2$$

and multiplying through we obtain:

(2.17)
$$\sigma_P{}^2 = \sum_{i=1}^{N} p_i \Big(\{w_1{}^2[r_{1,i} - E(r_1)]^2\} + \{w_2{}^2[r_{2,i} - E(r_2)]^2$$
$$+ 2w_1 w_2 [r_{1,i} - E(r_1)][r_{2,i} - E(r_2)]\} \Big)$$

Apply two expected value rules: (1) The expected value of a sum is the sum of the expected values. (2) The expected value of a constant times a random variable equals the constant times the expected value of the random variable. This yields

(2.18)
$$\sigma_P{}^2 = w_1{}^2 \sum_{i=1}^{N} p_i [r_{1,i} - E(r_1)]^2 + w_2{}^2 \sum_{i=1}^{N} p_i [r_{2,i} - E(r_2)] +$$
$$2w_1 w_2 \sum_{i=1}^{N} p_i [r_{1,i} - E(r_1)][r_{2,i} - E(r_2)]$$

The first right-hand term of equation 2.18 is the weight of security 1 squared times the variance of the returns of asset 1. The second term is the squared weight of asset 2 multiplied by the variance of security 2. The third term measures the interaction between the two securities. The expression $\sum p_i [r_{1,i} - E(r_1)][r_{2,i} - E(r_2)]$ represents the covariance between the two securities. The *covariance* measures the association between two random variables. Suppose that for a particular state (strong economy for example) high returns for asset 1 are associated with high returns for asset 2. In that case $[r_{1,i} - E(r_1)]$ and $[r_{2,i} - E(r_1)]$ will both be positive, and thus the product will also be positive. When the economy is weak, both terms will be negative, and the product will be positive.

On the other hand, a negative covariance indicates that the two assets are inversely related. The term $[r_{1,i} - E(r_1)]$ will be positive when $[r_{2,i} - E(r_2)]$ is negative, and vice versa, leading to a negative covariance. This was the case in our resort example. We can restate the two-security portfolio variance (equation 2.18) as

(2.19)
$$\sigma_P{}^2 = w_1{}^2 \, \sigma_1{}^2 + w_2{}^2 \, \sigma_2{}^2 + 2w_1 w_2 \, COV(r_1, r_2)$$

where $COV(r_1, r_2)$ is the covariance between the returns of securities 1 and 2.

It is sometimes helpful to standardize the covariance. The *correlation coefficient*, which measures the strength of association between two random variables, can be obtained by dividing by the covariance by the product of the two standard deviations:

(2.20)
$$\rho_{1,2} = \frac{COV(r_1, r_2)}{\sigma_1 \sigma_2},$$

where $\rho_{1,2}$ is the correlation coefficient between random variables 1 and 2. The correlation coefficient ranges between -1 and 1, with a correlation of 1 implying perfect positive correlation and -1 implying that the returns are perfectly negatively correlated. Equation 2.19, the portfolio variance for two assets, can now be restated as follows:

(2.21)
$$\sigma_P^2 = w_1^2 \sigma_1^2 + w_2^2 \sigma_2^2 + 2w_1 w_2 \rho_{1,2} \sigma_1 \sigma_2.$$

In a previous example in this chapter, the expected return for security 1 was 7.5% with a variance of 118.75%, and asset 2 had an expected return of 10% with a variance of 375.3%. Assume that the investor holds a portfolio consisting of 50% in asset 1 and 50% in security 2. The covariance between the assets will be high, as both are expected to suffer during recessions and prosper during booms. The covariance is

$$COV(r_1, r_2) = (-10 - 7.5)(-20 - 10)\,.25 +$$
$$(10 - 7.5)(15 - 10)\,.50 +$$
$$(20 - 7.5)(30 - 10)\,.25 = 200.$$

The correlation coefficient is found by dividing the covariance by the product of the standard deviations of the two assets: $200 \div (10.90)(18.37) = .999$. The portfolio variance is

$$\sigma_P^2 = .5^2\,(118.75) + .5^2\,(375.3) + 2\,(.5)(.5)\,(200) = 223.52 = 14.95\%$$

Notice that the standard deviation of the portfolio is greater than the standard deviation of asset 1 and less than that of asset 2. Note that if the correlation between the two securities were lower, the portfolio risk would be lower. We will see in Chapter 3 that if the correlation is low, the portfolio risk can be lower than the risk of either individual asset.

Portfolio Variance with Three Assets

The variance of a three-security portfolio is[10]

(2.22)
$$\sigma_p^2 = w_1^2\,\sigma_1^2 + w_2^2\,\sigma_2^2 + w_3^2\,\sigma_3^2 + 2w_1w_2\,COV(r_1,r_2)$$
$$+ 2w_1w_3\,COV(r_1,r_3) + 2w_2w_3\,COV(r_2,r_3).$$

More simply, the variance of a three-security portfolio is

(2.23)
$$\sigma_p^2 = \sum_{i=1}^{3}\sum_{j=1}^{3} w_i w_j COV(r_i, r_j).$$

This is a double summation. The i index starts and remains at 1 as the j index changes from 1 to 3. Then the i index changes to 2 and the j index again varies from 1 to 3. This process continues until the i index arrives at the final index number (3 in this case). Equation 2.23 yields the following:

---

[10] As in the previous derivation, we want the expected value of the squared deviations of the portfolio returns from the mean portfolio return.

$$E[r_{P,i} - E(r_P)]^2 = \sum_{i=1}^{N} p_i\{(w_1 r_{1,i} + w_2 r_{2,i} + w_3 r_{3,i}) - [w_1 E(r_1) + w_2 E(r_2) + w_3 E(r_3)]\}^2$$

Grouping terms for the individual stocks and factoring out the weights yields

$$\sigma_P^2 = \sum_{i=1}^{N} p_i [w_1(r_{1,i} - E(r_1)) + w_2(r_{2,i} - E(r_2)) + w_3(r_{3,i} - E(r_3))]^2$$

and multiplying through we obtain:

$$\sigma_P^2 = \sum_{i=1}^{N} p_i\Big(\{w_1^2[r_{1,i} - E(r_1)]^2\} + \{w_2^2[r_{2,i} - E(r_2)]^2\}$$
$$+ \{w_3^2[r_{3,i} - E(r_3)]^2\} + 2w_1w_2\,[r_{1,i} - E(r_1)][r_{2,i} - E(r_2)]$$
$$+ 2w_1w_3\,[r_{1,i} - E(r_1)][r_{3,i} - E(r_3)] + 2w_2w_3\,[r_{2,i} - E(r_2)][r_{3,i} - E(r_3)]\Big)$$

Applying two expected value rules gives

$$\sigma_P^2 = w_1^2\sum_{i=1}^{N} p_i[r_{1,i} - E(r_1)^2] + w_2^2\sum_{i=1}^{N} p_i[r_{2,i} - E(r_2)] + w_3^2\sum_{i=1}^{N} p_i[r_{3,i} - E(r_3)]$$
$$+ 2w_1w_2\sum_{i=1}^{N} p_i[r_{1,i} - E(r_1)][r_{2,i} - E(r_2)] + 2w_1w_3\sum_{i=1}^{N} p_i[r_{1,i} - E(r_1)][r_{3,i} - E(r_3)]$$
$$+ 2w_2w_3\sum_{i=1}^{N} p_i[r_{2,i} - E(r_2)][r_{3,i} - E(r_3)]$$

Simplifying further, we obtain equation 2.22.

$$w_1 w_1 \, COV(r_1, r_1) + w_1 w_2 \, COV(r_1, r_2) + w_1 w_3 \, COV(r_1, r_3)$$
$$+ \, w_2 w_1 \, COV(r_2, r_1) + w_2 w_2 \, COV(r_2, r_2) + w_2 w_3 \, COV(r_2, r_3)$$
$$+ \, w_3 w_1 \, COV(r_3, r_1) + w_3 w_2 \, COV(r_3, r_2) + w_3 w_3 \, COV(r_3, r_3).$$

This result collapses to equation 2.22 because the covariance between a return and itself is the variance of the returns.

The portfolio variance formula extends to any number of assets. Generalizing, the variance formula for a portfolio consisting of N assets is

(2.24)
$$\sigma_P^2 = \sum_{i=1}^{N} \sum_{j=1}^{N} w_i w_j COV(r_i, r_j).$$

OPPORTUNITY SETS

In the simplified two-period model of investment choice under certainty introduced in Chapter 1, the choice variable facing the investor was the number of dollars to spend in the current period. Although an infinite number of consumption patterns were available, graphic inspection of the corresponding linear opportunity set quickly summarized the consumption streams (opportunity sets) available to the investor. In the model of financial choice under outcome uncertainty, the mean and standard deviation of asset returns will summarize the alternatives available to an investor. We could use other, higher-order return distribution measures such as skewness, which assesses the symmetry of the distribution, and kurtosis, which measures the peakedness of the distribution. However, these measures are not necessary if asset returns are normally distributed and/or investors possess quadratic utility functions.[11] The normal probability distribution, which is bell-shaped and symmetric around the mean, plays a central role in statistical inference. Many natural phenomena, such as performance on standardized tests and the height of people, generate random variables with probability distributions that are approximated by a normal distribution. The normal distribution is not a single distribution but a family of distributions with different specifications of the mean and standard deviation. Because the mean and standard deviation perfectly describe a normal distribution, higher moments such as the skewness and kurtosis are not necessary. Since the normal distribution is so common, normal probability tables that approximate the area under the distribution associated with various deviations from the mean are available.[12] The

---

[11] Chapter 7 shows that investors who possess quadratic utility functions only utilize the mean and dispersion of the return distribution when selecting the optimal portfolio.

[12] From these tables we know that 68.26% of observations generated by a normal distribution will fall within one standard deviation from the mean and 95.44% of the observations will be between two standard deviations. For example, if it is assumed that IBM's yearly returns are normally distributed with a mean return of 10% with a standard deviation of 20%, there is a 68.26% chance that the yearly return will fall between −10% and 30%.

assumption of normality of returns greatly simplifies the asset allocation process and allows for graphical inspection of the opportunity set in a standard deviation–return space.

To illustrate the concept of the opportunity set under risk, assume that an investor is considering purchasing IBM, GM, and JP Morgan stock. The expected returns and standard deviations for the three risky assets are as follows:

	EXPECTED RETURN	STANDARD DEVIATION
IBM	18%	35%
GM	15	30
JP Morgan	12	25

The point marked IBM at the upper right portion of Figure 2.5 represents the risk and return combination of a fully invested position in IBM, and the points below and to the left depict the characteristics of GM and JP Morgan. A portfolio that is 33% invested each of the three stocks will have an expected return of 15% with a standard deviation of 17.31% (point *A* in Figure 2.5), assuming that the correlation between returns is zero. However, an investor is not restricted to these four portfolios; in reality, an infinite number of portfolios can be obtained by assigning different weights to the three risky stocks in the investment opportunity set. Because of the limitless number of possibilities, it would seem that selecting an optimal portfolio is an impossible task. However, Chapter 3 shows that many inferior portfolios can be eliminated, leaving a manageable set of superior portfolios. The key point of this chapter is that the risk and return of portfolios can be quantified using equations 2.14 and 2.24. No other information is necessary to summarize the investment choices available to the investor.

FIGURE 2.5

Opportunity Set for Three Equities and an Equally Weighted Portfolio of the Three Equities

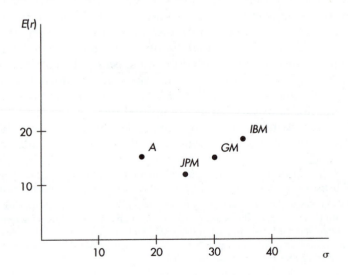

Questions and Problems

1. For a series of one-year holding period returns, what is the difference be-tween calculating the average return using the arithmetic and geometric methods? What are some problems with the arithmetic method?

2. Explain why the arithmetic annual mean returns for risky assets are always larger than the geometric mean returns in Exhibit 2.1.

3. Why must concepts from probability theory be used to analyze investment performance for risky assets? Why was probability theory not used when we analyzed the performance of risk-free assets in Chapter 1?

4. Investors enjoy returns with positive deviations from the mean and suffer from negative deviations. Why is the variance commonly used as a mea-sure of risk, as it weights both positive and negative deviations equally? Would another measure of risk, which only considers negative deviations from the mean of a risky asset, produce a superior measure of asset risk?

5. Suppose that an investor with $20,000 invests $14,000 in asset 1 and the re-mainder in security 2. What are the weights of the two assets?

6. Explain the concept of short selling. If an asset is shorted, will it have a positive or negative weight?

7. The portfolio expected return is a weighted average of the expected returns of the component assets. Is the portfolio variance a weighted average of the variances of the assets in the portfolio?

8. Why are the returns of most financial assets positively correlated? Provide examples of assets whose returns are highly positively and highly nega-tively correlated.

9. What is the general formula for the variance of a four-security portfolio?

10. Calculate the expected return and variance for the following asset:

RETURN	PROBABILITY
−30%	.05
0	.40
10	.40
30	.10
40	.05

11. The expected returns and variances for three assets are

ASSET	EXPECTED RETURN	VARIANCE
1	10%	.04
2	15	.09
3	17	.25

The correlations between the returns are $\rho_{12} = .20$, $\rho_{13} = .50$, $\rho_{23} = .30$. Calcu-late the portfolio expected return if the weight of asset 1 is .25 and asset 2, .60. Draw a graph of the opportunity set for these four portfolios in a standard deviation, expected return space.

SUMMARY

The existence of outcome uncertainty, or risk, implies that investors can no longer assign a specific payoff to an asset, as was done in Chapter 1 when we examined the theory of choice under certainty. Instead, the opportunity set must be characterized by risky assets whose payoffs are represented by a return distribution. Two important summary measures of a return distribution are its expected return or mean, a measure of central tendency, and its variance, a measure of the propensity of asset returns to deviate from the expected value.

The expected value of an individual security can be found by using subjective probability or by sampling previous returns. Using subjective probability, returns and probabilities for important states of nature (such as the health of the economy) are estimated. The security's expected value is a weighted average of the probabilities and the associated returns. Using sampled returns, the security's expected value is the sample's arithmetic average. Measures of return dispersion such as variance serve as an accepted proxy for security risk. The variance is the average of the squared deviations from the mean or expected value.

Based on these measures and security weights, the risk and return of a portfolio can be estimated. The portfolio's expected return is simply the weighted average of the component securities' expected returns. The portfolio's variance is more complicated because it depends on how the component securities covary over time.

Chapter 3 continues to explore the relation between risk and return for portfolios. With the expected return and risk measures defined in this chapter, we derive the minimum variance set, which is the opportunity set that exhibits the least risk for a given level of expected value. When this set is combined with a risk-free asset, an optimal portfolio is obtained.

REFERENCES

Fama, E. 1976. *Foundations of finance.* New York: Basic Books.

Ibbotson, R. and R. Sinquefield. 1982. *Stocks, bonds, bills, and inflation: Historical returns.* Charlottesville, Va: Financial Analysts Research Foundation. Updated in 1988 Quarterly Market Reports, Chicago, Ibbotson Associates.

Jones, C. and J. Wilson. 1989. Is stock price volatility increasing? *Financial Analysts Journal* Nov.–Dec., 20–26.

Malkiel, B. 1990. *A random walk down Wall Street.* New York: W. W. Norton.

Markowitz, H. 1952. Portfolio Selection. *Journal of Finance,* Dec., 77–91.

Markowitz, H. 1959. *Portfolio selection. Efficient diversification of investments.* New York: John Wiley & Sons.

Mendenhall, W., R. Scheaffer, and D. Wackerly. 1981. *Mathematical statistics with applications.* Boston: Duxbury Press.

Newbold, P. 1990. *Statistics for business and economics.* Englewood Cliffs, NJ: Prentice Hall.

Self-Test Problems

ST-1. Two assets have the following possible returns and probabilities:

ASSET 1		ASSET 2	
RETURN	PROBABILITY	RETURN	PROBABILITY
−5%	.20	−10%	.20
10	.50	15	.50
20	.30	25	.30

Calculate the portfolio expected return and variance for the weight of asset 1 equal to −2, 0, .25, and .75

ST-2. The monthly returns for two assets are given below:

	PERIOD			
	1	2	3	4
Security 1	3%	−3%	6%	−2%
Security 2	2	1	3	−1

Calculate the expected monthly return and variance for each asset and the covariance and correlation coefficients between the returns of the two assets.

Solutions to Self-Test Problems

ST-1. First calculate the expected returns of the two assets:

$E(r_1) = (.20)(-.05) + (.50)(.10) + (.30)(.20) = .10$
$E(r_2) = (.20)(-.10) + (.50)(.15) + (.30)(.25) = .13$

Calculate the variance and standard deviations of the two assets:

$\sigma_1^2 = (-.05 - .10)^2\ .20 + (.10 - .10)^2\ .50 + (.20 - .10)^2\ .30 = .0075$
$\sigma_1 = .087$
$\sigma_2^2 = (-.10 - .13)^2\ .20 + (.15 - .13)^2\ .50 + (.25 - .13)^2\ .30 = .0151$
$\sigma_2 = .1229$

The covariance between the returns of the two assets is

$COV(r_1,r_2) = (-.05 - .10)(-.10 - .13)\ .20$
$+ (.10 - .10)(.15 - .13)\ .50$
$+ (.20 - .10)(.25 - .13)\ .30 = .0105$

The correlation coefficient is $.0105 \div (.087)(.1229) = .982$.
The portfolio expected return is

$E(r_P) = .10w_1 + .13w_2$

The portfolio variance is

$$\sigma_p^2 = w_1^2 \, .0075 + w_2^2 \, .0151 + 2w_1w_2 \, .0105$$

The portfolio expected return and variance can be obtained for the weights of interest:

w_1	w_2	$E(r_p)$	σ_p^2
−1.00	2.00	0.160	0.02590
0.00	1.00	0.130	0.01510
0.25	0.75	0.123	0.01290
0.75	0.25	0.108	0.00908

ST-2. The expected returns are equal to

$$E(r_1) = (.03 - .03 + .06 - .02) \div 4 = 0.01$$
$$E(r_2) = (.02 + .01 + .03 - .01) \div 4 = 0.0125.$$

The variances are equal to

$$\sigma_1^2 = \frac{(.03 - .01)^2 + (-.03 - .01)^2 + (.06 - .01)^2 + (-.02 - .01)^2}{4 - 1}$$
$$= .0018.$$

$$\sigma_2^2 = \frac{(.02 - .0125)^2 + (.01 - .0125)^2 + (.03 - .0125)^2 + (-.01 - .0125)^2}{4 - 1}$$
$$= .00029.$$

The covariance between the returns of the two assets is

$$COV(r_1,r_2) = (.03 - .01)(.02 - .0125) + (-.03 - .01)(.01 - .0125) +$$
$$(.06 - .01)(.03 - .0125) + (-.02 - .01)(-.01 - .0125) \, / 4 - 1$$
$$= .0006.$$

CHAPTER 3

Efficient Portfolios

Introduction

In Chapter 2 we demonstrated that the opportunity set under uncertainty must be characterized by summary measures from a return distribution. Two important summary measures of a return distribution are its expected return, or mean, a measure of central tendency, and its variance, a measure of the propensity of asset returns to deviate from the expected value. The security's expected value is a weighted average of the probabilities and the associated returns. Measures of return dispersion such as the variance serve as an accepted proxy for security risk.

Based on these measures and security weights, the risk and return of the portfolio can be estimated. The portfolio's expected return is simply the weighted average of the component securities' expected returns. The calculation of the portfolio variance is more complicated because it must consider how the component securities covary over time.

In Chapter 3 we utilize portfolio expected return and risk concepts from Chapter 2 to investigate two important issues. First we examine the effect of diversification on portfolio risk. Second we explore decision rules for identifying superior portfolios available to the investor, given the risk and return characteristics of the component assets in the portfolio. Investors should confine their attention to this set of portfolios, called the efficient frontier, when constructing a portfolio of risky assets. We then examine optimal portfolio construction in the presence of a risk-free asset.

RISK REDUCTION PROPERTIES OF DIVERSIFICATION

In Chapter 2 we found that the expected return of a portfolio of assets is a weighted average of the expected returns of each component asset. Note that since the weights must sum to 1 ($w_1 + w_2 = 1$), we can restate the weight of asset 2 as $w_2 = 1 - w_1$. In the two-security case the expected portfolio return, $E(r_P)$, is

(3.1) $$E(r_P) = w_1 E(r_1) + (1 - w_1) E(r_2),$$

where w_1 and w_2 are the percentage of the portfolio invested in securities 1 and 2, respectively, and $E(r_1)$ and $E(r_2)$ are the expected returns of the two assets.

The portfolio variance is more difficult to calculate, since it must consider not only the component asset return variances but also covariance terms, which provide a measure of the interaction between the assets in the portfolio. The variance of a two-asset portfolio, σ_P^2, is

(3.2) $$\sigma_P^2 = w_1^2 \sigma_1^2 + (1 - w_1)^2 \sigma_2^2 + 2w_1(1 - w_1) \rho_{1,2} \sigma_1 \sigma_2,$$

where $\sigma_1^2, \sigma_2^2, \sigma_1, \sigma_2$ are the respective variances and standard deviations of the two assets and $\rho_{1,2}$ is the correlation coefficient between the returns of the two assets. The correlation coefficient multiplied by the product of the standard deviations is equal to the covariance between the two assets. The correlation coefficient ranges from −1 to 1.

To assess the effectiveness of diversification on portfolio risk, we examine how the portfolio return and its risk change for various degrees of comovement between the returns of the two assets in the portfolio. We consider the following four cases: (1) perfect positive correlation between asset returns, (2) perfect negative correlation between returns, (3) no correlation between returns, and (4) intermediate correlation (correlation coefficient of .5). In reality pairs of distinct assets with perfect positive and negative return correlations do not exist.[1] However, the returns of some assets approximate these extreme situations. Stock prices for firms in the same industry typically respond to the same macroeconomic and political forces such as consumer demand, currency changes, and political policy. Thus, Ford and General Motors equity price changes will be highly but not perfectly positively correlated. Another example of two highly correlated assets is futures contracts on indexes such as the Value Line and the Major

---

[1] An uninteresting case of two perfectly correlated assets is two identical securities, such as two shares of the same stock.

Market Index (MMI).[2] Although the Value Line index is a broad-based measure of equity market performance containing stock prices from more than 1700 U.S. firms and the MMI contains prices from only 20 very large, highly capitalized firms, the correlation coefficient between their futures returns is typically between .90 and .95.

Futures contracts can be used to induce a negative correlation between an asset and a futures contract on that asset. For example, a manager holding a diversified portfolio of equities might sell stock index futures contracts to protect the portfolio from stock price declines. In Chapter 16 we will investigate how a long position in equities combined with a short position in stock index futures will reduce portfolio risk.

An example of asset returns that have a correlation of approximately zero is equity and commodity prices. Expected company profits and the general level of interest rates are major determinants of stock prices, and supply and demand are the main determinants of commodity prices. Because these prices typically do not respond to the same variables, the association between their returns is approximately zero.

Stocks that are not in the same industry typically display intermediate correlation between returns (say .5), as they tend to respond similarly to the same economy-wide factors.

We will investigate how the portfolio return and risk are influenced by different degrees of association between the asset returns using an example of two assets with the following risk and expected return characteristics:

	EXPECTED RETURN	STANDARD DEVIATION
ASSET 1	20%	35%
ASSET 2	10	20

We first examine the portfolio risk and return in the case of perfect positive correlation between the returns, with short selling not allowed. We will investigate the effects of short selling on portfolio risk later in the chapter.

Perfectly Positively Correlated Assets

In the case of perfect positive correlation between asset returns, the two-asset portfolio variance is

(3.3) $$\sigma_P^2 = w_1^2\,\sigma_1^2 + (1-w_1)^2\,\sigma_2^2 + 2w_1(1-w_1)\,\sigma_1\sigma_2.$$

The right-hand side of equation 3.3 is in the form $X^2 + 2XY + Y^2$, which can be factored to $(X + Y)(X + Y)$. Thus we can rewrite equation 3.3 as follows:

(3.4) $$\sigma_P^2 = [w_1\,\sigma_1 + (1-w_1)\,\sigma_2]^2.$$

---

[2] See Chapter 16 for a discussion of futures contracts.

The resulting standard deviation is

$$\sigma_P = w_1\,\sigma_1 + (1 - w_1)\,\sigma_2. \tag{3.5}$$

This expression states that the portfolio standard deviation is a linear combination of the standard deviations of each asset in the portfolio. In our example, $\sigma_P = .35\,w_1 + .20(1 - w_1)$. To prove that the measure is linear, determine how the expected return changes as the portfolio standard deviation changes. From the chain rule of calculus:

$$\frac{dE(r_P)}{d\sigma_P} = \frac{dE(r_P)/dw_1}{d\sigma_P/dw_1} \tag{3.6}$$

The derivative of the expected return (equation 3.1) with respect to a change in the weight of asset 1 is

$$dE(r_P)/dw_1 = E(r_1) - \dot{E}(r_2). \tag{3.7}$$

The derivative of the portfolio standard deviation (equation 3.5) with respect to a change in the weight of asset 1 is

$$d\sigma_P/dw_1 = \sigma_1 - \sigma_2. \tag{3.8}$$

Plugging equations 3.7 and 3.8 into 3.6 gives the following slope:

$$\frac{E(r_1) - E(r_2)}{\sigma_1 - \sigma_2} = \frac{.20 - .10}{.35 - .20} = .67. \tag{3.9}$$

Thus the slope of the line illustrating possible combinations of risk and return in the case of perfectly correlated assets is constant. Risk and expected return characteristics for selected weights are calculated in Exhibit 3.1 and illustrated in Figure 3.1. The key point is that diversification does not reduce risk when the assets are perfectly correlated, because the portfolio standard deviation is simply a weighted average of

EXHIBIT 3.1

Risk and Return Combinations for Two Perfectly Correlated Assets

w_1	$E(r_p)$	σ_p
1.0	20%	35.0%
0.8	18	32.0
0.6	16	29.0
0.5	15	27.5
0.4	14	26.0
0.2	12	23.0
0.0	10	20.0

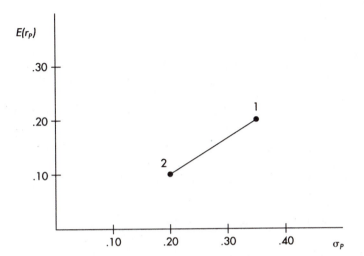

FIGURE 3.1
Risk and Return
Possibilities for Two
Perfectly Correlated
Assets

the standard deviations of the individual assets in the portfolio. This result should make sense intuitively. Because the assets move in tandem, diversification does not reduce portfolio risk.

Minimum-Variance Portfolio

Before discussing the return and risk combinations for assets with perfect negative correlation, we derive portfolio weights that will minimize the risk of a two-asset portfolio. This combination of w_1 and $1 - w_1$ produces the *minimum-variance portfolio* (MVP).[3] The starting point of the derivation of the MVP (given by equation 3.12b) is the general formula for portfolio variance, equation 3.2:

(3.10) $$\sigma_P^2 = w_1^2 \sigma_1^2 + (1 - w_1)^2 \sigma_2^2 + 2w_1(1 - w_1) \rho_{1,2}\sigma_1\sigma_2.$$

We want the weight of asset 1 that minimizes the portfolio variance (this will also minimize the standard deviation, which is the square root of the variance). To accomplish this task, obtain the derivative of the variance with respect to the weight of security 1 and set the resulting derivative to zero:

(3.11) $$\frac{d\sigma_P^2}{dw_1} = 2w_1 \sigma_1^2 - 2 \sigma_2^2 + 2w_1 \sigma_2^2 + 2 \rho_{1,2} \sigma_1 \sigma_2 - 4 w_1 \rho_{1,2} \sigma_1 \sigma_2 = 0.$$

Solving for the weight of asset 1 yields

(3.12a) $$w_1 (\sigma_1^2 + \sigma_2^2 - 2\rho_{1,2} \sigma_1\sigma_2) + \rho_{1,2} \sigma_1 \sigma_2 - \sigma_2^2 = 0, \quad \text{or}$$

---

[3] We derive the MVP for the three-security case in Chapter 4.

(3.12b)
$$w_1 = \frac{\sigma_2^2 - \rho_{1,2}\,\sigma_1\,\sigma_2}{\sigma_1^2 + \sigma_2^2 - 2\,\rho_{1,2}\,\sigma_1\,\sigma_2}.$$

In the case of two perfectly positively correlated assets with short sales not allowed, all funds will be invested in the less risky asset to obtain the minimum-variance portfolio. In this example the minimum-variance portfolio is obtained if all funds are invested in asset 2, the less risky asset.

Perfect Negative Correlation between Asset Returns

The benefits of diversification are easily demonstrated when the correlation between asset returns is equal to −1 because a risk-free portfolio consisting of two risky assets can be formed. The MVP can be simplified when the returns correlation is equal to −1:

(3.13)
$$w_1 = \frac{\sigma_2^2 + \sigma_1\sigma_2}{\sigma_1^2 + \sigma_2^2 + 2\sigma_1\,\sigma_2} = \frac{\sigma_2(\sigma_1 + \sigma_2)}{(\sigma_1 + \sigma_2)\,(\sigma_1 + \sigma_2)}$$
$$= \frac{\sigma_2}{(\sigma_1 + \sigma_2)}.$$

In this example the asset weights that will minimize the portfolio standard deviation are

$$w_1 = \frac{.20}{.35 + .20} = .3636$$

and

$$w_2 = 1 - .3636 = .6364.$$

Note that the greater weight is placed in asset 2, the lower-risk asset. The expected return for this portfolio is

(3.14a)
$$E(r_P) = .20(.3636) + .10(.6364) = .1364,$$

and the variance is

(3.14b) $\sigma_P^2 = (.3636)^2\,.1225 + (.6364)^2\,.04 + 2(.6364)(.3636)(-1)(.20)(.35) = 0.$

This example demonstrates the importance of incorporating the asset return interaction in the calculation of the portfolio risk. Although the portfolio contains two risky assets, a risk-free return of 13.64% is possible if the return correlation is equal to −1 because of the opposite movements of the asset returns. As illustrated in Figure 3.2, which graphs the risk and return combinations calculated in Exhibit 3.2, the risk of some portfolios

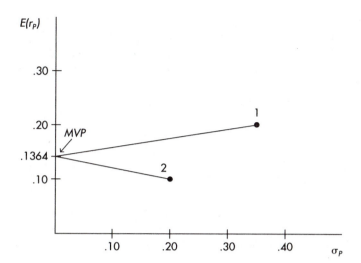

EXHIBIT 3.2

Risk and Return Combinations for Perfectly Inversely Correlated Assets

w_1	$E(r_p)$	σ_p
1.0	20%	35.0%
0.8	18	24.0
0.6	16	13.0
0.5	15	7.5
0.4	.14	2.0
0.2	12	9.0
0.0	10	20.0

is lower than the risk of any of the component assets when held in isolation if the return correlation is equal to −1.

We now investigate the slope of the two lines illustrated in Figure 3.2. The variance of a portfolio of two perfectly inversely related assets is

(3.15) $$\sigma_P^2 = w_1^2 \, \sigma_1^2 + (1 - w_1)^2 \, \sigma_2^2 - 2w_1(1 - w_1) \, \sigma_1 \, \sigma_2,$$

which can be factored as follows:

(3.16a) $$\sigma_P^2 = [w_1 \, \sigma_1 - (1 - w_1) \, \sigma_2]^2$$

or

(3.16b) $$\sigma_P = [w_1 \, \sigma_1 - (1 - w_1) \, \sigma_2]$$

or

$$-[w_1 \, \sigma_1 - (1 - w_1) \, \sigma_2].$$

The standard deviation is $[w_1 \sigma_1 + (1 - w_1) \sigma_2]$ if $w_1 > \sigma_2/(\sigma_1 + \sigma_2)$, which is represented by the line segment from point 1 to MVP in Figure 3.2, and $-[w_1 \sigma_1 + (1 - x_1) \sigma_2]$ if $w_1 < \sigma_2/(\sigma_1 + \sigma_2)$, the line segment MVP to portfolio 2. As in the case of perfect positive correlation, the slope of the line above the MVP is

$$(3.17) \qquad \frac{dE(r_P)}{d\sigma_P} = \frac{dE(r_P)/dw_1}{d\sigma_P/dw_1}$$

The derivative of the expected return (equation 3.1) with respect to a change in the weight of asset 1 is

$$(3.18) \qquad dE(r_P)/dw_1 = E(r_1) - E(r_2).$$

The derivative of the portfolio standard deviation (equation 3.16b) with respect to a change in the weight of asset 1 is

$$(3.19) \qquad d\sigma_P/dw_1 = \sigma_1 + \sigma_2.$$

The slope of the line segment from point 1 to MVP is

$$(3.20) \qquad \frac{E(r_1) - E(r_2)}{\sigma_1 + \sigma_2} = \frac{.20 - .10}{.35 + .20} = .182.$$

Using a similar procedure, the slope of the segment from point MVP to point 2 is

$$(3.21) \qquad \frac{E(r_1) - E(r_2)}{-(\sigma_1 + \sigma_2)} = \frac{.20 - .10}{-(.35 + .20)} = -.182.$$

Both line segments are linear.

No Correlation and Intermediate Positive Correlation between Asset Returns

Figure 3.3 displays the risk-return combinations (computed in Exhibit 3.3) for perfectly positively and negatively correlated assets. A return correlation between these two extremes will produce an intermediate curve such as curve *D*.

Specifically, assume that the correlation between asset returns is equal to 0, which implies no systematic relation between the returns. In this case the MVP simplifies:

$$(3.22) \qquad w_1 = \frac{\sigma_2^2}{\sigma_1^2 + \sigma_2^2}$$

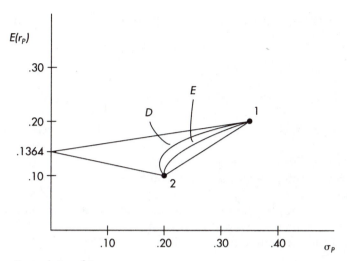

FIGURE 3.3

Risk and Return
Possibilities for Asset
Correlations of −1, 0,
.5, and 1

D-correlation of 0
E-correlation of .5

EXHIBIT 3.3

Risk and Return Combinations for Return Correlations of 0 and .5

w_1	$E(r_p)$	σ_p CORR = 0	σ_p CORR = .5
1.0	20%	35.00%	35.00%
0.8	18	28.28	30.20
0.6	16	22.47	25.94
0.5	15	20.16	24.11
0.4	14	18.44	22.54
0.2	12	17.46	20.42
0.0	10	20.00	20.00

The MVP in our example is $.0400 \div (.04 + .1225) = .246$. The expected return
of this portfolio is:

$$E(r_P) = .20(.246) + .10(.754) = .1246.$$

Variance and standard deviation are:

$$\sigma_P{}^2 = (.246)^2 .1225 + (.754)^2 .04 = .030.$$

$$\sigma_P = .1736.$$

Curve D illustrates the possible risk and return combinations in the case
of a correlation coefficient of zero.

Now assume a correlation of .57. The MVP is

$$w_1 = \frac{.04 - (.20)(.35)(.57)}{(.1225) + (.04) - (2)(.35)(.20)(.57)} = 0.$$

When the correlation is .57, there exist no combinations of the two securities that will be less risky than security 2 (the less risky asset). In general there will always be a correlation in which the combination of assets will not be less risky than the less risky asset.

Figure 3.3 shows the risk-return trade-off for the four cases. Diversification is more effective if the correlation is −1. However, diversification is still successful at lowering risk if the correlation between assets is higher, say .5. For example, the risk of owning an equally weighted portfolio (weight of .5 for both securities) with a correlation of 1 is 27.5% versus 24.11% if the correlation is .5 (Exhibits 3.1 and 3.3).

Opportunity Set with Short Selling

In the absence of short selling, the portfolio standard deviation decreases as the return correlation decreases; in the case of perfect negative correlation between asset returns, portfolio risk can be eliminated because of the opposite price movements. However, if one of two negatively correlated assets is sold short, the result is an increase in portfolio risk. For illustration assume that two perfectly negatively correlated securities in a portfolio have weights of 2 and −1. Suppose that price of asset 1 (with a weight of 2) increases substantially over the next quarter, resulting in a capital gain. Because of the perfect negative correlation between the assets, security 2 has declined in value. However, the investor will also realize a capital gain on this security because of its short position. If the positively weighted asset had declined in value, losses would have resulted for both securities. Thus, the risk of holding long and short positions of two perfectly negatively correlated assets is substantial because of their common price movements. Exhibit 3.4 further illustrates this aspect of short selling, presenting portfolio standard deviations and expected

EXHIBIT 3.4

Risk and Return Possibilities for Two Assets with Short Sales Allowed

w_1	w_2	$E(r_p)$	σ_p CORR = 1	σ_p CORR = −1
2.00	−1.00	30.0%	50.00%	90.00%
1.50	−0.50	25.0	42.50	62.50
1.25	−0.25	22.5	38.75	48.75
−0.25	1.25	7.5	16.25	33.75
−0.50	1.50	5.0	12.50	47.50
−1.00	2.00	0.0	5.00	75.00

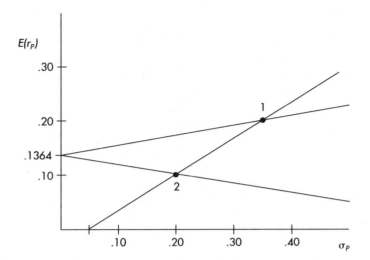

FIGURE 3.4

Risk and Return
Possibilities for
Perfectly Positively
and Negatively
Correlated Assets:
Short Sales Allowed

returns for various weighting schemes; these portfolios are plotted in Figure 3.4.

Short selling may increase or reduce the portfolio standard deviation if the assets are perfectly positively correlated. To illustrate we investigate two cases using the expected returns and standard deviations for the two assets introduced at the beginning of this chapter. In the first case, suppose the investor shorts $1,000 of the less risky asset, 2, and uses the proceeds, along with initial wealth of $1,000, to purchase $2,000 of security 1, resulting in weights of 2 and −1, respectively. The expected return of security 1 will double to 40% because the weight of asset 1 is equal to 2. Because asset 2 is shorted, the financing cost will be −10%, and the total expected return from this strategy is 30%.

Equation 3.5 presents the standard deviation of a perfectly correlated portfolio of assets. In this example the standard deviation of the portfolio is 35% × 2 − 20% = 50%.

In the second case the investor sells asset 1 and purchases the less risky security 2. When asset returns are perfectly positively correlated, it is reasonable to expect lower risk from selling asset 1 and buying security 2, the less risky asset. The expected return of stock 2 is the weight times the expected return, 2 × 10% = 20%. The financing cost is the expected return of security 1, −20%. Thus the expected return of the portfolio is 0% and the standard deviation is 20% × 2 − 35% = 5%. Figure 3.4 illustrates the possible risk and return combinations when short selling is allowed.

Therefore, if two assets are purchased (positive weights), portfolio risk is minimized when the asset correlation is equal to −1. The interaction term of equation 3.2 is negative because of the negative correlation, reducing portfolio risk. On the other hand, the risk is greater when an asset is shorted and the correlation is −1. The negative correlation coefficient is

COMMODITY FUTURES AS A DISTINCT ASSET CLASS

With over $7 trillion in assets, U.S. pension fund managers are searching for new methods of asset allocation consistent with risk diversification. These managers are examining the role of commodity futures as part of an aggregate portfolio of equities, bonds and Treasury bills. It appears that including commodity futures in a portfolio of financial assets is imprudent because of the risky nature of commodity futures. However, these instruments constitute a distinct asset class because of the low correlation between commodity performance and financial instrument returns. Thus, a portfolio consisting of financial assets and commodity futures could dominate (in a mean-variance sense) a portfolio strictly consisting of only financial assets.

Empirical research has expounded the benefits of diversification in commodity futures. In one of the first studies to compare the performance of commodity futures and financial asset returns, Bodie and Rosansky (1980) found that the mean return of a well diversified portfolio of commodity futures contracts over the period 1950–1976 was greater than the average risk-free interest rate. In addition, they found that a portfolio consisting of equities represented by the SP500 was not efficient. Including commodity futures would have produced a portfolio with a higher return and lower variance over this period.

As reported in the September 1989 issue of the New York Futures Exchange *NYFELine*, the Eastman Kodak Corporation pension fund has implemented these diversification concepts by investing in commodity futures as a part of its portfolio strategy. This $6.1 billion pension fund has dedicated approximately $50 million to a managed futures program, managed by Mount Lucas Investment Corporation.

multiplied by one positive weight and one negative weight, resulting in a positive interaction term and a higher portfolio variance.

OPTIMAL PORTFOLIO SELECTION

Having demonstrated that diversification gains effectiveness as the correlation between assets decreases, we turn our attention to the problem of optimal portfolio selection. Even with only a few securities an unlimited number of portfolios are available to an investor. Some portfolios are superior to others, and rational investors will restrict their attention to this set of optimal portfolios. We first discuss decision rules for selecting the set of optimal portfolios and properties of these portfolios. We then discuss optimal portfolio selection in the presence of a risk-free asset.

The Mean-Variance Rule and the Minimum-Variance Set

A popular decision rule developed for evaluating risky investment alternatives is the mean-variance rule, or the E-V rule (Markowitz, 1952). To evaluate risky alternatives in a mean and variance (or standard deviation) space, assume that asset returns are normally distributed, which implies that the mean and variance provide all relevant information about a risky asset. Alternatively, assume that investors possess quadratic utility functions (Chapter 7).

The E-V rule states that portfolio A is preferred to or *dominates* portfolio B if (1) the expected return of portfolio A is greater than or equal to the expected return of portfolio B *and* the variance (or standard deviation) of A is less than the variance of returns for portfolio B, or (2) the expected return of portfolio A is greater than the expected return of B and the variance of portfolio A is less than or equal to the variance of B. In symbols portfolio A is preferred to B by the E-V rule if

(3.23)
$$(1)\ E(r_A) \geq E(r_B)\ \text{and}\ \sigma_A^2 < \sigma_B^2.$$
$$(2)\ E(r_A) > E(r_B)\ \text{and}\ \sigma_A^2 \leq \sigma_B^2.$$

Figure 3.5 illustrates a set of investment opportunities. The investor can select any portfolio on or inside the hyperbola. Using the first E-V rule, portfolio K dominates portfolio L because K has a lower standard deviation for a given level of return. Therefore, rational investors will only select portfolios on the minimum-variance set. The *minimum-variance set* is a locus of risk and return combinations that minimizes the portfolio standard deviation for a given level of return. For assets that are not perfectly correlated, the curve above the MVP is concave and the part below the MVP is convex.[4]

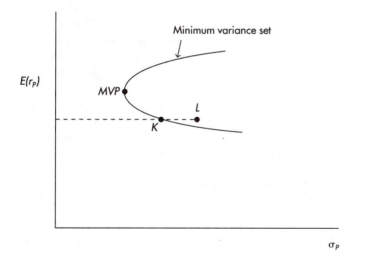

FIGURE 3.5

The Minimum Variance Set

[4] A curve is *concave* if we pick any pair of points F and G, join them by a straight line, and the line segment FG lies entirely below the curve (except at points F and G). If the curve is *convex*, the line segment will lie above the curve.

FIGURE 3.6

The Efficient
Frontier

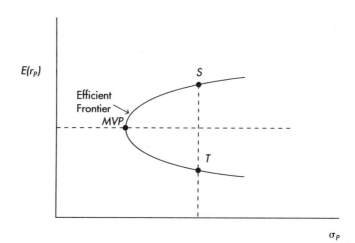

The Efficient Frontier

The minimum-variance set can be divided at the MVP into a top and lower half. The second E-V rule eliminates from consideration portfolios below the MVP. Investors prefer portfolios on the top half, called the *efficient frontier* because the return is greater for a given level of risk. In Figure 3.6 an investor prefers portfolio S to T because S has a greater return for the same level of risk. While both portfolios are on the minimum variance set, only S meets the criterion for the efficient frontier.

A rational investor will select an *efficient portfolio,* which is a portfolio on the efficient frontier. In the absence of a risk-free asset, individual preferences regarding risk and return determine the optimal portfolio. An extremely risk-averse investor will select a portfolio close to or on the MVP, while a more adventurous investor will select a portfolio with greater risk and return. Utility functions and indifference curves, discussed in Chapter 7, allow more systematic examination of the concept of optimal portfolio formulation. For now the important point is that the interaction between the efficient frontier and the individual's preferences for risk and return determine the optimal portfolio when a risk-free asset is not available.[5]

---

[5] The optimal portfolio formation problem is similar to the consumer choice problem in microeconomics. Consumers maximize their utility (satisfaction) subject to their budget constraint, which is determined by the individual's income and prices of goods. In a similar fashion, investors maximize utility subject to their constraint, the efficient frontier. We examine this problem in detail in Chapter 7.

The Efficient Frontier with Three Risky Assets

The minimum variance set will have the same hyperbolic shape with three or more assets as it did with two assets.[6] With two assets, risk and return characteristics of the individual securities are always included in the minimum variance set; however, with more than two assets, these points could fall inside the minimum-variance set. To illustrate the shape of the efficient frontier with three assets, consider the same two assets from the first part of this chapter, with expected returns of 20% and 10% for assets 1 and 2, respectively, and corresponding standard deviations of 35% and 20%. We now add a third risky asset with an expected return of 15% and a standard deviation of 25%.

Exhibit 3.5 presents assorted efficient portfolios (using techniques described in Chapter 4 for determining efficient portfolios), assuming a correlation of 0 between all asset returns. When held in isolation, security 1 has an expected return of 20% with a standard deviation of 35%. However, this portfolio is dominated by portfolio 8, which has approximately the same risk but a higher expected return, 21.69%. Asset 2 is dominated by portfolio 2, and security 3 is dominated by portfolio 5. This demonstrates that in a three-security portfolio the individual securities can lie inside the minimum variance set. That is, the expected return–standard deviation coordinates of the individual securities do not represent the coordinates of any portfolio on the minimum variance set.

We now turn our attention to optimal portfolio selection in the presence of a risk-free asset.

EXHIBIT 3.5

Efficient Portfolios

Portfolio	$E(r_p)$	σ_p	w_1	w_2	w_3
MVP	13.29%	14.26%	0.1660	0.5085	0.3254
1	16.54	18.91	0.4260	0.1186	0.4554
2	16.97	20.02	0.4630	0.0671	0.4726
3	17.53	21.58	0.5051	0.0000	0.4949
4	18.29	23.83	0.5659	−0.0912	0.5254
5	18.89	25.73	0.6143	−0.1639	0.5496
6	19.38	27.29	0.6532	−0.2223	0.5690
7	21.08	33.02	0.7895	−0.4267	0.6372
8	21.69	35.14	0.8385	−0.5001	0.6617
9	24.11	43.73	1.0316	−0.7898	0.7582
10	30.97	69.07	1.5810	−1.6140	1.0329

[6] The minimum variance set takes the shape of a hyperbola when graphed in an expected return–standard deviation space and is a parabola when drawn in an expected return–variance space.

Optimal Portfolio Selection with a Risk-Free Asset

We now add a risk-free asset to our analysis.[7] In this situation an investor can buy or sell risky assets and buy (lend funds) or sell (borrow money) a risk-free asset such as a short-term government bond with an interest rate of r_f. The expected return of the risky asset–bond portfolio is

$$(3.24) \qquad E(r_P) = w_1\, E(r_1) + (1 - w_1)\, r_f,$$

where w_1 is the percentage of the portfolio invested in the risky asset portfolio, $1 - w_1$ is the weight of the risk-free asset, $E(r_1)$ is the expected return of the risky asset portfolio, and r_f is the risk-free interest rate. The portfolio variance is

$$(3.25) \qquad \sigma_P^2 = w_1^2\, \sigma_1^2 + (1 - w_1)^2\, \sigma_f^2 + 2w_1(1 - w_1)\, \rho_{1,2}\, \sigma_1\, \sigma_f,$$

where σ_1^2 and σ_1 are the variance and standard deviation of the risky asset portfolio, respectively, and σ_f^2 and σ_f are the corresponding risk measures for the risk-free asset. However, since the return of the risk-free asset is certain, the standard deviation is 0: $\sigma_f = 0$. Thus the portfolio variance is simply the weight of the risky-asset portfolio squared multiplied by the variance of the portfolio:

$$(3.26) \qquad \sigma_P^2 = w_1^2\, \sigma_1^2$$

or

$$\sigma_P = w_1\, \sigma_1.$$

Given equations 3.24 and 3.26, we can determine the slope of the opportunity set when one asset is risk-free. As in previous cases, the change of the expected return with respect to a change in the portfolio standard deviation is needed to derive the slope of the opportunity set:

$$(3.27) \qquad \frac{dE(r_P)}{d\sigma_P} = \frac{dE(r_P)/dw_1}{d\sigma_P/dw_1}.$$

[7] Only governments can issue default-free bonds because of their ability to tax and control the money supply. In the United States, Treasury bills are generally viewed as a good proxy for the risk-free asset. Treasury bills are highly liquid non–interest bearing securities with an original maturity of one year or less. Treasury bills are offered by the Treasury Department in minimum denominations of $10,000, with multiples of $5,000 thereafter. Because of their short-term nature, Treasury bill prices are relatively insensitive to changes in the level of interest rates. (See Chapters 14 and 15 for a discussion of the effects of interest rate changes on bond prices.)

MANAGING FUNDS USING MODERN PORTFOLIO THEORY

Many of the ideas presented in the portfolio theory chapters were originally developed by Harry Markowitz, winner of the 1990 Nobel Prize for economic science. These ideas are now helping him manage funds invested in Japanese equities for Daiwa Securities Trust Co. According to an article appearing in *Wall Street and Technology*, his group at Daiwa, the global portfolio research department, manages $70 million in assets for Japanese individuals and U.S. institutions. Since inception the fund has outperformed the Tokyo Price Index (TOPIX) by approximately 10%.

The development of the procedures utilized to manage the portfolio began with back testing using data going back to 1970. The group tested various strategies using previous equity prices to select the optimal strategy. Markowitz compares this process to having a little man inside the computer to estimate the expected returns, variances, and covariances for the available assets. After the little man selected an efficient portfolio, transaction costs were computed, and the portfolio performance over a three-month period was monitored. Several methods were considered and the method with the superior performance in the back tests was selected to manage the actual portfolio. The group utilized several statistics to determine if a particular method's results were simply a result of chance or were repeatable. Of course the resulting optimal portfolios depend on the quality of the inputs and the expected returns, variances, and covariances of the securities.

Most of the analysis is performed on IBM RS/6000 workstations, personal computers, and Sun workstations.

The derivative of the expected return of the portfolio (equation 3.24) with respect to a change in the weight of the risky portion of the portfolio is

(3.28) $$dE(r_P)/dw_1 = E(r_1) - r_f.$$

The derivative of the portfolio standard deviation (equation 3.26) with respect to a change in w_1 is

(3.29) $$d\sigma_P/dw_1 = \sigma_1.$$

Plugging equations 3.28 and 3.29 into 3.27 reveals that the slope of the opportunity set is linear because the slope does not change as the weight is changed:

(3.30) $$\frac{E(r_P) - r_f}{\sigma_1}.$$

Figure 3.7 illustrates the linear opportunity set available to an investor in risky assets and a risk-free asset. The investor can invest in the risky portfolio Y, which has a standard deviation of σ_Y and an expected return of $E(r_Y)$ and borrow or lend at the risk-free rate, which delivers a certain

FIGURE 3.7

Risk and Return Possibilities from Risky Portfolio *Y* and a Risk-Free Asset

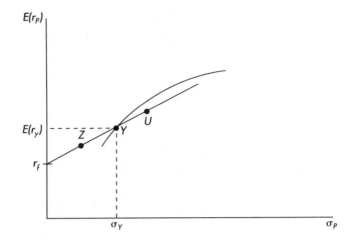

return (zero standard deviation) of r_f. The risk and return combinations of the two portfolios are represented by points Y and r_f in Figure 3.7. The two assets can be combined to form additional portfolios. Portfolio Z is equally weighted between the risky and risk-free assets. Its standard deviation is half the standard deviation of the risky asset, and its expected return equals the arithmetic average of the expected returns of the risky and risk-free assets. The investor can also borrow funds (sell bonds) to finance the purchase of the risky asset. This strategy, known as *margin trading*, increases the portfolio risk and return.[8,9] A margin portfolio consisting of a risky asset weight of 2 and a risk-free weight of –1 is represented by point U in Figure 3.7. The portfolio risk is twice the standard deviation of the risky asset portfolio.

The opportunity set consists of a line starting from r_f and running through point Y. The slope (rise over run) is $(E(r_Y) - r_f)/\sigma_Y$. To the left of point Y the investor is buying bonds (lending) and risky assets, and to the right of point Y the investor is selling bonds (borrowing) to finance the additional purchases of risky assets.

If a risk-free asset is present, some risky portfolios on the efficient frontier will be superior to others. As illustrated in Figure 3.8, the rational investor, who likes return and dislikes risk, will prefer opportunity set II

---

[8] Currently, the maximum amount that can be borrowed from a broker to finance stock purchases is 50%, which implies that an investor can borrow up to $50 to buy a stock worth $100. The Securities and Exchange Act of 1934 transferred to the Federal Reserve Board the authority to set maximum margin percentages. This percentage, which has changed numerous times since 1934, has ranged from 40 percent to 100 percent, with the last change occurring in 1974.

[9] For example, assume that an investor purchases $100 of a security, financed with $50 of debt and $50 of the investor's money. If the asset price increases by 10% to $110, the rate of return for the margin borrower is ($110 – $100)/$50 = 20%. On the other hand, a $10 decrease in the security price will result in a loss of 20%.

over I because set II delivers a higher return for a given level of risk. Similarly, opportunity set III dominates set II. In general the investor seeks to rotate counterclockwise the opportunity set (line) originating from point r_f. The most that this line can rotate is through point P^*, where the opportunity set is tangent to the efficient frontier. Therefore, P^* is the optimal risky portfolio. The slope of this line is $E[(r_{P^*}) - r_f]/\sigma_{P^*}$, and the Y-axis intercept is r_f. Thus, the equation of this line is $E(r_P) = r_f + [(E(r_{P^*}) - r_f)/\sigma_{P^*}]\sigma_P$, where $E(r_P)$ is the expected return of the portfolio of risky and risk-free assets and σ_P is the standard deviation of this portfolio.

Thus the important result of introducing a risk-free asset with unrestricted short selling is that all investors will select the same portfolio of risky assets, P^*. The selection of this portfolio of risky assets allows the individual to settle on the line originating from r_f and tangent to the efficient frontier, which is the opportunity set that maximizes portfolio return for a given a level of risk. This superior set of combinations of the risky assets and the risk-free asset is called the *capital market line*. Highly risk-averse investors will place most or all of their assets in bonds and leave a small percentage or nothing in the risky portfolio P^*, while less risk-averse investors will increase their expected risk and return by buying portfolio P^* on margin, placing them to the right of P^* on the capital market line.

Given the fact that investors evaluate portfolios on the basis of their expected returns and the standard deviations, the selection of the optimal portfolio of risky assets is independent of the individual's attitude toward risk, because all individuals willing to hold risky assets will settle on portfolio P^*. Thus the decisions of what risky portfolio to hold and the number of risk-free bonds to hold are not related. As you will see in Chapter 9, this *separation theorem,* developed by James Tobin (1958), plays a key role in determining equilibrium conditions in the capital market.

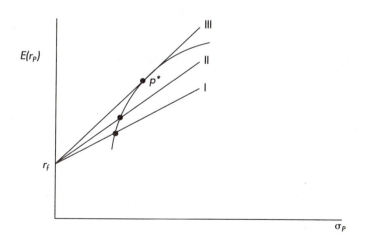

FIGURE 3.8

Risk and Return Possibilities for Three Risky-Asset Portfolios and a Risk-Free Asset

However, as will be demonstrated in Chapter 7, individual risk and return attitudes determine where each investor will settle along the capital market line.

Optimal Two-Security Risky Portfolio

As derived in Appendix 3, in the presence of a risk-free asset, the weights of the optimal two-risky security portfolio, P^*, are

$$\textbf{(3.31)} \quad w_{1^*} = \frac{[E(r_1) - r_f]\,\sigma_2{}^2 - [E(r_2) - r_f]\,COV(r_1,r_2)}{[E(r_1) - r_f]\,\sigma_2{}^2 + [E(r_2) - r_f]\,\sigma_1{}^2 - [E(r_1) - r_f + E(R_2) - r_f]\,COV(r_1,r_2)}$$

$$w_{2^*} = 1 - w_{1^*}.$$

Assume that asset 1 has an expected return of 15% with a standard deviation of 25%, and asset 2 has an expected return of 18% and a standard deviation of 35%. The correlation coefficient between the returns is .2 and the risk-free rate is 10%. The covariance is equal to $.2 \times .25 \times .35 = .0175$. The optimal weight of asset 1 is

$$w_{1^*} = \frac{(.15 - .10)\,.1225 - (.18 - .10)\,.0175}{(.15 - .10)\,.1225 + (.18 - .10)\,.0625 - (.15 - .10 + .18 - .10).0175}$$

$$= .5339$$

and

$$w_{2^*} = .4661.$$

The percentage of the risky-asset component of the portfolio invested in asset 1 is .5339, and the weight for asset 2 is .4661. Individual preferences determine the percentage of the total portfolio invested in risky and risk-free assets.

The expected return of the risky optimal portfolio is 16.39%, with a standard deviation of 25.05%. The equation for the capital market line is $10\% + [(16.39\% - 10\%)/25.05\%]\,\sigma_P$.

DIVERSIFICATION AND PORTFOLIO RISK

We now examine the relation between the portfolio variance and the number of assets held in the portfolio. Equation 3.32 gives the general formula for the variance of a portfolio of N assets:

$$(3.32) \qquad \sigma_P{}^2 = \sum_{i=1}^{N} \sum_{j=1}^{N} w_i w_j \, COV(r_i, r_j).$$

To investigate the relation between the number of assets in a portfolio and the variance of the portfolio, restate equation 3.32 as follows:

$$(3.33) \qquad \sigma_P{}^2 = \sum_{i=1}^{N} w_i^2 \sigma_i^2 + \sum_{i=1}^{N} \sum_{\substack{j=1 \\ i \neq j}}^{N} w_i w_j \, COV(r_i, r_j).$$

Assume that the assets in the portfolio are equally weighted, which implies that the weight of a particular asset is equal to $1 \div N$. We can restate equation 3.32:

$$(3.34) \qquad \sigma_P{}^2 = \sum_{i=1}^{N} (1/N)^2 \sigma_i^2 + \sum_{i=1}^{N} \sum_{\substack{j=1 \\ i \neq j}}^{N} (1/N)^2 \, COV(r_i, r_j).$$

There are N variance terms and $N(N-1)$ covariance terms. By factoring out $1 \div N$ from the variance term and $(N-1) \div N$ from the covariance term, we can rewrite equation 3.34 as follows:

$$(3.35) \quad \sigma_P{}^2 = (1/N) \sum_{i=1}^{N} (\sigma_i^2/N) + (N-1/N) \sum_{i=1}^{N} \sum_{\substack{j=1 \\ i \neq j}}^{N} COV(r_i, r_j)/N(N-1).$$

The summation of the variance of asset i divided by the number of assets is the average variance. The summation of the covariance terms divided by $N(N-1)$ is the average covariance. Replacing the summations with the averages, we can rewrite equation 3.35 as follows:

$$(3.36) \qquad \sigma_P{}^2 = 1/N \, \overline{\sigma_i^2} + (N-1/N) \, \overline{COV(r_i, r_j)}.$$

Equation 3.36 reveals the effect of diversification on portfolio risk. First assume that all risk is firm-specific, implying a 0 covariance among asset returns. In this case the portfolio variance is equal to $1 \div N$ multiplied by the average variance of the component assets. Because the portfolio variance approaches 0 as the number of assets in the portfolio increases, the risk can be eliminated by holding a large number of securities if the covariance terms among assets are equal to 0.

In reality assets are typically positively correlated as the investment performance is influenced by common factors such as interest rates, currency fluctuations, and economic performance. If the covariance terms are positive, the variance (first right-hand term of equation 3.36) goes to

FIGURE 3.9

Relation between the
Number of Securities
and the Portfolio
Standard Deviation

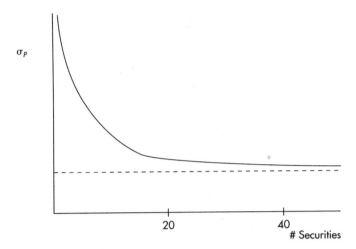

0 as N becomes large, but the second right-hand term approaches the average covariance. (As N becomes large, $(N - 1)/N$ approaches 1). Thus the source of portfolio risk in a diversified portfolio is the common movements among asset prices; while the firm-specific risk will be driven to 0 as the number of assets in the portfolio increases, the covariance terms cannot be diversified away.

Fama (1976) empirically investigated the relationship between portfolio risk and the number of securities in a portfolio. He calculated standard deviations for monthly returns for 50 randomly selected New York Stock Exchange stocks from July 1963 to June 1968. He then calculated the variance of portfolios consisting of one to fifty randomly selected securities. A single security with a standard deviation of approximately 11% was selected. Another security was randomly selected, and the standard deviation of the equally weighted portfolio was approximately 7.2%. Securities were added and portfolio risk was calculated until all fifty assets were selected. Fama found that "... most of the effects of diversification on the dispersion of the distribution of the portfolio return occur when the first few securities are added to the portfolio. Once the portfolio has twenty securities, further diversification has little effect." Figure 3.9 illustrates the hypothetical relationship between the number of securities in a portfolio and the portfolio standard deviation. The reduction of risk is substantial when increasing the number of assets from four to five, but a marginal reduction of risk occurs as the number of assets increases from 34 to 35.

SUMMARY

Diversification becomes more effective as the comovement between component assets is reduced; as a matter of fact, a riskless portfolio consisting of risky assets can be constructed if assets are perfectly negatively correlated. Investors can select from an infinite number of risky-asset portfolios. However, using the mean-variance selection criterion, investors will only select portfolios that maximize the expected return for a given level of risk. Thus the appropriate opportunity set is the set of portfolios that make up the efficient frontier. In the absence of a risk-free asset, risk and return preferences determine the optimal portfolio on the efficient frontier. Extremely risk-averse investors will select a portfolio close to or identical to the minimum variance portfolio, while less risk-averse investors will select a portfolio with greater risk and expected return.

An optimal risky portfolio is obtained when borrowing (and lending) at the riskless rate is possible. This optimal risky portfolio is identified by the tangency of a line starting at the fully invested risk-free portfolio and extending to the efficient frontier. This is the capital market line. Investors then select the percentage of the portfolio invested in the risky and risk-free assets. Thus there is a separation between investor risk aversion and the optimal risky portfolio. In other words, all investors faced with the same opportunity set will select the same risky assets and hold them in the same proportions. Less risk-averse investors will borrow money to finance the purchase of risky assets, and others will place more of their funds in the risk-free asset.

Next we utilize concepts from Chapters 2 and 3 to describe the construction of the efficient frontier in Chapter 4.

Questions and Problems

1. Provide examples of asset returns that are positively and negatively correlated. What is the normal case?

2. Explain why diversification does not reduce portfolio risk when the asset returns are perfectly positively correlated.

3. Explain the situation in which a risk-free portfolio of risky assets can be constructed.

4. How does short selling affect the risk and return of two assets that are perfectly positively correlated?

5. How is the optimal portfolio determined when a risk-free asset is not available? Explain the determination of the optimal portfolio in the presence of a risk-free asset.

6. What is the relation between the number of securities in a portfolio and the portfolio risk?

Questions 7–9 deal with two securities with expected returns of 16% and 12% and standard deviations of 50% and 30%, respectively.

7. If these two assets are perfectly positively correlated, what is the slope of the line illustrating possible combinations of risk and return?

8. What is the minimum variance portfolio with returns correlations equal to −1, 0, .5, and 1 with short sales not allowed?

9. Draw a graph illustrating the relation between the portfolio expected return and standard deviation for returns correlations of −1, 0, .5 and 1.

10. Utilize the E-V rule to select efficient portfolios.

			PORTFOLIOS			
	1	2	3	4	5	6
$E(r_P)$	10%	12%	8%	18%	18%	17%
σ_P	30%	28%	20%	40%	38%	35%

11. Assume that asset 1 has an expected return of 12% with a standard deviation of 30% and asset 2 has an expected return of 18% and a standard deviation of 50%. The correlation coefficient between the returns is equal to .4 and borrowing and lending at the risk-free interest rate of 8% is possible. What are the optimal weights of the two assets? What is the equation of the capital market line?

Self-Test Problems

ST-1. Assume that asset 1 has an expected return of 15% with a standard deviation of 30% and asset 2 has an expected return of 10% and a standard deviation of 20%. Calculate the portfolio expected return and standard deviation for various portfolios. Assume correlation coefficients of 1, 0, and −1. Also calculate the minimum variance portfolios, assuming short sales are not allowed.

ST-2. Asset 1 has an expected return of 10% with a standard deviation of 25%, and asset 2 has an expected return of 15% and a standard deviation of 35%. The correlation coefficient between the returns is .2 and the risk-free rate is 8%. What is the optimal portfolio of risky assets?

Solutions to Self-Test Problems

ST-1.	w_1	$E(r_P)$	σ_P CORR=1	σ_P CORR=0	σ_P CORR=^{2}−1
	0.00	10.00%	20.00%	20.00%	20.00%
	0.25	11.25	22.5	16.8	7.5
	0.50	12.50	25.0	18.0	5.0
	0.75	13.75	27.5	23.0	17.5
	1.00	15.00	30.0	30.0	30.0

When the correlation between returns is equal to 1, the MVP occurs when the weight of asset 1 is equal to 1. The weight of asset 1 that produces the MVP in the case of perfect negative correlation:

$$\frac{\sigma_2}{(\sigma_1 + \sigma_2)} = \frac{.20}{.30 + .20} = .40.$$

If the correlation coefficient is equal to 0, weight of asset 1 that gives the MVP:

$$\frac{\sigma_2^{\,2}}{\sigma_1^{\,2} + \sigma_2^{\,2}} = \frac{.04}{.09 + .04} = .3077$$

ST-2. The covariance between the returns is equal to $.2 \times .25 \times .35 = .0175$. The optimal weight of asset 1:

$$w_{1*} = \frac{[.10 - .08].1225 - [.15 - .08].0175}{[.10 - .08].1225 + [.15 - .08].0625 - [.10 - .08 + .15 - .08].0175}$$

$$= .233$$

and

$$w_{2*} = .767.$$

APPENDIX

3

Optimal Two-Risky-Security Portfolio

Our goal is to find the weights of the optimal two-security portfolio, P^*, consisting of risky assets 1 and 2, in the presence of a risk-free asset. The expected return of the risky asset component of the portfolio, $E(r_P)$, is

(3A.1) $$E(r_P) = w_1 E(r_1) + w_2 E(r_2),$$

where $E(r_1)$ is the expected return of asset 1 and $E(r_2)$ is the expected return of asset 2. The standard deviation is

(3A.2) $$\sigma_P = [w_1^{\,2} \sigma_1^{\,2} + (1 - w_1)^2 \sigma_2^{\,2} + 2w_1(1 - w_1) \rho_{1,2} \sigma_1 \sigma_2]^{1/2}.$$

We know that at the optimal risky portfolio, P^*, the slope of the capital market line is equal to the slope of the efficient frontier. Thus we set the slope of the capital market line equal to the slope of the efficient frontier at portfolio P^* and solve for the weight of asset 1.

The slope of the capital market line is $[E(r_{P*}) - r_f]/\sigma_1$. The slope of the efficient frontier changes as the weight of asset 1 changes. Using the chain rule of calculus, the slope of the efficient frontier at any risky portfolio P is

(3A.3)
$$\frac{dE(r_P)}{d\sigma_P} = \frac{dE(r_P)/dw_1}{d\sigma_P/dw_1}.$$

The derivative of the expected return with respect to a change in the weight of asset 1 is:

(3A.4)
$$dE(r_P)/dw_1 = E(r_1) - E(r_2)$$

The derivative of the portfolio standard deviation with respect to a change in the weight of asset 1 is:

(3A.5)
$$d\sigma_P/dw_1 = \frac{2w_1\,\sigma_1{}^2 - 2(1 - w_1)\,\sigma_2{}^2 + (2 - 4w_1)\,COV(r_1,r_2)}{2\,\sigma_P}$$

Substituting equations 3.4A and 3.5A into 3.3A produces

(3A.6)
$$\frac{dE(r_P)}{d\sigma_P} = \frac{\sigma_P\,E(r_1) - E(r_2)}{w_1\,\sigma_1{}^2 - (1 - w_1)\,\sigma_2{}^2 + (1 - 2w_1)\,COV(r_1,r_2)}.$$

Evaluating the change in the expected return with respect to a change in the portfolio standard deviation at portfolio P* gives

(3A.7)
$$\frac{dE(r_{P*})}{d\sigma_P} = \frac{\sigma_P\,E(r_1) - E(r_2)}{w_{1*}\,\sigma_1{}^2 - (1 - w_{1*})\,\sigma_2{}^2 + (1 - 2w_{1*})\,COV(r_1,r_2)}$$

where w_{1*} is the proportion of asset 1 in portfolio P*. Setting the slope of the capital market line equal to equation 3.7A and solving for w_{1*}, we obtain equation 3.31.

REFERENCES

Bodie, Z., and V. Rosansky. 1980. Risk and return in commodity futures, *Financial Analysts Journal*, May/June 1980, 27–39.

Copeland, T., and F. Weston. 1988. *Financial theory and corporate policy*. Reading, MA: Addison Wesley.

Evans, J., and S. Archer. 1968. Diversification and the reduction of dispersion. An empirical analysis. *Journal of Finance*, December, 761–767.

Fama, E. 1976. *Foundations of finance*, New York: Basic Books.

Markowitz, H. 1952. Portfolio selection. *Journal of Finance*, December, 77–91.

Markowitz, H. 1959. Portfolio selection. Efficient diversification of investments. New York: John Wiley and Sons.

Newbold, P. 1990. *Statistics for business and economics.* Englewood Cliffs, NJ: Prentice Hall.

Schwartzman, S. 1992. Daiwa taps Nobel know-how. *Wall Street and Technology,* August, 23–26.

Tobin, J. 1958. Liquidity preference as behavior toward risk. *Review of Economic Studies,* February, 65–86.

CHAPTER *4*

The Efficient Frontier

Introduction

Although an investor has an unlimited number of risky portfolios to choose from, the opportunity set can be substantially reduced by utilizing the mean-variance (E-V) decision rule, introduced in Chapter 3. The minimum-variance opportunity set, which is hyperbolic in an expected return–standard deviation space, is obtained by minimizing the portfolio standard deviation for a given level of expected return. The efficient frontier, which is the top half of the minimum-variance set, is obtained by maximizing the expected return for a given level of risk. Rational investors who employ only the expected return and standard deviation to analyze portfolios of risky assets will select a portfolio from the efficient frontier.

Graphical analysis, calculus, and nonlinear programming techniques can be implemented to estimate the minimum-variance set and efficient frontiers. In this chapter we systematically investigate the construction of the minimum-variance set and efficient frontier for three risky assets using the graphical approach originally developed by Harry Markowitz (1952, 1959). This approach is the easiest to understand. However, it can provide the minimum-variance set and efficient frontier for at most four risky assets. With a thorough understanding of the logic behind minimum variance set calculation using graphical analysis, you can move on to the more general calculus approach, which can deal with a large number of risky assets. In Appendix 4A we introduce the calculus framework (i.e., Lagrangian multiplier method) for determining the minimum-variance set for two risky assets and generalize this technique to N risky assets.

The calculus method cannot deal with constraints on the weights of the individual assets and with short-sale restrictions. Some institutions cannot short risky assets and may be restricted as to how much they can invest in particular assets. For instance, mutual funds are restricted by law from holding more than 5 percent of the shares of any one company. A nonlinear programming technique (i.e., quadratic programming) must be used to account for such constraints. We discuss this method in Appendix 4B.

The example we use to illustrate the graphical method consists of three risky assets with expected returns of

$$E(r_1) = 18\% \quad E(r_2) = 10\% \quad E(r_3) = 14\%$$

and the following covariance matrix:

		ASSET		
		1	2	3
A	1	.2500	.0000	.0500
S				
S	2	.0000	.0900	.0400
E	3	.0500	.0400	.2025
T				

The diagonal of this matrix gives the return variance of the assets. The standard deviation of asset 1 is .50, asset 2 is .30, and asset 3, .45. Correlation coefficients between the returns can be calculated with information provided by the covariance matrix. Using the fact that the correlation coefficient is equal to the covariance between the two returns divided by the product of their respective standard deviations, we obtain the following correlation coefficients between the asset returns:

$$\rho_{1,2} = .00/(.50)(.30) = .0000$$

$$\rho_{1,3} = .05/(.50)(.45) = .2220$$

$$\rho_{2,3} = .04/(.30)(.45) = .2963.$$

This information will allow us to calculate expected returns and variances for the portfolio.

CONSTRUCTION OF THE MINIMUM-VARIANCE SET

To construct the minimum-variance set using the graphical method, we must develop isomean and isovariance lines and graph them in a w_1, w_2 space. The minimum-variance set and efficient frontier can be determined by the interaction of these two lines. Initially we assume that short sales are permitted. Later in the chapter we analyze the graphical method assuming restrictions on short sales. We begin the graphical analysis by discussing the graphical depiction of the possible weights for a three-asset portfolio.

Possible Weights for a Three-Asset Portfolio

We start our analysis of the construction of the minimum-variance set and efficient frontier by examining and graphing the set of possible portfolio weights for three risky assets. Figure 4.1 plots possible weights for assets 1 and 2. Although the weight of asset 3 is not represented in Figure 4.1, it is implied by the weights of the first two assets. Conforming to the budget constraint, we know that $w_1 + w_2 + w_3 = 1$, which implies that the weight of asset 3 is equal to $1 - w_1 - w_2$.

At any portfolio along the *x*-axis, the weight of asset 2 is 0, and portfolios on the *y*-axis do not contain asset 1. On line segment *BD* the weight of asset 1 is 0. At point *B*, for example, all funds are invested in asset

FIGURE 4.1

Possible Weights for a Three-Asset Portfolio

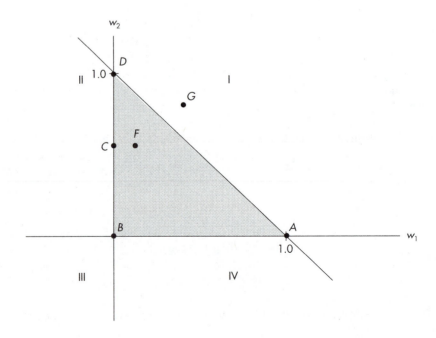

3. At point D the weight of asset 2 is 1, implying that no funds are invested in assets 2 and 3. Point C represents a weight of .50 for assets 2 and 3, with a corresponding weight of 0 for asset 1. A point on line segment DA suggests a weight of 0 for asset 3. Any point inside the triangle implies positive weights for all three assets. For instance, point F represents a portfolio in which the investor is 25% invested in asset 1, 50% invested in asset 2, and 25% in asset 3.

Points above the shaded triangle (point G for example) imply a short position in asset 3. Short positions of asset 1 are illustrated by portfolios located in quadrant II, and short positions of asset 2 are represented by points below the x-axis. If short sales are not allowed, legitimate points are located on or inside the shaded triangle; portfolios in the second and fourth quadrants are not possible due to this constraint.

Isomean Lines

An isomean line consists of a set of portfolios that deliver a given portfolio expected return. A family of these lines can be constructed, with each line representing a different expected return. To facilitate the graphing of these lines, derive the equation of the isomean lines. Restating the weight of asset 3 as $(1 - w_2 - w_3)$, the expected return of a three-asset portfolio is

(4.1) $$E(r_P) = w_1 E(r_1) + w_2 E(r_2) + (1 - w_1 - w_2) E(r_3).$$

Solving for the weight of asset 2 gives the following:

(4.2) $$w_2 = \frac{E(r_3) - E(r_P)}{E(r_3) - E(r_2)} + \frac{E(r_1) - E(r_3)}{E(r_3) - E(r_2)} w_1.$$

The first right-hand term of equation 4.2 is the intercept term (in a w_2, w_1 space), and the second right-hand term is the slope. The slope of the isomean lines in our example is $(18\% - 14\%) \div (14\% - 10\%) = 1$. The intercept is equal to $[14\% - E(r_P)]/(14\% - 10\%)$. Thus the intercept depends on the expected return of the portfolio. If the expected portfolio return is 12%, the intercept term is .5 and the equation of the isomean line is

(4.3) $$w_2 = .5 + 1w_1.$$

Equation 4.3 provides combinations of weights 1 and 2 (and implicitly the weight of asset 3) that deliver an expected portfolio return of 12%. One

FIGURE 4.2

Isoreturn Lines

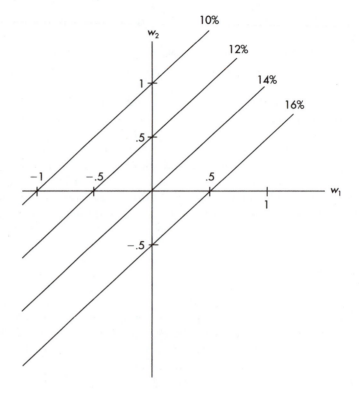

possible combination is $w_1 = .20$, $w_2 = .70$, and $w_3 = .10$, which satisfies the budget constraint. The expected return of this portfolio is

(4.4) $E(r_P) = 18\%(.20) + 10\%(.70) + 14\%(.10) = 12\%.$

The line labeled 12% in Figure 4.2 represents the isomean line for an expected portfolio return of 12%. A family of lines is also drawn, with each line representing a different portfolio return. The expected returns increase as the lines move southeast. Note that the slope of the isoreturn lines can be negative or positive. For example, if the expected returns of assets 2 and 3 are switched, $[E(r_2) = 14\%$ and $E(r_3) = 10\%]$, the slope of the isomean lines will be $(18\% - 10\%) \div (10\% - 14\%) = -2$. Here the returns increase as the lines move northeast.

Minimum-Variance Portfolio

It is helpful to find the MVP before proceeding further. We start our discussion of the derivation of the MVP with the variance of a three-security portfolio, again expressing the weight of asset 3 as $(1 - w_1 - w_2)$:

(4.5) $\quad \sigma_P^2 = w_1^2\sigma_1^2 + w_2^2\sigma_2^2 + (1 - w_1 - w_2)^2\sigma_3^2 + 2w_1w_2COV(r_1,r_2)$
$\quad\quad\quad + 2w_1(1 - w_1 - w_2)COV(r_1,r_3) + 2w_2(1 - w_1 - w_2)COV(r_2,r_3).$

To find the MVP, differentiate equation 4.5 with respect to w_1 and w_2 and set to zero, thus obtaining a minimum.[1]

(4.6a) $\quad \dfrac{d\sigma_P^2}{dw_1} = 2w_1[\sigma_1^2 + \sigma_3^2 - 2COV(r_1,r_3)] + 2w_2[\sigma_3^2 + COV(r_1,r_2)$
$\quad\quad\quad - COV(r_1,r_3) - COV(r_2,r_3)] + 2[COV(r_1,r_3) - \sigma_3^2] = 0$

(4.6b) $\quad \dfrac{d\sigma_P^2}{dw_2} = 2w_1 [\sigma_3^2 + COV(r_1,r_2) - COV(r_1,r_3) - COV(r_2,r_3)]$
$\quad\quad\quad + 2w_2[\sigma_2^2 + \sigma_3^2 - COV(r_2,r_3)] + 2[\sigma_3^2 - COV(r_2,r_3)] = 0.$

Insert covariances and variances from the example into equations 4.6a and 4.6b:

(4.7a) $\quad \dfrac{d\sigma_P^2}{dw_1} = 2w_1 [.25 + .2025 - 2(.05)] + 2w_2 (.2025 + 0 - .05 + .04)$
$\quad\quad\quad + 2(.05 - .2025) = 0$
$\quad\quad\quad = .705w_1 + .225w_2 - .305 = 0$

(4.7b) $\quad \dfrac{d\sigma_P^2}{dw_2} = 2w_2 (.2025 + 0 - .05 - .04) + 2w_2 (.09 + .2025 - .04)$
$\quad\quad\quad + 2(.2025 - .04) = 0$
$\quad\quad\quad = .225w_1 + .425w_2 - .325 = 0.$

To determine the MVP we must find the values of w_1 and w_2 by solving for the weight of asset 1 in equation 4.7a and plugging the result into equation 4.7b. Since the resulting equation is a function of w_2 only, we can solve for w_2 and then w_3. Equation 4.7a can be rewritten as

(4.8) $\quad\quad\quad\quad\quad\quad w_1 = (.305 - .225w_2)/.705.$

Plugging equation 4.8 into equation 4.7b yields

(4.9) $\quad\quad\quad\quad .225(.305 - .225w_2)/.705 + .425w_2 - .325 = 0.$

Thus w_2 is equal to .644. Plugging .644 for w_2 into equation 4.7a or 4.7b and solving for w_1 shows that the weight of asset 1 is equal to .227 and the resulting weight for asset 3 is .1289. Thus, the MVP in our example is identified by the following weights: $w_1 = .227$, $w_2 = .644$, $w_3 = .129$.

---

[1] The second derivative is positive, implying that the solution provides a minimum.

Isovariance Curves

An isovariance curve provides a locus of portfolios that provide the same portfolio variance. A family of isovariance curves, each containing a different level of portfolio variance, can be obtained. We can more conveniently restate equation 4.5, the variance of a three-asset portfolio, as follows:[2]

(4.10) $\sigma_P^2 = w_1^2[\sigma_1^2 - 2COV(r_1,r_3) + \sigma_3^2] + w_2^2[\sigma_2^2 - 2COV(r_2,r_3) + \sigma_3^2]$
$+ 2w_1w_2[COV(r_1,r_2) - COV(r_1,r_3) - COV(r_2,r_3) + \sigma_3^2]$
$+ 2w_1[COV(r_1,r_3) - \sigma_3^2] + 2w_2[COV(r_2,r_3) - \sigma_3^2] + \sigma_3^2.$

The portfolio variance in our example is

(4.12) $\sigma_P^2 = w_1^2[.25 - 2(.05) + .2025] + w_2^2[.09 - 2(.04) + .2025]$
$+ 2w_1w_2[0 - .05 - .04 + .2025] + 2w_1[.05 - .2025]$
$+ 2w_2[.04 - .2025] + .2025$

or

$\sigma_P^2 = .3525\ w_1^2 + .2125\ w_2^2 + .225\ w_1w_2 - .305\ w_1 - .325\ w_2 + .2025.$

Hence, to obtain a portfolio with a variance of 40%, for example, replace σ_P^2 with .40 and find solutions that satisfy this equation:

(4.13a) $.40 = .3525\ w_1^2 + .2125\ w_2^2 + .225\ w_1w_2 - .305\ w_1 - .325\ w_2 + .2025$

or

(4.13b) $0 = .3525\ w_1^2 + .2125\ w_2^2 + .225\ w_1w_2 - .305\ w_1 - .325\ w_2 - .1975.$

---

[2] Equation 4.10 is derived as follows. The variance of a three-asset portfolio is

(4.11) $\sigma_P^2 = w_1^2\ \sigma_1^2 + w_2^2\ \sigma_2^2 + (1 - w_1 - w_2)^2\ \sigma_3^2 + 2w_1w_2\ COV(r_1,r_2)$
$+ 2w_1(1 - w_2 - w_3)\ COV(r_1,r_3) + 2w_2(1 - w_1 - w_2)\ COV(r_2,r_3)$

$= w_1^2\ \sigma_1^2 + w_2^2\ \sigma_2^2 + (1 - 2w_1 - 2w_2 + 2w_1w_2 + w_1^2 + w_2^2)\ \sigma_3^2$
$+ 2w_1w_2\ COV(r_1,r_2) + (2w_1 - 2w_1^2 - 2w_1w_2)\ COV(r_1,r_3)$
$+ (2w_2 - 2w_2^2 - 2w_1w_2)\ COV(r_2,r_3)$

$= w_1^2\ \sigma_1^2 + w_2^2\ \sigma_2^2 + \sigma_3^2 - 2w_1\ \sigma_3^2 - 2w_2\ \sigma_3^2$
$+ 2w_1w_2\ \sigma_3^2 + w_1^2\ \sigma_3^2 + w_2^2\ \sigma_3^2 + 2w_1w_2\ COV(r_1,r_2)$
$+ 2w_1COV(r_1,r_3) - 2w_1^2\ COV(r_1,r_3) - 2w_1w_2\ COV(r_1,r_3)$
$+ 2w_2COV(r_2,r_3) - 2w_1w_2\ COV(r_2,r_3), - 2w_2^2\ COV(r_2,r_3)$

After the weights of the three assets are factored, equation 4.11 can be rewritten as equation 4.10.

GOLD AS INVESTMENTS FOR STOCK AND BOND PORTFOLIOS

The main contribution of modern portfolio theory is that the risk of a portfolio depends on the covariance of the assets under consideration, not the average risk of the individual components. Thus, merging an assortment of high-risk securities may result in a low-risk portfolio if the assets do not move in tandem. While gold is very risky as an individual asset, it may reduce the risk of a stock and bond portfolio, as the correlation between gold and financial assets is low. The correlation between equity and gold returns should be low, as corporate profits and the general level of interest rates determine stock prices, while supply and demand regulate gold prices. Jaffe (1989) investigates the risk and return characteristics of financial assets with a small portion of the portfolio devoted to gold. Jaffe finds that the correlation between gold and financial assets is not statistically different from zero.

Jaffe formulates various portfolios with and without an exposure to gold. For example, for the period 1970 to 1990 a portfolio consisting of 55% in common stocks, 15% in small stocks, 5% in Treasury bills, 10% in real estate, and 15% in foreign stocks delivers a 1.01% monthly geometric mean return (12.87% annualized return) with a standard deviation of 3.73%. When 10% of the portfolio is devoted to gold, the mean monthly return increases to 1.04% (13.24% annualized return) and the standard deviation is reduced to 3.51%. Other portfolios possess similar characteristics. Thus, a stock and bond portfolio with a small portion devoted to gold enhances the risk and return characteristics of the portfolio. Using concepts from this chapter, an efficient frontier with and without an exposure to gold can be computed. The efficient frontier for the portfolio with gold would dominate the portfolio without gold.

Suppose that our task is to graph equation 4.13b, thereby producing a set of weights that deliver portfolios with a variance of 40%. We start with an arbitrary value, say 0, for the weight of asset 2, and obtain the weight or weights that satisfy equation 4.13b. When w_1 is equal to 0, equation 4.13b is given by the following quadratic:

(4.14)
$$0 = .2125\, w_2^2 - .325\, w_2 - .1975.$$

Thus 1.995 and −.466 are two values of w_2 that satisfy equation 4.13b.[3] Hence two portfolios that deliver a portfolio variance of 40% are $w_1 = 0$, $w_2 = 1.995$, $w_3 = -.995$; and $w_1 = 0$, $w_2 = -.466$, $w_3 = 1.466$. These two portfolios are plotted in Figure 4.3 (points *A* and *B*). Notice that if these weights are plugged into equation 4.10, the resulting variance is .40.

We can repeat the process by changing w_1 or w_2 to obtain as many equal-variance portfolios as desired. Graphically, this would result in an

---

[3] We can find the roots of the quadratic equation $ax^2 + bx + c = 0$ using the well known formulas $x_1 = -b + \sqrt{b^2 - 4ac} \div 2a$ and $x_2 = -b - \sqrt{b^2 - 4ac} \div 2a$.

FIGURE 4.3

Isovariance Curves
of 30% and 40%

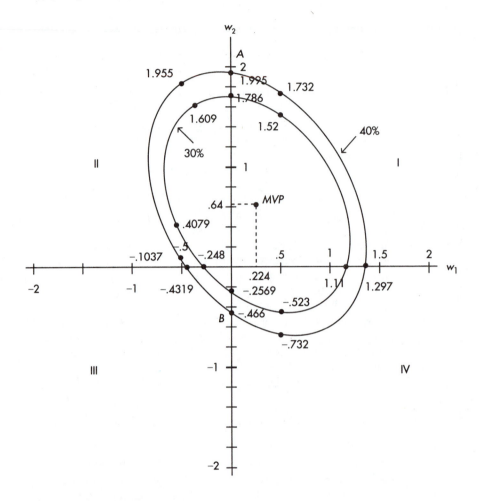

isovariance curve such as those shown in Figure 4.3. Exhibit 4.1 shows other weights that equate the portfolio variance to 40%. Once the 40% isovariance curve is traced, another curve with a different variance can be obtained with the same method. If a smaller variance is selected, 30% for example, the resulting curve will have a smaller diameter, fitting inside the curves with larger variances. As smaller variances are selected, the isovariance curves become tighter, eventually approaching the single point MVP, which is the minimum-variance portfolio.

The Critical Line

Determining the minimum variance set entails finding a number of portfolios that minimize portfolio variance for given levels of expected return. The process starts with selection of an arbitrary portfolio expected return. For that return you determine the portfolio weights that minimize the portfolio variance, subject to the budget constraint that the portfolio weights must sum to 1. (Initially we assume no restrictions to short selling, which implies that a given portfolio weight can vary from plus infinity to minus infinity. We consider constraints on short selling later in this chapter.) After that portfolio has been found, another expected return is selected and the process is repeated. This method is repeated a number of times until the entire minimum-variance set is determined.

This iterative process can be illustrated graphically for the three-security case by superimposing isomean lines and isovariance curves. In Figure 4.4 the parallel lines represent isomean lines, each with a different expected portfolio return, with higher returns to the southeast. These lines were derived from the expected return and covariance given earlier. Five isovariance curves also are shown, again based on the same input, with each curve representing a locus of portfolios that have the same variance. Note again that the ellipses get smaller as they converge to the point MPV.

Suppose that a computer algorithm is developed to find the minimum-variance set. The algorithm first selects an expected return, say 20.60%, as illustrated in Figure 4.4. On the 20.60% isomean line, suppose the algorithm initially selects point (portfolio) Z, which represents asset weights for the three securities. The algorithm uses the input covariance matrix, along with the weights of the three securities, to calculate the portfolio variance. The algorithm then tries to determine if a lower-variance portfolio can be found along the 20.60% isomean line.

Suppose that the algorithm selects portfolio Y, which is to the southwest of portfolio Z. The algorithm knows that it has moved in the wrong direction because portfolio Y will have a higher variance than Z; that is, Y is on a higher isovariance curve. Thus the next candidate selected will

EXHIBIT 4.1

Portfolios with 30% and 40% Variances

Variance	W_1	W_2	W_3
30%	1.11	0.00	−0.11
30	−0.25	0.00	1.25
30	0.00	1.79	−0.79
30	0.00	−0.26	1.26
30	0.50	1.52	−1.02
30	−0.50	1.65	−0.15
30	−0.50	0.41	1.09
40	1.30	0.00	−0.30
40	−0.43	0.00	1.43
40	0.00	2.00	−1.00
40	0.00	−0.47	1.47
40	0.50	1.73	−1.23
40	0.50	−0.73	1.23
40	−0.50	1.96	−0.46
40	−0.50	0.10	1.40

FIGURE 4.4

The Critical Line

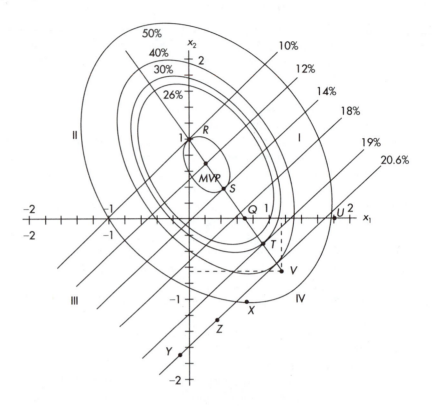

be in the northeasterly direction, say point X. Its portfolio variance is calculated and compared with the variance of portfolio Z. Portfolio X dominates Z because portfolio X possesses a lower variance, 50%.

Next suppose the algorithm selects portfolio V, at the tangency between the 20.60% isomean line and the 40% isovariance curve. Portfolio V replaces portfolio X as the superior portfolio because V exhibits a lower variance. The next candidate is portfolio U. The algorithm knows that it is moving in the incorrect direction because this portfolio has a higher variance than portfolio V. The algorithm then selects candidate portfolios between U and V, calculating the portfolio variances and comparing them with the variance of portfolio V, until it iterates back to portfolio V. The weights of portfolio V are $w_1 = 1.09$, $w_2 = -.59$, and $w_3 = .50$.

The selection of portfolio V as being on the minimum-variance set should make intuitive sense. At this tangency point the variance of the portfolio is minimized, given a portfolio return of 20.60%. A higher variance will result for a portfolio that is not located at the tangency.

The algorithm then selects another return, say 19%, and the process starts over. The algorithm will find the tangency between the 19% isomean line and the 30% isovariance curve at point T. Portfolio T therefore is also on the minimum-variance set and is graphed in Figure 4.4. The process continues until a number of portfolios on the minimum-variance set are obtained. The line crossing through these portfolios and the MVP is called the critical line. The *critical line* is the locus of portfolios that exhibit minimum variance for given levels of expected return.

Portfolios that are southeast of the MVP make up the efficient frontier because they maximize return for a level of portfolio variance. Examine portfolios R and S. Although both portfolios have the same variance, portfolio S has the higher expected return, 14%, and therefore is an efficient portfolio, dominating R in mean-variance space.

The critical line in Figure 4.4 passes through the first, second, and fourth quadrants. At point R the weight of assets 1 and 3 are 0, and asset 2 possesses a weight of 1. To the northwest of point R asset 1 is shorted and the weights of assets 2 and 3 are positive. At point Q the weight of asset 2 is 0, and assets 1 and 3 have positive weights. Below portfolio Q, asset 2 is shorted.

RESTRICTIONS ON SHORT SALES

Because some investors and financial institutions cannot short assets, implying that the minimum weight for an asset is 0, we now extend the graphical method to deal with constraints on short selling.

If short sales are not allowed, we are restricted to any point on or inside the triangle in the first quadrant in Figure 4.5. Portfolios to the northwest of point A and southeast of point B are not allowed because of

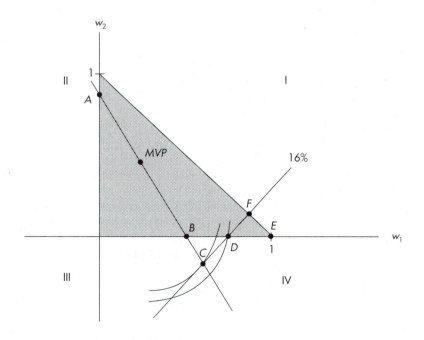

FIGURE 4.5

Minimum-Variance Portfolio with Short Sales Restrictions

the constraint. Efficient portfolios from MVP to portfolio B are legitimate because the portfolio weights are nonnegative.

To illustrate the effect of the short-sales restriction on efficient portfolio formulation, assume that an investor minimizes portfolio variance subject to a 16% expected portfolio return, represented by the isomean line in Figure 4.5. In the absence of restrictions on short sales, the optimal portfolio delivering a 16% return is C. However, this portfolio is not possible because of the constraint on short sales. Our goal is to find the asset weights that minimize the variance for a portfolio return of 16%, given that the weights are nonnegative. For a return of 16%, the portfolio that minimizes the variance subject to the constraint is portfolio D, which represents no investment in asset 2. Although portfolio C is preferred to D, D is the best portfolio for a 16% return given the constraint. Portfolio F also produces a 16% return, but it lies on a higher isovariance curve. Other efficient portfolios can be found, and the resulting efficient frontier is measured from MVP to B and from portfolio B to E.

Summary

The minimum-variance set provides the set of portfolios that minimize portfolio variance for a given portfolio expected return. The efficient frontier furnishes portfolios that maximize portfolio return for a given level of risk. The graphical method can be implemented to construct the minimum-variance set and efficient frontier for three risky assets. The method involves isomean lines and isovariance curves. The isomean lines illustrate various weights of the individual assets that produce a given portfolio expected return. The corresponding isovariance curves give a locus of portfolios that deliver a given portfolio variance. In combination the isomean and isovariance curves construct the minimum-variance set and efficient frontiers. Specifically, the MVP for a given level of expected return occurs at the tangency of the two curves. The critical line is the set of MVPs. The presence of short-sale restrictions acts as a constraint on this graphical method.

Appendix 4A explains the calculus method for efficient frontier determination. This method is more general than the graphical method because the calculus approach can calculate the minimum variance set for any number of risky assets. Appendix 4B explains the use of nonlinear programming to calculate the minimum variance set. Appendix 4C reviews matrix algebra concepts. Appendix 4D reviews the mathematics of constrained optimization.

Estimating efficient portfolios under the Markowitz framework is a difficult task when a realistic number of securities are considered. As demonstrated in Appendix 4A, approximating a variance-minimizing portfolio entails inverting an $N \times N$ matrix, where N is the number of securities under consideration. Of course, while inverting a 5×5 matrix is simple, inverting a 200×200 matrix is not a trivial assignment. In Chapter

5 we introduce the single-index model, which invokes a set of simplifying assumptions regarding the source of asset price changes. These assumptions greatly simplify the calculation of the expected portfolio return and portfolio variance. In Chapter 6 we utilize these assumptions to approximate portfolios on the minimum-variance set.

Questions and Problems

1. What does a point in Figure 4.1 represent? How is short sale of asset 1 portrayed graphically? How are positive weights for asset 3 represented?

2. What information does an isomean line provide? What is an isovariance curve?

3. Explain how the interaction of the isomean lines and isovariance curves provides the minimum-variance set. How is the efficient frontier determined?

4. In Figure 4.4, what portion of the critical line provides efficient portfolios?

5. Suppose that three assets have the following expected returns: $E(r_1) = 18\%$, $E(r_2) = 10\%$, $E(r_3) = 14\%$. What is the slope of the isomean lines? How will this slope change if assets 2 and 3 are switched? Provide several portfolios that deliver an expected return of 14%.

6. Three assets have the expected returns $E(r_1) = 20\%$, $E(r_2) = 12\%$, $E(r_3) = 16\%$ and the following covariance matrix:

	ASSET		
	1	2	3
1	0.20	0.00	0.02
2	0.00	0.10	0.04
3	0.02	0.04	0.18

Determine the MVP.

7. With information on the three assets from question 6, provide several portfolios that have a variance of 40%.

8. Using the calculus method outlined in Appendix 4A, determine several MVPs.

9. Suppose that because of external constraints the most that can be invested in asset 1 is 10%. Outline (in words) how the minimum variance set can be obtained.

Self-Test Problems

Three assets have the expected returns $E(r_1) = 22\%$, $E(r_2) = 10\%$, $E(r_3) = 17\%$ and the following covariance matrix:

	ASSET		
	1	2	3
1	.3600	.0200	.0000
2	.0200	.0225	.0400
3	.0000	.0400	.1225

ST-1. Construct several portfolios with a portfolio expected return of 15%.

ST-2. Construct portfolios with weights of $w_1 = 1$ and $w_1 = 0$ with a portfolio variance of .40.

ST-3. Use the calculus method to determine MVPs for expected returns of 15% and 20%.

Self-Test Answers

ST-1. The equation of an isomean line is

$$w_2 = \frac{E(r_3) - E(r_P)}{E(r_3) - E(r_2)} + \frac{E(r_1) - E(r_3)}{E(r_3) - E(r_2)} w_1.$$

The equation for the isomean line for an expected portfolio return of 15% is $w_2 = .2857 + .714\, w_1$.

Portfolios that have an expected return of 15% include

$$w_1 = 0,\, w_2 = .2857,\, w_3 = .7143.$$

$$w_1 = .5,\, w_2 = .6427,\, w_3 = -.1427.$$

ST-2. The portfolio variance in our example is

$$\sigma_P^2 = w_1^2[.36 - 2(0) + .1225] + w_2^2[.0225 - 2(.04) + .1225]$$
$$+ 2w_1 w_2[.02 - 0 - .04 + .1225] + 2w_1[0 - .1225]$$
$$+ 2w_2[.04 - .1225] + .1225$$

or

$$\sigma_P^2 = .4825\, w_1^2 + .065\, w_2^2 + .205\, w_1 w_2 - .245\, w_1 - .165\, w_2 + .1225.$$

Hence, to obtain portfolios with a variance of 40%, replace σ_P^2 with .40 and find solutions that satisfy the equation:

$$.40 = .4825\, w_1^2 + .065\, w_2^2 + .205\, w_1 w_2 - .245\, w_1 - .165\, w_2 + .1225$$

or

$$0 = .4825\, w_1^2 + .065\, w_2^2 + .205\, w_1 w_2 - .245\, w_1 - .165\, w_2 - .2775.$$

When w_1 is equal to 0, the above equation is given by the following quadratic:

$$0 = .065\, w_2^2 - .165\, w_2 - .2775.$$

Thus, −1.156 and 3.694 are two values of w_2 that satisfy the above equation. Hence, two portfolios that deliver a portfolio variance of 40% are $w_1 = 0$, $w_2 = -1.156$, $w_3 = 2.1556$; and $w_1 = 0$, $w_2 = 3.694$, $w_3 = -2.694$.

When $w_2 = 0$, the quadratic equation is

$$0 = .2375\, w_1^2 - .245\, w_1 - .2775.$$

The weights that satisfy this equation are $w_1 = 1.0536$ and $-.546$. Thus, two portfolios that deliver a portfolio variance of 40% are $w_1 = 1.0536$, $w_2 = 0$, $w_3 = -.05361$ and $w_1 = -.5459$, $w_2 = 0$, $w_3 = 1.5459$.

ST-3. To find portfolios that minimize the variance for expected returns of 15% and 20%, first set up the following matrix:

	A					**w**	**=**	**B**
0.72	0.040	0.00	0.22	1		w_1		0
0.04	0.045	0.080	0.10	1		w_2		0
0.00	0.080	0.245	0.17	1		w_3	=	0
0.22	0.100	0.170	0.00	0		λ_1		$E(r_P)$
1.00	1.000	1.000	0.00	0		λ_2		1

The inverse of the **A** matrix is equal to

$$\begin{bmatrix} 0.755 & 0.539 & -1.295 & 3.213 & -0.272 \\ 0.539 & 0.385 & -0.925 & -11.990 & 2.234 \\ -1.295 & -0.925 & 2.219 & 8.777 & -0.962 \\ 3.213 & -11.990 & 8.777 & -12.857 & 0.995 \\ -0.272 & 2.234 & -0.962 & 0.995 & -0.112 \end{bmatrix}$$

Portfolios on the minimum-variance set can be obtained by multiplying the inverse by the **B** vector. For a portfolio expected return of 15%, the weights that minimize the portfolio variance are: $w_1 = .21$, $w_2 = .44$, $w_3 = .35$. For an expected return of 20%, the weights are $w_1 = .37$, $w_2 = -.16$, $w_3 = .79$.

APPENDIX

4A

Calculus Method for Minimum-Variance Set Determination

Our goal is to determine the weights of a two-asset portfolio that minimize the portfolio variance for a particular expected rate of return. The two constraints are that (1) the portfolio expected return must equal the target return and (2) the weights of the two assets must sum to 1. The mathematical formulation of our problem is

minimize
$$\sigma_P^2 = w_1^2\,\sigma_1^2 + w_2^2\,\sigma_2^2 + 2w_1 w_2\,COV(r_1,r_2)$$
subject to

(4A.1)
$$w_1\,E(r_1) + w_2\,E(r_2) = E(r_{P^*})$$

or

$$w_1\,E(r_1) + w_2\,E(r_2) - E(r_{P^*}) = 0,$$

where $E(r_{P^*})$ is the target portfolio return and

(4A.2)
$$w_1 + w_2 = 1$$

or

$$w_1 + w_2 - 1 = 0.$$

We can use Lagrange multipliers to solve this constrained-optimization problem. This method is reviewed in Appendix 4D. Our task is to minimize the portfolio variance subject to two Lagrangian constraints. The Lagrangian objective function of the risk-minimization problem with two assets is

(4A.3)
$$L = w_1^2\,\sigma_1^2 + w_2^2\,\sigma_2^2 + 2w_1 w_2\,COV(r_1,r_2) + \lambda_1(w_1\,E(r_1)$$
$$+ w_2\,E(r_2) - E(r_{P^*})) + \lambda_2(w_1 + w_2 - 1) = 0.$$

The minimum-risk portfolio is determined by obtaining the derivatives of the Lagrangian objective function with respect to the weights of assets 1 and 2 and the two Lagrange multipliers. The resulting derivatives are set to 0 and the system of equations is solved for the weights of the portfolio. The partial derivatives are

(4A.4)
$$\frac{\delta L}{\delta w_1} = 2w_1\,\sigma_1^2 + 2\,COV(r_1,r_2)\,w_2 + \lambda_1\,E(r_1) + \lambda_2 = 0.$$

$$\frac{\delta L}{\delta w_2} = 2w_2\,\sigma_2^2 + 2\,COV(r_1,r_2)\,w_1 + \lambda_1\,E(r_2) + \lambda_2 = 0.$$

$$\frac{\delta L}{\delta \lambda_1} = w_1\,E(r_1) + w_2\,E(r_2) - E(r_{P^*}) = 0.$$

$$\frac{\delta L}{\delta \lambda_2} = w_1 + w_2 - 1 = 0.$$

These equations can be expressed in matrix form:

(4A.5)

$$
\underset{A}{\begin{bmatrix} 2\sigma_1^2 & 2COV(r_1,r_2) & E(r_1) & 1 \\ 2COV(r,r) & 2\sigma_2^2 & E(r_2) & 1 \\ E(r_1) & E(r_2) & 0 & 0 \\ 1 & 1 & 0 & 0 \end{bmatrix}}
\underset{w}{\begin{bmatrix} w_1 \\ w_2 \\ \lambda_1 \\ \lambda_2 \end{bmatrix}}
=
\underset{B}{\begin{bmatrix} 0 \\ 0 \\ E(r_{p*}) \\ 1 \end{bmatrix}}
$$

The solution of the **w** vector, $\mathbf{w} = \mathbf{A}^{-1}\,\mathbf{B}$, produces the weights of assets 1 and 2 that minimize the portfolio variance subject to the constraints.

To illustrate the determination of an MVP consisting of two assets, assume that asset 1 has an expected return of 20% and asset 2 has an expected return of 14%. The variance of asset 1 is .09, the variance of asset 2 is .04, and the covariance between the two returns is .02. We can find the weights that minimize the variance for a target portfolio return of 18% by plugging in the return and variance information to matrix 4A.5. The resulting matrix is

$$
\underset{A}{\begin{bmatrix} 0.18 & 0.04 & 0.20 & 1 \\ 0.04 & 0.08 & 0.14 & 1 \\ 0.20 & 0.14 & 0.00 & 0 \\ 1.00 & 1.00 & 0.00 & 0 \end{bmatrix}}
\underset{w}{\begin{bmatrix} w_1 \\ w_2 \\ \lambda_1 \\ \lambda_2 \end{bmatrix}}
=
\underset{B}{\begin{bmatrix} 0.00 \\ 0.00 \\ 0.18 \\ 1.00 \end{bmatrix}}
$$

and the inverse of matrix **A** is

$$
\mathbf{A}^{-1} = \begin{bmatrix} 0.0000 & 0.000 & 16.667 & -2.333 \\ 0.0000 & 0.000 & -16.667 & 3.333 \\ 16.6670 & -16.6670 & -50.000 & 7.667 \\ -2.3330 & 3.3330 & 7.667 & -1.247 \end{bmatrix}
$$

To obtain the w vector, multiply the inverse matrix by the *B* vector. The resulting weight vector is

$$
\mathbf{w} = \begin{bmatrix} .6706 \\ .3312 \\ -1.3330 \\ 0.1331 \end{bmatrix}
$$

Thus, the weight of asset 1 that will minimize the portfolio variance for an expected portfolio return of 18% is .6706, and the weight of asset 2 is .3312. This portfolio has an expected return of 18% and a variance of .0536. Another expected return can be selected to obtain another portfolio on the minimum variance set. This process is continued until the desired number of portfolios is obtained.

The calculus method can handle any number of assets. The general form of the matrix for N assets is

$$
\overset{\mathbf{A}}{\begin{bmatrix}
2\sigma_1^2 & 2COV(r_1,r_2) & \ldots & 2COV(r_1,r_N) & E(r_1) & 1 \\
2COV(r_2,r_1) & 2\sigma_2^2 & \ldots & 2COV(r_2,r_N) & E(r_2) & 1 \\
\cdot & \cdot & & \cdot & \cdot & \\
\cdot & \cdot & & \cdot & \cdot & \\
\cdot & \cdot & & \cdot & \cdot & \\
2COV(r_N,r_1) & 2COV(r_N,r_2) & \ldots & 2\sigma_N^2 & E(r_N) & 1 \\
E(r_1) & E(r_2) & \ldots & E(r_N) & 0 & 0 \\
1 & 1 & \ldots & 1 & 0 & 0
\end{bmatrix}}
\overset{\mathbf{w}}{\begin{bmatrix}
w_1 \\ w_2 \\ \cdot \\ \cdot \\ \cdot \\ w_N \\ \lambda_1 \\ \lambda_2
\end{bmatrix}}
=
\overset{\mathbf{B}}{\begin{bmatrix}
0 \\ 0 \\ \cdot \\ \cdot \\ \cdot \\ 0 \\ E(r_{P^*}) \\ 1
\end{bmatrix}}
$$

The weight vector is equal to $\mathbf{w} = \mathbf{A}^{-1}\,\mathbf{B}$.

APPENDIX

4B

Minimum-Variance Set Determination with Short Sales Not Allowed

To determine the minimum-variance set for risky assets under short-sales restrictions, minimize the portfolio variance subject to three constraints: (1) the weights of the portfolio must equal 1, (2) the expected portfolio return must equal a target return, and (3) the weights must be nonnegative. The calculus method cannot be used because the third constraint is an inequality, $w_i > 0$. At first glance this may look like a linear programming problem. However, although the constraints are linear, the objective function is not, because the portfolio variance contains squared and cross-product terms. Another technique, nonlinear or quadratic programming, must be implemented. Statistical packages that solve nonlinear programming problems using Kuhn-Tucker conditions are available. In the classic optimization problem with no restrictions on the sign of the choice variables and no inequalities in the constraints, the first-order condition for a local maximum or minimum is that the partial derivatives with respect to all of the choice variables must equal 0. Kuhn-Tucker conditions provide a similar set of conditions for the quadratic programming problem.[4]

Other constraints on the maximum or minimum values of the weights of the assets in the portfolio can be implemented using this framework. A portfolio manager may be faced with a regulation that forces him or her to diversify by holding no more than a certain percentage of the portfolio in any security. If short selling is not allowed and the maximum weight of any security is 10%, the relevant constraint is $0 < w_i < .10$.

---

[4]See Chiang (1974) for a discussion of quadratic programming techniques.

4C

Matrix Algebra Review

Matrix algebra allows us to summarize and find solutions to a set of linear equations. The general form of an $m \times n$ matrix, where n is the number of vertical columns and m is the number of horizontal rows, is

(4C.1)

$$
A = \begin{bmatrix}
a_{11} & a_{12} & \cdots & a_{1n} \\
a_{21} & a_{22} & \cdots & a_{2n} \\
\cdot & & & \cdot \\
\cdot & & & \cdot \\
\cdot & & & \cdot \\
a_{m1} & a_{m2} & \cdots & a_{mn}
\end{bmatrix}.
$$

Consider the following system of linear equations with two equations and two unknown variables, x and y.

(4C.2)
$$x - 3y = -3.$$

$$2x - 1y = 8.$$

This set of linear equations can be rewritten in matrix form:

(4C.3)
$$
\begin{matrix} A \end{matrix} \quad \begin{matrix} w \end{matrix} \quad = \quad \begin{matrix} B \end{matrix}
$$
$$
\begin{bmatrix} 1 & -3 \\ 2 & -1 \end{bmatrix} \begin{bmatrix} x \\ y \end{bmatrix} = \begin{bmatrix} -3 \\ 8 \end{bmatrix}
$$

Matrix **A** is multiplied by **w** to obtain equations 4C.2. To obtain the first equation of 4C.2, multiply matrix **A** and **w** and set the result equal to vector **B**. To multiply matrix **A** and **w**, take the first row of matrix **A** and multiply by vector **w**: $1\,x + -3\,y$ and set equal to -3. Then multiply the second row of matrix **A** by **w** to obtain $2\,x - 1\,y$ and set equal to 8. The result of the matrix multiplication is equations 4C.2.

We can use matrix algebra to solve for the unknown variables. If matrix **A** is an $n \times n$ matrix (if $n = m$, the matrix is said to be square), then the linear system **Aw** = **B** is a system of n equations and n unknowns. Our goal is to find the **w** vector. To accomplish this, multiply both sides by the inverse of matrix **A**, denoted as $\mathbf{A}^{-1}$: $\mathbf{A}^{-1}(\mathbf{Aw}) = \mathbf{A}^{-1}\,\mathbf{B}$. An $n \times n$ matrix is called nonsingular if there exists another $n \times n$ matrix $\mathbf{A}^{-1}$ such that $\mathbf{A}\,\mathbf{A}^{-1} = \mathbf{I}$, where **I** is an identity matrix. An identity matrix has diagonal elements equal to 1 and nondiagonal elements equal to 0. Because matrix **A** multiplied by the inverse of **A** is equal to the identity matrix, $\mathbf{A}^{-1}(\mathbf{Aw})$ can be simplified to **I w**. The identity matrix multiplied by matrix **w** is simply matrix **w**. Thus the solution of the linear system of equations, **w**, is equal to $\mathbf{A}^{-1}\,\mathbf{B}$.

The inverse of matrix **A** in the example at the beginning of this appendix is

(4C.4)
$$\mathbf{A}^{-1} = \begin{bmatrix} -.20 & .60 \\ -.40 & .20 \end{bmatrix}$$

The solution to the system of equations can be obtained by multiplying the inverse by matrix **B**:

(4C.5)
$$\mathbf{w} = \begin{bmatrix} -.20 & .60 \\ -.40 & .20 \end{bmatrix}\begin{bmatrix} -3 \\ 8 \end{bmatrix}$$

So x is equal to $(-.20 \times -3) + (.60 \times 8) = 5.4$, and y is equal to $(-.40 \times -3) + (.20 \times 8) = 2.8$.

4D

Lagrange Multipliers

The Lagrange multiplier technique is a popular method for solving constrained optimization problems.[5] Suppose that you wish to find the minimum or maximum of $f(x,y,z)$ subject to the constraint $g(x,y,z)$. We can introduce a fourth variable, λ, a Greek lowercase lambda and define a new function:

(4D.1) $$L = F(x,y,z,\lambda) = f(x,y,z) + \lambda g(x,y,z).$$

The variable λ is called a Lagrange multiplier. Our task is to find the critical points of the new function L by taking partial derivatives of each variable, setting each derivative equal to zero and solving for each variable.

To illustrate the use of Lagrange multipliers, assume that we want to maximize the function $x^2 + y^2$ subject to the constraint $x + 4y = 2$. The Lagrange function is

(4D.2) $$L = x^2 + y^2 + \lambda(2 - x - 4y).$$

The partial derivatives are

(4D.3) $$\frac{\partial L}{\partial x} = 2x - \lambda = 0$$

$$\frac{\partial L}{\partial y} = 2y - 4\lambda = 0$$

$$\frac{\partial L}{\partial \lambda} = 2 - x - 4y = 0.$$

We can express the partial derivatives in matrix form and solve for x, y, and λ.

(4D.4) $$\begin{bmatrix} 2 & 0 & -1 \\ 0 & 2 & -4 \\ -1 & -4 & 0 \end{bmatrix} \begin{bmatrix} x \\ y \\ \lambda \end{bmatrix} = \begin{bmatrix} 0 \\ 0 \\ -2 \end{bmatrix}$$

---

[5] For more information on mathematical techniques as applied to economics and finance problems, see Chiang (1974).

BASKET HEDGING

Immunizing portfolios against currency fluctuations has been a great concern for investors of international securities since the end of the Bretton Woods agreement in 1973. Since the breakdown of the Bretton Woods agreement, which provided a fixed exchange rate system, currency return volatility has increased dramatically. There are several strategies such as put and call insurance, option writing strategies, collars, and forward and futures hedging for immunizing portfolios against exchange rate changes. Possibly the simplest hedging instrument is a forward contract, which is an obligation to buy or sell a currency at a predetermined price at a future date. (See Chapter 16 for details of forward contracts.) Thus the manager of a U.S.-denominated portfolio with shares of U.S., Japanese, and U.K. securities could hedge each currency exposure by selling forward Japanese yen and British pound contracts to protect against currency depreciation. The forward contracts would lock in a future currency rate for the yen and pound, thereby protecting the security portfolio against currency declines. Hedging each currency exposure separately is called *matched hedging*.

Matched hedging is effective if the portfolio is exposed to a few major currencies such as the yen, pound, German mark, and Swiss frank. However, the matched hedging strategy is expensive to implement if the number of currency exposures is large because the difference between bid and ask spreads for minor currency forward contracts can be large.

Typically, a portfolio consisting of securities from many different countries can be effectively hedged using a few major currencies such as the yen, mark, and pound. Optimization theory is applied to determine the basket of major currencies that track the currency exposure of the entire portfolio. This hedging approach, called *basket hedging*, is very effective

in reducing portfolio risk because of the extremely high correlation between European Monetary System countries; for example, from 1983 to 1988, the correlation between monthly German mark returns and Belgian franc returns is .99 (Tucker, Madura, and Chiang 1991).

In practice, three major currencies are used to track the currency exposure of a portfolio. Only two currencies would result in large hedging errors, and four or more would result in an expensive and cumbersome hedge. The goal of basket hedging is to find the weights of the three currencies that minimize the variance of the basket minus the index, subject to the following two constraints: (1) the weights of the currencies, w_1, w_2, and w_3, must sum to 1, and (2) the weight of the portfolio that is being tracked, w_4 must equal −1. Thus our problem is as follows:

minimize

$$\sum_{i=1}^{4} \sum_{j=1}^{4} w_i w_j \, COV(r_i, r_j)$$

subject to

(1) $w_1 + w_2 + w_3 = 1$

(2) $w_4 = -1.$

This problem is similar to the determination of the minimum variance set discussed in Appendix 4A. The Lagrange equation is

$$L = \sum_{i=1}^{4} \sum_{j=1}^{4} w_i w_j \, COV(r_i, r_j) + \lambda_1(w_1 + w_2 + w_3 - 1) + \lambda_2(w_4 + 1).$$

BASKET HEDGING—*continued*

The partial derivatives are equal to

$$\partial L / \partial w_1 = 2w_1 \sigma_1^2 + 2\,COV(r_1,r_2)\,w_2 + 2\,COV(r_1,r_3)\,w_3 + 2\,COV(r_1,r_4)\,w_4 + \lambda_1 = 0$$

$$\partial L / \partial w_2 = 2w_2 \sigma_2^2 + 2\,COV(r_2,r_3)\,w_3 + 2\,COV(r_2,r_4)\,w_4 + 2\,COV(r_1,r_2)\,w_1 + \lambda_1 = 0$$

$$\partial L / \partial w_3 = 2w_3 \sigma_3^2 + 2\,COV(r_1,r_3)\,w_1 + 2\,COV(r_2,r_3)\,w_2 + 2\,COV(r_3,r_4)\,w_4 + \lambda_1 = 0$$

$$\partial L / \partial w_4 = 2w_4 \sigma_4^2 + 2\,COV(r_1,r_4)\,w_1 + 2\,COV(r_2,r_4)\,w_2 + 2\,COV(r_3,r_4)\,w_3 + \lambda_2 = 0$$

$$\partial L / \partial \lambda_1 = w_1 + w_2 + w_3 - 1 = 0$$

$$\partial L / \partial \lambda_2 = w_4 + 1 = 0.$$

These equations can be expressed in matrix form, $\mathbf{Aw = B}$:

$$\mathbf{A} = \begin{bmatrix} 2\sigma_1^2 & 2COV(r_1,r_2) & 2COV(r_1,r_3) & 2COV(r_1,r_4) & 1 & 0 \\ 2COV(r_2,r_1) & 2\sigma_2^2 & 2COV(r_2,r_3) & 2COV(r_2,r_4) & 1 & 0 \\ 2COV(r_1,r_3) & 2COV(r_2,r_3) & 2\sigma_3^2 & 2COV(r_3,r_4) & 1 & 0 \\ 2COV(r_1,r_4) & 2COV(r_2,r_4) & 2COV(r_3,r_4) & 2\sigma_4^2 & 0 & 1 \\ 1 & 1 & 1 & 0 & 0 & 0 \\ 0 & 0 & 0 & 1 & 0 & 0 \end{bmatrix} \quad w = \begin{bmatrix} w_1 \\ w_2 \\ w_3 \\ w_4 \\ \lambda_1 \\ \lambda_2 \end{bmatrix} \quad B = \begin{bmatrix} 0 \\ 0 \\ 0 \\ 0 \\ 1 \\ -1 \end{bmatrix}$$

Thus to calculate weights for a basket hedge, a covariance matrix for the returns of the three currencies that will be used for the hedge and the underlying portfolio is necessary. Assume that a portfolio manager desires to hedge a diversified portfolio of international securities worth $100 million. The following covariance matrix is obtained:

	GERMANY	U.K.	JAPAN	PORTFOLIO
GERMANY	.0100			
U.K.	.0096	.0144		
JAPAN	.0091	.0094	.0169	
PORTFOLIO	.0102	.0108	.0140	.0144

where the numbers down the diagonal are variances and off-diagonal terms are covariance terms.

The solution of the $\mathbf{w}$ vector, $\mathbf{w = A^{-1}B}$, produces the weights of the three currencies that minimize tracking error. The weights for the German, U.K., and Japanese forward contracts are $w_G = .340$, $w_{UK} = .124$, $w_J = .535$. Thus the number of contracts sold forward for a particular currency equals the currency weight resulting from the optimization problem (.340, .124, .535) times the market value of the portfolio ($100 million) divided by the forward price of the particular currency. See DeRosa (1991) for more detail on basket hedging and currency risk management.

The critical values are x, 2/17; y, 8/17; and λ, 4/17. Second-order conditions prove that the solution is a maximum.[6]

REFERENCES

Chiang, A. 1974. *Fundamental methods of mathematical economics.* New York: McGraw-Hill.

DeRosa, D. 1991. *Managing foreign exchange risk.* Chicago: Probus.

Evans, J., and S. Archer. 1968. Diversification and the reduction of dispersion. An empirical analysis. *Journal of Finance,* December, 761–767.

Fama, E. 1976. *Foundations of finance.* New York: Basic Books.

Francis, J., and S. Archer. 1979. *Portfolio analysis.* Englewood Cliffs, NJ: Prentice Hall.

Haugen, R. 1986. *Modern investment theory.* Englewood Cliffs, NJ: Prentice Hall.

Jaffe, J. 1989. Gold and gold stocks as investments for institutional portfolios. *Financial Analysts Journal,* March/April, 53–59.

Markowitz, H. 1952. Portfolio Selection. *Journal of Finance,* December, 77–91.

Markowitz, H. 1959. *Portfolio Selections. Efficient diversification of investments.* New York: John Wiley & Sons.

Tucker, A., J. Madura, and T. Chiang. 1991. *International financial markets.* St. Paul: West Publishing.

---

[6]Specifically, we need to evaluate the bordered Hession determinate $|H|$. The bordered Hession determinate for a two-variable Lagrange function is

$$H = \begin{vmatrix} 0 & f_x & f_y \\ f_x & L_{xx} & L_{xy} \\ f_y & L_{yx} & L_{yy} \end{vmatrix}$$

where f_x and f_y are the first partial derivatives of the objective function and $L_{xx}, L_{xy}, L_{yx},$ and L_{yy} are second derivatives of the Lagrange function. In our case the bordered Hession is

$$H = \begin{vmatrix} 0 & 1 & 4 \\ 1 & 2 & 0 \\ 4 & 0 & 2 \end{vmatrix} = -34 < 0.$$

Our solution is a maximum because this determinate is negative.

A Simplified Approach to Portfolio Formulation

CHAPTER *5*

The Single-Index Model

Introduction

The Markowitz framework, presented in Chapters 2 through 4, measures the expected return and variance of a portfolio of risky assets. The necessary inputs for the portfolio expected return and variance equations (equations 2.14 and 2.24) are the expected returns and variances of each of the component assets and a measure of association between asset returns. These inputs are generally obtained by sampling previous returns. Using these inputs and equations 2.14 and 2.24 and assuming that the variance is a reasonable measure of asset risk, you can implement the E-V rules to derive the set of efficient portfolios, those delivering the highest expected return for a given level of risk. Thus the output of this model is the set of efficient portfolios.

An elegant feature of the Markowitz model is that it makes no assumptions about the source of the comovement between the securities in the portfolio. In other words, the Markowitz model makes no assumptions regarding the correlation between asset returns and returns on the overall market or changes in inflation, for example. Therefore the resulting variance is a perfectly reliable and correct measure of the variability of the returns for the sample

101

period. Of course, whether this variance measure is accurate for future periods depends on the stability of the individual security variances and the covariances. Still, the key point is that no assumptions are made regarding the source of the common movements among asset prices.

Although the Markowitz model gives the correct value of the portfolio variance for the sample period, implementation of the model is problematic when a realistic number of securities are considered. In Chapter 4 we calculated efficient portfolios for three risky assets. This task was tractable because it entailed calculating the portfolio variance for just three assets with three correlation coefficients. However, portfolio managers typically consider hundreds of securities for inclusion in a portfolio. Such vast opportunity sets can frustrate the model's implementation. For instance, a portfolio manager considering a 200-security portfolio would need to calculate expected returns and variances for all 200 assets in addition to 19,900 correlation coefficients![1] Identifying the efficient set here is computationally difficult because the inverse of a 200×200 matrix is required each time a portfolio on the minimum variance set is calculated. Also, the Markowitz model requires that the number of observations in the time series be greater than the number of securities under consideration, which can be problematic when the number of assets is large. Thus, implementation of the Markowitz model is computationally burdensome for a realistic number of securities.

The purpose of this chapter is to introduce a model, based on a set of simplifying assumptions regarding the source of association between asset returns, that greatly reduces the computations necessary for calculation of the portfolio variance. This model, called the single-index model, assumes that the main source of movement for a security price is the price movement of the overall market; also, the correlation between asset returns is attributable to market movements. Although the single-index model, developed by William Sharpe (1963, 1964), is much more tractable than the Markowitz model, the resulting single-index risk measure is not as accurate. Keep in mind that this risk measure is only as good as the model's underlying assumptions.

THE SINGLE-INDEX MODEL

The single-index model assumes that security movements are related to changes in the overall market. We first explore this relation and the assumptions of this model. Using this framework, you can measure the expected return and variance of a security along with an estimate of the

---

[1] The number of correlation coefficients in a portfolio consisting of N assets is $N(N-1)$. However, because the correlation between assets i and j is equal to the correlation between assets j and i, the total number of correlation coefficients actually required is equal to $N(N-1) \div 2$.

covariance between two assets. Next we discuss the single-index measures of the portfolio expected return and variance in addition to limitations and problems with the model.

Assumptions of the Single-Index Model

The single-index model assumes that the main source of asset price fluctuations is the movement of the overall market, which can be proxied by an equity market index such as the SP500 or the Dow Jones industrial average. Figure 5.1 illustrates a plot of monthly returns for the market and a hypothetical asset for a sample period. The line running through the scatter plot (called the least-squares or characteristic line, estimated by regression analysis) is the line that minimizes the sum of squared errors of the returns, where an error is the difference between the actual and predicted returns. The equation of this line is

(5.1) $$r_i = a_i + b_i r_m + \epsilon_i,$$

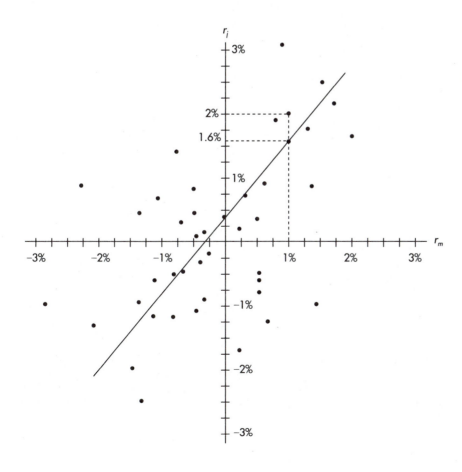

FIGURE 5.1

Relation between Market and Firm Security Returns

where r_i is the rate of return of asset i over a particular period; a_i is the rate of return that is independent of the market movement; b_i measures the sensitivity of asset i returns with respect to r_m ; r_m is the rate of return of the market index; and ϵ_i is the deviation of r_i from the return predicted by the model.

Equation 5.1 splits the return of an asset into two components. The first is a return independent of the movements of the overall market, and the second is the return related to the market. The slope term of equation 5.1, b_i, called the β-coefficient (read beta-coefficient), measures the sensitivity of the asset's returns with respect to the market returns. A β-coefficient of 1 implies that the asset price tends to move with the market, and a β-coefficient greater than 1 or less than 1 means that the asset fluctuates more or less than the market, respectively.

The least-squares line is also called the line of best fit.[2] However, this line is not perfect at predicting the asset returns. In Figure 5.1 the predicted monthly asset return conditional on a 1% market return is equal to 1.6%. The predicted return only considers economy-wide factors such as changes in aggregate U.S. output, changes in currency rates and inflation, and political policy. However, the actual return in this example is 2%. The difference between the actual and predicted returns, 0.4%, represents the firm-specific risk. For example, the firm might have received an unexpectedly large contract from the government or from a key buyer or benefited from an important judicial decision; this factor only influenced the price of this particular firm's stock. Examples of negative firm-specific risk are the death of a key manager, a fire at a production plant, and labor strikes. The difference between the actual and predicted return is attributable to the firm-specific events and is called the *residual*. The single-index model makes several important assumptions about the residuals and the source of the covariance between asset returns.

Regarding the residuals, the single-index model assumes that the expected value of a residual is 0. Figure 5.1 is consistent with this assumption. Here, the least-squares line is constructed so that the residuals are random; some of the residuals are positive and some are negative, but the expected value of the residual is $E(\epsilon_i) = 0$. Another assumption of the single-index model is that the residuals are uncorrelated with the market returns: $COV(\epsilon_i, r_m) = 0$. Thus, an extremely large change in the market return will have no impact on the magnitude of the error. Figure 5.2 plots a scatter diagram that adheres to this assumption. The final and possibly most critical and controversial assumption of the single-index model is that the residuals of assets are uncorrelated: $COV(\epsilon_i, \epsilon_j) = 0$. This suggests that the association between the returns of assets is attributable only to common market movements. Thus a high residual for, say, General Motors one day will not affect the residuals of other firms, including those in the

---

[2] We discuss estimation of the least-squares line later in this chapter.

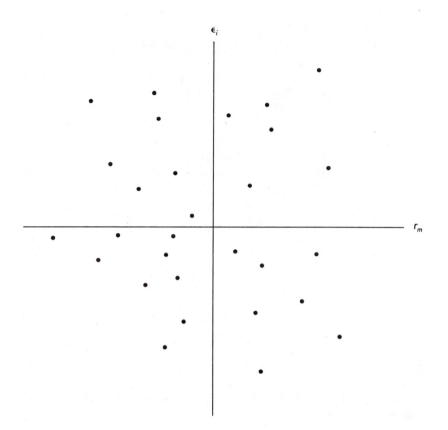

auto industry. We discuss the implications of this and other model assumptions later in this chapter.

Mean Return of a Security

The expected return or mean of a security can be expressed as the expected value of equation 5.1:

(5.2) $$E(r_i) = E(a_i + b_i r_m + \epsilon_i).$$

Since the expected value of the sum of random variables is equal to the sum of the expected values, we can rewrite equation 5.2 as

(5.3) $$E(r_i) = E(a_i) + E(b_i r_m) + E(\epsilon_i).$$

Since the intercept and β-coefficient are constants and the expected value of the residual is assumed equal to 0, we can rewrite equation 5.3 as

(5.4) $$E(r_i) = a_i + b_i E(r_m).$$

Equation 5.4 provides the expected return of a security under the single-index model. To illustrate the application of equation 5.4, assume that IBM exhibits a β-coefficient of 1.1, the intercept term is 0.5%, and the expected return of the market over the next month is 1.5%. The IBM expected return next month is therefore equal to $0.5\% + 1.1(1.5\%) = 2.15\%$.

Variance of a Security

Equation 5.9 provides the single-index model estimate of the variance of a security. This equation is derived as follows. The variance of security i, σ_i^2, is equal to $E[r_i - E(r_i)]^2$. Substituting using equations 5.1 and 5.4 yields

$$(5.5) \qquad \sigma_i^2 = E\{(a_i + b_i\, r_m + \epsilon_i) - [a_i + b_i E(r_m)]\}^2,$$

which is equal to

$$(5.6) \qquad \sigma_i^2 = E[b_i\, r_m + \epsilon_i - b_i E(r_m)]^2 = E\{b_i[r_m - E(r_m)] + \epsilon_i\}^2.$$

Equation 5.6 is in the form $(X + Y)^2$, where X is equal to $b_i[r_m - E(r_m)]$ and Y is equal to ϵ_i. Squaring the terms in equation 5.6 gives

$$(5.7) \qquad \sigma_i^2 = E\{b_i^2[r_m - E(r_m)]^2\} + 2b_i\, E\{[r_m - E(r_m)]\epsilon_i\} + E(\epsilon_i^2).$$

Factoring out b_i and applying the expected value operator to the random variables, we obtain

$$(5.8) \qquad \sigma_i^2 = b_i^2\, E\{[r_m - E(r_m)]^2\} + 2b_i\, E\{[r_m - E(r_m)]\, \epsilon_i\} + E(\epsilon_i)^2.$$

By assumption the residuals are unrelated to the market return. Thus we can rewrite equation 5.8 as follows:[3]

$$(5.9) \qquad \sigma_i^2 = b_i^2\, \sigma_m^2 + \sigma_{\epsilon i}^2,$$

where $\sigma_{\epsilon i}^2$ is the variance of the residuals. Equation 5.9 provides the variance of asset returns under the single-index model. It states that the variance of an asset comprises two elements. The first, measured by the first right-hand term of equation 5.9, is called the systematic risk or market risk. *Systematic risk* stems from economy-wide risk factors such as the health of the economy and unanticipated currency and interest rate changes that affect all investors. This risk is not diversifiable because it is

---

[3] Note that $E\{[r_m - E(r_m)]\}^2$ is equal to the variance of the market return, and $E(\epsilon_i)^2$ can be expressed as $E(\epsilon_i - 0)^2$ because the expected value of the residuals is equal to 0. Thus $E(\epsilon_i)^2$ is the variance of the residuals. Also, the covariance between the residuals and the market return can be written as $COV(\epsilon_i, r_m) = E\{(\epsilon_i - 0)\,[r_m - E(r_m)]\}$. This term is assumed to be zero.

present in all risky assets. The second right-hand term of equation 5.9 measures the *unsystematic* or *unique risk* of a security (loss of a key manager or a fire, for example). This risk is firm-specific and presumably can be diversified away.

Covariance between Two Assets

We now calculate the covariance between two assets under the single-index model (equation 5.12). The covariance between the returns of assets i and j is equal to

(5.10) $$COV(r_i, r_j) = E\{[r_i - E(r_i)][r_j - E(r_j)]\}.$$

Substituting equations 5.1 and 5.4 into 5.10 produces

(5.11) $$COV(r_i, r_j) = E\{(a_i + b_i r_m + \epsilon_i) - [a_i + b_i E(r_m)]\} \times$$
$$E\{(a_j + b_j r_m + \epsilon_i) - [a_j + b_j E(r_m)]\}.$$

In turn, equation 5.11 simplifies to:[4]

(5.12) $$COV(r_i, r_j) = b_i b_j \sigma_m^2.$$

An inspection of equation 5.12 reveals that the single-index model holds that the covariance between two assets is solely attributable to the movements of the market. To estimate the covariance between the returns of two assets you need only the variance of the market returns, which measures the magnitude of market changes, and β-coefficients, which measure the influence of market changes on the individual asset returns.

Expected Return and Variance of a Portfolio of Assets

The previous analysis demonstrated that the mean return of asset i is equal to $E(r_i) = a_i + b_i E(r_m)$ with a variance of $\sigma_i^2 = b_i^2 \sigma_m^2 + \sigma_{ei}^2$. We now measure the mean and variance of a portfolio of N assets under the single-index framework.

---

[4]Equation 5.11 can be rewritten as

$$COV(r_i, r_j) = E(\{b_i[r_m - E(r_m)] + \epsilon_i\} \{b_j[r_m - E(r_m)] + \epsilon_j\}).$$

After multiplying, we obtain

$$COV(r_i, r_j) = b_i b_j E\{[r_m - E(r_m)]^2\} + b_j E\{\epsilon_i[r_m - E(r_m)]\} + b_i E\{\epsilon_j[r_m - E(r_m)]\} + E(\epsilon_i \epsilon_j)$$

The first right-hand term consists of the β-terms of the two assets multiplied by the variance of the market returns. The second, third, and fourth right-hand terms are equal to zero by the assumptions invoked by the model.

Expected Return of a Portfolio.   The beta term for a portfolio of N assets, b_P, is simply a weighted average of the beta coefficients of the component securities:[5]

(5.13)
$$b_P = \sum_{i=1}^{N} w_i\, b_i.$$

For example, if asset 1 possesses a weight of .75 and a β-coefficient of 1.10, and asset 2 has a weight of .25 and a β-coefficient of .80, the portfolio β-coefficient is equal to .75 (1.10) + .25 (.80) = 1.025. Similarly, the portfolio intercept term is equal to a weighted average of the component intercept terms, $a_P = \Sigma\, w_i\, a_i$.[6] The portfolio residual, ϵ_P, is also a weighted average of the error terms of the securities in the portfolio, $\epsilon_P = \Sigma\, w_i\, \epsilon_i$. However, because we assume that each of the residual terms has an expected value of zero, the portfolio residual will also equal zero. Therefore equation 5.4 can be rewritten to express the expected portfolio return as follows:

(5.14)
$$E(r_P) = a_P + b_P E(r_m).$$

Thus, if the portfolio β-coefficient is equal to 1.025, the portfolio intercept is equal to 0.5%, and the expected annual market return is 10%, then the expected portfolio return under the single-index model is equal to 0.5% + 1.025(10%) = 10.75%.

---

[5] By definition, the slope (β) of the line relating the changes of the market index and the changes of the security portfolio is equal to $b_P = COV(r_P, r_m)/\sigma_m^2$. The covariance of portfolio and market returns is defined as

$$COV(r_P, r_m) = E\{[r_{P,i} - E(r_P)][r_{m,i} - E(r_m)]\}$$

In the two-security case $E(r_P) = w_1 E(r_1) + w_2 E(r_2)$, and $r_P = w_1 r_{1,i} + w_2 r_{2,i}$. Plugging these equations into the covariance formula for the portfolio and the market returns and rearranging, we obtain:

$$COV(r_P, r_m) = E\{w_1[r_{1,i} - E(r_1)][r_m - E(r_m)] + w_2[r_{2,i} - E(r_2)][r_m - E(r_m)]\}$$
$$= w_1 E[r_{1,i} - E(r_1)][r_m - E(r_m)] + w_2 E[r_{2,i} - E(r_2)][r_m - E(r_m)]$$

The first right-hand term of the above equation is the weight of asset 1 multiplied by the covariance of asset 1 and the market returns. The second right-hand term is the covariance between asset 2 returns and the market. Dividing the covariance terms by the market variance, we have

$$b_p = w_1\, b_1 + w_2\, b_2$$

In the N asset case the portfolio β is given by equation 5.13.

[6] From equation 5.4, we know that $a_p = E(r_P) - b_p E(r_m)$. The intercept term can be expressed as $\Sigma\, w_i\, E(r_i) - \Sigma\, w_i\, b_i\, E(r_m)$, or, $\Sigma\, w_i\, [E(r_i) - b_i E(r_m)]$. Because the term in brackets is defined as the intercept term for asset i, we have $a_P = \Sigma\, w_i\, a_i$. Thus the portfolio intercept is a weighted average of the intercepts of the component securities.

Portfolio Variance. The variance of security i in the single-index frame-work is equal to $b_i^2 \sigma_m^2 + \sigma_{\epsilon i}^2$, where the first term assesses the security's systematic risk and the second term is a measure of unsystematic risk (also called unique risk). Similarly, the variance of a portfolio of assets under the single-index model is equal to

(5.15)
$$\sigma_P^2 = b_P^2 \sigma_m^2 + \sigma_{\epsilon P}^2,$$

where b_P is the weighted β-coefficient of the portfolio, equal to $\Sigma\, w_i\, b_i$, and $\sigma_{\epsilon P}^2$ is the variance of the portfolio's residuals. Equation 5.15 provides the single-index model estimate of the Markowitz model portfolio variance. This estimator consists of three components: the weighted β-coefficient, the market variance, and the portfolio residual variance. We have dis-cussed the estimation of the first two components and now turn our at-tention to the estimation of the portfolio residual variance. In the next sec-tion we provide a comparison of the single-index and Markowitz models.

The calculation of the portfolio residual variance is similar to the calculation of the Markowitz model portfolio variance; variances for the residuals for each asset must be computed along with covariance terms between the residuals of the assets. The resulting portfolio residual variance is equal to

(5.16)
$$\sigma_{\epsilon P}^2 = \sum_{i=1}^{N} w^2 \sigma_{\epsilon i}^2 + \sum_{i=1}^{N} \sum_{\substack{j=1 \\ i \neq j}}^{N} w_i w_j\, COV(\epsilon_i, \epsilon_j).$$

However, one of the assumptions of the single-index model is that the covariance between the residual terms of different assets is equal to 0: $COV(\epsilon_i, \epsilon_j) = 0$. This assumption simplifies equation 5.16 considerably because the second right-hand term is equal to 0. Thus, to calculate the residual variance in this framework, the only necessary inputs are the weights of the assets and the variances of the residuals of each of the assets. Assuming that the residuals of different securities will have a covariance of 0, the covariance matrix of the portfolio residual variance will have positive values along the diagonal (the diagonal elements of a covariance matrix represent variances) but the off-diagonal terms will equal 0.

The portfolio's residual variance represents its unsystematic or diver-sifiable risk. An interesting question is what happens to the residual variance as the number of securities in the portfolio increases. To answer that question, assume that an investor holds an equally weighted portfolio, so the weight of each asset is equal to $1/N$. The portfolio residual variance is therefore equal to

(5.17)
$$\sigma_{\epsilon P}^2 = \sum_{i=1}^{N} (1/N)^2 \sigma_{\epsilon i}^2 = 1/N \sum_{i=1}^{N} (1/N)\, \sigma_{\epsilon i}^2 = 1/N\, \overline{\sigma_{\epsilon i}^2}.$$

FIGURE 5.3

Relation between the
Portfolio Variance
and the Number of
Securities in a
Portfolio

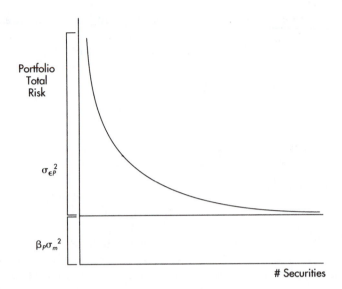

Thus the residual variance is equal to the weight of each security, $1/N$, multiplied by the average of the residual variances, $\sigma_{\epsilon i}^2$. As the number of securities becomes large, the portfolio residual variance will approach 0. For a diversified portfolio the single-index model portfolio variance estimate is essentially equal to the first right-hand term of equation 5.15, the portfolio β-coefficient squared times the market variance. Later we discuss the critical single-index model assumption that the residual terms are cross-sectionally independent.

Figure 5.3 portrays the relation between the portfolio's overall risk and the number of assets in the portfolio. The systematic or market risk is measured by the product of the portfolio β-coefficient and the market variance. The unsystematic risk, equal to $\sigma_{\epsilon P}^2$, declines as the number of assets in the portfolio increases.

COMPARISON OF MARKOWITZ AND SINGLE-INDEX MODELS

In the Markowitz framework the expected return of a portfolio of N assets is equal to

(5.18) $E(r_P) = w_1\, E(r_1) + w_2\, E(r_2) + \ldots + w_N\, E(r_N),$

and the portfolio variance equals

(5.19) $$\sigma_P^2 = \sum_{i=1}^{N} \sum_{j=1}^{N} w_i w_j\, COV(r_i, r_j).$$

Equations 5.18 and 5.19 are identical to equations 2.14 and 2.24, respectively. Because this model makes no assumptions about the source of comovements between asset returns, equation 5.19 provides the correct measure of the portfolio return variance for the given time frame. However, as noted in this chapter's introduction, equation 5.19 can be difficult to implement if the number of assets is large.

By contrast, the expected portfolio return under the single-index model is equal to

(5.20) $$E(r_P) = a_P + b_P E(r_m)$$

with a portfolio variance of

(5.21) $$\sigma_P^2 = b_P^2 \sigma_m^2 + \sigma_{\epsilon P}^2.$$

Equations 5.20 and 5.21 are identical to equations 5.14 and 5.15, respectively. In addition, the covariance between two assets is a function of the β-coefficients of the individual assets and the market variance:

(5.22) $$COV(r_i, r_j) = b_i b_j \sigma_m^2.$$

Equation 5.22 is identical to equation 5.12.

Now let us reexamine the task of the manager who must form efficient portfolios from a given opportunity set of 200 risky securities. As noted earlier, the following calculations must be made when utilizing the Markowitz model:

200 expected returns
200 variance terms
19,900 correlation coefficients

Estimating the expected returns and variances is a manageable task that can be performed by industry analysts who serve the manager. However, the main problem in implementing the Markowitz model is the number of correlations that must be calculated, 19,900 correlations in this example. This is an unwieldy task. Another major problem of implementing the Markowitz model is that securities analysts cannot focus their research efforts by specializing in particular industries but instead must be cognizant of the comovements between securities in all industries. Thus expected returns and variances for firms in, say, the auto industry must be calculated along with correlation coefficients between the auto firm returns and the returns of firms in other industries represented within the opportunity set.

In contrast, the single-index model requires fewer inputs and allows for specialization of effort by analysts. In the case of our 200-security portfolio, the calculation of the portfolio variance entails estimating β-coefficients of the 200 securities along with the variance of the market index. Therefore, the number of inputs necessary for the calculation of the single-index portfolio variance increases only linearly as the number of assets considered increases. If an additional security is contemplated, only two additional inputs, the β-coefficient and the residual variance of that security, are necessary. In contrast, in the case of the Markowitz portfolio variance, the number of calculations increases exponentially as the number of assets is increased. If an additional security is considered in a 200-security portfolio, correlations between that security and the existing 200 securities are necessary along with the variance of the proposed security. However, although the calculation of the portfolio variance in a single-index world is a tractable task, the resulting port-folio variance is only an estimate of the true portfolio risk and is only as accurate as the relevance of the underlying assumptions. We now turn our attention to the relation between the Markowitz model and single-index portfolio variance estimators (equations 5.19 and 5.21, respectively) to investigate the source of discrepancies between the portfolio variance estimates obtained by the two models. This dis-cussion is followed by a review of empirical studies exploring the relevance of the single-index model assumptions regarding the residuals.

Markowitz Model and Single-Index Portfolio Estimators

The single-index model is widely used to estimate the true portfolio variance, which is provided by the Markowitz model. Because the portfolio variance from the single-index model can differ from the variance from the Markowitz model, it is important to understand the source of discrepancies between the two variance measures.

Earlier in this chapter we found that the covariance between assets i and j under the single-index model is equal to the product of the estimated β-coefficient of the two securities and the variance of the market index plus the covariance between the residuals of the two assets:

(5.23) $$COV(r_i, r_j) = b_i b_j \sigma_m^2 + COV(\epsilon_i, \epsilon_j).$$

By invoking a single-index model assumption that the cross-sectional residual terms are equal to 0, we obtain equation 5.12. To investigate the effect of this assumption on the derivation of the single-index model variance estimator, we plug equation 5.23 into the Markowitz model portfolio variance estimator, equation 5.19, to obtain:[7]

(5.24) $$\sigma_P^2 = \sum_{i=1}^{N} \sum_{j=1}^{N} w_i w_j [b_i b_j \sigma_m^2 + COV(\epsilon_i, \epsilon_j)].$$

---

[7] This section follows the discussion contained in Hammer and Phillips (1992).

Equation 5.24 simplifies to

$$\textbf{(5.25)} \qquad \sigma_P{}^2 = \sum_{i=1}^{N} w^2 \sigma_{\epsilon i}{}^2 + (\sum_{i=1}^{N} w_i b_i)^2 \sigma_m{}^2 + \sum_{\substack{i=1 \\ i \neq j}}^{N} \sum_{j=1}^{N} w_i w_j [COV(\epsilon_i, \epsilon_j)].$$

The first right-hand term of equation 5.25 represents the variance of the residuals of the assets in the portfolio. The bracketed portion of the second right-hand term of equation 5.25 is the portfolio β-coefficient. Thus, the first two right-hand terms correspond to the single-index model portfolio variance estimate. We can rewrite equation 5.25 as follows:

$$\textbf{(5.26)} \qquad MM\ \sigma_P{}^2 = SIM\ \sigma_P{}^2 + \sum_{\substack{i=1 \\ i \neq j}}^{N} \sum_{j=1}^{N} w_i w_j\ COV(\epsilon_i, \epsilon_j),$$

where $MM\ \sigma_P{}^2$ is the Markowitz model portfolio variance measure and $SIM\ \sigma_P{}^2$ is the single-index model estimate of the portfolio variance. From equation 5.26, the equivalence of the variance estimators from the two models depends on the assumption that the residuals of the assets in the portfolio are uncorrelated.

If residuals are predominantly positively correlated, the single-index model will understate the true portfolio variance. This fact should be obvious from inspection of equation 5.16, the variance of portfolio residuals. The first right-hand term of equation 5.16 provides the variances of the residuals, and the second term represents the residual covariance terms. The single-index model assumes that the covariance terms are equal to 0. However, if these terms are in reality positive, the single-index model will understate the true variance by ignoring the common movements among the residuals.

On the other hand, the single-index model will overstate the true portfolio variance if the residuals are predominantly negative. By forcing the residuals to zero, the single-index variance estimator is ignoring the negative covariance terms, which leads to an overestimate of the true variance. The relation between security residuals is an empirical question that we now investigate.

Empirical Studies of Residual Covariances

Residuals of securities are not independent, since the performances of firms in the economy are interrelated. For example, suppose the U.S. government announces that automobile imports will be severely restricted. This news will likely lead to large positive residuals for not only the U.S. automobile producers General Motors, Ford, and Chrysler but also suppliers to these firms (such as tire, glass, and steel producers). In addition, publicly traded firms whose fortunes are tied to the health of the Michigan economy, such as local resorts, hotels, and hospitals, will also likely enjoy a positive residual because much of the economic activity in Michigan is linked to the auto industry.

However, one problem with the single-index model is that it rules out industry events by considering only systematic and unsystematic risk. In reality some information will affect only firms in a particular industry without impacting the overall market. Residuals among returns of firms in the same industry are typically positively correlated, as the stock prices tend to respond similarly to information.

King (1966) investigates the magnitude of industry effects on security variances using monthly returns from 1927 to 1960 for sixty-three New York Stock Exchange firms. After grouping the securities into industries and applying several factor analysis methods, King finds that industry affects are significant, accounting for 10 percent of the total security variance. He warns that the single-index model's assumption of cross-sectionally independent residual terms " . . . may be a dangerous simplification of the true relationships among residual yields." Thus the single-index model underestimates the portfolio variance because this model ignores the cross-sectional residual covariance terms.

Hammer and Phillips (1992) calculate the cross-sectional residual covariances from the single-index model for 1,653 firms using monthly return data from 1980 to 1989. They find that the single-index model assumption of independent residuals is violated, with 72 percent of the 1.4 million cross-sectional residual covariance statistics positive.

The single-index model assumption of independent residuals has been questioned in a number of academic studies. However, the consensus in the academic literature is that the correlation between residuals is mild, and therefore the Markowitz and single-index models produce efficient frontiers that plot in close proximity in an expected return–standard deviation space. In an early study of portfolio of selection models, Cohen and Pogue (1967) compare the solution sets obtained by the Markowitz, single-index, and multi-index models using monthly returns for 150 securities from 1947 to 1964. They conclude that " . . . ex post performance of the index models is not dominated by the Markowitz formulation." Also, " . . . the performance of the multi-index models is not superior to that of the single-index formulation, indicating the secondary importance of industry considerations for common stock portfolios."

ESTIMATING BETAS AND INTERCEPTS

This section presents the often-used least-squares approach for estimating the β and intercept terms required by the single-index model. We demonstrate the least-squares approach using monthly stock prices for two companies.

EXHIBIT 5.1

Prices and Returns for GE, First Chicago, and SP500

1989	GE Return	1st Chi. Return	SP500 Value	SP500 Return
Jan	—	—	275.31	—
Feb	9.66%	15.19%	297.09	7.91%
March	−6.74	4.40	287.11	−3.36
April	0.28	7.37	296.39	3.23
May	8.03	1.31	309.12	4.30
June	13.08	5.81	321.97	4.16
July	−5.65	0.31	319.23	−0.85
Aug	9.35	13.98	343.75	7.68
Sept	2.42	2.93	353.73	2.90
Oct	−4.94	−1.30	350.87	−0.81
Nov	0.00	−16.53	341.20	−2.76
Dec	14.22	−2.20	350.63	2.76

Monthly stock prices and returns during 1989 for General Electric and First Chicago along with SP500 index values appear in Exhibit 5.1. Casual inspection of the data reveals a positive association among the three returns; increases and decreases in the market are generally associated with price increases and decreases, respectively, for the two securities. Also, it appears that the fluctuations of the security prices are greater in absolute magnitude than the changes in the SP500.

Least-Squares Methodology

We can quantify the linear relation between security and market returns by utilizing the least-squares estimation technique to estimate the β-coefficient and the intercept. The β-coefficient and intercept from the least-squares technique together identify an equation (the line of best fit) for the line that minimizes the sum of the squared residuals.[8] As derived in Appendix 5, the least-squares solutions for the β-coefficient and intercept are given by

$$(5.27) \qquad b_i = \frac{COV(r_m, r_i)}{\sigma_m^2}$$

$$(5.28) \qquad a_i = \bar{r}_i - b_i \bar{r}_m,$$

where r_m is the rate of return of the market index, $\bar{r}_i$ is the mean of the asset returns, and $\bar{r}_m$ is the mean of the market index returns. The equation of the least-squares line is therefore $r_i = a_i + b_i r_m + \epsilon_i$. The least-squares model makes four assumptions about the residual term, ϵ_i: (1) The expected value

---

[8] This technique is called simple linear regression when one independent variable is utilized.

of the error term is equal to 0; some errors will be positive and some negative, but the errors cancel and the mean residual will equal 0. (2) The error term has a constant variance for all observations, which means that the residuals are not greater in absolute value for some observations than for others. (3) The residuals are uncorrelated. (4) The error terms are normally distributed. Given these assumptions about the residuals from the linear regression, the least-squares estimates have desirable properties. From the Gauss-Markov theorem, the least-squares estimates of the slope and intercept terms are unbiased estimators of the population parameters being estimated. (This implies that the expected value of the intercept and slope terms equals the estimated parameters.) Also, this theorem states that the least-squares estimates will have smaller standard errors than other linear, unbiased estimators. Also, the intercept and beta-coefficient will be normally distributed, which facilitates statistical inference.[9]

We can determine whether the estimated β-term is statistically different from zero. The applicable t statistic is equal to the β-coefficient divided by the standard error of the β. The standard error of the β-coefficient, $SE(b)$, is equal to the square root of $\sigma_\epsilon^2 / \Sigma[r_m - E(r_m)]^2$. The variance of the error term, σ_ϵ^2, has $N - m$ degrees of freedom, where N is the number of observations and m is the number of independent variables in the regression, including the intercept term.

Empirical Results

Exhibit 5.2 presents simple correlation coefficients between the returns. As expected, the correlations between the returns are positive, with a correlation between GE and the SP500 equal to .77 and a correlation of .74 between the SP500 and First Chicago.

The GE β-coefficient is equal to the covariance between GE and the market returns divided by the market variance. Since the market variance is equal to .00146, the GE β-coefficient is equal to .00225 ÷ .00146 = 1.54. Thus the GE returns fluctuate more than the SP500. The GE intercept term is equal to $a_{GE} = \bar{r}_{GE} - b_{GE}\bar{r}_m = .0361 - (1.54)(.02287) = .00088$. Thus the least-square line is equal to $.00088 + 1.54\ r_m$. Figure 5.4 illustrates the least-squares line for GE.

EXHIBIT 5.2

Correlation Coefficients between Returns

	SP500	GE	1st Chicago
SP500	1	.7697	.7425
GE		1	.3117
1st Chicago			1

[9] By virtue of the Gauss-Markov theorem, the least-squares estimators are said to be the best linear unbiased estimators (BLUE).

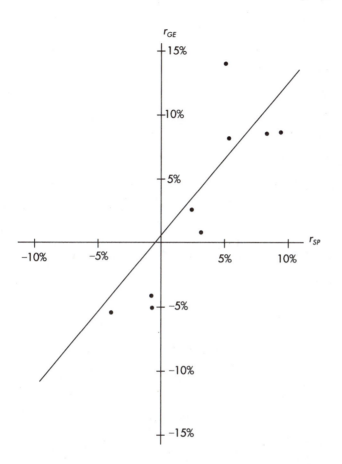

FIGURE 5.4

Least-Squares Line
for GE

The β-coefficient for First Chicago is equal to 1.66 and the intercept term is equal to −.0096. The least-squares line is illustrated in Figure 5.5.

We can determine if the β-coefficients are statistically different from zero. First, the standard error of the β-term must be calculated by dividing the sum of the squared residuals (.02339 for GE and .033 for First Chicago) by the degrees of freedom (the number of observations minus the number of independent variables including the intercept). The standard error is equal to the square root of this amount divided by the sum of the squared deviations of the SP500, .0146. Thus the standard error for the GE β-coefficient is equal to .4215. The t value for testing the hypothesis that the β-coefficient is equal to zero is the β-coefficient divided by the standard error: $1.54/.4215 = 3.65$. The standardized variable t_{N-2} will follow a t distribution with $N-2$ degrees of freedom. For example, if t_{N-2} is greater than 2.306, which is the 95 percent critical value, we can conclude at a high level of confidence that the estimated parameter value is different from the hypothesized value. Because the t value for the GE slope term is high relative to the critical value (3.65 versus 2.306), we reject the original hypothesis that the β-coefficient is equal to 0.

FIGURE 5.5

Least-Squares Line
for First Chicago

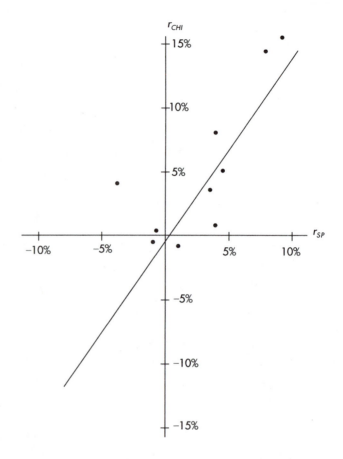

The t value for First Chicago's slope term is also high, at 3.32. The hypothesis that the β-coefficient is equal to 0 is also rejected.

In addition to testing for the statistical significance of the beta term, it is sometimes helpful to investigate the goodness of fit of the least-squares line. The coefficient of determination, or R^2 measures the goodness of fit of the regression line; specifically, the R^2 measures the proportion of the variability of the dependent variable that is explained by the independent variable. Some independent variables are more successful than others at explaining the dependent variable. For example, a regression relating shoe size (independent variable) to height (dependent variable) of a large sample of individuals will probably result in a high R^2 value because the residuals of the regression line will be small. In contrast, the R^2 from a regression with an independent variable of shoe size and a dependent variable of SAT scores for college students will likely be about 0.

The R^2 is equal to the variability of the security (or portfolio) explained by the market divided by the total security variance. The security variance attributable to market fluctuations is measured by β^2 times the market variance (the first right-hand term of equation 5.9), and the total security variance is provided by equation 5.9:

$$R^2 = \frac{b_i^2 \, \sigma_m^2}{b_i^2 \, \sigma_m^2 + \sigma_{\epsilon i}^2}.$$

The R^2 measure ranges between 0 and 1. An R^2 value of 1 means that the independent variable perfectly explains the fluctuations in the dependent variable, and an R^2 value of 0 implies that the independent variable has no explanatory value whatsoever.

For GE the β-coefficient is equal to 1.54, the residual variance is equal to .02339 ÷ 10 = .002339, and the market variance is equal to .00146. The R^2 is equal to $(1.54)^2(.00146)/\{[(1.54)^2(.00146)] + .002339\} = .59$. Thus the fluctuations in the SP500 explained approximately 59% of the fluctuations in GE returns during this period.

For First Chicago the R^2 value is slightly lower, $(1.66)^2 \, (.00146)/\{[(1.66)^2 \, (.00146)] + .0033\} = .55$.[10] These calculations are summarized in Exhibits 5.3 and 5.4.

Forecasting Ability of Beta-Coefficients

We have demonstrated how historical return information can be used to calculate the β-coefficient. Since the β-coefficient is utilized for portfolio construction and evaluation, an important question is how well the historical β-coefficients predict future ones. We shed more light on this subject by examining a study by Blume (1971). To improve the predictive ability of β-coefficients, models that incorporate accounting information such as financial structure, earnings performance, and dividend policy have been developed. We discuss several papers that evaluate the predictive performance of these models.

Blume (1971)

Blume's 1971 study addresses the predictive ability of β-coefficients. Using return information for all common stocks listed on the New York Stock Exchange from 1926 to 1968, Blume partitions his returns into six equal time periods. Using monthly return data, β-coefficients are calculated for each of the firms in the sample. The following procedure is utilized to randomly select portfolios of N securities to examine the stability of β-coefficients over time: The estimated β-coefficients are determined for each of the six-year periods and arranged in ascending order. Portfolios of

---

[10] The R-square value is equal to the squared correlation coefficient. For example, the correlation coefficient between SP500 and First Chicago returns is equal to .74, which is equal to the square root of the R-squared value, .5532.

EXHIBIT 5.3

Calculation of Beta and Intercept for GE

	Y	Y − Ȳ	(Y − Ȳ)²	X	(X − X̄)	(X − X̄) (Y − Ȳ)	ε	ε²
Feb	.0966	.0605	.0037	.0791	.0562	.0034	−.0258	.0007
March	−.0674	−.1035	.0107	−.0336	−.0565	.0059	−.0168	.0003
April	.0028	−.0333	.0011	.0323	.0094	−.0003	−.0478	.0023
May	.0803	.0442	.0019	.0430	.0201	.0009	.0134	.0002
June	.1308	.0947	.0090	.0416	.0187	.0018	.0658	.0044
July	−.0565	−.0926	.0086	−.0085	−.0314	.0029	−.0444	.0019
Aug	.0935	.0574	.0033	.0768	.0539	.0031	−.0254	.0006
Sept	.0242	−.0119	.0001	.0290	.0061	−.0001	−.0214	.0005
Oct	−.0494	−.0855	.0073	−.0081	−.0310	.0027	−.0329	.0011
Nov	.0000	−.0361	.0013	−.0276	−.0504	.0018	.0413	.0017
Dec	.1422	.1061	.0113	.0276	.0048	.0005	.0988	.0098

$\Sigma Y = .3971$
$E(Y) = .3971 / 11 = .0361$

$\Sigma (Y - E(Y))^2 = .05824$
$\sigma_Y^2 = .05824 / (11 - 1) = .0058$

$\Sigma X = .2517$
$E(X) = .2517 / 11 = .02287$

$\Sigma [X - E(X)]^2 = .0146$
$\sigma_X^2 = .0146 / (11 - 1) = .00146$

$\Sigma [X - E(X)] [Y - E(Y)] = .0225$
$COV (X,Y) = .0225 / (11 - 1) = .00225$

$\Sigma \epsilon^2 = .02339$

$$b_{GE} = \frac{COV(X,Y)}{\sigma_X^2} = \frac{.00225}{.00146} = 1.54$$

$a = \bar{Y} - \beta_i \bar{X} = .0361 - (1.54)(.02287) = .00088$

various sizes, ranging from one to one hundred securities are selected. Correlations are then calculated between the current-period β and the next-period β-coefficient for the portfolio.

Exhibit 5.5 presents correlation coefficients between β-coefficients from 1954 to 1961 with β-coefficients from 1961 to 1968. The results indicate that for individual securities past β-coefficients are poor predictors of future β-coefficients. For portfolios of one security, the correlation is .60, which implies that β-coefficients for individual securities derived from historical data explain only 36 percent of the variation of future β-coefficients.[11]

However, the predictive ability of the β-coefficients improves as the number of securities in the portfolio increases. With 50 securities the previous portfolio β-coefficient is almost a perfect predictor of the

---

[11] The coefficient of determination, which measures the percentage of the fluctuations of the dependent variable explained by the independent variable, is equal to correlation coefficient squared.

EXHIBIT 5.4

Calculation of Beta and Intercept for First Chicago

	Y	Y – Ȳ	(Y – Ȳ)²	X	(X – X̄)	(X – X̄) (Y – Ȳ)	ε	ε²
Feb	.1519	.1235	.0152	.0791	.0562	.0069	.0300	.0009
March	.0440	.0156	.0002	–.0336	–.0565	–.0009	.1095	.0119
April	.0737	.0453	.0021	.0323	.0094	.0004	.0296	.0009
May	.0131	–.0153	.0002	.0430	.0201	–.0003	–.0487	.0024
June	.0581	.0297	.0009	.0416	.0187	.0006	–.0014	.0000
July	.0031	–.0253	.0006	–.0085	–.0314	.0008	.0268	.0007
Aug	.1398	.1114	.0124	.0768	.0539	.0060	.0217	.0005
Sept	.0293	.0009	.0000	.0290	.0061	.0000	–.0093	.0001
Oct	–.0130	–.0414	.0017	–.0081	–.0310	.0013	.0101	.0001
Nov	–.1654	–.1938	.0376	–.0276	–.0504	.0098	–.1099	.0121
Dec	–.0220	–.0504	.0025	.0276	.0048	–.0002	–.0583	.0034

$\Sigma Y = .3126$
$E(Y) = .3126 / 11 = .0284$

$\Sigma [Y - E(Y)]^2 = .07345$
$\sigma_Y^2 = .05824 / (11 - 1) = .0073$

$\Sigma X = .2517$
$E(X) = .2517 / 11 = .02287$

$\Sigma [X - E(X)]^2 = .0146$
$\sigma_X^2 = .0146 / (11 - 1) = .00146$

$\Sigma [X - E(X)] [Y - E(Y)] = .0243$
$COV(X,Y) = .0225 / (11 - 1) = .00243$

$\Sigma \epsilon^2 = .0330$

$$b_{CH} = \frac{COV(X,Y)}{\sigma_X^2} = \frac{.00243}{.00146} = 1.66$$

$a = \bar{Y} - \beta_i \bar{X} = .0284 - (1.66)(.02287) = -.00956$

EXHIBIT 5.5

Correlations for β-Coefficients 1954–1961 with β-Coefficients 1961–1968

Number of Securities in Portfolio	Correlation Coefficient
1	.60
2	.73
4	.84
7	.88
10	.92
20	.97
35	.97
50	.98

Source: M. Blume, On the assessment of risk, *Journal of Finance*, March 1971, 1–10.

future-period β-coefficient. This result is not surprising, since low estimates of risk are canceled by high estimates. Blume's results suggest that " . . . naively extrapolated assessments of future risk for larger portfolios are remarkably accurate, whereas extrapolated assessments of future risk for individual securities and smaller portfolios are of some, but limited, value in forecasting the future."

In a recent study using monthly security returns from 1926 to 1985, Kolb and Rodriguez (1990) find that the distribution of β-coefficients is constant over both short- and long-run periods.[12]

Fundamental Betas

Rather than calculating β-coefficients from a history of returns, it is possible to estimate the risk of a company based on its fundamental characteristics. One of the first studies to relate accounting-determined and market-determined measures of risk is by Beaver, Kettler, and Scholes (1970). The purpose of their paper is twofold. First they examine the contemporaneous association between the β-coefficients and the accounting measures of risk. Second they determine which accounting measures can be utilized to predict the company risk. Of course the β-coefficient is the appropriate market-determined measure of risk. They utilize the following information to measure accounting risk: (1) Dividend payout ratio (dividends/earnings), (2) growth in earnings, (3) leverage, (4) liquidity, (5) asset size, (6) variability in earnings, and (7) covariability in earnings. They assert that firms with high payout ratios will have lower risk because a high ratio is indicative of the confidence of management regarding the level of future earnings. Firms with high levels of earnings growth should be riskier than lower-growth firms. Obviously, highly leveraged firms should have a higher β-coefficient because of greater default risk. Highly liquid firms should also have a lower β-coefficient. Beaver, Kettler, and Scholes assert that larger firms (as measured by total assets) will be less risky. Firms with volatile earnings and earnings that are highly correlated with the market should have a higher level of risk.

Using company β-coefficients and accounting information for 307 firms from 1947 through 1965, these authors generally find a high level of association between the market and accounting-based risk measures. Correlation coefficients have signs in predicted directions, with the exception of the liquidity measure. Because of the high degree of association between the β-coefficients and the accounting measures of risk, the researchers conclude that the " . . . evidence supports the contention that accounting measures of risk are impounded in the market-price based risk measure," and therefore a strategy of selecting portfolios according to the accounting risk measures " . . . is essentially equivalent to a strategy of

---

[12] See Bos and Newbold (1984), Collins, Ledolter, and Rayburn (1987) and Fabozzi and Francis (1978) for studies dealing with the stationarity of β.

ranking those same portfolios according the market-determined risk measure."

They also address the forecasting ability of the accounting risk measures. They determine the effectiveness of the period one (1947–1956) accounting risk measures in forecasting company β-coefficients in period two (1957–1965). After deleting several variables because of multicolinearity problems, they arrive at a final regression equation that includes the payout ratio, growth in earnings, and earnings variability. All of the independent variables are statistically significant and have the predicted signs. The independent variables are successful in predicting future market determined risk measures, explaining 44.7% of the fluctuations in the next-period β-coefficients. Because of the success of the accounting measures in forecasting β-coefficients, accounting ratios can be utilized when market information is not available, such as for a privately held firm going public.

Rosenberg and McKibben (1973)

Rosenberg and McKibben (1973) investigate the association between accounting- and market-based risk measures and β-coefficients. Their sample consists of accounting and market data from 1950 to 1971 for 578 securities. Thirty-two accounting ratios, market-based and market-valuation variables for the firms, are used as independent variables in a multiple regression model with the β-coefficient as the dependent variable. Accounting-based measures are generally similar to those used by Beaver, Kettler, and Scholes. Market-based variables include the historical β-coefficient, the ratio of annual volume for the security to the total volume for all securities, share turnover, and the share price. Market valuation variables include the dividend yield, earnings-price ratio, and the book value of the company.

Utilizing multiple regression analysis, Rosenberg and McKibben find a strong association between the independent variables and the company β-coefficients. Most of the variables have the anticipated sign and are statistically significant.

They next examine the forecasting performance of the variables over the period 1967 to 1970. Their results indicate that β-coefficients derived from historical returns are not useful in forecasting β-coefficients; the predictions based on historical returns are worse than the naive prediction that the company β-coefficient is equal to 1. In fact, " . . . the additional information provided by the historical beta, over and above that provided by the accounting descriptors, is small."

Academic research has demonstrated that accounting-based measures can improve the predictive ability of the market-based historical β-coefficients. Several finance consulting firms compute company β-coefficients on the basis of accounting and historical market information and sell this information to institutional investors. Portfolio managers use these "fundamental" β-coefficients for portfolio evaluation and asset allocation purposes. For example, portfolio managers who anticipate a bull market can purchase high–β-coefficient securities, and managers who track a market index can purchase securities with β-coefficients of 1. After completing several studies on fundamental β-coefficients, Rosenberg formed his own firm, Barr Rosenberg and Associates (BARRA), which provides an array of services to institutional investors, including fundamental β-coefficient information.

SUMMARY

By invoking some simplifying assumptions regarding the source of association between asset returns, the single-index model of Sharpe greatly reduces the computations necessary for portfolio variance calculation. This model assumes that the main source of movement for a security is the return of the overall market and that the association between asset returns is attributable to market movements. While the single-index model is much more tractable than the Markowitz model, the resulting risk measure is only an approximate measure that is as good as the relevance of the underlying assumptions.

The β-coefficient measures the sensitivity of asset price changes with respect to changes in the market index. Typically the β-coefficient is the slope term of the least-squares line. Empirical research indicates that accounting measures can be utilized to provide better predictions of β-coefficients.

In Chapter 6 we utilize the single-index-model assumptions to approximate portfolios on the investor opportunity set. We first utilize the single-index-model portfolio expected return and variance estimators to approximate portfolios on the minimum variance set. Then we discuss a model that approximates the optimal risky portfolio when borrowing and lending at the risk-free rate are possible.

Questions and Problems

1. What do the Markowitz and single-index models assume about the source of comovement between securities?

2. Why is the single-index model used to estimate the portfolio variance when the Markowitz model provides a correct measure of the portfolio variance?

3. Suppose that a portfolio consisting of 500 assets is considered. To utilize the Markowitz risk measure, how many correlation coefficients must be calculated? What inputs are necessary to calculate the single-index risk measure?

4. The number of assets under consideration increases from 500 to 501. Discuss the additional inputs necessary in the Markowitz and single-index frameworks.

5. If the β-coefficient for General Electric stock is equal to 1.2 and the intercept term is equal to 0.2%, what is the expected return for the stock if the expected market return is equal to 10%? Suppose the actual return is equal to 14%. What events might have caused the deviation of the actual and expected returns?

6. If the β-coefficient for IBM is equal to 1.05, the IBM residual variance is .02 and the market variance is .04, what is the single-index estimate of the variance of IBM stock?

7. Suppose that DuPont stock has a β of .85. What is the single-index model estimate of the covariance between DuPont and IBM returns? (See question 6 for IBM variance information.)

8. Below is return and variance information for four securities:

SECURITY	BETA	INTERCEPT	RESIDUAL VARIANCE
1	0.90	−.01	.030
2	1.10	.02	.025
3	1.60	.01	.015
4	1.05	.02	.020

What are the portfolio expected return and standard deviation if the weights for the securities are as follows: 1 − .40, 2 − .20, 3 − .35, 4 − .05. Assume that the market variance is equal to .04 and an expected return of 10%.

9. In the single-index framework, what happens to the portfolio residual variance as the number of securities in the portfolio increases?

10. Suppose that residuals tend to be positively correlated. Will the single-index model estimate of the portfolio variance be less than, equal to, or greater than the true portfolio variance? What if they are negatively correlated? Explain.

11. Monthly returns for the market portfolio, IBM, and Exxon are given below:

MONTH	SP500 RETURNS	IBM RETURNS	EXXON RETURNS
1	1.5%	0.5%	1.7%
2	0.0	0.2	−0.5
3	−2.0	−4.0	−3.0
4	−0.4	1.0	−0.6
5	2.3	1.5	4.0

Calculate the IBM and Exxon β and intercept terms and calculate the single-index variance, assuming an equally weighted portfolio and a market variance of .0625. Then use the above information to calculate the Markowitz variance.

12. How well do historical β-coefficients predict β-coefficients?

13. Can accounting information be utilized to forecast β-coefficients?

Self-Test Problems

Annual returns for the SP500, Goodyear, and McDonalds are provided below:

YEAR	SP500 RETURNS	GOODYEAR	McDONALDS
1	−5%	−10%	−5%
2	15%	7	10
3	25	40	30
4	−10	0	−20
5	25	20	25

ST-1. Calculate the β-coefficients for Goodyear and McDonalds.

ST-2. What is the single-index model covariance between the Goodyear and McDonalds returns? Compare this result with the actual covariance.

Self-Test Solutions

	$[r_{SP} - E(r_{SP})]^2$	$[r_{GY} - E(r_{GY})]^2$	$[r_{MC} - E(r_{MC})]^2$	$[r_{SP} - E(r_{SP})] \times [r_{GY} - E(r_{GY})]$	$[r_{SP} - E(r_{SP})] \times [r_{MC} - E(r_{MC})]$	$[r_{GY} - E(r_{GY})] \times [r_{MC} - E(r_{MC})]$
1	225	457.96	169	321	195	278.2
2	25	19.36	4	−22	10	−8.8
3	225	817.96	484	429	330	629.2
4	400	129.96	784	228	560	319.2
5	225	73.96	289	129	255	146.2
Σ	1100	1499.2	1730	1085	1350	1364

ST-1. $E(r_{SP}) = 50 \div 5 = 10\%$ $\sigma_{SP}^2 = 1100 \div (5-1) = 275$ $\sigma_{SP} = 16.58\%$

$E(r_{GR}) = 57 \div 5 = 11.4\%$ $\sigma_{GR}^2 = 1499.2 \div (5-1) = 374.8$ $\sigma_{GR} = 19.36\%$

$E(r_{MC}) = 40 \div 5 = 8\%$ $\sigma_{MC}^2 = 1730 \div (5-1) = 432.5$ $\sigma_{MC} = 20.80\%$

$COV(r_{SP}, r_{GR}) = 1085 \div (5-1) = 271.25$ $b_{GR} = 271.25 / 275 = .986$

$COV(r_{SP}, r_{MC}) = 1350 \div (5-1) = 337.50$ $b_{MC} = 337.50 / 275 = 1.23$

ST-2. The single-index model estimate of the covariance between Goodyear and McDonald's returns is equal to the product of the two β-coefficients and the market variance. Thus the covariance estimate is equal to $(1.23)(.986)(275) = 333.51$. The actual covariance is equal to $1364 \div 4 = 341$.

5

Derivation of Least-Squares Slope and Intercept Terms

Our goal is to find values of a and b for which the sum of squared errors is minimized. The sum of squared errors is equal to

(5A.1)
$$SS = \sum_{i=1}^{N} (y_i - a - bx_i)^2.$$

First obtain the intercept term by differentiating the equation 5A.1 with respect to a:

(5A.2)
$$\frac{\partial SS}{\partial a} = -2 \sum_{i=1}^{N} (y_i - a - bx_i) = -2\left(\sum_{i=1}^{N} y_i - Na - b \sum_{i=1}^{N} x_i\right).$$

Set equation 5A.2 equal to 0 and solve for a:

(5A.3)
$$\sum_{i=1}^{N} y_i - Na - b \sum_{i=1}^{N} x_i = 0.$$

Dividing equation 5A.3 by N gives the intercept term:

(5A.4)
$$a = \bar{y} - b\bar{x}$$

To find the least-squares solution for b, plug equation 5A.4 into equation 5A.1:

(5A.5)
$$SS = \sum_{i=1}^{N} ((y_i - \bar{y}) - b(x_i - \bar{x}))^2.$$

Differentiating equation 5A.5 with respect to b gives:

(5A.6)
$$\frac{\partial SS}{\partial b} = -2 \sum_{i=1}^{N} (x_i - \bar{x})[(y_i - \bar{y}) - b(x_i - \bar{x})]$$

$$= -2\left[\sum_{i=1}^{N} (x_i - \bar{x})(y_i - \bar{y}) - b \sum_{i=1}^{N} (x_i - \bar{x})\right].$$

This derivative must equal 0 for a minimum. Solving for b, we obtain

(5A.7)
$$b = \frac{\sum\limits_{1=1}^{N}(x_i - \bar{x})(y_i - \bar{y})}{\sum\limits_{i=1}^{N}(x_i - \bar{x})}.$$

We can divide the numerator and denominator by $N - 1$, which produces the covariance of the independent and dependent variables in the numerator and the variance of the independent variable in the denominator.

REFERENCES

Beaver, W., P. Kettler, and M. Scholes. 1970. The association between market determined and accounting determined risk measures. *Accounting Review,* Oct., 654–682.

Black, F., M. Jenson, and M. Scholes. 1972. The capital asset pricing model. Some empirical tests. In *Studies in the theory of capital markets,* M. Jenson, ed. New York: Praeger Publishers.

Blume, M. 1971. On the assessment of risk. *Journal of Finance,* March, 1–10.

Bos, T., and P. Newbold. 1984. An empirical investigation of the possibility of stochastic systematic risk in the market model. *Journal of Business,* Jan, 35–41.

Cohen, K., and J. Pogue. 1967. An empirical evaluation of alternative portfolio selection models. *Journal of Business,* July, 166–193.

Collins, D., J. Ledolter, J. Rayburn. 1987. Some further evidence on the stochastic properties of systematic risk. *Journal of Business,* July, 425–448.

Fabozzi, F., and J.C. Francis. 1978. Betas as a random coefficient. *Journal of financial and Quantitative analysis,* March, 101–116.

Fama, E. 1976. *Foundations of finance.* New York: Basic Books.

Hammer, J., and H. Phillips. 1992. The single-index model. Cross-sectional residual covariances and superfluous diversification. *International Review of Financial Analysis,* January, 39–50.

King, B. 1966. Market and industry factors in stock price behavior. *Journal of Business,* July, 139–170.

Kolb, R., and R. Rodriguez. 1990. Is the distribution of beta stationary? *Journal of Financial Research,* Winter, 279–284.

Malkiel, B., 1990. A random walk down Wall Street. New York: Norton.

Newbold, P. 1990. Statistics for business and economics. Englewood Cliffs, NJ: Prentice Hall.

Rosenberg, B., and J. Guy. 1976. Prediction of beta from investment fundamentals. *Financial Analysts Journal,* May-June, 60–72.

Rosenberg, B., and J. Guy. 1976. Prediction of beta from investment fundamentals: part 2. *Financial Analysts Journal,* July-Aug, 62–70.

Rosenberg, B., and W. McKibben. 1973. The prediction of systematic and specific risk in common stock. *Journal of Financial and Quantitative Analysis*, March, 317–333.

Sharpe, W. 1964. Capital asset prices. A theory of market equilibrium under conditions of risk. *Journal of Finance*, Sept, 425–442.

Sharpe, W. 1963. A simplified model of portfolio analysis. *Management Science*, January, 277–293.

6

The Efficient Frontier Revisited

Introduction

As discussed in Chapter 5, the single-index model invokes several simplifying assumptions regarding the source of asset movements that greatly facilitate the portfolio variance estimation task. While the Markowitz portfolio variance measure requires variances for the N securities under consideration and $N(N-1)/2$ correlation coefficients, the assumptions of the single-index model reduce the number of inputs to N beta-coefficients and residual variances.

Armed with the single-index model's portfolio return and variance estimators discussed in Chapter 5, we now can efficiently approximate the investor opportunity set in the presence and in the absence of a risk-free asset. The first half of this chapter employs the single-index model's portfolio return and variance measures and the Lagrange multiplier technique introduced in Appendix 4A to estimate portfolios on the minimum-variance set. This estimation requires a knowledge of basic calculus and matrix algebra, concepts reviewed in Appendixes 4C and 4D, respectively.

The second half of this chapter introduces a model developed by Elton, Gruber, and Padberg (1976; EGP henceforth), that implements the single-index model's assumptions to estimate the optimal risky portfolio when investors are able to borrow and lend at the risk-free rate. Recall from Chapter 3 that in the presence of a risk-free asset, a single optimal risky portfolio can be identified by the tangency between the efficient frontier and a line originating from the risk-free rate rotated counterclockwise.

This is a technical chapter utilizing matrix algebra and calculus concepts to compute efficient portfolios. It can be skipped without loss of continuity.

ESTIMATING EFFICIENT PORTFOLIOS USING THE MARKOWITZ MODEL

In Appendix 4A we utilized the Markowitz framework to determine portfolios on the minimum variance set. Specifically, the following optimization problem was solved using the Lagrange multiplier technique to obtain security weights that minimize the portfolio variance, σ_P^2 for a target rate of return, $E(r^*)$:

(6.1)
$$\sigma_P^2 = \sum_{i=1}^{N} \sum_{j=1}^{N} w_i w_j COV(r_i, r_j)$$

subject to

(1)
$$w_1 E(r_1) + w_2 E(r_2) + \ldots + w_N E(r_N) = E(r^*)$$

(2)
$$w_1 + w_2 + \ldots + w_N = 1.$$

The first constraint requires that the portfolio return equal the target return, $E(r^*)$, and the second constraint dictates that the sum of the asset weights equals 1, the so-called budget constraint.[1]

We now use a similar approach with the single index model variance measure to estimate portfolios on the minimum variance set. However,

---

[1] It is sometimes helpful to state this problem in matrix form. The portfolio variance can be rewritten as follows:

$$[w_1\, w_2 \ldots w_N] \begin{bmatrix} \sigma_1^2 & COV(r_1, r_2) & \ldots & COV(r_1, r_N) \\ COV(r_1, r_2) & \sigma_2^2 & \ldots & COV(r_2, r_N) \\ \cdot & \cdot & & \cdot \\ \cdot & \cdot & & \cdot \\ \cdot & \cdot & & \cdot \\ COV(r_N, r_1) & COV(r_N, r_2) & \ldots & \sigma_N^2 \end{bmatrix} \begin{bmatrix} w_1 \\ w_2 \\ \cdot \\ \cdot \\ \cdot \\ w_N \end{bmatrix}$$

continued

we first reformulate the single-index model expected portfolio return and variance estimators to facilitate use of the Lagrange multiplier technique.

When the number of assets under consideration (N) is small, estimating the minimum-variance set utilizing the Markowitz model and Lagrangian methodology is relatively simple. However, for a realistic number of securities this task becomes much more arduous.

Instead, the single-index model can be employed in conjunction with the Lagrangian technique to identify minimum-variance portfolios. Such an approach is simpler than the preceding optimization problem (which utilized the Markowitz model) when the number of assets is large. A principal objective of this chapter is to demonstrate how the single-index model can be used to identify the minimum-variance set. However, first we must reformulate the model's expected portfolio return and variance estimators to facilitate use of the Lagrangian multiplier technique.

SINGLE-INDEX MODELS PORTFOLIO EXPECTED RETURN AND VARIANCE MEASURES

Although we discussed the single-index model's portfolio expected return and variance measures in Chapter 6, we must rewrite these estimators in a more serviceable form before we utilize the Lagrange multiplier technique to obtain the variance-minimizing portfolio for a given portfolio return. We discuss first the portfolio expected return and then the portfolio variance.

---

[1]*Continued from previous page.*

The first constraint can be written as

$$[w_1 \, w_2 \ldots w_N] \begin{bmatrix} E(r_1) \\ E(r_2) \\ \cdot \\ \cdot \\ \cdot \\ E(r_N) \end{bmatrix} = E(r^*)$$

and the second constraint can be reformulated as follows:

$$[w_1 \, w_2 \ldots w_N] \begin{bmatrix} 1 \\ 1 \\ \cdot \\ \cdot \\ \cdot \\ 1 \end{bmatrix} = 1$$

Single-Index Model Portfolio Expected Return

As demonstrated in Chapter 5, the single-index model assumes that asset returns are related to the movement of the market index:

$$(6.2) \qquad r_i = a_i + b_i \, r_m + \epsilon_i,$$

where r_i is the return of asset i, a_i is the return that is independent of market movements, b_i is the beta measuring the effects of market movements on the asset returns, r_m is the return of the market index, and ϵ_i is the residual, which provides the difference between the predicted and actual returns.

The Markowitz portfolio return is equal to

$$(6.3) \qquad r_p = \sum_{i=1}^{N} w_i \, r_i \, .$$

Plugging equation 6.2 into equation 6.3, we obtain

$$(6.4) \qquad r_p = \sum_{i=1}^{N} w_i \, (a_i + b_i \, r_m + \epsilon_i),$$

which can be rewritten as follows:

$$(6.5) \qquad r_p = \sum_{i=i}^{N} w_i \, (a_i + \epsilon_i) + (\sum_{i=1}^{N} w_i \, b_i) \, r_m \, .$$

Thus the portfolio return can be thought of as N basic securities represented by the first right-hand term of equation 6.5 and an investment in the market index, represented by the second right-hand term of equation 6.5.

The return of the market index can be decomposed into two components, the expected market return and a random component:

$$(6.6) \qquad r_m = a_{N+1} + \epsilon_{N+1},$$

where a_{N+1} is the expected return of the market index and ϵ_{N+1} is the random error, which has a mean of 0. We will see later that the $N+1$ notation is used for convenience and greatly simplifies the task of computing efficient portfolios. Note that the variance of the market index, σ^2_{N+1}, is equal to the variance of ϵ_{N+1}. Also, for the sake of convenience, the portfolio beta, b_p, which is a weighted beta consisting of the betas of the assets in the portfolio, is denoted as w_{N+1}:

(6.7)
$$b_p = w_{N+1} = \sum_{i=1}^{N} w_i b_i.$$

Substituting equations 6.6 and 6.7 into 6.5 provides

(6.8)
$$r_p = \sum_{i=1}^{N} w_i (a_i + \epsilon_i) + w_{N+1} (a_{N+1} + \epsilon_{N+1})$$

$$= \sum_{i=1}^{N+1} w_i (a_i + \epsilon_i).$$

We are interested in the expected value of equation 6.8, the portfolio return:

(6.9)
$$E(r_p) = E \left[\sum_{i=1}^{N+1} w_i (a_i + \epsilon_i) \right].$$

Since the expected value of the residual term is equal to 0, the expected portfolio return is equal to

(6.10)
$$E(r_p) = \sum_{i=1}^{N+1} w_i a_i.$$

Equation 6.10 is equivalent to equation 5.14 of Chapter 5. To illustrate the use of the single-index model's portfolio expected return estimator (equation 6.10), assume that a portfolio of two securities is formed. Asset 1 has an intercept term (denoted as a_1) of .01 and a beta (b_1) of .9, and asset 2 possesses an intercept (a_2) of .02 and a beta (b_2) of 1.30. The expected return of the market index (a_3) is equal to .15. If the weights of securities 1 and 2 are .6 and .4, respectively, the portfolio beta is equal to $w_3 = (.6 \times .9) + (.4 \times 1.30) = 1.06$. Using equation 6.10, the expected portfolio return is equal to $(.6 + .01) + (.4 \times .02) + (.15 \times 1.06) = .014 + .159 = .173$. The sum of the first two left-hand terms provides the weighted intercept term.

Portfolio Variance

With the above notation we can also derive the portfolio variance. Substituting equations 6.8 and 6.10 into the portfolio variance equation, $\sigma_p^2 = E[r_p - E(r_p)^2]$, we obtain:

(6.11)
$$\sigma_p^2 = E[\sum_{i=1}^{N+1} w_i (a_i + \epsilon_i) - \sum_{i=1}^{N+1} w_i a_i]^2$$

$$= E[\sum_{i=1}^{N+1} w_i \epsilon_i]^2 = E[\sum_{i=1}^{N+1} w_i^2 \epsilon_i^2]$$

The expected value of ϵ_i^2 is equal to the residual variance of security i, since the expected value of the error term is 0. Thus equation 6.11 can be simplified to

(6.12)
$$\sigma_p^2 = \sum_{i=1}^{N+1} w_i^2 \sigma_{\epsilon i}^2,$$

where $\sigma_{\epsilon i}^2$ is the residual variance of security i. Note that equation 6.12 is identical to equation 5.15 of chapter 5: $\sigma_p^2 = b_p^2 \sigma_m^2 + \sigma_{\epsilon p}^2$; however, equation 6.12 presents the single-index model's portfolio variance in a more convenient form.

Equation 6.12 can be expressed in matrix form:

(6.13)
$$\sigma_p^2 = [w_1\, w_2 \dots w_{N+1}] \begin{bmatrix} \sigma_{\epsilon_1}^2 & 0 & . & . & . & 0 \\ 0 & \sigma_{\epsilon_2}^2 & . & . & . & 0 \\ . & . & & & & . \\ . & . & & & & . \\ . & . & & & & . \\ 0 & 0 & . & . & . & \sigma_{\epsilon_{N+1}}^2 \end{bmatrix} \begin{bmatrix} w_1 \\ w_2 \\ . \\ . \\ . \\ w_{N+1} \end{bmatrix}$$

Remember that w_{N+1} is the portfolio beta and $\sigma_{\epsilon_{N+1}}^2$ is the variance of the market index. Suppose that a two-asset portfolio is considered. Multiplying the matrices in equation 6.13, we obtain $\sigma_p^2 = w_1^2 \sigma_{\epsilon_1}^2 + w_2^2 \sigma_{\epsilon_2}^2 + w_3^2 \sigma_3^2$, which is equivalent to equation 5.15.

The computational advantage of the single-index model over the Markowitz method should be obvious if you examine the matrices in equation 6.13. Inverting the single-index portfolio variance matrix is a simple assignment, since the resulting inverse is simply a diagonal matrix with corresponding reciprocals along the diagonal.

ESTIMATING EFFICIENT PORTFOLIOS USING THE SINGLE-INDEX MODEL

Armed with more serviceable representations of the portfolio expected return and variance estimators (equations 6.10 and 6.12, respectively), we now reexamine the optimization problem whose solution provides portfolio weights that minimize the portfolio variance for a target portfolio return. Thus, the solution must produce weights that deliver the target expected portfolio return, the weights must sum to 1, and the portfolio beta must equal w_{N+1}. The problem is to minimize

$$\sigma_p^{\,2} = \sum_{i=1}^{N+1} w_i^{\,2}\, \sigma_{\epsilon_i}^2,$$

subject to

(1)
$$\sum_{i=1}^{N+1} w_i a_i = E(r_p^*)$$

(2)
$$\sum_{i=1}^{N} w_i = 1$$

(3)
$$\sum_{i=1}^{N} w_i b_i = w_{N+1}$$

or

$$\sum_{i=1}^{N} w_i b_i - w_{N+1} = 0.$$

The first constraint requires that the portfolio expected return equal the target return, $E(r_p^*)$. The second constraint dictates that the sum of the weights of assets 1 through N be equal to 1. The third constraint forces the portfolio beta to equal w_{N+1}.

If the number of assets is two, the problem is to minimize

(6.14)
$$\sigma_p^{\,2} = w_1^{\,2}\, \sigma_{\epsilon_1}^2 + w_2^{\,2}\sigma_{\epsilon_2}^2 + w_3^{\,2}\, \sigma_3^{\,2}$$

subject to

(1) $a_1\, w_1 + a_2\, w_2 + a_3\, w_3 = E(r_p^*)$
(2) $w_1 + w_2 = 1$
(3) $w_1\, b_1 + w_2\, b_2 - w_3 = 0.$

The Lagrange equation in the two-asset case is

(6.15) $L = w_1^{\,2}\, \sigma_{\epsilon_1}^2 + w_2^{\,2}\, \sigma_{\epsilon_2}^2 + w_3^{\,2}\, \sigma_3^{\,2} + \lambda_1\, [a_1\, w_1 + a_2\, w_2 + a_3\, w_3 - E(r_p^*)]$
$\quad + \lambda_2\, (w_1 + w_2 - 1) + \lambda_3\, (w_1\, b_1 + w_2\, b_2 - w_3) = 0.$

Derivatives of L with respect to each of the independent variables provide the following six first-order conditions:

(6.16)
$$\frac{\partial L}{\partial w_1} = 2w_1 \sigma_{\epsilon_1}^2 + \lambda_1 a_1 + \lambda_2 + \lambda_3 b_1 = 0$$

$$\frac{\partial L}{\partial w_2} = 2w_2 \sigma_{\epsilon_2}^2 + \lambda_1 a_2 + \lambda_2 + \lambda_3 b_2 = 0$$

$$\frac{\partial L}{\partial w_3} = 2w_3 \sigma_3^2 + \lambda_1 a_3 + 0 - \lambda_3 = 0$$

$$\frac{\partial L}{\partial \lambda_1} = a_1 w_1 + a_2 w_2 + a_3 w_3 - E(r_p^*) = 0$$

$$\frac{\partial L}{\partial \lambda_2} = w_1 + w_2 - 1 = 0$$

$$\frac{\partial L}{\partial \lambda_3} = w_1 b_1 + w_2 b_2 - w_3 = 0.$$

In matrix form this system of equations is

(6.17)
$$
\begin{matrix} & & \mathbf{A} & & & & & \mathbf{w} & = & \mathbf{B} \end{matrix}
$$

$$
\begin{bmatrix}
2\sigma_{\epsilon_1}^2 & 0 & 0 & a_1 & 1 & b_1 \\
0 & 2\sigma_{\epsilon_2}^2 & 0 & a_2 & 1 & b_2 \\
0 & 0 & 2\sigma_3^2 & a_3 & 0 & -1 \\
a_1 & a_2 & a_3 & 0 & 0 & 0 \\
1 & 1 & 0 & 0 & 0 & 0 \\
b_1 & b_2 & -1 & 0 & 0 & 0
\end{bmatrix}
\begin{bmatrix}
w_1 \\ w_2 \\ w_3 \\ \lambda_1 \\ \lambda_2 \\ \lambda_3
\end{bmatrix}
=
\begin{bmatrix}
0 \\ 0 \\ 0 \\ E(r_p^*) \\ 1 \\ 0
\end{bmatrix}
$$

where the first matrix is the **A** matrix, the second matrix is the **w** vector, and the vector to the right of the equal sign is the **B** matrix. The solution to the **w** vector, which provides the set of weights that minimizes the portfolio variance, is equal to $\mathbf{A}^{-1}\mathbf{B}$, where $\mathbf{A}^{-1}$ is the inverse of matrix **A**.[2]

To illustrate the use of the single-index model and the Lagrange multiplier method to obtain a portfolio on the minimum-variance set, assume that two securities are under consideration. The first security has a beta of .8, an intercept of .01, and a residual variance of .01. The second

---

[2]For example, a square matrix times its inverse produces an identity matrix, which is a matrix with 1s down the diagonal and 0s for off-diagonal terms. See Appendix 4C for a review of matrix algebra.

possesses a beta of 1.2, an intercept of .02 and a residual variance of .02. The expected market return is 15 percent and the variance of the market index is .04. We can obtain weights for assets 1 and 2 that minimize the portfolio variance for a target portfolio return of 25 percent by plugging the relevant information into the matrices presented in equation 6.17:

(6.18)

$$
\begin{array}{ccc}
\mathbf{A} & \mathbf{w} & \mathbf{B} \\
\begin{bmatrix}
0.02 & 0.00 & 0.00 & 0.01 & 1 & 0.8 \\
0.00 & 0.04 & 0.00 & 0.02 & 1 & 1.2 \\
0.00 & 0.00 & 0.08 & 0.15 & 0 & -1.0 \\
0.01 & 0.02 & 0.15 & 0.00 & 0 & 0.0 \\
1.00 & 1.00 & 0.00 & 0.00 & 0 & 0.0 \\
0.80 & 1.20 & -1.00 & 0.00 & 0 & 0.0
\end{bmatrix}
&
\begin{bmatrix}
w_1 \\ w_2 \\ w_3 \\ \lambda_1 \\ \lambda_2 \\ \lambda_3
\end{bmatrix}
=
\begin{bmatrix}
0.00 \\ 0.00 \\ 0.00 \\ 0.25 \\ 1.00 \\ 0.00
\end{bmatrix}
\end{array}
$$

Again, the weight vector (**w**) is equal to the product of $\mathbf{A}^{-1}\,\mathbf{B}$.

$$
\begin{array}{ccc}
\mathbf{A}^{-1} & \mathbf{B} & \mathbf{w} \\
\begin{bmatrix}
0.000 & 0.000 & 0.000 & -14.2857 & 2.857 & -2.143 \\
0.000 & 0.000 & 0.000 & 14.2857 & -1.857 & 2.143 \\
0.000 & 0.000 & 0.000 & 5.714 & .057 & -.143 \\
-14.286 & 14.286 & 5.714 & -14.857 & 1.857 & -1.771 \\
2.857 & -1.857 & .057 & 1.851 & -.302 & .284 \\
-2.143 & 2.143 & -.143 & -1.771 & .282 & -.282
\end{bmatrix}
&
\begin{bmatrix}
0.00 \\ 0.00 \\ 0.00 \\ 0.25 \\ 1.00 \\ 0.00
\end{bmatrix}
=
\begin{bmatrix}
-.714 \\ 1.714 \\ 1.486 \\ -1.857 \\ -.161 \\ -.161
\end{bmatrix}
\end{array}
$$

FUNDAMENTAL PORTFOLIO MANAGEMENT

We concentrate on quantitative portfolio management in this book. Quantitative models such as the Markowitz model, single-index model, the capital asset pricing model, and arbitrage pricing theory are utilized intensively by 30 percent of portfolio management firms to allocate assets across many distinct asset classes. However, the majority of equity portfolio managers continue to utilize non-quantitative techniques such as fundamental analysis to select stocks for inclusion in the portfolio. See Coggin (1989) for more detail on portfolio manager characteristics.

These fundamental analysis managers can be grouped into two categories. Value managers seek to purchase equities that are selling at a discount from fair value and sell securities that are expensive. Value managers typically utilize price/earnings ratios and book value ratios to select securities. Value managers typically possess securities with low betas, low price/earnings ratios, and high dividend yields.

Growth managers focus on companies with a high level of earnings growth. These managers purchase companies with high earnings growth with an expectation of continued high earnings growth. Portfolios of growth managers are characterized by high betas, high price/earnings ratios, and low dividend yields. Chapter 13, which deals with market efficiency, discusses the effectiveness and profitability of these management strategies.

TABLE 6.1

Efficient Portfolios

Portfolio	1	2	3	4
$E(r_p)$	17.50%	25%	30.00%	35.00%
σ_P	23.28%	39%	51.33%	64.22%
w_1	.36	−.71	−1.43	−2.14
w_2	.64	1.71	2.42	3.14

According to the single-index model, the weight of assets 1 and 2 should equal −.714 and 1.714, respectively, for a variance-minimizing portfolio with a 25% return. The portfolio β-coefficient is −.714(.8) + 1.714 (1.2) = 1.486. The portfolio variance is equal to $-.714^2(.01) + 1.714^2$ (.02) + 1.486^2(.04) = .1522, and the standard deviation is .390. The weighted intercept of this portfolio is .027; thus, the expected return of this portfolio is .027 + 1.486(.15) = .25.

Using the same methodology other portfolios on the minimum-variance set can be obtained. Table 6.1 presents several of these portfolios.

ESTIMATING THE OPTIMAL PORTFOLIO WHEN A RISK-FREE ASSET IS AVAILABLE

As demonstrated in Chapter 3, all investors will select the same portfolio of risky assets if borrowing and lending at the risk-free interest rate are possible. Equation 3.31 of Chapter 3 provides the optimal weights of risky securities 1 and 2 in the presence of a risk-free asset; although this equation, which is derived in Appendix 3, looks frightening, it is easily programmable. However, as in the computation of the Markowitz portfolio variance, determining the optimal risky portfolio is problematic when a realistic number of securities are considered.

Fortunately, EGP (1976) utilize the assumptions of the single-index model to develop a simple model for constructing the optimal risky portfolio in the presence of a risk-free asset that can be bought or sold. Their model can be implemented without the aid of a computer. Moreover, the solution obtained from their model is identical to the result that would be obtained using more complicated quadratic programming methods. We first discuss the criterion for evaluating the desirability of an asset and then utilize the EGP model to select the optimal portfolio with and without short-sales restrictions.

Criterion for Asset Performance Evaluation

To compute the optimal risky portfolio, the securities must first be ranked in terms of their relative attractiveness. The first step in assessing the desirability of a security is to measure its excess return, which is the return beyond the risk-free interest rate, $E(r_i) - r_f$, where $E(r_i)$ is the expected return of asset i and r_f is the risk-free interest rate. The performance measure must also incorporate the risk of the security. To illustrate the importance of including a risk measure in the performance measure, assume that securities 1 and 2 have expected returns of 12 percent and 14 percent, respectively, and the risk-free rate is 5 percent. Although security 2 has a higher excess return, 9 percent compared with 7 percent for security 1, security 2 may not be more desirable once risk is considered. We will see in Chapters 9 and 10 that the appropriate measure of market risk is the beta-coefficient. Suppose that the betas are .5 and 2 for securities 1 and 2 respectively. Since the risk for security 2 is substantially greater than that for asset 1, and the excess returns of the two securities are not dramatically different, asset 1 probably is the more desirable security.

The attractiveness of a security can be measured by its excess return over per unit of systematic risk: $E(r_i) - r_f / b_i$.[3] This ratio is 14 percent for asset 1 and 4.5 percent for asset 2. Thus asset 1 is the more desirable because it offers an excess return of 14 percent per unit of systematic risk.

Cutoff Ratio

The next step for obtaining the optimal risky portfolio is to rank the securities according to their ratios of excess return to beta. EGP develop a cutoff point, called C_0. Securities with ratios of excess return to beta that are greater than C_0 are included in the portfolio. When short selling is not allowed, securities with ratios less than C_0 are not included in the optimal portfolio. If short sales are allowed, securities with ratios less than C_0 are sold short.

$$(6.19) \qquad C_o = \frac{\sigma_m^2 \Sigma \dfrac{[(E(r_i) - r_f] b_i}{\sigma_{\epsilon i}^2}}{1 + \sigma_m^2 \Sigma (b_i^2 / \sigma_{\epsilon i}^2)},$$

where σ_m^2 is the market variance. C_0 adds securities to the portfolio if the analyst's estimate of the excess return is greater than the expected excess return on the security based on the performance of the optimal portfolio.[4]

---

[3]This measure is called the Treynor index. See Chapter 20 for more detail on this and other performance measures.

[4]C_0 can be rewritten as follows: $C_0 = b_{iP} [E(r_P) - r_f]/b_i$, where b_{iP} is the beta for security i based on a change in the optimal portfolio and $E(r_P)$ is the expected return of the optimal portfolio, and b_i is the beta-coefficient for security i with respect to a change in the market index. Assets are included in the optimal portfolio if the expected excess return to beta-coefficient is greater than the cutoff point, $[E(r_i) - r_f]/b_i > C_0$. Plugging the excess return to beta ratio into the new form of C_0, we obtain $E(r_i) - r_f > b_{iP} [E(r_i) - r_f]$. The left-hand side of this equation is the analyst's estimate of the excess return of security i, and the right-hand side is the excess return of the security based on the performance of the optimal portfolio.

Weights for each of the securities must be obtained once the securities are selected for inclusion in the optimal portfolio.

The weight of security i is

(6.20)
$$w_i = \frac{Z_i}{\sum_{i=1}^{N} Z_i}$$

where
$$Z_i = \frac{b_i}{\sigma_{\epsilon i}^2}\left[\frac{E(r_i) - r_f}{b_i} - C_0\right].$$

The second term determines the relative investment in a security, and the first expression scales the weights to ensure that the sum of the weights of all securities under consideration is equal to 1.

Determining the Optimal Risky Portfolio Using the EGP Model—No Short Sales Allowed

We provide an example of the determination of the optimal risky portfolio when short-sales restrictions exist using data provided in Table 6.2. Expected returns, beta-coefficients, and residual variances are provided for seven securities, and the securities are ranked according to the expected excess return over the beta-coefficient (column 4). In addition, the excess return over the residual variance (column 5) and the beta squared over the residual variance ratios (column 6) are calculated from data in the first three columns. The risk-free interest rate is 5 percent and the variance of the market index is 4 percent.

Our first task is to calculate C_0. The term $\Sigma\, b_i[E(r_i) - r_f]/\sigma_\epsilon^2$ is equal to column 5 times column 2: $1.00 + .0375 + .18 + .125 + 1.20 + .0665 + .6375 = 3.247$. Also, the sum of column 6 is equal to .4461. Thus, C_0 is equal to $4(3.247)/[1 + 4(.4461)] = 4.66$. Thus all securities that have an excess return to beta ratio greater than 4.66 will be included in the optimal portfolio. Thus, securities 1 through 5 will be included in the portfolio. Now the

TABLE 6.2

Return Information for Seven Securities

	$E(r_i)$	b_i	$\sigma_{\epsilon i}^2$	$(r_i - r_f)/b_i$	$(r_i - r_f)/\sigma_{\epsilon i}^2$	$b_i^2/\sigma_{\epsilon i}^2$
1	25%	1.50	30%	13.33	.667	.0750
2	8	.25	20	12.00	.150	.0031
3	15	.90	50	11.11	.200	.0162
4	10	.50	20	10.00	.250	.0125
5	20	2.00	25	7.50	.600	.1600
6	7	.50	15	4.00	.133	.0167
7	15	2.55	40	3.92	.250	.1625

weights must be determined for the five securities. The Z values are as follows:

$$Z_1 = 1.5/30 \, (13.33 - 4.66) = .434$$

$$Z_2 = .25/20 \, (12.00 - 4.66) = .092$$

$$Z_3 = .9/50 \, (11.11 - 4.66) = .043$$

$$Z_4 = .5/20 \, (10.00 - 4.66) = .1335$$

$$Z_5 = 2/25 \, (7.50 - 4.66) = .2272$$

The sum of the Z values is equal to .9297. The optimal weights are obtained by dividing the Z values by .9297:

$$w_1 = .434/.9297 = .4668$$

$$w_2 = .092/.9297 = .099$$

$$w_3 = .043/.9297 = .046$$

$$w_4 = .1335/.9297 = .1436$$

$$w_5 = .2272/.9297 = .2444.$$

Thus, security 1 should make up 46.68 percent of the optimal portfolio, asset 2 should account for 9.9 percent, and so on. This result is identical to the solution that would be obtained using more complex quadratic programming methods.

Determining the Optimal Risky Portfolio Using the EGP Model—Short Sales Allowed

We now reexamine the previous example assuming that short sales are allowed. As before, assets are ranked according to the excess return to beta ratio, and securities that possess a ratio greater than the cutoff point will be held long in the optimal portfolio. However, with short sales allowed, securities with a ratio less than the cutoff point will be held short; thus all securities under consideration will be held (with the exception of a security that has an excess return to beta ratio equal to C_0).

Z values will be calculated for all securities. If the proceeds of the short sales can be used as a source of funds, the weight of security i is as follows:

$$w_i = \frac{Z_i}{\sum\limits_{i=1}^{N} Z_i}$$

In this case the weights will sum to 1. If, however, the proceeds of the short sale cannot be used for investment, the scaling factor is equal to the sum of the absolute value of all of the Z values. In this example we assume that short-sale proceeds are available for investment, which is true for large institutional investors.

The Z values for the first five securities have been calculated. The Z value for asset 6 is $(.5/15) \times (4 - 4.66) = -.022$ and is $(2.55/40) \times (3.92 - 4.66) = -.047$ for asset 7. The sum of the Z values for the seven securities is .8607. The weights, obtained by dividing the individual Z values by .8607, are

$$w_1 = .434/.8607 = .5042$$

$$w_2 = .092/.8607 = .1069$$

$$w_3 = .043/.8607 = .0500$$

$$w_4 = .1335/.8607 = .1551$$

$$w_5 = .2272/.8607 = .2640$$

$$w_6 = -.022/.8607 = -.0256$$

$$w_7 = -.047/.8607 = -.0546$$

These weights deliver the optimal risky portfolio, according to the EGP model.

SUMMARY

The efficient frontier can be constructed using the single index model's estimator for the portfolio variance. The portfolio that minimizes the portfolio variance for a target portfolio return is obtained using the Lagrange multiplier technique. Three constrains exist. First, the target portfolio return must be achieved. Second, the weights must sum to 1. And third, the portfolio beta must equal the target beta. Inputs for the securities are obtained and plugged into the prescribed matrices and solved for the weights. The target return can be changed and another portfolio can be estimated.

The EGP model utilizes the single-index model's assumptions to approximate the optimal risky portfolio when borrowing and lending at the risk-free rate are possible. This tractable model provides a solution that is equivalent to the asset mix furnished by the more complex quadratic programming method. To utilize the EGP model, rank the assets according to their excess return to beta ratios. The cutoff ratio is obtained. If short selling is not allowed, assets that possess an excess return to beta ratio that is greater than the cutoff ratio are accepted. If short selling is allowed, securities will be held either long or short.

To solve an economic choice problem, the opportunity set must be combined with the preference function of the economic agent; we have devoted five chapters to obtaining the opportunity set under uncertainty for our investment choice problem. The goal of Chapter 7 is to provide a rigorous analysis of investor preferences. Armed with the opportunity set and preference information, you can identify a utility-maximizing portfolio, thus solving the choice problem.

REFERENCES

Blume, M. 1971. On the assessment of risk. *Journal of Finance*. March 1971, 1–10.

Coggin, T. D. 1989. Active equity management. In *Portfolio and investment management*, Frank J. Fabozzi, ed. Chicago: Probus Publishing Company.

Cohen, K., and J. Pogue. 1967. An empirical evaluation of alternative portfolio selection models. *Journal of Business* 166–193.

Elton, E., and M. Gruber. 1991. *Modern portfolio theory and investment analysis*, ed 4. New York: John Wiley & Sons.

Elton, E., M. Gruber, and M. Padberg. 1976. Simple criteria for optimal portfolio selection. *Journal of Finance*, December, 1342–1357.

Elton, E., M. Gruber, and M. Padberg. 1978. Simple criteria for optimal portfolio selection. Tracing out the efficient frontier. *Journal of Finance*. March, 296–302.

Sharpe, W. 1963. A simplified model of portfolio analysis. *Management Science*. January, 277–293.

Sharpe, W. 1964. Capital asset prices. A theory of market equilibrium under conditions of risk. *Journal of Finance* September, 425–442.

Questions and Problems

1. What inputs are necessary to estimate the efficient frontier using the single-index model?

2. What is an inverse of a matrix? How can we use the matrix approach to solve for a system of equations?

3. Why is it difficult to calculate minimum-variance portfolios using the Markowitz portfolio expected return and variance measures and the Lagrangian technique?

4. Suppose that a twenty-security portfolio is considered. How would you obtain the inputs necessary to estimate the efficient frontier under the Markowitz and single-index-model frameworks?

5. Why is the $N + 1$ notation used to reformulate the expected portfolio return and variance?

6. What are the advantages of the EGP model? What are the inputs to the model? What does the model provide?

7. What is the inverse of the following matrix?

$$\begin{bmatrix} 2 & 5 \\ 1 & 7 \end{bmatrix}$$

Multiply this matrix by its inverse. You should obtain an identity matrix.

8. The inputs for the single-index model's portfolio expected return measure are the intercept terms and the betas of each of the securities under consideration. If you are presented with only expected return and betas of the securities, how do you obtain the intercept information?

9. Suppose that two securities are considered. Security 1 has an intercept of .01, a beta of 1.4, and a residual variance of .02. Security 2 has an intercept of .015, a beta of .8, and a residual variance of .01. If the market variance is .04, what are the weights for the two securities that minimize the portfolio variance for a target portfolio return of 20 percent? Use Lotus 123 to calculate the inverse of the matrix. Input the square matrix and press /. Select D(ata), M(atrix), and I(nvert). Specify the input and output ranges, and the inverse of the matrix will follow.

10. Rework problem 9 and assume target portfolio returns of 10 percent and 30 percent.

11. Suppose that short sales are not allowed. How would you estimate minimum variance portfolios with data presented in problem 9?

12. Consider the following six assets:

	$E(r_i)$	b_i	$\sigma_{\epsilon i}^2$
1	20%	1.4	50
2	8%	0.7	15
3	15%	1.0	25
4	25%	1.3	40
5	10%	0.9	20
6	18%	1.2	30

If the risk-free interest rate is 5 percent and the market variance is 4%, what are the weights of the six securities that will provide the optimal risky portfolio? Use the EGP model and assume that short selling is not allowed.

13. Rework problem 12 assuming that short sales are allowed.

14. Rework problem 13 assuming a risk-free interest rate of 3 percent.

Self-Test Problems

ST-1.   Asset 1 has an expected return of 20%, a beta of 1.4, and a residual variance of .015. Asset 2 has an expected return of 13%, a beta of .9, and a residual variance of .010. Find the minimum variance portfolio corresponding to a target portfolio return of 18 percent. The expected market return is 13.5 percent and the market variance is equal to .04. Use Lotus 123 to calculate the inverse of the matrix. Input the square matrix and press /. Select D(ata), M(atrix), and I(nvert). Specify the input and output ranges, and the inverse of the matrix will follow.

ST-2.   An investor is considering four securities with the following betas and residual variances:

	$E(r_i)$	b_i	$\sigma_{\epsilon i}^2$
1	20%	5.0	30%
2	15%	3.0	15%
3	12%	1.5	3%
4	8%	0.8	1%

The risk-free interest rate is 5 percent and the market variance is 5 percent. Use the EGP model to determine the weights for the optimal portfolio, with and without short sales.

Solutions to Self-Test Problems

ST-1.   Although the intercept terms are not given, they can be obtained. We know that $E(r_i) = a_i + b_i E(r_i)$. Thus, the intercept for asset 1 is equal to $a_1 = .20 - (1.4 \times .135) = .011$. The intercept for asset 2 is $a_2 = .13 - (.9 \times .135) = .0085$. Plugging in the relevant information into the matrices of equation 6.17, we have

$$\begin{bmatrix} 0.030 & 0.0000 & 0.000 & 0.0110 & 1 & 1.4 \\ 0.000 & 0.0200 & 0.000 & 0.0085 & 1 & 0.9 \\ 0.000 & 0.0000 & 0.080 & 0.1350 & 0 & -1.0 \\ 0.011 & 0.0085 & 0.135 & 0.0000 & 0 & 0.0 \\ 1.000 & 1.0000 & 0.000 & 0.0000 & 0 & 0.0 \\ 1.400 & 0.9000 & -1.000 & 0.0000 & 0 & 0.0 \end{bmatrix} \begin{bmatrix} w_1 \\ w_2 \\ w_3 \\ \lambda_1 \\ \lambda_2 \\ \lambda_3 \end{bmatrix} = \begin{bmatrix} 0 \\ 0 \\ 0 \\ .18 \\ 1 \\ 0 \end{bmatrix}$$

Thus, $w_1 = .7142$ and $w_2 = .2857$. The portfolio beta equals 1.257, and the portfolio standard deviation is .2677.

ST-2.   In this problem, $\Sigma (b_j^2/\sigma_{\epsilon j}^2) = 25/30 + 9/15 + 2.25/3 + .64/1 = 2.8233$, and $\Sigma [(E(r_j) - r_f] b_j/\sigma_{\epsilon j}^2$ is equal to 10.4. Thus the cutoff point will equal $5[10.4/1 + 5(2.8233)] = 3.44$. The Z values:

$$Z_1 = (5/30)\ (3 - 3.44) = -.0733$$

$$Z_2 = (3/15)\ (3.33 - 3.44) = -.0213$$

$$Z_3 = (1.5/3)\ (4.66 - 3.44) = .6133$$

$$Z_4 = (.8/1)\ (3.75 - 3.44) = .248$$

If short sales are not allowed, only securities 3 and 4 will be held. The sum of the Z values equals .8613 and the weight of asset three equals .6133/.8613 = .712. The weight of asset 2 equals .248/.8613 = .288. If short sales are allowed, the sum of the Z values equals .7667. The optimal portfolio contains the four securities in the following proportions: $w_1 = -.0956$, $w_2 = -.0278$, $w_3 = .80$, and $w_2 = .3235$.

CHAPTER *7*

Maximizing Expected Utility

Introduction

As discussed in Chapter 1, a two-step procedure can be employed to solve problems of economic choice. First, agents derive the opportunity set for the assets under consideration, and second, the preferences of the agent must be identified. The interaction of the opportunity set and agent preferences reveals the optimal choice, that is, the solution to the economic choice problem. This two-step procedure was illustrated in Chapter 1 under perfect certainty.[1]

---

[1] The problem of choice in the absence of risk identified in Chapter 1 involved a single payoff, the risk-free interest rate. The opportunity set in this case was the money market line, which depicted the possible two-period consumption bundles available to the economic agent. Indifference curves revealed preferences regarding present versus future consumption. The interaction between the money market line and a family of indifference curves provided a utility-maximizing consumption stream.

This problem of economic choice is very similar to the consumer allocation problem of microeconomics. In the simple two-good setting, the consumer seeks to maximize utility, which is a function of the two goods, subject to the constraint, the budget line. The budget line illustrates the possible consumption bundles available to the consumer.

However, under outcome uncertainty, or risk, we argued that deriving the opportunity set (the first step) is more complicated than under perfect certainty. Indeed, we devoted Chapters 2 through 5 to obtaining the opportunity set under uncertainty for our economic choice problem, namely forming an optimal portfolio of financial assets. From these four chapters we concluded that in the presence of risky assets the opportunity set is given by the efficient frontier, and in the presence of both risky and risk-free assets it is given by the capital market line.

What we have not yet rigorously discussed, however, is the second step of our solution procedure, that is, how the preferences of economic agents can be identified. Indeed, to this point we have invoked only two assumptions regarding investor preferences: (1) that a high return is preferred to a low return and (2) that investors dislike risk. These minimal assumptions about investor preferences allowed us to draw two conclusions. First, in the absence of a risk-free asset a rational economic agent will select a portfolio on the efficient frontier. Second, when a risk-free asset is available, the risky component of the portfolio will contain the optimal risky portfolio, determined by the tangency of the efficient frontier and a line originating from the risk-free rate rotated counterclockwise as far as possible. Again, the opportunity set in the presence of risky and risk-free assets is the capital market line.

The goal of this chapter is to provide a more rigorous analysis of investor preferences. Focus your attention on the second step of the two-step procedure. Once it is completed, you can combine your knowledge of investor preferences and opportunity sets under uncertainty to identify optimal security portfolios and thus to solve the problem of economic choice. To meet this goal we investigate *utility theory*, which is the study of rational economic behavior. You will learn the important point that the optimal security portfolio will be the unique portfolio from the opportunity set that maximizes an investor's expected utility.

We begin our investigation with a discussion of the expected utility rule. In addition, we demonstrate that the expected utility framework leads to optimal results when the investor considers risky alternatives. The utility framework allows us to investigate risk-aversion, risk-neutrality, and risk-seeking behavior. Also, quadratic utility functions are discussed in detail along with a representation of appropriate indifference curves for a risk-averse investor in an expected return–standard deviation space.

UTILITY ANALYSIS

An economic agent must have a decision rule for evaluating alternatives under conditions of uncertainty. Early mathematicians believed that agents ranked risky investments by the expected-return criterion, selecting the alternative with the highest expected return. However, the St. Petersburg paradox, formulated by Swiss mathematician Nicolas

Bernoulli (1687–1759) in the early eighteenth century, illustrated the shortcomings of this decision rule. Later, Gabriel Cramer and Daniel Bernoulli (Nicolas's younger cousin) solved this paradox by discarding the expected-return rule in favor of the expected-utility criterion (Savage 1954). Von Neumann and Morgenstern (1947) revisited the expected-utility framework in the 1940s. Using a rigorous axiomatic approach, they demonstrated the superiority of the expected-utility criterion over not only the expected return method but over other possible decision methods. (See box for more on the development of the expected utility methodology.)

Below, we first apply utility theory to the problem of consumer choice. Because consumer goods are a source of satisfaction and are certain, rational economic agents select the consumption bundle that maximizes their total utility. This problem is similar to the situation introduced in Chapter 1, in which the investor allocated wealth over two periods by buying or selling a risk-free asset. When outcomes of the alternatives are known (utility from the consumption of an apple or an orange, for example), the outcomes are said to be *deterministic*.

However, because utility is a random variable for assets with uncertain payoffs, such as investments in stocks or foreign currencies, the expected-utility decision rule must be utilized to evaluate the alternatives. We introduce the expected-utility framework to analyze problems of choice under uncertainty, particularly as applied to the selection of risky portfolios of assets.[2]

Utility from Consumption

Utility is the satisfaction that an agent obtains from the consumption of goods and services. Utility is measured in units called utils to describe the level of satisfaction for a given choice.[3] Thus, one pizza might provide an individual with 10 utils and an apple 5 utils. Since we assume that rational agents prefer more utility over less, the individual will prefer a pizza over an apple, other things being equal.

A utility function describes the relation between an agent's utility level as measured in utils and the amounts of goods and services consumed. The general form of the utility function is:

(7.1) $$U = f(Q_1, Q_2, \ldots, Q_n),$$

where U is the total number of utils from a given set of goods and Q_1 is the quantity of good 1 consumed. Obviously, utility functions differ across

---

[2] The outcome is said to be *stochastic* when the outcomes are uncertain. An example of a stochastic outcome is an asset with an expected return of 10 percent with a standard deviation of 15 percent.

[3] We assume that utility is cardinal in nature, in other words, quantities of utility can be quantified and measured.

History of Expected-Utility Analysis

Early mathematicians believed that individuals faced with risky alternatives select the option that maximizes expected return. Although the expected-return rule is simple, it is not appropriate for all types of investors.

Problems with the expected-return criterion can be demonstrated by considering the St. Petersburg paradox, a classic problem formulated in the eighteenth century by Swiss mathematician Nicolas Bernoulli (1687–1759). Here is an adapted version of the problem: Suppose that a coin is tossed until one heads is obtained. You will receive $1 if heads is obtained on the first toss, $2 if heads is obtained on the second, $4 on the third, $8 on the fourth, and so on; thus, the payoff doubles with each additional toss. Therefore, if heads is obtained on the nth toss, the payoff is equal to 2^{n-1}. Obviously, you hope that heads appears only after a long series of tails. If heads is obtained after 10 tosses, the payoff is $512. How much would you be willing to pay for a chance to play this game?

Before answering this question, you should determine the expected value of the game. If heads is obtained on the first toss, an event with a probability of .5, a payoff of $1 results. To win $2, you need tails on the first toss and heads on the second toss. Since the two tosses are independent, the probability of this event is $(.5)(.5) = .25$. To obtain $4 from the game you need two tails followed by a heads. The probability of this occurrence is $(.5)(.5)(.5) = .125$. Thus the probability of a given result is equal to $1 \div 2^n$, where n is the number of coin tosses. The expected value of the St. Petersburg game is therefore:

$$.5(\$1) + .25(\$2) + .125(\$4) + .0625(\$8)$$
$$+ .03125(\$16) + \ldots$$
$$= \$.50 + \$.50 + \ldots = \infty$$

In other words, the expected value of the St. Petersburg game is infinite. While the probability terms decrease geometrically (½, ¼, ⅛, . . .), the payoffs increase at a geometric rate (1, 2, 4, 8, . . .), so that the expected value of

each toss is constant, namely $.50. An individual utilizing the expected-return criterion would be willing to pay an extremely large amount (say, $1 million) to participate in this game of chance. But would you be willing to pay a large amount to play this game? Probably not. Most individuals would be willing to pay only a few dollars to participate in this game. Thus the paradox: reasonable individuals would be willing to pay at most a few dollars to play a game with an expected payoff of infinity. This paradox occupied the best minds of the eighteenth century.

Rather than utilizing the expected-return criterion, Daniel Bernoulli and Gabriel Cramer (famous for developing Cramer's rule) attempted to solve the St. Petersburg paradox by focusing on expected utility. They were primarily interested in demonstrating the superiority of the expected-utility framework over the expected-return criterion.

Specifically, Bernoulli and Cramer argued that most individuals would be willing to pay only a few dollars to participate in the game because the game clearly exhibits tremendous risk. In other words, the amount that a risk-averse individual will pay is less than the expected return of the game, since risk represents a source of disutility. Bernoulli and Cramer contended that individuals would only pay up to an amount that would make them indifferent as to the utility derived from the certain dollar payment and the expected utility derived from the uncertain game of chance. The expected-utility framework was revisited in the 1940s by von Neumann and Morgenstern, who extended the Bernoulli and Cramer analysis to the general problem of decision making under uncertainty. Von Neumann and Morgenstern, using a rigorous axiomatic approach, demonstrated the superiority of the expected-utility criterion over not only the expected return method but other possible decision methods. Utility analysis is now employed in many fields, including economics, finance, and psychology, to analyze decision making under uncertainty.

individuals because tastes and preferences among agents are heterogeneous. However, despite somewhat disparate utility functions across agents, all utility functions tend to display three common characteristics. The first attribute, *insatiability*, is that individuals will prefer more of a commodity to less. Thus, five oranges will provide a consumer more utility than four oranges, and so on.

Although the total utility increases as additional units of a good are consumed, the additional or marginal utility from the consumption of additional units of a good decreases. To illustrate the second attribute, *diminishing marginal utility*, assume that an individual derives 10 utils from watching one hour of football, 18 utils from two hours, 24 units from three hours, and 27 utils from four hours. The total utility increases as the number of hours of football are watched, but the marginal utility decreases with each successive hour (10, 8, 6, 3).

The third common characteristic of all utility functions is *diminishing marginal substitutability:* to maintain a constant level of total utility, an agent must receive progressively greater quantities of good 2 as successive units of good 1 are removed. Suppose that an individual obtains 10 utils from a combination of 30 golf balls (good 1) and 30 tennis balls (good 2). Presumably the consumer holds this combination because it is the utility-maximizing mix, given budget constraints. The consumer might be equally satisfied with a combination of, say, twenty golf balls and forty-five tennis balls. Note that the agent must receive fifteen additional tennis balls to compensate for the loss of ten golf balls to maintain the original level of 10 utils. In general, the more of good 2 and less of good 1 that the consumer has, the more important a unit of good 1 is compared with a unit of good 2, and vice versa. If the individual receives fewer golf balls, say 10, the number of tennis balls must be increased substantially, say to 90, to maintain a constant level of utility. Thus there is a nonlinear trade-off between goods according to this common characteristic.

These three characteristics can be illustrated by assuming a two-good world. In that world the consumer's utility function is represented by $U = f(Q_1, Q_2)$, where Q_1 is the quantity of good 1 consumed and Q_2 is the quantity of good 2 consumed. In the utility function portrayed in Figure 7.1, the quantity of good 2 is held constant to illustrate the relation between the quantity of good 1 consumed and total utility. This figure depicts the principles of insatiability and diminishing marginal utility. The utility from the consumption of good 1, measured on the y-axis, increases as the quantity of good 1 increases. However, the curve demonstrating the relation between the quantity of good 1 and the corresponding utility increases at a decreasing rate. Thus, the marginal utility from the consumption of the first unit is greater than for the, say, fifth unit. The utility curve with respect to good 2 also assumes a concave shape.

We can also hold the total utility level constant and focus on combinations of goods 1 and 2 that provide a given level of utility. The locus of consumption bundles that provide a constant level of utility is

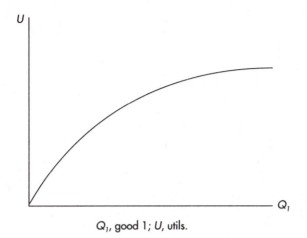

FIGURE 7.1
Relation between
Units of Good One
and Utility

Q_1, good 1; U, utils.

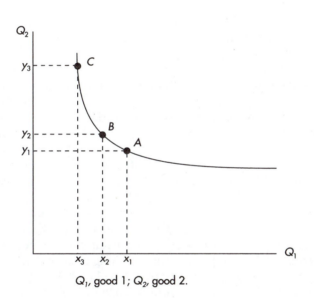

FIGURE 7.2
A Typical
Indifference Curve

Q_1, good 1; Q_2, good 2.

called an *indifference curve*. The equation for one indifference curve is $U_1 = f(Q_1, Q_2)$, where U_1 is a constant level of utility. Combinations of Q_1 and Q_2 for a given level of utility can be obtained and graphed in a Q_1, Q_2 space.

A typical indifference curve, illustrated in Figure 7.2, is convex, reflecting diminishing marginal substitutability among consumption goods. As the consumer gives up units of good 1, progressively more units of good 2 must be secured to maintain the utility level. From bundle A to B, the additional amount of good 2 necessary to maintain the original utility level is only $Y_2 - Y_1$. However, from point B to C, the additional amount of good 2 necessary is much greater, $Y_3 - Y_2$.

FIGURE 7.3

Utility Function
$U = x^{1/2}$

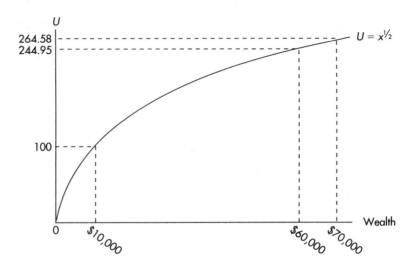

Utility from Wealth

Wealth also provides individuals with utility, since consumption is derived from wealth. However, although wealth derived from risky assets such as stocks and bonds is a source of utility, the uncertainty surrounding the actual return is a source of disutility for risk-averse investors. This is in contrast to goods and services, which provide no risk and therefore no disutility.

We can gain insight on the level of risk aversion for an agent by examining his or her utility function with respect to total wealth. The shape of this curve determines whether the individual is risk averse, risk neutral, or a risk seeker. Figure 7.3 provides a graph for an individual with the utility function $U = x^{1/2}$, where x is income and U is the corresponding utility. Total utility from wealth, as from consumption, generally increases at a decreasing rate, portraying the diminishing marginal utility principle. In this example the marginal utility from 0 to \$10,000 is equal to 100 utils. In contrast, as income increases from \$60,000 to \$70,000, utility increases from 244.95 to 264.58 utils, an increase of 19.63 utils. In this example the first \$10,000 is extremely important for the individual because this income is used to provide the necessities of life such as food and shelter. The marginal utility from \$60,000 to \$70,000 will be positive for rational agents but will be less than the first \$10,000.

Maximizing Expected Utility

Before investigating how expected utility can discriminate between risky alternatives, we investigate axioms of rational economic behavior. The expected-utility model, which allows us to evaluate decision making under uncertainty, follows from these axioms.

Axioms of Choice under Uncertainty

The expected-utility criterion is based on the following axioms concerning individual behavior under uncertainty (Fama and Miller 1972). From these axioms about rational behavior, the expected-utility model can be developed.

Axiom 1, Comparability.   Individuals have preferences among alternatives and can express them. Thus an individual considering alternatives x and y can (1) prefer x to y ($x > y$), (2) prefer y to x ($y > x$), or (3) be indifferent between the two alternatives ($x \sim y$).

Axiom 2, Transitivity.   If an individual prefers x to y and y to z, then the individual prefers x to z. In notational form, if $x > y$ and $y > z$, then $x > z$.

The first two axioms imply that individuals have preferences and are rational. By the first axiom a baseball fan will be able to rank teams in order of preference. By the second axiom, if the individual prefers the Cubs baseball team to the Dodgers and the Dodgers to the Mets, then the fan prefers the Cubs to the Mets.

Axiom 3, Independence (Substitution).   Suppose that an individual is indifferent between alternatives x and y. Now a third alternative, z, is introduced. The independence axiom states that the individual who is indifferent between x and y is therefore indifferent between the following two gambles: (1) a risky gamble between alternative x, with a probability of α and mutually exclusive alternative z, with a probability of $1 - \alpha$, and (2) a gamble between alternative y, with a probability of α, and the same mutually exclusive alternative z, with a probability of $1 - \alpha$.

In notational form, if $x \sim y$, then for any third prospect z, $G(x,z:\alpha) \sim G(y,z:\alpha)$, where $G(x,z:\alpha)$ represents a gamble in which the probability of obtaining x is α and z is $1 - \alpha$.

The independence axiom simply states that individual preferences for the outcomes of a gamble are not affected by the presence of risk. To illustrate, suppose that an individual is indifferent between attending a Mets baseball game and a Knicks basketball game. That individual would be indifferent between entering a lottery for $1 for a 1 in 10 chance of winning a ticket to a Knicks game and entering a lottery for $1 for the same 1 in 10 chance of winning a ticket to a Mets game. Although the individual might prefer not to play either lottery, the individual would be indifferent to the choice of the Mets or Knicks game if a lottery purchase was made. The key point is that the risk of the lottery and the uncertainty of the outcomes do not influence preferences for attending Knicks or Mets games.

Axiom 4, Measurability.   Suppose that an individual prefers x to y and y to z. There is a unique probability, α, that will make the individual indifferent between y and a gamble between x, with a probability α, and z, with probability $1 - \alpha$. Thus, if $x > y > z$, then $y \sim G(x,z:\alpha)$.

For illustration of axiom 4 assume that an individual prefers a new $60,000 Porsche automobile (alternative x) to a new $20,000 Honda (alternative y) and prefers a Honda to a used Volkswagen (alternative z). There exists a probability that would make the individual indifferent between a Honda and a gamble of either a Porsche or a used Volkswagen. One might argue that axiom 4 breaks down when the third alternative is a gruesome outcome such as death or dismemberment. For example, suppose that the first possibility is a Porsche, the second is a Honda, and the third is a poke in the eye with an ice pick. At first you might be unwilling to accept any gamble in which the third alternative is possible. However, suppose that the probability of receiving the third alternative is extremely small, say one in a trillion. Since the risks of everyday life, such as traveling in an automobile or plane or crossing the street, are higher, accepting the gamble is plausible.

Axiom 5, Ranking.   Suppose that x is preferred to y, which is preferred to z. Also, x is preferred to alternative u, which is preferred to z. The individual is indifferent to alternative y and a gamble between x, with a probability of α_1, and z, with a probability of $1 - \alpha_1$. Also, the individual is indifferent to alternative y and a gamble between x, with a probability of α_2, and u, with a probability of $1 - \alpha_2$. If $\alpha_1 > \alpha_2$, then y is preferred to u, and if $\alpha_1 = \alpha_2$, the individual is indifferent between y and u. In notational form, if $x > y > z$ and $x > u > z$, and $y \sim G(x,z:\alpha_1)$ and $u \sim G(x,z:\alpha_2)$, then $\alpha_1 > \alpha_2$ implies $y > u$, and $\alpha_1 = \alpha_2$ implies that $y \sim u$.

Expected Utility

Von Neumann and Morgenstern (1947) demonstrated that given these reasonable axioms regarding decision making under uncertainty, the expected-utility framework leads to optimal solutions for problems of economic choice under uncertainty. (See Appendix 7A for the proof.) The general formula for the expected utility of risky alternative x, $E[U(x)]$, is given by

(7.2)
$$E[U(x)] = \sum_{i=1}^{N} p(x_i)\, U(x_i),$$

where $p(x_i)$ is the probability of outcome x_i and $U(x_i)$ is its corresponding utility. The expected utility of a risky alternative is simply a weighted average of the possible utils and probabilities.

Suppose that a coin is tossed once. The participant wins $150 if heads results and $50 dollars if the result is tails. Would an individual with a utility function of $U = x^{1/2}$ pay $100, which is the expected payoff, to participate in such a gamble? To answer this question calculate the expected utility of the gamble and compare it with the utility of the participation price. The participant of this game will enjoy either $150^{½} = 12.25$ utils if the result is heads or $50^{½} = 7.07$ utils if the result is tails. Since the probability of obtaining a head is equal to .5, the expected utility of this gamble is equal to 12.25 (.5) + 7.07 (.5) = 9.66. This individual will not accept the gamble because the expected utility from the gamble, 9.66, is less than the utility of the initial investment, $100^{½} = 10$.

This situation is depicted in Figure 7.4, which illustrates the individual's concave utility function. The straight line under the utility function is the expected utility line. The *expected-utility line* provides expected payoff and utils corresponding to various probabilities of the gamble. For example, if the probability of receiving $150 is 1, the expected payoff is $150 and the expected utility is 12.25. At the other extreme, if the probability of receiving $50 is 1, the expected payoff is $50 and the expected utility will equal 7.07. As demonstrated above, the expected payoff equals $100 and the expected utility is 9.66 utils when the probability of receiving $150 is .5. On inspection the individual will reject this gamble because the expected utility is less than the utility of the $100 participation price.

When it comes to risky gambles, everyone has their price. To illustrate, suppose that the initial investment is reduced to $90. The individual now will accept the gamble because the expected utility from the gamble is greater than the utility of the participation price, $90^{½} = 9.49$ utils. We can find the maximum amount that the individual is willing to pay for the gamble by setting the expected utility equal to the utility function and solving for the participation price that ensures this equality. In this case, $9.66 = (x)^{½}$. Thus, x is equal to $93.32. At $93.32, the expected utility of the gamble is equal to the utility of the participation price. The maximum

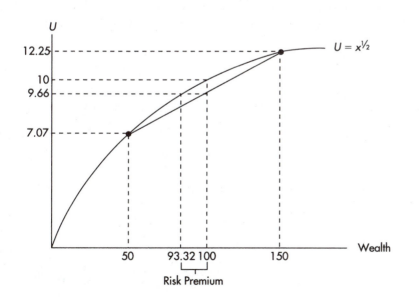

FIGURE 7.4
The Risk Premium

amount that an individual is willing to pay for a gamble is called the *certainty equivalent.* In other words, the certainty equivalent represents the participation price at which the agent is exactly indifferent between playing and not playing the game of chance. Any difference between the expected payoff and the certainty equivalent, $100 − $93.32 = $6.68 in our case, is called the *risk premium.* The certainty equivalent can be found graphically in Figure 7.4 by drawing a horizontal line at the expected utility level. The certainty equivalent is the point where this horizontal line intersects the utility function.

An individual with a concave utility function is said to be *risk averse* because the possible overall loss of $50 more than offsets the possible overall gain of $50. Risk averters are not gamblers because they will always reject a "fair gamble," a gamble in which the expected payoff is equal to the investment or participation price.

In contrast, a risk seeker will always accept a fair gamble. A risk seeker has a utility function that increases at an increasing rate, implying increasing marginal utility. This implies that the utility from the possible gain from the risky investment is greater than the utility from the certain participation price.

A utility function for a risk seeker is illustrated in Figure 7.5. A risk seeker with a utility function $U = x^2$ will be willing to accept the gamble described above. The expected utility from the gamble is equal to 150^2 $(.5) + 50^2(.5) = 12,500$ utils. The risk seeker will accept the gamble because the expected utility is greater than the utility of the participation price, $100^2 = 10,000$ utils. The certainty equivalent for this individual is equal to $12,500 = x^2$, or $111.80. In other words, a risk seeker would be willing to pay more to engage in a gamble than the gamble's expected payoff. This is clearly irrational behavior. (For instance, for the St. Petersburg paradox, in theory the risk seeker would be willing to pay more than an infinite number of dollars.) For this reason the risk premium for the

FIGURE 7.5

Utility Function for a Risk Seeker

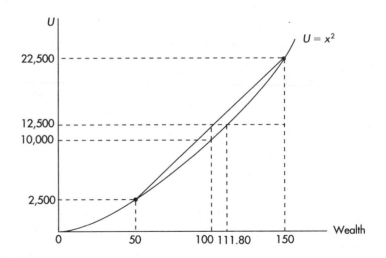

PROBLEMS WITH THE EXPECTED UTILITY FRAMEWORK

Von Neumann and Morgenstern, using reasonable assumptions and axioms regarding rational behavior by economic agents, demonstrated the superiority of the expected-utility decision rule. While these axioms have largely escaped empirical testing by economists, psychologists have studied whether individuals behave according to the theory. This body of research generally concludes that individuals do not behave in accord with these axioms. Probably the earliest and best known examples of systematic violations of the axioms of choice is the Allais paradox. Suppose that you are faced with the following two pairs of gambles. Which would you select?

a_1: 1.00 chance of $1 million
a_2: .10 chance of $5 million
       .89 chance of $1 million
       .01 chance of $0

and

a_3: .10 chance of $5 million
       .90 chance of $0
a_4: .11 chance of $1 million
       .89 chance of $0

A number of psychology researchers have found that the majority of subjects surveyed selected alternative a_1 for the first pair and a_3 for the second. For the first set of alternatives most subjects take the certain large amount of money (a_1) and avoid a gamble to obtain an even larger reward ($5 million). For the second pair subjects prefer the alternative with the greatest risk, a_3. These choices are inconsistent and violate the independence axiom (see Machina (1987) for more detail). For the first pair the utility of a_1 is greater than the utility of a_3.

$$U(\$1 \text{ million}) > .10\ U(\$5 \text{ million}) + .89\ U(\$1 \text{ million}) + .01\ U(\$0),$$

or

$$.11\ U(\$1 \text{ million}) > .10\ U(\$5 \text{ million}).$$

For the second pair,

$$.10\ U(\$5 \text{ million}) + .90\ U(\$0) > .11\ U(\$1 \text{ million}) + .89\ U(\$0),$$

or

$$.10\ U(\$5 \text{ million}) > .11\ U(\$1 \text{ million}).$$

Thus the selection of a_1 and a_3 is inconsistent.

Another problem with choice models is the framing phenomenon. Psychologists have found that alternative means of representing equivalent choice problems will lead to systematic differences in choice (Machina 1987). Tversky and Kahneman (1981) posit the following scenario:

Imagine that the United States is preparing for the outbreak of an unusual Asian disease, which is expected to kill 600 people. Two alternative programs to combat the disease have been proposed. Assume that the exact scientific estimate of the consequences of the programs are as follows:

If program A is adopted, 200 people will be saved.

If program B is adopted, there is a ⅓ probability that 600 people will be saved, and a ⅔ probability that no people will be saved.

Seventy-two percent of the subjects chose program A. A second group of subjects were given the same information, but the information was present in the following manner:

If program C is adopted, 400 people will die.

If program D is adopted, there is a ⅓ probability that nobody will die and ⅔ probability that 600 people will die.

Although the programs are simply restated, 78 percent of the subjects selected program D.

Thus the Allais paradox and the framing phenomenon are two violations of the axioms of choice under uncertainty.

FIGURE 7.6

Utility Function for a
Risk-Neutral
Investor

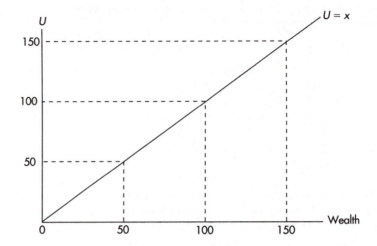

risk seeker is actually negative. In this example the risk premium is
$100 − $111.80 = −$11.80.

Finally, risk-neutral agents have a linear utility function, as presented
in Figure 7.6. Risk-neutral investors consider only the expected return of
risky alternatives and will select the investment that maximizes expected
return. In this example, assume that an investor has the linear utility
function $U = x$. The expected utility from the gamble is given by
$150(.5) + 50(.5) = 100$ utils. Thus the certainty equivalent of the gamble is
$100, and because the expected utility line coincides with the utility
function, there is no risk premium. The risk-neutral investor is willing to
accept a fair gamble. Again, it is clear that this is not rational economic
behavior. Thus early mathematicians who believed that individuals used
the expected-payoff criterion to select among risky alternatives implicitly
assumed that individuals were risk neutral. An important contribution of
the expected-utility criterion is that it explicitly recognizes that individuals
are commonly risk averse.

EQUILIBRIUM IN THE CAPITAL MARKET

Armed with knowledge of the opportunity set under uncertainty
(Chapters 2–5) and with the rigorous treatment of investor preferences
discussed above, we are prepared to solve our particular economic choice
problem, namely identifying optimal portfolios of financial securities. As
in the solution to the consumer choice problem, we must combine the
opportunity set and investor preferences to obtain an equilibrium risky
portfolio. In this section we first discuss the shape of indifference curves
for risk-averse investors, since these are the only rational agents worthy
of our consideration, and then discuss equilibrium in the capital market
with and without a risk-free asset.

Indifference Curves for Risk-Averse Investors

When analyzing utility from consumption, we simplified the analysis by assuming a two-good world. However, when investigating utility derived from investment in risky alternatives, the assumption that utility stems from just two sources is realistic. This is because it is generally assumed that investors utilize only the first two moments of the return distribution, expected return and standard deviation, when evaluating investments. Because we assume that the expected return and standard deviation adequately summarize risky investments, investor utility is a function of the expected return and the standard deviation, or $U = f\,[E(r),\ \sigma]$. The risk-averse investor obtains utility from higher returns and disutility from higher risk. Thus indifference curves for a risk-averse investor, illustrated in Figure 7.7, will have a positive *marginal rate of substitution* (MRS) for all levels of risk. The MRS of risk for return is the maximum amount of expected return the agent is willing to give up for an additional unit of risk to maintain a constant level of utility. In other words, the MRS represents the trade-off between risk and return needed to keep the agent utility neutral. A family of indifference curves (also known as an indifference map) is illustrated in Figure 7.7, with each curve associated with a different utility level. Because the investor obtains utility from return and disutility from risk, utility increases as the indifference curves move northwest. Thus indifference curve II is associated with a higher level of utility than curve I.

The shape of an indifference curve provides information on the degree of risk aversion. Figure 7.8 illustrates two indifference curves, I and II. Curve I represents an indifference curve for an extremely risk-averse individual, and curve II demonstrates an indifference curve for a less risk-averse individual. The indifference curves intersect at point A, corresponding to a portfolio standard deviation of σ_1 and an expected

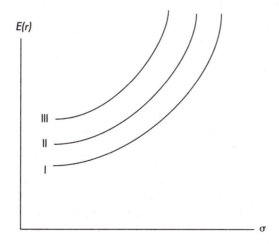

FIGURE 7.7

A Family of Indifference Curves for a Risk-Averse Investor

FIGURE 7.8

Indifference Curves
for Investors with
Different Degrees of
Risk Aversion

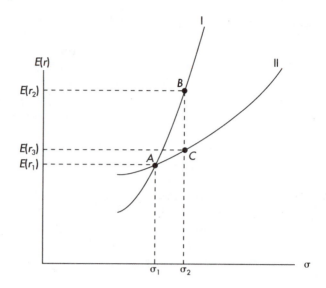

return of $E(r_1)$. We now determine indifference points when the standard deviation is increased to σ_2. To be indifferent between risk-return combinations A and B, the extremely risk-averse agent must receive a much higher level of return, $E(r_2)$, reflecting an extreme aversion to risk. In contrast, the less risk-averse agent need only be compensated with a much lower level of expected return, $E(r_3)$, to remain utility neutral (compare A and C). Thus, the steeper the indifference curve, the more risk-averse the investor.

Indifference curves for a risk seeker will exhibit a negative slope, resembling indifference curves illustrating preferences for normal goods in the classic consumer choice problem. The negative slope reflects the fact that both risk and return provide the risk seeker with utility. Of course, risk-neutral agents have horizontal indifference curves, as they ignore the dispersion of asset returns when making decisions under uncertainty. Because risk aversion is probably the most realistic depiction of the behavior of most investors, we will consider only risk aversion in our subsequent analysis.

Equilibrium

We now combine the opportunity set and preferences to determine the optimal portfolio of assets—that which maximizes the investor's expected utility. The utility-maximizing investor attains the highest indifference curve given the available investment opportunities.

We first assume that no risk-free asset is available. Therefore the optimal portfolio is obtained by combining the efficient frontier with a family of indifference curves for an investor, as illustrated in Figure 7.9. The equilibrium portfolio occurs at the tangency of the efficient frontier and the indifference curve (point C). At this point the MRS, which is the slope of the indifference curve, is equal to the slope of the efficient frontier, called the *marginal rate of transformation* (MRT). The MRS provides the amount of expected return that the agent is willing to give up for an addition unit of risk, and the MRT supplies the expected return that must be forgone for an additional unit of risk.[4]

To investigate the concept of investor equilibrium further, consider portfolio A in Figure 7.9. At this portfolio, which contains a high level of risk, the investor is willing to trade a large amount of expected return to reduce risk. However, the opportunity set requires the investor to trade in a lower amount of expected return for a lower level of risk. In other words, the investor will not settle on portfolio A because the MRS is greater than the MRT but instead will move in the direction of portfolio C. Because the same situation exists for portfolio B, the investor will continue moving toward portfolio C. Because of the low risk level at portfolio D, the investor is willing to increase risk substantially to increase the expected return (MRS is low). Equilibrium does not occur at portfolio D because the opportunity set requires the investor to trade in a lower amount of risk for expected return. In this situation the MRS is less than the MRT. Thus the investor is in equilibrium only at portfolio C, where the MRS is equal to the MRT. At this portfolio the agent has attained the highest indifference curve possible, given the efficient frontier constraint.

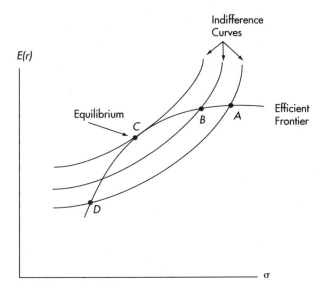

FIGURE 7.9

Equilibrium with No Risk-Free Asset

---

[4]In the consumer choice problem the opportunity set is the budget line, which provides combinations of two goods that can be purchased with a given income. The MRT is constant and equal to $-p_x/p_y$, where p_x (p_y) represents the price of good x (y). In contrast, in the risky-asset choice problem, the MRT is not constant.

Investors will obtain different equilibrium portfolios, depending on their unique utility functions and preferences regarding risk. As illustrated in Figure 7.10, an extremely risk-averse investor will select a portfolio close to the minimum-variance portfolio, portfolio *F*. A less risk-averse agent, represented by a flatter indifference curve, will choose portfolio *G*, a portfolio with a higher expected return and standard deviation.

As demonstrated in Chapter 3, all investors will hold the optimal risky portfolio if a capital market is present and investors are able to borrow and lend funds at the risk-free interest rate. Extremely risk-averse agents will place a high percentage of their assets in the risk-free asset, and less risk-averse agents will borrow funds at the risk-free interest rate to finance additional purchases of the optimal risky portfolio.

The relevant opportunity set, now that we have introduced the risk-free asset, is the capital market line (CML). Thus the CML is tangent to the efficient frontier. As demonstrated in Chapter 3, the slope and therefore the MRT of the capital market line is equal to $(E(r_{P*}) - r_f)/\sigma_{P*}$, where $E(r_{P*})$ is the expected return of the optimal risky portfolio, σ_{P*} is the risk of this portfolio, and r_f is the risk-free interest rate.

As before, the optimal portfolio is identified by combining the opportunity set (CML in this case) with the family of indifference curves. Portfolio *A* in Figure 7.11, which is attainable by borrowing funds and investing in the optimal risky portfolio, illustrates a utility-maximizing portfolio for a relatively non-risk-averse investor. At portfolio *A* the MRS for this investor is equal to the MRT, which is equal to the slope of the CML. When a capital market is present, the MRS will be the same for all investors, regardless of their preferences for risk.

FIGURE 7.10

Equilibrium for Extremely Risk-Averse and Less Risk-Averse Agents

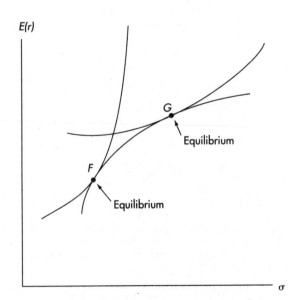

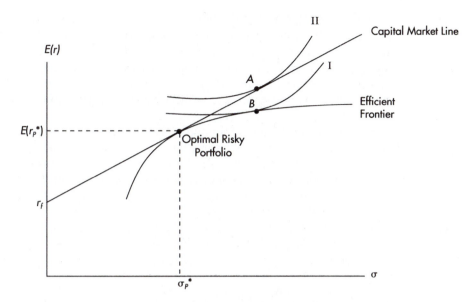

FIGURE 7.11

Equilibrium with and without a Capital Market

Finally, we now investigate the utility-maximizing positions with and without a capital market. In Figure 7.11 the utility-maximizing portfolio in the absence of a capital market is portfolio *B*. At this portfolio the individual resides on the highest indifference curve possible (curve I). Now suppose that a capital market is introduced. The equilibrium portfolio is portfolio *A*, attained by selecting the optimal risky portfolio and selling risk-free bonds. The investor is clearly better off with the introduction of a capital market because indifference curve II is now attainable. In general all portfolios on the CML dominate all portfolios on efficient frontier (with the exception of the optimal portfolio); in other words, the existence of a capital market enhances social welfare by allowing investors to attain higher levels of utility.

QUADRATIC UTILITY FUNCTIONS

In Chapter 2 we stated that investors utilize only the mean and variance to evaluate risky alternatives if one of the following conditions exist: (1) the asset returns are normally distributed, or (2) investors possess quadratic utility functions. We have discussed the first condition in detail in Chapter 2. We now focus on the second.

The quadratic utility function is used extensively in the academic literature. The quadratic utility takes the following form:

(7.3) $$U(x) = bx + cx^2,$$

where $U(x)$ is the utility of an economic agent derived from wealth, x is the wealth of the individual, and b and c are coefficients. The first derivative of the quadratic utility function is $b + 2xc$. Thus the first derivative, $b + 2xc$, is always positive if c is positive and negative if c is negative. However, a positive coefficient implies increasing marginal utility, which is not consistent with rational behavior. Thus we restrict our attention to quadratic utility functions with a negative c coefficient, which is consistent with diminishing marginal utility. The quadratic utility function declines after a certain level. The declining part of the quadratic utility function curve is not relevant in the decision-making process because this part of the curve violates the insatiability assumption (more wealth is preferred to less). The relevant part of the curve occurs when the first derivative is nonnegative: $b + 2cx > 0$, which implies that the total wealth (x) must be less than $-b/2c$, given that c is less than 0. Because of this constraint, the quadratic utility function is appropriate only for investments and games of chance with relatively modest possible returns.

The marginal utility of the quadratic utility function is simply the first derivative of equation 7.3:

(7.4)
$$\frac{dU(x)}{dx} = b + 2cx.$$

The change in the marginal utility with respect to changes in wealth is equal to the second derivative of equation 7.3:

(7.5)
$$\frac{d^2U(x)}{dx^2} = 2c.$$

Figure 7.12 depicts a utility function with the following equation: $U = 10{,}000x - .5x^2$. Note that the utility function declines and is not pertinent after a wealth level of $10,000.

FIGURE 7.12

Quadratic Utility Function

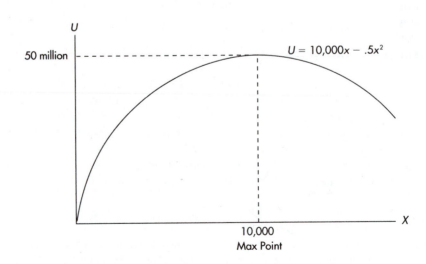

$U = 10{,}000x - .5x^2$

50 million

10,000
Max Point

We now demonstrate that investors with quadratic utility functions consider only the mean and variance of the risky alternative. Our task is to calculate the expected utility of the quadratic utility function:

(7.6) $$E\{[U(x)]\} = E[(bx + cx^2)]$$

$$= bE(x) + cE(x^2).$$

From Chapter 2, the variance of random variable x is equal to

(7.7) $$\sigma_x^2 = E[x - E(x)]^2 = E[x^2 - 2xE(x) + E(x)^2]$$

$$= E(x^2) - 2E(x)E(x) + E(x)^2$$

$$= E(x^2) - E(x)^2.$$

Therefore, $E(x^2)$ is equal to $\sigma_x^2 + E(x)^2$. Substituting this result into 7.6, we obtain

(7.8) $$E\{[U(w)]\} = bE(x) + c[\sigma_x^2 + E(x)^2]$$

$$= bE(x) + c\sigma_x^2 + cE(x)^2.$$

Equation 7.8 demonstrates that the expected utility is only a function of the expected return and the variance of returns. Higher moments, such as the skewness and the kurtosis of the return distribution, are not considered by the investor possessing a quadratic utility function.

Utility curves for investors with varying degrees of risk aversion can be traced out using equation 7.3. Assuming risk aversion ($c < 0$), a higher variance for a given level of return implies a lower level of expected utility. The magnitude of c determines the shape of the indifference curves. An extremely risk-averse investor (c negative and very low) will possess positively sloped and steep utility curves, and a less timid (but nevertheless risk-averse) agent will have indifference curves with a flatter slope.

The value of c for a risk-neutral individual will equal 0, implying that the variance is irrelevant when evaluating investment alternatives (see equation 7.8). A risk seeker obtains utility from risk; thus c will be positive.

Measuring Risk Aversion

The risk premium, which is the difference between the expected value of a risky alternative and the certainty equivalent, provides a measure of risk aversion. For a given gamble and income level, the higher the risk premium, the more risk-averse the economic agent. However, an interesting question is how an individual's attitude toward risk changes as total wealth changes. Ordinarily a millionaire is more likely to enter into a $1,000 gamble than is a destitute college student. Another relevant question is how the percentage invested in risky assets changes as wealth increases. In other words, is a millionaire more likely to place a higher percentage of his wealth in risky assets than an individual with less total wealth? To answer these questions, we utilize the following analysis.

Absolute Risk Aversion

Pratt (1964) and Arrow (1971) developed a measure that evaluates local risk aversion for a given level of wealth. Assume that an agent, with a utility function U and total wealth of x, is presented with a fair gamble z having an expected value of 0: $E(z) = 0$. Pratt and Arrow derive the risk premium that is necessary to make the agent indifferent between (1) the total wealth plus the risky gamble and (2) an amount received with certainty.

As derived in Appendix 7B, the Pratt-Arrow measure of local risk aversion is

(7.9)
$$\pi = (\tfrac{1}{2})\, \sigma_z^{\,2} \left[-\frac{U''(x)}{U'(x)} \right],$$

where π is the risk premium, $\sigma_z^{\,2}$ is the variance of the possible outcomes of the gamble, $U'(x)$ is the first derivative of the utility function (the marginal utility), and $U''(x)$ is the second derivative, which measures the change in the marginal utility with respect to changes in wealth.

To illustrate how the risk premium changes as wealth increases, assume that an agent with wealth of $10,000 has a logarithmic utility function, $U = \ln(x)$. The individual is considering two risky portfolios that will produce a dollar return over the next year of either $1,000 or $2,000, with each outcome equally likely; thus the end-of-period portfolio value will be $11,000 or $12,000 and the mean dollar return is $1500, with a standard deviation of $500. Therefore, the risk premium for this agent is $1/2(500^2)(1/11,500) = \$10.87$, which results in wealth of $11,489.13.[5] The agent is indifferent between a risky investment with a dollar return of $1,000 or $2,000 and a certain dollar return of $11,500 − $10.87 = $11,489.13. The investor will prefer the risky investment if its expected dollar return is greater than $1489.13.

Now assume that an individual with a logarithmic utility function and a portfolio value of $1 million is considering the same investment, implying an end-of-period portfolio value of either $1,001,000 or

---

[5] The first derivative of the logarithmic utility function is $1/x$ and the second derivative is $-1/x^2$. Thus the ratio of the second and first derivatives is $-1/x$.

$1,002,000. The agent's risk premium is $1/2(500)^2(1/1,001,500) = \$.1248$. Thus the millionaire will accept the gamble if the end-of-period expected wealth is greater than $1,001,499.88. Predictably, the millionaire is more likely to accept the investment because of the lower risk premium.

The risk premium presented in equation 7.9 is a measure of risk aversion. However, since $\frac{1}{2}\,\sigma_z^2$ is always positive, we can succinctly summarize the level of local risk aversion by focusing on the negative value of the second derivative of an individual's utility function relative to the first derivative. The absolute risk aversion (ARA) is defined as follows:

(7.10)
$$ARA = \frac{-U''(x)}{U'(x)}\,.$$

Decreasing ARA implies that agents hold more dollars in risky assets as wealth increases. This attribute seems to be consistent with rational economic behavior and is generally assumed by financial economists. However, we will see later in this chapter that the quadratic utility function exhibits increasing absolute risk aversion.

Relative Risk Aversion

The measure of relative risk aversion (RRA) shows how the percentage of total wealth invested in risky assets changes as wealth changes. The proportional size of the risk premium, p, is

(7.11)
$$p = \frac{1}{2}\,\sigma_z^2\left[-x\,\frac{U''(x)}{U'(x)}\right].$$

The RRA is defined as the ARA multiplied by total wealth:

(7.12)
$$RRA = \frac{-x\,U''(x)}{U'(x)} = -x\,(ARA).$$

Increasing RRA means that the investor will reduce the proportion of total wealth invested in risky assets as wealth increases. However, the agent will increase the risky asset percentage if the RRA is negative. Constant RRA (RRA equal to 1) implies that the percentage of wealth invested in risky assets remains constant as wealth increases. Although the consensus is that agents display negative ARA, no such agreement exists for RRA. As we will show in the next section, some popular utility functions display positive and constant RRA.

In the previous example the agents possessed logarithmic utility functions and the ARA was equal to $1/x$. Thus individuals possessing logarithmic utility functions will display constant relative risk aversion, as the RRA will equal 1: $[x\,(1/x) = 1]$.

ALTERNATIVE UTILITY FUNCTIONS

We now investigate properties of three commonly used utility functions: quadratic, logarithmic, and power functions.

The quadratic utility function, given by $U = bx + cx^2$, has several undesirable properties. First, to satisfy the insatiability assumption, the following condition must hold: $x \leq b/2c$. The second undesirable property is that the quadratic function displays increasing absolute risk aversion. To demonstrate this, take the first derivative of the ARA. The quadratic utility function has a first derivative of $(b - 2cx)$ and a second derivative of $-2c$. Thus, the ARA is equal to $2c/(b - 2cx)$. The ARA can be signed by observing its first derivative. The first derivative of the ARA of the quadratic function is equal to $4c^2/(b - 2cx)^2$, which is greater than 0 because $x \leq b/2c$.

The RRA of the quadratic function is simply the wealth times the ARA, $2xc/(b - 2cx)$. The first derivative of the RRA is $2c/(b - 2cx)^2$. Since this derivative is unambiguously positive, the quadratic function displays increasing relative risk aversion.

The logarithmic and power utility functions avoid these problems because these functions have less severe restrictions and can display negative absolute risk aversion. As noted before, the logarithmic function $U = ln(x)$ has an ARA of $1/x$. The derivative of the ARA is equal to $-1/x^2$. Because the second derivative is always negative, the logarithmic function exhibits decreasing absolute risk aversion. As noted above, a logarithmic function also implies constant RRA (RRA = 1). Thus investors with logarithmic utility functions do not vary their mix between risky and risk-free assets as total wealth changes.

The power function $U = x^c$, where $0 < c < 1$, also exhibits negative ARA and constant RRA. The ARA is equal to $(1 - c) \div x$ with a first derivative of $(c - 1)/x^2$. The RRA is equal to $(1 - c)$ and has a first derivative of 0.

SUMMARY

Because outcomes from risky assets are uncertain, economic agents must consult the expected utility framework rather than the expected return when identifying the best portfolio from the available opportunity set. Expected utility, which is a weighted average of the utility levels from each of the possible outcomes of a risky asset and the probabilities of occurrence, is utilized to rank alternatives.

The shape of the agent's utility function, which depicts the relation between wealth and total utility, determines if the individual is risk averse, risk neutral or risk seeking. Since we assume diminishing marginal utility, this curve will increase at a decreasing rate, illustrating risk aversion. The utility function will increase linearly for risk-neutral agents and will be convex for risk seekers. The risk premium for risk-averse investors and risk seekers will be positive and negative, respectively, because risk averse investors and risk seekers will always reject and accept, respectively, a fair gamble. Risk-neutral agents will always be indifferent to a fair gamble and possess a risk premium of 0.

The risk premium will change with income. We generally assume decreasing absolute risk aversion, as a wealthy individual is more likely to engage in a $1,000 gamble than a poor individual. However, the RRA, which provides information on the percentage of total assets invested in risky assets as income changes, is uncertain.

Three popular utility functions are the quadratic, logarithmic, and power functions. Although widely used, the quadratic function has a maximum value, violating the insatiability assumption. Thus restrictions must be placed on this function. Also, the quadratic function has positive ARA. The logarithmic and power functions possess less restrictive limitations and have negative ARA.

Armed with the knowledge of investor preferences provided by utility theory and the characteristics of the opportunity set under uncertainty, you can employ the two-step procedure originally detailed in Chapter 1 to identify portfolios of risky and risk-free assets that maximize expected utility. Also, the existence of a capital market enhances social welfare by allowing investors to attain higher levels of utility.

In Chapter 8 we utilize the Markowitz and single-index frameworks to analyze the impact of international diversification on the portfolio opportunity set.

REFERENCES

Arrow, K. J. 1971. *Essays in the theory of risk-bearing.* Amsterdam: North-Holland.

Bernoulli, D. 1954. Exposition of a new theory on the measurement of risk. *Econometrica.* January, 23–36.

Blume, M., and I. Friend. 1975. The asset structure of individual portfolios and some implications for utility functions. *Journal of Finance.* May, 585–603.

Debrew, G. 1959. *Theory of value.* New Haven: Yale University Press.

Fama, E. F., and M. H. Miller. 1972. *The theory of finance.* Hinsdale, IL: Dryden Press.

Friedman, M. 1976. *Price theory.* Chicago: Aldine.

Friedman, M., and L. J. Savage. 1948. The utility analysis of choices involving risk. *Journal of Political Economy.* August, 279–304.

Machina, M. J. 1987. Choice under uncertainty. Problems solved and unsolved. *Journal of Economic Perspectives.* Summer, 121–154.

Pratt, J. W. 1964. Risk aversion in the small and in the large. *Econometrica.* January-April, 122–136.

Roy, A. D. 1952. Safety first and the holding of assets. *Econometrica.* July, 431–449.

Savage, L. J. 1954. *The foundations of statistics.* New York: John Wiley & Sons.

Tversky, A., and D. Kahneman. 1981. The framing of decisions and the psychology of choice. *Science.* January, 453–458.

Von Neumann, J. and O. Morgenstern. 1947. *Theory of games and economic behavior.* Princeton, NJ: Princeton University Press.

Questions and Problems

1. Discuss the problems with the expected-return framework for selecting risky alternatives.

2. Consider the following investment opportunities:

INVESTMENT A		INVESTMENT B	
Outcome	Probability	Outcome	Probability
−$20	.33	−$500	.33
40	.33	10	.33
100	.33	1,000	.33

   Which alternative would you select if you utilized the expected-return criterion? Which alternative would you select if your utility function were $U = x^{1/2}$, $U = x$, or $U = x^2$.

3. Consider the following gamble:

OUTCOME	PROBABILITY
$50	.50
250	.50

   What is the certainty equivalent and risk premium if your utility function is $U = x^{1/2}$? Draw a graph illustrating the utility function, expected utility, and risk premium. Also do the same for the logarithmic function $U = \ln(x)$. Now assume a linear utility function, $U = 2x$, and graph the situation.

4. Prove graphically that a risk-averse investor will never enter into a fair gamble.

5. Demonstrate graphically that a risk-neutral investor makes investment decisions according to the expected-return criterion.

6. Draw an efficient frontier and possible equilibrium portfolios for risk-neutral and risk-averse investors.

7. One individual has $2 million and another has $10,000. Both are considering an investment that will pay either $3,000 or $2,000, with equal likelihood. If both agents have logarithmic utility functions, what is the maximum amount both are willing to pay for the gamble?

8. Discuss desirable and undesirable features of the quadratic, logarithmic, and power utility functions.

9. Distinguish between utility and expected utility. When do agents act to maximize their expected utility?

10. Explain the concepts of insatiability, diminishing marginal utility, and diminishing marginal substitutability.

11. Consider the following gambles:

	WIN	LOSE	PROBABILITY WIN
A	$102	$98	.5
B	110	90	.5
C	150	50	.5
D	200	0	.5

What are the certainty equivalents for each of the gambles for the utility functions $U = x^{1/2}$, $U = x^2$, and $U = x$?

$$7A$$

Derivation of the Expected Utility Rule[6]

Von Neumann and Morgenstern (1947) demonstrate that assuming the reasonable axioms of rational behavior presented earlier in this chapter, the expected-utility criterion leads to optimal solutions for problems of economic choice under uncertainty. To demonstrate that the expected-utility rule follows from these axioms, we must show that (1) the utility function is order preserving, or if $U(x) > U(y)$ then $x > y$ and if $U(x) = U(y)$ then $x \sim y$, and (2) the ordering of risky alternatives is according to expected utility, or $U[G(x,y,\alpha)] = \alpha U(x) + (1 - \alpha)U(y)$.

To demonstrate the first attribute, assume that the set S is bounded by two prospects a and b so that $a > b$ and for any prospect x in S, $a > x > b$. From axiom 4 we know that a probability value exists in which the individual is indifferent between (1) receiving with certainty alternative x and (2) a gamble yielding either outcome a with a probability $\alpha(x)$ or outcome b with a probability $1 - \alpha(x)$: $x \sim G[a,b:\alpha(x)]$. By axiom 4 the probability value $\alpha(x)$ is unique in S. There is also a unique probability value for gamble y such that $y \sim G[a,b:\alpha(y)]$. By axiom 5 we know that $\alpha(x)$ is order preserving because if $\alpha(x) > \alpha(y)$, then x is preferred to y. If the probabilities are equal, then the agent is indifferent between x and y.

Our next task is to demonstrate that investors use expected utility to rank risky alternatives. Remember that a and b are the upper and lower limits of a gamble, respectively, and x and y are stochastic alternatives that occur within the bounds of a and b. From the analysis above we know that

(7A.1) $x \sim G[a,b:\alpha(x)]$

and

(7A.2) $y \sim G[a,b:\alpha(y)]$.

Also, assume that outcome x has a probability of β and y has a probability of $1 - \beta$, or in notation, $G(x,y:\beta)$. To demonstrate that the expected-utility rule follows from these axioms, show that the function $\alpha(x)$ ranks risky alternatives according to expected utility.

---

[6]This appendix follows the treatment contained in Fama and Miller (1972).

First apply axiom 3 to *7A.1* and the risky gamble involving x and y:

(7A.3) $G(x,y:\beta) \sim G\{G[a,b:\alpha(x)], y:\beta]\}.$

This situation is illustrated below:

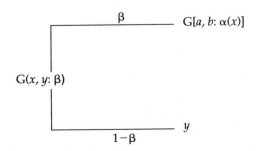

The agent is indifferent between $G(x,y:\beta)$ and a gamble in which (1) the agent obtains either gamble $G[a,b:\alpha(x)]$ with probability β or alternative y with a probability $1-\beta$. Now applying axiom 3 to equations 7A.2 and 7A.3, we obtain:

(7A.4) $G\{G[a,b:\alpha(x)], y:\beta\} \sim G[G(a,b:\alpha(x)), G(a,b:\alpha(y)):\beta].$

Applying the transitivity axiom to equations 7A.3 and 7A.4, we have:

(7A.5) $G(x,y:\beta) \sim G[G(a,b:\alpha(x)), G(a,b:\alpha(y)):\beta].$

The right-hand expression of equation 7A.5 is a compound gamble in which the individual obtains the gamble $G[a,b:\alpha(x)]$ with probability β or gamble $G[a,b:\alpha(y)]$ with probability $1-\beta$:

The above figure shows that the probability of obtaining outcome a is $\beta \; \alpha(x) + (1 - \beta) \; \alpha(y)$ and the probability of obtaining b is $\beta[1 - \alpha(x)] + (1 - \beta) \; [1 - \alpha(y)]$. Because of this fact we can restate equation 7A.5 as follows:

(7A.6) $\qquad\qquad G(x,y:\beta) \sim G(a,b:\beta \; \alpha(x) + (1 - \beta) \; \alpha(y)).$

From axiom 4, $G(x,y:\beta) \sim G[a,b:\alpha(G(x,y:\beta))]$. Because axiom 4 tells us that the probability $\alpha(G(x,y:\beta))$ is unique, we finally have

(7A.7) $\qquad\qquad \alpha(G(x,y:\beta)) = \beta \; \alpha(x) + (1 - \beta) \; \alpha(y).$

Thus the ranking of a and b is according to expected utility. In general the expected utility is a weighted average of the possible utility levels from risky alternatives and their corresponding probabilities.

APPENDIX

7B

Derivation of Absolute and Relative Risk Aversion Measures

To derive the ARA measure, assume an agent with total assets equal to x and a utility function U. The agent is considering a risky gamble z in which the expected value of z is 0. We are interested in the risk premium, $\pi(x,z)$, that would make the individual indifferent between accepting the gamble and taking a certain amount:

(7B.1) $\qquad\qquad E[U(x + z)] = U[x + E(z) - \pi(x,z)],$

where $E[U(x + z)]$ is the expected utility of the current wealth and $U[x + E(z) - \pi(x,z)]$ is the utility of the wealth plus the expected value of the gamble minus the risk premium. Pratt (1964) expands the utility function around x on both sides of equation 7A.1 using a Taylor's series approximation. Expanding the right-hand side of equation 7B.1, we obtain

(7B.2) $\qquad\qquad U(x) - \pi \; U'(x) + \text{higher-order terms.}$

The Taylor's series expansion of the left-hand side of equation 7B.1 provides

(7B.3) $\qquad\qquad E[U(x) + zU'(x) + \tfrac{1}{2} z^2 \; U''(x)] + \text{higher order terms.}$

Equation 7B.3 can be simplified because the first term, $U(x)$, is not a random variable and the expected value of z^2 is equal to the variance of z. Thus, equation 7B.3 can be rewritten as follows:

(7B.4) $U(x) + \tfrac{1}{2}\sigma_z^2\, U''(x) + \text{higher-order terms.}$

Assuming that higher-order terms are equal to 0, equating equations 6A.2 and 6A.4 and solving for the risk premium, we obtain the local risk premium:

(7B.5) $\pi = \tfrac{1}{2}\sigma_z^2[-U''(x)/U'(x)],$

which is identical to equation 7.9. The relative risk aversion measure is derived in a similar manner.

CHAPTER

International Diversification

Introduction

Our earlier analysis, principally contained in Chapters 2 through 4, showed that portfolio performance is enhanced *ex ante* with an expanded investment opportunity set. It should not be surprising, therefore, to discover that portfolio performance is enhanced if the opportunity set expands to include overseas securities, provided that such securities do not merely duplicate purely domestic investment opportunities. We will soon provide evidence that international securities markets provide nonredundant investment opportunities.

The extent of the new opportunities offered by international diversification is vast, even from a U.S. perspective. The size of the non–U.S. equity market recently has been estimated at over $4.2 trillion, or over 60 percent of the world's total equity market. Exhibit 8.1 presents the world's organized equity markets and some of their institutional characteristics. Furthermore, the U.S. bond market constitutes less than half of the world bond market when measured in nominal dollar value outstanding. Of course, from a non–U.S. perspective the opportunities offered by overseas investment are even greater. For instance, Germany accounts for less than 4 percent of the world equity market and less than 8

EXHIBIT 8.1

World Equity Markets

Stock Exchange	Number of Companies Listed	Market Capitalization ($ millions)	Average Daily Volume (millions of shares)	Trading Hours (local time)
Australia	1,506	164,930	102.8	10:15–12:15 2:00–3:15
Belgium	340	50,535	N/A	
Canada (Montreal)	1,188	368,917	5.36	9:30–4:00
Canada (Toronto)	N/A			
Canada (Vancouver)	2,334	4,515	14.0	6:30–1:30
France	888	244,998	N/A	10:00–5:00
Hong Kong	308	71,697	N/A	10:00–12:30 2:30–3:30
Italy	211	135,428	N/A	10:00–1:45
Japan (Osaka)	N/A	2,747,948	118.9	9:00–11:00 1:00–3:00
Japan (Tokyo)	N/A	3,191,191	1,040.0	9:00–11:00 1:00–3:00
South Korea	N/A	57,007	9.7	9:40–11:40 1:20–3:20
Mexico	309	N/A	32.9	10:30–11:30
Netherlands	572	91,720	N/A	10:00–4:30
New Zealand	387	15,208	6.5	9:30–11:00 2:15–3:30
Norway	137	13,090	N/A	10:00–3:00
Singapore	326	N/A	N/A	10:00–12:30 2:30–4:00
Switzerland (Basel)	483	N/A	N/A	9:10–1:30
Switzerland (Geneva)	494	100,032	N/A	9:00–1:15
Switzerland (Zurich)	2,914	125,403	N/A	9:30–1:15
Taiwan	N/A	92,008	354	9:00–12:00
United Kingdom	2,656	2,659,707	N/A	9:00–5:00
United States	1,681	2,400,000	161	9:30–4:00
West Germany	741	186,601	7,354	11:30–1:30

SOURCE: *Institutional Investor*, March 1989, pp. 197–204.

percent of the world bond market. Belgium accounts for less than 2 percent of each market, and Canada accounts for less than 3 percent of each market.

Based in part on the principles developed by contemporary portfolio theory and in part on advancements in communications technology,

Shares Owned by Individuals (percent)	Shares Owned by Institutions or Funds (percent)	Restrictions on Foreign Ownership
10	90	Only on strategic industries such as uranium.
N/A	N/A	
52	48	Some financial institutions are subject to a maximum limit of equity that can be held by nonresidents.
N/A	N/A	See Montreal exchange.
80	20	None
30	20	Investors in countries outside the European Community cannot hold more than 20% of equity without approval.
N/A	N/A	None
N/A	N/A	None
N/A	N/A	None
23.6	72	None
68	29.3	Nonresidents can invest in stocks only through mutual funds and convertible bonds.
58.33	41.67	N/A
N/A	N/A	None
N/A	N/A	Foreigners must have approval for ownership of 24% or more.
22.5	15	Limits are imposed on foreign ownership of stocks.
25	75	Restrictions apply for stocks in some industries.
N/A	N/A	No restrictions for bearer shares, but ownership of registered shares is normally restricted to residents.
N/A	N/A	See Basel exchange.
10	N/A	See Basel exchange.
40.7	50.1	Foreign investors are required to apply for a remittance permit.
20	80	None
N/A	N/A	None
N/A	N/A	None

investors are increasingly availing themselves of the opportunities offered by foreign markets. For example, Exhibit 8.2 reports the gross volume of sales and purchases of domestic stocks by nonresidents for four nations for a recent period. The exhibit shows increasing growth in such transactions through time. Figure 8.1 displays the growth in foreign trading of U.S.

EXHIBIT 8.2

Cross-Border Stock Transactions

	United States[a]	Japan[b]	Germany[c]	Canada[d]
1980	75.2	26.2	6.8	12.4
1981	75.5	43.7	6.9	9.2
1982	79.9	34.6	6.3	5.2
1983	134.1	71.5	13.4	8.4
1984	122.6	778.3	12.4	8.8
1985	159.0	81.9	36.9	11.9
1986	277.5	201.6	77.9	20.2
1987	481.9	374.7	76.8	45.7
1988	618.4	503.7	71.2	51.9
1989	746.9	516.4	68.6	63.1
1990	881.0	498.2	61.4	69.7
1991	1,036.3	387.0	88.0	82.5

Source: *FRBNY Quarterly Review*, Summer 1992, p. 23.
[a]U.S. Treasury international capital data.
[b]Japanese Ministry of Finance.
[c]Deutsche Bundesbank, *Balance of Payments Statistics, Statistical Supplements to the Monthly Reports of the Deutsche Bundesbank*, series 3.
[d]Statistics Canada, *Security Transactions with Non-Residents and Quarterly Estimates of the Canadian Balance of International Payments*.

FIGURE 8.1

Foreign Trading of
U.S. Stocks

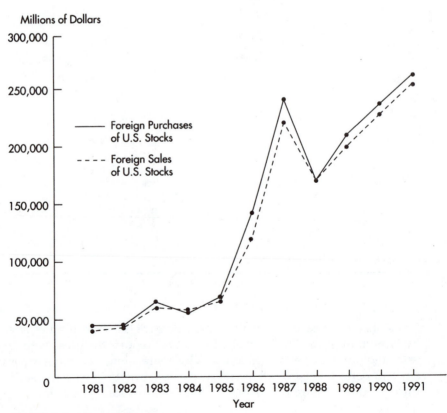

SOURCE: Federal Reserve Bulletin, various issues.

stocks during the 1980s and early 1990s. Increasing international diversification is also evidenced by the advent of international mutual funds, the advent of American depository receipts, the lengthening of exchange trading sessions to capture overseas volume, the growth of international mergers and acquisitions (over $200 billion in cross-border mergers and acquisitions in 1990 and 1991), and the listing of domestic stocks for trading on overseas security exchanges. Over 25 percent of the stocks listed for trading in Paris, Zurich, Singapore, and Frankfurt are foreign stocks. In 1991, 2,709 stocks were listed outside home market exchanges (includes Europe, Asia/Pacific, and North America), and in the first half of 1992 over $10.4 billion of stocks (179 deals) were issued outside home markets.

Given that the theory of international diversification represents a simple extension of our earlier analysis, this chapter focuses on the empirical evidence regarding such diversification and on methods for constructing international portfolios. We begin with an analysis of the computation of risk and returns from foreign investments, followed by a presentation of empirical evidence regarding the risk and returns from international diversification for a recent period. A brief discussion of foreign exchange risk and country risk is then provided, followed by a summary of empirical literature that compares international and purely domestic portfolio performance. The chapter concludes with a discussion of various methods used for constructing international portfolios.

COMPUTING RISK AND RETURNS FROM FOREIGN INVESTMENTS

Computing risk and returns from foreign investments differs from computing those of domestic investments because of accompanying exchange rate changes. It is convenient to divide the return to the domestic investor, $1 + R_D$, into a component due to the return in the home market, $1 + R_F$, and a component due to the exchange return, $1 + R_E$:

(8.1)
$$(1 + R_D) = (1 + R_F)(1 + R_E).$$

For instance, if the value of a share of a British stock rises to £30 in time 1 from £25 in time 0, and if the $/£ exchange rate declines to $1.75/£ from $2.00/£ (a dollar appreciation), then the one-period return on the U.S. investor's purchase of the British stock is 5 percent:

$$(1 + R_D) = (30/25)(1.75/2.00), \text{ or } R_D = .05.$$

Simplifying equation 8.1 gives

(8.2)
$$R_D = R_F + R_E + R_F R_E.$$

Here we have $R_D = (.20) + (-.125) + (.20)(-.125) = .05$. The cross-product term $R_F R_E$ is typically much smaller than R_F or R_E, so it is often ignored. Thus the domestic return is approximately equal to the sum of the home market return and the exchange return. Invoking this approximation provides the following mean and standard deviation of return on a foreign security:

(8.3) $$R_D = R_F + R_E,$$

(8.4) $$\sigma_D = [\sigma^2_F + \sigma^2_E + 2\sigma_{FE}]^{1/2}$$

where σ_{FE} is the covariance of the home market and exchange returns. Thus, by ignoring the cross-product term, we treat the foreign security as a type of two-asset portfolio. From our earlier Markowitz analysis, it should be clear that σ_D is less than the sum of σ_F and σ_E, principally because there is less than perfect positive correlation between R_F and R_E. Indeed, empirically σ_{FE} is close to 0 and sometimes negative.

EMPIRICAL RISK AND RETURN ESTIMATES

The justification for and benefits of international diversification depend on the correlations between markets and the risk and return of each market. After all, if foreign securities are merely duplicates of domestic securities, then access to foreign markets does not truly expand the opportunity set. In this section we provide some empirical estimates of risk and return from international diversification for a recent period, employing the formulas presented in the last section. Empirically, we find that there is ample justification for engaging in foreign investment, especially with respect to equities. Independent studies confirm our findings.

Correlations among Foreign Markets

Exhibit 8.3 provides correlations among the world's major equity markets for the period 1986–1990. We used monthly returns for value-weighted market indices. These indices capture a large percentage of the capitalized value of their nation's equity market and tend to be the most cited: the SP500 (U.S.), the FT-SE100 (U.K.), the NIKKEI 225 (Japan), and so on. The correlations exhibit some anticipated properties: higher correlations for nations that are geographically proximate to one another (Germany and France, U.S. and Canada), and higher correlations for the Netherlands due to the multinational flavor of most Dutch companies (Philips, AKZO, and Royal Dutch–Shell). The overall average correlation reported in Exhibit 8.3 is .532.[1] This is substantially lower than the correlations among intra-

---

[1] Excluding the crash month of October 1987, the average correlation is .389.

EXHIBIT 8.3

Correlations among International Stock Markets, 1986–1990

	Canada	France	Germany	Japan	Netherlands	Switzerland	United Kingdom
France	0.431						
Germany	0.345	0.562					
Japan	0.295	0.438	0.352				
Netherlands	0.594	0.604	0.696	0.390			
Switzerland	0.522	0.651	0.801	0.401	0.711		
United Kingdom	0.691	0.558	0.467	0.356	0.690	0.580	
United States	0.773	0.490	0.413	0.277	0.654	0.571	0.572

country indices, such as the SP500 and Dow Jones Industrial Average (DJIA), which are commonly over .90. Other studies report similar correlations: Eun and Resnick (1988) found an average correlation of .41 across international equity markets for the period 1973–1982, and Solnik (1988) reports an average correlation of .35 for the period 1971–1986.[2]

Similar correlations have been found for international bond markets. For example, Chollerton, Pieraerts, and Solnik (1986) report an average correlation coefficient of .43 for the long-term bond indices of major industrialized nations. Solnik (1988) reports an average correlation coefficient between the U.S. dollar bond market and foreign bond market of .254 for the period 1971–1985. This result contrasts with the high correlations found for intracountry bond indices or fixed-income mutual funds. For instance, the correlation between two typical U.S. bond mutual funds is well above .90.

These low correlations between world equity markets and world debt markets constitute strong justification for engaging in international diversification. They suggest that foreign markets do not offer merely redundant investment opportunities to those available domestically. Common world factors affect the prices of firm stocks and bonds worldwide, but national or regional factors play a more important role in determining asset prices, thus causing substantial independence between markets. These latter factors include domestic fiscal and monetary policy, domestic regulations on trade flow, capital controls, and the like. Finally, many other researchers provide additional evidence of nonduplicative worldwide security markets; for example, Roll (1988) found that 26

---

[2] Early studies of the correlations among major international markets include Levy and Sarnat (1970) and Lessard (1973). Also see Eun and Resnick (1984). For tests of the stability of correlation coefficients over time, see Maldonado and Saunders (1981), Shaked (1985), and Jorion (1985). For recent examinations of possible gains from international diversification in emerging markets, see Bailey and Stulz (1990) and Cheung and Ho (1991).

Another method of examining the dependence of markets is to measure their degree of comovement over a short period. Several researchers have examined the transmission of prices and volatility from one market to another on a daily, overnight, or even hourly basis. See, for example, Hilliard (1979), Becker, Finnerty, and Gupta (1990), and Becker, Finnerty and Tucker (1992).

INTEGRATION AMONG EEC EQUITY MARKETS

With the removal of import tariffs and a common agricultural policy of price supports and production management between member nations of the European Economic Community (EEC) in the late 1960s, the EEC completed an important step toward the creation of a unified or "common" market. The total integration of EEC trading and markets was scheduled for completion by year-end 1992, when the last of all nontariff barriers were to be removed. Such nontariff barriers included divergent national product standards, differential rates of value-added taxes and excise duties, and other barriers such as custom controls.

To the extent that the stock markets of EEC members are effected by economic conditions and their economies become more integrated, their market returns should become more highly correlated. Thus diversification across EEC markets should become less attractive.

The exhibit below reports the correlation coefficients among some EEC stock markets (based on indices measured in local currency units) for two separate periods: 1981–1985 (top cell) and 1986–1990 (bottom cell). Given that stock prices are driven by expectations of future performance, the anticipated effects of EEC integration have been capitalized in these reported values. As the exhibit demonstrates, the vast majority of correlations among stock markets have increased significantly. European markets are becoming more integrated, implying that international portfolios may have to be rebalanced to replace some EEC securities with non-EEC securities.

	Belgium	Denmark	France	Ireland	Netherlands	Spain	United Kingdom
Denmark	−.16						
	.31						
France	.19	−.22					
	.62	.44					
Ireland	−.17	.01	.15				
	.70	.49	.71				
Netherlands	.19	.49	−.11	.15			
	.26	.47	.40	.14			
Spain	.19	.56	.09	−.20	.56		
	.04	.64	.44	.13	.58		
UK	.16	.33	.07	.57	.42	.17	
	.70	.30	.73	.69	.29	.19	
WG	−.08	.20	−.06	.60	.79	.10	.57
	.67	.59	.78	.62	.48	.42	.75

national stock market indices all moved in the same direction in just one month during a recent ten-year period, namely the crash month of October 1987.

Foreign Market Standard Deviations of Returns

Risk depends on the standard deviations of returns as well as the correlation coefficients. Exhibit 8.4 presents the annualized standard deviations of returns for our eight national stock market indices for the period 1986–1990. The column Home Market Risk presents the standard deviations when returns are calculated in the indices' home currency. The column Exchange Risk reports the standard deviations of percentage exchange rate changes, where the exchange rates are defined as the U.S. dollar price of a unit of foreign currency. As discussed in the previous section, the total risk to the domestic (U.S.) investor, σ_D, is lower than the mere sum of the home market risk, σ_F, and the exchange risk, σ_E (equation 8.4). Thus the standard deviations presented under the column Total Risk are lower than the sum of the corresponding standard deviations presented in the first and second columns of Exhibit 8.4. For instance, the total risk for an investment in the FT-SE100, from a U.S. perspective, is .2316. This is substantially less than the sum of the U.K. home market risk (.2108) and the $/£ exchange risk (.1155).

Exhibit 8.4 demonstrates that for the period 1986–1990, the U.S. equity market was less volatile than most other equity markets (stated in their own currencies). The higher risk of foreign investments is even more pronounced after the effects of exchange risk are included (again assuming a U.S. perspective). Eun and Resnick (1988) and Solnik (1988) report similar results. Also, the total risk of the U.S. bond market was less than the total risk of most foreign bond markets for the period, once the effects of exchange risk were incorporated. Independent studies report a similar result. For example, Salomon Brothers reported a standard deviation of monthly dollar returns equal to 3.48 percent for the U.S.

EXHIBIT 8.4

Risk from a U.S. Perspective

Equity Markets	Home Market Risk (σ_F)	Exchange Risk (σ_E)	Total Risk (σ_D)
Canada	.2217	.0513	.2482
France	.2380	.1351	.2608
Germany	.2005	.1307	.2314
Japan	.1930	.1461	.2470
Netherlands	.2118	.1302	.2289
Switzerland	.1707	.1392	.2099
United Kingdom	.2108	.1155	.2316
United States	.1821	NA	.1821

EXHIBIT 8.5

Diversification across International Equity Markets

Proportion Invested in World Index	Total Risk
0.00	.1821
0.10	.1727
0.20	.1668
0.30	.1609
0.40	.1581
0.50	.1573
0.60	.1586
0.70	.1625
0.80	.1687
0.90	.1769
1.00	.1856

government bond index and 3.18 percent for the world bond index for the period 1978–1983.

Exhibit 8.5 demonstrates the *ex post* risk reduction benefits of combining a value-weighted world portfolio (excluding U.S. stocks) and the corresponding U.S. stock index for the period 1986–1990. The exhibit reports the standard deviations under various percentages of foreign investment. It appears that the minimum risk is achieved with a 50 percent to 60 percent investment in the U.S. portfolio and a 40 percent to 50 percent investment in the value-weighted world portfolio. Total risk is reduced by about 14 percent from a U.S. perspective.[3] Risk reduction from international bond market diversification was also evident for the period.

Exhibit 8.5 suggests that international equity diversification would have reduced risk for the period 1986–1990. Would risk have been reduced in another period? Will risk likely be reduced in the future from international diversification? The answers to these questions depend of course on the correlation between the world portfolio and the U.S. stock index as well as the standard deviation of each index. Given that other researchers (e.g., Eun and Resnick and Solnik) have reported similar correlations and standard deviations while employing different sample periods, it is reasonable to conclude that risk reduction through international diversification will continue to be effective.[4]

---

[3] From Exhibit 8.5, the total risk of the value-weighted world portfolio (excluding U.S. stocks) was .1856 (a proportion in the world index of 100 percent). This suggests that from a foreign perspective, risk can be reduced by diversifying into the U.S. stock market.

[4] Exhibit 8.5 suggests that risk reduction through international diversification is available at the market index level. There is also compelling evidence that similar diversification benefits can be achieved by investing in fewer foreign securities. Specifically, Solnik (1974) found that with as few as thirty stocks spread equally across the U.S. and major European stock markets, the risk for a U.S. investor is about half of that of a comparably sized purely domestic stock portfolio.

Returns from International Diversification

Risk reduction is not the sole motive for engaging in overseas investment. Higher expected returns arising from faster-growing economies or from currency gains may also motivate international investment. For instance, from 1960 to 1990 the real gross domestic product of Japan grew at 7.1 percent per annum, and the U.S. rate was just 3.2 percent.

In terms of returns, foreign equity markets generally outperformed the U.S. market for most of the past three decades, including the period 1986–1990. Exhibit 8.6 reports the average annual returns from January 1986 through December 1990 for our same eight countries. The difference between the home market return and return to U.S. investor is attributable to exchange rate changes (equation 8.2). Four of the seven foreign markets had greater home-country returns than the United States, and the average non–U.S. equity index had a return of .1640 in its home country. Also, the dollar generally depreciated during this period, especially with respect to the Japanese yen, thus making the foreign returns to the U.S. investor even more attractive after repatriation. Thus any reasonable method of international equity diversification would have both lowered risk (Exhibit 8.5) and increased returns for the period 1986–1990. Solnik (1988) reports similar results for a sample of seventeen equity markets for the period 1971–1985. Ibbotson, Siegel, and Love (1985), using annual data from 1964–1985, also report superior performance for non–U.S. equities. Their results are presented in Exhibit 8.7. They also indicate that foreign bond markets outperformed the U.S. bond market for the period. An internationally diversified long-term bond portfolio also would have both lowered risk and increased returns for the period 1986–1990, principally because of the appreciation of the Japanese bond market and the Japanese yen.[5]

EXHIBIT 8.6

Equity Market Returns, 1986–1990

Market	Home Country	To U.S. Investor
Canada	.1202	.1135
France	.1811	.1591
Germany	.1352	.1607
Japan	.1901	.2823
Netherlands	.2016	.2108
Switzerland	.1034	.1294
United Kingdom	.2165	.2102
United States	.1716	.1716

[5] Later in this chapter we present a summary of the evidence regarding the performance of international mutual funds vis-à-vis purely domestic (U.S.) mutual funds.

EXHIBIT 8.7

World Capital Market Annual Returns, 1964–1985

	Compound Return	Standard Deviation
Equities		
United States	8.81	16.89
Foreign		
Europe	7.83	15.58
Asia	15.14	30.74
Other	8.14	20.88
Foreign Total	9.84	16.07
Equities Total	9.08	15.28
Bonds		
United States		
Corporate	5.35	9.63
Government	5.91	6.43
United States Total	5.70	7.16
Foreign		
Corporate Domestic	8.35	7.26
Government Domestic	5.79	7.41
Crossborder	7.51	5.76
Foreign Total	6.80	6.88
Bonds Total	6.36	5.50
Cash Equivalents		
United States	6.49	3.22
Foreign	6.50	7.10
Cash Total	6.38	2.92

Source: R. Ibbotson, L. Siegel, and K. Love, World wealth: Market values and returns, *Journal of Portfolio Management*, Fall 1985. This copyrighted material is reprinted with permission form *The Journal of Portfolio Management*, 488 Madison Avenue, NY, NY 10022.

Summary of Empirical Results

The results of this section strongly suggest that risk can be reduced through international diversification. Also, it is likely that international diversification will continue to reduce risk in the foreseeable future. The results of this section also suggest that recent return performance has been enhanced through international diversification, at least from a U.S. viewpoint. However, this *ex post* result was principally attributable to the performance of the Japanese market during the late 1980s. There is no reason to believe that foreign markets will produce greater future *unexpected* returns than the U.S.[6] In addition, historic returns from international diversification have been less than purely domestic returns

---

[6] Indeed, as an interesting case study of how mean-variance analysis can fail in practice, note that the Japanese equity market has suffered a substantial devaluation since our sample data ended in 1990. Funds that invested in Japanese companies were among the best-performing funds from 1986 through 1990, but by December 1992 they exhibited an average loss of about 22 percent. This bear market, like the great bear and bull markets of history, illustrates the limitations of standard portfolio analysis and reminds us that there is not a magic formula for investment and portfolio formation.

from a non–U.S. perspective (e.g., Japan). Still, there is no reason to believe that future unexpected returns from international portfolios will be less than purely domestic returns, so international diversification clearly presents benefits on an *ex ante* basis: risk reduction without sacrificing expected return.

RISK AND IMPEDIMENTS OF FOREIGN INVESTMENT

Investment in foreign securities entails some risks and impediments that are not associated with purely domestic investment. These risks and impediments are analogous to those observed in the context of foreign direct investment (Korbin 1979). In this section we briefly discuss these risks and impediments. Before doing so, however, we want to emphasize that the advantages of international diversification clearly appear to exceed the limited disadvantages described here. The costs and difficulties associated with foreign investment are not sufficient to explain, for example, why many private firms exhibit an international balance sheet but also exhibit a parochial pension plan. For example, U.S. pension funds currently hold less than 10% of their assets in foreign equities, which represent about 60% of the world market portfolio.

Exchange Risk

As demonstrated in Exhibit 8.5, the total risk of a portfolio can be reduced through international diversification despite the added exchange rate risk. To better represent such added risk, consider Figure 8.2, which portrays the recent behavior of the Morgan Stanley capital international world index (MSWI) expressed in three different currencies: the U.S. dollar, Japanese yen, and British pound. Expressing the index in this manner demonstrates the impact of currency changes on global investments made by U.S., Japanese, and U.K. investors during this period. The index in dollars was the only gainer, up 2.2 percent; the index in yen and pounds lost 6.5 percent and 12.7 percent, respectively.

Exchange rate risk can be reduced through a variety of methods, including diversifying across several national currencies and transacting in currency forward, futures, option, and swap markets. Such methods are described in detail in Chapters 16 through 19.[7] Several researchers have examined the efficiency and benefits of alternative currency hedging techniques (Madura and Reiff 1985, Eun and Resnick 1988, and Black

---

[7] Some debate exists as to whether investors should be concerned with exchange rate risk. In theory investors care about purchasing power risk, not nominal dollar risk. Yet for various reasons it is commonly argued that exchange risk management is fruitful. In a sense exchange rates are real variables, not nominal ones, and as such have a specific influence on the portfolio choices of the nationals of each country. See Adler and Dumas (1983) for a related discussion.

FIGURE 8.2

The Morgan Stanley
World Index in
Three Currencies

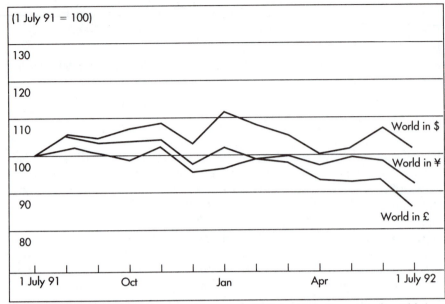

SOURCE: Morgan Stanley Capital International Perspectives, 1992. Reprinted with permission from *Global Finance* magazine, August 1992.

1990). Empirically, most researchers find benefits from hedging international portfolios against exchange risk. For example, based on an analysis of stock indices for six major countries for the period January 1974 to October 1985, Madura and Reiff (1985) reported that a strategy of hedging exchange risks reduced overall portfolio risk by 50 percent with no offsetting decrease in portfolio returns. Of course, the effect of eliminating exchange gains or losses on expected returns will vary across countries and over time. Eun and Resnick (1988) demonstrated that international portfolios hedged *ex ante* outperformed their unhedged counterparts. Perold and Schulman (1988) report similar hedging benefits.

Country Risk

The term *country risk* has various meanings. It has been defined as generally as any deviation from interest rate parity (Aliber 1973), but mainly it is used to describe phenomena such as the imposition of capital controls on foreign investments and the expropriation of investor wealth by a foreign central government. For example, the U.S. government froze all Iraqi assets held in the U.S. immediately after the start of Desert Shield in late 1990. Country risk is not typically considered important when investing in industrialized nations, such as those listed in Exhibit 8.6. It is relevant, however, when contemplating investment in less developed and less politically stable economies, such as Hong Kong today.

EXCHANGE RATE RISK: LIVE AND LEARN

Below is a letter from A. Keith Brodkin, president of MFS Worldwide Governments Trust, to the shareholders as of June 30, 1991. MFS Worldwide Governments Trust is a load mutual fund that specializes in the management of government bonds, issued principally in the United States, Canada, and Europe. The fund's total net assets are about $172 million, and the fund has provided an average net asset value change (including reinvested dividends) of about 15.5% per year since its inception over ten years ago. The letter highlights how exchange rate risk can substantially affect the performance of an international investment. For the first half of 1991 the fund's net realized loss on investments was $756,540. The fund's realized loss on currency transactions was $715,045, accounting for nearly 95% of the total net loss. As the letter indicates, the fund's management intends to hedge a significant portion of its foreign bond holdings against currency fluctuations for the remainder of 1991.

Dear Shareholders:

The bond market rally in most major foreign markets, which began late in 1990, continued through the first six months of 1991. Interest rates in countries such as France, Denmark, Australia and New Zealand dropped sharply, reflecting very weak economic activity and a reduction in inflation. In contrast, U.S. Treasury bond yields rose in recent months, fueled by investors' concerns that the United States is about to embark upon a business recovery which will bring a new round of inflationary pressures.

While the Trust was well-positioned outside of the United States to benefit from these rising bond prices, its overall performance was adversely impacted by the dramatic upward move of the U.S. dollar during the spring, and the fact that only a portion of our foreign bond exposure was hedged back into U.S. dollars. Concerns about developments in Eastern Europe, as well as a general slowdown in economic growth in Western Europe, led to a 20% decline in the value of the German mark relative to the U.S. dollar. Because other currencies in the european monetary system are tied very closely to the German mark, they also experienced similar declines.

Portfolio Strategy

We maintain a positive outlook for world bond markets. Based on our belief that the U.S. will experience a mild economic recovery, with further declines in inflation, we expect U.S. Treasury bond yields to fall below 8% over the next year. However, we continue to favor the Australian and Canadian bond markets over the United States, as well as those of several European countries, such as Denmark, France and Ireland, because we believe sluggish growth patterns and relatively low inflation levels should lead to even greater declines in long-term interest rates. We have hedged a significant portion of these holdings back into United States dollars to reduce the impact of currency fluctuations on portfolio performance for the balance of this year.

We appreciate your support and welcome any questions or comments you may have.

Respectfully,

A. Keith Brodkin
President
July 29, 1991

It is generally conceded that country risk is not readily diversifiable. After all, if a foreign government expropriates your wealth, it is not likely that another government will appropriate wealth to you. Still, there are ways for international investors and portfolio managers to track and price country risk. Country risk has been quantified, and country risk indices do exist. The best known indices include Haner's business environmental risk information index, Haendel, West, and Meadow's political system stability index, Business International's country assessment service, and *Euromoney* magazine's country risk index. These indices in part reflect economic indicators such as GNP and interest rates and in part reflect expert opinion on political turmoil and attitude toward foreign investors. Presumably, a portfolio manager can employ such indices to help make decisions on where to invest overseas and may employ them to help determine foreign asset prices, perhaps by incorporating a country risk index in the kind of multifactor pricing models described in Part 2.

Impediments. There are several impediments to foreign investment, many of which are surmountable:

- Unfamiliarity with foreign markets. Cultural differences, different languages and trading procedures, and different accounting procedures and time zones all represent impediments to foreign investment.
- The costs of obtaining firm-specific data or sometimes even macroeconomic data are high for some foreign countries. In addition, the quality of these data, if available, is often uneven.
- Limits on foreign investment. Institutional investors in most countries can only hold limited proportions of foreign assets in their portfolios.
- Liquidity. Some foreign markets have relatively low liquidity or thin trading volume. Price manipulation may be of greater concern for these markets.[8]
- Costs. Brokerage commissions and other transaction costs historically have been much greater in foreign nations than in the U.S. A typical bid-ask spread for a foreign stock is about 100 basis points. This may be why foreign investors tend to hold their national securities for longer periods on average than U.S. investors. It also partially explains why fees charged by international money managers are commonly greater than those charged by domestic managers, although these higher fees also reflect the added costs of data collection, research, and communications accompanying overseas investment. Still, the deregulation of capital markets worldwide is serving to lower these costs. Especially noteworthy was the Big Bang of 1986, which dramatically reduced

---

[8] Evidence regarding the efficiency of foreign securities markets is mixed. See Ang and Pohlman (1978), Officer (1975), Roux and Gilbertson (1978), Kato and Schallheim (1985), Jaffe and Westerfield (1985), and many others. See Hawawini (1988) for a summary.

commissions in London as well as opened up the London Stock Exchange to foreign investment firms. This event was similar to the deregulation of commissions in the U.S. in 1975. Besides brokerage commissions, a potential cost of foreign investment is the withholding of taxes by most stock markets. However, the tax is only on dividend income, may be reclaimable, or may be claimed as a tax credit in the home country.

STUDIES OF INTERNATIONAL MUTUAL FUND PERFORMANCE

The previous empirical analysis and related studies suggested that international portfolios could have outperformed purely U.S. portfolios for most of the past thirty years. An interesting question is, Did they? Several researchers have addressed this question by comparing the past performance of international mutual funds (IMFs), such as the Fidelity overseas fund, the Putnam international equities fund, and the Scudder international fund, with that of domestic mutual funds, such as the Vanguard index fund. Perhaps the most comprehensive of these studies was performed by Essayyad and Wu (1988), who assessed the performance of eighteen IMFs over the period 1977–1984. Fifteen of the funds had a greater mean monthly return than the SP500 for the period. In addition, sixteen of the eighteen IMFs exhibited a lower coefficient of variation (defined as standard deviation of returns divided by mean return) than the SP500, indicating a lower level of risk per unit of return. Finally, the average percentage of variation in returns of the eighteen IMFs explained by SP500 movements was only 24 percent, confirming that IMF return patterns differ substantially from U.S. market returns—a desirable attribute for foreign diversification. Rao and Aggarwal (1987) and Eun, Kolodny, and Resnick (1991) report similar findings.

Another study of the performance of IMFs was conducted by Cumby and Glen (1990), who examined a sample of fifteen U.S.-based IMFs between 1982 and 1988 with two different performance measures. They found no evidence that the IMFs, either individually or as a whole, outperformed a broad, value-weighted international equity index (namely the often-quoted MSWI) over the sample period. This result parallels that of several studies which find that domestic mutual funds do not in general outperform a domestic stock index (on a risk-adjusted basis) such as the SP500. The results of Cumby and Glen suggest that active management of IMFs does not yield superior performance. Relatedly, they found some evidence that the IMFs outperformed the U.S. index for the period but that this result was most likely due to the benefits of international diversification rather than any superior performance by fund managers.

AROUND-THE-CLOCK GLOBAL SECURITY TRADING

A major deregulatory event known as the Big Bang that occurred on the London Stock Exchange (LSE) in October 1986 further facilitated progress toward around-the-clock trading. A computerized network called SEAQ (pronounced "see-yak") was established. SEAQ is similar to the NASDAQ over-the-counter system in the United States. International traders conduct trading through a telecommunications network. In addition, the LSE began to allow investment firms that trade in the United States and Japan to trade in London. Consequently, the large investment firms that trade on the New York and Tokyo exchanges have created a nearly 24-hour market, using the NYSE from 9:30 a.m. to 4:00 p.m. Eastern time, the Tokyo Stock Exchange (TSE) from 7:00 p.m. to 1 a.m. Eastern time, and the LSE from 4:00 a.m. to 10:30 a.m. Eastern time. Shares that are traded on each exchange can be bought or sold almost any time of the day. As more companies have their stocks listed on the various exchanges, stock market trading will be almost continuous.

Relatedly, the NYSE recently took its first step toward 24-hour trading. Beginning June 13, 1991, the NYSE offers two types of after-hours trading: (1) from 4:15 p.m. to 5:00 p.m. Eastern time, trades will be executed at the 4:00 p.m. closing prices; and (2) a session from 4:00 p.m. to 4:15 p.m. Eastern time will be only for program trades of baskets of stocks. The trade must include 15 stock issues and be worth at least $1 million. To date, however, volume in these after-hours sessions has been limited.

CONSTRUCTING INTERNATIONAL PORTFOLIOS

Strategies for constructing international portfolios (international asset allocation) are somewhat analogous to those for constructing domestic portfolios. For instance, a passive investor who decides to diversify internationally can hold an international index fund—the so-called passive international approach. The investor could replicate the MSWI by constructing an appropriate value-weighted portfolio of international securities. This approach is analogous to holding a domestic index fund (the passive domestic approach).

There are two possible justifications for engaging in the passive international approach, one empirical and the other theoretical. Empirically, if studies suggest that IMFs do not on average outperform a broad international index, then holding an international index fund may be judicious. The results of Cumby and Glen (1990) provide empirical support for the passive approach. These researchers found that IMFs, either individually or as a whole, underperformed the MSWI. The theoretical argument for engaging in the passive international approach parallels the theoretical argument motivating the passive domestic approach. Namely, if expected return is related to a market index and if security prices are in equilibrium, then investors should only be compensated for systematic risk. To eliminate nonsystematic risk, investors should hold an index fund. Thus, if securities are in equilibrium and the CAPM holds, the investor should hold an index fund.[9] Moreover, even if asset prices are not in equilibrium but the investor has no forecasting expertise, again the investor should hold an index fund. Analogously, if expected returns were determined by an international CAPM whose market index was a value-weighted international index, then the investor should hold a value-weighted international index fund such as the MSWI. Thus there is a theoretical argument for holding an international index fund that parallels the rationale for holding a domestic index fund in a segregated, closed economy. However, there is little empirical evidence that supports an international version of the CAPM. Solnik (1988) and Jacquillat and Solnik (1978) find that the variation of asset returns is principally explained by the domestic market index and not a world market index. This result holds even for the stock returns of domestically based multinational corporations. Consequently, the better justification for engaging in a passive international approach lies in the empirical work on IMF performance, such as that of Cumby and Glen (1990).[10]

Another asset allocation approach for an international investor who cannot forecast expected returns is to minimize total risk. Solnik and Noetzlin (1982) refer to this technique as the extrapolative approach. Here the construction of the minimum-risk international portfolio is based on the historical covariance matrix of international asset returns. This approach is effective if the covariance structure is stable intertemporally. Researchers (especially Jorion 1985) support such stability. For instance, the correlation coefficients among regional nations, such as the United States and Canada, remain high through time while the opposite holds for geographically dispersed nations (e.g., the United States and Japan). Empirically, Solnik and Noetzlin find that the extrapolative approach outperforms the passive international approach as well as the simplified approach. They define the simplified approach as one that allocates an equal amount of investment to all securities, thus it assumes equal correlations among all security pairs.

A final approach to international asset allocation is the active international approach. Here the asset allocation strategy differs from world market capitalization weights. It is analogous to the active approach in a domestic setting and thus is largely based on the belief that security prices are not in equilibrium and that forecasting ability obtains.[11] The

---

[9] This concept was discussed loosely in Chapter 1 and will be more apparent after the discussion of asset pricing in Part 2.

[10] Some contend that a value-weighted international index such as the MSWI may not be sufficiently diversified, since one country, Japan, currently accounts for about 50 percent of the index. Japan is overweighted because Japanese firms commonly hold large percentages of the stocks of other Japanese firms, creating a type of double accounting. An index using the value of a country's equity assets may be more appropriate.

[11] Interestingly, Solnik and Noetzlin (1982) find that the world market portfolio does not lie on the efficient frontier, implying that internationally, market portfolios are inefficient.

VANGUARD'S EUROPE FUND

In 1990 the Vanguard Group offered a new type of no-load index mutual fund called the Vanguard Europe fund. The fund's origination was motivated by Vanguard's overall policy directive to become a leading index fund manager; by theory and evidence on the benefits of international diversification; and by investor demand for European stocks, which were exhibiting lower price/earnings and price–to–cash flow ratios than U.S. and Japanese equities. Indeed, by year-end 1990 European stocks had an average price/earnings ratio of 14.4 and price–to–cash flow ratio of 6.5. For U.S. stocks these ratios were 19.5 and 9, respectively; for Japanese stocks, the ratios were 35.6 and 12.4.

The Vanguard Europe fund is designed to mirror the risk-return profile of the Morgan Stanley Capital International European Free Index (MSCIEFI), a type of value-weighted index consisting principally of large capitalized European stocks. On August 13, 1992, the Vanguard Europe fund exhibited the following approximate weightings: 39 percent in U.K. stocks, 15 percent in German stocks, 13 percent in French stocks, 7 percent in Swiss stocks, 7 percent in stocks of the Netherlands, 5 percent in Spain and Italy, and the remaining 9 percent spread over Belgium, Sweden, Denmark, Austria and Norway.

The fund's manager is Gus Sauter, who also oversees other index funds offered by Vanguard. Sauter's compensation is based in part on how closely he tracks the performance of the MSCIEFI and on the fund's total operating expenses. Currently, the fund's total operating expenses are remarkably low at 0.33 percent per year. By contrast, the average general equity fund has an annual expense ratio of 1.3 percent of investor assets. The current Vanguard Europe fund totals a bit over $242 million.

Sauter employs computerized software to help track the MSCIEFI. The proprietary software is designed to signal him when portfolio rebalancing is required due to changes in the value-determined weights of the MSCIEFI. In addition, the software discloses how futures contracts on different national stock indexes can be employed so that the fund remains fully invested. In order to track the MSCIEFI as closely as possible, Sauter wants to minimize his actual cash holdings; that is, he seeks to be fully funded. Yet, he needs to have a means of low-cost rebalancing to maintain tracking with the index. Employing index futures contracts avoids having to be less than fully funded, yet provides a means to track the index, at least over short intervals, without having to trade the stocks. For instance, suppose that U.K. stocks exhibit a relative appreciation but that the appreciation may be transitory. Since the stocks appreciated, the value-determined weight in U.K. stocks will have increased. However, rather than selling other national stocks to purchase more U.K. stocks or maintaining a cash holding to purchase the stocks, Sauter can employ U.K. futures contracts to modify the fund's overall composition temporarily. Such techniques are discussed more thoroughly in Chapter 16.

The Vanguard Group does not conduct any foreign exchange rate forecasting and the fund does not engage in any currency risk management. In addition, the fund's portfolio turnover rate is substantially lower than the average fund's portfolio turnover rate, which is about 90 percent per year. Since the fund's inception in 1990, its total annualized return has been about 5.07 percent. This return figure assumes that all dividend payments have been reinvested and reflects repatriation of foreign cash flows into U.S. dollars.

decision concerning how much to invest in each international security depends on asset risk, expected return, and covariance.[12] Thus, the only fundamental difference between the active international approach and the active domestic approach is that the former entails an element of exchange exposure. As discussed earlier in the chapter, there are methods to eliminate such exposure. Still, investors may believe that exchange rates are not in equilibrium. For instance, key players in currency markets are central banks, which are not profit maximizers. The evidence regarding the efficiency of the currency market is very mixed. Here the accompanying reduction in expected return associated with exchange rate hedging may lead the investor to remain unhedged. As shown by Black (1990), assuming some exchange exposure can lead to an increase in expected return.

SUMMARY

It is commonly argued that international investment lowers risk by eliminating nonsystematic volatility without sacrificing expected return—an important free lunch. For this argument to obtain, world capital markets must not be duplicates. Evidence reported in this chapter and by numerous researchers suggests that world markets are indeed independent. While world markets may be more alike today than just a few years ago as a result of innovations in communications technology, worldwide capital market deregulation, and the advent of new financial products linking international markets, it is likely that world capital markets will continue to behave (somewhat) independently of one another. Indeed, it is likely that world markets will never be completely alike or redundant. Thus, international diversification should continue to improve the risk-adjusted performance of a domestic portfolio for the foreseeable future.

Evidence indicates that international portfolios have dominated purely domestic U.S. portfolios—especially equity portfolios—for the past 30 years. This evidence is based on market indices and passive management strategies, so active international market and security selection may have further improved international performance. There are risks and added costs and impediments associated with international diversification, but these factors are negligible in light of the substantial risk-return advantages offered by such investment.

Based on this evidence and on the tenets of modern portfolio theory, domestic investors are increasingly availing themselves of the opportunities offered by foreign investment. International portfolio investment

---

[12] In practice managers often select a portfolio within each country and then engage in country selection. Since nondomestic factors appear to be relatively unimportant in determining asset prices, as shown by Solnik (1988) and Jacquillat and Solnik (1988) and as discussed above, this approach may be judicious.

has been a mainstay in European markets and is becoming a more prevalent practice in the United States. Portfolio managers can engage in international investment in ways that are similar to domestic portfolio construction.

REFERENCES

Adler, M., and B. Dumas. 1983. International portfolio choice and corporate finance. A synthesis. *Journal of Finance.* June, 925–984.

Agmon, T. 1973. Country risk. The significance of the country factor for share-price movements in the United Kingdom, Germany, and Japan. *Journal of Business.* January, 24–32.

Agmon, T., and D. Lessard. 1977. Investor recognition of corporate international diversification. *Journal of Finance.* September, 1049–1055.

Aliber, R. 1973. The interest rate parity theorem: A reinterpretation. *Journal of Political Economy.* December, 1451–1459.

Ang, J., and R. Pohlman. 1978. A note on the price behavior of Far Eastern stocks. *Journal of International Business Studies.* Spring.

Arnott, A., and N. Henrikkson. 1989. A disciplined approach to global asset allocation. *Financial Analysts Journal.* March-April, 17–28.

Bailey, W., and R. Stulz. 1990. Benefits of international diversification: The case of Pacific basin stock markets. *Journal of Portfolio Management.* Summer, 57–61.

Becker, K., Finnerty, J., and M. Gupta. 1990. The intertemporal relation between the U.S. and Japanese stock markets. *Journal of Finance.* September, 1297–1306.

Becker, K., J. Finnerty, and A. Tucker. 1992. The intraday interdependence structure between the U.S. and Japanese equity markets. *Journal of Financial Research.* Spring, 27–37.

Biger, N. 1979. Exchange risk implications of international portfolio diversification. *Journal of International Business Studies.* 10: 64–74.

Black, F. 1990. Equilibrium exchange rate hedging. *Journal of Finance.* 45: 899-908.

Chamberlain, T., C. Cheung, and C. Kwan. 1990. International investment and currency risk. *Journal of Economics and Business.* 42: 141–152.

Cheung, Y., and Y. Ho. 1991. The intertemporal stability of the relationships between the Asian emerging markets and the developed equity markets. *Journal of Business Finance and Accounting.* 18:235–254.

Chollerton, K., P. Pieraerts, and B. Solnik. 1986. Why invest in foreign currency bonds? *Journal of Portfolio Management.* Summer, 4–8.

Cumby, R., and J. Glen. 1990. Evaluating the performance of international mutual funds. *Journal of Finance.* June, 497–521.

Errunza, V. 1977. Gains from portfolio diversification into less developed countries' securities. *Journal of International Business Studies.* Fall/Winter, 83–99.

Essayyad, M., and H. Wu. 1988. The performance of U.S. international mutual funds. *Quarterly Journal of Business and Economics.* Autumn, 32–46.

Eun, C., R. Kolodny, and B. Resnick. 1991. U.S. based international mutual funds: A performance evaluation. *Journal of Portfolio Management.* Spring, 88–94.

Eun, C., and B. Resnick. 1984. Estimating the correlation structure of international share prices. *Journal of Finance.* December, 1311–1324.

Eun, C., and B. Resnick. 1988. Exchange rate uncertainty, forward contracts, and international portfolio selection. *Journal of Finance*. March, 197–215.

Eun, C. and S. Shim. 1989. "International Transmission of Stock Market Movements." *Journal of Financial and Quantitative Analysis* 24:241–256.

Grauer, R., and N. Hakansson. 1987. Gains from international diversifications: 1968–85 returns on portfolios of stocks and bonds. *Journal of Finance*. July, 721–738.

Grubel, H. 1968. Internationally diversified portfolios: Welfare gains and capital flows. *American Economic Review*. December, 89–94.

Hawawini, G. 1988. Market efficiency and equity pricing. International evidence and implications for global investing. In *Global investing. A guide to international security analysis and portfolio management*. P. Aron, ed. New York: John Wiley & Sons.

Hilliard J. 1979. The relationship between equity indices on world exchanges. *Journal of Finance*. March, 103–114.

Ibbotson, R., L. Siegal, and K. Love. 1985. World wealth: Market values and returns. *Journal of Portfolio Management*. Fall, 4–23.

Jacquillat, B., and B. Solnik. 1978. Multinationals are poor tools for diversification. *Journal of Portfolio Management*. Winter, 8–12.

Jaffe, J., and R. Westerfield. 1985. Patterns in Japanese common stock returns: Day of the week and turn of the year effects. *Journal of Financial and Quantitative Analysis*. June, 261–272.

Jorion, P. 1985. International portfolio diversification with estimation risk. *Journal of Business*. July, 258–278.

Jorion, P. 1989. Asset allocation with hedged and unhedged foreign stocks and bonds. *Journal of Portfolio Management*. 49–54.

Kato, K., and J. Schallheim. 1985. Seasonal and size anomalies in the Japanese stock market. *Journal of Financial and Quantitative Analysis*. June, 243–260.

Korbin, S. 1979. Political risk: A review and reconsideration. *Journal of International Business Studies*. 67–80.

Lessard, D. 1973. International portfolio diversification: A multivariate analysis for a group of Latin American countries. *Journal of Finance*. June, 619–633.

Levy, H., and A. Lerman. 1988. The benefits of international diversification in bonds. *Financial Analysts Journal*. September–October, 56–64.

Levy, H., and M. Sarnat. 1970. International diversification of investment portfolios. *American Economic Review*. September, 668–675.

Logue, D. 1982. An experiment in international diversification. *Journal of Portfolio Management*. 22–27.

Madura, J. 1985. International portfolio construction. *Journal of Business Research*. Spring, 87–95.

Madura, J., and W. Reiff. 1985. A hedge strategy for international portfolios. *Journal of Portfolio Management*. 11:70–74.

Maldonado, R., and A. Saunders. 1981. International portfolio diversification and the inter-temporal stability of international stock market relationships, 1957–78. *Financial Management*. Autumn, 54–63.

Makin, J. 1978. Portfolio theory and the problem of foreign exchange risk. *Journal of Finance*. May, 517–534.

McDonald, J. 1973. French mutual fund performance: Evaluation of internationally diversified portfolios. *Journal of Finance*. December, 1161–1180.

Officer, R. 1975. Seasonality in Australian capital markets. *Journal of Financial Economics*. March, 29–52.

Perold, A., and E. Schulman. 1988. The free lunch in currency hedging. Implications for investment policy and performance standards. *Financial Analysts Journal*. May–June, 45–50.

Rao, R., and R. Aggarwal. 1987. Performance of U.S.-based international mutual funds. *Akron Business and Economic Review*. Winter, 89–106.

Roll, R. 1988. The international crash of October 1987. *Financial Analysts Journal*. 44:19–35.

Ross, S., and M. Walsh. 1983. A simple approach to the pricing of risky assets with uncertain exchange rates. In *The internationalization of financial markets and national economic policy*. R. Hawkins, R. Levich, and C. Wihlborg, eds. Greenwich, CT: JAI Press.

Roux, F., and B. Gilbertson. 1978. The behavior of share prices on the Johannesburg stock exchange. *Journal of Business, Finance, and Accounting*. Summer, 223–232.

Rugman, A. 1976. Risk reduction by international diversification. *Journal of International Business Studies*. Fall–Winter, 75–80.

Saunders, A., and R. Woodward. 1977. Gains from international portfolio diversification: U.K. evidence 1971–75. *Journal of Business Finance and Accounting*. 4:299–309.

Shaked, I. 1985. International equity markets and the investment horizon. *Journal of Portfolio Management*. Winter, 80–84.

Solnik, B. 1974. Why not diversify internationally? *Financial Analysts Journal*. July–August, 48–54.

Solnik, B. 1988. *International investments*. Reading, MA: Addison-Wesley.

Solnik, B., and B. Noetzlin. 1982. Optimal international asset allocation. *Journal of Portfolio Management*. Fall, 11–21.

Stulz, R. 1984. Pricing capital assets in an international setting: An introduction. *Journal of International Business Studies*. 15:55–74.

Subrahmanyam, M. 1975. On the optimality of international capital market integration. *Journal of Financial Economics*. March, 3–28.

Tapley, M. ed. 1986. *International Portfolio Management*. London: Euromoney Publications.

Thomas, L. 1988. Currency risks in international equity portfolios. *Financial Analysts Journal*. March–April, 68–70.

Vertin, J. ed. 1984. *International Equity Investing*. Homewood, IL: Dow Jones-Irwin.

Watson, J. 1980. The stationarity of inter-country correlation coefficients: A note. *Journal of Business, Finance, and Accounting*. Spring, 297–303.

Questions and Problems

1. Would a portfolio of German stocks generate the same returns to a U.S. investor as to a British investor or a German investor? Explain.

2. It is often asserted that world financial markets are becoming more alike. Discuss some possible reasons for this trend. Also discuss the consequence of this trend for international diversification.

3. Would you expect the correlations of stock returns to be higher between U.S. and industrialized countries' stocks or between United States and

lesser developed countries' (LDC) stocks? Why? What implications would this finding have for constructing an optimal international portfolio?

4. In some years the stock returns of LDC countries such as Mexico have been very high. Does this necessarily imply that U.S. investors would have earned superior returns by investing in Mexican stocks? Does it mean that Mexican investors who bought Mexican stocks would have increased their purchasing power more than U.S. investors who bought U.S. stocks?

5. A study by Jacquillat and Solnik (1978) assessed the sensitivity of returns on MNCs to various national stock index returns. Summarize their results and offer implications for (1) investors who employ MNC stocks as a substitute for direct foreign security investment and (2) the theoretical justification underlying the passive approach to international asset allocation.

6. Review the components that determine the volatility of unhedged foreign asset returns and hedged foreign asset returns. Why would you normally expect unhedged returns to be more volatile? Under what conditions could unhedged returns be less volatile?

7. An IMF offered to U.S. investors contained stocks of firms from 10 different west European countries. Is the exchange rate risk of this IMF substantially less than that of an IMF concentrated on the stocks of a single west European country? Explain.

8. What is the principal limitation of using historical correlations to construct international stock portfolios? Does empirical evidence suggest that this limitation is profound?

9. Using the same risk-return space, draw a representative domestic efficient frontier and a representative world efficient frontier. Discuss why the difference between these frontiers arises.

10. From Exhibit 8.4 explain why the reported total risk is less than the sum of the corresponding home market risk and exchange risk for each national equity market.

11. From Exhibit 8.5 the minimum-risk portfolio exhibits a proportion of at least 50 percent in the U.S. market. Why do you suppose that this proportion is so large? (Hint: Recall the results of Jacquillat and Solnik.)

12. Should we anticipate that foreign asset markets will exhibit greater future abnormal returns than U.S. markets? If not, why should we anticipate any future benefit from engaging in international diversification?

13. Summarize the empirical literature on the performance of international mutual funds.

14. Discuss the theoretical rationale for engaging in the passive approach to international portfolio construction. Also discuss the empirical motivation for such an approach.

15. Using the long-term risk and return figures listed in Exhibit 8.7, describe the rationale for diversifying a U.S. dollar bond portfolio into foreign currency bonds.

16. Describe the concept of country risk and how international portfolio managers can account for this risk.

17. Describe the Big Bang and its consequences for international security trading.

18. What is the principal difference between an active domestic asset allocation strategy and an active international asset allocation strategy?

19. In practice active international portfolio managers often construct a portfolio within each country and then select a subset of such portfolios—so called country selection. In theory this strategy is suboptimal, as portfolios should be formed on the basis of all possible covariance pairings. Defend this strategy.

20. Assume you purchased a German stock today for DM50 per share, and it pays no dividends. You expect the mark to appreciate from today's spot rate of $0.55 to $0.62 in one year. You also expect the stock to be worth DM59 in one year. What is your expected return on the investment?

21. A U.S. portfolio manager considers purchasing a Mexican stock that is expected to increase in price by 130 percent in one year. However, the peso is expected to depreciate against the dollar by 40 percent over the year. What is the expected return on the stock from the manager's perspective?

22. A U.S. investor purchases a French stock for FF200 and expects the stock to be worth FF280 at the end of one year. What would be the return if the investor's expectations were correct and a one-year forward sale of francs was negotiated as of the day of the stock investment at a forward discount of 3 percent?

Self-Test Problems

ST-1 through ST-3 refer to the following information about U.S. and U.K. market returns and beginning-of-period $/£ exchange rates:

(1) PERIOD	(2) U.S. RETURN	(3) U.K. RETURN	(4) $/£ EXCHANGE RATE
1	8%	6%	$2.00
2	14	2	1.80
3	2	-4	1.80
4	11	8	1.70
5	14	17	1.60
6	5	6	1.60
7	-	-	1.90

ST-1. What is the average return in each market from the perspective of a U.S. investor and from the perspective of a U.K. investor?

ST-2. What is the covariance of the home market and exchange returns from each investor's perspective?

ST-3. What is the standard deviation of return of each market from each investor's perspective?

Solutions to Self-Test Problems

ST-1. The exchange returns for the U.S. investor are

PERIOD	EXCHANGE RETURN	PERIOD	EXCHANGE RETURN
1	−10.00%[a]	4	−5.88%
2	0.00	5	0.00
3	−5.55	6	18.75

[a]Example: ($1.80 − $2.00)/($2.00).

The exchange returns for the U.K. investor are

PERIOD	EXCHANGE RETURN	PERIOD	EXCHANGE RETURN
1	11.11%[a]	4	6.25%
2	0.00	5	0.00
3	5.88	6	−15.79

[a]Example: [(1/$1.80) − (1/$2.00)]/(1/$2.00). Notice that the sum of the exchange returns to the two investors does not equal 0 due to Jensen's inequality.

The average return in the U.S. market to the U.S. investor is simply 9 percent, or $(8\% + 14\% + \ldots + 5\%)/6$. Likewise, the average return in the U.K. market to the U.K. investor is 5.83 percent. Invoking equation 8.3, the average return in the U.K. market to the U.S. investor is the average of the sum of corresponding U.K. market returns and exchange returns to the U.S. investor, or

$5.39\% = [(6\% - 10\%) + (2\% - 0\%) + \ldots + (6\% + 18.75\%)]/6$. Similarly, the average return in the U.S. market to the U.K. investor is $10.24\% = [(8\% + 11.11\%) + (14\% + 0\%) + \ldots + (5\% - 15.79\%)]/6$.

ST-2. First note that the average return to a U.S. investor is −0.4467 percent and that the average exchange return to a U.K. investor is 1.2417 percent. Thus the covariance of the home market returns and exchange returns (σ_{FE}) from the U.S. investor's perspective is .0013, or $[(6\% - 5.83\%)(-10\% + 0.4467\%) + (2\% - 5.83\%)(0\% + 0.4467\%) + \ldots + (6\% - 5.83\%)(18.75\% + 0.4467\%)]/(6 - 1)$. Likewise, the covariance of the home market returns and exchange returns from the U.K. investor's perspective is .0005, or $[(8\% - 9\%)(11.11\% - 1.2417\%) + \ldots + (5\% - 9\%)(-15.79\% - 1.2417\%)]/(6 - 1)$. Standard deviations are computed in an analogous fashion.

ST-3. First note that the standard deviation of returns of the U.S. market is .0490 and that the standard deviation of the returns of the U.K. market is .0694. Thus the standard deviation of the U.S. market from the U.S. investor's perspective is simply .0490, while the standard deviation of the U.K. market from the U.K. perspective is simply .0694. Also, the standard deviation of exchange returns (σ_E) for the U.S. investor is .1016, while it is .0935 for the U.K. investor. Thus, invoking equation 8.4, the standard deviation of the U.K. market to the U.S. investor is .1332, or $[(.0694)^2 + (.1016)^2 + 2(.0013)]^{\frac{1}{2}}$. Notice that this is less than .0694 + .1016. Likewise, the standard deviation of the U.S. market to the U.K. investor is .1102, or $[(.0490)^2 + (.0935)^2 + 2(.0005)]^{\frac{1}{2}}$. Notice that this is less than .0490 + .0935.

PART TWO

Equilibrium Asset Pricing and Market Efficiency

IN PART 1 THE MARKOWITZ MEAN-VARIANCE OPTIMIZATION TECHNIQUE showed how a rational investor would seek to maximize utility in terms of expected return and risk. Models of asset pricing attempt to depict the theoretical equilibrium relationship between expected return and risk in capital markets whose investors price assets in a rational manner under conditions of uncertainty. Asset pricing models owe their origin to the Markowitz principles discussed in Part 1, that is, how markets determine prices when all investors seek mean-variance efficient portfolios; hence, the models have been around for only about thirty years.

The usefulness of asset pricing models is obvious: If a model correctly depicts how prices are determined in capital markets, then such an understanding provided by the model helps in the portfolio analysis process, such as whether or not the return on a security or a portfolio is accurately predictable and whether it is possible to identify an undervalued or overvalued (i.e., mispriced) security. Several asset pricing theories that depict the intuitive relation between risk and return (i.e., higher expected return to compensate for higher risk) have been developed and tested empirically. However, a precise measure of risk in capital markets remains elusive. There is to date no generally accepted and robust asset pricing model that provides an accurate and definitive risk-return relation. Nevertheless, though the theoretical models have not provided all the answers, they provide useful insight into the behavior of real-world capital markets and have changed the ways in which Wall Street analyzes risk and return. According to a well-known investment practitioner, commentator, and founding editor of the *Journal of Portfolio Management*, Peter L. Bernstein, "theory opened the path out of the wasteland left by the crash of '74. Theory lent form and elegance to substance and authority to usage. . . . The line between practitioner and academic theorist has become increasingly blurred. . . . Practitioners—today often academics—are constantly engaging in cooperative explorations with theoreticians, enlarging and elevating human knowledge as they seek new answers to the old questions."[1]

Thus familiarity with and a keen appreciation of asset pricing theories are requisites for the modern investment analyst or portfolio manager. Part 2 of this book therefore presents the major asset pricing models that have had an impact on capital markets and portfolio management over the past two decades or so. Following the presentation of each model we discuss how it can be applied in practical investment analysis, and more important, we emphasize the difficulties and limitations associated with the use of each model in practice.

Chapter 9 presents the pioneer asset pricing model, the original or traditional capital asset pricing model (CAPM), which has been the best known and has generated the most controversy. Chapter 10 provides brief discussions of the major extensions of the CAPM and alternative models and highlights the main differences between them and the original CAPM. Chapter 11 addresses the main contemporary alternative to the CAPM, the arbitrage pricing theory (APT). Chapter 12 provides a summary of the empirical tests of the

---

[1]Bernstein (1992c, pp. 17–18). Bernstein provides an interesting historical account of the effect of theoretical developments by academicians on Wall Street in his book *Capital ideas: The improbable origins of modern Wall Street*, New York: The Free Press, 1992.

main asset pricing models discussed in Chapters 9, 10, and 11, that is, how well actual data fit the models and to what extent the models correctly depict the behavior of capital markets. Closely related to asset pricing is the concept of market efficiency, which is covered in Chapter 13.

Thus, after studying Part 2, you will gain (1) an understanding of asset pricing models in general, (2) an appreciation of the important linkage between theories of asset pricing and practical portfolio analysis, (3) comprehension of why you would or would not use the models in practice, and (4) if you decide to use them, how to do so with a clear understanding of their limitations and the pitfalls associated with blind and mechanical application of the models in practice. ■

CHAPTER *9*

The Capital Asset Pricing Model

Introduction

Any theory of capital asset pricing attempts to provide a model that depicts the manner in which capital assets are priced in financial markets. Sharpe (1964), Lintner (1965), and Mossin (1966) each independently developed a model of asset pricing that largely evolved from the concepts of optimal portfolio selection discussed in Chapter 7. The resulting CAPM depicts the relationship between the expected return of an asset and its risk under conditions of market equilibrium and in a capital market whose investors all undertake optimal portfolio selection while using the Markowitz mean-variance framework.

Several extensions of the CAPM have been proposed. These later models attempt to be more realistic by relaxing some of the more restrictive assumptions of the original CAPM. In this chapter we focus on the original CAPM. Extensions and alternative models are addressed in Chapters 10 and 11.

Derivation of the CAPM

Several simplifying assumptions are invoked in the derivation of the original CAPM, as follows:[1]

1. All assets are marketable.
2. Capital markets are perfect: (a) All assets are infinitely divisible, that is, fractions of assets can be traded. (b) All investors are price takers, that is, no one investor can influence the market by buying or selling actions. (c) Taxes and transaction costs do not exist or alternatively do not affect the investment decision. (d) Unlimited borrowing and short selling are allowed, without margin requirements. (e) Information is costlessly available to every investor, and all investors possess the same information.
3. A risk-free interest rate exists at which all investors can undertake unlimited borrowing or lending.
4. All investors are risk averse and seek to maximize expected utility over one-period horizons (Chapter 7).
5. Investors have homogenous expectations: (a) They possess the same investment horizons, and their estimates of the expected returns, variances (or standard deviations), and covariances of risky assets are identical. (b) They all base their portfolio selection decisions on Markowitz mean-variance optimization. In other words, all investors perceive investment alternatives and arrive at portfolio decisions in exactly the same manner.

The derivation of the original CAPM follows from these assumptions and the mean-variance analysis of Chapter 7, and so the capital market line (CML) described in Chapters 3 and 7 is an appropriate starting point. The derivation that follows uses Sharpe's (1964) method. (For readers not interested in the derivation of the CAPM, the final form is equation 9.10). The CML as shown in Figure 3.8 is the line that represents the different possible combinations of the risk-free asset and the portfolio of risky assets (point P^*) that an investor may choose to hold, depending on risk preferences. If all investors possessed homogenous expectations, then the set of efficient portfolios and CML they face would be the same, since all investors would be using the same values of expected returns, variances, and covariances. The optimal portfolio of risky assets, P^*, is therefore the same for all investors. In accordance with the separation theorem (discussed in Chapter 7), depending on individual risk preference, the investor determines the position on the CML by borrowing or lending at the risk-free rate, r_f, and investing a proportion of wealth in P^*. Market equilibrium requires that for each risky asset there be a market-clearing

---

[1] As in much of economic modeling, making simplifying assumptions is necessary given the complexity of capital markets; this enables the achievement of simpler and more manageable models. Thus if conditions in reality do not deviate substantially from these assumptions, then the model is a good and workable approximation to reality and should possess reasonable and demonstrable validity. The implications of these seemingly unrealistic assumptions will be discussed later in this chapter.

price. By assumption, all investors hold P* and the riskless asset in some proportion. Therefore, *in equilibrium,* the portfolio P* must now consist of *all* risky assets, held by every investor. (If an asset was not included in this portfolio implying that no one wanted to hold it, then markets would not clear.) This portfolio is usually called the *market portfolio*; in theory it consists of all risky assets in the world, that is, assets ranging from financial securities such as bonds and stocks to nonfinancial assets such as real estate, collectibles, human capital, consumer durables, and the like, which exist in all countries of the world.

We shall label the market portfolio M. (It replaces P* of Figure 3.8.) Each asset's proportion, w_i, in this portfolio is given by

$$w_i = \frac{\text{total market value of asset } i}{\text{total market value of all assets in the market}}$$

Figure 9.1 depicts the capital market line and the market portfolio. As in Chapter 3, the slope of the capital market line, $r_f\,ML$ (which is analogous to line III in Figure 3.8), is

(9.1)
$$\frac{E(r_M) - r_f}{\sigma_M},$$

where $E(r_M)$ is the expected return of the market portfolio and σ_M is the standard deviation of the market portfolio. Similarly, the equation of line $r_f\,ML$ is

(9.2)
$$E(r_P) = r_f + \frac{E(r_M) - r_f}{\sigma_M}\sigma_P$$

where $E(r_P)$ is the expected return on a portfolio located at any point, P, on $r_f\,ML$, and σ_P is the standard deviation of this portfolio.

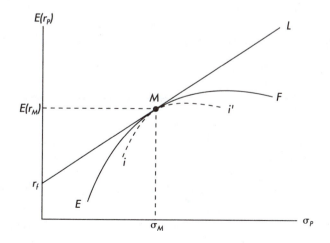

FIGURE 9.1

The Capital Market Line and the Market Portfolio

Based on equation 9.2, the relationship between the risk of any risky asset i and its expected return, $E(r_i)$, can be derived. Consider that portfolio P consists of a proportion w_i invested in asset i and a proportion $(1 - w_i)$ invested in the market portfolio, M. From equations 3.24 and 3.25, the expected return and standard deviation of this portfolio are, respectively,

$$(9.3) \qquad E(r_P) = w_i \, E(r_i) + (1 - w_i) \, E(r_M)$$

and

$$(9.4) \qquad \sigma_P = [w_i^2\sigma_i^2 + (1 - w_i)^2\sigma_M^2 + 2w_i(1 - w_i) \, COV(r_i, r_M)]^{1/2}$$

Alternative feasible portfolios consisting of i and M lie along the curve iMi', with each portfolio's position depending on the value of w_i. However, the optimal combination of i and M is attainable at point M, the market portfolio (which by definition consists of asset i as well as all other risky assets). As in equation 3.6, the slope of the tangent to line iMi' at any point is

$$(9.5) \qquad \frac{dE(r_P)}{d\sigma_P} = \frac{dE(r_P)}{dw_i} \left/ \frac{d\sigma_P}{dw_i} \right.$$

From equation 9.3,

$$(9.6) \qquad \frac{dE(r_P)}{dw_i} = E(r_i) - E(r_M),$$

and from equation 9.4,

$$(9.7) \qquad \frac{d\sigma_P}{dw_i} = \frac{w_i\sigma_i^2 - \sigma_M^2 + w_i\sigma_M^2 + (1-2w_i) \, COV(r_i,r_M)}{\sigma_P}.$$

Therefore, equation 9.5 can be expressed as equation 9.6 divided by equation 9.7:

$$(9.8) \qquad \frac{dE(r_P)}{d\sigma_P} = \frac{E(r_i) - E(r_M)}{w_i\sigma_i^2 - \sigma_M^2 + w_i\sigma_M^2 + (1-2w_i) \, COV(r_i,r_M)} \sigma_P.$$

At M, $w_i = 0$, $\sigma_P = \sigma_M$, and the slope of the tangent to iMi' (equation 9.8) is equal to the slope of the CML, equation 9.1. Therefore,

$$(9.9) \qquad \frac{dE(r_P)}{d\sigma_P} = \frac{[E(r_i) - E(r_M)]\sigma_M}{COV(r_i,r_M) - \sigma_M^2} = \frac{E(r_M) - r_f}{\sigma_M},$$

from which

(9.10)
$$E(r_i) = r_f + [E(r_M) - r_f]\frac{COV(r_i, r_M)}{\sigma_M^2}.$$

Equation 9.10 is the original CAPM equation. Simply put, it states that the equilibrium expected return on any risky asset, *i*, consists of the risk-free rate plus a risk premium (the second term in equation 9.10), which depends on the covariance of the asset's return with that of the market portfolio. Equation 9.10 is more commonly expressed in a somewhat more compact form:

(9.11)
$$E(r_i) = r_f + [E(r_M) - r_f]\beta_i,$$

where

(9.12)
$$\beta_i = [COV(r_i, r_M)]/\sigma_M^2$$

Note that the term, $E(r_M) - r_f$, which is the expected *market risk premium*, and σ_M^2, the variance of the market portfolio return, are the same for determining the expected return for every asset; thus, β_i is unique to asset *i* by virtue of the covariation between the asset's return and that of the market portfolio. Therefore, β_i (the *market beta* of asset *i*) is a measure of this covariance risk, or the *systematic* or *market* risk of asset *i*.[2] The terminology stems from the underlying concept that the market portfolio contains all assets in the market and is a fully diversified portfolio in which all *unsystematic* or *diversifiable* risk (Chapter 3) has been diversified away. Thus, according to the CAPM, the relevant measure of the risk of an asset is its contribution to the systematic risk of an investor's portfolio as defined by its beta rather than the inherent variance in the asset's total return. Only the undiversifiable portion of risk is rewarded in returns; the diversifiable portion is not *priced*, since every investor can achieve full diversification. This result, of course, is consistent with the principle of portfolio diversification that motivated the development of the CAPM.

THE CAPM RISK-RETURN RELATIONSHIP: THE SECURITY MARKET LINE

The elegance of the CAPM (equation 9.10 or 9.11) arises from the simplicity with which expected return is related to risk, namely, in a linear fashion. As illustrated in Figure 9.2, equation 9.11 plots as a straight line $(r_f S)$; the

---

[2] The β used here is not the same as the beta *b* of the single-index model of Chapter 5, even though the two can be related under certain assumptions. This is discussed later in this chapter.

FIGURE 9.2

Security Market
Line

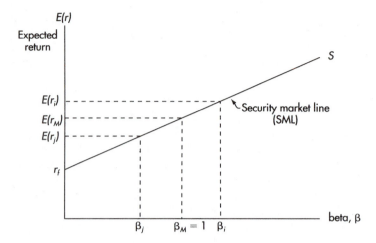

security market line (SML), with expected return, $E(r_i)$, on the y-axis and β_i on the x-axis.[3] The slope of the SML is equal to $[E(r_M) - r_f]$. The SML should not be confused with the CML of Figure 9.1, however. The SML depicts the expected return–risk relationship for *any asset or portfolio i*, which need not be on the efficient frontier, but the CML is valid *only for efficient portfolios*. Note also that the x-axis of the CML is the standard deviation of portfolio return, while it is beta for the SML.

From equation 9.11, the beta of the market portfolio, or an asset or portfolio whose return has perfect positive correlation with that of the market portfolio, is 1. This is shown in Figure 9.2, where for $\beta = 1$, the expected return is that of the market portfolio, $E(r_M)$. Since the market portfolio consists of all risky assets, a beta of 1 is usually considered average. Thus, if an asset or portfolio has a beta less than 1, such as β_j in Figure 9.2, it has lower systematic or market risk than average, and therefore its expected return, $E(r_j)$, is proportionately lower than that of the market portfolio, $E(r_M)$. Reciprocally, an asset with a beta greater than 1, such as β_i, has an expected return, $E(r_i)$, that is higher than $E(r_M)$. For a security that has no systematic risk (i.e., $\beta = 0$; the security's covariance with the market portfolio is 0), the expected return is equal to the risk-free rate, r_f. (The short-term U.S. Treasury bill rate is often considered the nearest approximation to the true risk-free rate.) Risky securities have a β greater than 0; therefore its expected return should include a risk premium over the riskless rate that is directly proportional to the risk (β) of the security. Thus, the CAPM is intuitively appealing in the sense that higher expected return relates directly to higher risk.

As an illustration of pricing with the CAPM, suppose that stock D has a beta of 0.65, and stock G has a beta of 1.34. The expected return on the

---

[3] The x-axis variable could also be $COV(r_i, r_M)$ instead of β_i, in accordance with equation 9.10, but β_i is more commonly used. The SML will be the same linear shape, since the difference is only in the scaling.

market portfolio, $E(r_M)$, is 10%, and the risk-free rate of interest is 5%. From equation 9.11, the expected return on each of the stocks is as follows:

$$E(r_D) = 5 + 0.65(10 - 5) = 8.25\%$$

$$E(r_G) = 5 + 1.34(10 - 5) = 11.7\%.$$

The difference between the expected returns of the two stocks reflects the differences in their risks: because D has lower systematic risk than the market average, its expected return (8.25 percent) is lower than that of the market; it consists of a risk premium of only 3.25 percent—that is, 8.25% − 5%, or 0.65(10 − 5)—in addition to the risk-free rate of return. Stock G, however, has a higher expected return commensurate with its higher beta, providing a risk premium of 6.7 percent over the risk-free rate. (Note that the market risk premium over the risk-free rate is 5 percent, or 10% − 5%.)

The expected return–beta relationships of these two stocks are depicted in Figure 9.3. Securities such as stock D with beta less than one are sometimes called *defensive* securities, and those with beta greater than one (such as stock G) are *aggressive* securities.

It is evident from this example and discussion that any application of the CAPM in practical portfolio analysis requires that (1) the model be valid in real-world capital markets and (2) the market portfolio be identifiable and its return and the betas for securities be measurable with reasonable accuracy. We examine these issues, which have generated much discussion and controversy about the usefulness of the model in practice, shortly, but first we examine how the CAPM can be utilized in practical investment analysis.

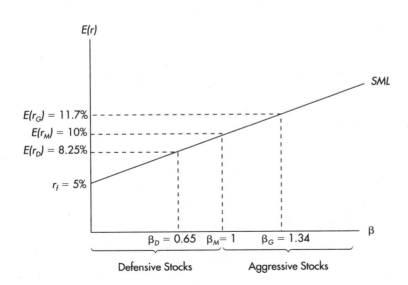

FIGURE 9.3

SML Illustration: Defensive and Aggressive Stocks

APPLICATION OF THE CAPM IN INVESTMENT SELECTION

The applicability of the CAPM in practical investment management arises only because of the likelihood that in reality there are significant deviations from the model due to inefficiencies in the capital market. If the model held exactly, or even approximately, as the theory stipulates, all investors would hold the market portfolio or an approximation of it and lend or borrow at the risk-free rate in accordance with their risk preferences. This would make active portfolio management irrelevant. (Changes in an investor's portfolio will be necessary only if personal risk preferences change, prompting a move to a different point on the CML.) Thus, according to the CAPM (equation 9.11), market forces would ensure that security prices adjust so that in equilibrium each asset plots on the security market line of Figure 9.2. However, in the presence of inefficiencies or disequilibrium a security would plot off the SML, as do stocks A and B in Figure 9.4. A and B are said to be *mispriced* because they provide returns (and sell at prices) different from those predicted by the CAPM. Thus, if it is believed that assets are priced in equilibrium according to the CAPM, then the model can be used to profit from the mispricing of a security due to temporary disequilibrium or inefficiencies.

If the return on a security over a period t conforms with the CAPM, then the return can be depicted as follows:

(9.13)
$$r_{it} = \alpha_i + r_{ft} + \beta_i[r_{Mt} - r_{ft}] + \epsilon_{it,}$$

where r_{it} is the rate of return of asset i over period t; r_{ft} is the riskless rate of return over period t; and r_{Mt} is the rate of return of the market portfolio over period t.

FIGURE 9.4

Mispricing and the Security Market Line

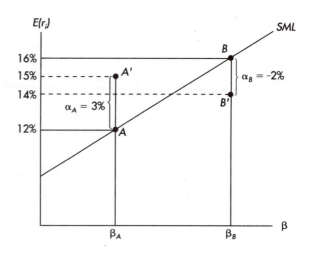

Taking expectations of both sides of equation 9.13, the expected return of asset *i* over a period is given by

(9.14) $$E(r_i) = \alpha_i + r_f + \beta_i[E(r_M) - r_f].$$

Therefore, if the CAPM holds, α (alpha) should be 0; that is, equation 9.14 becomes equation 9.11. Thus mispricing of a security can be measured by its alpha value, i.e., the extent to which it plots off the SML. For example, in Figure 9.4, if the estimate of the expected return of security A (which could be obtained by using fundamental analysis, the firm's financial statements and growth prospects, and/or historical price data) is 15 percent, and the equilibrium (SML) expected return is 12 percent, A's alpha is 3 percent, the vertical distance *AA'*. Similarly, security B's alpha is –2 percent, the distance *B'B*. Security A (positive alpha) is underpriced, or undervalued, because given its risk (beta), it provides a higher return than it should, but B (negative alpha) is overpriced, or overvalued, because it provides a lower return than it should. An alpha of 0, of course, means that the security plots on the SML and is correctly priced. Therefore, use of the CAPM involves identification of mispriced securities by the investor or analyst, leading to appropriate investment decisions; that is to say, buy a security if it is underpriced ($\alpha > 0$) and sell a security if it is overpriced ($\alpha < 0$). In an efficient market such buying and selling of mispriced securities will quickly lead to restoration of equilibrium. That is, according to the CAPM the securities will become correctly priced and will lie on the SML until disequilibrium occurs again.

The CAPM concept is also applicable in asset allocation strategies for both passive and active portfolio management. In passive management the investor seeks an appropriate mix of risk-free securities (such as Treasury bills) and a market portfolio of risky assets, in accordance with personal risk-return preferences. The portfolio is not altered unless the investor's preferences change. In active management the investor makes forecasts about the direction of asset prices and rebalances the portfolio to take advantage of such changes to obtain maximum profit if the forecasts turn out to be correct. (Such active management is known as market timing, or in contemporary parlance, tactical asset allocation.) Using the CAPM concept, an investor or portfolio manager who wishes to undertake market timing makes forecasts of the expected return on the market portfolio, $E(r_M)$, and the risk-free rate, r_f, and obtains reliable estimates of the betas of securities. Then a portfolio can be formed or rebalanced based on the forecasts of the direction of the market. For example, if the forecast is that the market trend will be upward, that is, $E(r_M) - r_f$ will increase, the composition of the portfolio can be changed to increase its β by increasing the proportion of risky assets in the portfolio and/or increasing the β of the risky portion of the portfolio by including securities with higher betas while keeping the proportion of risk-free assets to risky assets the same. This strategy provides a higher expected return according to equation 9.11

and ensures that if the forecast is correct, a higher portfolio return will be obtained. Conversely, a bearish forecast of the direction of the market requires that the portfolio be rebalanced to have a low beta.

Validity of the CAPM

Several of the assumptions underlying the derivation of the CAPM may be adjudged unrealistic, thus raising concerns about the validity of the model. However, as is commonly noted in the relation between theory and practice in finance and economics, if the predictions of a model such as the CAPM reflect an accurate depiction of the real world, then whether or not the assumptions are realistic is not of much importance. Therefore, for the CAPM the test is whether or not in practice (1) beta is the relevant measure of the risk of a capital asset and (2) security returns actually conform to the expected return–risk relationship depicted by the model. In this regard the evidence on the CAPM, from the numerous empirical studies conducted since its inception, is mixed at best. Some tests of the CAPM, especially the earliest ones, provide some support for the model, though not conclusively, while others do not. A summary of the empirical tests of the original and alternative forms of the CAPM as well as other asset pricing models is presented in Chapter 12.

The lack of unequivocal empirical validation of the CAPM may be attributed to two major reasons.

First, capital markets are very complex, and many of the assumptions underlying the CAPM are violated in the real world; therefore a simple model such as the CAPM, though it depicts a logical expected return–risk relationship in a market constituted of rational risk-averse investors, may not adequately capture the complexities of the asset pricing process. Several studies have analyzed the effects of relaxation of some of the CAPM assumptions to conform more closely to reality. Unfortunately, analysis becomes intractable if all the assumptions are relaxed at the same time; hence most of the studies examine relaxation of only one or two assumptions. The violations that have been most examined are multi-period investment decision-making process of investors; the presence of frictions (transaction costs, taxes, restrictions on short sales, etc.) in capital markets; the heterogeneity in investors' investment horizons and objectives; heterogeneity in expectations about means, variances and covariances of returns;[4] relaxation of the strong, unrealistic mean-variance

---

[4] An argument for a good approximation to homogeneity in expectations in the real-world has been advanced by some as follows: financial markets, especially in more recent times, are largely dominated by a relatively small group of institutional investors or money managers who trade in large volumes of securities and exert a major influence on the determination of prices; these institutional traders have access to similar information, use similar techniques for analysis, are usually in regular contact with each other, and may therefore arrive at beliefs and expectations that are largely similar.

assumption, which is inconsistent with investor preferences; the nonexistence of a riskless asset or constant risk-free rate; differences in borrowing and lending rates; and nonmarketability of certain assets, such as human capital.

In some cases relaxation of an assumption does not alter the CAPM significantly, while in some other cases, it necessitates an extension or alternative form of the model. Some of these are presented in Chapter 10.[5]

Second, there are limitations to the statistical techniques available for undertaking the empirical tests, so that the tests are unable to provide conclusive results. (This is discussed in Chapter 12.)

The initial empirical validation of the CAPM provided by some of the early studies and the model's simple, logically appealing risk-return relation endeared the CAPM and the beta concept to some professional portfolio managers in the 1970s. Even though there has always been much controversy as to whether the CAPM is of any use in practical investment management, the beta concept is still utilized by some portfolio managers and several investment firms. Firms such as Value Line and Merrill Lynch compute, publish, and sell beta estimates of several firms. Also, some corporations have used the CAPM and beta, in many cases inappropriately, in corporate financial decisions such as in the determination of the cost of capital in project valuation.

However, as far back as the late 1970s, questions have been raised regarding the model's validity and the legitimacy of using beta in practical investment management. Richard Roll (1977, 1978, 1980, 1981) questioned the validity of the CAPM empirical tests, argued that it was impossible to test the CAPM (Chapter 12), and highlighted the misapplications and incorrect conclusions that could result from simplistic applications of the model. Roll's critique, along with the skepticism of some other academics and investment practitioners, prompted an *Institutional Investor* article, "Is Beta Dead?" (Wallace 1980). Since then, however, tests of the CAPM and related models have continued, still without a resolution of the issues, and controversy and misunderstanding remain among academicians and practitioners regarding testability and practical applications of the model. Fama and French (1992) have again revived the controversy. They found that there was no significant relationship between expected return and beta, thus raising doubts once more about the empirical validity of the CAPM and the use of beta.[6] Not surprisingly, their results have again led to questions about the demise of beta.[7] (See the box titled "Is this the Night of the Living Beta?") However, Amihud, Christensen, and Mendelson (1992) claim that Fama and French's results are flawed because of the

---

[5] There is a large body of literature of studies on the effect of relaxation of the assumptions of the CAPM. A complete discussion of this literature is beyond the scope of this book.

[6] Fama and French's study is discussed in detail in Chapter 12.

[7] Fama and French's results substantiated those of numerous previous studies that also found little or no significant relation between expected return and beta in the context of the CAPM (cf. Chen, Roll, and Ross 1986, and Lakonishok and Shapiro 1986).

IS THIS THE NIGHT OF THE LIVING BETA?

In July 1980 *Institutional Investor* asked the controversial—albeit esoteric—question, "Is beta dead?" The answer: Not yet, though it certainly was under attack at the time. Nonetheless, the influence of beta—a measure of a stock's price volatility relative to the market's—would mushroom in the 1980s as it became accepted in finance classes and boardrooms as financial orthodoxy.

So here it is 1992, and beta is reportedly on its deathbed once again. This time the most devastating blow has been struck by the University of Chicago's Eugene Fama and Kenneth French, whose recent study argues that long-term equity returns depend not on beta but on far more mundane factors, such as a company's size or its book-to-market-equity ratio.

In fact, Fama and French conclude that the commonly accepted relationship between beta and return doesn't exist at all. Says Fama, whose earlier work provided part of beta's empirical underpinning: "People have found that the [correlation between higher betas and higher returns] is much flatter than expected by CAPM. We've found it to be *completely* flat."

The tangled tale of beta begins with Harry Markowitz. In his 1952 doctoral dissertation at the University of Chicago, Markowitz showed that the covariance among stocks in a portfolio (the correlation of returns) can be used to achieve maximum return for the degree of risk being taken on. Markowitz used a technique called mean-variance analysis to construct an "efficient" portfolio—one that provides the highest return for a given level of risk.

Markowitz's work paved the way for the development of the capital asset pricing model in the mid-1960s by Stanford University's William Sharpe and others. CAPM was designed to predict the expected return for an individual stock or portfolio by adding risk-free return, usually the rate on short-term Treasuries, to risk-adjusted market return. The latter is calculated by multiplying the average market return by the beta for that stock or portfolio.

Beta measures systematic—that is, market—risk. (Theorists assume that unsystematic risk, which results from factors unique to a particular company, can be eliminated through portfolio diversification.) If a stock's price is more volatile than the overall market, it will have a beta greater than 1; if it's less volatile, the beta will be less than 1. According to CAPM, a high-beta stock has a greater expected return than a low-beta stock.

CAPM has become more than just a tool for investment managers; it's widely used today to make corporate capital-allocation decisions, which, given lagging U.S. productivity, has caused it to draw fire from some quarters. "CAPM combines so many strands of theoretical innovation that it remains the keystone of investment theory, theories of market behavior and the allocation of capital in both private and public enterprises," writes Peter Bernstein, the founding editor of *The Journal of Portfolio Management*, in his recent book, *Capital Ideas.*

According to Alfred Rappaport, chairman of financial advisory firm Alcar Group and an adjunct professor at Northwestern University's Kellogg Graduate School of Management, between one half and two thirds of large U.S. companies use CAPM in some form to find the hurdle rate for capital budgeting. A public corporation generally uses the model in one of two ways: by plugging in its actual beta to determine the cost of equity for the entire company or by assigning a proxy beta for calculating individual rates for its various divisions. (That proxy is derived by using a

Is This the Night of the Living Beta?—*Continued*

beta from a publicly listed company or group of companies in the same industry as the division being looked at.)

Almost from their birth, beta and CAPM have been intensely debated. "I was saying fifteen years ago that you shouldn't necessarily expect to find any relation between beta and expected return," says Richard Roll, a finance professor at the University of California at Los Angeles. "CAPM requires the true market index to be Markowitz-efficient [that is, to have minimum variance for its expected return]; then it follows mathematically. The trouble is that no truly Markowitz-efficient market index has ever been used to test CAPM." The true market index, adds Roll, "should include all the assets in the world," which would be all but impossible.

Although the Fama-French study crunched data that includes all nonfinancial shares traded on the New York Stock Exchange, the American Stock Exchange and Nasdaq between 1963 and 1990, it still failed to achieve a Markowitz-efficient market index, according to Roll. His conclusion: The paper proves nothing.

Case closed? Hardly. Fischer Black, co-inventor (with Myron Scholes) of the option pricing theory and a partner at Goldman, Sachs & Co., disagrees with Roll. To Black, people have focused so much effort on finding holes in CAPM that they have begun "data mining." "If you dig long enough," he explains, "you'll find almost any results you want." Adds Black: "There's no evidence that beta is not a good measure of risk. The only question is whether it is a good indicator of expected return." In fact, Black argues, Fama-French's conclusions have been in the literature for years. Black himself published a study in 1972 with Scholes and then–University of Rochester

professor Michael Jensen in which they showed that the actual return of stocks was flatter than expected under CAPM.

Still, the conventional wisdom about beta lives on. "We've kind of always known that beta was not an adequate measure of risk [vis-á-vis return]," says Fama, "but we've simply never faced it." Stanford's Sharpe, who calls the work of Fama and French "a neatly done study," admits that "if you reject the idea that beta is relevant for return, then you would reject CAPM too." However, he adds, "I wouldn't. I don't like going into the world without some theory."

Despite all this theoretical jousting, most finance professors will continue to teach beta and CAPM. "It's taught because it's the simplest form of a theory that gives a relation between risk and return—not because it's correct," says Roll. "Everybody agrees that there's a relation between risk and return; they disagree about how to incorporate it into a model. Teaching starts with CAPM and goes on to a multi-factor model for measuring risk, such as the arbitrage pricing theory." APT, which calculates expected return by incorporating several dimensions of systematic risk, including inflation and interest rates, was developed in 1976 by Yale University economist Stephen Ross and quickly championed by Roll. The two men now have their own money management firm which markets APT (*Institutional Investor*, November 1991).

But should CAPM be used in the real world? Columbia University Law School professor Louis Lowenstein contends in his 1991 book, *Sense and Nonsense in Corporate Finance*, that "very few of the corporate managements who use CAPM, or who rely on consultants who use it, understand it well enough or realize what a mischievous piece of work it is."

Continued

IS THIS THE NIGHT OF THE LIVING BETA? — *Continued*

Alcar's Rappaport agrees that there are problems, though he faults not the model but the practitioners. "Corporate finance people develop a hurdle rate using CAPM," he explains, "but unfortunately they compare that rate with results that are accounting-based, such as return on earnings." That, he adds, is "like mixing apples and oranges and not even coming up with fruit."

Lowenstein goes further, denying that there is any quantifiable way to measure risk directly. "The very notion of 'measurable risk,'" he writes, "seems like an oxymoron." Lowenstein argues that CAPM by definition takes into account only systematic risk, whereas a company must be more concerned with its unique risks. Even CAPM pioneer

Sharpe agrees that "what you ought to think of is how sensitive a project is to economic issues."

The fact is, despite "the death of beta," many companies will continue to use CAPM to make capital-budgeting decisions. "Corporations are misusing CAPM if they are actually plugging numbers into it," says Roll, "because it's probably not very accurate." But, he adds with a mordant chuckle, "It's no more grievous than the way companies forecast their own cash flow."

Source: Michael Peltz, *Institutional Investor*, June 1992, p. 42. This copyrighted material is reprinted with permission from Institutional Investor, Inc. 488 Madison Avenue, New York, New York 10022.

inappropriateness of their statistical methodology; Amihud et al report that their tests using an alternative methodology showed a significant return–beta relationship and conclude that "beta is alive and well."

Underlying the controversy over the CAPM and beta is the unresolved question of how the market portfolio (and its return) and beta are measured. Because the market portfolio in theory should consist of all risky assets in the world and includes components such as human capital that are difficult to measure correctly and/or are nonmarketable, the true Markowitz-efficient market portfolio is impossible to identify or measure (even approximately) for purposes of testing the CAPM. Roll and Ross (1992), akin to Roll's 1977 critique (Chapter 12), assert that since (1) it is all but impossible to identify a mean-variance efficient market index as an appropriate proxy for the market portfolio and (2) the empirical tests are prone to error due to statistical limitations posed by the very nature of the data utilized (such as in the estimation of beta), the empirical findings of CAPM tests really cannot tell us conclusively whether or not the model is valid. They conclude that if the model "cannot tell us about average returns, then it is not of practical value for a variety of applications including the computation of the cost of capital and the construction of investment portfolios."

Thus the available evidence indicates that while the CAPM provides a simple and intuitive theoretical construct about the risk-return relation in free markets whose investors are risk averse, it does not provide a precise depiction of the relation, and beta cannot be regarded as *the* measure of risk in capital markets. In essence there appears to be little or no justification for using the model in investment analysis, such as the identification of mispriced securities using alphas discussed in the previous section. (There is no reason to believe that the SML equation is valid, and even if it were, it is virtually impossible to identify the true security market line or even a reasonable approximation.)

However, even though a quantitative measure of risk and an appropriate risk-return model remain elusive, there is still an argument for the application of the concept of the CAPM and in particular beta in practical portfolio management. What is critical is that blind mechanical application of the CAPM should be avoided, and the limitations associated with using betas should be well understood. This issue is discussed in the next section.

THE MARKET PORTFOLIO, THE MARKET FACTOR, AND TWO BETAS

It is evident from the preceding discussion that even if the CAPM were valid, its use in investment selection would be critically dependent on (1) the identification of the market portfolio, (2) the estimation or prediction of its expected return, and (3) the estimation of beta. As noted earlier, in the strictest sense the market portfolio is not identifiable or measurable, and so surrogates have to be employed in the analysis. In early applications and tests of the CAPM, because much of the work was concentrated on stocks, stock market indices such as the Standard and Poor's 500 stock index were used as proxies for the market portfolio. Market betas were estimated by undertaking regressions of the returns of individual securities or portfolios on the returns of a market index (the market factor), as described in Chapter 5. The estimate of b in equation 5.1 is then used as a proxy for β in the CAPM. Obviously, a market index is not representative of the theoretical market portfolio of the equilibrium CAPM. However, the use of a stock market index as the proxy for the market portfolio is the norm, so much so that it has led to the mistaken notion, among some academics and practitioners alike, that the beta of the single-index model (b in equation 5.1, when r_M is the return on the market index) and that of the CAPM (β in equation 9.11) are the same.[8] However, though the two betas are clearly not the same, arguments have been put forward to justify the use of market indexes as adequate surrogates for the market portfolio and for the measurement of beta.

---

[8] In some texts and articles the Greek letter β is used to denote both betas. Though such texts may note the distinction between the two betas, confusion is still possible. For this reason, we deliberately use two different symbols, b and β.

Rosenberg (1981) argues that it is not particularly important whether the market index is a good approximation of the true market portfolio; since we do not know the true market portfolio, for purposes of investment strategy it is reasonable to "separate assets into broad homogenous classes or 'markets' and to use an index of approximate outstandings of more prominent securities in each market as a surrogate for the total market."[9] This implies that if the analysis involves stocks, a stock market index is adequate as a market portfolio proxy, while for bonds a bond market index would be appropriate, and so on.

Movements of the aggregate stock market to a certain extent reflect changes in investors' expectations about the performance of the economy. Therefore, stock market movements mirror investor perceptions about changes in the values of capital assets in general, and market indexes are likely to be highly correlated with the "true" market portfolio.

The usefulness of market indices and betas in investment management is expressed by Bernstein (1981) as follows: "Is beta dead? The question is ridiculous. As long as individual securities continue to move up and down in sympathy with—or as part of—broad market movements, portfolio managers must be concerned about the sensitivity of their portfolios to the general market, the stability of that relationship, and the accuracy of the measurement tools that they employ."

Similarly, Roll and Ross (1992) note about market indexes (whether they are mean-variance efficient or not): "Despite problems with the [CAPM], market value weighted index proxies are of considerable interest in their own right because they reflect averages of investor holdings. Whether or not such indices produce betas that are cross-sectionally related to average returns, their own returns serve as a benchmark for investment comparisons. Beating or trailing a value-weighted index has become the most widely-accepted criterion of investment performance. It is obviously an appropriate criterion relative to the wealth-weighted average returns of other investors."

These arguments do not make a case for the validity of the CAPM; rather they do so for the use of market indices and beta more in the context of the single-index, or market, model, which is essentially an empirical model that does not necessarily have anything to do with the CAPM, though they can be related under certain assumptions (Jensen 1979, pp. 27–29; Rosenberg 1981). An often overlooked fact is that the single-index model and the concept of beta as a measure of covariance risk preceded the CAPM—the former was postulated by Markowitz (1959) and Sharpe (1963) as a model of the nature of covariance between securities; the CAPM is a theory based on equilibrium and mean-variance efficiency assumptions.[10] Therefore, the use of betas estimated using market indexes in the context of the CAPM represents an implicit acceptance that (a) the

[9] Similar arguments are made by Stambaugh (1982) and Brown and Brown (1987).

[10] See Markowitz (1984) for a detailed discussion of the distinction between the two betas.

CAPM is valid, and (b) the market index is an adequate surrogate of the theoretical market portfolio. As noted earlier, neither of these conditions has been (and perhaps cannot be) substantiated by empirical tests (Chapter 12).

In any case, the use of market indexes and betas in investment practice, whether in the context of the CAPM or the market model, is subject to limitations, and therefore it is essential to exercise caution.

Even if a market index is considered to be an adequate proxy, it is difficult to measure its expected return, since stock market movements are quite difficult to predict. A measure of expected return frequently used is the average historical return over a long time. However, this assumes that the probability distribution generating the *ex post* returns is stationary over time and that the sample averages in the past will be the same in the future. This procedure may be highly error prone and inefficient especially if the time interval over which average returns are computed is not very long. See, for example, Carleton and Lakonishok (1985) on difficulties in measuring the market return.

The appeal of the market beta is that it reflects the risk of an asset or stock in relation to the movements of the stock market, which is to a certain degree driven by economic factors. In this context differences in beta across firms are assumed to reflect fundamental characteristics, such as a firm's industry or its financial leverage position, which in turn determine the manner in which changes in economy-wide factors influence the stock's performance.[11] Thus an analyst could attempt to predict a firm's beta based on information obtained about the firm and its industry in addition to forecasts about the economy. Two approaches that have been examined (Beaver, Kettler, and Scholes 1970 and Rosenberg and McKibben 1973) in predicting such fundamental betas from company characteristics (such as accounting data) were discussed in Chapter 5. Rosenberg and Guy (1976a, 1976b) also present an estimation technique based on forecasts of the effects of future macroeconomic conditions on a firm depending on its industry and firm-specific characteristics, such as financial leverage and variability of earnings. Also, as discussed in Chapter 5, betas can be calculated from historical returns. However, betas calculated using only historical returns suffer from the problem of nonstationarity—betas, especially for individual stocks, may change from period to period in response to structural changes in the factors responsible for price movements such as monetary policy regimes, business cycles, interest rate cycles, market psychology, institutional factors, and industry and firm characteristics. Numerous studies have examined the nonstationarity of betas, and the degree of nonstationarity has been determined to be

---

[11] The relationships between the single-index model beta and firm-specific, industry, and macroeconomic variables are examined by Beaver, Kettler, and Scholes (1970), Rosenberg and McKibben (1973), Rosenberg and Marathe (1976), Rosenberg and Guy (1976a, 1976b), Fabozzi and Francis (1979), Francis and Fabozzi (1979), and Abell and Krueger (1989).

dependent on several factors: (1) the number of securities in a portfolio; (2) the assumed holding period for calculating returns (weekly, monthly, annually, etc.); (3) the number of observations or the length of time over which the estimation is made; and (4) the method of portfolio construction (Blume 1971, 1975; Levy 1971; Alexander and Chervany 1980; Fabozzi and Francis 1978; Francis and Fabozzi 1979; Francis 1979; Tole 1981; Kolb and Rodriguez 1990). The evidence on nonstationarity does not recommend the use of a security's historical beta without adjustment, which is tantamount to an assumption that the beta in a future period will be the same as in a past period. Thus, as an alternative to adjusting betas based on fundamental industry or firm-specific factors, historic betas can be adjusted based on the identification of a statistically determined model of beta tendencies over time. For example, Reilly and Wright (1988) examine betas as adjusted by Merrill Lynch and Value Line according to the following equations:

Merrill Lynch

$$\text{adjusted beta} = 0.33743 + 0.66257 \text{ (unadjusted beta)}$$

Value Line

$$\text{adjusted beta} = 0.35 + 0.67 \text{ (unadjusted beta)}$$

Note that the equations are based on data covering certain time periods, and therefore there is no reason to believe that the equations will hold for future periods. Thus, by virtue of their being forecasts, estimated betas are subject to uncertainty and measurement error. No one method of estimation is consistently accurate in its forecast; while one method may provide better forecasts than another during one period, the opposite can occur in another period.[12] Also, betas computed from historical data may differ according to (1) the return interval used (i.e., weekly, monthly, annual), and (2) the period over which the estimation is done. Statman (1981) and Reilly and Wright (1988) report that betas for individual securities calculated using weekly returns (as done by Value Line) over a five-year estimation period (i.e., 260 weekly observations) were significantly different from those computed from monthly returns (as done by Merrill Lynch) over the same five-year period. Similarly, Levy (1981), using data for a 20-year period, found differences in beta values computed for different investment horizons ranging from one month (240 observations) to 30 months (8 observations). Carleton and Lakonishok (1985) also report differences in monthly, quarterly, and annual betas for industry portfolios for data covering the same period. Thus the use of measured

---

[12] See, for example, a comparison of betas from investment information firms by Harrington (1983).

betas in selecting investments may be appropriate only when the holding periods match the return interval used in the computation of the betas. Also, there is no "correct" estimation period for the computation of betas, though a five-year period is commonly used. Other factors that may influence the reliability of firm betas estimated over a certain period include the frequency of trading of the security and the amount of information available about a security during the period (Scholes and Williams 1977, Dimson 1979, and Clarkson and Thompson 1990).

The foregoing suggests that there are several possible sources of measurement error (or estimation risk) in the estimation of betas. This result implies that decisions, even assuming that the CAPM or market model is valid, are prone to error, and wrong decisions can be made. Clearly, if the market index, the SML, and beta are incorrectly measured, investment analysis using the CAPM, such as the use of alpha (Figure 9.4), could be erroneous and meaningless. Carleton and Lakonishok (1985), for example, show how blind use of historical estimates can lead to erroneous results (box, "An Illustration of the Limitations of Using Historical Estimates").

Clearly, application of the CAPM and beta in practical portfolio management should be undertaken with caution in view of the numerous limitations discussed so far. There is no strong reason to believe that the use of betas or the CAPM leads to superior portfolio selection compared with alternative approaches such as traditional or fundamental investment analysis, technical analysis, or even naive portfolio selection strategies.[13] Thus, the CAPM or beta concept can at best be regarded as one of several possible techniques that may be useful in investment analysis and that may at times lead to good results but just like any other technique cannot assure large profits.

SUMMARY

The original CAPM, as the pioneering theory of capital asset pricing, provides a theoretical framework for examining the behavior of capital asset prices in regard to the relationship between risk and return. Even though there is not much evidence to substantiate its validity and the testability of the theory is still debatable, the empirical implications of the CAPM paved the way for the numerous tests that have provided a vast amount of useful empirical evidence about the behavior of capital markets today (Chapters 12 and 13). However, the usefulness of the model in practical portfolio management is arguably limited. Extensions of the CAPM as well as alternative models, some of which claim to be superior

---

[13] Some academics and practitioners discount the usefulness, in practical portfolio management, of beta or the CAPM entirely. See for example Vandell (1981), Schneller (1983), and Dreman (1992), and Hulbert (1992).

AN ILLUSTRATION OF THE LIMITATIONS OF USING HISTORICAL ESTIMATES

The following is an excerpt from Carleton and Lakonishok (1985):

The CAPM relates return to risk as follows:

$$E(R_i) = R_f + [E(R_M) - R_f]\beta_i,$$

where:

$E(R_i)$ = the expected return on company i,
R_f = the risk-free rate,
$E(R_M)$ = the expected return on the market portfolio, and
β_i = the company's systematic risk, or beta.

The task, under the CAPM, is to determine the company's beta. Our confidence in choice of any given historical data representation to estimate the market risk premium is at this point somewhat shaken, however. A natural step may be to examine the return experiences of similar firms, given that we are not sure about how to determine a market risk premium, hence expected return. In addition, even in the CAPM framework, it may be appropriate to look at groups of companies or industries, rather than at individual companies.

Thus, rather than concentrate on various issues critical in the case of individual securities (such as measurement error and coefficient instability), we will focus our analysis on the industry level. This will facilitate the presentation of results and enable us to demonstrate better the possible reason for differences in return experiences.

We grouped the sample companies into 15 industries based on their two-digit Standard Industrial Classification codes. The exhibit above gives the number of companies in each industry. The next exhibit provides for each industry annual geometric returns, arithmetic returns and standard deviations of returns for

Industry Classifications

Industry	SIC Code
1. Mining	10-14
2. Construction	15-17
3. Food	20-21
4. Textile	22-23
5. Paper	24-27
6. Chemicals	28
7. Petroleum	29
8. Rubber	30-31
9. Metals	32-34
10. Machinery	35-39
11. Transportation	40-49
12. Wholesale Trade	50-51
13. Retail Trade	52-59
14. Finance	60-67
15. Services	70-89

the 1926–80 period. Three beta coefficients, three intercept (alpha) coefficients, and three coefficients of determination (R-squares) are also presented. The exhibit on p. 230 shows the same results for the 1971–80 period. These coefficients were estimated from the following regression:

$$R_{it} - R_{ft} = \alpha_i + \beta_i(R_{Mt} - R_{ft}) + e_{it},$$

where R_{it}, R_{ft} and R_{Mt} are the period t returns for industry i (each security received the same weight), the risk-free rate (Treasury bill returns), and the return on the market portfolio (equally weighted Fisher index), respectively. Thus the differences between the three sets of coefficients result from differences in the estimation intervals (monthly, quarterly, or annual). For the 1971–80 period, 10 of the 15 industries exhibit differences in betas of at least 0.1. For the mining industry, the monthly beta is 0.83, the annual 0.63; for the petroleum industry, the quarterly beta is 0.50, the annual 0.73. Assuming an annual risk premium of

9 · *The Capital Asset Pricing Model* 229

AN ILLUSTRATION OF THE LIMITATIONS OF USING
HISTORICAL ESTIMATES—*Continued*

Returns and Risk Measures by Industries, 1926–1980

Industry	Geo. Mean[a]	Arith. Mean[a]	Stan. Dev.[a]	Beta (1)[b]	Beta (3)[b]	Beta (12)[b]	Alpha (1)[a,b]	Alpha (3)[a,b]	Alpha (12)[a,b]	R^2 (1)[b]	R^2 (3)[b]	R^2 (12)[b]
Mining	16.1	21.7	38.7	1.02	1.10	1.03	3.54[c]	2.91[d]	4.10	0.87	0.92	0.78
Construction	7.2	20.1	62.0	1.43	1.72	1.53	−3.17	−6.09	−4.80	0.60	0.78	0.66
Food	11.9	15.0	27.6	0.75	0.71	0.80	1.33[d]	1.45[d]	0.83	0.92	0.94	0.92
Textile	10.6	16.8	38.7	1.04	1.13	1.11	−1.69[d]	−2.22[c]	−1.93	0.90	0.95	0.89
Paper	13.0	18.4	37.6	1.01	1.07	1.10	0.60	0.12	−0.12	0.92	0.96	0.93
Chemicals	12.7	16.1	28.6	0.86	0.82	0.83	1.33[d]	1.61[c]	1.55[c]	0.92	0.96	0.92
Petroleum	14.7	18.9	31.3	0.80	0.74	0.81	4.28[c]	4.35[c]	4.65[c]	0.71	0.82	0.73
Rubber	10.6	16.8	39.2	1.06	1.10	1.12	−1.94	−2.02[d]	−2.10	0.89	0.95	0.89
Metals	12.2	17.8	38.9	1.11	1.13	1.13	−0.72	−0.96	−1.30	0.96	0.98	0.93
Machinery	12.5	18.4	37.6	1.09	1.07	1.11	−0.24	0.04	−0.40	0.97	0.98	0.96
Transportation	10.4	14.5	29.9	0.99	0.95	0.81	−1.33	−0.68	0.37	0.89	0.91	0.80
Wholesale Trade	11.4	16.7	35.9	0.83	0.91	1.02	1.33	0.28	−0.82	0.69	0.84	0.89
Retail Trade	10.7	16.3	36.1	0.90	0.87	1.01	−0.60	−0.28	−1.03	0.88	0.91	0.86
Finance	11.4	15.8	30.1	0.99	0.94	0.85	−0.60	0.00	1.02	0.94	0.95	0.84
Services	13.0	19.9	40.6	1.04	1.03	1.09	0.84	1.45	1.47	0.86	0.91	0.79
Average	11.9	17.5	36.8	0.99	1.02	1.02	0.24	0.08	0.10	0.86	0.92	0.85

[a]Annualized percentages.

[b]The number in parentheses is the length of the estimation interval—monthly, quarterly, or yearly.

[c]Statistical significance of 5 per cent for a two-tailed test.

[d]Statistical significance of 10 per cent for a two-tailed test.

about 8 percent, a 0.1 difference in betas will create a 0.8 percent difference in expected returns; not much in the abstract, perhaps, but one that translates into $1.9 million per year in earnings for a firm like Duke Power if beta is used to determine its return on book equity.

The coefficients of determination at the industry level are extremely high. For the 1926–80 period, the averages across industry are 0.86, 0.92 and 0.85 for the monthly, quarterly, and annual intervals, respectively. Although there is some indication of a better fit for quarterly data, the differences are not large enough to decide on the basis of statistical fit

that quarterly data should be used to estimate betas.

We should note that these results probably underestimate the impact of estimation intervals on betas of individual companies. We used intervals of one month or longer. Betas estimated from daily or weekly data are subject to biases caused by trading patterns; there are no biases in estimated betas for NYSE securities when monthly data are used. Furthermore, our betas are estimated at the level of industries, not individual securities; differences due to beta estimation intervals are partially suppressed when industry aggregates are employed.

Continued

An Illustration of the Limitations of Using Historical Estimates—*Continued*

Returns and Risk Measures by Industry, 1971–1980

	Geo. Mean[a]	Arith. Mean[a]	Stan. Dev.[a]	Beta (1)[b]	Beta (3)[b]	Beta (12)[b]	Alpha (1)[a,b]	Alpha (3)[a,b]	Alpha (12)[a,b]	R^2 (1)[b]	R^2 (3)[b]	R^2 (12)[b]
Mining	24.8	29.4	38.2	0.83	0.70	0.63	12.42[c]	13.43[c]	17.54	0.55	0.51	0.23
Construction	20.1	26.6	41.4	1.21	1.29	1.31	5.79[d]	6.01	6.65	0.86	0.88	0.83
Food	12.6	15.0	25.1	0.81	0.81	0.83	0.24	0.80	−0.15	0.92	0.92	0.91
Textile	7.6	14.3	41.9	1.13	1.17	1.34	−5.41[c]	−5.14[d]	−6.11	0.87	0.88	0.86
Paper	11.6	15.0	28.6	0.99	1.03	0.96	−1.33	−1.61	−1.64	0.94	0.96	0.95
Chemicals	13.7	15.4	20.0	0.81	0.77	0.66	1.33	1.29	1.94	0.86	0.91	0.91
Petroleum	20.7	24.4	31.5	0.69	0.50	0.73	9.25[d]	10.42[d]	10.16	0.49	0.40	0.45
Rubber	11.6	16.4	33.5	1.01	1.02	1.10	−1.45	−1.33	−1.53	0.88	0.89	0.90
Metals	14.8	17.3	25.0	1.01	0.94	0.83	1.33	1.89	2.02	0.94	0.95	0.93
Machinery	16.2	21.2	34.1	1.15	1.18	1.17	2.30	0.08	2.47[c]	0.96	0.96	0.99
Transportation	10.9	13.4	24.3	0.72	0.68	0.82	−0.84	−0.76	−1.83	0.87	0.87	0.97
Wholesale Trade	12.7	17.7	34.0	1.19	1.24	1.13	−1.09	−1.16	−0.50	0.94	0.94	0.92
Retail Trade	8.4	14.4	38.9	1.13	1.26	1.15	−4.91	−5.01[d]	−5.62	0.92	0.94	0.86
Finance	8.9	13.4	30.3	1.06	1.05	1.00	−4.41[d]	−4.06[d]	−3.46	0.89	0.92	0.91
Services	15.2	22.1	38.6	1.28	1.38	1.28	1.09	1.15	2.78	0.94	0.95	0.93
Average	14.0	18.4	32.4	1.00	1.00	1.00	0.84	0.96	1.52	0.86	0.86	0.84

[a]Annualized percentages.

[b]The number in parentheses is the length of the estimation interval—monthly, quarterly, or yearly.

[c]Statistical significance of 5 per cent for a two-tailed test.

[d]Statistical significance of 10 per cent for a two-tailed test.

According to the CAPM, the theoretical intercept, or alpha, should be zero; estimated deviations from zero should be attributable to conventional estimation problems; and the intercept should be irrelevant in generating industry or company expected returns. Given that our beliefs in CAPM are somewhat shaken, however, the question is whether to retain or discard the intercept when expected returns are being generated.

For the 1926–80 period and the monthly intercept, a two-tailed test shows two intercepts to be different from zero at the 5 percent significance level and three at the 10 percent level; 10 intercepts are not significantly different from zero. One approach to the develop

ment of an expected industry rate of return would be to discard the intercepts, especially the 10 that are not significantly different from zero, statistically. We feel that this procedure errs. What we want for an expected return estimate is an unbiased point estimate; if the regression equation were correctly specified, retaining estimated beta while discarding estimated alpha would obviously produce bias in estimated expected rate of return.

Unfortunately, the size of the intercepts indicates that the effect on expected industry returns is substantial. For the rubber industry, for example, the monthly intercept is −1.94 percent per year. Also, the results indicate that differences in estimation intervals produce

---

in their depiction of asset pricing and in their usefulness in portfolio selection, have followed the CAPM. Some of these extensions and alternative models are examined in the next chapter.

Questions and Problems

1. Explain the relation between risk and return as depicted by the CAPM.
2. Differentiate between the capital market line and the security market line.
3. What features of the CAPM make it appealing as an asset pricing model?
4. What is meant by the market portfolio?
5. Why is it difficult to measure the return on the market portfolio?
6. What is the difference between the beta of the single-index model of Chapter 7 and the beta of the CAPM?
7. Differentiate between aggressive and defensive securities.
8. Discuss the relevance of a security's alpha in regard to security selection using the SML.

9. Outline the major limitations you would take into consideration when using the CAPM for investment selection.

10. If you are an investment analyst, and you are provided with a list of historical betas for a number of firms, what are the issues you would consider before deciding whether or not to use the betas for your portfolio selection?

11. On the first day of your job as a security analyst, one of your new colleagues tells you, "I pick stocks solely on the basis of betas." What would you say?

12. You have a diversified portfolio with a beta of 1. If you forecast that a huge bull market is imminent and you want to rebalance your portfolio, should you increase or decrease the beta of your portfolio? Explain.

13. The beta of ABC Corp. is 1.15. The risk-free rate of interest is 4 percent. The expected market return is 8 percent.
    (a) What should be the equilibrium expected return of ABC's stock?
    (b) Sketch the security market line for ABC's stock.

14. The stock of The Mikey Corporation has a beta of 0.90. The expected return on the market portfolio is 10 percent and the market risk premium is 6 percent. Calculate the expected return on this security.

15. Assume MMI, Inc., has a stable beta of 0.95. The expected market return is 6 percent and the risk-free rate is 3 percent. Your projections show that the stock will provide a return of 8 percent. According to the CAPM, is MMI's stock undervalued or overvalued? Explain through calculations and graphically.

16. Isicorp has a historical beta of 1.2. However, you think this beta should be adjusted according to the Value Line adjustment equation given in the chapter. The one-month Treasury bill rate is 3.5 percent. The expected market return is 9 percent. Based on your analysis of information on Isicorp, you think that the company's stock will provide a return of 12 percent. You believe in CAPM equilibrium.
    (a) Calculate the firm's alpha.
    (b) Should you invest in this security? Why?

Self-Test Problems

ST-1. The expected return on the market portfolio is 8 percent and the market risk premium is 5 percent. Calculate the expected return on a security if
    (a) Its historical beta is 0.85.
    (b) Its fundamental beta is 1.05.

ST-2. You have computed the historical beta of a portfolio to be 1.12. Calculate the adjusted betas using (1) the Value Line adjustment equation and (2) the Merrill Lynch adjustment equation.

ST-3. TBIO Inc.'s stock has a beta of 1.5. The expected market return is 10 percent and the risk-free rate is 5 percent. You calculate that the stock will provide a return of 11 percent. Using the CAPM, is TBIO's stock undervalued or overvalued?

Solutions to Self-Test Problems

ST-1.

Market risk premium = expected market return − risk-free rate

$$5\% = 8\% - \text{risk-free rate.}$$

Therefore,

$$\text{risk-free rate} = 8\% - 5\% = 3\%$$

From equation 9.11,

(1) Using the historical beta,

$$\text{Expected return on security} = 3\% + (5\%)(0.85) = 7.25\%$$

(2) Using the fundamental beta,

$$\text{Expected return on security} = 3\% + (5\%)(1.05) = 8.25\%$$

Note: This problem shows how analysis can be different if there is reason to believe that a firm's risk as measured by beta is likely to differ from what was obtained in the past.

ST-2. (1) Value Line:

$$\text{Adjusted beta} = 0.35 + 0.67\,(1.12) = 1.1004$$

(2) Merrill Lynch:

$$\text{Adjusted beta} = 0.33743 + .66257\,(1.12) = 1.07951$$

ST-3. From equation 9.11,

$$\text{Equilibrium expected return} = 5 + (10 - 5)(1.5) = 12.5\%$$

Therefore, since the security will provide a return of only 11 percent, which is less than the return it should provide given its beta (12.5 percent), the security is overpriced. The security's alpha is negative, as evident from equation 9.14:

$$11 = \alpha + 5 + (10 - 5)(1.5)$$
$$\alpha = 11 - 12.5 = -1.5\%$$

REFERENCES

Abell, J. D., and T. M. Krueger. 1989. Macroeconomic influences on beta. *Journal of Economics and Business* 41:185–193.

Alexander, G. J., and N. L. Chervany. 1980. On the estimation and stability of beta. *Journal of Financial and Quantitative Analysis* 15:123–137.

Alexander, G. J., and J. C. Francis. 1986. *Portfolio Analysis*. Englewood Cliffs, NJ: Prentice Hall.

Amihud, Y., B. J. Christensen, and H. Mendelson. 1992. Further evidence on the risk-return relationship. Working paper, Stern School of Business, New York University, November.

Beaver, W., P. Kettler, and M. Scholes. 1970. The association between market determined and accounting determined risk measures. *Accounting Review* 45:654–682.

Bernstein, P. L. 1981. Dead—or alive and well? *Journal of Portfolio Management*. Winter, 4.

Bernstein, P. L. 1992a. If beta is dead, where is the corpse? *Forbes*. July 20, 343.

Bernstein, P. L. 1992b. The great beta deβate. *Journal of Portfolio Management*. Fall, 1.

Bernstein, P. L. 1992c. How improbable are the origins of modern Wall Street? or The miraculous importance of three little words. *Financial Analysts Journal*. September-October, 15–18.

Blume, M. 1971. On the assessment of risk. *Journal of Finance*. March, 26:1–10.

Blume, M. 1975. Betas and their regression tendencies. *Journal of Finance*. June, 30:785–795.

Blume, M. 1979. Betas and their regression tendencies: Some further evidence. *Journal of Finance*. March, 34:265–267.

Brealey, R. A. 1990. Portfolio theory versus portfolio practice. *Journal of Portfolio Management*. Summer, 6–10.

Brown, K. C., and G. D. Brown. 1987. Does the composition of the market portfolio *really* matter? *Journal of Portfolio Management*. Winter, 26–32.

Carleton, W. T., and J. Lakonishok. 1985. Risk and return on equity: The use and misuse of historical estimates. *Financial Analysts Journal*. January-February, 38–47.

Carvell, S., and P. Strebel. 1984. A new beta incorporating analysts' forecasts. *Journal of Portfolio Management*. Fall, 81–85.

Clarkson, P. M., and R. Thompson. 1990. Empirical estimates of beta when investors face estimation risk. *Journal of Finance* 45:431–453.

Cox, J., J. Ingersoll, and S. Ross. 1985. An intertemporal general equilibrium model of asset prices. *Econometrica*. March, 53:363–384.

Dimson, E. 1979. Risk measurement when shares are subject to infrequent trading. *Journal of Financial Economics* 7:197–226.

Dreman, D. 1992. Bye-bye to beta. *Forbes*. March 30, 148.

Fabozzi, F., and J. C. Francis. 1978. Beta as a random coefficient. *Journal of Financial and Quantitative Analysis*. March, 13:101–116.

Fabozzi, F., and J. C. Francis. 1979. Industry effects and the determinants of beta. *Quarterly Review of Economics and Business*. Autumn, 19:61–74.

Fama, E. 1991. Efficient capital markets II. *Journal of Finance*. December, 46:1575–1617.

Fama, E., and K. French. 1992. The cross-section of expected stock returns. *Journal of Finance*. June, 47:427–465.

Francis, J. C. 1979. Statistical analysis of risk coefficients for NYSE stocks. *Journal of Financial and Quantitative Analysis.* December, 14:981–997.

Francis, J. C., and F. Fabozzi. 1979. The effects of changing macroeconomic conditions on the parameters of the single index model. *Journal of Financial and Quantitative Analysis.* June, 14:351–360.

Harrington, D. R. 1983. Whose beta is best? *Journal of Portfolio Management.* July-August, 67–72.

Hulbert, M. 1992. Beta is dead. *Forbes.* June 22, 239.

Jensen, M. C. 1979. Tests of capital market theory and implications of the evidence. In *Handbook of Financial Economics.* J. L. Bicksler, ed. Amsterdam: North Holland Publishing Company.

Klemkosky, R. C., and J. D. Martin. 1975. The adjustment of beta forecasts. *Journal of Finance.* September, 1123–1128.

Kolb, R. W., and R. J. Rodriguez. 1989. The regression tendencies of betas. A reappraisal. *Financial Review* 24:319–334.

Kolb, R. W., and R. J. Rodriguez. 1990. Is the distribution of betas stationary? *Journal of Financial Research* 13:279–283.

Lakonishok, J., and A. C. Shapiro. 1986. Systematic risk, total risk, and size as determinants of stock market returns. *Journal of Banking and Finance.* March, 10:115–132.

Lee, C. F., and S. Rahman. 1991. New evidence on of timing and the security selection skill of mutual fund managers. *Journal of Portfolio Management.* Winter, 61–68.

Levy, H. 1981. The CAPM and the investment horizon. *Journal of Portfolio Management.* Winter, 32–40.

Levy, H. 1984. Measuring risk and performance over alternative investment horizons. *Financial Analysts Journal.* March-April, 61–68.

Levy, R. 1971. On the short-term stationarity of beta coefficients. *Financial Analysts Journal.* November-December, 55–62.

Lindahl-Stevens, M. 1978. Some popular uses and abuses of beta. *Journal of Portfolio Management.* Winter, 13–17.

Lintner, J. 1965. The valuation of risky assets and the selection of risky investments in stock portfolios and capital budgets. *Review of Economics and Statistics.* February, 47:13–37.

Markowitz, H. 1983. Nonnegative or not nonnegative: A question about CAPMs. *Journal of Finance.* May, 283–295.

Markowitz, H. 1984. The "two beta" trap. *Journal of Portfolio Management.* Fall, 12–20.

Merton, R. C. 1973. An intertemporal capital asset pricing model. *Econometrica.* September, 41:867–887.

Mossin, J. 1966. Equilibrium in a capital market. *Econometrica.* October, 34:768–783.

Pettit, R. R., and R. Westerfield. 1974. Using the capital asset pricing model and the market model to predict security returns. *Journal of Financial and Quantitative Analysis.* September, 9:579–605.

Peltz, M. 1992. Is this the night of the living beta? *Institutional Investor.* June, 42–43.

Reilly, F. K., and D. J. Wright. 1988. A comparison of published betas. *Journal of Portfolio Management.* Spring, 64–69.

Roll, R. 1977. A critique of the asset pricing theory's tests. *Journal of Financial Economics* 4:129–176.

Roll, R. 1978. Ambiguity when performance is measured by the security market line. *Journal of Finance* 33:1051–1069.

Roll, R. 1980. Performance evaluation and benchmark errors I. *Journal of Portfolio Management*. Summer, 5–12.

Roll, R. 1981. Performance evaluation and benchmark errors II. *Journal of Portfolio Management*. Winter, 17–22.

Roll, R., and S. Ross. 1992. On the cross-sectional relation between expected returns and betas. Working paper #21, Yale School of Organization and Management, May.

Rosenberg, B. 1981. The capital asset pricing model and the market model. *Journal of Portfolio Management*. Winter, 5–16.

Rosenberg, B. 1985. Prediction of common stock betas. *Journal of Portfolio Management*. Winter, 5–14.

Rosenberg, B., and J. Guy. 1976a. Prediction of beta from investment fundamentals: Part one. *Financial Analysts Journal*. May-June, 60–72.

Rosenberg, B., and J. Guy. 1976b. Prediction of beta from investment fundamentals: Part two. *Financial Analysts Journal*. July-August, 62–70.

Rosenberg, R., and V. Marathe. 1976. Common factors in security returns: Microeconomic determinants and macroeconomic correlates. *Proceedings: Seminar on the Analysis of Security Prices*. University of Chicago Graduate School of Business.

Rosenberg, B., and W. McKibben. 1973. The prediction of systematic and specific risk in common stock. *Journal of Financial and Quantitative Analysis*. March, 317–333.

Rudd, A., and B. Rosenberg. 1980. The "market model" in investment management. *Journal of Finance*. May, 35:597–606.

Samuelson, P. A. 1989. The judgement of economic science on rational portfolio management: Indexing, timing, and long-horizon effects. *Journal of Portfolio Management*. Fall, 4–12.

Schneller, M. I. 1983. Are better betas worth the trouble? *Financial Analysts Journal*. July-August, 74–77.

Scholes, M., and J. Williams. 1977. Estimating betas from nonsynchronous data. *Journal of Financial Economics* 5:309–327.

Sharpe, W. 1963. A simplified model for portfolio analysis. *Management Science*. January, 277–293.

Sharpe, W. 1964. Capital asset prices: A theory of market equilibrium under conditions of risk. *Journal of Finance*. September, 366–383.

Sharpe, W. 1978. Major investment styles. *Journal of Portfolio Management*. Winter, 68–74.

Sharpe, W. 1984. Factor models, CAPMs and the APT. *Journal of Portfolio Management*. Fall, 21–25.

Sharpe, W. 1992. Asset allocation: Management style and performance measurement. *Journal of Portfolio Management*. Winter, 7–19.

Sharpe, W. 1991. Capital asset prices with and without negative holdings. *Journal of Finance*. June, 46:489–509.

Sharpe, W., and G. Alexander. 1990. *Investments*. Englewood Cliffs, NJ: Prentice Hall.

Stambaugh, R. 1982. On the exclusion of assets from tests of the two-parameter model. *Journal of Financial Economics*. 10:235–268.

Statman, M. 1981. Betas compared. Merrill Lynch vs. Value Line. *Journal of Portfolio Management*. Winter, 41–44.

Tole, T. M. 1981. How to maximize stationarity of beta. *Journal of Portfolio Management*. Winter, 45–49.

Vandell, R. F. 1981. Is beta a useful measure of security risk? *Journal of Portfolio Management*. Winter, 23–31.

Vasicek, O. 1973. A note on using cross-sectional information in Bayesian estimation of security betas. *Journal of Finance*. December, 28:1233–1239.

Wallace, A. 1980. Is beta dead? *Institutional Investor*. July, 23–30.

Alternative Forms of the CAPM and Multi-Factor Asset Pricing Models

Introduction

This chapter discusses some of the alternative asset pricing models that have followed the development of the CAPM. The models, as either extensions of the CAPM (Chapter 9) or alternative specifications of asset pricing, relax some of the restrictions of the original CAPM. While the CAPM provides a simple and elegant depiction of the risk-return relation, the deficiencies highlighted in Chapter 9 and the rather weak empirical support (Chapter 12) for the model led to the development of these models, which attempt to be more realistic in their assumptions and more amenable to empirical testing.

Numerous extensions to the CAPM as well as alternative asset pricing models have been proposed, so only the major ones which have gained the widest appeal and which provide the most unique insights are presented.[1] The differences between these alternative versions and the original CAPM are highlighted. The models examined are the zero-beta CAPM, the multiperiod and multibeta versions of the CAPM, the consumption-based CAPM, and international asset pricing models. The arbitrage pricing model falls under the general class of multifactor asset pricing models; however, because it has evolved as *the* alternative to the CAPM both as a theory of asset pricing and in applications in portfolio management, it is discussed separately in Chapter 11.

The primary purposes of this chapter are (1) to familiarize you with a few of the alternative asset pricing models and (2) to serve as a transitional chapter between the traditional CAPM and the more recent multibeta/APT models. Therefore, we do not go into detail on the derivation of the models. Also, the models discussed in this chapter that have gained acceptance in terms of practical applicability in portfolio management are the multibeta models. In the empirical and practical context, they are no different from the APT model of Chapter 11; therefore, to avoid redundancy, numerical examples and discussions of practical applications are deferred until Chapter 11.

THE ZERO-BETA CAPM

The zero-beta CAPM, derived by Black (1972), relaxes the assumption that a risk-free asset exists and investors can borrow or lend at the risk-free rate.[2] In Black's model the risk-free rate is replaced by a zero-beta portfolio, which is a portfolio whose return is uncorrelated with the market portfolio return; that is, its systematic risk or beta is zero. However, the portfolio is not entirely risk-free, since it has some individual variance of return. The zero-beta portfolio lies on the efficient frontier and is also a minimum-variance portfolio. The risk-return relationship is depicted in Figure 10.1.

The Black model is also predicated on the mean-variance efficiency of the market portfolio in equilibrium, as in the original CAPM. Furthermore, it hinges on the requirement that short selling of risky securities be unrestricted, which allows the zero-beta portfolio to be constructed from a combination of risky assets through borrowing and short selling. (Construction of such a portfolio is possible only when there are no

---

[1] See Copeland and Weston (1988) , Alexander and Francis (1986), and Elton and Gruber (1984) for references and reviews of several CAPM extensions such as on the existence of (1) imperfections or frictions in markets, (2) heterogeneity in expectations, and (3) the nonmarketability of certain assets. More recent articles include among others Merton (1987), Kazemi (1988), Lee, Wu, and Wei (1990), Sharpe (1991), Levy and Samuelson (1992), and Smith (1993).

[2] Mayers (1973) also derives a version of the CAPM that incorporates the absence of a riskless asset and the existence of nonmarketable assets.

FIGURE 10.1

The Zero-Beta
CAPM

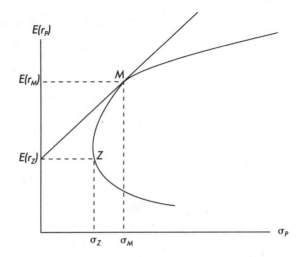

restrictions on short selling, since most securities have positive correlations and it is virtually impossible to construct a portfolio that is uncorrelated with the market portfolio or a proxy entirely from long positions in assets.)

In the zero-beta CAPM, the equilibrium expected return on an asset i, $E(r_i)$, is given by

(10.1)
$$E(r_i) = E(r_z) + [E(r_M) - E(r_z)]\beta_i,$$

where $E(r_z)$ is the expected return on the zero-beta portfolio.

Thus, the zero-beta CAPM has the same linear relationship as the original CAPM (equation 9.11), and the measure of systematic risk is the same market portfolio beta.[3] The application of the model is therefore similar to that of the original CAPM except that the expected return on the zero-beta portfolio, which is higher than the risk-free rate, has to be estimated.

By virtue of its relaxation of the risk-free asset assumption and the findings by some studies (Black, Jensen, and Scholes 1972 and Fama and MacBeth 1973) that the empirical evidence was more consistent with the zero-beta version than the original CAPM (Chapter 12), the zero-beta CAPM gained some acceptance as an alternative CAPM. However, it still suffers from the other restrictions of the CAPM discussed in Chapter 9, in particular the assumption of unrestricted short selling. Other variants of the model consider further relaxations such as (1) that there is risk-free borrowing and lending but at different interest rates (the risk-free borrowing rate is higher than the risk-free lending rate); (2) that investors can invest at the risk-free rate but cannot borrow at a risk-free rate; (3) that

---

[3] The model is sometimes also called the two-factor model, since in addition to the market portfolio there is a second factor, the zero-beta portfolio.

there is risk-free lending but there are margin requirements on risk-free borrowing; and (4) that there are no risk-free assets and short selling is prohibited. (Alexander and Francis 1986, Chapter 8, and Fama 1976, Chapter 8.) Sharpe (1991) has recently reexamined the CAPM where no short selling is allowed.

THE MULTIPERIOD CAPM

The multiperiod or intertemporal version of the CAPM, initially derived by Merton (1971, 1972, 1973) relaxes the unrealistic assumption in the original CAPM of a one-period investment horizon.[4] In this version investors make their utility-maximizing portfolio decisions by considering not only the returns on alternative assets over just one period but also returns that may be available in subsequent periods. That is, their portfolio decisions are geared toward maximizing the expected utility of lifetime consumption. In addition, it is assumed that trading in assets takes place continuously over time. Also, the investor knows at each point in time the stochastic processes of the changes in the investment opportunity set over the investment horizon. The returns and the changes in the opportunity set are also assumed to follow continuous-time stochastic processes.[5] The model relaxes the mean-variance assumption of the single-period CAPM but retains some other assumptions of the original CAPM: (1) investor expectations are homogeneous; (2) all assets are marketable; (3) assets have "limited liability" (i.e., an asset's value is never below zero); markets are perfect or frictionless, with no transaction costs, no taxes, no restrictions on short sales, and infinitely divisible assets); (4) markets are competitive, and each investor is a price-taker; and (5) the capital market is always in equilibrium. However, while the original CAPM assumes that asset returns have a normal distribution, the stochastic process of the model, a diffusion process (Chapter 17), assumes that returns have a log-normal distribution.

Under these assumptions Merton derived a general continuous-time intertemporal equilibrium model. With the additional assumptions that (1) the investment opportunity set is constant over time, and (2) a riskless asset exists and the risk-free rate is nonstochastic over time, Merton derived the CAPM equation, 9.11, of Chapter 9:[6]

$$E(r_i) = r_f + [E(r_M) - r_f]\beta_i$$

[4] Several other multiperiod versions of asset pricing models have since followed (e.g., Long 1974, Breeden 1979, and Cox, Ingersoll, and Ross 1985).

[5] While the assumption of a continuous-time process is not exactly realistic, Merton argued that "for well-developed capital markets, the time intervals between successive market openings is sufficiently small to make the continuous-time assumption a good approximation."

[6] Merton's derivation, which uses stochastic calculus, is mathematically advanced and is beyond the scope of this book.

Thus a continuous-time analog of the security market line of the single-period (static) CAPM is derived in a multiperiod (dynamic) framework under some less restrictive assumptions; however, this is facilitated by the unrealistic assumption that the investment opportunity set is constant over time, which is analogous to the assumption that investors are single-period utility maximizers in the static CAPM. Therefore, the greater appeal of the multiperiod framework is the more realistic case that the investment opportunity set changes over time. This leads to the multibeta version of the CAPM, discussed next.

THE MULTIBETA CAPM

The multibeta CAPM (Merton 1973) evolved from the relaxation of the assumption that the investment opportunity set and the riskless rate are constant over time. That is, the investment opportunity set changes stochastically over time, which is more consistent with reality. For example, the interest rate, an indicator of the investment opportunity set, changes stochastically over time. Under the assumption that the change in the risk-free rate alone captures changes in the investment opportunity set (i.e., it is an instrumental variable), Merton showed that investors' portfolio decisions will be in accordance with a three-fund separation theorem (analogous to the two-fund theorem of Chapter 7). This states that, under certain assumptions, given a set of n risky assets and the riskless asset, investors would be indifferent between choosing portfolios from among the original $(n + 1)$ assets or from three portfolios ("mutual funds") constructed from these assets. The three funds are: (1) the riskless asset, (2) the market portfolio, and (3) a portfolio whose returns are perfectly negatively correlated with changes in the investment opportunity set (in this case, changes in the riskless rate), that is, one that provides a hedge against unfavorable intertemporal shifts in the efficient frontier. The resulting multibeta CAPM in this framework expresses the expected return on an asset i as

(10.2) $$E(r_i) = r_f + [E(r_M) - r_f]\beta_{Mi} + [E(r_N) - r_f]\beta_{Ni},$$

where $E(r_N)$ is the expected return on the hedge portfolio, N, and β_{Ni} is asset i's beta with respect to the hedge portfolio, just as β_{Mi} is the market portfolio beta.

Thus there are two systematic risks, one reflecting the asset's covariation with the market portfolio and the other reflecting the asset's covariation with the hedge portfolio, that is, the risk of unfavorable (unexpected) shifts in the investment opportunity set. The expected excess return over the risk-free rate, $[E(r_N) - r_f]$, is the premium for bearing this risk.

If one variable does not adequately capture the investment opportunity set and k state variables are required, there are $k + 2$ funds instead of three, and equation 10.2 generalizes to[7]

(10.3)
$$E(r_i) = r_f + [E(r_M) - r_f]\beta_{Mi} + [E(r_{s1}) - r_f]\beta_{s1i}$$
$$+ \ldots\ldots\ldots + [E(r_{sk}) - r_f]\beta_{ski},$$

where $[E(r_{sj})]$ is the expected return on asset j representing the jth state variable, and β_{sji} is the beta of asset i associated with changes in the state variable j.

Equation 10.3 shows that each asset's expected return will depend on the degree of its covariation with the market portfolio as well as its covariances with various hedge portfolios that hedge against the k pervasive sources of uncertainty in the economy. Note that even if an asset's market beta is zero, its expected return will not necessarily be equal to the risk-free rate, r_f, unless its betas associated with all the other state variables are all zero. Also, the expected return on a zero-beta portfolio (as defined earlier) could replace the riskless rate, r_f, in equation 10.3 if there is no riskless asset.

By virtue of the assumption of optimal diversification, the state variables are essentially economy-wide or marketwide and influence the returns on all assets in the market. There is as yet no specific set of variables identified as the state variables in equation 10.3. Richard (1979) suggests variables such as disposable income, prices of goods, the change in the money supply, and wage rates. Some studies have examined variables such as the slope of the term structure of interest rates, consumption expenditures, economy-wide default risk, inflation, the short-term interest rate, real final sales, industrial production, and oil prices (e.g., Ferson and Harvey 1991; Shanken 1990; Burmeister and McElroy 1988; Chen, Roll, and Ross 1985; and Chan, Chen, and Hsieh 1985). As will be evident from Chapter 12, empirical investigations to determine if there is a set of appropriate state variables are still evolving.

Other multibeta asset pricing models similar to that presented above have been developed under varying sets of assumptions. For example, some make the same continuous-time assumption as Merton (Breeden 1979; Cox, Ingersoll, and Ross 1985). Others derive discrete-time models (Long 1974, Sharpe 1977, and Bossaerts and Green 1989). The arbitrage pricing models (Ross 1976, Connor 1984, Connor and Korajczyk 1989, and Reisman 1992), which are discussed in Chapter 11, also fall under the general class of multibeta pricing models and are not much different empirically from some of the models discussed in this chapter, but some of them are derived under certain uniquely different assumptions. (In some models the CAPM is shown to be a special case of the APT.)

---

[7] The derivation of the model with k state variables was undertaken by Richard (1979).

Long's (1974) multiperiod model relates stock returns to the market portfolio, inflation, and the term structure of interest rates in a relation similar to equation 10.3. Sharpe (1977) decomposes the market beta of the original CAPM into a number of betas associated with portfolios or factors that may represent economic variables. In this model each portfolio or factor contributes to the market's expected excess return over the riskless rate in proportion to the overall risk of the market. Thus this multibeta model differs somewhat from equation 10.3 in that the market portfolio itself does not feature in the model, but all the betas are assumed to be related to the market beta.[8]

While the multibeta CAPMs relax some of the more unrealistic assumptions of the traditional CAPM, they also still retain some of the same underlying assumptions as the original CAPM and in some models the concept of a market portfolio. For this reason these models are also subject to some of the limitations and criticisms of the original CAPM discussed in Chapter 9. In particular, to facilitate use of the multibeta CAPM in practice, the market beta and the betas associated with other factors or state variables have to be estimated. Hence the problems of identification of factors or state variables and estimation of betas discussed in Chapter 9 also apply. This issue is examined in greater detail in the next chapter.

Because the empirical and practical implications of the multibeta CAPM and the APT are virtually the same (Fogler 1982, Sharpe 1984, and Shanken 1985), the treatment of the estimation of betas and the use of the models for practical investment management is deferred until Chapter 11 after the APM is introduced.[9]

The Consumption-Based CAPM

Breeden (1979) extended Merton's model by developing a multiperiod continuous-time model in which the multibeta pricing model reduces to a single-beta model whose beta is derived from aggregate consumption rather than the market portfolio or several state variables. Breeden argued that in equilibrium the marginal utility of consumption must equal the marginal utility of wealth and so the optimal portfolio and consumption decisions of individuals will be such that the expected return on an asset,

---

[8] In this sense the model is closer to the APT. As will be discussed in Chapter 11, there is little difference, especially in an empirical context, between a multibeta form of the CAPM such as Sharpe's and the equilibrium arbitrage pricing theory (Shanken 1985).

[9] This deferment is also partly because the APT is generally perceived to be *the* multifactor model, while the CAPM is usually thought of as a single-factor model, even though the multibeta versions of the original CAPM were conceptualized or developed before or about the same time as the APT (e.g., Rosenberg 1974, Stone 1974, Rosenberg and Guy 1976, and Sharpe 1977).

$E(r_i)$, can be expressed as a linear asset pricing relation (the consumption-based CAPM) as follows:

(10.4) $$E(r_i) = r_f + [E(r_C) - r_f]\beta_{iC}$$

where $E(r_C)$ is the expected growth rate in per capita aggregate consumption (or the expected return on an asset that is perfectly correlated with aggregate consumption), and β_{iC} is the consumption beta of asset i. This is a measure of systematic risk defined in the same manner as the market beta, that is, a measure of the asset's covariance with the change in aggregate consumption:

(10.5) $$\beta_{iC} = [COV(r_i, r_C)] / VAR (r_C)$$

The consumption beta is therefore the slope or coefficient of the regression of the asset's return on the growth rate of per capita consumption (similar to the market model beta in Chapter 5).

Thus, in relation to the multibeta model discussed in the previous section, the hedging of shifts in consumption and investment opportunities defined by many state variables is collapsed into just one variable, aggregate real consumption. Breeden argues that individuals will adjust their consumption and investment decisions in response to changes in the state variables, which are captured adequately by changes in aggregate consumption. Therefore, the consumption beta is argued to be as good a measure of systematic risk as the market beta because the growth rate in aggregate consumption is argued to be proportional to the market portfolio return.

The appeal of the consumption CAPM (CCAPM) when it was developed as an alternative to both the original and multibeta CAPMs was that it is more amenable to empirical testing because it overcomes the problem of identifying (1) several state variables that are not observable and/or (2) the unobservable market portfolio or an adequate proxy, since consumption data are generally available and "the consumption measures available cover a greater fraction of the true consumption variable than the fraction that the market portfolio measures cover of the true market portfolio" (Breeden 1979). However, there have been difficulties with regard to suitability of the available consumption data as well as questions about testability of the model in general (Cornell 1981; Breeden, Gibbons, and Litzenberger 1989; Ferson and Harvey 1992; and Fama 1992). These are discussed in the context of empirical tests of the model in Chapter 12.

The use of the CCAPM follows the same lines as for the original CAPM. Historical consumption betas may be estimated from regressions of security returns on per capita growth rate in aggregate real consumption, as with market betas. However, perhaps because of the problems associated with consumption data and the relatively slow pace of empirical work on the model (there is no evidence that consumption betas can perform better than market betas), the CCAPM has not gained widespread appeal in investment practice. The empirical evidence to date does not provide strong support for the CCAPM compared with the traditional CAPM and the multibeta models (Mankiw and Shapiro 1986; Chen, Roll, and Ross 1986).

INTERNATIONAL ASSET PRICING MODELS

The extension of asset pricing theory to an international setting follows from the concept of international portfolio diversification discussed in Chapter 8. With financial markets becoming increasingly globalized, if investors are able to diversify internationally, then the principle of optimal portfolio selection can be extended to an international context. An international asset pricing model has to take into account numerous problems not encountered in developing the one-country, or domestic, models discussed thus far: (1) Because there are barriers to international investment, the concept of one world capital market in which prices are freely determined is not tenable. (2) Countries have different currencies, and the influence of exchange rate movements has to be considered. (3) Investors in different countries do not have the same tastes and do not consume the same basket of goods; also, while some goods are traded internationally, others are not. (4) Inflation rates change stochastically and are different across countries. (5) Investors in different countries face different investment opportunity sets. For these reasons, extension of the CAPM to the international context becomes much more complex, particularly in regard to homogeneity of expectations and the portfolio choices of investors. Inevitably, international asset pricing models have to make simplifying assumptions about these problems in addition to the assumptions of the domestic CAPM.

Solnik (1974) pioneered the derivation of an equilibrium international asset pricing model based on Merton's (1973) intertemporal CAPM.[10] He developed the following pricing relationship analogous to the original CAPM in the framework of an integrated one-world capital market:

(10.6)
$$E(r_i) = r_{fi} + [E(r_{WM}) - r_{fW}]\beta_{Wi}$$

where $E(r_{WM})$ is the expected return on the world market portfolio; r_{fi} is the risk-free rate of the country of security i; r_{fW} is the average international risk-free rate; and β_{Wi} is the international systematic risk of security i, which reflects the asset's covariance with the world market portfolio.

[10] Grauer, Litzenberger, and Stehle (1976) also derive a model of international asset pricing under different assumptions.

Clearly, the concept of a world market portfolio in a segregated world capital market is not realistic. It is also subject to the problems discussed in Chapter 9 of the market portfolio. In an alternative approach, Stulz (1981b) extended Breeden's (1979) consumption-based CAPM to the international context. In this model, analogous to Breeden's asset pricing relation (equation 10.4), an asset's expected return is related to its covariance with changes in world real consumption, rather than a world market portfolio. Other models have sought to relax the assumption that there is a fully integrated international capital market by incorporating barriers in international CAPMs (Black 1974; Stulz 1981a; Errunza and Losq 1985, 1989; Eun and Janakiraman 1986; Gultekin, Gultekin, and Penanti 1989; and Hietala 1989).

Multibeta versions of international asset pricing models have been developed in the context of the arbitrage pricing model; these models are examined in Chapter 11. The difficulties involved in the empirical testing of the various versions of the international asset pricing models are discussed in Chapter 12.

SUMMARY

Alternative asset pricing models are (1) extensions of the original CAPM achieved by relaxing some assumptions and/or (2) models of a different form that are derived using alternative approaches and assumptions. Multibeta pricing models extend the intuition of the original CAPM (i.e., the expected return–systematic risk relation) by linking asset prices to the investment opportunity set as defined by economic state variables, either in lieu of or in addition to the market portfolio. This linkage provides a more realistic and appealing framework for asset pricing and overcomes some of the deficiencies of the CAPM of Chapter 9. The performance of these alternative models compared with that of the original CAPM, in an empirical sense and in applications in investment management, is discussed in the next two chapters.

Questions

1. What are the key similarities and differences between the original CAPM of Chapter 9 and (1) the zero-beta CAPM and (2) the consumption-based CAPM?

2. Explain the difference between Black's zero-beta portfolio and a riskless asset.

3. Why is a multiperiod asset pricing model preferable to a single-period model?

4. What differentiates multibeta asset pricing models from single-beta models?

5. What is the possible relationship between the consumption-based CAPM and a multifactor model?

6. Do the extensions or alternative forms of the CAPM overcome the problems and limitations of the original CAPM?

7. What are the major problems involved in extending asset pricing models to the international context?

REFERENCES

Alexander, G. J., and J. C. Francis. 1986. *Portfolio Analysis.* Englewood Cliffs, NJ: Prentice Hall.

Black, F. 1972. Capital market equilibrium with restricted borrowing. *Journal of Business* 45:444–455.

Black, F. 1974. International capital market equilibrium with investment barriers. *Journal of Financial Economics* 1:337–352.

Black, F., M. Jensen, and M. Scholes. 1972. The capital asset pricing model: Some empirical findings. In *Studies in the theory of capital markets,* M. Jensen, ed. New York: Praeger.

Bonser-Neal, C., G. Brauer, R. Neal, and S. Wheatley. 1990. International investment restrictions and closed-end country fund prices. *Journal of Finance* 45:523–548.

Bossaerts, P., and R. Green. 1989. A general equilibrium model of changing risk premia. Theory and tests. *Review of Financial Studies,* vol 2, 467–493.

Breeden, D. T. 1979. An intertemporal asset pricing model with stochastic consumption and investment opportunities. *Journal of Financial Economics* 7:265–296.

Breeden, D. T., M. R. Gibbons, and R. H. Litzenberger. 1989. Empirical tests of the consumption-oriented capital asset pricing model. *Journal of Finance* 44:231–262.

Burmeister, E., and M. McElroy. 1988. Joint estimation of factor sensitivities and risk premia for the APT. *Journal of Finance* 43:721–733.

Chan, K. C., N. Chen, and D. Hsieh. 1985. An exploratory investigation of the firm size effect. *Journal of Financial Economics* 14:451–471.

Chen, N., R. Roll, and S. A. Ross. 1986. Economic forces and the stock market. *Journal of Business* 59:383–403.

Connor, G. 1984. A unified beta pricing theory. *Journal of Economic Theory* 34:13–31.

Connor, G., and R. Korajczyk. 1989. An intertemporal equilibrium beta pricing model. *Review of Financial Studies* 2:373–392.

Copeland, T., and J. F. Weston. 1988. *Financial Theory and Corporate Policy.* Reading, MA: Addison-Wesley.

Cornell, B. 1981. The consumption-based asset pricing model: A note on potential tests and applications. *Journal of Financial Economics* 9:103–108.

Cox, J., J. Ingersoll, and S. Ross. 1985. An intertemporal general equilibrium model of asset prices. *Econometrica* 53:363–384.

Elton, E., and M. Gruber. 1984. Non-standard CAPMs and the market portfolio. *Journal of Finance* 39:911–924.

Errunza, V., and E. Losq. 1985. International asset pricing under mild segmentation. Theory and test. *Journal of Finance* 40:105–124.

Errunza, V., and E. Losq. 1989. Capital flow controls, international asset pricing and investor's welfare: a multicountry framework. *Journal of Finance* 44:1025–1038.

Eun, C., and S. Janakiraman. 1986. A model of international asset pricing with a constraint on the foreign equity ownership. *Journal of Finance* 41:847–914.

Fama, E. 1976. *Foundations of finance.* New York: Basic Books.

Fama, E. 1991. Efficient capital markets II. *Journal of Finance* 46:1575–1617.

Fama, E., and K. French. 1992. The cross-section of expected stock returns. *Journal of Finance* 47:427–465.

Fama, E., and J. MacBeth. 1973. Risk, return and equilibrium: Empirical tests. *Journal of Political Economy* 81:607–635.

Ferson, W. 1992. Theory and empirical testing of asset pricing models. Working paper, University of Chicago Graduate School of Business. In *The finance handbook,* R. Jarrow, W. T. Ziemba, and V. Maksimovic, eds. Amsterdam: North Holland Publishing Co (in press).

Ferson, W., and C. Harvey. 1991. The variation of economic risk premiums. *Journal of Political Economy* 99:385–415.

Ferson, W., and C. Harvey. 1992. Seasonality and consumption-based asset pricing. *Journal of Finance* 47:511–552.

Fogler, H. 1982. Common sense on CAPM, APT, and correlated residuals. *Journal of Finance* 36:325–335.

Grauer, F., R. Litzenberger, and R. Stehle. 1976. Sharing rules and equilibrium in an international capital market under uncertainty. *Journal of Financial Economics* 3:233–256.

Gultekin, M. N., N. B. Gultekin, and A. Penanti. 1989. Capital controls and international capital market segmentation: The evidence from the Japanese and American stock markets. *Journal of Finance* 44:849–870.

Harvey, C. 1991. The world price of covariance risk. *Journal of Finance* 46:111–158.

Hietala, P. K. 1989. Asset pricing in partially segmented markets. Evidence from the Finnish markets. *Journal of Finance* 44:697–718.

Isimbabi, M. J. 1992. Comovements of world securities markets, international portfolio diversification, and asset returns. In *Recent developments in international banking and finance.* vol 6, S. J. Khoury, ed.

Jarrow, R. A. 1988. *Finance Theory.* Englewood Cliffs, NJ: Prentice Hall.

Kazemi, H. 1988. A multiperiod asset-pricing model with unobservable market portfolio: A note. *Journal of Finance* 43:1015–1024.

Korajczyk, R., and C. Viallet. 1989. An empirical investigation of international asset pricing. *Review of Financial Studies* 2:553–585.

Lee, C. F., C. Wu, and K. C. J. Wei. 1990. The heterogenous investment horizon and the capital asset pricing model: Theory and implications. *Journal of Financial and Quantitative Analysis* 25:361–376.

Levy, H., and P. A. Samuelson. 1992. The capital asset pricing model with diverse holding periods. *Management Science* 38:1527–1542.

Long, J. B. 1974. Stock prices, inflation, and the term structure of interest rates. *Journal of Financial Economics* 1:131–170.

Mankiw, N. G., and M. D. Shapiro. 1986. Risk and return: Consumption beta versus market beta. *The Review of Economics and Statistics* 48:452–459.

Mayers, D. 1973. Nonmarketable assets and the determination of capital asset prices in the absence of a riskless asset. *Journal of Business* 46:258–267.

Mayers, D., and E. Rice. 1979. Measuring portfolio performance and the empirical content of asset pricing models. *Journal of Financial Economics* 4:3–28.

Merton, R. C. 1971. Optimum consumption and portfolio rules in a continuous-time model. *Journal of Economic Theory* 3:373–413.

Merton, R. C. 1972. An analytic derivation of the efficient frontier. *Journal of Financial and Quantitative Analysis* 7:1851–1872.

Merton, R. C. 1973. An intertemporal capital asset pricing model. *Econometrica* 41:867–887.

Merton, R. C. 1987. A simple model of capital market equilibrium with incomplete information. *Journal of Finance* 42:483–510.

Reisman, H. 1992. Intertemporal arbitrage pricing theory. *Review of Financial Studies* 5:105–122.

Richard, S. F. 1979. A generalized capital asset pricing model. In *Portfolio theory. 25 years after.* E. Elton and M. Gruber, eds. Amsterdam: North Holland.

Rosenberg, B. 1974. Extra-market components of covariance in security returns. *Journal of Financial and Quantitative Analysis.* March, 263–274.

Rosenberg, B., and J. Guy. 1976. Prediction of beta from investment fundamentals. Part one. *Financial Analysts Journal.* May-June, 60–72.

Ross, S. 1976. The arbitrage theory of capital asset pricing. *Journal of Economic Theory* 13:341–360.

Shanken, J. 1985. Multi-beta CAPM or equilibrium-APT? A reply. *Journal of Finance* 40:1189–1196.

Shanken, J. 1990. Intertemporal asset pricing: An empirical investigation. *Journal of Econometrics* 45:99–120.

Sharpe, W. 1977. The capital asset pricing model: A multi-beta interpretation. In *Financial decision making under uncertainty.* H. Levy and M. Sarnat, eds. New York: Academic Press.

Sharpe, W. F. 1991. Capital asset prices with and without negative holdings. *Journal of Finance* 46:489–509.

Solnik, B. 1974. An equilibrium model of the international capital market. *Journal of Economic Theory* 8:500–524.

Solnik, B. 1988. *International investments.* Reading, MA: Addison-Wesley.

Smith, R. T. 1993. Heterogenous beliefs and learning about the expected return in a market for a short-lived asset. *The Financial Review* 28:1–24.

Stone, B. K. 1974. Systematic interest rate risk in a two-index model of returns. *Journal of Financial and Quantitative Analysis* 9:709–721.

Stulz, R. 1981a. On the effects of barriers to international investment. *Journal of Finance* 36:923–934.

Stulz, R. 1981b. A model of international asset pricing. *Journal of Financial Economics* 9:383–406.

Stulz, R. 1984. Pricing capital assets in an international setting: An introduction. *Journal of International Business Studies.*

C H A P T E R *11*

The Arbitrage Pricing Model

Introduction

The arbitrage pricing theory (APT), originally developed by Ross (1976a,b), attempts to provide a model that explains asset pricing better than the original CAPM. Over the past decade the APT has emerged as the alternative theory of asset pricing to the CAPM. The appeal of the APT is that it is a more general model whose derivation is based on more intuitive and less restrictive underlying assumptions than the original CAPM. However, the CAPM and the APT are not inconsistent, and the original CAPM can be obtained as a special case of the more general APT under certain conditions.

In this chapter we present the basic APT model and discuss how the model can be applied in investment practice. As with the CAPM, we also highlight some of the limitations of the model in investment management applications. As will be seen, in an empirical sense and for practical applications there is no significant difference between the APT and the multibeta models discussed in Chapter 10.

251

The APT Model

The APT assumes that investors believe homogeneously that asset returns are randomly generated according to a k-factor model, which can be depicted as follows:

$$\textbf{(11.1)} \qquad r_i = E(r_i) + \beta_{i1}F_1 + \ldots\ldots + \beta_{ik}F_k + e_i,$$

where r_i is the (random) return on asset i; $E(r_i)$ is the expected return on asset i; F_j is systematic (common) factor j ($j = 1, \ldots, k$); β_{ij} is a measure of the sensitivity of asset i to factor j; and e_i is the idiosyncratic component of return, unique to asset i.

In the factor model of equation 11.1, it is assumed that there are k systematic factors that are mainly responsible for the movements in the prices of all assets. These factors are common to all assets; the components of return due to unsystematic factors such as firm-specific or industry events are represented by e_i. The difference between the actual return realized on asset i, r_i, and the expected return, $E(r_i)$, is due to the influence of the k factors, $F_1, F_2, \ldots, F_k$. Since $E(r_i)$ at the beginning of a period already incorporates expectations, the k factors are largely unanticipated, that is, their influence on returns arises from unanticipated events or surprises. If the factors are all zero, that is, there are no surprises during a period, then the actual return will be equal to the expected return. The k factors are random; therefore the expected value of each factor is 0: $E(F_j) = 0$. Similarly, the expected value of the idiosyncratic component of return is 0: $E(e_i) = 0$. Also, since the idio-syncratic component of return for each asset is unique to that asset, e_i is independent of e_j for all i and j: $E(e_i, e_j) = 0$; $i \neq j$. Similarly, the factors are assumed to be independent of each other [$E(F_i, F_j) = 0$, $i \neq j$] and independent of e_i: $E(e_i, F_j) = 0$ for all i and j.

The systematic factors would be expected to be related to fundamental economic factors such as economic activity, interest rates, and inflation, which have economy-wide effects on all assets or firms to varying degrees. However, the APT does not address the question of how many factors there are and what the factors are. This issue is addressed in empirical tests of the APT in Chapter 12.

In the derivation of the original APT other assumptions include the following:
1. Asset markets are perfectly competitive and frictionless.
2. All investors have homogenous beliefs that returns are generated according to the model depicted in equation 11.1.
3. Investors have monotonically increasing concave utility functions.
4. The number of assets existing in the capital market from which portfolios are formed is much larger than the number of factors.

Ross's derivation was based on the intuition that (1) in an efficient market, and consistent with market equilibrium, no riskless arbitrage profit opportunities can exist and (2) only a few common factors are priced for large, well-diversified portfolios.[1] The resulting pricing relation expresses the expected return on an asset i in a linear relationship with the k-factor risks as follows:

(11.2) $$E(r_i) = \lambda_0 + \beta_{i1}\lambda_1 + \beta_{i2}\lambda_2 + \ldots\ldots + \beta_{ik}\lambda_k$$

where λ_j is the risk premium required by investors per unit of the risk due to factor j as measured by the β_{ij}. A zero-beta asset or portfolio, that is, one with no sensitivities to all the k factors (the β_{ij}s are all 0) and hence no systematic risk, will have an expected zero-beta rate of return, λ_0. Alternatively, λ_0 may denote the riskless rate of return if a riskless asset exists.

Thus in the APT pricing relation (equation 11.2), the expected return on an asset is dependent on its sensitivities to each of the k risk factors (the β_{ij}s) and the risk premium associated with each of the factors. The β_{ij}s (factor coefficients, or factor loadings) are proportional to the covariance of the asset's return with the factors, much the same as the market beta is a measure of the covariance of an asset's return with the market portfolio in the CAPM (Chapter 9). In a large market with many assets from which well-diversified portfolios can be formed, the influence of unsystematic factors such as firm-specific or industry characteristics represented by the idiosyncratic component of return, e_i in equation 11.1, are assumed to be fully diversifiable. Thus the risk of an asset or portfolio, hence its expected return, is defined primarily by the effect of the k factors, and cross-sectional variations in asset returns result from the differences in the sensitivities of assets to each of the factors depending on the assets' characteristics.

From equation 11.2 a portfolio, $p1$, which has unit sensitivity only to factor 1 and no sensitivity to any other factor (i.e., $\beta_{i1} = 1$, $\beta_{i2} = \beta_{i3} = \ldots = \beta_{ik} = 0$), will have its expected return given by

(11.3) $$E(r_{p1}) = \lambda_0 + \lambda_1,$$

from which derives

(11.4) $$\lambda_1 = E(r_{p1}) - \lambda_0.$$

That is, the risk premium for factor 1 can be interpreted as the expected excess return over the riskless rate or the zero-beta rate on the portfolio

---

[1] Subsequent refinements and extensions of the APT have used different sets of assumptions and/or different logic to arrive at alternative derivations of the APT pricing relation (Huberman 1982; Chamberlain and Rothschild 1983; Dyvbig 1983; Grinblatt and Titman 1983; Connor 1984; Ingersoll 1984; Wei 1988; Reisman 1988, 1992a; Connor and Korajczyk 1989; Shanken 1992; Handa and Linn 1991). For a concise treatment of various approaches to deriving the APT, see Jarrow (1988).

that has unit systematic risk on factor *1* and no systematic risk on all other factors. A portfolio such as *p1* is a *pure factor,* or *factor-mimicking,* portfolio.

Equation 11.2 can therefore be rewritten in terms of expected return on the *k* pure factor portfolios as follows:

(11.5) $E(r_i) = \lambda_0 + \beta_{i1}[E(r_{p1}) - \lambda_0] + \beta_{i2}[E(r_{p2}) - \lambda_0] + \ldots + \beta_{ik}[E(r_{pk}) - \lambda_0],$

which expresses the expected excess return on an asset *i* in terms of the expected excess returns on the pure factor portfolios and the respective βs.

With equation 11.5 the expected return on an asset can be calculated if the expected return on the pure factor portfolios and the λ_0 are known. For example, suppose there are three systematic risk factors and the expected returns on the pure factor portfolios of these factors are 10 percent, 13 percent, and 15 percent, respectively. If λ_0 is assumed to be the risk-free rate and it is 4 percent, then from equation 11.4 the expected risk premiums on the three factors are, respectively,

$$E(r_{p1}) - \lambda_0 = 10\% - 4\% = 6\%$$
$$E(r_{p2}) - \lambda_0 = 13\% - 4\% = 9\%$$
$$E(r_{p3}) - \lambda_0 = 15\% - 4\% = 11\%.$$

Assume that $\beta_{i1} = 0.50$, $\beta_{i2} = -2.00$ and $\beta_{i3} = 1.60$ for a security. Then according to equation 11.5, the expected return on this security is

$$E(r_i) = 4\% + 0.5(6\%) + -2.00(9\%) + 1.60(11\%) = 6.6\%.$$

As evident from this example, determining the expected return on a security depends on (1) precise estimation of the βs, and (2) identification of systematic factors and estimation of the expected returns on the pure factor portfolios. These issues are discussed in relation to the validity and practical applicability of the APT model later in this chapter.

Construction of a Pure Factor Portfolio

With a large and diverse set of assets with different βs, it is possible to find assets that can be combined to form portfolios with either unit sensitivities or no sensitivities to certain factors ($\beta_{ij} = 1$ or $\beta_{ij} = 0$) by investing in assets whose βs are known in appropriate proportions. For example, assume there are only two systematic risk factors and that four assets, A, B, C, D, have sensitivities to these factors as follows:

| | ASSETS | | | |
	A	B	C	D
β_1	0.50	−1.90	−3.30	3.00
β_2	0.70	−2.90	2.30	−0.40

If the investor forms a portfolio by investing 10 percent of available wealth in A, 10 percent in B, 20 percent in C, and 60 percent in D, the weighted sensitivity of this portfolio to factor *1* will be one:

$$\beta_{p1} = 0.1(0.50) + 0.1\ (-1.90) + 0.2\ (-3.30) + 0.6\ (3.00) = 1$$

The sensitivity of this portfolio to factor 2 will be zero:

$$\beta_{p2} = 0.1(0.70) + 0.1\ (-2.90) + 0.2\ (2.30) + 0.6\ (-0.40) = 0$$

Therefore it is theoretically possible to construct from a large number of assets a portfolio that has unit sensitivity to one factor, no sensitivities to all other factors, and negligible idiosyncratic return—that is, a "pure factor" portfolio.

A One-Factor APT

Even though the APT in a general sense implies the existence of more than one systematic factor, a one-factor APT pricing relation is conceivable. For example, it may be believed that one economic factor (e.g., a measure of business or economic activity such as GNP) or a market factor (such as movements in the SP500) captures all the significant sources of risk relevant for asset pricing. If this one factor is F_1, then equation 11.5 becomes

(11.6) $$E(r_i) - \lambda_0 = \beta_{i1}[E(r_{p1}) - \lambda_0]$$

or

(11.7) $$E(r_i) = \lambda_0 + \beta_{i1}[E(r_{p1}) - \lambda_0]$$

Equation 11.7 can be depicted graphically, as shown in Figure 11.1. The expected return on asset i, $E(r_i)$, corresponds to β_{i1}, and when $\beta_1 = 1$, the expected return is that of the factor 1 portfolio. When $\beta_1 = 0$, the expected return is λ_0, as shown.

However, much of the empirical evidence on the APT so far suggests the existence of more than one factor (see Chapter 12); hence the APT is usually perceived as a multifactor model. (The discussion in this chapter generally assumes a multibeta APT pricing relation.)

When there is more than one factor, Figure 11.1 becomes a hyperplane with additional axes corresponding to the other factor betas in a multibeta pricing relation. You may have noticed that Figure 11.1 is somewhat similar to the security market line of the CAPM (Figure 9.2). Indeed, the APT is consistent with the original CAPM (Chapter 9) and its multibeta extensions (Chapter 10), as discussed next.

FIGURE 11.1

Expected Return in a
One-Factor APT
Model

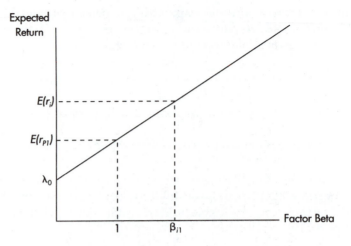

THE RELATION BETWEEN THE APT AND THE CAPM

If the single factor in the preceding discussion is assumed to be represented by the market portfolio (defined either as the true market portfolio or the market factor or a proxy such as the SP500 index, as discussed in Chapter 9) whose expected return is $E(r_M)$, then equation 11.7 can be rewritten as

(11.8) $$E(r_i) = \lambda_0 + \beta_{iM}[E(r_M) - \lambda_0],$$

which is the same as equation 10.1, the pricing relation for the zero-beta CAPM, where $\lambda_0 = E(r_z) =$ the expected return on the zero-beta portfolio.

Alternatively, if a riskless asset exists and r_J is the return on this asset, then r_J can replace λ_0 and equation 11.7 can also be written as

(11.9) $$E(r_i) = r_F + \beta_{iM}[E(r_M) - r_F],$$

which is the same as equation 9.11, the original CAPM equation. Thus, the CAPM equation is arrived at via the more general APT pricing relation. Note that this is achieved under the different set of assumptions of the APT. Also, equation 11.9 does not require $E(r_M)$ to be the expected return on the mean-variance efficient market portfolio, as does the CAPM. $E(r_M)$ can therefore be the expected return on a market index if it is considered that market movements reflect unexpected changes in any systematic factors that influence asset returns.

At the time of its development, proponents of the APT argued that the APT was superior to the original CAPM because (1) the underlying assumptions of the APT are less restrictive and more realistic and (2) the

APT's empirical implications make it more amenable to empirical testing than the CAPM.[2] Such arguments are in regard to the following:

1. While both theories make the realistic assumptions that investors prefer more wealth to less and that they are risk averse, the quadratic utility assumption of the original CAPM (Chapter 7) is much more restrictive.

2. The APT does not require the assumption of multivariate normal distribution of returns, as does the original CAPM. In the APT no assumptions are made about the probability distribution of returns, and investors are not assumed to select portfolios on the basis of expected return and variance or standard deviation. Therefore, with the APT there is no drawback in empirical tests due to the nonnormality that is sometimes observed in the empirical distribution of security returns.

3. The APT does not require the existence of the market portfolio. Hence the difficulties associated with the market portfolio as discussed extensively in Chapter 9, such as identification of the market portfolio or a suitable proxy and the requirement that it be mean-variance efficient, are avoided. Thus $E(r_M)$ in equation 11.9 need not be the expected return on the true market portfolio but rather the expected return on a portfolio (e.g., a market index) that is considered to be the adequate proxy for the underlying systematic risk factors. Thus the CAPM derived in this manner may be perceived to be more consistent with the intuition that has made the CAPM a popular model, that is, the observed tendency for asset prices to move together. This is manifested as the empirical phenomenon of common variation in asset returns captured in a single or market factor, as depicted in the single-index, or market, model (Chapter 5).

4. The APT does not require the restrictive assumption of the existence of a risk-free asset and a riskless rate at which lending and borrowing are undertaken.

5. The APT is more general than the original single-beta CAPM in the sense that it explicitly allows for several risk factors. This may be considered more realistic than the original CAPM's single beta, since one measure may not fully capture systematic risk factors. (Obviously, this distinction does not apply to the multibeta versions of the CAPM).

6. While the original CAPM is a one-period model, the APT holds as a multiperiod model. Again, this distinction does not apply to the multiperiod CAPM versions discussed in Chapter 9.

However, in certain respects the APT also makes certain assumptions

---

[2]See for example, Roll and Ross (1980). The APT, especially the claim that it is more empirically testable, has, however, been criticized. See, for example, Shanken (1982, 1985).

and arrives at implications similar to those of the CAPM, namely: (1) the assumption of perfect and frictionless asset markets; (2) the assumption that investors have homogeneous expectations; (3) the linear relation between return and risk; and (4) the notion that security return prices are solely based on nondiversifiable risk.

Most of the above distinctions apply only when the original CAPM and the original APT are being compared. More recent theoretical work on asset pricing, such as the studies cited in footnote 1, has tended to blur such distinctions, following the development of more general multibeta asset pricing models that use different sets of assumptions. These in many cases are less restrictive than those of the original models, and from them the original CAPM and APT models can be obtained as special cases. For example, Handa and Linn (1991) derive the APT under the assumption that investors have heterogenous beliefs about asset returns, and Wei (1988) derives a model that seeks to unify the CAPM and APT; in it the market portfolio is one of the factors in a multibeta asset pricing relation. Shanken (1985), Connor (1984), Sharpe (1984), Jarrow and Rudd (1983), and Grinblatt and Titman (1987) discuss the theoretical and/or empirical consistencies and equivalence of the CAPM and the APT.

It can also be seen that the APT equation, 11.2 or 11.5, is equivalent to the multiperiod CAPM equation, 10.3. The state variables in the latter can be represented by the APT factors. This equivalence illustrates the empirical consistencies between the multibeta versions of the CAPM and the APT. Hence the use of the APT in portfolio management discussed shortly applies to multibeta asset pricing models in general.

WHAT ARE THE APT FACTORS?

The APT does not say anything about the nature of the pervasive factors or how many there are. This issue has therefore been the subject of empirical tests. Because the APT makes the underlying assumption that the factors are pervasive, the factors should represent economy-wide sources of risk that influence the performance of firms and therefore returns. Empirical researchers have used two major approaches in attempts to determine the nature and number of factors (Chapter 12):

1. *Factor analysis* and *principal component analysis* are statistical procedures used to extract factors from the historical returns of a group of securities.
2. A set of economic and financial factors judged to represent pervasive sources of risk are examined in relation to asset returns using regression analysis to determine if they provide evidence consistent with the model.

In the first approach the factors extracted are in the form of security returns. In the second approach the factors are proxied by economic and financial variables. Some of the variables that have been examined include the following:

1. Indicators of real economic activity, for example consumption expenditure, industrial production, gross national product, money supply, and growth rate of final sales or profits.
2. Short-term and long-term interest rate changes.
3. Inflation.
4. Oil price changes.
5. A stock market index.

While empirical tests have found combinations of some of these variables to be consistent with the APT and multibeta asset pricing models in general, no specific set of factors has been determined to be the one that absolutely and consistently explains cross-sectional variations in expected returns. Because the APT is a relatively new model, only a few empirical studies (Chapter 12) have been undertaken, and the empirical literature on multifactor asset pricing models is still evolving. However, it is not surprising that the variables listed above should be found to be significant in determining expected returns, since they influence the performance of all firms. Unexpected news about the above economic variables usually affects security prices, consistent with equation 11.1.

APPLICATION OF THE APT AND MULTIBETA PRICING MODELS IN PORTFOLIO MANAGEMENT

The application of the APT and multibeta pricing models in general in investment practice parallels that of the original CAPM. As pointed out in Chapter 9, if asset prices conformed to the equilibrium model, then each asset would be priced according to the model, and there would be no reason to undertake active portfolio management. Thus practical application of the model rests on the presumption that in disequilibrium the market prices of certain securities are not the equilibrium prices in accordance with the asset pricing model; that is, the securities are mispriced. The actions of investors seeking to profit from such disequilibrium will therefore result in prices adjusting to their equilibrium level. For instance, in the example given earlier, the equilibrium expected return on the security is 6.6 percent, according to the APT. However, the investor who arrives at the conclusion that the security's current price is such that its expected return is, say, 8 percent, can undertake transactions to profit from the mispricing, as discussed in Chapter 9.

Obviously, the application of the APT in this manner is subject to limitations similar to those discussed for the CAPM in Chapter 9: to determine the equilibrium expected return on a security, the β-coefficients for each factor and the expected returns on pure factor portfolios (the λs) have to be estimated. The problem of estimating the βs and λs parallels that of the estimation of the market beta and the expected market return in the CAPM. Though the problems associated with identification of the market portfolio and estimation of its return do not arise in the APT, the factor betas are measured with error. Also, temporal structural changes in the economy may result in temporal differences in the relative degrees of the influence of the factors, and so the βs and λs associated with economic and financial factors may vary significantly from period to period.[3] Therefore, the prediction of factor coefficients and the risk premiums, even when the "correct" set of factors can be ascertained, is subject to significant error. Furthermore, the set of factors may change from period to period, for example, over stages of the business cycle, different monetary policy regimes, and different inflationary or interest rate environments. Thus, in the absence of a specific set of factors that holds for every period, an investor or analyst may have to determine the appropriate set of factors for the investment horizon being considered. Since more than one β is being estimated in a multibeta model, the problem of estimation error and nonstationarity of the coefficients may be even more pronounced than in the case of the one-factor (market) beta CAPM. Thus, the application of the APT should be undertaken with the same caution and judgment discussed extensively in Chapter 9.

In an alternative (passive) approach to the use of the APT in portfolio management, the investor could construct a portfolio with the desired optimal exposures to each of the systematic risk factors, given that a set of APT factors has been identified. This strategy is appropriate for large portfolios containing several different assets, because it takes advantage of the fact that different types of assets and portfolios have different degrees of sensitivity to the factors. For example, bonds and stocks at certain times may have opposite sensitivity to interest rate changes; utility stocks are highly sensitive to interest rates compared with the average stock; similarly, some retail stocks have higher than average sensitivity to inflation, and such sensitivity may be opposite to that of gold or petroleum stocks; cyclical stocks are more sensitive to changes in the business cycle than others such as utility or food stocks.[4] Thus, as the example on the construction of pure factor portfolios shows, with a large number of diverse assets to choose from, portfolios can be constructed to achieve the desired exposures to the systematic factors by holding long and short positions in the different assets in appropriate proportions. Because of the size of such a portfolio, the idiosyncratic component of risk will be diversified away.

In an active portfolio management strategy, a portfolio may be changed periodically depending on the investor or portfolio manager's forecasts of *unanticipated* movements in a factor. For example, if the average or

---

[3] Ferson and Harvey (1991) provide some evidence on the variation of βs and risk premiums over time.

[4] See Berry, Burmeister, and McElroy (1988) for an analysis of the sensitivities of several industry groups to risk factors.

consensus forecast is that the inflation rate will be 3 percent (expected inflation rate) and the investor thinks that it will be 1 percent, the unanticipated change in inflation forecast by the investor will be –2 percent. A portfolio strategy to take advantage of the unanticipated change if the investor's forecast turns out to be correct can be designed by reconstituting the portfolio to have the appropriate inflation beta.

Clearly, while the APT's more general nature and use of factors make it more intuitively appealing than the CAPM, its usefulness in investment practice is subject to the limitations of an equilibrium model, as is the CAPM. The APT's practical appeal lies in the strategic design of portfolios to take advantage of movements in factors, but this approach can be accomplished with the use of general factor models, which are not equilibrium models and do not require the factors to be pervasive. In any case the identification of the systematic APT factors is still a subject of ongoing empirical research (Chapter 12), and the estimation of λs and βs as well as determination of the desired exposure to factor risks for different investors constitute major difficulties in the application of the APT and multibeta models in practical investment management.[5]

INTERNATIONAL ARBITRAGE PRICING THEORY

As is the case with the (international) CAPM (Chapter 10), the APT has been extended to the international framework (Solnik 1983; Ross and Walsh 1982; Levine 1989; and Ikeda 1991). As with the international CAPM, several additional assumptions are made in the derivation of the international APT (IAPT) about differences in currencies, investor preferences, inflation rates, and exchange rate uncertainty. In the same way as the one-country APT does not require the identification of a market portfolio, the IAPT avoids the problem of identification of a world market portfolio required in the case of the international CAPM.

The IAPT pricing relation is similar to equation 11.2, and where national, industry and firm-specific factors are assumed to be completely diversifiable in the context of an integrated world capital market, the βs and λs are associated with only pervasive international factors. However, primarily because of barriers across countries, national factors dominate security returns and the relative influence of international factors is limited. The IAPT and indeed international asset pricing models in general are not much more than theoretical concepts. Empirical research on the influence of international factors in asset pricing (Chapter 12) is limited and is still evolving.

---

[5] See Brealey (1990) for a detailed discussion of the difficulties of applying theoretical equilibrium models such as the APT in investment practice.

Summary

The APT, originally developed as an alternative to the CAPM, is more general and utilizes less restrictive assumptions than the original CAPM. However, the APT and CAPM are not inconsistent. For purposes of practical investment management, the APT and other multibeta pricing models provide more flexibility than the CAPM with respect to the application of an equilibrium model, because the APT factors are relatable to actual economic and financial variables. Nevertheless, the difficulties associated with utilizing an equilibrium model in investment practice apply to the APT as they do the CAPM, and therefore, as with the CAPM, the APT has to be used with caution and judgment as one of many tools in undertaking prudent investment management.

Questions and Problems

1. In what ways are the underlying assumptions of the APT different from those of the original CAPM?

2. Explain how the APT can be consistent with the original CAPM.

3. Explain how the multibeta CAPM of Chapter 10 can be equivalent to the general APT model.

4. Why are the APT factors necessarily associated with unanticipated changes?

5. Why would you expect the APT factors to be related to fundamental economic variables?

6. Explain what is meant by
   1. a pure factor portfolio
   2. a zero-beta portfolio.

7. Describe how the APT may be utilized in practical investment management.

8. What are the major difficulties and limitations associated with the use of an equilibrium model such as the APT in portfolio practice?

9. The factor betas for four assets representing their sensitivities to two factors are as follows:

	A	B	C	D
Factor 1	1.20	−1.60	−1.30	3.00
Factor 2	−3.70	0.90	−0.30	1.05

Assume if you invest, respectively, 20 percent, 30 percent, 40 percent, and 10 percent of your wealth in these assets, compute the betas of the two factors for the portfolio consisting of the four assets.

10. An APT model consists of a market factor and an interest rate factor. The expected return on the market portfolio is 7 percent and the expected return on the pure factor portfolio for unanticipated interest rate changes is 5

percent. If the expected zero-beta rate of return is 3 percent, calculate the equilibrium expected return on a security with a market beta of 1.5 and an interest rate beta of −0.50.

11. In a four-factor APT model, the factor betas for a security are 1.2, −1.5, 1.1, and 2.8, respectively. The expected returns of the pure factor portfolios for the factors are 8 percent, 5.5 percent, 7.5 percent, and 8.6 percent. If the risk-free rate is 4.5 percent, calculate
   (1) the expected risk premiums for each of the factors.
   (2) the equilibrium expected return on the security.

Self-Test Problems

ST-1. Assume that in a three-factor APT model, the factor betas for a security are −0.8, 3.5, and 1.5 respectively. If the risk-free rate is 4 percent and the expected returns of the pure factor portfolios are 5 percent, 6 percent, and 4.5 percent, calculate
   1. the expected risk premiums for each of the factors.
   2. the equilibrium expected return on the security.

ST-2. The sensitivities to unanticipated inflation for three assets are represented by their factor betas as follows:

X	Y	Z
−1.8	2.0	0.55

If you invested equal amounts in the three assets, what would be the inflation beta of the portfolio made up of the three assets?

Answers to Self-Test Problems

ST-1. (1) From equation 11.4, the expected risk premiums are

Factor 1: 5% − 4% = 1%
Factor 2: 6% − 4% = 2%
Factor 3: 4.5% − 4% = 0.5%

(2) Using equation 11.5, the equilibrium expected return on the security is

4% + (−0.8)(1) + (3.5)(2) + (1.5)(0.5) = 10.95%.

ST-2. The weighted inflation beta of the portfolio is

(1/3)(−1.8) + (1/3)(2.0) + (1/3)(0.55) = 0.25.

REFERENCES

Beenstock, M., and K. Chan. 1988. Economic forces in the London stock market. *Oxford Bulletin of Economics and Statistics*, 50, 27-39.

Berry, M., E. Burmeister, and M. McElroy. 1988. Sorting out risks using known APT factors. *Financial Analysts Journal* 44:29–42.

Bossaerts, P., and R. Green. 1989. A general equilibrium model of changing risk premia: Theory and tests. *Review of Financial Studies* 2:467–493.

Brealey, R. A. 1990. Portfolio theory versus portfolio practice. *Journal of Portfolio Management.* Summer, 6–10.

Burmeister, E., and M. McElroy. 1988. Joint estimation of factor sensitivities and risk premia for the APT. *Journal of Finance* 43:721–733.

Burmeister, E., and K. Wall. 1986. The APT and macroeconomic factor measures. *Financial Review* 21:1–20.

Chamberlain, G., and M. Rothschild. 1983. Arbitrage, factor structure, and mean variance analysis on large asset markets. *Econometrica* 51:1281–1304.

Chan, K. C., N. Chen, and D. Hsieh. 1985. An exploratory investigation of the firm size effect. *Journal of Financial Economics* 14:451–471.

Chen, N., R. Roll, and S. A. Ross. 1986. Economic forces and the stock market. *Journal of Business* 59:383–403.

Connor, G. 1984. A unified beta pricing theory. *Journal of Economic Theory.* December, 34:13–31.

Connor, G., and R. Korajczyk. 1989. An intertemporal equilibrium beta pricing model. *Review of Financial Studies* 2:373–392.

Cox, J., J. Ingersoll, and S. Ross. 1985. An intertemporal asset pricing model. *Econometrica* 53:363–384.

Dyvbig, P. 1983. An explicit bound on individual assets' deviation from APT pricing in a finite economy. *Journal of Financial Economics* 12:483–496.

Ferson, W. 1992. Theory and empirical testing of asset pricing models. Working paper, University of Chicago Graduate School of Business.

Ferson, W., and C. Harvey. 1991. The variation of economic risk premiums. *Journal of Political Economy* 99:385–415.

Grinblatt, M., and S. Titman. 1983. Factor pricing in a finite economy. *Journal of Financial Economics* 12:497–507.

Grinblatt, M., and S. Titman. 1987. The relation between mean-variance efficiency and arbitrage pricing. *Journal of Business* 60:1–40.

Handa, P., and S. Linn. 1991. Equilibrium factor pricing with heterogeneous beliefs. *Journal of Financial and Quantitative Analysis.* March, 26:11–22.

Harvey, C. 1991. The world price of covariance risk. *Journal of Finance* 46:111–158.

Huberman, G. 1982. A simple approach to arbitrage pricing theory. *Journal of Economic Theory.* October, 28:183–191.

Huberman, G. 1987. Arbitrage pricing theory. In *The New Palgrave: A Dictionary of Economics.* London: Macmillan.

Huberman, G., S. Kandel, and R. Stambaugh. 1987. Mimmicking portfolios and exact arbitrage pricing. *Journal of Finance.* March, 42:1–10.

Ikeda, S. 1991. Arbitrage pricing under exchange risk. *Journal of Finance* 46:447–456.

Ingersoll, J. 1984. Some results in the theory of arbitrage pricing. *Journal of Finance* 39:1021–1040.

Jarrow, R. A. 1988. *Finance theory.* Englewood Cliffs, New Jersey, Prentice Hall.

Jarrow, R. A., and A. Rudd. 1983. A comparison of APT and CAPM. *Journal of Banking and Finance* 7:295–303.

John, K., and H. Reisman. 1991. Fundamentals, factor structure, and multibeta models in large asset markets. *Journal of Financial and Quantitative Analysis.* March, 26:1–10.

Korajczyk, R., and C. Viallet. 1989. An empirical investigation of international asset pricing. *Review of Financial Studies.* 2:553–585.

Levine, R. 1989. An international arbitrage pricing with PPP deviations. *Economic Inquiry* 27:587–599.

McElroy, M., and E. Burmeister. 1988. Arbitrage pricing theory as a restricted nonlinear multivariate regression model. *Journal of Business and Economic Statistics.* January, 6:29–42.

Merton, R. 1973. An intertemporal capital asset pricing model. *Econometrica* 41:867–887.

Reisman, H. 1988. A general approach to the APT. *Econometrica* 56:473–476.

Reisman, H. 1992a. Intertemporal arbitrage pricing theory. *Review of Financial Studies* 5:105–122.

Reisman, H. 1992b. Reference variables, factor structure, and the approximate multibeta representation. *Journal of Finance.* September, 47:313–321.

Roll, R., and S. A. Ross. 1980. An empirical investigation of the arbitrage pricing theory. *Journal of Finance.* December, 35:1073–1103.

Roll, R., and S. A. Ross. 1984. The arbitrage pricing approach to strategic portfolio planning. *Financial Analysts Journal.* May-June.

Ross, S.A. 1976a. The arbitrage theory of capital asset pricing. *Journal of Economic Theory* 13:341–360.

Ross, S.A. 1976b. Risk, return, and arbitrage. In *Risk and Return in Finance,* vol 1. I. Friend and J. L. Bicksler, eds. Cambridge, MA: Ballinger.

Ross, S.A., and M. Walsh. 1982. A simple approach to the pricing of risky assets with uncertain exchange rates. *Research in International Business and Finance* 3:39–54.

Shanken, J. 1982. The arbitrage pricing theory. Is it testable? *Journal of Finance.* December, 37:1129–1140.

Shanken, J. 1985. Multi-beta CAPM or equilibrium-APT? A reply. *Journal of Finance.* September, 40:1189–1196.

Shanken, J. 1992. The current state of the arbitrage pricing theory. *Journal of Finance.* September, 47:1569–1574.

Sharpe, W. 1984. Factor models, CAPMs and the ABT. *Journal of Portfolio Management.* Fall, 21–25.

Sharpe, W. 1982. Factors in New York Stock Exchange returns. *Journal of Portfolio Management.* Summer, 5–19.

Shukla, R., and C. Trzcinka. 1991. Research on risk and return. Can measures of risk explain anything? *Journal of Portfolio Management.* Spring, 15–21.

Solnik, B. 1983. International arbitrage pricing theory. *Journal of Finance* 38:449–457.

Wei, K. 1988. An asset-pricing theory unifying the CAPM and APT. *Journal of Finance.* September, 43:881–892.

CHAPTER *12*

Empirical Tests of Asset Pricing Models

Introduction

This chapter discusses the results of several empirical tests of the capital asset pricing model and the arbitrage pricing theory and the implications of these results for portfolio and risk management. A formidable problem here involves setting up an effective method for testing, or test methodology. As we shall see, various conceptual and statistical problems are inherent in tests of asset pricing models. In addition, we must always be concerned about the possibly contaminating effects of the inevitable real-world violations of the model's assumptions. However, it is a widely accepted premise in economics that the assumptions of a model, however unrealistic, are not important if the model explains or predicts economic behavior well. The usefulness of an asset pricing model depends critically on whether it can explain or predict expected returns on securities. With this in mind, let us turn to our discussion of the empirical evidence.

Empirical Tests of the CAPM

Basic Predictions

The principal empirically testable predictions of the CAPM include the following:

1. The expected return on an asset or portfolio is positively related to the beta of the asset or portfolio, and the cross-sectional relationship between expected return and beta is linear (as represented by the SML).

2. Beta is the only measure of risk that is priced in the market. Thus, unsystematic risk is unrelated to expected returns. Furthermore, other characteristics, such as the size of a firm or the firm's price/earnings ratio, are argued to be unrelated to expected returns once beta is controlled.

3. The intercept of the estimated SML is the risk-free rate.

We will briefly discuss each of these predictions in turn.

Prediction 1 is central to the CAPM. It is certainly bold, since it asserts *jointly* that (1) essentially all investors hold the market portfolio, and consequently the contribution of a given security to the risk of any investor's portfolio is related to its systematic risk as measured by beta; (2) investors recognize (or behave as if they recognize) that beta is the only relevant measure of the riskiness of a stock in their portfolio; (3) collectively investors determine the equilibrium prices of all stocks, and thus their expected returns, according to this measure of risk; and (4) the equilibrium relationship between beta and expected return is linear.

Prediction 2 effectively rules out the possibility that other variables are employed by the market to determine expected returns. In particular, a security's unsystematic risk should be unrelated to the security's expected return. Other security characteristics, such as the size of a firm, the firm's price/earnings ratio, and the ratio of the firm's market value to its book value (known as the firm's q ratio), should also be unrelated to expected returns once beta is controlled.

Prediction 3 states that the return on the risk-free asset (e.g., the return on U.S. Treasury bills) should lie on the SML. This is important not only because of the large volume of "risk-free" assets outstanding in the market, but also because it leads to a simple process of combining investments in the market portfolio with the risk-free asset to create portfolios that have any desired level of beta risk. For example, given that the market portfolio has a beta of 1 and that the risk-free asset has a beta of 0 and lies on the SML, a portfolio divided evenly between the market portfolio and the risk-free asset will have a beta of .5 and thus should have the same expected return as any other security or portfolio that has a beta of .5.

Measurement Problems

Selecting a Proxy for the Market Portfolio: The Roll Critique.   Since the market portfolio essentially includes all assets, it is unobservable. Thus in order to test the CAPM researchers must choose a proxy for the market portfolio. The returns on stocks are then regressed on the returns on this proxy portfolio to obtain estimates of beta. Most of the early tests used a value-weighted portfolio of stocks such as those listed on the NYSE and the AMEX. However, in 1977 Richard Roll published an important critique of tests of the CAPM in which he argued that the model is essentially untestable because of the unobservability of the true market portfolio. He argued that estimates of beta are sensitive to the selection of a market portfolio proxy, and thus beta estimates obtained using a given proxy are biased relative to the true beta. While other researchers have argued that the CAPM can be effectively tested if proper care is given to the selection of a market portfolio proxy (Stambaugh 1982), Roll's critique remains an important consideration in interpreting results of empirical tests of the CAPM.

Measuring Beta.   In addition to the problem of the sensitivity of beta estimates to the choice of a market portfolio proxy, there are several serious statistical problems associated with estimating beta. Estimates of the beta of individual securities, β_i, are usually obtained using the following market model regression:

(12.1)
$$R_{it} = \alpha_i + \beta_i R_{Mt} + \epsilon_{it},$$

where R_{it} and R_{Mt} are the period t returns on stock i and the market portfolio proxy, respectively. The first problem associated with this approach is that given the substantial volatility of individual stock returns, the estimates of beta generally have large standard errors. Using monthly returns it is not uncommon for the standard error of β_i to be in excess of .5. Because of this problem, tests of the CAPM are often performed on portfolios of stocks rather than on individual stocks, as discussed later.

Another problem concerns the stability of beta over time. It is unrealistic to assume that the beta of any firm is constant through time. A firm's beta may change as it grows from a fledgling to a large, relatively stable firm, or its beta may change if the firm changes its product mix through diversification. Changes in the firm's financial leverage will also affect the beta of the firm's equity. Thus, since the researcher must use some amount of historical data to estimate a firm's beta, several questions arise. How much past information should be used? Should we use only the most recent data, since these data are most likely to reflect the firm's current status? Unfortunately, using fewer data generally results in larger standard errors of the estimate of beta. Furthermore, can we be reasonably sure that an estimate of beta based on historical data is a reliable estimate of the *ex ante* (forward-looking) beta that we assume the market is using to price securities?

Not surprisingly, a large body of research has developed to examine the issue of the stability of beta through time. A study by Blume (1975) is perhaps the most widely known study of this kind. Blume estimated the betas of firms using monthly data for each of two consecutive seven-year periods. He found that relative to the estimate obtained for the earlier period, the subsequent beta tended to regress toward a value of 1, which is, of course, the overall mean level of beta. Specifically, Blume regressed beta estimates of firms in the second period, β_{i2}, against their corresponding values in the first period, β_{i1}, and obtained the following estimated regression equation:

(12.2)
$$\beta_{i2} = .343 + .677 \, \beta_{i1}$$

This equation indicates that a firm observed to have a beta greater (less) than 1 in the first period tends to have a lower (higher) beta in the subsequent period. For example, if firm i is observed to have a beta of 2 in the first period, the equation predicts its beta in the second period will be $.343 + .677(2) = 1.697$. In contrast, if firm i had a beta of .5 in the first period, its predicted beta for the second period is $.343 + .677(.5) = .682$.

There are at least two reasons why betas have this regression tendency. First, as firms grow and diversify, their performance relative to the economy may become more stable. While a firm is young and relatively small, its beta may be high; later, as the firm matures, its beta decreases. Second, the phenomenon may simply reflect measurement error. Since all betas are measured with error, estimates observed at the extremes (that is, high or low) are more likely to reflect the extremes of statistical errors than other observations. But since a statistical error in the same direction and for the same firm is unlikely to be repeated in the next sampling period, the regression tendency will be observed. Many security firms have adopted Blume's adjustment technique in reporting betas to their customers. For instance, consider the excerpt from Merrill Lynch's publication *Security Risk Evaluation* (Exhibit 12.1).

Results of Empirical Tests of the CAPM

Sharpe and Cooper (1972) conducted one of the first empirical tests of the CAPM—a cross-sectional test. Using all of the stocks on the NYSE for the period 1931–1967, they calculated the betas of each stock annually using monthly returns for the previous five years. Each year the stocks were separated into deciles according to their estimated beta, and the returns on portfolios of the stocks in each decile were calculated for the next year. Finally they calculated the average return on each decile's portfolio. Their results are displayed in Exhibit 12.2 and Figure 12.1 on page 272. The average portfolio returns are positively related to their average betas, and

EXHIBIT 12.1

A Sample of Beta Estimates, Adjusted Betas, and Other Statistics, Using Monthly Returns for 7/88–6/93.

Ticker Symbol	Security Name	93/09 Close Price	Beta	Alpha	R-SQR
IDIR	Integrated Direct Inc.	0.805	0.39	−0.38	0.06
ISLS	Intelligent Surgical Laser I	2.250	3.39	−11.06	0.00
IRTI	Integrated Res Technologies	3.281	1.54	2.22	0.00
ITG	Integra Finl Corp	48.000	0.87	0.49	0.22
IN	Integon Corp	26.375	1.22	2.98	0.02
ISYS	Integral Sys Inc Md	13.500	0.95	0.65	0.11
IDTI	Integrated Device Technology	18.500	2.20	0.12	0.20
ICST	Integrated Circuit Sys Inc	17.500	2.07	4.81	0.05
IHS	Integrated Health Svcs Inc	26.875	1.86	1.41	0.16
ITLB	Integrated Labs Inc	4.625	0.03	−0.44	0.04
IPEC	Integrated Process Equip Cor	11.000	−0.31	5.10	0.09
IPECU	Integrated Process Equip Cor Unit	16.500	1.80	3.99	0.01
INTS	Integrated Sys Inc	9.750	1.34	−0.55	0.13
IDCC	Intek Diversified Corp	1.141	0.88	1.97	0.00
INTC	Intel Corp	70.750	1.46	1.98	0.23
ITPX	Inteleplex Corp	0.258	0.21	1.52	0.02
ITR	Intelcom Group Inc	19.000	3.99	6.10	0.01
INAI	Intellicorp Inc	4.500	0.72	2.20	0.00
INEL	Intelligent Electrs Inc	22.125	2.83	3.03	0.27
IT	Intelogic Trace Inc	2.625	0.46	2.15	0.01
ICL	Intellicall Inc	12.750	1.69	0.56	0.11
ITAS	Inter Active Svcs Inc	0.266	3.11	2.61	0.01
ITSY	Intellisys Inc	0.625	0.41	−7.54	0.06
INS	Intelligent Sys Corp New	1.625	1.27	−1.40	0.08
IPR	Inter-City Prods Corp Ord	2.625	0.78	−1.95	0.01
IFG	Inter Regl Finl Group Inc	29.500	1.36	1.05	0.23
INTL	Inter Tel Inc	6.125	0.16	3.20	0.02
IITCF	Intera Information Tech Corp Class A	7.625	1.95	−0.94	0.14
INNN	Interactive Network Inc	8.500	−1.29	4.38	0.03
ISB	Interchange Finl Svcs S B N	17.375	0.31	0.17	0.01

Source: Merrill Lynch, Pierce, Fenner, & Smith, Inc. *Security Risk Evaluation*, September, 1993.

the relationship is nearly perfectly monotonic. As illustrated in Figure 12.1, the relationship is also nearly perfectly linear. The equation for the fitted SML shown is

(12.3)
$$E(R_j) = 5.55 + 12.72\ \beta_j$$

This equation was fitted by regression, and the adjusted R^2 of the regression was .95, indicating that 95 percent of the variation of expected returns on these portfolios was explained by beta. Note, however, that the intercept of the regression, 5.55 percent, was considerably in excess of the

Resid Std Dev-N	Std. Err.		Adjusted Beta	Number of Observ
	Of Beta	Of Alpha		
22.35	2.65	5.35	0.60	19
19.02	3.34	6.11	2.58	12
48.07	1.68	6.40	1.36	60
5.87	0.20	0.78	0.91	60
8.56	1.01	2.05	1.15	19
8.97	0.40	1.44	0.97	40
16.00	0.56	2.13	1.80	60
20.86	1.36	4.17	1.71	27
12.45	0.75	2.38	1.57	29
13.84	1.08	2.83	0.36	28
9.91	1.74	3.09	0.13	13
11.02	1.93	3.43	1.56	13
11.99	0.50	1.89	1.22	42
27.53	0.96	3.67	0.92	60
9.62	0.34	1.28	1.30	60
43.43	1.74	6.82	0.48	43
34.24	4.30	8.67	2.98	18
23.43	0.82	3.12	0.82	60
16.86	0.59	2.25	2.21	60
28.22	0.99	3.76	0.65	60
16.86	0.59	2.25	1.46	60
53.93	2.82	9.32	2.40	36
28.03	3.02	6.67	0.61	18
14.63	0.51	1.95	1.18	60
15.21	0.64	2.44	0.86	41
9.06	0.32	1.21	1.24	60
20.78	0.73	2.77	0.44	60
17.19	0.71	2.69	1.63	43
27.11	1.98	6.09	−0.52	22
7.00	0.24	0.93	0.54	60

average risk-free rate for the period under study, which was less than 2 percent.

Fama and MacBeth (1974) conducted an alternative cross-sectional test of the CAPM by running the following regression with estimated portfolio data for the period 1935–1968:

(12.4)
$$E(R_P) = \gamma_0 + \gamma_1 \beta_P + \gamma_2 \beta_P^2 + \gamma_3 \sigma_{eP},$$

where $E(R_P)$ and β_P are the expected return and beta of the portfolio and σ_{eP} is the standard deviation of the error term in the time series regression

EXHIBIT 12.2

Empirical Results of Tests of the CAPM, 1931–67

Decile	Average Annual Return	Portfolio Beta
10	22.67	1.42
9	20.45	1.18
8	20.24	1.14
7	21.77	1.24
6	18.49	1.06
5	19.43	0.98
4	18.88	1.00
3	14.99	0.76
2	14.63	0.65
1	11.58	0.58

Source: W. Sharpe and G.M. Cooper, "Risk-Return Class of New York Stock Exchange Common Stocks: 1931–1967, *Financial Analysts Journal* 28:46–52.

FIGURE 12.1

An Empirical Estimation of the SML Using Data for 1931–1967.

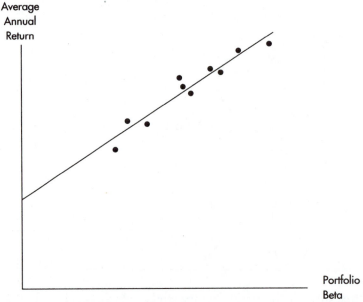

SOURCE: W. Sharpe and G. M. Cooper. 1972. Risk-Return Class of New York Stock Exchange Common Stocks: 1931–1967. *Financial Analysts Journal* 28:46–52.

used to calculate β_P; σ_{eP} is thus a measure of nonsystematic risk. According to the CAPM, the coefficient γ_0 should be equal to the average risk-free rate and γ_1 should be positive. The coefficient of β_P^2, γ_2, measures the extent to which the relationship between β_P and expected returns is nonlinear, and the coefficient of σ_{eP}, γ_3, measures the extent to which nonsystematic risk is priced in the market. According to the CAPM, γ_2 and γ_3 should be 0. Consistent with the CAPM, Fama and MacBeth found that γ_1 was positive and γ_2 and γ_3 were near 0. However, the value of γ_0 was greater than the average return on Treasury bills for the period of analysis.

Black, Jensen, and Scholes (1972) conducted an alternative type of test of the CAPM, known as a time series test. They subtracted the risk-free rate of return from the raw returns on each stock to obtain excess returns and likewise calculated excess returns on a market portfolio to obtain the following alternative market model:

(12.5)
$$R_{it} - R_{ft} = \delta_i + \beta_i(R_{Mt} - R_{ft}) + e_{it}.$$

Using this model, they obtained estimates of δ_i and β_i for each firm by regression using sixty monthly return observations. They then ranked each security by its beta and formed ten portfolios of stocks based on the decile rankings of the stocks by beta, with portfolio 1 containing the 10 percent of stocks with the highest betas, portfolio 2 containing the 10 percent of stocks with the next highest betas, and so on. Finally, they regressed the monthly excess returns on each of these portfolios on the excess return on the market portfolio proxy for periods subsequent to the initial sixty-month period to obtain estimates of δ_P and β_P for each portfolio. According to the CAPM, the intercept δ_P should be 0 for each portfolio, and of course the higher-beta portfolios should provide higher expected returns.

The results of their tests are summarized in Exhibit 12.3. Note that the average (monthly) returns increase monotonically and by similar increments as we move from the lowest- to the highest-beta portfolios, providing additional support for two of the critical predictions of the CAPM, namely, that expected returns should increase with beta and that the relationship should be linear. However, while the average value of δ_P

EXHIBIT 12.3

Summary of Time Series Tests of the CAPM

Portfolio	Monthly Average Return	β_P	δ_P	$t(\delta_P)$
1 (Highest Risk)	0.0213	1.56	−0.0008	−0.4
2	0.0177	1.38	−0.0019	−2.0
3	0.0171	1.25	−0.0006	−0.8
4	0.0163	1.16	−0.0002	−0.2
5	0.0145	1.06	−0.0005	−0.9
6	0.0137	0.93	0.0006	0.8
7	0.0126	0.85	0.0005	0.7
8	0.0115	0.75	0.0008	1.2
9	0.0109	0.63	0.0019	2.3
10 (Lowest Risk)	0.0091	0.50	0.0020	1.9
The Market	0.0142	1.00	0.0000	—

β_P, Estimated beta; δ_P, estimated intercept; $t(\delta_P)$, t-value of the intercept.

Source: F. Black, M. C. Jensen, and M. Scholes, "The Capital Asset Pricing Model: Some Empirical Tests." In M. C. Jensen, ed. *Studies in the Theory of Capital Markets* (New York: Praeger, 1972).

is close to 0 across all portfolios, there remains a systematic relationship between δ_P and the beta of the portfolio. Low-risk portfolios have positive δ_P values, and high-risk portfolios have negative δ_P values. These results indicate that low-beta stocks provide higher expected returns than predicted by the CAPM and high-beta stocks provide lower expected returns than predicted by the CAPM. As such, these results are similar to the results of the cross-section tests, namely, that the risk-free rate implied by the SML is greater than the actual risk-free rate.

To gain an assessment of the economic significance of these results, consider the value of δ_P for the low-risk portfolio, $\delta_{10} = .002$, which indicates that low-beta stocks provide a per annum expected return of approximately $.0020 \times 12 = .024$, or 2.4 percent beyond that predicted by the CAPM. In contrast, the highest-beta stocks provide a per annum expected return of approximately $-.0008 \times 12 = -.0096$, or .96 percent less than that predicted by the CAPM.

In summary, the results of early tests of the CAPM indicate that (1) expected returns are positively related to beta and the relationship appears to be linear, (2) unsystematic risk is not priced in the market, and (3) the intercept of the estimated SML is substantially in excess of the risk-free rate. Thus, overall results of the empirical tests provide partial support for the CAPM.

Recently Fama and French (1992) conducted yet another test of the CAPM. Their analysis was motivated by evidence from other empirical studies indicating that (1) expected returns on stocks are inversely related to the size of the firm as measured by the product of price per share times number of shares outstanding (see Chapter 13), and (2) beta and firm size are also inversely related. Given this evidence, the question arises: Is firm size just a proxy for beta, or are expected returns on stocks actually related to firm size for some other reason (e.g., investors demand higher returns on small firms because they are less liquid and thus impose higher transaction costs (Amihud and Mendelson [1986])? The study of Fama and French represented an attempt to disentangle the effects of firm size and beta on expected returns.

Using data for the period 1963–1990, Fama and French sorted NYSE, AMEX and NASDAQ stocks into portfolios annually on the basis of size (measured as the log of market value of equity, in millions of dollars), and for each size category calculated the average return, the average beta, and the average size of the stocks in each portfolio. Then they repeated the analysis, sorting on the basis of prior-period, or "preranking," beta instead of size. Their results are summarized in Exhibit 12.4 on page 276. The top part provides results for portfolios ranked by size. Note that average returns are inversely related to firm size: The smallest 5 percent of firms (category 1A) provide an average return of 1.64 percent per month, and the largest 5 percent of firms (category 10B) provide an average return of .9 percent per month. Thus there is a strong inverse relationship between firm size and average returns. Note, however, that the (postranking) betas are also inversely related to firm size: the smallest firms (category 1A) have the highest average beta, 1.44, and the largest firms (category 10B) have the smallest average beta, .9. Thus the evidence suggests that there exists a very tight relationship among firm size, beta, and average returns.

The question is, therefore, is size or beta driving expected returns? The second part of Exhibit 12.4 provides some direct evidence on this issue. Here firms are sorted annually by preranking beta, and statistics are calculated. The important evidence here is that there is virtually no relationship between average returns and beta: the lowest-beta stocks (category 1A) provided an average return of 1.2 percent per month, and the highest-beta stocks (category 10B) provided an average return of 1.18 percent. Thus the results suggest that firm size rather than beta is the dominant factor. Fama and French also sorted stocks by size and beta simultaneously and obtained similar results.

Fama and French extended their analysis to explore additional variables that according to previous research are related to expected returns. They examined size, price-earnings ratio, book-to-market equity ratio (BE/ME), and leverage. Although all of these variables were found to be related to expected returns, size and BE/ME were dominant. The final portion of Exhibit 12.4 shows the results of a sorting of stocks by BE/ME. The firms with the smallest BE/ME ratio, category 1A, provided the smallest average returns, .3 percent per month, and firms with the largest BE/ME ratios, categories 10A and 10B, provided the largest average returns, 1.92 percent and 1.83 percent per month, respectively. In summary, the results of Fama and French indicate not only that the central tenet of the CAPM (the positive relationship between expected return and beta) is unsupported by the data but also that other variables are much stronger predictors of expected returns.

TESTS OF VARIANTS OF THE CAPM

A common finding of the empirical tests of the CAPM just discussed is that the intercept term of the estimated SML is greater than the risk-free rate. Interestingly, this finding is consistent with the prediction of the zero-beta form of the CAPM discussed in Chapter 11. Furthermore, if the zero-beta form of the CAPM is the true characterization of market equilibrium, but tests of the type of Black, Jensen, and Scholes (BJS) are conducted using the estimated risk-free rate, then we should expect the intercept term δ_P to be positive for low-beta portfolios and negative for high-beta portfolios. Of course, this is precisely the result BJS obtain. Thus the evidence more strongly supports the zero-beta form of the CAPM than the standard form.

Another assumption of the CAPM is that taxes have no effect on equilibrium prices. However, until recently the tax rate on dividends has been higher than the tax rate on (realized) capital gains, suggesting that firms that pay higher dividends must provide higher expected returns to

EXHIBIT 12.4

Properties of Portfolios of NYSE, AMEX and NASDAQ Stocks
Stocks Formed on Size, Beta, and Book-to-Market Equity (BE/ME), 1963-1990

Average monthly returns, average post-ranking betas, average size (log of market value of equity in millions of dollars) and ln (BE/ME) are calculated for sorted portfolios. Portfolios are formed by separating firms into deciles according to size, beta, or BE/ME; then the firms in the smallest and largest deciles are split into two categories.

	1A	1B	2	3	4	5
			Portfolios Formed on Size			
Avg. Return	1.64	1.16	1.29	1.24	1.25	1.29
Avg. Postranking β	1.44	1.44	1.39	1.34	1.33	1.24
ln (ME)	1.98	3.18	3.63	4.10	4.50	4.89
ln (BE/ME)	−0.01	−0.21	−0.23	−0.26	−0.32	−0.36
			Portfolios Formed on Preranking Beta			
Avg. Return	1.20	1.20	1.32	1.26	1.31	1.30
Avg. Postranking β	0.81	0.79	0.92	1.04	1.13	1.19
ln (ME)	4.21	4.86	4.75	4.68	4.59	4.48
ln (BE/ME)	−0.18	−0.13	−0.22	−0.21	−0.23	−0.22
			Portfolios Formed on BE/ME			
Avg. Return	0.30	0.67	0.87	0.97	1.04	1.17
Avg. Postranking β	1.36	1.34	1.32	1.30	1.28	1.27
ln (ME)	4.53	4.67	4.69	4.56	4.47	4.38
ln (BE/ME)	−2.22	−1.51	−1.09	−0.75	−0.51	−0.32

Source: E. Fama and K. R. French. "The Cross-Section of Expected Stock Returns," *Journal of Finance* 47:427–465.

compensate investors for greater taxes imposed (unless by some means such as the dividend clientele equilibrium suggested by Black and Scholes (1974) and Miller and Scholes (1978), differential taxation is effectively neutralized). Litzenberger and Ramaswamy (1979) conducted a test of a tax-adjusted version of the CAPM. Their results indicate that there is a positive though nonlinear relationship between expected returns and dividend yields, consistent with the tax-adjusted CAPM.

Finally, a number of empirical tests of the consumption-based CAPM discussed in Chapter 11 have been conducted. These include the works of Hansen and Singleton (1982, 1984), Breeden, Gibbons and Litzenberger (1989), and Ferson and Harvey (1991), among others. Unfortunately, tests of this model are fraught with even greater conceptual, statistical, and data availability problems than the standard CAPM. The results of these tests

6	7	8	9	10A	10B
1.17	1.07	1.10	0.95	0.88	0.90
1.22	1.16	1.08	1.02	0.95	0.90
5.30	5.73	6.24	6.82	7.39	8.44
−0.36	−0.44	−0.40	−0.42	−0.51	−0.65
1.30	1.23	1.23	1.33	1.34	1.18
1.26	1.32	1.41	1.52	1.63	1.73
4.36	4.25	3.97	3.78	3.52	3.15
−0.22	−0.25	−0.23	−0.27	−0.31	−0.50
1.30	1.44	1.50	1.59	1.92	1.83
1.27	1.27	1.27	1.29	1.33	1.35
4.23	4.06	3.85	3.51	3.06	2.65
−0.14	0.03	0.21	0.42	0.66	1.02

have been generally disappointing, yielding little empirical support for the predicted pricing relationships.

EMPIRICAL TESTS OF THE ARBITRAGE PRICING MODEL

Empirical tests of the arbitrage pricing model discussed in Chapter 11 involve determining whether (1) there exist a few systematic or nondiversifiable factors that explain asset returns according to the assumed return generating model (i.e., whether the factor betas or coefficients.(*b*s) of the factors (*F*s) in equation 11.1 are significant), and (2) the factors are priced, that is, whether risk premiums are associated with the factor betas.

As noted in Chapter 11, the APT does not make any assertions about the number and the nature or identity of the factors. However, though not

BETTING ON BETA IS BUNK, RESEARCHERS SAY

A widely held theory that some of the most volatile stocks are the best long-term performers is bunk, say two University of Chicago business professors.

Their conclusions about the so-called beta coefficient as a predictor of stock-market yields could have a significant impact on investment strategies and corporate financing decisions, said Kenneth R. French, one of the professors.

The findings appear to challenge the Nobel Prize-winning theories of retired Stanford University Professor William F. Sharpe, whose capital-asset pricing model has been a staple of business education for 20 years.

Capital-asset pricing links a stock's price to its volatility relative to the stock market as a whole. Sharpe's model says stocks that are expected to have sharper short-term advances and declines than the general market should yield above-average returns in the long run.

A stock's relative volatility is known in the investment community as its beta coefficient or simply its beta.

French said he and Professor Eugene F. Fama studied 50 years' worth of data on thousands of stocks and concluded that stocks with high betas did not provide higher average returns and those with low betas did not provide lower average returns.

The researchers did find, though, that companies with high book values relative to their stock-market price provided better returns than those with low book values relative to market price. Book value refers to a company's hypothetical per share price as figured by accountants.

Fama and French also found that small companies tend to do better by their investors than large companies, a long-accepted principle among investment experts.

Sharpe, winner of the 1990 Nobel Memorial Prize in Economic Science for theories based on beta, said the Chicago study does not contradict his views, which he said concern future—as opposed to historical—investment returns. He said his theories are based on predicted beta, which is derived from a number of factors, including past performance, company size and book-to-market ratios.

The Fama-French paper "is saying that beta as a sole variable is dead and I don't dispute that," Sharpe said in a telephone interview from his office in Los Altos, Calif. He said capital-asset pricing remains a sound model.

"If it were true that stocks with high market risk looking forward don't have higher expected returns, why on God's green Earth would anybody hold them?" he said.

French said groups of stocks with historically high beta coefficients include those of companies involved in petroleum refining, electronic components and land development.

In practice, capital-asset pricing "still has some merit for how I should build a portfolio in the future," said Gilbert Beebower, executive vice president in charge of advanced investment concepts at SEI Corp., a Wayne, Pa.-based investment services company.

But he said no investment theory works all the time: "It's hard to find people who consistently over time are always the winner."

Source: The Buffalo News/Wednesday, April 1, 1992.

relevant as a direct test of the theory, some empirical studies have also sought to ascribe some economic interpretation to the factors. If the important factors affecting stock returns can be identified, the APT becomes relevant for strategic portfolio management, as demonstrated in Chapter 11.

The early empirical tests of the APT used the factor analysis technique to determine the factors present in the return-generating process of common stocks. Factor analysis extracts common factors that are unobservable variables derived from the covariation among stock returns; the common factor model equation in factor analysis is much like equation 11.1 (Johnson and Wichern 1988, Chapter 9).

The factor analysis study by Roll and Ross (1980) found that three or at most four common factors are important for pricing. Subsequent and similar studies by Chen (1983), Brown and Weinstein (1983), Kryzanowski and To (1983), Cho (1984), Cho, Elton and Gruber (1984), Lehman and Modest (1988), Conway and Reinganum (1988), and others used various versions of the factor analysis technique and obtained results suggesting that the number of factors ranges anywhere between one and six. While results of these studies provide evidence in support of the APT, especially when compared with the CAPM, the tests are admittedly weak and inconclusive. Some other tests that also use factor analysis, for example, Reinganum (1981), Cho and Taylor (1987), and Gultekin and Gultekin (1987), did not find support for the APT pricing relation.

The results from the factor analysis studies are in general questionable because the technique has statistical limitations and the number of factors is indeterminate. For example, the number of factors may vary with sample size (i.e., the number of stocks in a portfolio) and the number of time series observations and for the same sample may differ across subperiods. Furthermore, different versions of the technique do not always produce consistent results. (See Dhrymes, Friend, and Gultekin (1984), Dhrymes, Friend, Gultekin, and Gultekin (1985a,b), Kryzanowski and To (1983), Raveh (1985), Ehrhardt (1987), and Conway and Reinganum (1988) for discussions of these problems.) Thus the factor structure that is determined with a given set of assets may not be stable across other subsets of assets or across time. This problem may explain the differences in the results of the various studies. Dhrymes and associates (1984, 1985a,b) question the general validity of the empirical results obtained from the factor analysis techniques.

As an alternative to factor analysis, the principal component analysis technique, which also extracts factors, or components, from the covariation of returns, was suggested by Chamberlain and Rothschild (1983).[1]

---

[1] One major difference between factor analysis and principal component analysis is that the former assumes that the idiosyncratic components of the common factor structure are uncorrelated with each other, while the latter allows them to be correlated with each other. See Johnson and Wichern (1988) for a discussion of differences between the two techniques.

continued

Using this approach, studies by Trzcinka (1986), Connor and Korajczyk (1988), Brown (1989), and Shukla and Trzcinka (1990) find that as many as five pervasive factors could be present but in general the evidence that one factor was predominant is strong. This finding is consistent with the dominance of a market factor in stock returns, for example, as found by King (1966). The studies (Connor and Korajczyk 1988, Brown 1989) that detected one dominant factor find that it is highly correlated with or identify the factor as the equally weighted market index; however, Brown cautions that "this empirical evidence is also consistent with a k-factor model ($k > 1$), where each factor is equally important and is priced in an APT context." Noting the limitations of the statistical procedures in producing reliable inferences, Brown concludes that "mechanical application of purely statistical procedures to determining the number of pervasive factors in equity returns may lead to false inferences."

These results indicate that neither the factor analysis nor the principal component analysis technique can be said to be superior to the other in determining the number of factors and testing for pricing. Shukla and Trzcinka (1990) compare both methodologies in their tests and conclude that "the power of either methodology is an empirical issue which should be examined in specific circumstances. It may be that factor analysis is superior to principal component analysis, but the results of this study are a clear indication that the superiority of any technique must be decided on a case-by-case basis."

Another problem with testing the APT via factor analysis is that the factors derived from the techniques cannot be directly interpreted as economic factors, and therefore lack relevance for many investors. However, it is possible to draw limited inferences from the analysis of the correlations between the extracted factors and economic variables. Some recent studies (cf. Chew 1993) have regressed the extracted factors on various macroeconomic variables to determine whether the factors do indeed have economic relevance. These early results show promise in that the factors appear to be related to macroeconomic variables. Unfortunately, the relationships appear to be unstable.

An alternative approach to testing the APT that has been investigated is the a priori selection of economic variables as factors based on economic theory and intuition and determining the degree to which the set of factors explains the cross-sectional variation in returns according to the APT's

---

[1]*continued from p. 279*
One of the underlying assumptions of the return generating factor model (equation 11.1) used to derive the APT by Ross (1976) is that the idiosyncratic components of returns that are not explained by the common factors are uncorrelated across securities (i.e., the returns follow an exact factor structure), thus making the use of factor analysis the appropriate technique for extracting factors. However, Chamberlain and Rothschild (1983) showed that assuming only an approximate factor structure, in which the idiosyncratic components of the returns are allowed to be weakly correlated, is sufficient for Ross's result. Thus principal component analysis ("computationally and conceptually simpler than factor analysis") becomes appropriate for the empirical analysis.

pricing relation. Such tests are not necessarily tests of the APT per se but rather of the general multibeta asset pricing models of the type discussed in Chapter 10 (Merton 1973; Cox, Ingersoll, and Ross 1985), of which the APT is one. Nevertheless, the pioneering work by Chen, Roll, and Ross (CRR) (1986) was motivated by the APT and is therefore generally associated with the model.

CRR considered the following five economic factors as candidates for explaining the return generating structure of common stocks:

1. Monthly growth rate in U.S. industrial production (MP)
2. Changes in expected inflation (DEI)
3. Unanticipated inflation (UI)
4. Unanticipated changes in default risk premiums (UPR), measured as the difference between the return on a portfolio of corporate bonds rated "Baa and under" and the return on a portfolio of long-term U.S. government bonds
5. Unanticipated changes in the slope of the term structure of interest rates (UTS), measured as the difference between the return on a portfolio of long-term U.S. government bonds and the one-month U.S. Treasury bill return, that is, the unanticipated return on long-term government bonds[2]

First CRR examined the correlations of these variables with each other and with returns on a value-weighted index of NYSE stocks for the period 1953–1983 and for various subperiods. The results are displayed in Exhibit 12.5. Note that the signs of the coefficients are fairly stable through time, though by no means are they constant. The signs of the correlations of the macro variables with stock returns are also generally as expected. For example, the correlation of stock returns with *MP* is always positive, and the correlation of stock returns with *UI* is always negative. Of course, the correlation of a macro variable with stock returns must be reasonably stable if the variable is to be useful in a test of asset pricing.

The second stage of CRR's analysis involved a regression of returns on portfolios of stocks on the macro variables:

(12.6) $R = a + b_{MP}\,MP + b_{DEI}\,DEI + b_{UI}\,UI + b_{UPR}\,UPR + b_{UTS}\,UTS + e$

Since there are five independent variables in this model, it was not practical to form portfolios based on each of the slope coefficients in the regression in a manner analogous to tests of the CAPM. Instead CRR formed portfolios on the basis of firm size, which they know to be strongly related to average returns (see Chapter 13), to obtain the desired dispersion of expected returns without biasing the tests. Each year the slope coefficients for each portfolio were estimated using monthly data for

---

[2]They also investigated the equally weighted and value-weighted stock market indexes, percentage changes in real per capita consumption, and changes in oil prices, but did not find them to be significant.

EXHIBIT 12.5

Correlation Matrix for Macroeconomic Variables

	EWNY	VWNY	MP	DEI	UI	UPR	UTS
1953–1983							
VWNY	.916						
MP	.103	.020					
DEI	−.163	−.119	.063				
UI	−.163	−.112	−.067	.378			
UPR	.105	.042	.216	.266	.018		
UTS	.227	.248	−.159	−.394	−.103	−.752	
1953–1972							
VWNY	.930						
MP	.147	.081					
DEI	−.130	−.122	.020				
UI	−.081	−.021	−.203	.388			
UPR	.265	.214	.213	.068	.072		
UTS	.110	.108	−.059	−.210	−.041	−.688	
1973–1977							
VWNY	.883						
MP	.022	.118					
DEI	−.314	−.263	.004				
UI	−.377	−.352	−.004	.505			
UPR	.341	.231	.227	.032	.289		
UTS	.217	.313	−.350	−.280	−.026	−.554	
1978–1983							
VWNY	.937						
MP	.092	−.010					
DEI	−.143	−.073	.169				
UI	−.055	−.024	−.168	.375			
UPR	.275	−.319	.248	.458	.259		
UTS	.424	.431	−.277	−.512	−.239	−.890	

VWNY, return on the value-weighted NYSE index; EWNY, return on equally weighted NYSE index; MP, monthly growth rate in industrial production; DEI, change in expected inflation; UI, unanticipated inflation; UPR, unanticipated change in the risk premium (Baa and under return – long-term government bond return); UTS, unanticipated change in the term structure (long-term government bond return – Treasury-bill rate).

Source: N. Chen, R. Roll, and S. A. Ross, "Economic Forces and the Stock Market," *Journal of Business* 59(1986): 391.

the trailing five years, and these estimates were used as independent variables to explain returns for each of the next twelve months. The process was repeated each year, yielding a time series of estimates of the risk premium associated with each macro variable. The average of these risk premiums was then computed, and a *t* test was applied to determine whether risk associated with each macro variable was priced by the market. The results are displayed in Exhibit 12.6. Note that all of the

EXHIBIT 12.6

Economic Variables and Pricing (Percent per Month $\times$ 10), Multivariate Approach

	MP	DEI	UI	UPR	UTS	Constant
1958–84	13.589	–.125	–.629	7.205	–5.211	4.124
	(3.561)	(–1.640)	(–1.979)	(2.590)	(–1.690)	(1.361)
1958–67	13.155	.006	–.191	5.560	–.008	4.989
	(1.897)	(.092)	(–.382)	(1.935)	(–.004)	(1.271)
1968–77	16.966	–.245	–1.353	12.717	–13.142	–1.889
	(2.638)	(–3.215)	(–3.320)	(2.852)	(–2.554)	(–.334)
1978–84	9.383	–.140	–.221	1.679	–1.312	11.477
	(1.588)	(–.552)	(–.274)	(.221)	(–.149)	(1.747)

MP, monthly growth rate in industrial production; DEI, change in expected inflation; UI, unanticipated inflation; UPR, unanticipated change in the risk premium (Baa and under return – long-term government bond return); UTS, unanticipated change in the term structure (long-term government bond return – Treasury-bill rate); t statistics are in parentheses.

Source: N. Chen, R. Roll and S. A. Ross, "Economic Forces and the Stock Market," *Journal of Business* 59 (1986): 396.

variables are significant in at least one subperiod (that is, the *t* statistic is greater than 2 in absolute value), and for a given macro variable the sign of the average risk premium is generally the same across the subperiods. The results therefore suggest that these macro variables are associated with relatively stable risk premiums in the stock market.

Similar results have been reported by Burmeister and Wall (1986), Berry, Burmeister, and McElroy (1988), and McElroy and Burmeister (1988). They used variables very similar or identical to CRR's variables except that they substituted *unanticipated change in the growth rate of real final sales* (constructed from GNP data) for CRR's industrial production variable.

The findings of these studies are generally consistent with economic intuition—the factors found to be priced are systematic in that they reflect factors that influence all firms to varying degrees depending on their characteristics. The variables are implicitly incorporated in the traditional discounted cash flow valuation formula: changes in industrial production (or real final sales) and unanticipated inflation influence the expected cash flows of firms, and term structure and default risk as well as inflation influence the discount rate (Chen, Roll, and Ross 1986; Roll and Ross 1984b; and Burmeister and Wall 1986). There are, of course, several other macroeconomic variables that may be found to be significant in pricing, for example the money supply, GNP, and other measures of economic activity.[3] The degree to which any variable captures economic risk factors better than others is an empirical issue, though some variables can be argued to be more appropriate than others; changes in the money supply,

---

[3] Kim and Wu (1987) and Beenstock and Chan (1988) (on the London Stock Exchange) use several other macroeconomic variables to test the APT.

for example, are arguably well reflected in inflation or interest rate changes.

Burmeister and McElroy (1988) further extended their earlier tests by using alternative econometric techniques to test a six-factor APT model consisting of the following:

1. Unexpected inflation
2. Unanticipated change in the growth rate of real final sales
3. Change in the 30-day Treasury bill rate
4. The monthly return on a portfolio of twenty-year corporate bonds
5. The monthly return on a portfolio of twenty-year government bonds
6. The monthly return on the SP500

The authors referred to the first three factors as measured, or observed, factors, and the last three are unobserved factors; that is, they are proxies for unobservable risk factors. Variables 4 and 5 together reflect the risk measures of variables 3 and 4 used by CRR and by Burmeister and Wall. The SP500 return was included to represent a residual market factor, which could be regarded as a proxy for factors not captured by the other five factors. The inclusion of the market factor also enabled the authors to conduct tests of the CAPM empirically nested within the APT, which is in turn nested within a more general linear factor model of stock returns. Their tests rejected the CAPM in favor of the APT.

Finally, several recent studies have shown that the CPR variables can actually explain the size effect (Chan, Chen, and Hsieh 1985 and He and Ng 1993). However, He and Ng's (1993) analysis indicates that the CPR variables cannot explain the relationship between book-to-market value and expected returns.

Tests such as these on the APT and multibeta pricing models in general (Chan, Chen, and Hsieh 1985; Ferson and Harvey 1991) provide much more empirical meaning to the models and usefulness in investment practice. However, there is not yet enough empirical evidence to bring about general acceptance of a particular set of factors that best explains consistent cross-sectional variations in returns across all securities or that constitutes definitive tests of the models. Also, the relation between macroeconomic variables and the factors extracted through factor analysis or principal component analysis is yet to be investigated extensively in empirical work. Several other approaches continue to be explored in attempts to facilitate empirical tests that will provide reliable inferences on the APT and other multibeta models (Huberman, Kandel, and Stambaugh 1987; Connor and Korajczyk 1989; Bossaerts and Green 1989; McCulloch and Rossi 1990; Reisman 1992; John and Reisman 1991; and Shanken 1992a,b). However, the tests suffer from the usual limitation of joint tests, that is, the factors determined or chosen are correctly identified—they are the "true" factors—and they are priced according to the asset pricing relation.

IMPLICATIONS OF THE EMPIRICAL TESTS FOR PORTFOLIO AND RISK MANAGEMENT

CAPM-Related Tests

Early tests of the CAPM provided considerable support for a beta-based approach to portfolio and risk management, and this approach is still widely used today. However, recent evidence, particularly that of Fama and French (1992), casts doubt on the usefulness of beta as a measure of priced risk in the market, at least with regard to its role as the sole measure of risk. Variables such as firm size and book-to-market ratio have been shown to predict expected returns on stocks effectively. Unfortunately, theories showing why these variables should explain expected returns have not yet been developed. As a result we are in the curious position of being able to manipulate the expected returns on portfolios, but we do not know whether these portfolios are efficient in the sense that they provide expected returns commensurate with the risk they impose. Thus the challenge for theoreticians, as well as practicing portfolio managers, is to determine whether portfolios constructed on the basis of variables such as beta, size and/or book-to-market represent efficient portfolios. Given the recent development of indexes of small- and medium-sized firms (called small-cap and mid-cap indexes), it appears that the market recognizes the importance of the relationship between asset returns and size.

APT-Related Tests

Empirical tests of the APT using factor analysis tell us that one major common factor and a few minor common factors affect stock returns. However, the usefulness of this information for portfolio and risk management is severely limited because (1) the factors have no economic identification, and (2) the factors appear to be unstable across groups of stocks and through time. These concerns notwithstanding, factor analysis may be useful in creating hedge portfolios, that is, portfolios designed to limit investors' exposure to one or more of the major common risk factors of the market. If such portfolios can be constructed, the approach may be most useful in terms of eliminating investors' exposure to factors that appear *not* to be priced in the market—that is, to limit investors' exposure to risk that is not compensated.

An advantage of APT analyses based on macroeconomic variables as factors is, of course, that the factors are observable. Thus portfolio managers can develop forecasts of the values of such variables and design portfolios that are projected to provide the greatest return-to-risk performance based on the forecasts, the sensitivities of each stock to the variable, and the historical risk premiums associated with each variable. Alternatively, portfolios could be designed to limit an investor's exposure to risk associated with certain macro variables if, say, the investor is already highly exposed to that risk factor because of other assets held. Overall, the various APT-related analyses promise to provide the portfolio manager with better means to assess and control the riskiness and the expected return of a portfolio than is available through standard Markowitz-type portfolio analysis and the CAPM. However, many problems must be solved before this promise is fully realized.

SUMMARY

Empirical tests of the CAPM generally support the theory, but not unequivocally so. Early tests of the CAPM support two of its principal predictions: (1) Expected returns on stocks are positively related to beta and the relationship between expected returns and beta is linear; and (2) nonsystematic risk is not priced in the market. However, these studies indicate that the intercept of the estimated SML is substantially greater than the risk-free rate. This result is inconsistent with the standard form of the CAPM but is consistent with a two-factor (zero-beta) form of the CAPM. Empirical tests of the consumption-based CAPM have not been supportive of this version. More recently, empirical analyses indicate that expected returns on stocks are closely related to firm size, that firm size is closely related to beta, and that once firm size is controlled, the relationship between expected returns and beta is very weak. Thus while the CAPM may be useful to portfolio managers, its limitations and other variables such as firm size and book-to market ratio should be recognized in order to obtain a full picture of the risk-return relationship prevalent in the market.

Empirical tests of the APT are hampered by problems of identification and stability of the factors. However, to the extent that stable factors can be identified, portfolio managers have a powerful tool to tailor portfolios to suit the specific needs of investors with regard to risk exposure and expected return.

Questions and Problems

1. List and discuss the principal empirically testable predictions of the CAPM.

2. Discuss the problems associated with empirically testing the CAPM. Include in your discussion problems in estimating betas and problems in selecting a market portfolio proxy.

3. A stock is observed to have a beta of 1.67 during the past five years. Using Blume's estimated equation (12.2), estimate the stock's future beta.

4. Discuss the test methodology and empirical results of both the cross-sectional and time series tests of the CAPM. Which predictions are upheld and which are not?

5. Based on the results of empirical tests of the CAPM, would you rather hold a well-diversified portfolio of stocks with a beta of .5 or hold equal proportions of a market portfolio proxy and the risk-free asset (also with a beta of .5)? How would you exploit this situation in an arbitrage strategy?

6. Discuss Fama and French's (1992) empirical evidence on the importance of beta, size, and book-to-market ratio in explaining expected returns on stocks.

7. Discuss the various approaches taken by researchers to test the APT, including factor analysis, principal components, and direct selection of macroeconomic factors.

8. Empirical tests of the APT via factor analysis have fairly consistently found a single predominant factor and several minor factors, and the predominant factor is generally highly correlated with returns on an equally weighted index of all stocks. Do these results suggest that a simple single-index model, and thus the simple view of the CAPM, suffices to characterize the market? Why or why not?

9. Discuss the implications of CAPM-related empirical research and APT-related empirical research for portfolio and risk management.

REFERENCES

Amihud, Y., and H. Mendelson. 1986. Asset pricing and the bid-ask spread. *Journal of Financial Economics* 17:223–249.

Beenstock, M., and K. Chan. 1988. Economic forces in the London stock market. *Oxford Bulletin of Economics and Statistics*.

Berry, M., E. Burmeister, and M. McElroy. 1988. Sorting out risks using known APT factors. *Financial Analysts Journal*. March/April.

Black, F., M. C. Jensen, and M. Scholes. 1972. The capital asset pricing model. Some empirical tests. In *Studies in the theory of capital markets*, M. C. Jensen, ed. New York: Praeger.

Black, F. and M. Scholes. 1974. The effects of dividend yield and dividend policy on common stock prices and returns. *Journal of Financial Economics* 1:1–22.

Blume, M. 1975. Betas and their regression tendencies. *Journal of Finance* 10:785–795.

Bossaerts, P. and R. Green. 1989. A general equilibrium model of changing risk premia: theory and tests. *Review of Financial Studies*, 467–493.

Breeden, D. T. 1979. An intertemporal asset pricing model with stochastic consumption and investment opportunities. *Journal of Financial Economics*. September, 7:265–296.

Breeden, D. T., M. R. Gibbons, and R. H. Litzenberger. 1989. Empirical tests of the consumption-oriented capital asset pricing model. *Journal of Finance* 44:231–262.

Brown, S. 1989. The number of factors in security returns. *Journal of Finance* 44:1247–1262.

Brown, S., and M. Weinstein. 1983. A new approach to testing asset pricing models: the bilinear paradigm. *Journal of Finance* 38:711–743.

Burmeister, E. and M. McElroy. 1988. Joint estimation of factor sensitivities and risk premia for the APT. *Journal of Finance* 43:721–733.

Burmeister, E., and K. Wall. 1986. The APT and macroeconomic factor measures. *Financial Review* 21:1–20.

Chamberlain, G., and M. Rothschild. 1983. Arbitrage, factor structure, and mean variance analysis on large asset markets. *Econometrica* 51:1281–1304.

Chan, K. C., N. Chen, and D. Hsieh. 1985. An exploratory investigation of the firm size effect. *Journal of Financial Economics* 14:451–471.

Chen, N. 1983. Some empirical tests of the theory of arbitrage pricing. *Journal of Finance* 38:1393–1414.

Chen, N. 1991. Financial investment opportunities and the macroeconomy. *Journal of Finance* 46:529–554.

Chen, N., R. Roll, and S. A. Ross. 1986. Economic forces and the stock market. *Journal of Business* 59:383–403.

Chen, S-J. 1993. Identifying macroeconomic factors in the context of the arbitrage pricing theory. Statistical effects or structural changes. Presented at the Midwest Finance Association meeting, Indianapolis.

Cho, D. C. 1984. On testing the arbitrage pricing theory: inter-battery factor analysis. *Journal of Finance* 39:1485–1502.

Cho, D., E. Elton, and M. Gruber. 1984. On the robustness of the Roll and Ross arbitrage pricing theory. *Journal of Financial and Quantitative Analysis* 19:1–10.

Cho, D., C. Eun, and L. Senbet. 1986. International arbitrage pricing theory. An empirical investigation. *Journal of Finance.* June, 41:313–329.

Cho, D. C., and W. Taylor. 1987. The seasonal stability of the factor structure of stock returns. *Journal of Finance* 42:1195–1211.

Christofi, A. C., and G. Philippatos. 1987. An empirical investigation of the international arbitrage pricing theory *Management International Review.* January, 27:13–22.

Connor, G. 1984. A unified beta pricing theory. *Journal of Economic Theory* 34:13–31.

Connor, G. 1989. Notes on the arbitrage pricing theory. In *Theory of valuation,* S. Bhattacharya and G. Constantinides, eds. Rowman and Littlefield. Lanham, MD.

Connor, G., and R. Korajczyk. 1988. Risk and return in an equilibrium APT: Application of a new test methodology. *Journal of Financial Economics* 21:255–289.

Connor, G., and R. Korajczyk. 1989. An intertemporal equilibrium beta pricing model. *Review of Financial Studies* 2:373–392.

Conway, D., and M. Reinganum. 1988. Stable factors in security returns. Identification using cross-validation. *Journal of Business and Economic Statistics* 6:1–28.

Corhay, A., G. Hawanini, and P. Michel. 1987. Seasonality in the risk-return relationship. Some international evidence. *Journal of Finance* 42:49–68.

Cornell, B. 1981. The consumption-based asset pricing model: A note on potential tests and applications. *Journal of Financial Economics* 9:103–108.

Cox, J., J. Ingersoll, and S. Ross. 1985. An intertemporal general equilibrium model of asset prices. *Econometrica* 53:363–384.

Dhrymes, P. J. 1984. The empirical relevance of arbitrage pricing models. *Journal of Portfolio Management* 35:35–44.

Dhrymes, P. J., I. Friend, and N. B. Gultekin. 1984. A critical reexamination of the empirical evidence on the arbitrage pricing theory. *Journal of Finance* 39:323–346.

Dhrymes, P. J., I. Friend, N. Gultekin, and M. Gultekin. 1985a. New tests of the APT and the implications. *Journal of Finance* 40:659–674.

Dhrymes, P. J., I. Friend, N. Gultekin, and M. Gultekin. 1985b. An empirical investigation of the implications of arbitrage pricing theory. *Journal of Banking and Finance* 9:73–99.

Ehrhardt, M. C. 1987. A mean-variance derivation of a multi-factor equilibrium model. *Journal of Financial and Quantitative Analysis* 11:227–236.

Fama, E. F. 1990. Stock returns, expected returns, and real activity. *Journal of Finance.* September, 45:1089–1108.

Fama, E., and J. MacBeth. 1974. Tests of the multiperiod two-parameter model. *Journal of Financial Economics.* May, 1:43–66.

Fama, E., and K. R. French. 1992. The cross-section of expected stock returns. *Journal of Finance.* June, 47:427–466.

Ferson, W. 1992. Theory and empirical testing of asset pricing models. Working paper, University of Chicago Graduate School of Business. In *The finance handbook,* Forthcoming, Jarrow, R.A., W. T. Ziemba, and V. Maksimovic, eds. North Holland, Amsterdam.

Ferson, W., and C. Harvey. 1991. The variation of economic risk premiums. *Journal of Political Economy* 99:385–415.

Ferson, W., S. Kandel, and R. Stambaugh. 1987. Tests of asset pricing with time-varying risk premiums and market betas. *Journal of Finance* 42:201–220.

Gultekin, M. N., and N. B. Gultekin. 1987. Stock return anomalies and tests of the APT. *Journal of Finance* 42:1213–1224.

Gultekin, M. N., N. B. Gultekin, and A. Penanti. 1989. Capital controls and international capital market segmentation: The evidence from the Japanese and American stock markets. *Journal of Finance* 44:849–870.

Hamao, Y. 1988. An empirical examination of the arbitrage pricing theory: Using Japanese data. *Japan and the World Economy* 1:45–61.

Hansen, L., and K. Singleton. 1982. Generalized instrumental variables estimation of nonlinear rational expectation models. *Econometrica* 50:1269–1286.

Hansen, L., and K. Singleton. 1984. Stochastic consumption, risk aversion, and the temporary behavior of asset returns. *Journal of Political Economy* 91:249–265.

Harvey, C. 1991. The world price of covariance risk. *Journal of Finance* 46:111–158.

He, J., and L. Ng, 1993. Economic forces, fundamental variables, and equity returns. Working paper, University of Texas, Austin.

Hietala, P. K. 1989. Asset pricing in partially segmented markets: Evidence from the Finnish markets. *Journal of Finance* 44:697–718.

Huberman, G. 1982. A simple approach to arbitrage pricing theory. *Journal of Economic Theory* 28:183–191.

Huberman, G. 1987. Arbitrage pricing theory. In *The new Palgrave. A dictionary of economics.*

Huberman, G., S. Kandel, and R. Stambaugh. 1987. Mimmicking portfolios and exact arbitrage pricing. *Journal of Finance* 42:1–10.

Ikeda, S. 1991. Arbitrage pricing under exchange risk. *Journal of Finance* 46:447–456.

Isimbabi, M. J. 1992. Comovements of world securities markets, international portfolio diversification, and asset returns. In *Recent Developments in International Banking and Finance,* vol 6, S. J. Khoury, ed.

Jaffe, J., and R. Westerfield. 1985. Patterns in Japanese common stock returns. Day of the week and turn-of-the-year effects. *Journal of Financial and Quantitative Analysis* 20:261–272.

John, K., and H. Reisman. 1991. Fundamentals, factor structure, and multibeta models in large asset markets. *Journal of Financial and Quantitative Analysis* 26:1–10.

Johnson, R. A., and D. W. Wichern. 1988. *Applied Multivariate Statistical Analysis.* Englewood Cliffs, NJ: Prentice Hall.

Kandel, S. 1984. On the exclusion of assets from tests of the mean variance efficiency of the market portfolio. *Journal of Finance* 39:63–75.

Kandel, S., and R. Stambaugh. 1989. A mean-variance framework for tests of asset pricing models. *Review of Financial Studies* 2:125–156.

Kim, M., and C. Wu. 1987. Macroeconomic factors and stock returns. *Journal of Financial Research.* Summer, 10:87–98.

King, B. 1966. Market and industry factors in stock price behavior. *Journal of Business* 39:139–190.

Korajczyk, R., and C. Viallet. 1989. An empirical investigation of international asset pricing. *Review of Financial Studies* 2:553–585.

Kryzanowski, L., and M. To. 1983. General factor models and the structure of security returns. *Journal of Financial and Quantitative Analysis* 18:31–52.

Lehman, B., and D. Modest. 1988. The empirical foundations of the arbitrage pricing theory. Empirical tests. *Journal of Financial Economics* 21:213–254.

Levine, R. 1989. An international arbitrage pricing with PPP deviations. *Economic Inquiry* 27:587–599.

Litzenberger, R. H., and K. Ramaswamy. 1979. The effect of personal taxes and dividends on capital asset prices: Theory and empirical evidence. *Journal of Financial Economics* 163–195.

MacKinlay, A., and M. Richardson. 1991. Using generalized method of moments to test mean-variance efficiency. *Journal of Finance* 46:511–527.

McCulloch, R., and P. Rossi. 1990. Posterior, predictive, and utility-based approaches to testing the arbitrage pricing theory. *Journal of Financial Economics* 28:7–38.

McElroy, M., and E. Burmeister. 1988. Arbitrage pricing theory as a restricted nonlinear multivariate regression model. *Journal of Business and Economic Statistics* 6:29–42.

Merton, R. 1973. An intertemporal capital asset pricing model. *Econometrica.* September, 867–887.

Miller, M. H., and M. S. Scholes. 1978. Dividends and taxes. *Journal of Financial Economics* 6:333–364.

Raveh, A. 1985. A note on factor analysis and arbitrage pricing theory. *Journal of Banking and Finance* 9:317–321.

Reinganum, M. 1981. The arbitrage pricing theory. Some empirical results. *Journal of Finance* 36:313–321.

Reisman, H. 1988. A general approach to the APT. *Econometrica* 56:473–476.

Reisman, H. 1992. Intertemporal arbitrage pricing theory. *Review of Financial Studies* 5:105–122.

Reisman, H. 1992. Reference variables, factor structure, and the approximate multibeta representation. *Journal of Finance* 47:313–321.

Roll, R. 1977. A critique of the asset pricing theory's tests. *Journal of Financial Economics* 4:129–176.

Roll, R., and S. A. Ross. 1980. An empirical investigation of the arbitrage pricing theory. *Journal of Finance.* December, 35:1073–1103.

Roll, R., and S. A. Ross. 1984. A critical re-examination of the empirical evidence on the arbitrage pricing theory. A reply. *Journal of Finance* 39:347–350.

Roll, R., and S. A. Ross. 1984. The arbitrage pricing approach to strategic portfolio planning. *Financial Analysts Journal.* May–June, 40:14–26.

Ross, R. 1976. The arbitrage theory of capital asset pricing. *Journal of Economic Theory* 13:341–360.

Ross, R. 1984. Reply to Dhyrmes: APT *is* empirically relevant. *Journal of Portfolio Management.* Fall, 54–56.

Ross, R., and M. Walsh. 1982. A simple approach to the pricing of risky assets with uncertain exchange rates. *Research in International Business and Finance* 3:39–54.

Shanken, J. 1982. The arbitrage pricing theory. Is it testable? *Journal of Finance* 37:1129–1140.

Shanken, J. 1985. Multi-beta CAPM or equilibrium-APT? A reply. *Journal of Finance.* September, 40:1189–1196.

Shanken, J. 1985b. Multivariate tests of the zero-beta CAPM. *Journal of Financial Economics* 14:327–348.

Shanken, J. 1986. On the exclusion of assets from tests of the mean variance efficiency of the market portfolio: An extension. *Journal of Finance.* June, 331–337.

Shanken, J. 1987. Multivariate proxies and asset pricing relations. Living with the roll critique. *Journal of Financial Economics* 18:91–110.

Shanken, J. 1990. Intertemporal asset pricing. An empirical investigation. *Journal of Econometrics* 45:99–120.

Shanken, J. 1992a. The current state of the arbitrage pricing theory. *Journal of Finance* 47:1569–1574.

Shanken, J. 1992b. On the estimation of beta-pricing models. *Review of Financial Studies* 5:1–33.

Sharpe, W. 1984. Factor models, CAPMs and the APT. *Journal of Portfolio Management.* Fall, 21–25.

Sharpe, W. 1982. Factors in New York Stock Exchange returns. *Journal of Portfolio Management.* Summer, 5–19.

Sharpe, W., and G. M. Cooper. 1972. Risk-return class of New York Stock Exchange common stocks: 1931–1967. *Financial Analysts Journal.* March–April, 28:46–52.

Shukla, R., and C. Trzcinka. 1990. Sequential tests of the arbitrage pricing theory: A comparison of principal components and maximum likelihood factors. *Journal of Finance* 45:1541–1564.

Stambaugh, R. F. 1982. On the exclusion of assets from tests of the two-parameter model: A sensitivity analysis. *Journal of Financial Economics* 10:237–268.

Trzcinka, C. 1986. On the number of factors in the arbitrage pricing model. *Journal of Finance* 41:345–368.

Wei, K. 1988. An asset-pricing theory unifying the CAPM and APT. *Journal of Finance* 43:881–892.

CHAPTER *13*

Market Efficiency: Theory and Evidence

Introduction

We have all heard the expressions "There's no free lunch," and, regarding a so-called bargain, "You get what you pay for." Such expressions are common in our language for the simple reason that we live in a competitive world populated by and large by well-informed, economically self-interested people. Consequently, the price of any asset tends to reflect its true equilibrium value, that is, its value in relation to other assets. Since we should expect no less competition in the securities market, are there any bargains among securities? This issue has attracted an enormous amount of theoretical and empirical research, guided principally by the tenets of the *efficient market hypothesis.*

The efficient market hypothesis is one of the most important and pervasive as well as controversial concepts in the modern theory of finance (Fama 1970, 1991). This is because the hypothesis addresses in the most general terms the consequences of competition in the financial markets in determining the equilibrium values of financial assets. Efficient market assumptions underlie all of the valuation models discussed in this book. Furthermore, reliance on the efficient market hypothesis has allowed researchers to conduct effective empirical tests of other hypotheses, primarily in the context of event studies. But perhaps the most important implication of the hypothesis is that the market price of any security reflects the true, or rational, value of the security; thus in an efficient market investors are assured that the securities they purchase are fairly priced. (By the same token, it implies that there are no bargains in the security markets.)

The first section of this chapter discusses the efficient market hypothesis, its implications, its relationship to valuation models, and its importance in empirical tests of other hypotheses in finance. The second section discusses practical limitations to achieving market efficiency. The next three sections discuss results of empirical tests of the efficient market hypothesis, other evidence that raises questions about the efficiency of financial markets, and implications of market efficiency for portfolio management.

THE EFFICIENT MARKET HYPOTHESIS

The financial press regularly reports new information about the state of the economy (such as the latest GDP growth rate), as well as news about individual firms (such as a firm's latest earnings). In addition, professional analysts' forecasts of such variables are frequently reported, and these forecasts also represent new information. Even a novice investor understands that such information affects the values of financial assets. The efficient market hypothesis helps us to understand how and when such information is impounded into the prices of securities.

As a general definition the capital market is said to be efficient if security prices fully reflect all available information. The key issues associated with this definition are (1) in what sense market prices "fully reflect" information; and (2) what information is being reflected. Regarding the latter issue, the efficient-market hypothesis can be applied to any of three important types of information. The market is said to be *weak form efficient* if all information contained in historical prices is fully reflected in current prices. Alternatively stated, weak form efficiency concerns the question of whether past returns predict future returns, or the question of return *predictability*. The market is *semistrong form efficient* if all publicly available information is fully reflected in current prices, and the market is *strong form efficient* if all information, whether public or private, is fully reflected in current prices. Later we will discuss the importance of each of these forms.

Regarding the first issue, the market price of a security at time t, P_t, fully reflects an information set of a given type available at time t, I_t, if P_t is based on rational expectations of the time $t + 1$ value of the security, conditional on I_t, $E[P_{t+1} \mid I_t]$, discounted at an equilibrium discount rate that is also based on I_t, $r(I_t)$:[1]

(13.1) $$P_t = E[P_{t+1} \mid I_t] / [1 + r(I_t)].$$

$E[P_{t+1} \mid I_t]$ is said to be a *rational* expectation if the market's assessment of the distribution of $P_{t+1} \mid I_t$ is the true distribution of $P_{t+1} \mid I_t$, which is not directly observable. Thus, if the market is efficient with respect to I_t, the true expected return on the security, given I_t, is equal to the equilibrium expected return $r(I_t)$. Conversely, if the market is not efficient, the true expected return on the security is not equal to $r(I_t)$, and in effect the security is mispriced.

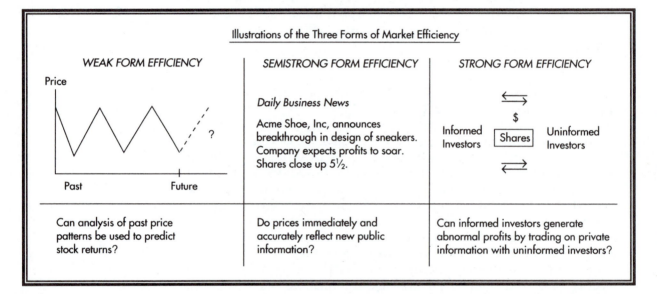

Illustrations of the Three Forms of Market Efficiency

WEAK FORM EFFICIENCY	SEMISTRONG FORM EFFICIENCY	STRONG FORM EFFICIENCY
Can analysis of past price patterns be used to predict stock returns?	Do prices immediately and accurately reflect new public information?	Can informed investors generate abnormal profits by trading on private information with uninformed investors?

To illustrate the above, suppose the market's expectation of the price of stock A one year from today, $E[P_{t+1}]$, is $50, and the current equilibrium expected return on the stock, r_t, is 10 percent. Thus the equilibrium price of the stock is $P_t = E[P_{t+1}]/(1 + r_t) = \$50/1.10 = \$45.45$. If the market's expectation of P_{t+1} is correct (that is, the market's expectation coincides with the true expected price), then the current price of the stock, $45.45, implies an expected return of 10 percent. But suppose the market incorrectly assesses the true expected price of the stock next year, which is, say, $55. In this case the current price implies a true expected return of approximately 21 percent ($= [55 - 45.45]/45.45$), which is greater than the equilibrium expected return. In this case, the price of the stock should be $55/1.10 = \$50$ to provide the equilibrium expected return of 10 percent.

According to the above discussion, if the market is efficient with respect to a given type of information, no investor can use that information in a

---

[1] Note that P_{t+1} includes any distributions such as a dividend to be received between time t and $t + 1$.

trading scheme to generate abnormal returns, that is, returns consistently in excess of the equilibrium expected return $r(I_t)$. The implications of this statement can be further illustrated by examining each form of market efficiency.

Weak Form Efficiency

As you recall, the market is weak form efficient if current prices fully reflect all information contained in historical prices. This implies that no investor can devise a trading rule based on past price patterns to earn abnormal returns. Interestingly, Wall Street is replete with "technical analysts" who claim they can predict price changes on the basis of past price patterns. If the market is weak form efficient, their claims are bogus.

To see how competition leads to weak form efficiency, consider the case of a stock that exhibits return reversals on a weekly basis. That is, if the return on the stock is positive (negative) in a given week, its return in the next week tends to be negative (positive). To simplify the case, let's assume that the stock provides an average return of 2 percent during even-numbered weeks and −1.5 percent during odd-numbered weeks. Thus, for the passive buy-and-hold investor, the stock provides an average return of approximately 13 percent per annum ($= 2 \times 26 - 1.5 \times 26$). However, an astute investor could sell the stock at the end of each of the even-numbered weeks, hold the proceeds in cash, or better, marketable securities such as Treasury bills, through the odd-numbered week, and then repurchase the stock at the end of the odd-numbered week. The average return to this strategy would be at least 26 percent per annum, plus interest on the marketable securities. (The average return may be further enhanced if the investor also sells the stock short during the odd-numbered weeks.)

However, note that the sale of the stock at the end of each even-numbered week would tend to exert downward pressure on the stock price at that time, which would tend to reduce the return for the week. Likewise, purchases of the stock at the end of each odd-numbered week would tend to raise the price of the stock, thereby increasing the return for the week. Thus, if a sufficing number of investors (or a single investor with sufficient funds) engaged in this strategy, their actions would tend to smooth the expected returns across the weeks, and the return on the stock might no longer be predictable. Of course, a practical limitation to arbitrage strategies such as this is that they involve greater transaction costs and possibly greater risk. These limitations to arbitrage, and thus the achievement of market efficiency, are discussed in more detail later.

It is often argued that weak form efficiency implies that stock prices must follow a random walk; that is, stock returns are serially uncorrelated and have a constant mean. The rationale for this argument is that stock returns should not be predictable in a competitive market. Indeed, this view led to many of the early tests of weak form efficiency and also influences our interpretation of the various anomalies in stock returns that have been documented, both of which are discussed later. However, it is clear from equation 13.1 that market efficiency does not imply that stock returns follow a random walk—the equilibrium expected return at any time t, $r(I_t)$, is simply rationally based on the information set available at time t, and thus changing information sets over time can lead to time-varying, and as some would argue, even serially correlated equilibrium expected returns. Thus in assessing the efficiency of the market on the basis of the observed behavior of stock returns, and observed *predictability* of returns in particular, one must judge whether the observed behavior is rational. Given the subjectivity of judgments of rational behavior, it is not surprising that the question of whether the market is efficient is so hotly debated.

Semistrong Form Efficiency

Of course, to consider the market efficient with respect to a given type of information, the condition must hold at all times t, $t + 1$, and so on. Over time the set of information available to the market changes as new information arrives, so new rational expectations, and thus new prices, develop. For example, $P_{t + 1}$ will reflect information set $I_{t + 1}$, and $P_{t + 1}$ will deviate from the price that was previously expected to prevail at $t + 1$, $E[P_{t + 1} \mid I_t]$, to the extent that new information alters market expectations. Thus, the *ex post* realized return on the security from time t to time $t + 1$, $[(P_{t + 1} - P_t) / P_t]$, may be higher or lower than the expected return $r(I_t)$ depending on the new information that arrives at time $t + 1$. Nevertheless, the new price $P_{t + 1}$ is also based on rational expectations given $I_{t + 1}$. This leads to the important implication that in an efficient market the price of a security will change immediately and rationally in response to new information. In other words, in responding to new information the market will neither delay nor overreact or underreact.

Since the market's response to new information plays such an important role in empirical tests of the efficient market hypothesis as well as other hypotheses in finance, additional discussion is warranted. Let us focus on semistrong form efficiency, in which I_t includes all publicly available information. Consider the case of a firm that will publicly announce its latest earnings next period, at time $t + 1$. At time t the market develops rational expectations of the firm's earnings, and these expectations are impounded into $E[P_{t + 1} \mid I_t]$ and thus P_t. At time $t + 1$, when the earnings are announced, the new information will determine $P_{t + 1}$, and $P_{t + 1}$ will deviate from $E[P_{t + 1} \mid I_t]$. Thus the realized return on the stock for the period $(t, t + 1)$ will deviate from $r(I_t)$ to the extent that the actual earnings deviate from expected earnings. However, at time t the market anticipates the implication of each of the possible values of the firm's upcoming earnings for the value of $P_{t + 1}$, and in fact these anticipations play an integral role in determining $E[P_{t + 1} \mid I_t]$ and thus P_t. Thus when the actual earnings are announced at time $t + 1$, the market responds immediately and rationally to the new information. In fact, only if on a continuing basis market responses are immediate and rational can market prices at any time *t* fully reflect the information set available at time *t*, I_t.

Strong Form Efficiency

Strong form efficiency applies the most rigorous standard that prices fully reflect all new information, public or private. Private information may be generated by insiders such as a firm's management or by analysts who either generate private information through investigation or have superior ability to process publicly available information. (The SEC prohibits insider trading for short-term (six months) profit, but insiders are otherwise allowed to buy or sell their firm's stock as long as they do not possess information that they have a fiduciary duty to disclose.) Although it is difficult to imagine how market prices could fully reflect private information, note that to obtain abnormal profits, the holder of private information must trade in the market. To the extent that market participants can identify the trader as an insider or a superior analyst, the trader's private information may be at least partially revealed as the trader attempts to buy or sell shares, and market prices will adjust accordingly. Of course the trader then has an incentive to conceal his or her identity to maximize the returns on the proprietary information.

MARKET EFFICIENCY AND EQUILIBRIUM PRICING MODELS

Returning to equation 13.1, note that $r(I_t)$ is defined as an equilibrium discount rate. The efficient market hypothesis does not specify the process by which equilibrium expected returns are generated. Thus, any model of equilibrium expected returns, such as the CAPM or APT, can be used to determine $r(I_t)$, and in this sense the efficient market hypothesis is consistent with any such model. This consistency represents an important unification of finance theory but also has an unfortunate consequence: empirical tests of either the efficient market hypothesis or any equilibrium pricing model are necessarily joint tests of both. For example, if results of empirical tests support the CAPM, they also support the efficient market hypothesis. On the other hand, if the results fail to support the CAPM, both the CAPM and the efficient market hypothesis are brought into question. Similarly, tests of the efficient market hypothesis require a model of the return-generating process, so interpretations of empirical results must always be taken with a caveat.

The situation is further complicated when researchers conduct empirical tests of other hypotheses in an event study framework. Consider the case of a firm issuing additional shares of stock. Several competing theories exist about the effect of issuing new shares on the market value of a firm's stock (Miller and Rock 1985; Myers and Majluf 1984).

Researchers have tested these theories in event studies by examining abnormal returns on issuing firms' shares around the date on which the firm announces that it will issue new shares. Based on the evidence, the researchers make conclusions about one or more of these theories, but in doing so they must assume that the market is semistrong form efficient, so the valuation effects are captured on the announcement date, and that they have used the correct return generating process in calculating abnormal returns. As such, the researchers are conducting a joint test of the theory, the efficient market hypothesis, and the return generating process that they selected. Despite this limitation, event studies have been an important tool in advancing finance theory.

PRACTICAL LIMITATIONS TO ACHIEVING MARKET EFFICIENCY

Market efficiency with respect to any given type of information is the direct result of competition among investors, who bear costs to gather information and to trade on such information and whose compensation for doing so comes only in the form of abnormal returns. Thus we are presented with a paradox: if the market is efficient, no one can obtain abnormal profits, but without the possibility of obtaining abnormal profits, no one will incur the cost of gathering and processing the very information that is to be fully reflected in market prices in an efficient market (Grossman and Stiglitz 1980).

To resolve this paradox we must realize that market efficiency is a continuum, and absolute market efficiency as defined in the previous section is but an extreme point on this continuum. In practice the point of equilibrium on this continuum will be determined by the market for information described above. That is, investors will cease to gather and process information when the marginal cost of doing so is equal to the marginal benefit–abnormal profits. Given this perspective, it is clear that market efficiency will vary across securities according to the relative costs and benefits associated with gathering and processing information. For example, it may be generally more costly to gather and process information on small firms than on large firms, and total potential abnormal profits may be smaller as well. As a result the market may be less efficient for small firms than for large firms.

To illustrate the above point, let us focus on transaction costs. Those who compete in the market for information on a given stock must engage in trades to realize abnormal profits and therefore must incur transaction costs that reduce their net profits. Thus, other things being equal, markets in which transaction costs are higher will tend to be less efficient. (Note that the market for transaction services is also competitive.) For example, suppose it has been observed that a given stock tends to have higher returns at the turn of each calendar month. If the size of the abnormal returns on these days is insufficient to cover the round-trip transaction costs required to capture the abnormal returns, the regularity will persist. Alternatively, if the abnormal returns exceed round-trip transaction costs, short-term traders will start to purchase the stock just prior to the turn of the month and sell it after realizing the abnormal returns. However, their actions en masse will tend to raise the price of the stock prior to the turn of the month and lower the price later, which will tend to reduce the abnormal returns at the turn of the month. Their activity will cease when the abnormal returns are reduced to the level of round-trip transaction costs.

EMPIRICAL TESTS OF THE EFFICIENT MARKET HYPOTHESIS

Our discussion of empirical tests of the efficient market hypothesis initially focuses on each form of the hypothesis introduced earlier. Following this is a discussion of documented evidence of stock return anomalies and seasonalities that are difficult to reconcile with market efficiency.

Weak Form Tests

Since weak form efficiency implies that abnormal returns cannot be obtained by trading on the basis of past price patterns, tests of weak form efficiency have focused on the power of past price changes (or returns) to predict future price changes (or returns). Runs tests have been used to determine whether nonrandom patterns of persistent returns or reversals occur in stock prices. A runs test simply involves counting the number of consecutive returns of the same sign, which are then compared with the expected number of consecutive returns for a series of random numbers of the same sample size. A significant difference in actual versus expected numbers indicates nonrandomness. Results of early runs tests (Fama 1965) failed to find evidence of nonrandomness in daily stock returns.

Filter rules are mechanical trading rules. A commonly employed filter is the following: if the price of a stock rises x percent, buy and hold the stock until the price drops at least x percent from a previous high, at which time sell. Such rules can be tested for various values of x. If stock prices fluctuate randomly, filter rules should not yield abnormal returns. On the other hand, if patterns do exist, it may be possible to earn substantial profits following such rules. Empirical tests indicate that profitable rules can be devised but that they are not profitable after considering even conservative transaction costs (Fama and Blume 1966).

Additional tests are designed to determine whether stock returns are autocorrelated. That is, the correlation of current returns, R_t, with returns at various lags τ, $R_{t-\tau}$, ($\tau = 1,2$, etc.) are calculated. If for any lag τ the autocorrelation is statistically different from 0, then returns are predictable, and as it is argued, such evidence indicates that the market is weak form inefficient. On the other hand, if the autocorrelations are zero, then returns are not predictable and the evidence is consistent with weak form efficiency.

At least two problems are associated with such tests. First, implicit in the design is the assumption that expected returns are constant over time, an assumption not required by the efficient market hypothesis. For example, *expected returns* may vary slowly but substantially over time and nevertheless may be consistent with rational asset pricing (think of interest rates in this regard). If so, returns over short periods may indeed be predictable (i.e., returns may be autocorrelated) and nevertheless the market may be weak form efficient. Second, linear tests like autocorrelation would fail to capture any possible nonlinear (i.e., more complex) relationship between current and past returns. If only nonlinear relationships existed, the finding of insignificant autocorrelations would be erroneously interpreted as evidence in support of weak form market efficiency.

Fama (1965) calculated autocorrelations of daily returns on the firms included in the Dow Jones Industrial Average for the period 1959–1963. Shown in Exhibit 13.1 are the sample autocorrelations that Fama reported for various daily lags. All of the correlations are small, and most are statistically insignificant. Other researchers have obtained similar results using daily, weekly, and monthly returns on individual stocks. Although the results are not conclusive because of the criticisms noted above, they are consistent with weak form efficiency.

In contrast, autocorrelation tests using portfolios have reached a different conclusion. Numerous studies have documented positive autocorrelations of daily stock index returns ranging from about .2 for portfolios of large firms to .4 for portfolios of small firms (Conrad and Kaul 1989). Fisher (1966) has argued that index return autocorrelation is due at least in part to nonsynchronous trading. Spurious positive autocorrelation in portfolio returns is induced if the returns on the individual stocks in the portfolio are based on prices observed at different points in time across the stocks. However, Lo and MacKinlay (1988) and Conrad and Kaul (1988) find reliable autocorrelations of *weekly* returns on indexes of NYSE stocks. Conrad and Kaul argue that these results are not spurious but are due to time-varying equilibrium expected returns, indicating that short-horizon returns are to a certain extent predictable.[2]

---

[2] However, Ogden (1993) argues that it is unlikely that short-horizon index return autocorrelation is due to time-varying expected returns simply because the variability and persistence of expected returns required to induce the observed level of autocorrelation is too large (for instance, large negative expected returns must often exist and persist for some time). He argues that the phenomenon is due to the nonsynchronous incorporation of marketwide information into the stocks in the index. That is, the incorporation of new marketwide information is immediate for some stocks, while for others it is delayed. This in turn is due to information processing and transaction costs that inhibit arbitrage trading that would otherwise lead to the immediate impoundment of information into the prices of all stocks.

EXHIBIT 13.1

Sample Autocorrelations of Daily Return on the Dow-Jones Industrials for Lags $\tau = 1, 2, \ldots 10$

| STOCK | \multicolumn{10}{c}{LAG (τ)} | | | | | | | | | | τ |
	1	2	3	4	5	6	7	8	9	10	
Allied Chemical	.017	−.042	.007	−.001	.027	.004	−.017	−.026	−.017	−.007	1223
Alcoa	.118*	.038	−.014	.022	−.022	.009	.017	.007	−.001	−.033	1190
American Can	−.087	−.024	.034	−.065*	−.017	−.006	.015	.025	−.047	−.040	1219
AT&T	−.039	−.097*	.000	.026	.005	−.005	.002	.027	−.014	.007	1219
American Tobacco	.111*	−.109*	−.060*	−.065*	.007	−.010	.011	.046	.039	.041	1283
Anaconda	.067*	−.061*	−.047	−.002	.000	−.038	.009	.016	−.014	−.056	1193
Bethlehem Steel	.013	−.065	.009	.021	−.053	−.098*	−.010	.004	−.002	−.021	1200
Chrysler	.012	−.066*	−.016	−.007	−.015	.009	.037	.056*	−.044	.021	1692
Du Pont	.013	−.033	.060*	.027	−.002	−.047	.020	.011	−.034	.001	1243
Eastman Kodak	.025	.014	−.031	.005	−.022	.012	.007	.006	.008	.002	1238
General Electric	.011	−.038	−.021	.031	−.001	.000	−.008	.014	−.002	.010	1693
General Foods	.061*	−.003	.045	.002	−.015	−.052	−.006	−.014	−.024	−.017	1408
General Motors	−.004	−.056*	−.037	−.008	−.038	−.006	.019	.006	−.016	.009	1446
Goodyear	−.123*	.017	−.044	.043	−.002	−.003	−.035	−.014	−.015	−.007	1162
International Harvester	−.017	−.029	−.031	.037	−.052	−.021	−.001	.003	−.046	−.016	1200
International Nickel	.096*	−.033	−.019	.020	.027	.059*	−.038	−.008	−.016	.034	1243
International Paper	.046	−.011	−.058*	.053*	.049	−.003	−.025	−.019	−.003	−.021	1447
Johns Manville	.006	−.038	−.027	−.023	−.029	−.080*	.040	.018	−.037	.029	1205
Owens Illinois	−.021	−.084*	−.047	.068*	.086*	−.040	.011	−.040	.067*	−.043	1237
Procter and Gamble	.099*	−.009	−.008	.009	−.015	.022	.012	−.012	−.022	−.021	1447
Sears	.097*	.026	.028	.025	.005	−.054	−.006	−.010	−.008	−.009	1236
Standard Oil (Calif.)	.025	−.030	−.051*	−.025	−.047	−.034	−.010	.072*	−.049*	−.035	1693
Standard Oil (N. J.)	.008	−.116*	.016	.014	−.047	−.018	−.022	−.026	−.073*	.081*	1156
Swift and Co.	−.004	−.015	−.010	.012	.057*	.012	−.043	.014	.012	.001	1446
Texaco	.094*	−.049	−.024	−.018	−.017	−.009	.031	.032	−.013	.008	1159
Union Carbide	.107*	−.012	.040	.046	−.036	−.034	.003	−.008	−.054	−.037	1118
United Aircraft	.014	−.033	−.022	−.047	−.067*	−.053	.046	.037	.015	−.019	1200
U.S. Steel	.040	−.074*	.014	.011	−.012	−.021	.041	.037	−.021	−.044	1200
Westinghouse	−.027	−.022	−.036	−.003	.000	−.054*	−.020	.013	−.014	.008	1448
Woolworth	.028	−.016	.015	.014	.007	−.039	.013	.003	−.088*	−.008	1445

*Sample autocorrelation is at least two standard deviations to the left or to the right of its expected value under the hypothesis that the true autocorrelation is zero.

Source: Eugene F. Fama, "The Behavior of Stock Market Prices," *Journal of Business* 38 (1965): 72.

Predictability has also been documented in long-horizon portfolio returns. Using returns on portfolios of NYSE stocks for the period 1926–1985, Fama and French (1988a) find negative autocorrelations of three- to five-year returns in the range of −.25 to −.4, and a similar result for a value-weighted index of NYSE and AMEX stocks for the period 1926–1986 (Poterba and Summers 1988). Fama and French (1988b) find that lagged aggregate dividend yields often explain more than 50 percent of the variation in subsequent two- to four-year index returns! Fama and French (1989) argue that time variation in expected returns captured by variables such as aggregate dividend yields is consistent with modern intertemporal asset pricing models (Merton 1973) as well as the original consumption-smoothing hypothesis (Friedman 1957):

> ... asset-pricing models predict that consumption depends on wealth rather than current income. When income is high in relation to wealth, investors want to smooth consumption into the future by saving more. If the supply of capital-investment opportunities is not also unusually large, higher desired savings lead to lower expected security returns. Conversely, investors want to save less when income is temporarily low. Again, without an offsetting reduction in capital-investment opportunities, lower desired savings tend to push expected returns up ... " (p. 42).

Evidence of long-horizon predictability has also been documented for individual securities. DeBondt and Thaler (1985, 1987) find that extreme losers (winners) among individual NYSE stocks over a three- to five-year period tend to have positive (negative) abnormal returns in subsequent years. Their results are depicted in Figure 13.1. Since these results indicate that abnormal returns are predictable, the evidence is inconsistent with weak form efficiency. DeBondt and Thaler attribute these results to market

FIGURE 13.1

Average of Sixteen Three-Year Test Periods between January 1933 and December 1980. Length of Formation Period: Three Years

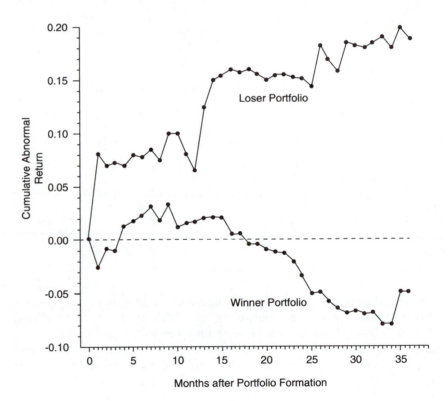

overreaction to bad (good) news about these firms. As such, the results may also suggest that the market is semistrong form inefficient. Chan (1988), Ball and Kothari (1989), and others argue that these results may be due to failure to properly measure abnormal returns (i.e., to adjust for risk). However, using alternative measures of risk, Chopra, Lakonishok, and Ritter (1992) find results similar to those of DeBondt and Thaler. Conrad and Kaul (1993) argue that the phenomenon is due to biases in computed returns—specifically, biases induced when monthly returns are cumulated over long intervals.

Semistrong Form Tests

Tests of semistrong form efficiency focus on the market's response to the public release of new information. If the market is semistrong form efficient, price changes associated with new information should be immediate and rational; that is, the market should neither overreact nor underreact.

The bulk of the empirical evidence pertaining to semistrong efficiency has been generated in the context of event studies. In a typical event study, the researcher focuses on a given news event associated with a firm, such as the firm's announcement of its quarterly earnings, and examines the abnormal returns on the firm's stock around the announcement date. Market efficiency is tested by determining whether the market response is immediate and rational. Of course, event studies are also undertaken with the primary purpose of testing hypotheses about the valuation effect of the news itself, so in such studies market efficiency is assumed. Nevertheless, the substantial event study literature that has developed in the past twenty years also provides evidence on semistrong form efficiency.

The basic methodology for event studies was developed by Fama, Fisher, Jensen, and Roll (FFJR) (1969). They examined the effect of a stock split on the price of a firm's stock. FFJR calculated abnormal returns on each stock in their sample for each month from thirty months before to thirty months after the month of the split using the single-index model (see Chapter 5). The abnormal return on stock i for period t is calculated as

(13.2) $$e_{i,t} = R_{i,t} - (\hat{a}_i + \hat{b}_i R_{M,t}),$$

where $R_{i,t}$ and $R_{M,t}$ are the returns on the stock and a proxy for the market portfolio, and $\hat{a}_i$ and $\hat{b}_i$ are estimates of the market model parameters. They then computed the cross-sectional average of the abnormal returns on the stocks for each month relative to the split month, and cumulative average abnormal returns (CARs) were calculated from these averages. The results of their analysis are displayed in Figure 13.2. Note the buildup of CARs up to month 0, the split month, and the absence of additional abnormal returns after the split month. The buildup of abnormal returns prior to

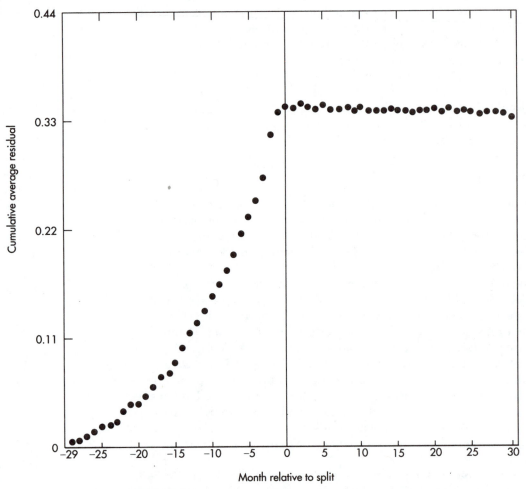

FIGURE 13.2
CARs for Stock Splits

announcement is consistent with the hypothesis that firms tend to split their shares after an unusually positive performance of their stock, which in turn is a rational market response to unusually good news about the firm's prospects. The absence of additional cumulative abnormal returns after the announcement is consistent with semistrong form efficiency.

Following the pioneering study of FFJR, refinements have been made in the data and methodology used in event studies. Most notably, the development and widespread dissemination of the University of Chicago's Center for Security Prices (CRSP) tapes containing daily returns has allowed researchers to gauge market responses to events on a daily basis. Hundreds of event studies have now been conducted, focusing on many different types of events. These studies generally document a swift and unbiased market reaction to new information. As such, the discussion in most event studies focuses mainly on the hypothesis being tested, thereby assuming semistrong form efficiency. A few examples of event studies include Ball and Brown (1968) and Beaver (1968), who studied the market's response to earnings announcements, and Pettit (1972), Aharony and Swary (1980), and Asquith and Mullins (1983), who studied the market's response to dividend announcements. See Jensen and Ruback (1983) for a review of evidence of the valuation effects of announcements of mergers and takeovers and Smith (1986) for a review of evidence of the valuation effects of announcements of new security issues.

Other evidence, however, appears to be inconsistent with semistrong form efficiency. Ball (1978) and Joy and Jones (1979) review evidence indicating that the market appears to *underreact* to announcements of unexpectedly high and low earnings. That is, firms announcing unexpectedly high (low) earnings subsequently experienced positive (negative) abnormal returns on average. This phenomenon has been dubbed postannouncement drift. The evidence indicates that underreaction is more substantial for smaller firms; hence, some researchers have argued that the greater transaction costs associated with smaller firms inhibit the impoundment of new information such as that contained in earnings reports. However, Foster, Olson, and Shevlin (1984) and others argue that these results may be attributable to the method used to estimate the market's expected earnings prior to the earnings announcement (e.g., analysts' forecasts). When Foster, Olson, and Shevlin use an alternative method to assess earnings expectations, the postannouncement drift disappears.

Strong Form Tests

Tests of strong form efficiency focus on private information. The market is strong form efficient if for example insiders cannot earn abnormal profits on their trades. Insiders must report their purchases and sales of their firm's stock to the SEC, and the SEC reports this information to the public at a later date. Jaffe (1974) and Lorie and Niederhoffer (1968) studied purchases and sales of insiders and the subsequent abnormal returns on their firms' stocks. The researchers found a tendency of these firms to provide positive abnormal returns following insider purchases and negative abnormal returns following insider sales. However, Seyhoun (1986) provides evidence indicating that insider buying is more prominent in small firms and insider selling is more prominent in large firms. Seyhoun's evidence, combined with evidence that small firms generally provide higher risk-adjusted returns than large firms (see the discussion in the next section), may partially explain the insider trading results, albeit by deference to another phenomenon that is difficult to explain.

Security analysts and many professional portfolio managers also generate private information. For example, on a weekly basis the Value

Line investment survey ranks 1700 common stocks according to assessments of the stocks' return prospects. The stocks are divided into five groups. Stocks in group 1 have the strongest return prospects, and stocks in group 5 have the weakest prospects. Studies by Copeland and Mayers (1982), Stickel (1985) and others indicate that Value Line has some ability to predict abnormal returns over short horizons. In addition, Lloyd-Davies and Canes (1978) find evidence that security analysts' recommendations published in the *Wall Street Journal*'s "Heard on the Street" column are followed by abnormal returns of about 1 percent for recommended purchases and –2 percent for recommended sales. These results appear to be inconsistent with strong form efficiency.

Finally, a number of researchers have studied the performance of mutual funds for evidence that their management has the ability to generate abnormal returns through stock selection (Jensen 1968, Henriksson 1984, Chang and Lewellen 1984, Ippolito 1989). The results generally indicate that at best active managers generate abnormal returns that are barely sufficient to cover additional expenses incurred. Thus this evidence is consistent with strong form efficiency.

RETURN ANOMALIES AND SEASONALITIES

Among the most intriguing empirical studies in finance are those that document evidence of anomalies and seasonalities in returns on stocks and other assets. Among the stock return anomalies and seasonalities discovered are (1) the price/earnings effect, a negative relationship between a firm's price/earnings ratio and risk-adjusted expected returns; (2) the size and January effects, a tendency of small firms to provide positive risk-adjusted returns, particularly in January and especially at the turn of the year; (3) the monthly effect, a tendency of stock index returns to be higher at the turns of calendar months; (4) the holiday effect, relatively high stock index returns on the last trading day before a holiday; and (5) the weekend effect, negative average stock index returns on Mondays. Each of these return anomalies suggests that stock returns are predictable, and therefore their existence suggests that the stock market is weak form inefficient.

The Price/Earnings Effect

Basu (1977) was first to document evidence that price/earnings ratios have marginal power to explain cross-sectional variations in expected returns on stocks even after controlling for risk by means of the CAPM beta (β). Ball (1978) provides a possible explanation. He argues that price/earnings is a proxy for risk; that is, if stocks have the same earnings but one is riskier, the riskier stock will have a lower price and thus a lower price/earnings

EFFICIENT MARKET THEORY LIVES!

What distinguishes journalism from mere reporting is the search for Deeper Meaning. And, since few events are immune from this search, it's hardly a surprise that the Oct. 19 stock-market crash has attracted all sorts of Deeper Meaningfulness. What is rather surprising, however, is how far from the mark most of these commentaries are. Consider this portentous offering in the April 18 issue of Business Week:

"The October 19 cataclysm marks the failure of the most pervasive belief in economics today: an unquestioning faith in the wisdom of markets. . . . The intellectual core of the free-market paradigm was the efficient market theory [EMT]. . . . Then came Bloody Monday. The EMT can't explain it." Similar pronouncements have appeared in The Wall Street Journal, London's Financial Times and elsewhere.

Actually, of course, Adam Smith had never heard of the Efficient Market Theory and many true capitalists on Wall Street bitterly oppose it. Indeed, you don't have to swear fealty to this rather abstruse view of how financial markets work to believe that the U.S. Postal Service is never going to outperform Federal Express.

But in any case, much of this Deeper Meaning interpretation about the failure of the EMT proceeds from a misunderstanding of what, exactly, the EMT is.

How Perfection is Achieved

So, what is it? A perfectly efficient market is one where the price of every security equals its investment value at all times. (For the financially literate, that means that the market price of a stock equals the present value of its future

prospects.) This perfection is achieved when all investors have access to all currently available information about the future, all are good analysts, all follow market prices and all adjust their stock positions accordingly. In short, a perfectly efficient market is one where an amazing amount of information is fully and immediately reflected in prices.

Great, but pie-in-the-skyish. You know, for example, that your brother-in-law wouldn't recognize a piece of information if it flew up his nose. Thus, as a concession to a world made up of brothers-in-law and brokers, the EMT comes in three flavors: the "strong" form that argues that all current information, public and private, is reflected in stock prices; the "semi-strong" form that says that only publicly available info is; and the "weak" form which restricts what is known to the basic trade-off between return and risk reflected in prices of securities. Financial economists—particularly those who have brothers-in-law—don't believe in the strong form.

It's fairly easy to make a case that what happened in October supports the weak form of EMT. What happened was simple. There was a sudden wave of new information, all of it bad, and all of it threatening to swamp U.S. corporate earnings. Stock prices responded—just like they're supposed to—by collapsing. One finance academic called this process "a massive reformation of investor expectations." Indeed, even before the washout on Monday, Oct. 19, the market was busily digesting the news and reflecting these reforming expectations.

Directly before the Crash, late Tuesday on Oct. 13, the Democrats on the House Ways and Means Committee agreed to tax changes that would make corporate takeovers less attractive. Eeeek! Corporate takeovers had been

Continued

Efficient Market Theory Lives!—*Continued*

the mighty engine pushing up the market; news of a takeover, or rumors of one, enhance not only the future prospects of the target company, but (and more immediately) the price of the stock as well. Even if only for the short term.

So that was bad news. But worse, early Wednesday morning on Oct. 14, the trade figures for August were announced and—eeek!—the deficit was larger than expected. That not only depressed the dollar but goosed up interest rates: Treasury-bond yields pierced the psychologically sensitive 10% barrier. Little wonder this information drove the Dow down 95 points by the close of trading Wednesday.

Even worse, consider what happened on Thursday, Oct. 15. Not only did Chemical Bank raise its prime lending rate, but Treasury Secretary James Baker threw a tantrum over West Germany's monetary policy. Specifically, Mr. Baker suggested that he might go Germany one better in dumping on the dollar. His hint that the U.S. would not defend the dollar against the depressing impact of Bonn's events seemed to confirm fears that Wednesday's higher interest rates were not a random blip on the inflation screen. Result? The Dow slid 57 points more.

On Friday, Oct. 16, more of the same. Reports of an Iranian attack on a U.S.-flagged oil tanker didn't help any. Pessimism spread as the news spread, and the Dow dived 108 points.

Over the weekend, the news got even grimmer. Mr. Baker continued to publicly threaten the Germans—double-eek! In fact, it was reported that he was ready to let the dollar drop even more. Indeed, it had gotten to the point where brothers-in-law all over the world realized that the dollar might keep falling. That, of course, would push up U.S. interest rates and inflation, and render corporate earnings—politely put—weak. Who would want to hold stocks in this kind of environment?

Indeed, by Monday morning, Oct. 19, the bad news was zipping around the world, communicated by falling stock prices, which, in turn, constituted its own bad news. (Actually, foreign investors who had the most to lose from a falling dollar had started the dumping action Sunday night.) It's no stretch at all to say that what happened on Black Monday was the utterly predictable result of the fact that information flows have become so good, so instantaneous. Unfortunately, but just as predictably, the group of investors seeking to respond to all this distressing information and adjust their portfolio holdings accordingly—that is, dump their stocks—became so large that they swamped the trading technology. Resulting illiquidity made an orderly retreat from the market impossible.

After October, of course, the tenor of information changed again. The news was surprisingly good. Interest rates subsided, inflation anxieties were quelled, the dollar remained fairly stable, unemployment continued to behave and takeover activity resumed. Consumer spending remained steady and GNP figures weren't too bad. Thus—no hocus-pocus about it—corporate earnings seemed likely to be strong. And, of course, lower stock prices meant investors could purchase these improved, future prospects "cheap." Investors seeking to adjust their portfolio holdings accordingly—that is, buy stocks—lifted the Dow some 200 points back from its October low.

As with all academic debate, needless to say, there's an element of game-playing. Critics can complain that it's easy to discover reasons for events after the fact and ultimately impossible to prove how much effect these factors, or any others, really had.

Efficient Market Theory Lives!—*Continued*

But other aspects of EMT should not be forgotten. EMTers maintain that stock prices do fluctuate around the underlying market valuation. That much (or all?) of a 500-point down move could be called a "fluctuation" is a disturbing thought. But there's nothing in EMT to preclude it.

Proof Is in the Investing

The proof of the EMT is in the eating, or, more precisely, in the investing. If markets are efficient, and any price movements left over are random and hence unpredictable, equity investors will not in the long run be able to beat a strategy of buying and holding a diversified portfolio of stocks. They just won't be able to find information that is not already reflected in prices. They may luck out, and beat the market in the short run, but eventually they will regress to the mean.

The evidence is very powerful that this is exactly what happens. For example, Forbes columnist Mark Hulbert, proprietor of a Washington-based monitoring service, reports that only a dozen or so of the 100 investment-newsletter portfolios he has monitored since 1980 have been able to beat the market—and not by much. Big institutional investors do about as well. There has been no decisive change in performance since the Crash.

The market isn't perfectly efficient. Some advisers did beat it. Many of them exploited one or another of the marginal "anomalies" that researchers have known and puzzled about for years, such as the slight tendency of stocks with low "price-earnings ratios" (the market price of the stock relative to the company's profits per share) to go up more than average.

But as dramatic as the Crash was—and it was—it did not deck the Efficient Market Theory as properly understood, or lay bare the ruins of capitalism. Deeper Meanings to the contrary, look no further than the old Wall Street saying: When the market wants to go down, it does.

---

ratio as well as a higher expected return. Thus, if β is an imperfect measure of risk (e.g., we need a multifactor asset-pricing model) or β is measured with error, the price/earnings ratio will capture part of the relevant risk of a stock and thus will have power to explain expected returns.

The Size and January Effects

Banz (1981) was among the first researchers to document the size effect. Banz showed that CAPM risk-adjusted returns are negatively related to firm size. The differential is especially large in comparing the smallest firms with the largest firms—19.8 percent per year. Other researchers have argued that this result occurs because β is an imperfect measure of risk (Chan, Chen, and Hsieh 1985; Chan and Chen 1988) or because β estimates are downward biased for small firms due to statistical problems (Roll 1981, Reinganum 1981), or because of methodological problems (Chan and Chen 1988). It is also interesting to note that the size and price/earnings effects are related; small firms tend to have low price/earnings ratios (Reinganum 1981, Basu 1983).

Rozeff and Kinney (1976) first documented that average stock index returns are higher in January than in other months. They obtained their results using an equally weighted index of NYSE stocks, which of course gives a greater collective weight to the more numerous small firms in the index. Later research determined that this weighting was critical, since January returns on value-weighted indexes, which give much greater collective weight to large firm stocks, are not as large. Thus the January effect is largely confined to small-firm stocks and is therefore related to the size effect. Keim's (1983) analysis indicates that the lion's share of the annual average excess returns earned by small firms is realized in January, and about one-quarter of the size effect is realized in the first five trading days in January, when average returns on small firm stocks approach 1 percent per day.

The principal explanation that has emerged in the literature to explain the January effect is the tax-loss selling hypothesis (Branch 1977, Roll 1983, Reinganum 1983, Ritter 1988). Proponents of this hypothesis argue that in December investors tend to sell stocks that have experienced losses in the current year to realize capital losses and thus reduce their tax liability. The resulting temporary price pressure depresses the prices of these 'losers' in December, and when their prices rebound to equilibrium levels in January, the result appears as high January returns. It is argued that small-firm stocks are particularly susceptible to tax-loss selling effects, in part because it is more likely that small-firm stocks are held by individual investors (as opposed to institutional investors such as mutual funds and pension funds), who are the prime candidates for tax-loss selling, and also because small firm stocks, being much more volatile, are more likely to be losers (as well as winners, of course).

Evidence consistent with the tax-loss selling hypothesis is displayed in Figure 13.3, which is based on a study by Rozeff (1986). Shown are the average January returns on portfolios of stocks arranged by size and separated into two groups according to whether returns on the portfolio during July–November of the previous year were positive (winning years) or negative (tax-losing years), for the period 1926–1982. For each size decile, average January returns are higher in tax-losing years than in winning years, evidence consistent with the tax-loss selling hypothesis. However, even in the winning years the average January returns are much higher for small-firm stocks than for large-firm stocks. Thus a substantial portion of the January effect appears to be unrelated to tax-loss selling. Although the effect does not appear to be due to seasonal shifts in risk (Keim and Stanbaugh 1986), other explanations for the phenomenon include seasonally high cash flows (such as dividends and bonuses) received by investors, who use this cash to purchase stocks in January (Ogden 1990), and year-end window dressing by institutional investors, who tend to dump losing small-firm stocks in December, prior to annual performance review, and repurchase such stocks in January (Haugen and Lakonishok 1988).

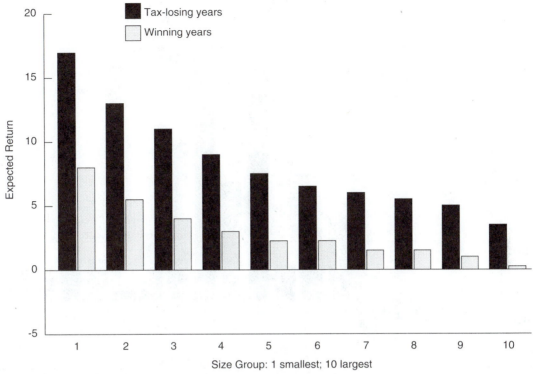

FIGURE 13.3

Average Returns in January by Firm Size for Stocks with Positive
Returns ("Winners") or Negative Returns ("Losers") in the Previous
July–November Period, 1922–1982

Source: R. Haugen and Lakonishok. 1988. *The Incredible January Effect.* Homewood: Dow Jones Irwin.

The Monthly Effect

Ariel (1987) examined average returns on both value-weighted and
equally weighted indices of NYSE and AMEX stocks for each of the
trading days of the calendar month. His results for the period 1963–1981
indicate that both indices provide relatively high average returns each day
of the half-month period beginning on the last trading day of the calendar
month and relatively low or negative average returns on the other days
of the calendar month. Ariel also shows that this monthly effect is not
merely a manifestation of the January effect or other anomalies. Lakonishok and Smidt (1988) calculated daily returns on the Dow Jones
Industrial Average for the ninety-year period 1897–1986 and calculated
average returns on the index sorted by trading day of the calendar month.
They found relatively large positive average returns for each of four
consecutive trading days beginning with the last trading day and
extending through the first three trading days of the calendar month. The

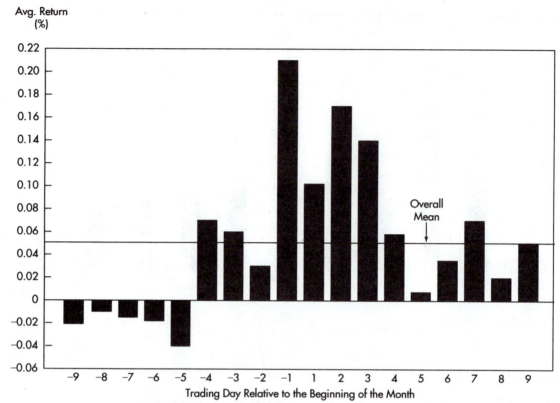

FIGURE 13.4

Average Percent Returns on Stocks for Nine Trading Days before and after the Beginning of the Calendar Month, Based on the CRSP Value Weighted Index for 1967–1991.

total return realized on these four trading days over the ninety-year period accounted for slightly more than 100 percent of the total return on the index for the period, indicating that the average return realized on the remaining trading days of the month was negative. Figure 13.4 shows the average daily return on a value-weighted index of NYSE and AMEX stocks for each trading day from nine trading days before the turn of the calendar month through nine trading days after the turn of the calendar month computed for the twenty-five-year period 1967–1991. The average returns on trading days –1, +1, +2, and +3 relative to the turn of the month are the largest, substantially above the overall average daily return.

Ogden (1990) provides an explanation for this turn-of-the-month phenomenon. He argues that the effect is due to an aggregate concentration of cash payments to investors at the turn of the month. He documents evidence that the bulk of payments of dividends, interest, and principal on securities are made on these days and argues that such infusions of cash increase investors' demand for stocks, thus raising their prices. As Ogden also points out, because of transaction costs it is unlikely that an investor can realize abnormal profits by buying stocks just before the end of the month and selling after the third or fourth trading day of the next month. (Berkowitz, Logue, and Noser [1988] estimate the average cost of a round-trip transaction on the NYSE to be about .46 percent.)

The Holiday Effect

Lakonishok and Smidt (1988), Ariel (1990), and others have recently documented evidence that stock index returns tend to be higher on the last trading day before a holiday. Ariel's results for the period 1963–1982 indicate that the average preholiday return on a value-weighted portfolio, 0.364 percent, is fourteen times the mean daily return for the remaining days of the year, 0.026 percent, and approximately one-third of the total market return for the period 1963–1982 was earned on eight trading days that each year fall before holidays. Ariel suggests that major clienteles of investors may for whatever reason prefer to increase their purchases of stock prior to a holiday.

The Weekend Effect

A number of studies have calculated average stock index returns sorted by day of the week and have found that average returns on Monday are negative (Cross 1973, French 1980, Gibbons and Hess 1981). Examining intraday stock index returns, Harris (1986) found that much of Monday's negative return occurs between Friday's market close and Monday's market open; hence the anomaly is referred to as the weekend effect. Average returns on a value-weighted portfolio of NYSE and AMEX stocks for the period 1963–1990 are shown by day of the week in Exhibit 13.2.

Lakonishok and Levi (1982) argue that the weekend effect is partially due to the effect of settlement procedures on the NYSE. Since 1968 the NYSE has allowed investors five business days to present payment for purchases of stock. (Prior to 1968 the settlement period was four business days.) Allowing for an extra day for the check to clear (settlement is in

EXHIBIT 13.2

Average Percent Daily Stock Index Returns by Day of the Week, 1967–1991

Index[1]	All Days	Monday	Tuesday	Wednesday	Thursday	Friday
Value-Weighted	0.0420	−0.0980	0.0444	0.1113	0.0506	0.0958
(Std. Dev.)	(0.8903)	(1.1100)	(0.8143)	(0.8557)	(0.8147)	(0.8172)
Equal-Weighted	0.0708	−0.1280	0.0076	0.1412	0.1129	0.2135
(Std. Dev.)	(0.8244)	(0.0173)	(0.7423)	(0.7967)	(0.7590)	(0.7425)

[1] Index returns are obtained from the University of Chicago's Center for Research in Security Prices (CRSP) files, which includes all NYSE and AMEX common stocks.

clearing house funds, which become available as federal funds on the next business day), the total delay between purchase and payment is therefore six business days. For a normal week (i.e., ignoring holiday market closings) this implies that for Monday through Thursday the delay is eight calendar days and for Friday the delay is eleven calendar days. Thus, Lakonishok and Levi argue that since on Fridays an investor can earn an extra three days of interest on the funds that will be used to pay for stock, closing prices on Friday should be slightly higher than on Monday; hence a weekend effect. However, Lakonishok and Levi's empirical analysis indicates that their hypothesis can explain only a small fraction of the weekend effect.

More recently Lakonishok and Maberly (1990) show that individuals tend to increase their selling activity relative to buying activity on Mondays, and this may also contribute to the weekend effect. Their results are consistent with Osborne's (1962) argument that there is a day-of-the-week effect in the processing of information by individual investors. Individuals may have a slight tendency to make excessive purchases of stocks during the week (on the advice of predominantly buy-oriented brokers) and wait until the weekend to sort out their financial situation. They then realize that they need to sell some shares and therefore become net sellers on Monday.

IMPLICATIONS OF MARKET EFFICIENCY FOR PORTFOLIO MANAGEMENT

The extent to which the financial markets are informationally efficient has important implications for portfolio management. Consider the extremes first. If financial markets are highly efficient, an assumption made in models such as the CAPM, then portfolio management essentially involves the development of optimally diversified portfolios along the lines of the theories discussed elsewhere in this text. For example, the essential conclusion of the CAPM is that an efficient strategy for an investor is relatively passive—simply buy and hold risky assets in a portfolio with weights equal to the value of each asset relative to the total value of all assets, and combine this portfolio with holdings of the risk-free asset according to risk tolerance, as discussed in Chapter 1.

On the other hand, if financial markets are extremely inefficient, investors may be better off identifying and holding underpriced assets and avoiding (or selling short) assets that are overpriced. In effect, portfolio management would be active and might involve both market timing and security selection. While much of modern portfolio theory would still be relevant in an inefficient market, (that is, an investor might optimally diversify among the underpriced stocks identified), many of the conclusions of equilibrium models would be rendered ineffectual.

Of course, the type of active strategy employed depends on the type of inefficiency exhibited in the market. Specifically, if the market is weak form inefficient, then technical analysis may be useful to uncover profitable trading rules. If the market is semistrong form inefficient, then buying or selling at the time that information is released to the public (i.e., to take advantage of market overreaction or underreaction) may provide abnormal returns. Finally, if the market is strong form inefficient, an investor may obtain abnormal profits by trading on privately generated information.

It is important to consider the general consequences of an active portfolio management strategy in greater detail. Note that even if the securities market is inefficient, investors considering an active portfolio management strategy designed to earn abnormal profits must account for the additional risk and transaction costs that are likely to be associated with the strategy. For example, an investor who chooses to hold only a small subset of all available securities (i.e., those that are identified as underpriced by some criteria) is likely to hold a portfolio that is relatively risky, since the portfolio is not widely diversified. Furthermore, active strategies generally involve high transaction costs, since the investor is likely to sell stocks that are no longer underpriced in favor of other stocks that are underpriced. Consequently, if the investor follows an active strategy that is bogus, the portfolio will perform poorly because (1) it is likely to be exposed to risk that is not compensated in the market (although it should be noted that some strategies are explicitly designed to *reduce* risk for a given level of expected return); and (2) the net return on the portfolio will be lower because of greater transaction costs.

Thus, before embarking on an active strategy, the investor should thoroughly examine the legitimacy of the strategy in terms of its ability to generate superior risk-adjusted returns net of transaction costs (perhaps via testing using past data) relative to passive portfolios. And, of course, given the substantial economies of scale with respect to transaction costs, any given strategy is more likely to succeed if it is carried out on a larger scale. For these reasons, increasing attention is being given to transaction cost management (Wagner and Banks 1992, Gennotte and Jung 1992). We reiterate the point that the market is competitive with regard to information gathering and processing. Thus, as in any other competitive market, of all investors engaged in active strategies, only those who are talented and can control costs will succeed.

The state of competition in financial markets no doubt falls between the extremes described above. Financial market structures appear to reflect aspects of behavior consistent with both efficient and inefficient markets. Primary illustrations of this point are the simultaneous existence of both actively and passively managed investment companies (mutual funds) and of both full-service brokers, who offer security selection advice as well as transactions services, and discount brokers, who generally offer only transactions services. Also note that even in an efficient market, full-service brokers provide valuable services, including financial planning, risk estimation and management, liquidity management, and the like.

Summary

The efficient market hypothesis addresses in the most general terms the role of competition in determining the equilibrium values of financial assets. As such, the hypothesis underlies all equilibrium asset-pricing models. The hypothesis states that security prices fully reflect all available information. However, given the costs associated with gathering and processing information and trading, it is unlikely that such absolute efficiency is achievable. Thus it is more useful to depict market efficiency on a continuous scale than as an absolute. Differences in the relative costs of information and trading across securities are likely to lead to differences in the observed efficiencies of various securities markets.

The empirical evidence on market efficiency is mixed. Regarding weak form efficiency, many tests have uncovered nonrandom patterns and seasonalities in stock returns. However, it is unlikely that an investor can realize abnormal returns by exploiting the patterns and seasonalities analyzed thus far, because of the added transaction costs involved. Similarly, some empirical evidence indicates that the market overreacts or underreacts to new firm-specific information. However, it is possible that the results of these studies suffer from biases in measures of risk or biases in the returns themselves. In any event, it is unclear whether investors can realize abnormal returns by trading to exploit the market's reaction to new information, again because of the transaction costs involved. Thus, subject to the constraints of transaction costs, the market appears to be weak form and semistrong form efficient. Finally, a limited number of studies indicate that the market is not strong form efficient.

The extent to which the market is efficient has important implications for portfolio management. Greater efficiency is generally associated with a more passive and more diversified portfolio, while inefficiency implies more active and selective portfolio management. Investors considering an active portfolio management strategy in pursuit of abnormal profits linked to market inefficiency must account for the additional risk and transaction costs that are likely to be associated with the strategy.

Questions and Problems

1. Define the efficient market hypothesis and describe the three forms of the hypothesis.
2. Explain how a competitive market would tend to drive out return reversals on a given stock.

3. Explain why the market may be less efficient for small-firm stocks than for large-firm stocks.

4. Evidence that professional analysts can realize consistent abnormal returns would refute which form of the efficient market hypothesis?

5. Evidence of abnormal returns on stocks for several years after an extreme earnings announcement potentially refutes which form of the efficient market hypothesis? Provide explanation for this phenomenon that is consistent with market efficiency.

6. Discuss the joint hypothesis nature of event studies designed to measure the market's reaction to new information.

7. What is the paradox associated with market efficiency? How is it resolved?

8. Why should market efficiency be viewed as a continuum rather than an absolute?

9. Discuss the various stock return anomalies and seasonalities that have been documented by researchers. Can they be reconciled with market efficiency?

10. On a daily basis the *Wall Street Journal* provides information on the dividend yield, price/earnings ratio, 52-week high and low closing prices, and the most recent closing price, of each of thousands of stocks on the NYSE, AMEX and other exchanges. Based on the evidence discussed in the chapter, of what use might this information be to an investor?

11. What are the implications of market efficiency for portfolio management? (Include in your discussion a focus on active versus passive portfolio management, the effect of transaction costs, the choice of full-service brokers versus discount brokers, and the choice of mutual funds versus self-selected stocks.)

12. Discuss the role of portfolio theory in an inefficient market.

13. Calculate daily returns on a major stock index such as the Dow Jones Industrial Average or the SP500 index for several recent months, and use these returns to calculate the one-day lag autocorrelation of returns on the index. Compare your results to evidence discussed in the text and provide one or more explanations for the results.

REFERENCES

Aharony, J., and I. Swary. 1980. Quarterly dividend and earnings announcements and stockholders' return. An empirical analysis. *Journal of Finance* 35:1–12.

Ariel, R. 1990. High stock returns before holidays. Existence and evidence on possible causes. *Journal of Finance*. December.

Ariel, R. 1987. A monthly effect in stock returns. *Journal of Financial Economics* 18:161–174.

Asquith, P., and D. Mullins. 1983. The impact of initiating dividend payments on shareholders' wealth. *Journal of Business* 56:77–96.

Ball, R. 1978. Anomalies in relationships between securities' yields and yield-surrogates. *Journal of Financial Economics* 6:103–126.

Ball, R., and P. Brown. 1968. An empirical evaluation of accounting income numbers. *Journal of Accounting Research* 6:159–178.

Ball, R., and S. Kothari. 1989. Nonstationary expected returns. Implications for tests of market efficiency and serial correlations in returns. *Journal of Financial Economics* 25:51–74.

Banz, R. 1981. The relationship between return and market value of common stocks. *Journal of Financial Economics* 9:3–18.

Basu, S. 1977. Investment performance of common stocks in relation to their price-earnings ratios. A test of the efficient market hypothesis. *Journal of Finance* 32:663.

Basu, S. 1983. The relationship between earnings' yield, market value and return for NYSE common stocks: further evidence. *Journal of Financial Economics* 12:129–156.

Beaver, W. 1968. The information content of annual earnings announcements. *Journal of Accounting Research* 6(suppl):67–92.

Berkowitz, S.A., D.E. Logue, and E.A. Noser, Jr. 1988. The total cost of transactions on the NYSE. *Journal of Finance* 43:97–112.

Branch, B. 1977. A tax loss selling rule. *Journal of Business* 50:198–207.

Chan, K. 1988. On the contrarian investment strategy. *Journal of Business* 61:147–163.

Chan, K., and N. Chen. 1988. An unconditional asset-pricing test and the role of firm size as an instrumental variable for risk. *Journal of Finance* 43:309–325.

Chan, K. C., N-F. Chen and D. A. Hsieh. 1985. An exploratory investigation of the firm size effect. *Journal of Financial Economics* 14:451–471.

Chang, E., and W. Lewellen. 1984. Market timing and mutual fund investment performance. *Journal of Business* 57:57–72.

Chopra, N., J. Lakonishok, and J. R. Ritter. 1992. Measuring abnormal performance. Do stocks overreact? *Journal of Financial Economics* 31:235–268.

Conrad, J., and G. Kaul. 1988. Time-variation in expected returns. *Journal of Business* 61:409–425.

Conrad, J., and G. Kaul. 1989. Mean reversion in short horizon expected returns. *Review of Financial Studies* 2:225–240.

Conrad, J., and G. Kaul. 1993. Long-term market overreaction or biases in computed returns? *Journal of Finance* 48:39–63.

Copeland, T., and D. Mayers. 1982. The value line enigma: A case study of performance evaluation issues. *Journal of Financial Economics* 10:289–321.

Cross, F. 1973. The behavior of stock prices on Fridays and Mondays. *Financial Analysts Journal* 29:67–69.

DeBondt, W., and R. Thaler. 1985. Does the stock market overreact? *Journal of Finance* 40:793–805.

DeBondt, W., and R. Thaler. 1987. Further evidence on investor overreaction and stock market seasonality. *Journal of Finance* 42:557–581.

Fama, E. 1965. The behavior of stock market prices. *Journal of Business* 38:34–105.

Fama, E. 1970. Efficient capital markets: A review of theory and empirical work. *Journal of Finance* 25:383–417.

Fama, E. 1991. Efficient capital markets. II. *Journal of Finance* 46.

Fama, E., and M. Blume. 1966. Filter rules and stock market trading. *Journal of Business* 39:226–241.

Fama, E., L. Fisher, M. Jensen, and R. Roll. 1969. The adjustment of stock prices to new information. *International Economic Review* 10:1–21.

Fama, E., and K. French. 1988a. Permanent and temporary components of stock prices. *Journal of Political Economy* 96:246–273.

Fama, E., and K. French. 1988b. Dividend yields and expected stock returns. *Journal of Financial Economics* 22:3–25.

Fama, E., and K. French. 1989. Business conditions and expected returns on stocks and bonds. *Journal of Financial Economics* 25:23–29.

Fisher, L. 1966. Some new stock-market indexes. *Journal of Business* 39:191–225.

French, K. 1980. Stock returns and the weekend effect. *Journal of Financial Economics* 8:55–69.

Foster, G., C. Olson, and T. Shevlin. 1984. Earnings releases, anomalies, and the behavior of security returns. *Accounting Review* 59:574–603.

Friedman, M. 1957. *A Theory of the Consumption Function.* Princeton: Princeton University Press.

Gennotte, G., and A. Jung. 1992. Commissions and asset allocation. *Journal of Portfolio Management.* Fall, 12–17.

Gibbons, M., and P. Hess. 1981. Day of the week effect and asset returns. *Journal of Business* 54:3–27.

Grossman, S., and J. Stiglitz. 1980. On the impossibility of informationally efficient markets. *American Economic Review* 70.

Harris, L. 1986. A transaction data study of weekly and intradaily patterns in stock returns. *Journal of Financial Economics* 16:99–117.

Haugen, R., and J. Lakonishok. 1988. *The incredible January effect.* Homewood: Dow Jones Irwin.

Henriksson, R. 1984. Market timing and mutual fund performance. An empirical investigation. *Journal of Business* 57:73–96.

Ippolito, R. 1989. Efficiency with costly information: A study of mutual fund performance. *Quarterly Journal of Economics* 1–23.

Jaffe, J. 1974. Special information and insider trading. *Journal of Business* 47:410–428.

Jensen, M. 1968. The performance of mutual funds in the period 1945–1964. *Journal of Finance* 23:389–415.

Jensen, M. C., and R. S. Ruback. 1983. The market for corporate control: The scientific evidence. *Journal of Financial Economics II.* April, 5–50.

Joy, O. M., and C. P. Jones. 1979. Earnings reports and market efficiencies: an analysis of the contrary evidence. *Journal of Financial Research* 2:51–63.

Keim, D. 1983. Size-related anomalies and stock return seasonality: Further empirical evidence. *Journal of Financial Economics* 12:12–32.

Keim, D., and R. Stanbaugh. 1986. Predicting returns in the stock and bond markets. *Journal of Financial Economics* 17:357–390.

Lakonishok, J., and M. Levi. 1982. Weekend effects on stock returns. A note. *Journal of Finance.* June, 37:883–889.

Lakonishok, J., and J. Maberly. 1990. The weekend effect: Trading patterns of individual and institutional investors. *Journal of Finance* 45:231–243.

Lakonishok, J., and S. Smidt. 1988. Are seasonal anomalies real? A ninety year perspective. *Review of Financial Studies* 1:435–455.

Lloyd-Davies, P., and M. Canes. 1978. Stock prices and the publication of second-hand information. *Journal of Business* 51:43–56.

Lo, A., and C. MacKinlay. 1988. Stock market prices do not follow random walks: Evidence from a simple specification test. *Review of Financial Studies* 1:41–66.

Lorie, J., and V. Niederhoffer. 1968. Predictive and statistical properties of insider trading. *Journal of Law and Economics* 11:35–53.

Malkiel, B. 1991. *A random walk down Wall Street.* New York: W. W. Norton.

McConnell, J., and C. Muscarella. 1985. Corporate capital expenditure decisions and the market value of the firm. *Journal of Financial Economics* 14:399–422.

Merton, R. C. 1973. An intertemporal capital asset pricing model. *Econometrica* 41:867–887.

Miller, M., and K. Rock. 1985. Dividend policy under asymmetric information. *Journal of Finance*. September, 1031–1051.

Myers, S., and Majluf. 1984. Corporate financing and investment decisions when firms have information that investors do not have. *Journal of Financial Economics* 13:187–221.

Ogden, J. 1990. Turn-of-month evaluations of liquid profits and stock returns: A common explanation for the monthly and January effects. *Journal of Finance* 45:1259–1272.

Ogden, J. 1993. A critique of three explanations for positive autocorrelation of short-horizon stock index returns. Working paper, State University of New York, Buffalo.

Osborne, M. F. M. 1962. Periodic structure in Brownian motion of the stock market. *Operations Research* 10:345–379.

Pettit, R. 1972. Dividend announcements, security performance, and capital market efficiency. *Journal of Finance* 27:993–1007.

Poterba, J. M., and L. H. Summers. 1988. Mean reversion in stock prices. *Journal of Financial Economics* 22:27–59.

Reinganum, M. 1981. Misspecification of capital asset pricing: Empirical anomalies based on earnings yields and market values. *Journal of Financial Economics*.

Reinganum, M. 1983. The anomaly stock market behavior of small firms in January: Empirical tests for tax loss effects. *Journal of Financial Economics* 12:89–104.

Ritter, J. 1988. The buying and selling behavior of individual investors at the turn of the year. *Journal of Finance* 43:701–717.

Roll, R. 1981. A possible explanation of the small firm effect. *Journal of Finance* 36:879–888.

Roll, R. 1983. Vas ist das? The turn-of-the-year effect and the return premium of small firms. *Journal of Portfolio Management* 9:18–28.

Rozeff, M. 1986. Tax-loss selling: Evidence from December stock returns and share shifts. Proceedings of the CRSP seminar on the analysis of security prices. May, 9–45.

Rozeff, M., and W. Kinney. 1976. Capital market seasonality: The case of stock returns. *Journal of Financial Economics* 3:379–402.

Seyhoun, N. 1986. Insiders' profits, costs of trading, and market efficiency. *Journal of Financial Economics* 16:189–212.

Smith, C. 1986. Investment banking and the capital acquisition process. *Journal of Financial Economics* 15:3–29.

Stickel, S. 1985. The effect of value line investment survey rank changes on common stock prices. *Journal of Financial Economics* 14:121–144.

Wagner, W. H., and M. Banks. 1992. Increasing portfolio effectiveness via transaction cost management. *Journal of Portfolio Management*. Fall, 6–11.

PART THREE

Interest Rates, Bond Valuation, and Bond Portfolio Management

IN PART 3, CONSISTING OF CHAPTERS 14 AND 15, WE ANALYZE THE PRICING of bonds and the management of bond portfolios. Chapter 14 discusses theories and models for the valuation of debt securities, as well as empirical evidence. Chapter 15 discusses various techniques and strategies for the management of bond portfolios, including both passive and active strategies, and discusses the managerial implications of new innovations in the bond market. ∎

Interest Rates and the Valuation of Debt Securities: Theory and Evidence

Introduction

Many different types of debt securities are issued in the United States and international financial markets. As shown in Exhibit 14.1, the collective volume of outstanding debt securities in the United States is measured in trillions of dollars. Debt securities are categorized by issuer and maturity, such as short- and long-term bank CDs, U.S. Treasury bills, notes, and bonds, domestically issued corporate commercial paper, notes and bonds, internationally issued euronotes and eurobonds, and municipal bond issues called serial issues that carry a series of maturities. Debt securities are also distinguished by characteristics such as risk of default, tax status, and premature retirement provisions. These characteristics, as well as fundamental macroeconomic factors such as inflation, real investment opportunities, and the investors' time

EXHIBIT 14.1

Aggregate Balances Outstanding of Major Debt Instruments, 1983–1991.

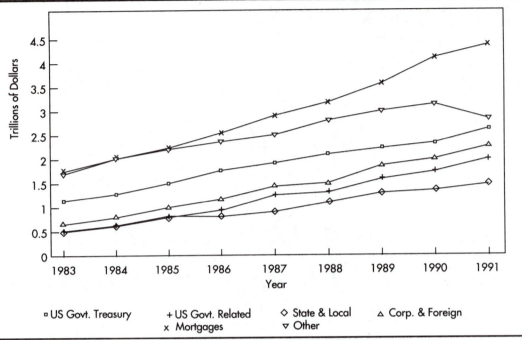

Source: Federal Reserve Bulletin, various issues.

preference for consumption, determine the values of and returns on debt securities. This chapter discusses theories and models of the valuation of debt securities, focusing on these characteristics and factors, and also discusses related empirical evidence. Chapter 15 discusses techniques and strategies for the management of bond portfolios.

THE CLASSICAL THEORY OF INTEREST

The classical theory of interest (Fisher 1930) focuses on the macroeconomic factors that determine the general equilibrium level of the interest rate in the economy, abstracting from the specific characteristics of any individual debt security. The equilibrium interest rate is determined by the aggregate supply and demand for funds in the debt market. Virtually all economic entities, including governments, businesses, financial institutions, and individuals, contribute to both the supply and demand for funds. The resulting aggregate supply and demand determines the equilibrium nominal interest rate as well as the equilibrium volume of debt securities outstanding.

The aggregate demand for funds is affected by many factors. For example, consider the demand for funds in the business sector. Assuming that firms evaluate their investment opportunities according to the net present value (NPV) rule, other things being equal, the number of profitable investments is a negative function of the discount rate, of which the nominal interest rate is an important component. Thus at higher interest rates fewer investments are profitable and the business sector's demand for funds is lower. Other factors such as technological breakthroughs that increase the profitability of real investment opportunities also affect demand, thus the equilibrium interest rate. The aggregate supply of funds is also affected by many factors. Two important determinants of the supply of funds are the wealth of individual investors and their propensity to invest their current income.

Inflation is an important macroeconomic factor that affects both the supply and demand for funds. Fisher (1930) developed a precise theoretical relationship between the nominal interest rate and inflation. Fisher argued that an underlying equilibrating process determines a real rate of interest, R, that would prevail in the absence of inflation, and that in the presence of inflation the equilibrium nominal interest rate, r, would adjust to provide investors a real rate of R. Given inflation at rate i, the nominal interest rate required to provide investors with a real return of R is the solution to equation 14.1:

(14.1)
$$1 + r = (1 + R)(1 + i).$$

Note that for the investor to be fully compensated for inflation, both principal and real interest, $(1 + R)$, must be adjusted for inflation. Solving equation 14.1 for r yields

(14.2)
$$r = R + i + Ri.$$

Given modest rates of inflation and real interest, the cross-product term, Ri, is small and is often ignored, leaving the approximate formula

(14.3)
$$r \approx R + i.$$

According to this relationship a change in the inflation rate causes an approximately equal change in the equilibrium nominal interest rate. For example, if the equilibrium real rate of interest is 2 percent and the inflation rate is 3 percent, the equilibrium nominal rate is $2\% + 3\% = 5\%$, and if the inflation rate rises to 6%, the new equilibrium nominal interest rate will be $2\% + 6\% = 8\%$.

Empirical Evidence on Inflation and Interest Rates

In the empirical counterpart to Fisher's equation, the nominal interest rate, r, is approximately equal to a real rate, R, plus the *expected* rate of inflation, $E(i)$:

(14.4) $r \approx R + E(i).$

A number of approaches can be used to examine this relationship empirically. One simple method is to subtract from the current interest rate the most recent *realized* inflation rate, used as a proxy for current expected inflation. The difference is an estimated real rate. Ibbotson and Siegel (1991) used this approach to extract estimated real rates from nominal interest rates on default-free debt securities using annual data for the period 1961–1990 for each of several countries. Their results for Germany, Japan, the United Kingdom, and the United States are displayed in Figures 14.1 through 14.4, respectively.

Note that the inflation rates in all countries were relatively low throughout the 1960s, peaked in the 1970s or early 1980s, and subsided throughout the 1980s. While the estimated real rates on both short- and long-term debt securities are generally positive, low or negative real rates were realized when the inflation rates peaked. This evidence suggests that real interest rates and inflation rates are negatively correlated.

Does this evidence indicate that the bond market is irrational with respect to inflation expectations? Perhaps, but not necessarily. For instance, throughout this period market expectations of inflation may have been represented by a weighted average of past inflation rates (i.e.,

FIGURE 14.1

Germany: Real Interest Rates and Inflation

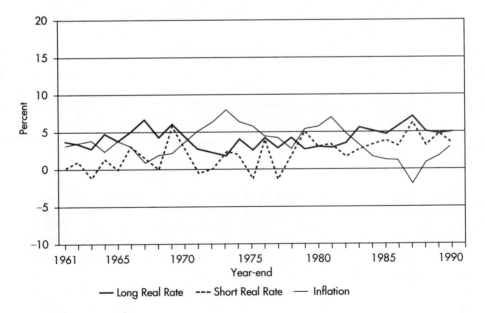

— Long Real Rate   --- Short Real Rate   — Inflation

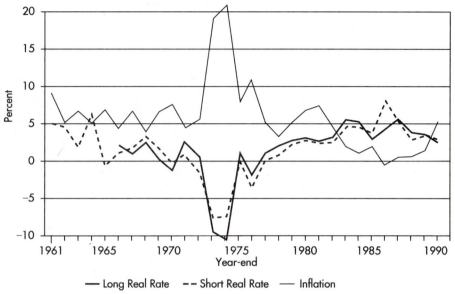

FIGURE 14.2

Japan: Real Interest Rates and Inflation

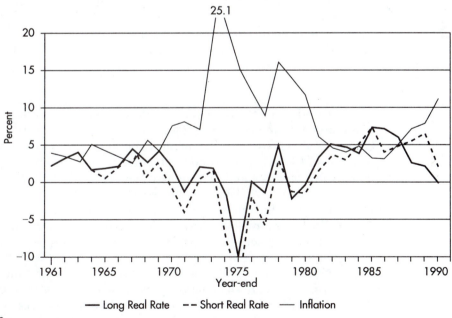

FIGURE 14.3

United Kingdom: Real Interest Rates and Inflation

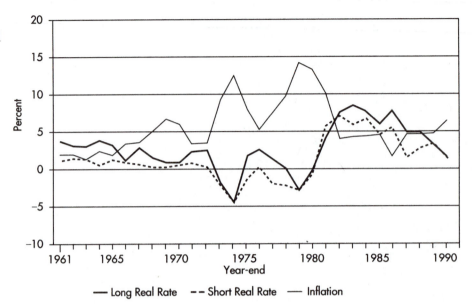

not just the most recent year), and these expectations, along with a given
real rate, may have been impounded into nominal interest rates. This
characterization of market expectations may explain why negative real
rates appear ex post when the inflation rate is rising and large positive real
rates appeared when the inflation rate subsequently subsided.

Another approach to testing the relationship between interest rates and
inflation is to regress the realized inflation rate in period t, i_t, on the
one-period nominal interest rate at the end of the previous period, r_{t-1}:

(14.5) $$i_t = \gamma_0 + \gamma_1 r_{t-1} + e_t,$$

where γ_0 and γ_1 are the regression intercept and slope coefficient, respectively, and e_t is an error term. Equation 14.5 tests the assertion that r_{t-1}
contains a forecast of the inflation rate in period t. Furthermore, comparing
equations 14.4 and 14.5 and noting that $E(e_t) = 0$, if the Fisher effect holds
empirically, then γ_0 should be equal to the negative of the real rate and γ_1
should be equal to 1. Fama (1975) tested this regression using monthly
inflation rates and one-month U.S. Treasury bill rates for the period
1953–1971. His estimate of γ_1 was .98, which is very close to value of 1
predicted by the Fisher equation, and the estimate of γ_0 was −.0007, corresponding to a real rate of about 1 percent per annum ($1.0007^{12} - 1 = .0084$).
Thus Fama's evidence indicates that Treasury bill rates generally comprise
an unbiased estimate of inflation plus an average real rate of about 1
percent, consistent with Fisher's equation. In a subsequent study Fama
and Gibbons (1982) again found that γ_1 is approximately 1, but they also
found that the real rate and the inflation rate were negatively correlated.

The question remains whether this result is (1) spurious (i.e., simply an artifact of the sample data), (2) is the rational consequence of intertemporal equilibria in the bond market, or (3) is evidence of market inefficiency.

CHARACTERISTICS OF DEBT SECURITIES

In addition to the fundamental factors discussed above, four principal characteristics govern the valuation of specific debt securities: maturity, default risk, taxation, and premature retirement or conversion provisions. We will discuss the effects of each of these characteristics on the value, yield, and expected return on a bond for the most part separately. However, to obtain a complete valuation of any debt security it is necessary to account simultaneously for all of these characteristics, including all possible interactive effects.

Debt Maturity and the Term Structure of Interest Rates

The term structure of interest rates defines the relationship between the interest rate or yield on a debt security and its maturity. Our discussion of term structure theory focuses on the pricing of default-free securities, but the concepts developed apply to all debt securities.

Interest Rate Measures.   We begin the discussion with several measures of interest rates on debt securities of various maturities. The first measure is the spot rate, denoted as $s_{0,n}$. $s_{0,n}$ is the per-period interest rate in effect at time 0 that applies to a pure-discount bond that matures in n periods. A pure-discount bond provides one payment at maturity, with no interim payments. Defining the payment at maturity as M_n and the current price as $P_{0,n}$, the spot rate $s_{0,n}$ is the solution to equation 14.6.

(14.6)
$$P_{0,n} = \frac{M_n}{(1 + s_{0,n})^n}$$

For example, if the price of a pure discount bond promising \$1 at the end of four years is $P_{0,4} = 0.8072$, then $s_{0,4} = (M_n/P_{0,n})^{1/4} - 1 = 0.055$, or 5.5 percent per annum.

In a perfect market, given spot rates for all maturities, you can determine the value of any default-free bond with fixed payments. For example, a bond that pays periodic coupon interest in the amount C and a principal payment in the amount M_n after n years can be viewed as a portfolio of pure-discount bonds, and its price can be determined as

(14.7)
$$P_{0,n} = \sum_{t=1}^{n} \frac{C}{(1 + s_{0,t})^t} + \frac{M_n}{(1 + s_{0,n})^n}.$$

However, a second pricing formula, the yield to maturity, is more often applied to coupon-bearing bonds. Denoting as y_n the yield on an n-period bond, y_n is found using equation 14.8:

(14.8)
$$P_{0,n} = \sum_{t=1}^{n} \frac{C}{(1 + y_n)^t} + \frac{M_n}{(1 + y_n)^n}.$$

For example, consider a bond with a coupon rate of 11.625 percent per annum that matures in twenty years. If the price of the bond is \$133.67 per \$100 of par value, its yield, found by trial and error using equation 14.8, is $y_{20} = 6.89\%$. Note that for a given bond, price and yield are inversely related; as the yield rises, the price of the bond falls. In the case of the pure discount bond (i.e., when $C = 0$), $y_n = s_{0,n}$, while for coupon bonds y_n is a weighted average of the spot rates in equation 14.7.

Spot rates and yields are extractions. That is, we observe the payments associated with debt securities and their market prices, and with these we extract spot rates and yields via equation 14.6, 14.7 or 14.8. While the monetary cost and benefits of a given debt-security investment are represented by its price and future payments, respectively, spot rates and yields provide important measures of return that are more readily comparable across securities.

Yield quotations on coupon-bearing bonds, as well as spot rate-quotes on U.S. Treasury bills and strips, are available daily in publications such as the *Wall Street Journal*. Exhibit 14.2 provides an example of these quotes for October 31, 1993. U.S. Treasury strips are pure-discount bonds representing a claim to a single coupon or principal payment of a Treasury note or bond. Various investment banking firms purchase Treasury coupon issues and then sell pro rata claims on each payment to investors. Treasury strips, also known as bullet bonds, are popular with investors because they provide a single payment at a given future date with no interim payments such as coupons that would have to be reinvested and because they have much longer maturities than Treasury bills, the longest of which matures in 52 weeks.

Comparisons of bonds of different maturities are further facilitated with the *forward rate*, which is extracted from the spot rates of bonds with different maturities. Consider two pure-discount bonds, both of which provide a payment of \$1 at maturity. The first bond matures in one year, and the second bond matures in two years. The current price of the one-year bond is 0.9434, implying that $s_{0,1} = 0.06$, and the current price of the two-year bond is 0.8734, implying that $s_{0,2} = 0.07$. Although the two-year bond clearly provides a higher per-period interest rate, a more explicit comparison can be made by calculating the marginal benefit of extending the investment horizon from one to two years. This can be done by splitting $s_{0,2}$ into two one-year components, $s_{0,1}$ and $f_{1,2}$, where the latter is an implicit forward rate:

(14.9)
$$s_{0,2} = [(1 + s_{0,1})(1 + f_{1,2})]^{1/2} - 1.$$

EXHIBIT 14.2

Prices and Yields on U.S. Treasury Bills, Notes, Bonds and Strips for September 30, 1993

TREASURY BONDS, NOTES & BILLS

Thursday, September 30, 1993

Representative Over-the-Counter quotations based on transactions of $1 million or more.

Treasury bond, note and bill quotes are as of mid-afternoon. Colons in bid-and-asked quotes represent 32nds; 101:01 means 101 1/32. Net changes in 32nds. n-Treasury note. Treasury bill quotes in hundredths, quoted on terms of a rate of discount. Days to maturity calculated from settlement date. All yields are to maturity and based on the asked quote. Latest 13-week and 26-week bills are boldfaced. For bonds callable prior to maturity, yields are computed to the earliest call date for issues quoted above par and to the maturity date for issues below par. *-When issued.

Source: Federal Reserve Bank of New York.

U.S. Treasury strips as of 3 p.m. Eastern time, also based on transactions of $1 million or more. Colons in bid-and-asked quotes represent 32nds; 101:01 means 101 1/32. Net changes in 32nds. Yields calculated on the asked quotation. ci-stripped coupon interest. bp-Treasury bond, stripped principal. np-Treasury note, stripped principal. For bonds callable prior to maturity, yields are computed to the earliest call date for issues quoted above par and to the maturity date for issues below par.

Source: Bear, Stearns & Co. via Street Software Technology Inc.

GOVT. BONDS & NOTES

Rate	Maturity Mo/Yr	Bid	Asked	Chg.	Ask Yld.
7 1/8	Oct 93n	100:04	100:06	-1	0.86
6	Oct 93n	100:07	100:09	....	2.11
7 3/4	Nov 93n	100:17	100:19	-1	2.46
8 5/8	Nov 93	100:21	100:23	-2	2.24
9	Nov 93n	100:22	100:24	....	2.33
11 3/4	Nov 93n	101:01	101:03	....	2.05
5 1/2	Nov 93n	100:12	100:14	....	2.63
5	Dec 93n	100:15	100:17	....	2.73
7 5/8	Dec 93n	101:04	101:06	....	2.58
7	Jan 94n	101:02	101:04	....	2.90
4 7/8	Jan 94n	100:18	100:20	....	2.90
6 7/8	Feb 94n	101:11	101:13	....	2.94
8 7/8	Feb 94n	102:02	102:04	-1	2.94
9	Feb 94	102:04	102:06	....	2.89
5 3/8	Feb 94n	100:29	100:31	....	2.95
5 3/4	Mar 94n	101:09	101:11	....	2.96
8 1/2	Mar 94n	102:20	102:22	....	2.92
7	Apr 94n	102:00	102:02	....	3.05
5 3/8	Apr 94n	101:06	101:08	-1	3.16
7	May 94n	102:08	102:10	-1	3.17
9 1/2	May 94n	103:25	103:27	-1	3.14
13 1/8	May 94n	105:31	106:01	-2	3.14
5 1/8	May 94n	101:06	101:08	....	3.19
5	Jun 94n	101:07	101:09	-1	3.23
8 1/2	Jun 94n	103:25	103:27	....	3.20
8	Jul 94n	103:18	103:20	-1	3.26
4 1/4	Jul 94n	100:22	100:24	-1	3.32
6 7/8	Aug 94n	102:30	103:00	-1	3.33
8 5/8	Aug 94n	104:14	104:16	-1	3.30
8 3/4	Aug 94	104:16	104:20	-1	3.28
12 5/8	Aug 94n	107:28	107:30	-1	3.24
4 1/4	Aug 94n	100:24	100:26	....	3.33
4	Sep 94n	100:18	100:20	-1	3.35
8 1/2	Sep 94n	104:30	105:00	-1	3.32
9 1/2	Oct 94n	106:01	106:03	-2	3.43
4 1/4	Oct 94n	100:26	100:28	....	3.41
6	Nov 94n	102:22	102:24	-1	3.46
8 1/4	Nov 94n	105:05	105:07	....	3.44
10 1/8	Nov 94	107:06	107:08	-1	3.44
11 5/8	Nov 94n	108:27	108:29	-1	3.42
4 5/8	Nov 94n	101:07	101:09	-1	3.49
4 5/8	Dec 94n	101:09	101:11	-1	3.51
7 5/8	Dec 94n	104:30	105:00	-1	3.47
8 5/8	Jan 95n	106:07	106:09	-1	3.57
4 1/4	Jan 95n	100:26	100:28	-1	3.57
3	Feb 95	100:02	101:02	-4	2.21
5 1/2	Feb 95n	102:14	102:16	-2	3.61
7 3/4	Feb 95n	105:14	105:16	-1	3.59
10 1/2	Feb 95	109:03	109:05	-2	3.57
11 1/4	Feb 95n	110:03	110:05	-2	3.56
3 7/8	Feb 95n	100:09	100:11	-2	3.62
3 7/8	Mar 95n	100:08	100:10	-3	3.66
8 3/8	Apr 95n	106:28	106:30	-4	3.67
3 7/8	Apr 95n	100:07	100:09	-3	3.69
5 7/8	May 95n	103:09	103:11	-3	3.72
8 1/2	May 95n	107:11	107:13	-4	3.73
10 3/8	May 95	110:09	110:11	-4	3.72
11 1/4	May 95n	111:22	111:24	-2	3.69
12 5/8	May 95	113:27	113:31	-4	3.64
4 1/8	May 95n	100:19	100:21	-2	3.71
4 1/8	Jun 95n	100:18	100:20	-3	3.75
8 7/8	Jul 95n	108:22	108:24	-3	3.75
4 1/4	Jul 95n	100:24	100:26	-3	3.78
4 5/8	Aug 95n	101:14	101:16	-3	3.78
8 1/2	Aug 95n	108:12	108:14	-3	3.77
10 1/2	Aug 95n	112:00	112:02	-3	3.74
3 7/8	Aug 95n	100:01	100:03	-3	3.82
3 7/8	Sep 95n	99:31	100:01	-3	3.86
8 5/8	Oct 95n	109:07	109:09	-3	3.83
5 1/8	Nov 95n	102:16	102:18	-3	3.85
8 1/2	Nov 95n	109:10	109:12	-3	3.84
9 1/2	Nov 95n	111:11	111:13	-4	3.83
11 1/2	Nov 95	115:10	115:14	-4	3.83
9 1/4	Jan 96n	111:11	111:13	-3	3.97
7 1/2	Jan 96n	107:21	107:23	-5	3.99
4 5/8	Feb 96n	101:10	101:12	-5	4.01
7 7/8	Feb 96n	108:18	108:20	-3	4.02
8 7/8	Feb 96n	110:25	110:27	-4	4.02
7 1/2	Feb 96n	107:26	107:28	-4	4.03
7 3/4	Mar 96n	108:18	108:20	-5	4.07
9 3/8	Apr 96n	112:17	112:19	-4	4.09
7 5/8	Apr 96n	108:15	108:17	-4	4.10
4 1/4	May 96n	100:10	100:12	-4	4.10
7 3/8	May 96n	107:29	107:31	-4	4.13
7 5/8	May 96n	108:21	108:23	-4	4.13
7 7/8	Jun 96n	109:26	109:28	-2	4.03
7 7/8	Jul 96n	109:17	109:19	-8	4.18
7 7/8	Jul 96n	109:21	109:23	-3	4.19
4 3/8	Aug 96n	100:15	100:17	-4	4.18
7 1/4	Aug 96n	108:04	108:06	-5	4.23
7	Sep 96n	107:24	107:26	-5	4.19
8	Oct 96n	110:14	110:16	-5	4.27
6 7/8	Oct 96n	107:12	107:14	-4	4.27
7 1/4	Nov 96n	108:15	108:17	-5	4.29
6 1/2	Nov 96n	106:12	106:14	-5	4.30
6 1/8	Dec 96n	105:13	105:15	-4	4.30
8	Jan 97n	110:31	111:01	-4	4.36
6 1/4	Jan 97n	105:24	105:26	-4	4.35
6 3/4	Feb 97n	107:12	107:14	-5	4.38
6 7/8	Mar 97n	107:29	107:31	-5	4.39
8 1/2	Apr 97n	113:04	113:06	-5	4.42
6 7/8	Apr 97n	107:30	108:00	-6	4.43
8 1/2	May 97n	113:10	113:12	-6	4.45
6 3/4	May 97n	107:19	107:21	-5	4.46
6 3/8	Jun 97n	106:16	106:18	-7	4.45
8 1/2	Jul 97n	113:23	113:25	-6	4.50
5 1/2	Jul 97n	103:16	103:18	-6	4.48
8 5/8	Aug 97n	114:11	114:13	-6	4.52
5 5/8	Aug 97n	103:27	103:29	-3	4.52
5 1/2	Sep 97n	103:13	103:15	-5	4.54
8 3/4	Oct 97n	115:07	115:09	-4	4.56
5 3/4	Oct 97n	104:09	104:11	-5	4.57
8 7/8	Nov 97n	115:28	115:30	-6	4.58
6	Nov 97n	105:07	105:09	-5	4.59
6	Dec 97n	105:08	105:10	-6	4.61
7 7/8	Jan 98n	112:15	112:17	-7	4.62
5 5/8	Jan 98n	103:26	103:28	-7	4.63
8 1/8	Feb 98n	113:18	113:20	-7	4.64
5 1/8	Feb 98n	101:26	101:28	-7	4.65
5 1/8	Mar 98n	101:27	101:29	-5	4.65
7 7/8	Apr 98n	112:30	113:00	-6	4.66
5 1/8	Apr 98n	101:23	101:25	-7	4.69
9	May 98n	117:22	117:24	-8	4.68
5 3/8	May 98n	102:21	102:23	-8	4.72
5 1/8	Jun 98n	101:20	101:22	-7	4.72
8 1/4	Jul 98n	114:25	114:27	-7	4.74
5 1/4	Jul 98n	102:04	102:06	-5	4.74
9 1/4	Aug 98n	119:09	119:11	-8	4.75
4 3/4	Aug 98n	99:28	99:30	-7	4.76
4 3/4	Sep 98n	99:27	99:29	-7	4.77
7 1/8	Oct 98n	110:11	110:13	-7	4.77
3 1/2	Nov 98	100:00	101:00	....	3.29
8 7/8	Nov 98n	118:09	118:11	-8	4.79
6 3/8	Jan 99n	107:03	107:05	-7	4.82
8 7/8	Feb 99n	118:23	118:25	-9	4.86
7	Apr 99n	110:02	110:04	-8	4.89
8 1/2	May 94-99	103:10	103:18	-3	2.62
9 1/8	May 99n	120:17	120:19	-8	4.89
6 3/8	Jul 99n	107:03	107:05	-11	4.94
8	Aug 99n	115:12	115:14	-12	4.94
6	Oct 99n	105:08	105:10	-11	4.97
7 7/8	Nov 99n	115:02	115:04	-12	4.98
6 3/8	Jan 00n	107:06	107:08	-12	5.02
7 7/8	Feb 95-00	105:16	105:20	+8	3.61
8 1/2	Feb 00n	118:24	118:26	-14	5.01
5 1/2	Apr 00n	102:26	102:28	-11	4.98
8 7/8	May 00n	121:10	121:12	-14	5.04
8 3/8	Aug 95-00	108:01	108:05	-2	3.80
8 3/4	Aug 00n	120:31	121:01	-17	5.08
8 1/2	Nov 00n	119:26	119:28	-17	5.13
7 3/4	Feb 01n	115:20	115:22	-14	5.16
11 3/4	Feb 01	140:07	140:11	-10	5.11
8	May 01n	117:13	117:15	-13	5.19
13 1/8	May 01	149:22	149:26	-16	5.14
7 7/8	Aug 01n	116:28	116:30	-10	5.22
8	Aug 96-01	109:29	110:01	-2	4.24
13 3/8	Aug 01	152:12	152:16	-14	5.17
7 1/2	Nov 01n	114:20	114:22	-10	5.25
15 3/4	Nov 01	169:08	169:12	-9	5.17
14 1/4	Feb 02	160:19	160:23	-15	5.20
7 1/2	May 02n	114:30	115:00	-10	5.31
6 3/8	Aug 02n	106:31	107:01	-11	5.37
11 5/8	Nov 02	144:18	144:22	-14	5.36
6 1/4	Feb 03n	105:29	105:31	-13	5.43
10 3/4	Feb 03	138:25	138:29	-10	5.40
10 3/4	May 03	139:13	139:17	-16	5.42
5 3/4	Aug 03n	102:22	102:24	-11	5.39
11 1/8	Aug 03	142:27	142:31	-17	5.44
11 7/8	Nov 03	149:05	149:09	-18	5.47
12 3/8	May 04	154:29	155:01	-14	5.47
13 3/4	Aug 04	166:29	167:01	-17	5.48
11 5/8	Nov 04	149:29	150:01	-18	5.54
8 1/4	May 00-05	116:17	116:21	-9	5.24
12	May 05	154:12	154:16	-20	5.57
10 3/4	Aug 05	144:03	144:07	-19	5.60
9 3/8	Feb 06	132:29	133:01	-19	5.63
7 5/8	Feb 02-07	113:02	113:06	-13	5.63
7 7/8	Nov 02-07	115:21	115:25	-14	5.64
8 3/8	Aug 03-08	120:05	120:09	-15	5.66
8 3/4	Nov 03-08	123:12	123:16	-13	5.67
9 1/8	May 04-09	127:01	127:05	-17	5.68
10 3/8	Nov 04-09	138:08	138:12	-19	5.67
11 3/4	Feb 05-10	150:04	150:08	-20	5.69
10	May 05-10	136:01	136:05	-19	5.70
12 3/4	Nov 05-10	160:29	161:01	-21	5.70
13 7/8	May 06-11	172:17	172:21	-24	5.71
14	Nov 06-11	175:16	175:20	-24	5.72
10 3/8	Nov 07-12	142:21	142:25	-19	5.87
12	Aug 08-13	159:26	159:30	-23	5.89
13 1/4	May 09-14	175:01	175:05	-33	5.85
12 1/2	Aug 09-14	167:15	167:19	-31	5.89
11 3/4	Nov 09-14	159:28	160:00	-30	5.92
11 1/4	Feb 15	159:11	159:13	-29	6.20
10 5/8	Aug 15	152:09	152:11	-29	6.22
9 7/8	Nov 15	143:13	143:15	-26	6.23
9 1/4	Feb 16	135:29	135:31	-25	6.24
7 1/4	May 16	111:22	111:24	-20	6.27
7 1/2	Nov 16	114:23	114:25	-20	6.28
8 3/4	May 17	130:08	130:10	-24	6.27
8 7/8	Aug 17	131:28	131:30	-24	6.28
9 1/8	May 18	135:14	135:16	-21	6.27
9	Nov 18	134:03	134:05	-24	6.28
8 7/8	Feb 19	132:21	132:23	-20	6.28
8 1/8	Aug 19	123:06	123:08	-21	6.29
8 1/2	Feb 20	128:08	128:10	-20	6.29
8 3/4	May 20	131:21	131:23	-21	6.28
8 3/4	Aug 20	131:24	131:26	-23	6.28
7 7/8	Feb 21	120:18	120:20	-20	6.29
8 1/8	May 21	124:00	124:02	-19	6.28
8 1/8	Aug 21	124:02	124:04	-19	6.28
8	Nov 21	122:19	122:21	-19	6.27
7 1/4	Aug 22	113:03	113:05	-16	6.26
7 5/8	Nov 22	118:06	118:08	-19	6.26
7 1/8	Feb 23	112:03	112:05	-19	6.22
6 1/4	Aug 23	102:29	102:31	-19	6.03

U.S. TREASURY STRIPS

Mat.	Type	Bid	Asked	Chg.	Ask Yld.
Nov 93	ci	99:21	99:21	....	2.98
Feb 94	ci	98:28	98:28	+1	3.10
May 94	ci	98:00	98:01	-1	3.28
Aug 94	ci	97:04	97:05	-2	3.38
Nov 94	ci	96:05	96:06	....	3.51
Nov 94	np	96:06	96:07	-1	3.50
Feb 95	ci	95:06	95:07	....	3.62
Feb 95	np	95:05	95:06	-1	3.65
May 95	ci	94:06	94:07	-1	3.72
May 95	np	94:04	94:06	-2	3.75
Aug 95	ci	93:05	93:06	-1	3.81
Aug 95	np	93:03	93:05	-2	3.84
Nov 95	ci	92:02	92:04	-2	3.91
Nov 95	np	92:02	92:04	-2	3.91
Feb 96	ci	90:30	91:00	-2	4.03
Feb 96	np	90:30	91:00	-2	4.03
May 96	ci	89:22	89:24	-2	4.18
May 96	np	89:22	89:24	-2	4.18
Aug 96	ci	88:18	88:21	-3	4.25
Nov 96	ci	87:15	87:18	-3	4.31
Nov 96	np	87:15	87:18	-3	4.31
Feb 97	ci	86:11	86:14	-3	4.39
May 97	ci	85:02	85:05	-3	4.49
May 97	np	85:02	85:05	-3	4.49
Aug 97	ci	83:29	84:00	-4	4.57
Aug 97	np	83:29	84:00	-4	4.57
Nov 97	ci	82:23	82:26	-4	4.64
Nov 97	np	82:23	82:26	-4	4.64
Feb 98	ci	81:16	81:19	-5	4.72
Feb 98	np	81:15	81:18	-5	4.72
May 98	ci	80:13	80:16	-6	4.76
May 98	np	80:13	80:16	-4	4.76
Aug 98	ci	79:06	79:10	-5	4.82
Aug 98	np	79:05	79:08	-5	4.84
Nov 98	ci	78:03	78:07	-6	4.86
Nov 98	np	78:03	78:07	-5	4.86
Feb 99	ci	76:27	76:31	-5	4.94
Feb 99	np	76:25	76:29	-5	4.96
May 99	ci	75:21	75:25	-6	5.00
May 99	np	75:20	75:24	-7	5.01
Aug 99	ci	74:19	74:24	-6	5.03
Aug 99	np	74:18	74:22	-6	5.04
Nov 99	ci	73:13	73:18	-7	5.09
Nov 99	np	73:13	73:18	-7	5.09
Feb 00	ci	72:13	72:17	-3	5.11
Feb 00	np	72:14	72:19	....	5.10
May 00	ci	71:08	71:13	-5	5.16
May 00	np	71:07	71:11	-6	5.17
Aug 00	ci	70:05	70:10	-8	5.20
Aug 00	np	70:05	70:10	-8	5.20
Nov 00	ci	69:01	69:06	-7	5.25
Nov 00	np	69:01	69:06	-8	5.25
Feb 01	ci	68:01	68:06	-7	5.27
Feb 01	np	68:00	68:04	-7	5.28
May 01	ci	66:31	67:03	-10	5.31
May 01	np	66:31	67:03	-9	5.31
Aug 01	ci	65:28	66:01	-9	5.35
Aug 01	np	65:27	65:31	-9	5.36
Nov 01	ci	64:24	64:29	-11	5.40
Nov 01	np	64:23	64:27	-9	5.41
Feb 02	ci	63:15	63:20	-7	5.48
May 02	ci	62:18	62:23	-6	5.49
May 02	np	62:15	62:20	-8	5.51
Aug 02	ci	61:16	61:21	-8	5.53
Aug 02	np	61:15	61:20	-8	5.54
Nov 02	ci	60:13	60:18	-8	5.58
Feb 03	ci	59:10	59:15	-6	5.63
Feb 03	np	59:12	59:17	-6	5.62
May 03	ci	58:09	58:14	-10	5.67
Aug 03	ci	57:09	57:14	-10	5.70
Nov 03	ci	56:08	56:14	-10	5.74
Feb 04	ci	55:03	55:08	-6	5.81
May 04	ci	54:04	54:09	-8	5.84
Aug 04	ci	53:08	53:13	-8	5.86
Nov 04	ci	52:11	52:17	-8	5.88
Nov 04	bp	52:20	52:26	-10	5.83
Feb 05	ci	51:08	51:14	-8	5.94
May 05	ci	50:09	50:14	-8	5.98
May 05	bp	50:13	50:18	-8	5.96
Aug 05	ci	49:14	49:19	-5	6.00
Aug 05	bp	49:21	49:27	-8	5.96
Nov 05	ci	48:13	48:19	-8	6.05
Feb 06	ci	47:19	47:24	-8	6.07
Feb 06	bp	48:26	48:31	-9	5.86
May 06	ci	46:26	47:00	-14	6.08
Aug 06	ci	46:02	46:08	-8	6.09
Nov 06	ci	45:08	45:14	-7	6.11
Feb 07	ci	44:04	44:09	-10	6.19
May 07	ci	43:11	43:16	-10	6.21
Aug 07	ci	42:20	42:25	-10	6.22
Nov 07	ci	41:27	42:01	-9	6.24
Feb 08	ci	40:28	41:01	-10	6.30
May 08	ci	40:06	40:11	-10	6.31
Aug 08	ci	39:11	39:16	-10	6.35
Nov 08	ci	38:19	38:25	-10	6.37
Feb 09	ci	37:25	37:30	-10	6.41
May 09	ci	37:01	37:06	-14	6.44
Aug 09	ci	36:07	36:12	-16	6.48
Nov 09	ci	35:19	35:24	-14	6.49
Nov 09	bp	36:14	36:19	-23	6.34
Feb 10	ci	34:27	35:00	-10	6.52
May 10	ci	34:08	34:13	-12	6.53
Aug 10	ci	33:20	33:26	-8	6.54
Nov 10	ci	33:03	33:08	-8	6.54
Feb 11	ci	32:11	32:16	-6	6.58
May 11	ci	31:21	31:26	-8	6.61
Aug 11	ci	31:01	31:06	-10	6.63
Nov 11	ci	30:14	30:19	-10	6.65
Feb 12	ci	29:28	30:01	-8	6.66
May 12	ci	29:13	29:18	-6	6.66
Aug 12	ci	28:28	29:01	-6	6.67
Nov 12	ci	28:13	28:18	-6	6.67
Feb 13	ci	27:25	27:30	-8	6.70
May 13	ci	27:08	27:13	-8	6.71
Aug 13	ci	26:26	26:31	-8	6.71
Nov 13	ci	26:12	26:17	-6	6.71
Feb 14	ci	25:30	26:03	-1	6.71
May 14	ci	25:15	25:20	-3	6.72
Aug 14	ci	25:01	25:06	-3	6.72
Nov 14	ci	24:19	24:23	-4	6.73
Feb 15	ci	24:06	24:10	-4	6.73
Feb 15	bp	24:09	24:14	-4	6.71
May 15	ci	23:27	23:31	-3	6.72
Aug 15	ci	23:14	23:19	-3	6.72
Aug 15	bp	23:17	23:22	-3	6.70
Nov 15	ci	23:03	23:08	....	6.71
Nov 15	bp	23:06	23:11	....	6.69
Feb 16	ci	22:23	22:28	-3	6.71
Feb 16	bp	22:26	22:31	-3	6.69
May 16	ci	22:11	22:16	-3	6.71
May 16	bp	22:16	22:21	-1	6.68
Aug 16	ci	21:31	22:04	-3	6.71
Nov 16	ci	21:20	21:25	-3	6.71
Nov 16	bp	21:31	22:03	-4	6.64
Feb 17	ci	21:07	21:12	-4	6.72
May 17	ci	20:28	21:00	-4	6.72
May 17	bp	20:29	21:02	-6	6.71
Aug 17	ci	20:15	20:20	-6	6.73
Aug 17	bp	20:21	20:26	-3	6.69
Nov 17	ci	20:04	20:09	-6	6.73
Feb 18	ci	19:29	20:01	-4	6.71
May 18	ci	19:18	19:23	-4	6.71
May 18	bp	19:21	19:26	-4	6.69
Aug 18	ci	19:08	19:13	-4	6.71
Nov 18	ci	18:30	19:02	-6	6.71
Nov 18	bp	19:01	19:05	-4	6.69
Feb 19	ci	18:21	18:26	-3	6.70
Feb 19	bp	18:24	18:29	-3	6.68
May 19	ci	18:12	18:16	-4	6.70
Aug 19	ci	18:02	18:06	-4	6.70
Aug 19	bp	18:05	18:09	-3	6.68
Nov 19	ci	17:25	17:29	-4	6.70
Feb 20	ci	17:15	17:20	-4	6.70
Feb 20	bp	17:18	17:22	-4	6.68
May 20	ci	17:09	17:13	-4	6.68
May 20	bp	17:12	17:16	-4	6.66
Aug 20	ci	17:00	17:04	-4	6.68
Aug 20	bp	17:03	17:07	-4	6.66
Nov 20	ci	16:23	16:27	-4	6.68
Feb 21	ci	16:16	16:20	-2	6.67
Feb 21	bp	16:20	16:24	-1	6.64
May 21	ci	16:08	16:13	-1	6.66
May 21	bp	16:14	16:18	-1	6.62
Aug 21	ci	16:01	16:05	-1	6.65
Aug 21	bp	16:08	16:12	+2	6.60
Nov 21	ci	15:30	16:03	-4	6.61
Nov 21	bp	16:03	16:07	-4	6.58
Feb 22	ci	16:00	16:04	-4	6.54
May 22	ci	15:24	15:28	-4	6.54
Aug 22	ci	15:16	15:20	-4	6.54
Aug 22	bp	15:18	15:23	-3	6.52
Nov 22	ci	15:08	15:12	-5	6.54
Nov 22	bp	15:12	15:16	-4	6.51
Feb 23	ci	15:24	15:28	-6	6.37
Feb 23	bp	15:31	16:03	-6	6.32

TREASURY BILLS

Maturity	Days to Mat.	Bid	Asked	Chg.	Ask Yld.
Oct 07 '93	3	2.56	2.46	-0.16	2.49
Oct 14 '93	10	2.60	2.50	-0.20	2.54
Oct 21 '93	17	2.71	2.61	-0.15	2.65
Oct 28 '93	24	2.46	2.36	-0.12	2.40
Nov 04 '93	31	2.76	2.72	-0.05	2.76
Nov 12 '93	39	2.88	2.84	-0.02	2.89
Nov 18 '93	45	2.89	2.85	-0.01	2.90
Nov 26 '93	53	2.90	2.86	-0.01	2.91
Dec 02 '93	59	2.91	2.89	....	2.94
Dec 09 '93	66	2.93	2.91	-0.01	2.97
Dec 16 '93	73	2.94	2.92	....	2.98
Dec 23 '93	80	2.94	2.92	....	2.98
Dec 30 '93	**87**	**2.92**	**2.90**	**-0.01**	**2.96**
Jan 06 '94	94	2.95	2.93	....	2.99
Jan 13 '94	101	2.96	2.94	-0.01	3.01
Jan 20 '94	108	2.98	2.96	....	3.03
Jan 27 '94	115	2.99	2.97	+0.01	3.04
Feb 03 '94	122	3.00	2.98	-0.02	3.05
Feb 10 '94	129	3.02	3.00	-0.01	3.07
Feb 17 '94	136	3.03	3.01	....	3.09
Feb 24 '94	143	3.03	3.01	-0.02	3.09
Mar 03 '94	150	3.04	3.02	-0.01	3.10
Mar 10 '94	157	3.05	3.03	....	3.11
Mar 17 '94	164	3.05	3.03	-0.01	3.12
Mar 24 '94	171	3.06	3.04	....	3.13
Mar 31 '94	**178**	**3.04**	**3.02**	**-0.02**	**3.11**
Apr 07 '94	185	3.09	3.07	....	3.16
May 05 '94	213	3.12	3.10	+0.01	3.19
Jun 02 '94	241	3.14	3.12	+0.01	3.22
Jun 30 '94	269	3.15	3.13	....	3.23
Jul 28 '94	297	3.21	3.19	+0.02	3.30
Aug 25 '94	325	3.24	3.22	+0.02	3.34
Sep 22 '94	353	3.25	3.23	+0.02	3.35

Source: The Wall Street Journal, September 30, 1993, p. C14. Reprinted by permission of *The Wall Street Journal*,

In the present example, $f_{1,2} = [(1.07)^2 / (1.06)] - 1 = .0801$. Thus, the investor receives a marginal rate of about 8 percent by extending the maturity of the bond from one to two years.

Generalizing, any forward rate $f_{t-i,t}$ can be calculated given spot rates $s_{0,t-i}$ and $s_{0,t}$ and using equation 14.10:

(14.10)
$$f_{t-i,t} = \frac{(1 + s_{0,t})^t}{(1 + s_{0,t-i})^{t-i}} - 1.$$

Given the prevalence of yield quotes on coupon bonds, many analysts calculate forward rates by substituting yields for the spot rates in Equation 14.10. Be forewarned: the discrepancy between forward rates calculated using yields and spot rates can be substantial.

Yield Curves. A yield curve is a graphical depiction of the term structure of interest rates for a given type of security. An example of a yield curve, constructed from the yields on U.S. Treasury strips shown in Exhibit 14.2, is provided in Figure 14.5. Note that the yield curve slopes upward; that is, Treasury securities with longer maturities have higher yields. The upward-sloping yield curve is typical; flat and downward-sloping yield curves are observed less frequently. To demonstrate the factors that determine spot rates, forward rates, and the slope of the yield curve, we now discuss various theories of the term structure of interest rates.

Term Structure Theories. Four theories have been developed to explain the term structure of interest rates: the pure expectations theory, the liquidity preference theory, the market segmentation theory, and the preferred habitat theory. Each is discussed below. The analysis focuses on spot rates rather than yields because spot rates are the fundamental units used to price all default-free debt securities.

The pure expectations theory. The pure expectations theory (Fisher 1930, Lutz 1940) is based on simple concepts of choice and expectation. Consider an investor who wishes to invest $1 for two periods. The investor can simply purchase two-period pure-discount bonds with a total value of $1 and realize a total return of $1(1 + s_{0,2})^2$ at the end of period 2. Alternatively, the investor can initially purchase one-period pure-discount bonds totaling $1 in value, realize a total return of $1(1 + s_{0,1})$ at the end of the first period, and then purchase new one-period pure-discount bonds with a total value of $1(1 + s_{0,1})$ and realize a total return of $1(1 + s_{0,1})(1 + s_{1,2})$ at the end of period 2. However, at time 0 the investor does not know the one-period rate, $s_{1,2}$, that will prevail at time 1. That is, at time 0 the rate $s_{1,2}$ is a random variable. Thus, the investor's total return on this rollover strategy is uncertain. However, at time 0 the investor can

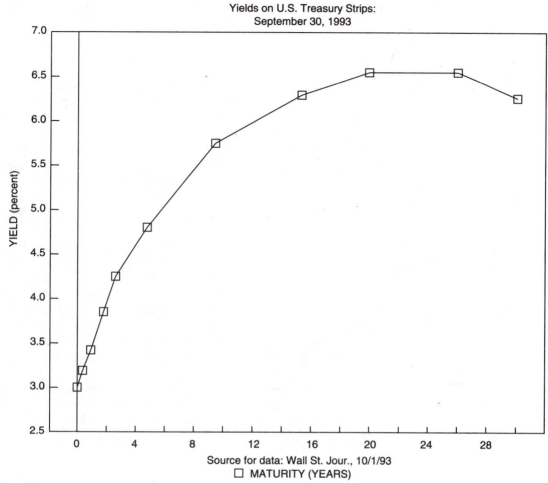

FIGURE 14.5

Treasury Yield Curve for September 30, 1993.

Source: The *Wall Street Journal*, October 1, 1993. Reprinted by permission of *The Wall Street Journal*,
© 1993 Dow Jones & Company, Inc. All rights reserved worldwide.

develop an expectation of $s_{1,2}$. We will denote this expectation as $E_0(s_{1,2})$ where the subscript on E indicates that the assessment of expectation is made at time 0. As a result, the investor's expected total return from the rollover strategy is $\$1(1 + s_{0,1})[1 + E_0(s_{1,2})]$.

According to the pure expectations theory, investors prefer the investment strategy that provides the highest expected total return for a given investment horizon. Applying this rule to the present case, investors will prefer the two-period bond if $(1 + s_{0,2})^2 > (1 + s_{0,1})[1 + E_0(s_{1,2})]$ and will prefer the rollover strategy if $(1 + s_{0,2})^2 < (1 + s_{0,1})[1 + E_0(s_{1,2})]$. Since the former case implies an excess demand for two-period bonds and the latter case implies an excess demand for one-period bonds, equilibrium is reached only when

(14.11) $$(1 + s_{0,2})^2 = (1 + s_{0,1})[1 + E_0(s_{1,2})].$$

For example, if the current one-period spot rate is $s_{0,1} = .06$ and the current expectation of the one-period spot rate one period from now is $E_0(s_{1,2}) = 0.07$, the equilibrium current spot rate on two-period bonds is $s_{0,2} = [(1.06)(1.07)]^{1/2} - 1 = .065$.

More generally, according to the pure expectations theory, the equilibrium spot rate on an n-period bond is determined by equation 14.12:

(14.12) $$(1 + s_{0,n}) = \{(1 + s_{0,1})[1 + E_0(s_{1,2})][1 + E_0(s_{2,3})] \ldots [1 + E_0(s_{n-1,n})]\}^{1/n}.$$

That is, $s_{0,n}$ is the geometric mean of current and expected future one-period spot rates. Equation 14.12 states that an n-period bond is priced to provide the same total return to maturity as an investor expects to receive with a rollover strategy involving one-period bonds to the same horizon. In fact, the most general statement of the pure expectations theory is that in equilibrium all conceivable investment strategies that involve continuous investment to a given horizon (but that may involve buying and selling bonds of various maturities at any time) provide the same expected total return.

Note that since the above statement applies to any given investment horizon, it applies to a one-period horizon. Thus according to the pure expectations theory the expected return on any n-period bond in the first period, denoted as $E_0(_n r_{0,1})$, is equal to the one-period spot rate $s_{0,1}$:

(14.13) $$E_0(_n r_{0,1}) = s_{0,1} \text{ for all } n.$$

To illustrate this point we return to the previous example, in which $s_{0,1} = .06$; $s_{0,2} = .065$; and $E_0(s_{1,2}) = .07$. Assume an investor who has a one-period horizon chooses to purchase a two-period pure discount bond with a \$1 payoff at maturity and plans to sell it after one period. The current price of the bond is $.8817 = \$1/(1.065)^2$. After one period the former two-period bond will be a one-period bond, and its price will be $\$1/(1 + s_{1,2})$. If the expected value of $s_{1,2}$, .07, is realized, the bond's price will be $\$.9346 = \$1/(1.07)$ and the investor will have realized a return of $_2 r_{0,1} = .06 = (.9346/.8817) - 1$ in the first period, which is equal to $s_{0,1}$. Note, however, that if the realized value of $s_{1,2}$ is greater (less) than the expected value of .07, the investor's return will be less (greater) than .06, as we will illustrate later.

Finally, the pure expectations theory provides us with a straightforward interpretation of forward rates. A comparison of equations 14.9 and 14.11 reveals that

(14.14) $f_{1,2} = E_0(s_{1,2}).$

By extension,

(14.15) $f_{t-1,t} = E_0(s_{t-1,t})$ for all t.

That is, according to the pure expectations theory forward rates are unbiased expectations of corresponding future spot rates.

The liquidity preference theory.   The liquidity preference theory (Hicks 1946) derives its name from the argument that lenders are generally averse to holding a long-term debt security because of the loss of liquidity involved. However, this is much less a concern in well-functioning financial markets, whose investors can sell the security at any time at a competitive price and with only a small transaction cost. Instead, an investor's aversion to holding long-term default-free debt stems primarily from the fact that the *volatility* of short-term returns on a bond generally increases with the bond's maturity; that is, longer-term bonds are more risky.

To illustrate the riskiness of short-term returns on multiperiod bonds, we return to the previous numerical example. Given $s_{0,1} = .06$ and $E_0(s_{1,2}) = .07$, under the pure expectations hypothesis $s_{0,2} = .065$, and the expected return on the two-period bond in the first period is $.06 = s_{0,1}$. If, however, the realized value of $s_{1,2}$ is greater (less) than $E_0(s_{1,2}) = .07$, then the first-period return on the two-period bond will be less (greater) than .06. To see this, assume the following binomial distribution of $s_{1,2}$, assessed at time 0:

(14.16) $s_{1,2} = \begin{cases} .04 \text{ with probability } .5 \\ .10 \text{ with probability } .5. \end{cases}$

Given this distribution, $E_0(s_{1,2}) = .5(.04) + .5(.10) = .07$, as before. If at time 1, $s_{1,2} = .04$, the price of a one-period pure-discount bond will be ($\$1/1.04$) $= .9615$, and an investor who purchased a two-period bond at time 0 realizes a return of $(.9615/.8817) - 1 = .0905$. Alternatively, if $s_{1,2} = .10$ is realized, the price of a one-period bond will be .9615, and the return on the two-period bond in the first period is $(.9091/.8817) = .0311$. Thus, the expected first-period return on the two-period bond is $.5(.0905) + .5(.0311) = .0608$, which differs only slightly from $s_{0,1}$ due to a minor statistical effect known as Jensen's inequality.[1]

If investors are averse to the interest rate risk illustrated above (that is, if interest rate risk is systematic), investors will demand compensation for bearing the risk associated with multiperiod bonds. That is, the expected return on a multiperiod bond must exceed the expected return on a

---

[1] Given any random variable X, $E(\frac{1}{x}) > \frac{1}{E}(x)$ according to Jensen's inequality. In the present context, $x = 1 + r$, where r is random.

one-period bond. The resulting expected return *premium* will be impounded into the price of the multiperiod bond, driving its price lower than it would be in a pure expectations equilibrium. However, because the maturity and thus the interest-rate risk of any bond changes as the bond approaches maturity, an important question as to the behavior of the expected return premiums on bonds with various maturities emerges.

We begin to answer this question by referring again to our example. Assume as before that $s_{0,1} = .06$ and $E_0(s_{1,2}) = .07$, but now the equilibrium price of a two-period bond is .8700 instead of .8817, as it was under pure expectations. As a result, $s_{0,2} = (1/.8700) - 1 = .0721$, which exceeds the value of $s_{0,2}$ under pure expectations (.065). Now we calculate the expected return on the two-period bond in the first period, using the binomial process for $s_{1,2}$ given in equation 14.16. Note that after period 1 a two-period bond becomes a one-period bond and must have the same price as other one-period bonds. Thus, if $s_{1,2} = 0.04$, then the price of the bond will be .9615, and the realized return on the two-period bond in the first period will be $(.9615/.87) - 1 = .1052$. If instead $s_{1,2} = .10$, the return will be $(.9091/.87) - 1 = .0449$. Since each of these outcomes has a probability of .5, the expected return on the two-period bond in the first period is $E_0(_2r_{0,1}) = .5(.1052) + .5(.0449) = .0751$. Thus, the two-period bond is priced to provide an expected return premium of $.0751 - .06 = .0151$, or 1.51 percent, in the first period. Of course, based on the discussion above, the expected return on the two-period bond in the second period is simply .07, or $.5(.04) + .5(.10)$. With these first- and second-period expected returns we can recalculate the original price of the two-period bond: $\$1/[(1.0751)(1.07)] = .8693$, which differs slightly from the actual original price of .8700 only because of Jensen's inequality.

As the example illustrates, the entire expected return premium on a two-period bond is assigned to the first period. This is reasonable because the bond's return is risky only in the first period. (Stated differently, none of the expected-return premium on a two-period bond can be assigned to the second period because the bond will then be a one-period bond and must be priced accordingly.) Denoting as $E_0(_np_{0,1})$ the expected return premium on an n-period bond in the first period, the expected return on an n-period bond in the first period can be expressed as

(14.17) $E_0(_nr_{0,1}) = s_{0,1} + E_0(_np_{0,1}).$

In the present example,

$$E_0(_2r_{0,1}) = .06 + .0151 = .0751.$$

Under the liquidity preference theory, the spot rate on a two-period bond can be decomposed into expected returns in the first and second periods:

(14.18) $s_{0,2} = \{[1 + s_{0,1} + E_0(_2p_{0,1})] \, [1 + E_0(s_{1,2})]\}^{\frac{1}{2}} - 1.$

In this example, $s_{0,2} = .0721$, and the right-hand side of equation 14.18 is $\{[1 + 0.06 + .0151]\ [1 + 0.07]\}^{1/2} - 1 = .0725$. The slight discrepancy is again due to Jensen's inequality. In general the spot rate on an n-period bond can be expressed as

(14.19) $$s_{0,n} = \{[1 + s_{0,1} + E_0({}_np_{0,1})]\ [1 + E_0(s_{1,2}) + E_0({}_{n-1}p_{1,2})] \cdots$$
$$[1 + E_0(s_{n-2,n-1}) + E_0({}_2p_{n-2,n-1})]\ [1 + E_0(s_{n-1,n})]\}^{1/n} - 1.$$

The right-hand side of equation 14.19 is the geometric mean of the sequence of expected total returns (including sequential premiums) from the first period to maturity, minus 1.

Finally, if expected return premiums are embedded in the spot rates on multiperiod bonds as shown in equations 14.18 and 14.19, forward rates calculated via equations 14.9 and 14.10 can no longer be interpreted as unbiased expectations of future one-period spot rates, as was the case under the pure expectations theory (recall equations 14.14 and 14.15). Instead, forward rates contain both expectations of a future spot rate and an expected return premium. Comparing equations 14.9 and 14.18, we can see that $f_{1,2}$ is approximately equal to the sum of the expected one-period spot rate at time 1 and the expected return premium on a two-period bond in the first period:

(14.20) $$f_{1,2} \approx E_0(s_{1,2}) + E_0({}_2p_{0,1}).$$

As such, $f_{1,2}$ captures the expected return on a two-period bond in the second period—$E_0(s_{1,2})$—and the premium portion of the expected return on the two-period bond in the first period—$E_0({}_2p_{0,1})$. Not surprisingly, the information contained in forward rates is often misunderstood. For example, some interpret equation 14.9 as indicating that the expected return on a two-period bond in the first period is $s_{0,1}$ and in the second period is $f_{1,2}$, which is incorrect. Forward rates extracted via equation 14.10 for longer-term bonds are even more complex, as you can determine by using equation 14.19 to substitute into equation 14.10. Although $f_{t-1,t}$ always contains information about $E_0(s_{t-1,t})$, the terms representing the expected return premiums do not readily cancel.

The Cox-Ingersoll-Ross model of the term structure. Recently Cox, Ingersoll, and Ross (1981, 1985) (CIR) developed a popular general equilibrium theory of the term structure of interest rates. Their model assumes perfect markets and incorporates real production functions in the economy as well as investors' wealth and risk aversion to determine equilibrium values for all assets, including default-free bonds. The theory is capable of incorporating both interest-rate expectations and risk premiums in pricing bonds. Although a full discussion of their theory is beyond the scope of this text, we will highlight their contribution to our understanding of the term structure. More generally, the CIR model is introduced to illustrate one of the many recently developed general equilibrium models of the term structure.[2]

To illustrate the characteristics of their equilibrium, CIR assume a simple setting in which the term structure of interest rates is completely defined in terms of one factor, and the movements of this factor through time are perfectly correlated with the short-term default-free rate of interest, r. Working with continuous-time mathematics, CIR then assume that r obeys the following autoregressive process, or elastic random walk:

$$(14.21) \qquad\qquad dr = k(\theta - r)dt + \sigma\sqrt{r}dz,$$

where dr is the change in r over the next instant of time, dt, and dz is an Ito process, which has a standard normal distribution defined over dt. According to equation 14.21, changes in r over time contain an expectation component, $k(\theta - r)dt$, and a random component, $\sigma\sqrt{r}dz$. Given $k > 0$, the expectation component specifies that if r is above (below) its usual level, θ, r is expected to fall (rise) by an amount proportional to the current deviation from the normal rate, $\theta - r$. The random component specifies that the variance of unexpected changes in the interest rate is proportional to the level of r, or $\sigma^2 r$.

Given the process in equation 14.21, CIR derive the following closed-form model for the price of a default-free pure discount bond with maturity n:

$$(14.22) \qquad\qquad P = Ae^{-Br}$$

where

$$A = \left[\frac{2\gamma e^{(k + \lambda + \gamma)n/2}}{(\gamma + k + \lambda)(e^{\gamma n} - 1) + 2\gamma}\right]^{2\kappa\theta/\sigma^2}$$

$$B = \frac{2(e^{\gamma n} - 1)}{(\gamma + k + \lambda)(e^{\gamma n} - 1) + 2\gamma}$$

and

$$\gamma = ((k + \lambda)^2 + 2\sigma^2)^{\frac{1}{2}}.$$

In this model, λ is the market risk premium parameter; $\lambda < 0$ implies positive interest rate risk premiums. Specifically, the instantaneous expected return on the bond is

$$(14.23) \qquad\qquad r + \lambda r(\partial P/\partial r)/P,$$

---

[2] For a recent review of one-factor term structure models, see Hull and White (1993).

where $\partial P / \partial r$ is the partial derivative of P with respect to r. Thus, expected return premiums are proportional to the interest elasticity of the bond, which generally increases with maturity, n. Figure 14.6 shows three simulated yield curves generated by the CIR model using $k = .5$, $\theta = .08$, $\sigma = .1$, $\lambda = -.2$, and $r = .04, .08$, and $.12$. Note that when $r < \theta$, the yield curve slopes upward, reflecting expectations of rising rates; when $r = \theta$ the yield curve is approximately flat (with a slight upward slope reflecting the term premium); and when $r > \theta$ the yield curve slopes downward, reflecting expectations of falling rates.

The single-factor structure of the CIR model may be too restrictive to explain the behavior of the entire term structure of interest rates. More sophisticated models that incorporate two or more interest rate factors have been developed, and they appear to have some power to explain the behavior of both short-term and long-term interest rates (Brennan and Schwartz 1979, Longstaff and Schwartz 1992).

The market segmentation and preferred habitat theories.   According to the market segmentation theory (Culbertson 1957), the market for debt securities actually consists of a number of separate markets defined by debt maturity. For instance, separate markets for short-term, medium-term and long-term debt may exist. There is a separate set of lenders and borrowers for each maturity segment, and the equilibrium interest rate in each segment is determined by separate supply and demand schedules. These separate equilibriums are illustrated in Figure 14.7.

Proponents of this theory argue that many major market participants restrict their borrowing or lending to a particular segment of the maturity spectrum because of the nature of their business activity. For example, life

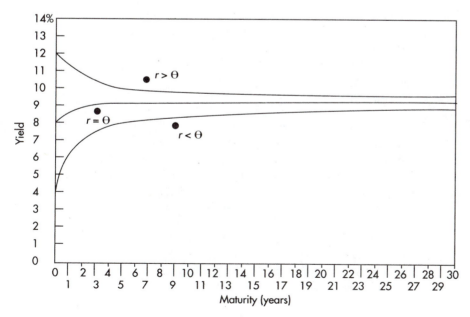

FIGURE 14.6

Simulated Term Structures Using the Cox, Ingersoll, and Ross Model

FIGURE 14.7

Separate
Equilibriums under
the Market
Segmentation Theory

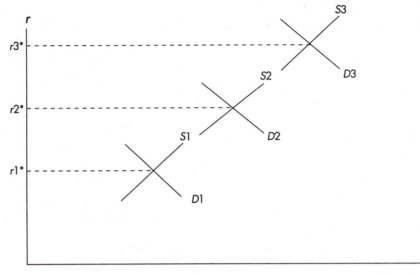

insurance companies generally purchase long-term debt as a means of matching the maturity of their assets with their generally long-term liabilities (i.e. claims), and commercial banks tend to purchase short-term debt to match the maturities of their liabilities (i.e., deposits). Such maturity matching minimizes both transaction costs and interest rate risk. Critics argue that other risk-neutral borrowers will choose the debt maturity that minimizes expected long-term costs and other risk-neutral lenders will choose the debt maturity that maximizes expected returns, and as a result the supply and demand curves depicted in Figure 14.7 will shift until an expectations-based equilibrium (with possible expected-return premiums for longer maturities) is reached.

The preferred-habitat theory (Modigliani and Sutch 1966) is a blend of the pure expectations, liquidity preference, and market segmentation theories and is essentially an arbitrage approach to the term structure. According to this theory, lenders have preferred maturity habitats; that is, they prefer to invest in bonds with a given maturity because that maturity matches the timing of planned expenditures, in a manner similar to the segmentation theory. As noted above, maturity matching minimizes interest rate risk and transaction costs. However, according to this theory lenders will choose bonds with shorter or longer maturities if the lender can realize sufficient additional expected return (to the habitat horizon) that outweighs the additional transaction costs and interest rate risk. Similarly, borrowers may deviate from their maturity habitat if the expected reduction in borrowing costs (to the habitat horizon) outweighs the additional transaction costs and risk.

Empirical evidence on the term structure of interest rates.   Our analysis of empirical evidence concerning the term structure of interest rates focuses initially on two hypotheses, the pure expectations hypothesis and the liquidity premium hypothesis. According to the pure expectations hypothesis, bonds of all maturities should provide the same expected return for a given holding period, and the liquidity premium hypothesis posits that the expected one-period return on a bond should increase with its maturity.

Fama (1984) conducted an extensive empirical analysis of the returns on U.S. Treasury securities for the 30-year period 1953–1982. Fama calculated monthly return premiums above the one-month Treasury bill rate on multiperiod securities. Results of this analysis are displayed in Exhibit 14.3. Panel A shows the average percent monthly return premiums on Treasury bills with maturities of two to twelve months (P2 through P12). The evidence indicates that for the full period as well as most subperiods, the average return premiums are positive and increase with maturity through about nine months and then plateau. Most of these premiums are statistically significant. These results indicate that multiperiod Treasury bills provide reliable premiums that generally increase with maturity, and as such the evidence is consistent with the liquidity premium hypothesis.

However, the evidence for Treasury bills contrasts with the evidence for Treasury bonds, shown in panel B. Here the average premiums are reliably positive only for bonds with maturities of less than one year. Average premiums on intermediate-term bonds are positive but insignificant, and the average premiums on long-term bonds are negative though insignificant. The latter evidence is consistent with the pure expectations hypothesis.

It is difficult to reconcile the overall evidence in Exhibit 14.3 with either hypothesis. However, note that the sample period in Fama's study ended in 1982, which in retrospect was the start of a decade-long rally in bond prices due to a precipitous decline in interest rates for all maturities. During this period long-term bonds provided unprecedented returns and return premiums. Evidence of bond returns in this period is provided in Exhibit 14.4 on page 343. This exhibit shows the average annual returns on Treasury securities for the ten-year period subsequent to Fama's analysis, 1983–1992. The average returns increase monotonically with maturity except for the longest-maturity category. Note, however, that the higher average returns on the longer-term securities are also associated with higher risk; Exhibit 14.4 also shows the standard deviations of the annual returns, which increase with maturity. This evidence is consistent with the liquidity premium hypothesis.

Empirical tests of the segmentation and preferred habitat hypotheses generally focus on either (1) changes in the relative aggregate supplies of debt, particularly Treasury debt, of various maturities, or (2) discontinu-

EXHIBIT 14.3

Average Monthly Return Premiums on Multiperiod U.S. Treasury Bills (Panel A) and Longer-Term U.S. Treasury Notes and Bonds (Panel B) for Various Periods

	Panel A: Average monthly return premiums on Treasury bills				
Bill	N = 211 8/64–12/82	N = 101 8/64–12/72	N = 110 1/73–12/82	N = 56 1/73–12/77	N = 54 1/78–12/82
			Average premiums		
P2	0.032	0.028	0.035	0.016	0.056
P3	0.057	0.045	0.067	0.042	0.094
P4	0.063	0.046	0.078	0.056	0.101
P5	0.074	0.061	0.086	0.065	0.108
P6	0.073	0.066	0.079	0.062	0.097
P7	0.069	0.071	0.067	0.060	0.074
P8	0.088	0.084	0.091	0.083	0.100
P9	0.089	0.086	0.092	0.082	0.102
P10	0.057	0.025	0.086	0.077	0.096
P11	0.064	0.066	0.063	0.066	0.059
P12	0.074	0.103	0.047	0.040	0.054
			t statistics for average premiums		
P2	6.40	6.97	4.03	2.70	3.38
P3	6.40	7.17	4.21	3.42	3.15
P4	4.70	5.18	3.23	2.78	2.26
P5	4.14	5.12	2.64	2.43	1.78
P6	3.34	4.35	2.01	1.92	1.32
P7	2.75	3.68	1.50	1.58	0.90
P8	3.04	3.86	1.76	1.95	1.04
P9	2.59	3.27	1.49	1.69	0.88
P10	1.49	0.83	1.26	1.41	0.75
P11	1.54	2.09	0.83	1.10	0.42
P12	1.61	2.87	0.57	0.59	0.36

		Panel B: Average monthly return premiums on Treasury notes and Treasury bonds						
Portfolio Number	Maturity Range (Months)	N = 360 1953-82	N = 60 1953-57	N = 60 1958-62	N = 60 1963-67	N = 60 1968-72	N = 60 1973-77	N = 60 1978-82
				Average premiums				
1	M<6	0.036	0.017	0.045	0.002[a]	0.040	0.051	0.063
2	6≤M<12	0.042	0.032	0.082	−0.008	0.062	0.049	0.034
3	12≤M<18	0.048	0.039	0.095	−0.013	0.069	0.062[a]	0.034
4	18≤M<24	0.037	0.042	0.099	−0.036	0.072	0.040	0.002
5	24≤M<30	0.026	0.066	0.086	−0.053	0.060	0.050	−0.053
6	30≤M<36	0.034	0.050	0.117	−0.066	0.093	0.053	−0.044
7	36≤M<48	0.012	0.046	0.120	−0.082	0.041	0.028	−0.080
8	48≤M<60	−0.024	0.043	0.059	−0.133	0.030	−0.029	−0.112
9	60≤M<120	−0.012	0.052	0.085	−0.118	0.083	0.017	−0.190
10	M ≅ 240	−0.128	0.015	0.001	−0.331	−0.032	−0.054	−0.068
				t statistics for average premiums				
1	M<6	3.86	1.52	3.42	0.18	2.34	2.62	1.38
2	6≤M<12	1.97	1.73	3.23	−0.50	1.54	1.07	0.32
3	12≤M<18	1.47	1.29	1.94	−0.46	1.09	0.85	0.22
4	18≤M<24	0.88	0.96	1.60	−0.89	0.78	0.45	0.01
5	24≤M<30	0.53	1.19	1.20	−1.10	0.56	0.49	−0.22
6	30≤M<36	0.60	0.78	1.33	−1.25	0.74	0.46	−0.16
7	36≤M<48	0.18	0.65	1.14	−1.20	0.28	0.22	−0.26
8	48≤M<60	−0.32	0.45	0.46	−1.61	0.18	−0.20	−0.32
9	60≤M<120	−0.13	0.43	0.62	−1.11	0.39	0.10	−0.46
10	M ≅ 240	−0.99	0.08	0.01	−1.84	−0.09	−0.20	−0.66

Source: E. F. Fama, "Term Premiums in Bond Returns." *Journal of Financial Economics* 13 (1984): pp 535-536.

EXHIBIT 14.4

Means and Standard Deviations of Annual Returns on U.S. Treasury
Securities with Various Maturities, 1983–1992

Maturity	Mean Return (%)	Standard Deviation (%)
91 days (T-bills)	7.70	1.98
1–3 years	9.74	3.00
3–5 years	10.97	4.97
5–7 years	11.65	6.57
7–10 years	12.10	8.13
10–15 years	13.03	9.79
15+ years	13.00	10.60

Source: Merrill Lynch Capital Markets, New York, 1993.

ities in yields across the maturity spectrum. Overall, the evidence is mixed.
For example, Elliot and Echols (1976) and Roley (1981) found evidence
consistent with the market segmentation hypothesis, while Pesando
(1978), Van Horne (1980) and Lang and Rasche (1977) found little or no
evidence consistent with the hypothesis. Most of these studies focused on
long-term Treasury yields. In contrast, Ogden (1987b) analyzed the
short-term Treasury bill market for evidence of short-horizon preferred
maturity habitats. Ogden argued that corporations have a preferred
maturity habitat at the turn of each calendar month because the bulk of
their payments of dividends on equity, and interest and principal on debt,
are due at the turn of the month. Thus corporate treasurers prefer to invest
idle cash in Treasury bills due to mature at the end of the month, when the
firm's payments are due, than in Treasury bills with longer or shorter
maturities, other things being equal. The resulting excess demand for
month-end Treasury bills would generally raise their prices and lower
their yields relative to other Treasury bills. Ogden's evidence is consistent
with these arguments. An example of this month-end preferred habitat in
Treasury bill yields is provided in Figure 14.8, which shows Treasury bills
yields for January 31, 1991. Note that the yield on the Treasury bill that
matures at the end of the calendar month is substantially lower than the
yields on adjacent-maturity Treasury bills.

Default Risk

The second principal characteristic governing the valuation of specific
debt securities is default risk. The term *default risk* refers to uncertainty
about a borrower's ability to make the contracted payments on a debt
security and the effect of default on realized returns. The only debt
securities that are truly free of default risk are those issued by a
government that also has the power to tax and to print money, such as U.S.
Treasury securities. Corporate bonds, municipal bonds, and other debt
securities bear varying levels of default risk. We now analyze the effects
of default risk on the price, yield, and expected return on a debt security.

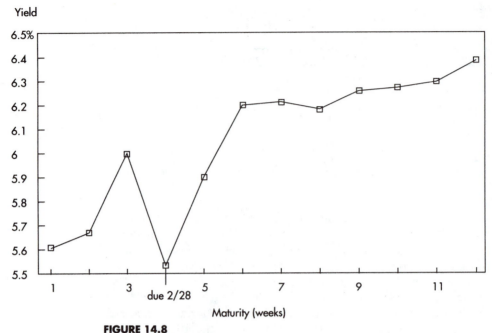

FIGURE 14.8

Yields on U.S. Treasury Bills for January 31, 1991
Source: Data from the *Wall Street Journal*, February 1, 1991.

For simplicity, our analysis will focus on default-risky pure-discount bonds, but the analysis can easily be adapted to default-risky coupon bonds. We begin by distinguishing between the promised yield and the expected return on a default-risky bond. Denoting as $P_{0,n}$ the current price of an n-period default-risky pure-discount and M_n the promised payment at maturity, the yield to maturity on the bond is the value of y_n that solves equation 14.24:

(14.24)
$$P_{0,n} = \frac{M_n}{(1 + y_n)^n}.$$

For example, suppose a firm issues a ten-year pure-discount bond with a promised payment of $M_n = \$1000$ at maturity, and the price of the bond is $P_{0,10} = \$385.50$. Then $y_n = (1000/385.5)^{1/10} - 1 = .1$, or 10 percent.

Note that in equation 14.24 we use the promised payment, M_n, to compute y_n. Since M_n is the maximum amount that the investor can receive from the firm (and the investor will receive this amount only if the firm does not default), y_n is the highest return to maturity that the investor can realize. Denoting as m_n the *realized* payment at maturity (noting that $m_n \leq M_n$), the *realized return to maturity* on the bond, $_nr_{0,n}$, is the solution to equation 14.25:

$$P_{0,n} = \frac{m_n}{(1 + {}_n r_{0,n})^n} \cdot$$

(14.25)

In the present example, if the firm does not default, then $m_{10} = M_{10} = 1000$, and ${}_{10}r_{0,10} = y_{10} = 10\%$. However, suppose the firm defaults and the investor receives only $m_{10} = \$300$. Then ${}_{10}r_{0,10} = (300/385.5)^{1/10} - 1 = -.0248$, or -2.48 percent.

Assume that there are S possible payoffs at maturity on an n-period default-risky pure-discount bond, each denoted as $m_{n,s}$, and each with an associated probability denoted as $q_{n,s}$. Then the expected return to maturity on the bond, $E({}_n r_{0,n})$, can be calculated using equation 14.26:

(14.26)

$$E({}_n r_{0,n}) = \sum_{s=1}^{S} q_{n,s} \left\{ \left(\frac{m_{n,s}}{P_{0,n}} \right)^{1/n} - 1 \right\}$$

Equation 14.26 illustrates that default risk can be defined in terms of the probability of a loss (i.e., loss = promised payment − actual payment). Equation 14.26 shows that the discrepancy between promised yield and expected return to maturity, $y_n - E({}_n r_{0,n})$, increases with default risk. Returning to the previous example, assume there are two possible payoffs ($S = 2$): $m_{10,1} = 1000$ with probability $q_{10,1} = 0.8$ and $m_{10,2} = 300$ with probability $q_{10,2} = 0.2$. Then, assuming $P_{0,10} = \$385.50$ as before:

$$E({}_{10} r_{0,10}) = .8(.1000) + .2(-.0248) = .0750,$$

or 7.5 percent. Note the discrepancy between the promised yield and the expected return to maturity: $y_n - E({}_n R_{0,n}) = .1000 - .0750 = .0250$, or 2.5 percent.

We can also demonstrate that the promised yield on a bond with a given maturity increases with its default risk and that this is true whether investors are neutral or averse to default risk. We begin by denoting the promised yield and expected return to maturity on an n-period default-free pure discount bond as $y_n^* = E({}_n r_{0,n}^*)$. We will initially assume that investors are default-risk neutral and therefore demand the same expected return for default-risky and default-free bonds. Thus, using the example above, investors require $y_{10}^* = E({}_{10} r_{0,10}^*) = .075$ for a ten-year default-free pure discount bond. Using equation 14.23, this implies that the price of the default-free bond is \$485.19, or $\$1,000/(1.075)^{10}$, which is, of course, greater than the price of the default-risky bond, \$385.50. Thus, $y_n > y_n^*$, and $E({}_{10} r_{0,10}^*) = E({}_{10} r_{0,10})$. If instead investors are risk averse, they will pay a price *less than* \$385.50 for the default-risky bond to incorporate a risk premium; that is, $E({}_{10} r_{0,10}) > E({}_{10} r_{0,10}^*)$. For example, if the price of the default-risky bond is \$360, equation 14.25 can be used to determine that the expected return on the bond will be $E({}_{10} r_{0,10}) = .8 (.1076) + .2(-.0181) = .0825$ or 8.25 percent. In this case the promised yield on the bond rises to 11.07 percent, or $.1107 = (100/350)^{1/10} - 1$. Thus, in either case, $y_n > y_n^*$; that is, the promised yield on the default-risky bond is greater than the promised yield on the default-free bond. However, the expected return on the default-risky bond is greater than the expected return on the default-free bond only in the risk aversion case.

The relationships between promised yield, expected return, and default risk established in the above discussion are illustrated qualitatively in Figure 14.9. The figure illustrates that promised yields increase monotonically with default risk, while expected returns may or may not increase with default risk, depending on whether investors demand a premium for bearing default risk. However, whether or not investors demand a risk premium, the discrepancy between promised yield and expected return, $y_n - E({}_n r_{0,n})$, is positive for all bonds except default-free bonds, and the discrepancy increases with default risk. Note also that the difference between the promised yields on a default-risky bond and a default-free bond, $y_n - y_n^*$, which is a popular measure of the risk premium on a default-risky bond, is always an upward-biased estimate of the true risk premium, $E({}_n r_{0,n}) - y_n^*$, and this bias also increases with default risk.

This analysis focuses on yields, expected returns, and expected return premiums *to maturity*. Another important return measure for a bond is the holding-period return, obtained by holding a bond for a length of time that does not extend to the bond's maturity. Denoting as $P_{0,n}$ and $P_{t,n-t}$ the

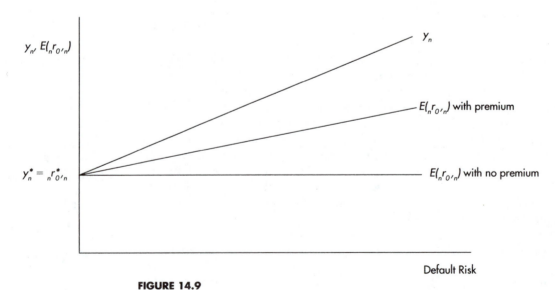

FIGURE 14.9

Promised Yields and Expected Returns to Maturity on *n*-Period Default-Risky Bonds by Default Risk

values of a pure-discount bond at the beginning and end of a holding period of t periods, the per period holding return, $h_{0,t}$, is

(14.27)
$$h_{0,t} = (P_{t,n-t}/P_{0,n})^{1/t} - 1.$$

Using the previous example, suppose the investor purchases the ten-period bond at the price $P_{0,10} = \$385.50$ and sells it four periods later at $P_{4,6} = \$606$. Then $h_{0,t} = (606/385.50)^{\frac{1}{4}} - 1 = .1197$, or 11.97 percent. Note that holding period returns, unlike returns to maturity, can exceed the originally promised yield to maturity.

Contingent Claims Analysis of Default-Risky Debt.   Corporate debt is a contingent claim. That is, the payoff on the debt is contingent on the future value of the firm. Recent advances in the pricing of options, which are also contingent claims, has led to powerful pricing models for default-risky debt. Black and Scholes (1973) and Merton (1974) have shown that in a perfect market the stock of a levered firm constitutes a call option on the assets of the firm, where the face value and maturity of the debt represent the exercise price and expiration date of the option. We discuss the pricing of options in detail in Chapter 17. However, because of the substantial and growing application of contingent claims analysis to the pricing of corporate debt (Ramaswamy and Sundaresan 1986, Ogden 1987c), a brief discussion here is warranted.

To illustrate the contingent claims pricing of corporate debt in the simplest setting, we will assume (1) the capital market is perfect, (2) the default-free interest rate, r, is constant, and (3) the firm has outstanding only two securities: non-dividend-paying equity and a single issue of pure-discount debt, which promises to pay the amount M_n on the maturity date, n. It is also assumed that returns on the firm's assets, with value V, can be described by the stochastic differential equation 14.28:

(14.28)
$$dV/V = \alpha dt + \sigma dz,$$

where α is the per annum expected rate of return on the firm's assets, σ is the per annum standard deviation of the firm's returns, and dz is a standard Ito process. (Thus in the contingent claims model the variance of the firm's returns, σ^2, is invariant to firm size; that is, the variance of dV/V is assumed constant.) Next, we must establish several boundary conditions that are necessary to solve for the values of the securities. For instance, if on the maturity date $V_n < M_n$, the shareholders will default and bondholders will take over the firm, in which case the value of the shares, E_n, will be zero, and the value of the debt, D_n, will be $D_n = V_n$. Alternatively, if $V_n \geq M_n$, the shareholders will payoff the debt, so $D_n = M_n$ and $E_n = V_n - M_n$. Also, if at any time $t < n$ the value of the firm goes to zero ($V_t = 0$), the value of both the debt and the equity will also be zero ($D_t = 0$ and $E_t = 0$).

EXHIBIT 14.5

Yield Premiums on Ten-Year Pure Discount Debt Calculated with the Black-Scholes Model (risk-free yield is 10 percent)

D/V	$\sigma = .20$	$\sigma = .40$
0.05	0.43%	0.63%
0.10	0.47	1.06
0.15	0.51	1.58
0.20	0.54	2.18
0.25	0.58	2.88
0.30	0.64	3.66
0.35	0.78	4.46
0.40	0.90	5.35
0.45	1.10	6.28
0.50	1.34	7.15
0.55	1.68	8.34
0.60	2.01	9.50
0.65	2.45	10.90
0.70	2.99	12.47

Given these conditions, the current value of the firm's equity, E, can be determined as a function of V, σ^2, r, M_n and n, using the Black-Scholes model discussed in Chapter 17. Then, since the value of the firm is equal to the sum of the values of the outstanding claims, the value of the debt, D, is found as

(14.29)
$$D = V - E.$$

Our focus is on the implications of the model for the pricing of the firm's debt. Consider a firm with assets that have a value of $1,000. Assume that $\sigma = 0.35$, $r = 0.10$, and the firm has outstanding debt that matures in ten years ($n = 10$) and has a face value of $1,200. Under these conditions the value of the equity is $647.35 and the value of the debt is $1,000 − $647.35 = $352.65. Thus the promised yield on the debt is $y_n = (1200/352.65)^{1/10} - 1 = 0.1303$, and the yield premium on the debt is $y_n - y_n^* = 0.1303 - 0.10 = 0.0303$, or 3.03 percent. The ratio of debt to firm value, D/V, is .353. As Merton (1974) argues, σ and D/V are the relevant measures of risk for a bond with a given maturity; bond risk increases monotonically with each of these risk measures. Exhibit 14.5 shows yield premiums derived from the model that correspond to various values of σ and D/V, given $n = 10$ and $r = .10$ as in the above example. Note that the yield premiums increase with both σ and D/V.

Empirical Evidence on Default Risk

Historical perspective.   Throughout the century the supply of publicly issued low-risk, or investment-grade, corporate bonds, as defined below, has generally grown with the economy. However, the history of publicly issued high-risk, or speculative-grade, bonds is irregular. Early in this century, public issuance of high-risk corporate debt was fairly common. However, during the Great Depression a great number of firms defaulted on their bonds, even bonds formerly designated as low risk. In the succeeding several decades, the market for new public corporate bonds was generally restricted to investment-grade bonds. Of course, throughout this period high-risk bonds existed, as the financial condition of some of the firms that had originally issued investment-grade debt deteriorated. These bonds are called fallen angels. But most smaller and high-risk firms were de facto restricted to raising debt funds through private placements with financial institutions.

In the latter 1970s the public new-issue high-risk corporate bond market reemerged, led by Michael Milken and the ill-fated investment banking firm Drexel Burnham Lambert. Throughout most of the 1980s volume in the junk bond market, as it came to be known, surged. As a result many smaller and high-risk firms found a new source of debt funds: the public bond market. Unfortunately, liquidity in this market depended heavily on Drexel Burnham Lambert's willingness to act as a dealer, and when Drexel faltered and entered bankruptcy, the junk bond market also faltered. Weakness in the economy in 1990 also contributed to substantial losses in many outstanding junk bonds, and the new-issue junk bond market virtually disappeared. However, by 1992 the prices of outstanding junk bonds generally recovered, and the new-issue junk bond market emerged once again.

Bond ratings.   A number of firms provide credit rating classifications for default-risky bonds. The leading bond rating firms are Moody's Investor Service and Standard and Poor's Corporation (S&P). For bonds with the highest credit quality (and thus the lowest assessed risk of default), Moody's provides a rating of Aaa and S&P provides a rating of AAA. For bonds of lower credit quality, the following rating classifications are assigned, listed in descending order of credit quality: Aa, A, Baa, Ba, B, Caa, Ca, and C for Moody's; AA, AA, A, BBB, BB, B, CCC, CC, and C for S&P. S&P also includes the classification D for bonds in default. In addition, both Moody's and S&P include rating modifiers for most of their ratings classifications. For bonds that are in the upper, middle, and lower ranges of credit quality within a given classification, Moody's adds the modifiers 1, 2 and 3, respectively (e.g., B1). S&P provides corresponding modifiers + and – for bonds in the upper and lower ranges within a given classification (e.g., B+). Bonds with Moody's (S&P) ratings of Baa (BBB) or above are investment-grade bonds, and bonds with lower ratings are speculative-grade, or junk, bonds. These designations are important because many financial institutions are prohibited from investing in speculative-grade bonds. S&P's bond ratings and their definitions are displayed in Exhibit 14.6.

Empirical evidence.   We now discuss the results of several types of empirical analyses of default-risky bonds. We first discuss evidence of the

EXHIBIT 14.6

Standard and Poor's Debt Rating Definitions

A Standard & Poor' corporate or municipal debt rating is a current assessment of the creditworthiness of an obligor with respect to a specific obligation. This assessment may take into consideration obligors such as guarantors, insurers, or lessees.

The debt rating is not a recommendation to purchase, sell, or hold a security, as it does not comment on market price or suitability for a particular investor.

The ratings are based, in varying degrees, on the following considerations:

(1) Likelihood of default. The rating assesses the obligor's capacity and willingness as to timely payment of interest and repayment of principal in accordance with the terms of the obligation.

(2) The obligation's nature and provisions.

(3) Protection afforded to, and relative position of, the obligation in the event of bankruptcy, reorganization, or other arrangement under bankruptcy laws and other laws affecting creditors' rights.

Likelihood of default is indicated by an issuer's senior debt rating. If senior debt is not rated, an implied senior debt rating is determined. Subordinated debt usually is rated lower than senior debt to better reflect relative position of the obligation in bankruptcy. Unsecured debt, where significant secured debt exists, is treated similarly to subordinated debt. (See page 49 for more details regarding secured debt.)

Long-term rating definitions

AAA   Debt rated 'AAA' has the highest rating assigned by S&P. Capacity to pay interest and repay principal is extremely strong.

AA   Debt rated 'AA' has a very strong capacity to pay interest and repay principal and differs from the highest rated debt only in small degree.

A   Debt rated 'A' has a strong capacity to pay interest and repay principal, although it is somewhat more susceptible to the adverse effects of changes in circumstances and economic conditions than debt in higher rated categories.

BBB   Debt rated 'BBB' is regarded as having an adequate capacity to pay interest and repay principal. It normally exhibits adequate protection parameters, but adverse economic conditions or changing circumstances are more likely to lead to a weakened capacity to pay.

Dept rated 'BB', 'B', 'CCC', 'CC', and 'C' is regarded as having predominantly speculative characteristics with respect to capacity to pay interest and repay principal. 'BB' indicates the least degree of speculation and 'C' the highest degree of speculation. While such debt will likely have some quality and protective characteristics, these are outweighed by large uncertainties or major risk exposures to adverse conditions.

BB   Debt rated 'BB' has less near-term vulnerability to default than other speculative grade debt. However, it faces major ongoing uncertainties or exposure to adverse business, financial, or economic conditions that could lead to inadequate capacity to meet timely interest and principal payments.

B   Debt rated 'B' has greater vulnerability to default but presently has the capacity to meet interest payments and principal repayments. Adverse business, financial, or economic conditions would likely impair capacity or willingness to pay interest and repay principal.

CCC   Debt rated 'CCC' has a current identifiable vulnerability to default, and is dependent on favorable business, financial, and economic conditions to

EXHIBIT 14.6

Standard and Poor's Debt Rating Definitions (*continued*)

meet timely payment of interest and repayment of principal. In the event of adverse business, financial, or economic conditions, it is not likely to have the capacity to pay interest and repay principal.

CC The rating 'CC' is typically applied to debt subordinated to senior debt which is assigned an actual or implied 'CCC' rating.

C The rating 'C' is typically applied to debt subordinated to senior debt which is assigned an actual or implied 'CCC-' debt rating.

D Debt is rated 'D' when the issue is in payment default, or the obligor has filed for bankruptcy. The 'D' rating is used when interest or principal payments are not made on the date due, even if the applicable grace period has not expired, unless S&P believes that such payments will be made during such grace period.

Plus (+) or minus (−): The ratings from 'AA' to 'CCC' may be modified by the addition of a plus or minus sign to show relative standing within the major rating categories.

If an issuer's actual or implied senior debt rating is 'AAA', its subordinated or junior debt is rated 'AAA' or 'AA+'. If an issuer's actual or implied senior debt rating is lower than 'AAA' but higher than 'BB+', its junior debt is typically rated one designation lower than the senior debt rating. For example, if the senior debt rating is 'A', subordinated debt normally would be rated 'A-'. If an issuer's actual or implied senior debt rating is 'BB+' or lower, its subordinated debt is typically rated two designations lower than the senior debt rating.

Investment and speculative grades

The term "investment grade" was originally used by various regulatory bodies to connote obligations eligible for investment by institutions such as banks, insurance companies, and savings and loan associations. Over time, this term gained widespread usage throughout the investment community. Issues rated in the four highest categories, 'AAA', 'AA', 'A', 'BBB', generally are recognized as being investment grade. Debt rated 'BB' or below generally is referred to as speculative grade. The term "junk bond" is merely a more irreverent expression for this category of more risky debt. Neither term indicates which securities S&P deems worthy of investment, as an investor with a particular risk preference may appropriately invest in securities that are not investment grade.

Ratings continue as a factor in many regulations, both in the U.S. and abroad, notably in Japan. For example, the Securities and Exchange Commission (SEC) requires investment-grade status in order to register debt on Form-3, which, in turn, is how one offers debt via a Rule 415 shelf registration. The Federal Reserve Board allows members of the Federal Reserve System to invest in securities rated in the four highest categories, just as the Federal Home Loan Bank System permits federally chartered savings and loan associations to invest in corporate debt with those ratings, and the Department of Labor allows pension funds to invest in commercial paper rated in one of the three highest categories. In similar fashion, California regulates investments of municipalities and county treasurers, Illinois limits collateral acceptable for public deposits, and Vermont restricts investments of insurers and banks. The New York and Philadelphia Stock Exchanges fix margin requirements for mortgage securities depending on their rating, and the securities haircut for commercial paper, debt securities, and preferred stock that determines net capital requirements is also a function of the ratings assigned.

(continued)

EXHIBIT 14.6

Standard and Poor's Debt Rating Definitions (*continued*)

Short term rating definitions

A Standard & Poor's short term rating is a current assessment of the likelihood of timely payment of debt with an original maturity of no more than 365 days, such as commercial paper. It is also assigned to remarketed long term debt with a provision that allows the holder to put the debt back to the company in less than one year, in addition to the usual long term rating. (Medium term note programs are assigned long term ratings.)

Ratings are graded into several categories, ranging from 'A-1' for the highest quality obligations to 'D' for the lowest.

A-1 This highest category indicates that the degree of safety regarding timely payment is strong. Debt determined to possess extremely strong safety characteristics is denoted with a plus sign (+) designation.

A-2 Capacity for timely payment on issues with this designation is satisfactory. However, the relative degree of safety is not as high as for issues designated 'A-1'.

A-3 Debt carrying this designation has an adequate capacity for timely payment. It is, however, more vulnerable to the adverse effects of changes in circumstances than obligations carrying the higher designations.

B Debt rated 'B' is regarded as having only speculative capacity for timely payment.

C This rating is assigned to short-term debt obligations with a doubtful capacity for payment.

D This rating indicates that the obligation is in payment default.

CreditWatch and Rating Outlooks

An S&P rating evaluates default risk over the life of a debt issue, incorporating an assessment of all future events to the extent they are known or considered likely. But S&P also recognizes the potential for future performance to differ from present expectations. Rating outlooks and CreditWatch listings address this possibility by focusing on the scenarios that could result in a rating change.

CreditWatch highlights potential changes in ratings of bonds, commercial paper, and other fixed-income securities. Issues appear on CreditWatch when an event or deviation from an expected trend has occurred or is expected and additional information is necessary to take rating action. For example, the issuer is placed under such special surveillance as the result of mergers, recapitalizations, regulatory actions, or unanticipated operating developments. Such rating reviews normally are completed within 90 days, unless the outcome of a specific event is pending. A listing does not mean a rating change is inevitable. However, in some cases, it is certain that a rating change will occur and only the magnitude of the change is unclear. Wherever possible, a range of alternative ratings that could result is shown. CreditWatch is not intended to include all issues under review, and rating changes will occur without the issues appearing on CreditWatch. An issuer cannot automatically appeal a CreditWatch listing, but analysts are sensitive to issuer concerns and the fairness of the process.

A rating outlook is assigned to all long-term debt issues–except for structured finance–and also assesses potential for change. It is distinguished from CreditWatch in that the outlook has a longer time frame and incorporates trends or risks with less certain implications for credit quality. An outlook is not necessarily a precursor of a rating change or a CreditWatch listing.

CreditWatch designations and outlooks may be "positive", which indicates a rating may be raised, or "negative", which indicates a rating may be lowered. "Developing" is used for those unusual situations in which future events are so unclear that the rating potentially may be raised or lowered. "Stable" is the outlook assigned when ratings are not likely to be changed, but should not be confused with expected stability of the company's financial performance.

Source: Standard and Poor's Corporate Finance Criteria, 1992.

relationships between a firm's bond rating and (1) various variables related to default risk, and (2) the yield premium on the bond. We then discuss evidence on the probability of default and the losses to investors upon default. This is followed by a discussion of evidence concerning the overall return performance of default-risky debt. Our focus is on recent empirical analyses, many of which coincide with the recent emergence of the junk bond market. For earlier empirical analyses of default-risky bonds, we refer the reader to classic studies by Hickman (1958) and Fisher (1959).

Bond ratings and default risk variables.   A number of studies demonstrate that bond ratings are closely related to both firm characteristics and bond indenture provisions. These in turn are logically related to a firm's likelihood of default (West 1973; Pinches and Mingo 1973; Kaplan and Urwitz 1979; Reilly and Joehnk 1976; and Kidwell, Marr, and Ogden 1989). Higher bond ratings are generally associated with firms that are larger and that have lower debt ratios, more stable earnings, higher fixed-charge coverage ratios and higher current ratios. Higher bond ratings are also associated with bonds that have higher payment priority (e.g., mortgage versus subordinated debenture) and that have a sinking fund.[3] These variables typically explain 60 percent to 90 percent of the variation in bond ratings. As an example of the findings of such studies, Exhibit 14.7 displays the results of Kidwell, Marr, and Ogden's (1989) analysis of the ratings on 192 newly issued utility company bonds. The dependent variable in the analysis is the firm's S&P bond rating, converted to a numerical value (AAA = 1, AA = 2, etc.). Ordinal probit analysis rather than standard regression is used in recognition of the ordinal nature of the dependent variable. The coefficients of all of the independent variables have the expected signs and most are statistically significant, and the estimated R^2 is approximately 76 percent; over 70 percent of the bonds in their sample are correctly classified.

Earlier we introduced the contingent claims pricing model for default-risky debt. Simulations from this model indicated that for a firm with a simple capital structure consisting of equity and a single issue of debt, and for a given maturity of the debt, the firm's return standard deviation, σ, and its leverage ratio, D/V, are sufficient to determine the default risk of the debt. Ogden (1987a) tested this model on a sample of fifty-seven publicly traded firms with simple capital structures consisting primarily of common equity and one issue of debt. He found that both σ and D/V are important determinants of bond ratings, and together they explain approximately 79 percent of the variation in the S&P ratings of the bonds issued by these firms, suggesting that the contingent claims model is very useful in assessing default risk. When Ogden added firm size as an additional explanatory variable, the explanatory power increased to almost 86 percent. The latter results are consistent with the results of

---

[3]Sinking funds are discussed later in this chapter.

EXHIBIT 14.7

Coefficient Estimates and Summary Statistics from Ordinal Probit Analysis of Utility Bond Ratings. Dependent Variable is S&P Bond Rating Converted to a Numerical Value (AAA = 1, AA = 2, etc.)

Explanatory Variables[a]	Regression 1		Regression 2	
	Coefficient	t-value	Coefficient	t-value
CONSTANT	10.395	3.75***	10.932	3.86***
SUB	0.460	2.81***	0.518	2.99***
TYPE	−0.487	−1.62	−0.587	−1.88*
ASSETS	−0.185	−1.62	−0.262	−2.13**
DEBT	3.781	0.91	4.301	1.01
FCOV	−9.397	−9.27***	−9.372	−9.16***
FCOVA	−3.181	−4.26***	−2.901	−3.79***
FCOVP	−2.074	−2.74***	−2.036	−2.69**
FSD	0.758	0.37	0.758	0.36
CUR	−1.013	−2.31**	−1.063	−2.41**
CHCUR	−0.992	−2.63**	−1.093	−2.84***
SF			−1.383	−1.83*
Estimated R^2	0.755		0.764	
Sample size	192		192	
Percent correctly categorized	72.4		70.9	

[a]Explanatory variables are defined as follows: SUB = a zero-one variable with value 1 (0) for subordinated (nonsubordinated) issues; TYPE = a zero-one variable with value 1 (0) for electric (gas) utilities; ASSETS = the natural logarithm of issuer's total assets; DEBT = the ratio of total debt to total asssets; FCOV = the natural logarithm of issuer average fixed coverage ratio; FCOVA = the change in issuer fixed coverage ratio data; FSD = the standard deviation of issuer fixed coverage ratio; CUR = issuer average current ratio; CHCUR = the change in issuer current ratio over the past two years.
*Significant at the 0.10 level.
**Significant at the 0.05 level.
***Significant at the 0.01 level.

Source: D. S. Kidwell, M. W. Marr, and J. P. Ogden, "The Effects of a Sinking Fund on the Reoffering Yields of New Public Utility Bonds", *Journal of Financial Research* 12 (1989): p. 12.

previous studies noted above and indicate that the contingent claims model, which is invariant to firm size, does not adequately capture a component of default risk that is (inversely) related to firm size.

Yield premiums and default risk.   According to the earlier discussion of default-risky debt, the yield premium on a default-risky bond, the difference between the yield on the bond and the yield on default-free debt with the same maturity, should unambiguously increase with the default risk of the bond. Using bond ratings as a proxy for default risk, we can observe the relationship between default risk and yield premiums empirically. As part of his analysis of default-risky debt, Altman (1989) computed the yearly averages of yields on U.S. Treasury bonds and corporate bonds with various S&P ratings for the period 1972–1987. His results are displayed in Exhibit 14.8. For each year average yields increase monotonically as rating quality falls, as expected. Note the very large average yield premiums on junk bonds: For the years 1982–1987, average yield premium on CCC-rated bonds over Treasuries was 7.24 percent. However, recall that these are *promised* yields, not expected returns. Thus, the more important evidence concerns the risk of default, losses upon default, and ultimately the return performance of risky debt.

Probability of default and default losses. Fons and Kimball (1991) report that 350 out of more than four thousand issuers defaulted on bonds rated by Moody's in the twenty-one-year period 1970–1990. They also report the rating history of these defaulting issues for the years prior to and including the year of default. Their results are displayed in Exhibit 14.9. Note that in the year of default only one issuer had an investment-grade rating (they identify this issuer as Manville Corporation); the rest had

EXHIBIT 14.8

Average Yields to Maturity for Various S&P Bond Rating Categories, 1973–1987.

Year	Treasury Bond	AAA	AA	A	BBB	BB	B	CCC
1973	7.15	7.56	7.71	7.87	8.40	NR*	NR	NR
1974	8.13	8.33	8.56	8.65	9.37	NR	NR	NR
1975	8.28	8.64	8.89	9.31	10.12	NR	NR	NR
1976	7.88	8.36	8.37	8.81	9.45	NR	NR	NR
1977	7.76	8.12	8.34	8.48	8.87	NR	NR	NR
1978	8.57	8.74	8.93	9.05	9.53	NR	NR	NR
1979	9.27	9.53	9.80	10.01	10.62	11.66	13.16	NR
1980	11.22	11.66	12.02	12.31	13.09	14.15	14.98	NR
1981	13.20	13.91	14.32	14.60	15.50	16.54	17.33	NR
1982	12.51	13.32	13.73	14.19	15.45	16.32	17.76	21.86
1983	11.09	11.66	11.86	12.17	12.79	13.63	14.61	18.62
1984	12.34	12.43	12.94	13.25	13.97	14.99	15.53	17.71
1985	10.74	10.94	11.41	11.66	12.16	13.65	14.52	16.75
1986	8.16	9.02	9.40	9.64	10.19	11.79	12.82	15.98
1987	8.76	9.32	9.66	9.92	10.42	11.46	12.96	16.12

*NR = not relevant due to small samples and unreliable data.

Source: E. I. Altman, "Measuring Corporate Bond Mortality and Performance," *Journal of Finance* 44 (1989): p. 919.

EXHIBIT 14.9

Rating History of 350 Defaulting Issuers

		Rating at Default	Calendar Years Prior to Default							
			1	2	3	4	5	10	15	20
Invest. Grade	Aaa	0	0	0	0	1	2	2	2	1
	Aa	0	2	2	4	7	6	0	1	2
	A	1	1	6	15	12	10	13	5	4
	Baa	0	14	28	30	33	28	30	24	13
Spec. Grade	Ba	39	97	138	119	102	94	47	26	23
	B	215	197	134	98	67	49	19	17	7
	Cs	95	39	15	11	11	10	8	7	3

Source: J. S. Fons and A. E. Kimball, "Corporate Bond Defaults and Default Rates 1970–1990," *Journal of Fixed Income* 1 (1991): 41.

EXHIBIT 14.10

Total New Issue Amounts of Corporate Bonds by S&P Bond Rating, 1971–1986 in Millions of Dollars

Bond Rating	1971	1972	1973	1974	1975	1976	1977	1978	1979	1980	1981	1982	1983	1984	1985	1986
AAA	5125	3179	4046	7420	11,348	9907	11,046	7967	10,400	10,109	11,835	6197	3920	2350	9016	14,438
AA	5467	4332	3670	8797	9654	9560	7494	7374	5910	10,497	11,748	14,597	14,110	18,291	23,223	46,978
A	6688	4745	4254	8388	12,752	8103	5236	5330	6489	12,195	12,432	13,315	5516	12,252	23,381	34,173
BBB	2139	1198	937	1248	2367	2938	1558	1513	1225	2595	3900	5738	5827	5194	11,068	21,993
BB	292	258	105	250	20	397	579	408	359	418	290	1378	2894	4698	2041	7098
						(10)	(15)	(10)	(8)	(9)	(6)	(16)	(24)	(23)	(23)	(37)
B	112	101	140	18	27	59	526	1029	917	879	894	1122	3713	6485	5945	21,260
						(3)	(17)	(39)	(33)	(28)	(15)	(24)	(46)	(68)	(77)	(133)
CCC	0	0	0	0	14	75	78	34	91	25	0	145	285	1901	1668	4668
						(1)	(5)	(1)	(3)	(1)	(0)	(2)	(5)	(9)	(14)	(40)
Total Rated	19,823	13,813	13,152	26,121	36,182	31,039	26,517	23,655	25,391	36,718	41,099	42,492	36,205	51,171	76,342	150,608

Source: E. I. Altman, "Measuring Corporate Bond Mortality and Performance," *Journal of Finance* 44 (1989): 914.

speculative-grade ratings. However, one year prior to their default a total of seventeen issuers had investment-grade ratings; two years prior to their default thirty-six issuers had investment-grade ratings, and so on. Thus the evidence indicates that the rating agencies have substantial short-term but limited long-term ability to predict default.

Exhibit 14.10 shows the total values of new issues of corporate bonds by S&P bond rating and the total number of new junk bonds for each year from 1971 to 1986, reported by Altman (1989). Due to the indicated changes in the number of bonds of a given class over time, to obtain a meaningful assessment of the probability of default for a given class of bonds, it is important to focus on (1) the relative rather than absolute frequency of default and especially (2) the cumulative default rate, or mortality rate, over time. Altman's calculations of the annual and cumulative mortality rates by rating class are shown in Exhibit 14.11. Both the yearly and cumulative mortality rates generally increase as rating quality falls, as expected. Note the high longer-term cumulative default rates of speculative-grade bonds; for example, after ten years, approximately one-third (31.91 percent) of the bonds originally rated B defaulted.

EXHIBIT 14.11

Mortality Rates by Original S&P Bond Rating, 1971–1987

Original Rating	Years After Issuance									
	1	2	3	4	5	6	7	8	9	10
AAA										
Yearly	0.00%	0.00%	0.00%	0.00%	0.00%	0.13%	0.00%	0.00%	0.00%	0.00%
Cumulative	0.00%	0.00%	0.00%	0.00%	0.00%	0.13%	0.13%	0.13%	0.13%	0.13%
AA										
Yearly	0.00%	0.00%	1.81%	0.39%	0.14%	0.00%	0.00%	0.00%	0.13%	0.00%
Cumulative	0.00%	0.00%	1.81%	2.20%	2.33%	2.33%	2.33%	2.33%	2.46%	2.46%
A										
Yearly	0.00%	0.31%	0.39%	0.00%	0.00%	0.06%	0.12%	0.00%	0.04%	0.00%
Cumulative	0.00%	0.31%	0.71%	0.71%	0.71%	0.77%	0.89%	0.89%	0.93%	0.93%
BBB										
Yearly	0.04%	0.25%	0.17%	0.00%	0.45%	0.00%	0.17%	0.00%	0.23%	0.84%
Cumulative	0.04%	0.29%	0.46%	0.46%	0.91%	0.91%	1.07%	1.07%	1.30%	2.12%
BB										
Yearly	0.00%	0.62%	0.64%	0.31%	0.29%	4.88%	0.00%	0.00%	0.00%	0.00%
Cumulative	0.00%	0.62%	1.25%	1.56%	1.84%	6.64%	6.64%	6.64%	6.64%	6.64%
B										
Yearly	1.98%	0.92%	0.74%	4.24%	4.16%	4.98%	3.62%	4.03%	8.47%	4.33%
Cumulative	1.98%	2.88%	3.60%	7.69%	11.53%	15.94%	18.98%	22.24%	28.83%	31.91%
CCC										
Yearly	2.99%	2.88%	3.97%	22.87%	1.37%	N/A	N/A	N/A	N/A	N/A
Cumulative	2.99%	5.78%	9.52%	30.22%	31.17%	N/A	N/A	N/A	N/A	N/A

Mortality rates are adjusted for defaults and redemptions.

Source: E. I. Altman, "Measuring Corporate Bond Mortality and Performance," *Journal of Finance* 44 (1989): 915.

Altman also provides evidence of the losses incurred by investors upon default for his sample. Shown in Exhibit 14.12 are the average prices per $100 of original par value after default by rating class for the bonds that defaulted in the period 1971–1987. Losses tend to be greater for lower-rated bonds. For example, for the five AAA-rated bonds that defaulted, bondholders lost on average 21.33 percent of their principal ($100–$78.67), while for the twelve CCC-rated bonds, bondholders lost on average 58.85 percent of principal. Thus the evidence indicates that the probability of default and the losses upon default are substantially greater for lower-rated bonds.

Return performance.   The evidence this far indicates that lower-rated bonds have substantially higher promised yield premiums but also have a higher probability of default and incur greater losses upon default. The question remains whether, given the greater default risk, high-risk bonds have greater average returns. Altman calculated the return spreads earned by the bonds in his sample over Treasury bonds for the period 1971–1987. The results of his calculations are shown by rating class and number of years after issuance in Exhibit 14.13. The return spreads are measured in cumulative basis points (1 basis point = .01 percent). Note that every entry in the exhibit is positive, indicating that on average the bonds in each rating class provided a positive return spread over Treasuries for every return horizon from one to ten years. Furthermore, for every given return horizon the return spreads tend to increase as bond rating falls. This evidence indicates that the market provides an expected return premium for default risk. Note, however, that Altman's sample period ends in 1987 and thus does not extend to the period associated with Drexel Burnham Lambert's demise, the subsequent recession, or the reemergence of the junk bond market.

EXHIBIT 14.12

Average Prices of Bonds after Default by Original S&P Bond Rating, 1971–1987

Original Rating	Average Price After Default (Per $100)	Number of Observations
AAA	78.67	5
AA	79.29	13
A	45.90	19
BBB	45.30	22
BB	35.71	13
B	42.56	64
CCC	41.15	12
C	10.00	2
NR	31.18	23
Arithmetic Average or Total	44.58	173

Source: E. I. Altman, "Measuring Corporate Bond Mortality and Performance," *Journal of Finance* 44 (1989): 916.

EXHIBIT 14.13

Return Spreads on Corporate Bonds over Treasury Bonds in Basis
Points by S&P Rating Category, 1971–1987

Years After Issuance	Bond Rating at Issuance						
	AAA	**AA**	**A**	**BBB**	**BB**	**B**	**CCC**
1	45	76	104	171	326	382	519
2	100	168	223	366	684	861	1174
3	165	243	367	609	1129	1460	2062
4	246	359	556	923	1710	1746	496
5	344	515	782	1250	2419	2160	1561
6	457	710	1047	1700	2648	2676	NA
7	598	949	1366	2286	3585	3365	NA
8	772	1246	1778	2911	4725	4058	NA
9	987	1591	2278	3721	6073	3673	NA
10	1245	2028	2885	4577	7637	4467	NA

Source: E. I. Altman, "Measuring Corporate Bond Mortality and Performance," *Journal of Finance* 44 (1989): 918.

Taxation of Bonds

The third principal characteristic governing the valuation of specific debt
securities is taxes. In evaluating any investment investors are ultimately
concerned with after-tax returns. Regarding bonds, investors are concerned with the taxation of coupon income and capital gains. Assuming
that capital gains or losses are realized at maturity, the after-tax yield
to maturity on an *n*-period bond, y'_n, can be calculated using equation
14.30:

$$(14.30) \qquad P_{0,n} = \sum_{t=1}^{n} \frac{C(1-T)}{(1+y'_n)^t} + \frac{M_n - (M_n - P_{0,n})G}{(1+y'_n)^n}$$

where T and G are the tax rates on coupon income and capital gains,
respectively. However, if the bond is purchased at a premium $(P_{0,n} > M_n)$,
the capital loss may be amortized over the life of the bond and deducted
from ordinary income, in which case y'_n is calculated using equation 14.31:

$$(14.31) \qquad P_{0,n} = \sum_{t=1}^{n} \frac{C(1-T) + T(P_{0,n} - M_n)/n}{(1+y'_n)^t} + \frac{M_n}{(1+y'_n)^n}$$

Coupon interest on most state and local government bonds, known as
municipal bonds, is exempt from federal income taxation, and coupon
income on other bonds is taxed at the ordinary income tax rate. Also, states
with income taxation generally exempt the coupon income of bonds
issued by municipalities within the state from state taxes. Due to this
favorable tax treatment, the price of a municipal bond will be higher, and
thus the pretax yield will be lower, than that of a taxable bond with the

same coupon rate, maturity, and default risk. However, in equilibrium the bonds should provide the same after-tax yield to the marginal investor. Consider an n-period municipal bond and an n-period corporate bond of equal risk, both of which have a current price equal to their maturity value (i.e., $P_{0,n} = M_n$). In equilibrium the yield on the municipal bond, $y_{n,mun.}$, and the yield on the corporate bond, $y_{n,corp.}$, must have the following relationship

$$(14.32) \qquad y_{n,mun.} = y_{n,corp.}(1 - T),$$

where T is the tax rate on ordinary income for the marginal investor. For example, if $y_{n,corp.} = 0.100$ and $T = 0.31$, then $y_{n,mun.} = 0.100(1 - 0.31) = 0.069$. Rearranging equation 14.32, one can solve for the equilibrium implied tax rate that is operating across the taxable and tax-exempt bond markets:

$$(14.33) \qquad T = 1 - (y_{n,mun.}/y_{n,corp.}).$$

In the preceding example, $T = 1 - (.069/.100) = 0.31$ or 31 percent. Figure 14.10 shows implied marginal tax rates for the period 1970–1991 obtained by using the average yields on long-term Aaa-rated public utility and municipal bonds. The implied tax rate fluctuated between 21 percent and 39 percent over this period.

Premature Retirement and Conversion Provisions

The last characteristic influencing the pricing of specific debt issues is their specific provision(s). Most long-term corporate bond indentures contain one or more provisions for the premature retirement of the bonds, including call, sinking fund, and put provisions. Most municipal bonds and some U.S. Treasury bonds also are callable. In addition, some corporate bonds may be converted into common stock. Each of these provisions represents an option held either by the issuer (in the case of call and sinking fund provisions) or the investor (in the case of the conversion and put provisions) to retire or convert bonds prior to maturity at preset prices. We will analyze the effects of each of these provisions on the value, yield, and expected return on a bond.[4]

The Call Provision.   The call provision on a bond is an option held by the issuer that allows the issuer to retire all or part of the issue prior to maturity at a prespecified price or set of prices. Thus callable bonds are

---

[4] For additional insight about the values of these provisions, see Chapter 17, which discusses option pricing.

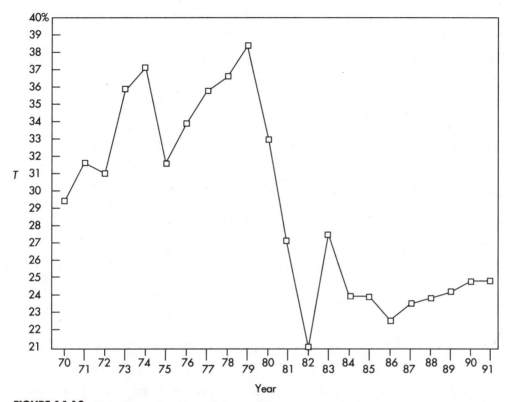

FIGURE 14.10

Implied Tax Rate, T, Operating between the Taxable and Tax-Exempt
Bond Markets, 1970–1991

also contingent claims. In this case the contingency is whether the issuer
will retire the bond prior to maturity at the call price. This will rationally
occur if the uncalled value of the bond exceeds the call price, and this in
turn depends on a number of factors, including the movement of interest
rates. We will focus on the features of the typical call provision included
in most long-term fixed-coupon corporate bond indentures, although
similar features are associated with many municipal bonds and some U.S.
Treasury bonds.

Note that the issuing firm usually sets the coupon rate, C, on a new
bond such that the initial market price of the bond, $P_{0,n}$, is equal to the
bond's maturity, or par, value. The initial *call price* is then fixed at $P_{0,n} + C$,
and call prices in future years follow a declining scale, reaching par value
at maturity. The amount of the call price in excess of par value at any time
is the *call premium*. Superimposed on this call price schedule is a *deferment
period*, usually five to ten years beginning on the date of issuance, during

FIGURE 14.11

Features of the Typical Call Provision on Long-Term Corporate Bonds

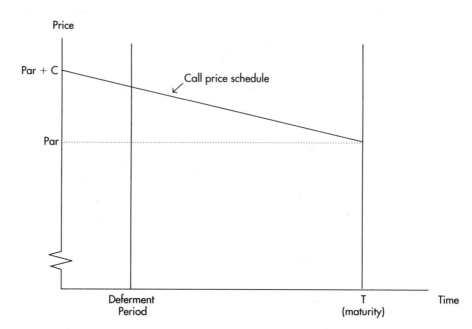

which time the bonds cannot be called.[5] Those features of the call premium are illustrated in Figure 14.11.

The callable bond contract can be viewed as involving the investor's purchase of a noncallable equivalent bond from the issuer and the issuer's purchase of a call option on the bond from the investor. Thus the market value of the callable bond, P^{cb}, is equal to the value of the noncallable equivalent bond, P^{ncb}, minus the value of the call option, P^{co}:

(14.34)
$$P^{cb} = P^{ncb} - P^{co}.$$

The value of the call option on a bond depends on the probability that the management of the firm that has issued the bond, acting in the interest of the firm's shareholders, will call the bond. This will occur if and when the present value of expected payments on the bond (accounting for possible future calls) exceeds the current call price. In general this situation will occur when the required yield on the firm's debt has fallen (which causes the present value of future payments to rise), because of either a decline in the general level of interest rates or a decline in the default risk premium on the firm's debt. Given this decision rule for the management of the issuing firm, the market value of the bond will never exceed the current call price after the deferment period. And in general the value of

---

[5] Some bonds are not redeemable and others are not refundable during the deferment period. If the bond is not redeemable, it is not callable under any circumstances during the deferment period. Nonrefundable bonds can be called during the deferment period for purposes other than to refund at a lower interest rate.

the call provision to the firm increases as (1) interest rates fall or are expected to fall, (2) interest rate volatility rises, (3) the call price decreases, (4) the deferment period becomes shorter, or (5) the bond's maturity increases.

To illustrate the valuation of the call provision, consider a two-period default-free bond with face value of $100 and with a coupon rate of 7 percent per period. We will assume that the pure expectations theory holds, with $s_{0,1} = .06$, $s_{0,2} = .065$, and $E_0(s_{1,2}) = .07$ as in our previous examples, and with the distribution of $s_{1,2}$ given by equation 14.14. If the bond is noncallable, its value is simply

(14.35) $$P^{ncb} = \$7/(1.06) + \$107/(1.065)^2 = \$100.94,$$

and its yield is $y^{ncb} = .0648$.

Now assume that the bond is callable after one period at a call price of $101. If, at time 1, $s_{1,2} = .04$, the uncalled value of the bond will be $107/1.04 = \$102.88$, so the issuer will call the bond and the investor will receive the first coupon payment of $7 and the call price of $101, for a total of $108. If $s_{1,2} = .10$, then the uncalled value of the bond will be $107/1.10 = \$97.27$, so the issuer will not call the bond, and the investor will receive the first coupon payment of $7 and will have a one-period bond with a value of $97.27, for a total value of $104.27. Under the pure expectations theory, the callable bond will be priced to provide an expected return in the first period equal to $s_{0,1} = .06$. Since each of the outcomes at time 1 has a probability of .5, the price of the callable bond is the solution to equation 14.36:

(14.36) $$0.06 = 0.50 \left(\frac{\$108 - P^{cb}}{P^{cb}}\right) + 0.50 \left(\frac{104.27 - P^{cb}}{P^{cb}}\right),$$

or $P^{cb} = \$100.13$. The yield on the callable bond is $y^{cb} = .0693$. The value of the call option is

(14.37) $$P^{co} = P^{ncb} - P^{cb} = \$100.94 - \$100.13 = \$0.81.$$

Note that the callable bond and its noncallable equivalent provide the same *expected return* in both periods even though the *yield* on the callable bond is 45 basis points higher ($y^{cb} - y^{ncb} = .0693 - .0648 = .0045 = .45\%$). It is a common misconception that since the callable bond has a higher yield, it has a higher expected return. This misconception is supported by the argument that the callable bond must provide a return premium due to the "risk" of a call. In fact, the callable bond is *less* risky than its noncallable counterpart. In the present example the standard deviations of the first-period returns on the noncallable and callable bonds are 3.93 percent and 2.63 percent respectively.

The Sinking Fund Provision.   Present in most long-term corporate bond indentures, the sinking fund provision requires the issuer to retire a specified portion of the issue each year, usually after a deferment period of five to ten years. As much as 95 percent of the issue may be scheduled for retirement prior to the bond's stated maturity via the sinking fund provision.[6] Although the sinking fund requirement itself is not optional (and in fact failure to retire bonds under this requirement constitutes an event of default), the firm can choose either of two means of retiring bonds to satisfy the requirement. The firm can choose (1) to make a cash payment to the trustee of the issue, who will use the money to retire bonds selected by lottery at the sinking fund call price, which is usually par value, or (2) to purchase bonds in the open market and present these bonds to the trustee. As such, the sinking fund also represents a contingency that has been modeled via contingent claims analysis (Ho and Singer 1984).

The effect of a sinking fund on the value of a corporate bond is complex. Researchers have argued that the orderly retirement of bonds via the sinking fund reduces the default risk and enhances the liquidity of the issue, and thus the sinking fund increases the value of the issue. On the other hand, the choice of means by which the firm can retire the bonds imparts a valuable option to the firm. That is, when a sinking fund payment is due, if the market price of the bonds is greater than par value, the firm's management, acting in the interest of the shareholders, will choose to retire bonds by lottery at par value, but if the market price of the bonds is less than par value, the firm will purchase bonds in the open market. As such, the sinking fund is similar *in effect* to a call provision applicable to a portion of the issue each year, and in this respect the sinking fund provision reduces the value of the bonds.

The situation is further complicated if accumulators are present in the bond market. An accumulator is an investor (or group of investors) who attempts to purchase all or most of the outstanding supply of a sinking fund bond issue whose market value has become substantially discounted from its par value. If successful, the accumulator eliminates the firm's option to make open market purchases to satisfy the sinking fund requirement, thus forcing the firm to purchase the bonds by lottery at par value, resulting in a profit for the accumulator (Kalotay 1981, Dunn and Spatt 1984, Ho and Singer 1984, Ogden 1988).

The Put Provision.   A small proportion of corporate bond issues in recent years have included a put provision, which allows the investor to present the bonds to the firm for premature retirement at a specified put price, usually par value, following an initial deferment period. The putable bond contract can be viewed as involving the investor's purchase of both a

---

[6]Some sinking fund provisions allow the issuer to accelerate the rate of retirement via the sinking fund provision, and a few allow the firm to choose from among several of the firm's bond issues the specific bonds to be retired to satisfy the requirement.

nonputable equivalent bond and a put option on the bond. Thus the value of the putable bond, P^{pb}, is equal to the value of a nonputable equivalent, P^{npb}, plus the value of the put option, P^{po}:

(14.38)
$$P^{pb} = P^{npb} + P^{po}.$$

Investors will exercise the put option when the present value of the expected future payments on the bond (accounting for any possible future exercise of the put option) is less than the put price. In general this situation will occur when the required yield on the firm's debt has risen because of an increase either in the general level of interest rates or in the default risk premium on the firm's debt. Thus the value of the put provision increases as (1) interest rates rise or are expected to rise, (2) interest rates become more volatile, (3) the put price increases, (4) the deferment period is shortened, or (5) the bond's maturity increases.

Convertible Bonds. The convertible bond includes an option that allows the investor to convert the bond into a fixed number of shares of the issuer's common stock. Thus the conversion option represents yet another contingency associated with some bond contracts. Contingent claims analysis allows the value of the convertible bond to be expressed as the sum of the values of a nonconvertible equivalent bond plus the value of the conversion option (Constantinides 1984). Thus from an investment perspective the convertible bond is a hybrid, taking on some of the risk and return characteristics of both a bond and a stock.

To illustrate the basic valuation of convertible bonds, consider a bond with a *conversion ratio* of 16, which means that the holder has the option to convert each bond, with a par value of $1,000, into 16 shares of common stock. The corresponding *conversion price* is $62.50 = $1,000/16, meaning that the investor must relinquish $62.50 in bond par value for each share. Now suppose the bond provides a coupon rate of 6 percent and matures in twenty years, and comparable straight (i.e., nonconvertible) bonds are selling for $864 per $1,000 par value. If the price of the firm's stock is greater (less) than $54 ($864/16), the bond's *conversion value*, the total stock value received upon conversion of one bond, will be greater (less) than its straight bond value (also called the floor value), and the conversion option is said to be in the money (out of the money). Given that the investor can either retain the bond or convert at any time, the value of the convertible bond is equal to *at least* the greater of (1) the value of its straight bond equivalent, and (2) its conversion value.

In general the value of the convertible bond will exceed both its straight bond value and its conversion value. To see this, consider the two relevant cases in which the bond is either out of the money or in the money. If the bond's conversion option is out of the money, the rational investor will not exercise the option. However, since the option has some potential for paying off (i.e., if the stock price rises sufficiently), the option has a positive (or at least nonnegative) value, and thus the value of the convertible bond will generally exceed the value of its straight bond equivalent by an amount equal to the value of the option. Alternatively, if the conversion option is in the money, the value of the bond must be at least equal to its conversion value. However, the investor may have greater value by holding than by immediately exercising the conversion option. This is because the bond-plus-option nature of the convertible bond provides a floor value, represented by the value of the straight-debt component, that is removed when the bond is converted. Thus retaining the conversion option allows the investor to realize upside potential if the stock price rises while retaining the floor value. Also note that upon conversion coupon payments cease and are replaced by dividends (if any). Contingent claims analysis indicates that immediate conversion of an in-the-money convertible bond is optimal if the stock's dividend yield exceeds the current yield on the bond, which is simply the ratio of the coupon rate to the price of the bond. Note that if at any time it is optimal to convert a bond, the market price of the bond is likely to be very close to the conversion value. Finally, it is important to note that convertible bonds are also generally callable. Thus, the firm has the option to retire the bonds at a prespecified call price. In the event of a call, however, bondholders have the option to convert their bonds rather than to accept the call price. Thus, if the conversion value is greater than the call price, management's actions are tantamount to forcing conversion.

Empirical Evidence on Premature Retirement and Conversion Privileges. Empirical evidence indicates that the yield premium required for callability varies through time and is generally highest when interest rates are high and are expected to fall (Jen and Wert 1967, 1968; Van Horne 1980; Kidwell 1976). Regarding the sinking fund, empirical evidence indicates that the effect of a sinking fund on a bond's yield depends on the general level of interest rates and the bond's default risk (Dyl and Joehnk 1979; Kalotay 1981; and Kidwell, Marr, and Ogden 1989), consistent with the theoretical arguments discussed earlier. Kidwell, Marr, and Ogden (1989) examined the effect of the sinking fund on the yields on a sample of new public utility bonds for the period 1977–1982. The results of their analysis are displayed in Exhibit 14.14. Note that the yield premium is positive and quite large for low-risk bonds issued when interest rates are high (over 50 basis points) but is actually negative for high-risk bonds issued when interest rates are low (–19 basis points).

Chatfield and Moyer (1986) provide an empirical analysis of the effect of the put provision on corporate bonds. Their results indicate that the put provision lowers bond yields by as much as 89 basis points. Finally, Brennan and Schwartz (1980) provide an empirical analysis of a contingent claims pricing model for convertible bonds. They find that the market generally prices the conversion option embedded in such bonds in accordance with their model.

EXHIBIT 14.14

The Estimated Effect of a Sinking Fund on the Yield on New-Issue Public Utility Bonds for Different Interest Rate Environments and Default Risk, 1977–1982

Sample Stratification		
Interest Rate Level (Long-Term U.S. Treasury Yield)	Default Risk	Effect of Sinking Fund on Yield (Basis Points)
<8.5%	Low	−12.6 (t = −2.43)
<8.5	High	−19.0 (t = −2.21)
>11.0	Low	50.9 (t = 2.05)
>11.0	High	5.8 (t = 0.28)

Adapted from D. S. Kidwell, M. W. Marr, and J. P. Ogden, The Effects of a Sinking Fund on the Reoffering Yields of New Public Utility Bonds, *Journal of Financial Research* 12 (1988): 12.

Mortgage-Backed Securities.   Mortgage-backed securities are debt securities of various types that are secured by portfolios, or pools, of mortgages, primarily home mortgages. As indicated in Exhibit 14.1, the aggregate volume of mortgages in the United States is larger than any other debt market. Yet until recently capital market investors have had limited means to invest in mortgages because although they are large in the aggregate, individual mortgages are much smaller than corporate, municipal, or Treasury issues, and there was virtually no secondary market for them. The limited access of major investors in the mortgage market, in turn, limited the aggregate supply of funds to the mortgage market. Thus, in keeping with its long-standing commitment to home ownership and growth in the housing market, the U.S. government began to foster development of the mortgage-backed securities market.

In 1970 the Government National Mortgage Association (GNMA, or Ginnie Mae), began purchasing individual mortgages and selling securities, known as pass-through securities, backed by these mortgages. Pass-throughs remit, or pass through, all interest and principal payments on the pool of mortgages to investors on a pro rata basis. Soon afterward the Federal National Mortgage Association (Fannie Mae) and the Federal Home Loan Mortgage Corporation (Freddie Mac) joined in the issuance of pass-through securities. Mortgage-backed securities were immediately popular with investors, in part because payments were guaranteed by one of the above agencies of the U.S. government.

However, investors' interest in pass-through securities was limited because of the uncertainty of the payments on the securities, which in turn was due to uncertainty surrounding prepayments on the underlying mortgages. Mortgage borrowers may at any time pay the balance on the mortgage, generally without penalty. This privilege is tantamount to a call provision held by the borrower to retire the mortgage at its par value (i.e., paying the remaining principal balance). Based on our discussion of the call provision, it is rational for borrowers to retire their mortgages if market interest rates fall below the interest rate on the mortgage. Thus, when interest rates fall, the payments on a pass-through security accelerate, and the investor loses the opportunity to earn interest at the previous rate. Furthermore, many mortgage borrowers retire their mortgages early for other reasons. For instance, a homeowner who decides to move to another residence generally sells the previous home, and given the due-on-sale clauses on virtually all mortgages, the homeowner must retire the mortgage. Such random prepayments on mortgages add more uncertainty to an investment in mortgage-backed securities.

Particularly in response to these problems with pass-through securities, the mortgage industry developed a new type of mortgage-backed security, the collateralized mortgage obligation (CMO). CMOs are generally backed by a previously issued pass-through security. The payments on the pass-through security are broken down into a series of classes, called tranches, that vary in terms of maturity and risk. The typical CMO has four tranches. The first three tranches receive interest as it accrues on the mortgages, and the fourth tranch, known as a Z bond, initally receives no interest. The first tranch receives all principal payments until it is entirely paid. Then the second tranch begins to receive principal payments until it is entirely paid, at which time the third tranch begins to receive principal payments. Cash payments on the Z bond begin only after the first three tranches are retired. The tranches stratify the risk of the pass-through security so that the first tranch has the lowest risk and the fourth tranch has the highest risk. Some CMO structures include securities that have a claim to only the interest portion of the mortgage payments (interest-only securities or IOs), or only the principal portion of the mortgage payments (principal only securities or POs).

The risk tailoring provided by the CMO structure allows the issuers of mortgage-backed securities to appeal to a much broader group of investors. Today CMOs are the dominant form of mortgage-backed security and are sold principally in a specific form called the real estate mortgage investment conduit, or REMIC. At present over half of the home mortgages originated in the United States are securitized in this manner. (For more information on the markets for, and pricing of, mortgage-backed securities, see Bartlett 1989.)

Floating Rate Bonds.   The unprecedented levels and volatility of interest rates in the late 1970s and early 1980s spawned many developments in the bond market, including floating-rate bonds. The standard floating-rate bond issued by a firm pays coupon interest at a rate that varies with the interest rate on a specified short-term security, such as U.S. Treasury bills, or a specified interest rate quotation such as the London interbank offered rate (LIBOR). A constant spread is added to adjust for default risk, differences in liquidity, and so on. Because the floating-rate bond is essentially always paying the current market interest rate, its price is much more stable as interest rates change over time than is the case for a fixed-coupon bond, and this is its primary appeal to investors. Thus from a theoretical perspective if the market demands a liquidity premium as compensation for the *price risk* of a long-term fixed-coupon bond, then the liquidity premium required for a long-term floating-rate bond should be small or zero. However, many floating-rate bonds specify a maximum or minimum interest rate (*cap* and *floor*, respectively). For these bonds interest rate risk is not completely eliminated.

Other, more exotic floating-rate bonds have also emerged recently, or may be constructed using swaps (Chapter 18). Some financial institutions have issued inverse floaters, or yield curve notes (Ogden 1987a), which pay interest at a rate that varies inversely with short-term interest rates. And some firms with low credit ratings have issued reset notes, or rating-sensitive notes, whose coupon interest varies with the firm's credit risk (Ogden and Moon 1993). Finnerty (1988) lists recent innovations in the bond market and provides rationales for the development of new types of bonds. Innovations in the bond market are discussed further in Chapter 15.

SUMMARY

The value, yield, and expected return on a bond are determined by many macroeconomic factors such as inflation and investment opportunities, characteristics of the issuer such as default risk, and characteristics of the bond issue itself such as maturity, taxation, and premature retirement and conversion provisions. Ultimately the effects of these factors and characteristics must be combined to determine the overall value of a bond. Empirical evidence indicates that investors demand a liquidity premium for investing in longer-term bonds, though the liquidity premium appears to vary through time. Evidence also indicates that investors demand a premium for bearing default risk. Recent innovations in the bond market such as the development of floating-rate bonds and mortgage-backed securities have greatly enhanced investment opportunities but have also added to the complexity of the valuation process.

Questions and Problems

1. If investors expect the rate of inflation to be 5 percent next year and they demand a real rate of return of 2 percent, what should be the observed nominal interest rate on one-year bonds?

2. Summarize the evidence on the relationship between interest rates and inflation. Is the Fisher equation valid? Does the market rationally impound inflation expectations into interest rates?

3. We observe the following spot interest rates:

$$s_{0,1} = 0.04, \ s_{0,2} = 0.05, \ s_{0,3} = 0.06$$

Compute the price and yield to maturity on a three-year bond that provides annual coupon payments at a rate of 8 percent per annum.

4. Given the spot rate information from problem 3, compute the forward rates $f_{1,1}$ and $f_{2,1}$. According to the pure expectations theory, what do these forward rates represent?

5. Given $s_{0,1} = 0.06$, $s_{0,2} = 0.065$, and $s_{0,3} = 0.07$ and the assumption that investors expect the one-year rate in the future to be equal to the current one-year rate (i.e., $s_{0,1} = E_0(s_{1,2}) = E_0(s_{2,3}) = \dots$), what is the expected return premium on two- and three-year bonds in the first year?

6. Does the pure expectations hypothesis or the liquidity premium hypothesis better explain the empirical evidence on the returns on default-free securities of various maturities? What about other theories?

7. Compute the promised yield to maturity and expected return to maturity on a default-risky pure-discount bond given the following information:

$$n = 5 \text{ years}$$

$$P_{0,5} = \$567$$

$$M_5 = \$1000$$

$$m_{5,1} = \$1000 \text{ with probability } 5,1 = 0.8$$

$$m_{5,2} = \$250 \text{ with probability } 5,2 = 0.2$$

8. If five-year U.S. Treasury bonds provide a yield to maturity of 5.5 percent, what is the expected return premium on the bond in problem 6?

9. (This problem requires the use of the Black-Scholes model.) Compute the value of and yield premium required on the pure-discount debt of a firm given the following values: $V = \$2,000$, $r = 0.05$, $\sigma = 0.30$, $T = 5$ years, $M_5 = \$1,000$.

10. Discuss the empirical evidence on rates of default, yields, and realized returns on corporate bonds. Do you conclude from the evidence that default-risky bonds are priced to provide an expected returns premium for the risk of default? Do you think this market is efficient?

11. The yields on high-grade corporate and municipal bonds are 9 percent and 7.2 percent, respectively. What is the implied tax rate operating across these markets?

12. Discuss the factors that determine the effect of a call provision in a bond's yield.

13. Discuss the factors that determine the effect of a sinking fund provision on a bond's yield.

14. Discuss the factors that determine the effect of a put provision on a bond's yield.

15. Discuss the effect of a conversion option on the risk and expected return on a corporate bond.

16. You have the following information on a convertible bond issue:

FRANKLIN, INC.
8½% Due 12/31/2005

Bond Rating (Moody's)	Baa
Market Price of Bond (per $1,000 par)	$990.00
Market Price of Common Stock	57.00
Conversion Ratio	14.75
Dividend Yield on Common Stock	5.50%
Coupon Rate on Bond	6.50%
Estimated Floor Price	$775.00

Calculate the conversion value of the bond. Is the bond's conversion option in the money or out of the money? If you purchased this bond, what factors would you monitor over time in order to determine whether early conversion is optimal?

17. Describe (1) pass-through mortgage-backed securities and (2) collateralized mortgage obligations (CMOs).

REFERENCES

Altman, E. I. 1989. Measuring corporate bond mortality and performance. *Journal of Finance* 44:909–922.

Asquith, P., D. W. Mullins, Jr., and E.D. Wolff. Original issue high yield bonds. Aging analyses of defaults, exchanges, and calls. *Journal of Finance* 44:923–952.

Bartlett, W. W. 1989. Mortgage-backed securities: products, analysis, trading. Englewood Cliffs, N.J.: Prentice Hall.

Black F., and M. Scholes. 1973. The pricing of options and corporate liabilities. *Journal of Political Economy* 81:637–59.

Boardman, C. M., and R. W. McNally. 1981. Factors affecting seasonal corporate bond prices. *Journal of Financial and Quantitative Analysis* 16:207–226.

Brennan, M. J., and E. S. Schwartz. 1979. A continuous time approach to the pricing of bonds. *Journal of Banking and Finance* 3:133–155.

Brennan, M. J., and E. S. Schwartz. 1980. Analyzing convertible bonds. *Journal of Financial and Quantitative Analysis* 15:907–929.

Campbell, J. Y. 1986. A defense of traditional hypotheses about the term structure of interest rates. *Journal of Finance* 14:183–193.

Chatfield, R. E., and R. C. Moyer. 1986. "Putting" away bond risk. An empirical examination of the value of the put option on bonds. *Financial Management* 15:26–33.

Constantinides, G. M. 1984. Warrant exercise and bond conversion in competitive markets. *Journal of Financial Economics* 13:371–98.

Cox, J. C., J. E. Ingersoll, Jr., and S. A. Ross. 1981. A reexamination of traditional hypotheses about the term structure of interest rates. *Journal of Finance* 36:769–799.

Cox, J. C., J. E. Ingersoll, Jr., and S. A. Ross. 1985. A theory of the term structure of interest rates. *Econometrica* 53:385–407.

Culbertson, J. M. 1957. The term structure of interest rates. *Quarterly Journal of Economics* 71:485–517.

Dunn, K. B., and C. S. Spatt. 1984. A strategic analysis of sinking fund bonds. *Journal of Financial Economics* 13:399–423.

Dyl, E. A., and M. D. Joehnk. 1979. Sinking funds and the cost of corporate debt. *Journal of Finance* 36:887–893.

Elliot, J. W., and M. E. Echols. 1976. Market segmentation, speculative behavior, and the term structure of interest rates. *Review of Economics and Statistics* 58:40–49.

Fama, E. F. 1975. Short-term interest rates as predictors of inflation. *American Economic Review* 65:269–282.

Fama, E. F. 1976. Forward rates as predictors of future spot rates. *Journal of Financial Economics* 3:361–377.

Fama, E. F. 1984. Term premiums on bond returns. *Journal of Financial Economics* 13:509–528.

Fama E. F., and M. R. Gibbons. 1982. Inflation, real returns and capital investment. *Journal of Monetary Economics* 9:297–323.

Finnerty. 1988. Financial engineering in corporate finance: an overview. *Financial Management* 17:14–33.

Fisher, I. 1930. *The theory of interest.* New York: MacMillan.

Fisher, L. 1959. Determinants of risk premiums in corporate bonds. *Journal of Political Economy* 67:217–237.

Fons, J. S. 1987. The default premium and corporate bond experience. *Journal of Finance* 42:81–97.

Fons, J. S., and A. E. Kimball. 1991. Corporate bond defaults and default rates 1970–1990. *Journal of Fixed Income* 1:36–47.

Friedman, B. M. 1979. Interest rate expectations versus forward rates. Evidence from an expectations survey. *Journal of Finance* 34:965–973.

Hickman, W. B. 1958. *Corporate bond quality and investor experience.* Princeton: Princeton University Press; New York: National Bureau of Economic Research.

Hicks, J. R. 1946. *Value and capital,* ed 2. London: Oxford University Press.

Ho, T., and R. F. Singer. 1984. The value of corporate debt with a sinking fund provision. *Journal of Business* 57:315–336.

Ho, T., and R. F. Singer. 1982. Bond indenture provisions and the risk of corporate debt. *Journal of Financial Economics* 10:375–406.

Hull, J., and A. White. 1993. One-factor interest-rate models and the valuation of interest-rate derivative securities. *Journal of Financial and Quantitative Analysis* 28:235–254.

Ibbotson, R. G., and L. B. Siegel. 1991. The world bond market: Market values, yields and returns. *Journal of Fixed Income* 1:90–99.

Jaffe, D. M. 1975. Cyclical variations in the risk structure of interest rates. *Journal of Monetary Economics* 1:309–325.

Jen, F. C., and J. E. Wert. 1966. Imputed yields of a sinking fund bond and the term structure of interest rates. *Journal of Finance* 21:697–713.

Jen, F. C., and J. E. Wert. 1967. The effect of call risk on corporate bond yields. *Journal of Finance* 22:637–651.

Jen, F. C., and J. E. Wert. 1968. The deferred call provision and corporate bond yields. *Journal of Financial and Quantitative Analysis* 3:157–169.

Johnson, R. E. 1967. Term structures of corporate bond yields as a function of risk of default. *Journal of Finance* 22:318–321.

Kalotay, A. J. 1981. On the management of sinking funds. *Financial Management* 10:34–40.

Kaplan, R. S., and G. Urwitz. 1979. Statistical models of bond ratings. A methodological inquiry. *Journal of Business* 52:231–261.

Kidwell, D. S. 1976. The inclusion and exercise of call provisions by state and local governments. *Journal of Money, Credit and Banking* 8:391–398.

Kidwell, D. S., M. W. Marr, and J. P. Ogden. 1989. The effects of a sinking fund on the reoffering yields of new public utility bonds. *Journal of Financial Research* 12:1–14.

Lang, R. W., and R. H. Rasche. 1977. Debt-management policy and the own price elasticity of demand for U.S. government notes and bonds. *Economic Review at the Federal Reserve Bank of St. Louis* 59:8–22.

Longstaff, F. A., and E. S. Schwartz. 1992. Interest rate volatility and the team structure. A two-factor general equilibrium model. *Journal of Finance* 47:1259–1282.

Lutz, F. A. 1940. The structure of interest rates. *Quarterly Journal of Economics* 55:36–63.

Merton, R. C. 1974. On the pricing of corporate debt: The risk structure of interest rates. *Journal of Finance* May 29:449–470.

Modigliani, F., and R. C. Sutch. 1966. Innovations in interest rate policy. *American Economic Review* 56:178–197.

Nelson, C. R., and G. W. Schwert. 1977. Short-term interest rates as predictors of inflation: On testing the hypothesis that the real rate of interest is constant. *American Economic Review* 67:478–486.

Ogden, J. P. 1987a. An analysis of yield curve notes. *Journal of Finance* 42:99–110.

Ogden, J. P. 1987b. The end of the month as a preferred habitat: A test of operational efficiency in the money market. *Journal of Financial and Quantitative Analysis* 22:329–344.

Ogden, J. P. 1987c. Determinants of the ratings and yields on corporate bonds: Tests of the contingent claims model. *Journal of Financial Research* 10:329–339.

Ogden, J. P. 1988. A rational for the sinking fund provision in a quasi-competitive corporate bond market. *Journal of Business Research* 16:197–208.

Ogden, J. P., and T. Moon. 1993. An analysis of reset notes and rating-sensitive notes. *Journal of Financial Engineering* 2:175–194.

Park, S. Y., and M. R. Reinganum. 1986. The puzzling price behavior of treasury bills that mature at the turn of the calendar months. *Journal of Financial Economics* 16:267–283.

Pesando, J. E. 1978. On the efficiency of the bond market. *Journal of Political Economy* 86:1057–1076.

Pinches, G. E., and K. A. Mingo. 1973. A multivariate analysis of industrial bond ratings. *Journal of Finance* 28:1–32.

Reilly, F. K., and M. D. Joehnk. 1976. The association between market-determined risk measures for bonds and bond ratings. *Journal of Finance* 31:1387–1403.

Ramaswamy K., and S. M. Sundaresan. 1986. Valuation of floating-rate instruments. *Journal of Financial Economics* 17:251–272.

Roley, V. V. 1981. The determinants of the treasury yield curve. *Journal of Finance* 36:1103–1126.

Smith, C., and J. Warner. 1979. On financial contracting: An analysis of bond covenants. *Journal of Financial Economics* 7:115–161.

Stiglitz, J. E. 1970. A consumption-oriented theory of the demand for financial assets and the term structure of interest rates. *Review of Economics Studies* 37:321–350.

Van Horne, J. C. 1980. The term structure of interest rates: A test of the segmented markets hypothesis. *Southern Finance Journal* 47:1129–1140.

Van Horne, J. C. 1980. Called bonds: How did the investor fare? *Journal of Portfolio Management* 6:58–61.

West, R. R. 1973. Bond ratings, bond yields and financial regulations: Some findings. *Journal of Law and Economics* 16:159–168.

Yun, Y-S. 1984. The effects of inflation and income taxes on interest rates: Some new evidence. *Journal of Financial and Quantitative Analysis* 18:425–448.

CHAPTER 15

Bond Portfolio Management

Introduction

This chapter introduces various techniques and strategies that practitioners currently use to manage bond portfolios. At the outset you should recognize that much of the portfolio theory discussed earlier in the text can be applied to the management of bond portfolios and that indeed bonds are often part of a well-diversified portfolio that also includes equities. However, a specific focus on bond portfolio management techniques is necessary, not only because bonds differ in fundamental aspects from equities, a point emphasized in the previous chapter, but also because bond portfolios are often designed to fulfill specific investment objectives, again because of their distinguishing characteristics. The bulk of the analysis focuses on the management of the two fundamental sources of risk associated with bonds—interest rate risk and default risk. Regarding both of these sources of risk, we focus on risk management in the contexts of both passive and active management strategies. The chapter concludes with a discussion of the roles of new types of debt-related securities in bond portfolio management.

Measuring Interest Rate Risk

Bond portfolio managers have long been concerned with the effects of changes in interest rates on the performance of their portfolios. This concern was heightened in the late 1970s and early 1980s, when interest rates and interest rate volatility rose to unprecedented levels, only to fall again in subsequent years. From an analysis of the basic bond pricing formula, as well as the empirical evidence discussed in Chapter 14, interest rate risk is generally positively related to the maturity of a given debt instrument.

Duration As a Measure of Interest Rate Risk

The most widely used measure of the interest rate risk of a bond is *duration*, developed by Macaulay (1938). Starting with the basic formula for the price of a bond, P, given its cash flows, C_t, and yield, y, which can be written as

(15.1)
$$P = \sum_{t=1}^{n} C_t (1 + y)^{-t},$$

we initially calculate the sensitivity of the bond's price to its yield by calculating the derivative of P with respect to $(1 + y)$:

(15.2)
$$\frac{dP}{d(1 + y)} = \sum_{t=1}^{n} - tC_t (1 + y)^{-t-1}$$

Then, by multiplying both sides of equation 15.2 by $(1 + y)/P$ and taking absolute values, we obtain the bond's *elasticity* with respect to $(1 + y)$, which is the bond's duration, D:

(15.3)
$$D = \left| \frac{dP/P}{d(1 + y)/(1 + y)} \right| = \frac{\sum_{t=1}^{n} tC_t (1 + y)^{-t}}{P}.$$

To illustrate the duration measure in equation 15.3, consider first the case of pure discount bonds. Since a pure discount bond provides only one payment at maturity, C_T, the numerator of the duration formula is simply $nC_T(1 + y)^{-t}$, which is equal to n times the price of the bond. Thus, for a pure discount bond, $D = nP/P = n$; that is, the duration of a pure discount bond is equal to the bond's maturity. For this reason the duration of a bond is interpreted in terms of *years*. Thus a U.S. Treasury strip with four years to maturity has a duration of four years. Of course the formula is more

Concept of 'Duration' Helps Investors Measure the Interest-Rate Risk of Bonds

Duration: Bond yield vs. risk

Duration is a money manager's tool to measure the trade-off of risk and reward. It reflects the effect interest rates have on prices of bonds of varying maturities and shows why longer-term investments typically have higher yields. Simply put, each year of duration equals the chance for a 1% gain or loss of principal for every 1% of rate movement. Here's a look at various bond mutual funds, their current yields and duration.

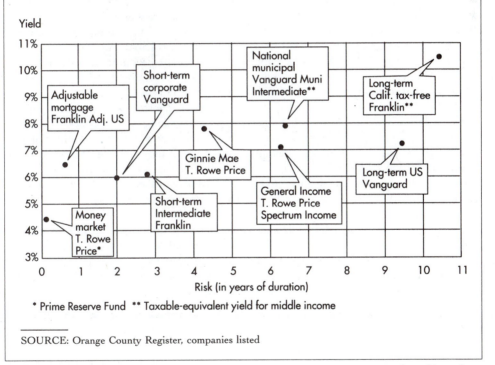

* Prime Reserve Fund ** Taxable-equivalent yield for middle income

SOURCE: Orange County Register, companies listed

Knight-Ridder Tribune

As short-term savings rates hit lows not seen in two decades, longer-term bonds have become an investment fancy.

But bonds—unlike short-term bills from the U.S. Treasury or money market mutual funds—are filled with risks that can zap an investor's principal.

The most obvious risk is default, meaning that the bond issuer can't pay. And many savers understand that investing in bonds is only as

(continued)

Concept of 'Duration' Helps Investors Measure the Interest-Rate Risk of Bonds — *continued*

safe as the company or government issuing it. That's why credit ratings for bonds exist.

But what is far more difficult to understand is a second type of risk: how the price of a bond can change. That happens through the daily trading of bonds on the open market, where prices are based on how the bond's coupon rate — or the interest it pays annually — compares with prevailing interest rates.

To help gauge this risk, experts use a measurement called "duration." And they suggest savers watch it as well.

"In my business, duration is the most critical decision we make," said John Hague of Pacific Investment Management Co. in Newport Beach, Calif., that manages more than $30 billion in bonds.

"People need a way to know that the (potential) price change could be greater than the yield they extended to get" by buying longer-term bonds, he added.

After a more than decade-long drop in interest rates, few investors can recall how devastating rising rates can be on bond investments.

Though complex, duration is relatively simple to follow.

"It helps you better understand the risks involved," said Rob Shumacher, a bond portfolio manager for Kemper Securities in Chicago.

Duration is measured in years. Each year represents an expected 1 percent change in bond prices for every full 1 percent move in interest rates. An investor owning an intermediate-bond fund with a duration of 5 years, for example, could lose 5 percent of his principal if 5-year interest rates go up 1 percent.

Longer-term portfolios, very popular in today's low-rate climate, are even riskier, with durations approaching 10 years. That means a 1 percent rise in rates could wipe out 10 percent of principal. And zero coupon bonds, sold at deep discounts to have interest paid through price appreciation, are the riskiest on the duration scale.

"Many investors are not as aware of price volatility of longer-term bonds as they should be," said Jerome Jacobs, bond manager for Vanguard Funds in Valley Forge, Pa. "People tend to ignore risk factors to preserve income."

Rising rates can be devastating on long-bond values. In the rate spike of the early 1980s, some U.S. Treasury bonds traded for 50 cents on the dollar. And in 1987, a steep rise in rates cut 20 percent off bond prices within a six-week period.

Of course, interest-rate volatility in bonds is a two-way street.

---

complex for coupon bonds. In such cases the numerator is the sum of the present values of the cash flows, C_t, each weighted by the length of time until it is received, t. As a result the duration of a coupon bond reflects the fact that such a bond can be seen as a portfolio of pure discount bonds with payoffs corresponding to each of the payments of the bond. Thus the duration of a coupon bond is always less than the stated maturity of the bond, since its duration is a weighted average of the duration of its payments. For example, the duration of a four-year 10 percent coupon bond that is selling at its par value of $100 (and thus $y = 0.10$) is

CONCEPT OF 'DURATION' HELPS INVESTORS MEASURE THE INTEREST-RATE RISK OF BONDS—*continued*

Falling rates can provide the added bonanza of capital gains. The higher the duration, the greater the chance for a loss—or a gain. And volatility allowed bond managers to post double-digit returns for investors in a low-rate environment last year.

Duration should not be confused with average maturity, a number more often quoted when discussing bond portfolios, experts note. Average maturity does not distinguish between the types of interest payments being made to investors. Many money managers view average maturity as useless other than as a very simple way to compare portfolios.

But duration is no cure-all for managing risk in bond investments.

Of course, it does not reflect credit risks or currency risks. Many bond funds, for example, use broad holdings of government and corporate issues from around the globe in an attempt to maximize returns. This, however, increases risk as well—risk not calculated through duration.

Also remember that interest rates do not move in tandem. In the current cycle, short-rates have tumbled steeply while longer rates have modestly declined. Savers using duration must measure risk by comparing rate movements of an equal maturity.

An additional shortcoming is that duration tabulation is partly an estimate and subject to the faults and biases of the money manager calculating it.

This is particularly worrisome in two areas—mortgage-backed securities and callable bonds. A duration calculation involving such securities must estimate the likelihood of the mortgages being repaid or the bonds being repurchased by the issuer. It is hard to predict such events, which can dramatically change an investor's return.

And finally, duration does not weigh external changes that affect bond prices. Those include the supply of bonds or new tax rules favoring one type of bond investment over another.

Those who plan to hold their bonds to maturity can ignore duration and interest-rate risks. They'll get 100 cents on the dollar when they turn in their investments. That's why zero-coupon bonds are so popular despite, according to duration measurements, they're among the most volatile bonds around.

$$D = \frac{\$10(1)(1.10)^{-1} + \$10(2)(1.10)^{-2} + \$10(3)(1.10)^{-3} + \$110(4)(1.10)^{-4}}{100}$$

$$= 3.49 \text{ years.}$$

Note that by the definition of duration, this bond has the same interest elasticity as a pure discount bond with 3.49 years to maturity. It is also clear that for a given maturity, the higher the bond's coupon interest, the shorter its duration. Figure 15.1 shows durations by maturity for bonds with various coupon rates.

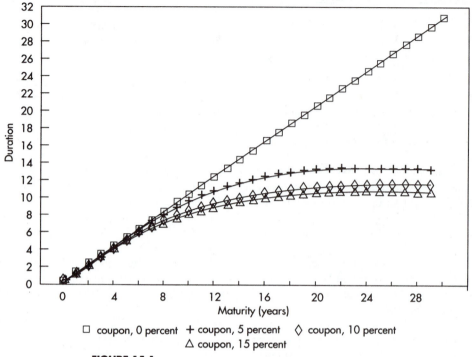

FIGURE 15.1

Durations of Various Bonds by Maturing (Yield is 10 Percent)

Problems with the Duration Measure

In practice, using duration as a measure of interest rate risk is fraught with perils (see feature item). The most serious problem is a consequence of the model itself. Since the model does not distinguish between yields of bonds with different maturities, its predictions regarding the relative change in the prices of bonds with different maturities will be precisely realized only when we observe small parallel shifts in a flat yield curve; that is, when the yields on all bonds are equal and move in tandem over time. Although yields on bonds of various maturities are positively correlated, they are not perfectly correlated. Furthermore, short-term yields are more volatile than long-term yields, and nonflat yield curves are more the norm than flat yield curves (with upward-sloping yield curves predominating). Fisher and Weil (1971) developed an alternative duration-based immunization design that does not require a flat yield curve, but their model does depend on parallel shifts in the yield curve.

Convexity

Another problem with duration arises because of the convex relationship between the price of a bond and its yield. Recall that duration is related to the first derivative of the price of a bond with respect to its yield, which is negative. For small percentage changes in the bond's yield, duration provides a good approximation of the corresponding percentage change in the price of the bond. However, this approximation is increasingly biased for large changes in the yield, due to *convexity*, which is formally defined as the second derivative of price with respect to yield, or equivalently, the first derivative of duration with respect to yield.

To illustrate the problem of convexity, we return to the previous example, in which a four-year 10 percent coupon bond selling at its par value, and thus, because $y = 10$ percent, has a duration of 3.49 years. Using duration, if the yield on the bond falls to 9.5 percent, the price of the bond is predicted to rise by $D[-\Delta y/(1 + y)] = 3.49(.005/1.10) = .01586$, or 1.586 percent, to a price of $101.59. The actual new price of the bond will be $101.60, indicating a prediction error of only 1 cent. However, if the yield falls to 5 percent, the price is predicted to rise by $3.49(.05/1.10) = .1586$, or 15.86 percent, to $115.86. However, the actual new price of the bond will be $117.73, or $1.87 higher than predicted. This represents a substantial error, 10.55 percent ($1.87/$17.73). Given errors of this magnitude, analysts often adjust their duration-based estimates for the effect of convexity (Yawitz 1989, Sullivan and Kiggins 1989).

Portfolio managers face other problems using duration, notably the uncertain maturities on bonds that have call, put, or sinking fund provisions or are subject to default risk. Ogden's (1987b) empirical analysis shows that call provisions, sinking fund provisions, and default risk have substantial effects on the interest rate sensitivity of corporate bonds. His evidence indicates that all three factors have a negative impact on interest rate sensitivity. Call and sinking fund provisions have a greater negative effect when the market price of the bond is high relative to the call price or sinking fund price, and bonds with lower credit ratings have substantially smaller interest rate risk. It is important to account for the effects of these additional factors on interest rate sensitivity.

Despite the problems noted above, duration is an effective measure of relative interest rate risk, at least for longer-term, noncallable, default-free fixed-income bonds such as Treasury bonds. To see this, consider the measure *relative duration*, the ratio of the durations of any two bonds, A and B: D_A/D_B. Assuming that both bonds have the same yield, using equation 15.3 we can see that the relative duration of the bonds is equal to the ratio of the percentage changes in their prices (in response to a given change in yield):

(15.4)
$$D_A/D_B = \frac{[dP_A/P_A]/[d(1 + y)/(1 + y)]}{[dP_B/P_B]/[d(1 + y)/(1 + y)]} = \frac{dP_A/P_A}{dP_B/P_B}.$$

According to equation 15.4, the duration measure specifies that the ratio of the percentage changes in the prices of any two bonds (i.e., their relative duration) should be constant as interest rates change (over a short horizon) or equivalently that the percentage changes in the prices of the two bonds should be perfectly correlated. Now, over a short horizon the return on a bond is almost completely determined by the percentage change in its price (i.e., its capital gain or loss), so the effectiveness of duration as a measure of relative interest rate risk can be assessed by examining the correlations of the returns on bonds of various maturities over short horizons. Bond returns should be perfectly correlated.

We calculated the correlations of quarterly returns on Merrill Lynch's Treasury indexes, introduced in Chapter 14, for the 15-year period 1978–1992. The results are displayed in Exhibit 15.1. With only one minor exception the correlations are greater than .9. These results indicate that for these indices duration is an effective measure of relative interest rate risk. We can also use these data to calculate the relative durations of the various indexes using the following regression:

(15.5) $$R_{Lt} = a + b\,R_{St} + e_t,$$

where R_{Lt} and R_{St} are the returns on a longer-term bond index and a shorter-term bond index, respectively. The estimate of relative duration is the slope coefficient, b (i.e., $b \approx D_L/D_S$). The estimates of relative duration for the Merrill Lynch indexes are shown in brackets in Exhibit 15.1. All of the relative duration estimates are greater than 1, and the estimates

EXHIBIT 15.1

Correlation of Returns and Relative Durations for Merrill Lynch's Treasury Bond Indices, computed from quarterly data, 1977–1992

Index Maturity (years)	Index Maturity (years)					
	1-3	3-5	5-7	7-10	10-15	15+
1–3	1.00	0.97 [1.79]	0.94 [2.25]	0.93 [2.67]	0.90 [3.11]	0.87 [3.50]
3–5		1.00	0.99 [1.29]	0.98 [1.54]	0.96 [1.83]	0.94 [2.08]
5–7			1.00	0.99 [1.21]	0.98 [1.47]	0.97 [0.98]
7–10				1.00	0.99 [1.22]	0.98 [1.41]
10–15					1.00	0.99 [1.17]
15+						1.00

Source of returns data: Merrill Lynch Capital Markets, New York, 1993.

Relative duration, shown in brackets, is the slope coefficient from a regression of the returns on the longer-maturity index on the returns on the shorter-term index.

increase with the discrepancy in the maturities of the bond indexes, as expected. The estimates indicate that for example returns on the fifteen-plus-year index are 3.5 times as sensitive to changes in interest rates than are returns on the one- to three-year index.

MANAGING INTEREST RATE RISK

The various techniques commonly used to manage interest rate risk can be divided into passive and active strategies. Managers are more likely to depend on passive strategies if they believe that the bond market is semistrong form efficient. Active strategies are used if the manager believes that either (1) the bond market is inefficient, or (2) while the market may be efficient, equilibrium returns, and particularly return premiums, vary sufficiently through time to warrant an active strategy that may lead to a higher reward-to-risk ratio through time.

Passive Interest Rate Risk Management

Buy-and-Hold Strategy.   The epitome of passive bond management is the buy-and-hold strategy. Here the manager initially purchases a portfolio of bonds that provide the desired risk and return characteristics, based on empirical evidence such as that provided in Chapter 14. Then, as bonds mature or are redeemed, new bonds are purchased so as to maintain the initial characteristics of the portfolio.

Generally the passive portfolio is designed to replicate the performance of a given bond index or set of indexes. Perhaps the most widely followed indices of the Treasury bond market are the Lehman Treasury index and Merrill Lynch's Treasury indices. The Merrill Lynch indices document returns on three-month Treasury bills as well as Treasury securities with maturities of one to three years, three to five years, five to seven years, seven to ten years, ten to fifteen years, and fifteen-plus years, in addition to combinations such as the one- to ten-year and ten-plus-year Treasuries. (Average returns and standard deviations of most of these indices for the period 1983–1992 are shown in Exhibit 14.4). Indices of the broader bond market include Salomon Brothers broad investment grade (BIG) index, the Lehman Brothers aggregate index, and the Merrill Lynch domestic master index. The broad market indices include governments, corporates, mortgage-backed securities, and other bonds. All of these indexes are market-value-weighted indices of total returns. Since it is generally impractical to replicate any of these indices precisely, relative portfolio performance is subject to *tracking error* between the portfolio and the index. However, if the bonds in the portfolio closely correspond to those in the index, tracking error is generally very small, often only a few basis points.

Immunization.   In many instances the bond manager is responsible for ensuring that the bond portfolio can provide a particular pattern of future cash flows. For example, a pension fund manager may have used actuarial tables to estimate the cash flows that the fund is expected to disburse in future years. In this case, the manager is concerned about the effects of uncertain future interest rates on the fund's performance and thus the ability of the fund to meet future obligations. Given interest rate uncertainty, the fund may be exposed to two types of risk: *price risk* and *reinvestment rate risk*. Price risk occurs when the manager invests in long-term bonds even though some of the future obligations of the fund will be due in the short term. When the short-term obligations become due, some of the long-term bonds must be sold at a price that is unknown when the bonds are purchased. Thus over time the fund is exposed to risk regarding the adequacy of the proceeds from bond sales to meet ongoing obligations. Reinvestment rate risk occurs when the manager purchases short-term bonds even though some of the future obligations of the fund are due in the long term. In this case the manager must plan to reinvest the proceeds of maturing bonds in new bonds at future interest rates that are unknown. Hence the fund is exposed to risk that the total payoff on this rollover strategy may be inadequate to meet distant future obligations.

A portfolio is said to be *immunized* if both of those sources or risk are eliminated or offset. The two techniques most widely used to immunize portfolios are cash-flow matching or *dedication*, and duration-based immunization.

Dedication.   In some circumstances immunization can be achieved by purchasing bonds that provide future payoffs exactly matching the timing and amount of future obligations. That is, each of the future payoffs on the portfolio is dedicated to meet a specific future obligation. A simple example of a dedication strategy was discussed in Chapter 14: a corporate treasurer may invest idle cash in Treasury bills that mature at the end of the calendar month, when obligations such as dividends and interest and principal payments are commonly due. Dedication strategies to meet longer-term obligations have been made easier recently with the availability of U.S. Treasury strips. However, dedication strategies to meet longer-term obligations may be less effective because (1) the amount and timing of distant future obligations may not be precise and generally can be only estimated, and (2) the most common form of bond investment is the coupon bond, which provides multiple scheduled payments that add to the difficulty of designing a dedication strategy. In these more general circumstances a duration-based immunization strategy may be more effective.

Duration-based immunization.   Under ideal conditions the duration measure can be used to achieve immunization. The procedure is relatively straightforward: *purchasing bonds whose collective duration is equal to the duration of the cash flow requirements will result in complete immunization.* For example, suppose a manager wishes to provide for cash flow equal to $100 per year for each of the next twenty years. If current level of interest rate is 10 percent, these cash flows have a duration of 7.51 years. Thus the manager should choose a portfolio of bonds that collectively has a duration of 7.51 years. However, given the problems with duration discussed earlier, immunization using duration may not provide complete elimination of risk.

Active Interest Rate Risk Management

Active interest rate risk management strategies inevitably involve market timing; that is, trying to determine whether bond returns over a short investment horizon will be high or low. Market timing in turn requires effective forecasts of changes in interest rates. Interest rate forecasts are generally of two types. The first type of forecast concerns the general level of interest rates; that is, whether the entire yield curve will shift up or down in the near term. The second type of forecast concerns twists in the yield curve, that is, whether short-term interest rates will fall while long-term interest rates rise, or vice versa. With either type of forecast, the goal is to invest in bonds with maturities that are likely to provide the highest short-term expected return or return premium per unit of risk. The analyst will generally forecast interest rates to a particular horizon date; hence this type of forecasting is referred to as *horizon analysis*.

Given the tremendous competitiveness of the bond market, it is at best extremely difficult to forecast the direction of interest rates. Some analysts adopt a *fundamental approach* to forecasting interest rates. They examine such factors as fiscal and monetary policies and expectations of the growth rate of GDP. Regarding fiscal policy, credible Congressional action to reduce the federal budget deficit substantially is generally bullish for the bond market for two reasons. First, expectations of the supply of Treasury securities will be lowered, and second, a fiscal policy of restrained spending or increased taxes is likely to reduce economic activity, at least in the short term, and interest rates are generally positively related to business activity. Monetary policy has its greatest impact on short-term interest rates. An expansionary monetary policy will generally lower short-term interest rates and will tend to spur economic activity. However, this will generally lead to higher inflation in the future, so long-term interest rates may not fall and in fact may rise. A stringent monetary policy will tend to have opposite effects. Given the effect of monetary policy on interest rates, a great many analysts follow every pronouncement of the Fed governors on current monetary policy. These analysts are called Fed watchers.

Other bond analysts adopt a *technical* approach. They follow recent trends in interest rates, interest rate spreads, and so on, for clues to the future course of interest rates. Technical forecasting may involve simply charting relationships among interest rates or sophisticated time series analyses.

Forecasters must be concerned not only about the accuracy of their forecasts but also the timing of their trades. For instance, a positively sloped yield curve may be interpreted as indicating that interest rates will rise. To benefit from the ensuing rate increase, the investor should shorten the duration of the portfolio. However, shortening the maturities of the bonds in the portfolio locks in lower yields to maturity. If the rate increase takes a long time to develop, or never materializes, realized returns on the portfolio will actually be lower than if the strategy was not undertaken.

Regardless of the approach, forecasters are not always correct. For this reason they use various techniques to limit their exposure to risk. Forecasters use a myriad of hedging vehicles, including interest rate futures, options, and swaps, to reduce risk while trying to capture higher returns. (These hedging techniques are discussed later in the chapter.) Over time the successful strategies lead to superior performance, and unsuccessful strategies are modified or scrapped.

Quasi-Active Strategies

Some analysts employ quasi-active management strategies, so called because they either do not depend heavily on interest rate forecasts or because they are explicitly a mix of active and passive strategies. Two examples of quasi-active strategies are *riding the yield curve* and *contingent immunization.*

Riding the Yield Curve.   The strategy of riding the yield curve relies on the predominance of the upward-sloping yield curve and the assumption that the average change in the yields on bonds of all maturities is zero. The strategy involves purchasing bonds with a given initial maturity and yield and holding them until their maturity shortens to a designated point. The bonds are then sold and the proceeds are used to purchase new bonds with the same initial maturity. When the bonds are sold, they generally have a lower yield than when they were purchased, and thus the investor realizes a capital gain.

The success of this strategy clearly depends on the existence of liquidity premiums that tend to increase with maturity. In other words, it is assumed that the yield curve slopes upward because the yields on longer-term bonds contain larger liquidity premiums. Therefore, the long-term success of this strategy can be determined by examining the average returns on bonds of various maturities, which was presented for Treasury securities in Chapter 14. As you recall, the evidence indicates that reliable liquidity premiums are present in Treasury securities with maturities of up to about one year, but the liquidity premiums of longer-term bonds are less reliable. Thus it is not surprising that the strategy of riding the yield curve is most popular among managers of short-term securities. It is also important to note that this strategy generates greater transaction costs and generally greater risk than most passive investment strategies.

Bond Managers Beat the Pack
By Finding Market Inefficiencies

Looking at the performance of professional bond-market investors, it's easy to understand why many people recommend "indexing"—simply buying a portfolio of bonds whose performance tracks some market gauge.

During the past 10 years, nearly three out of four bond managers failed to beat the Salomon Brothers Broad Investment Grade Bond Index, according to SEI, an investment research company. The average bond mutual fund returned just 10.76% a year in that period, 1.22 percentage points behind the index, according to Morningstar Inc.

But a handful of fixed-income managers do manage to pull away from the pack. The $170 million Managers Intermediate Mortgage Securities Fund posted an impressive average annual return of 13.19% during the past five years, while Pacific Investment Management Co.'s $3.4 billion PIMCO Total Return Fund had annual returns of 12.61%. The funds not only beat the five-year index return of 11.36%, but kept risks in check—which earned them top five-star ratings from Morningstar.

How did they do it? In part, by exploiting the free lunches, or "inefficiencies," they say are left on the table by other bond-market investors. "Basically, all our excess return is a result of inefficiencies in the marketplace," says Worth Bruntjen, who runs the Managers Intermediate Mortgage fund.

As he and some other pros see it, the bond market is chock full of such free lunches. The trick is being able to spot them—and having the flexibility to profit from them.

"The inefficiencies arise because a lot of bond investors are subject to artificial constraints, which make them appear irrational," says Frank Rabinovitch, a managing director at PIMCO. "It's not that they are irrational, it's just that their regulatory, tax, advertising or accounting environment makes them act that way."

For example, many big investors are compulsive buyers of one-year securities. "A lot of regulations and accounting rules draw an arbitrary line at 12 months," says Mr. Bruntjen. "Money-market funds, for instance, aren't allowed to buy securities that mature in more than one year," while accounting rules pressure banks to likewise stick with one-year securities.

'Bad Values'

But one-year securities "tend to be particularly bad values," says Thomas Klaffky, managing director at Salomon Inc. Since 1980, returns on one-year paper have been about 0.5 percentage point less than they should have been for that level of risk, Salomon research shows.

Individuals who don't face such restraints could get a better deal for the same average risk with a mixed portfolio of two-year and six-month securities. "That way, you avoid buying something that's being bid up by everyone else," says Mr. Klaffky.

Usually, though, exploiting such inefficiencies requires sophisticated analytical tools and very low trading costs. That generally puts them out of the reach of small investors, unless they participate indirectly through mutual funds.

To identify such funds, investors should look for bond managers with records of good returns but not bloated risks. They should also be sure their chosen funds' main goal is high total return, including price appreciation, and not just yield.

In today's low interest-rate environment, many investors and mutual funds are compelled to reach for yield at almost any price.

(continued)

BOND MANAGERS BEAT THE PACK
BY FINDING MARKET INEFFICIENCIES—*Continued*

That can lead them to make poor tradeoffs between risk and return, which damages them in the long run.

For example, many issues of long-term corporate bonds are "callable" after 10 years—that is, they allow the company to redeem the bonds at a pre-specified price in 10 years. Investors get hurt when their bonds are called, since that only happens when future rates are lower than today's; suddenly, investors would lose the higher income that they thought they'd locked up long term.

To compensate investors for that risk, callable bonds offer higher yields than non-callable bonds. The problem is, they don't offer enough extra yield for the risk. "People are so hungry for yield, they're not being careful," says Mr. Rabinovitch. The yield premium would have to be 0.45 to 0.5 percentage point—roughly three times today's levels—before long-term callable bonds would be worth the extra risk, he says.

The flip side of this situation is that "putable" bonds are chronically cheap. Putable bonds give investors the right to sell the bond back to the issuer at a pre-specified price some time in the future. That right protects investors against a future bear market by limiting their potential losses. To pay for that insurance, investors get a lower yield on putable bonds than on normal bonds. The secret is, the yield give-up typically isn't as great as it should be to pay for the bear-market protection.

Why do putable bonds sell so cheaply? Mostly because both issuers and buyers are distracted by short-term goals. Issuers are "happy as long as they can borrow at a lower rate because it makes them look good," says Mr. Rabinovitch. But because most buyers are reluctant to accept lower yields, he says, putable bonds' yields end up being higher than is warranted, given their reduced risk.

Another case of yield-driven inefficiency is a volatile security called an "interest-only" strip, or IO. IOs are created from mortgage-backed bonds; as the name suggests, IOs receive only the interest cash flows that are "stripped" from the mortgage securities. When interest rates fall and homeowners refinance their mortgages, the underlying mortgages that support IOs evaporate, and IOs' yields plummet. When that happens, IOs' prices plunge, too.

Indeed, after the past year's refinancing boom, yields on some IOs are actually negative—that is, if homeowners keep refinancing at today's pace, prices of IOs in today's market would exceed the present value of all their future cash flows.

Those awful yields make IOs very unappetizing to today's yield-starved investors, so prices are down to 20 cents on the dollar or lower. What's more, regulatory changes for banks, thrifts and insurers essentially have put IOs off-limits to most of those institutions.

But because so many buyers see IOs as leprous, their risk/return tradeoffs have changed. Prepayments aren't likely to maintain today's pace forever, so the potential returns on some IOs far outweigh the risks, says Mr. Rabinovitch.

With little downside risk, and potential gains of 50% or more, "these poor-yield, good return characteristics make IOs an excellent addition to total return portfolios—something that's not possible for yield-oriented managers," Mr. Rabinovitch says. Even so, "IOs aren't a prudent bet for more than 1% to 2% of a portfolio because their characteristics are too weird."

Source: Wall Street Journal, July 20, 1993, pp. C1, C9. Reprinted by permission of *The Wall Street Journal,* © 1993 Dow Jones & Company, Inc. All rights reserved worldwide.

Contingent Immunization.   Contingent immunization is a strategy that combines forecast-based bets on the course of interest rates with a passive immunization strategy (Leibowitz and Weinberger 1981). In this strategy, the manager establishes a minimum acceptable rate of return which is slightly below the rate that could be obtained with a completely immunized portfolio. Then, subject to this constraint the manager engages in limited active bond trading. If the active strategy proves successful, realized returns on the portfolio exceed those of the passive portfolio. However, if the strategy fails the portfolio still provides the minimum return because either (a) the portfolio's exposure to the active strategy is sufficiently limited throughout the planning period, or (b) upon realizing a critical level of losses by a given date, the active strategy is abandoned and the entire portfolio is immunized. The active strategy may involve buying and selling bonds or trading in interest rate futures or swap contracts according to interest rate forecasts.

Managing Default Risk

Managing a portfolio of default-risky bonds is considerably more complex than managing default-free bonds, because default-risky bonds are subject to both interest rate risk and default risk. Furthermore, default-risky bonds are more likely to contain call and sinking fund provisions. The discussion here focuses on managing default risk, but ultimately the manager must deal with the complexities of interest rate and default risk simultaneously.

As with any portfolio, the manager of a portfolio of default-risky bonds must address two basic questions: (1) How much risk should the portfolio be exposed to? (2) Should the management be passive or active? In addressing the first question, the manager may begin by reviewing empirical evidence, such as that discussed in Chapter 14, on the risk and return performance of bonds in each rating category, and use these data to decide the general mix of bond quality that best suits the objections of the portfolio. Some institutional investors, such as insurance companies, are restricted by law to include only investment-grade debt in their portfolios, while the stated purpose of some bond mutual funds may be to invest exclusively in junk bonds. In other situations the manager may have more flexibility, in which case fixed percentages of total funds may be invested in risk-free bonds, investment-grade bonds and speculative-grade bonds.

Passive Default-Risk Management

Perhaps the simplest passive investment strategy involves simply choosing bonds according to their credit ratings and engaging in a buy-and-hold strategy, updating only when bonds mature, default, are called, or undergo a change in their rating class. Of course this strategy relies on the credit analysis of rating agencies such as S&P or Moody's, both in terms of their ability to access credit worthiness and the timeliness of their rating classifications. Substantial empirical analysis, discussed earlier, indicates that bond yield premiums are in general closely associated with default risk. However, additional evidence (Weinstein 1987) indicates that the market generally reacts to changes in an issuer's creditworthiness well in advance of a rating change. Thus, the evidence indicates that bond ratings, at least for outstanding issues, are often stale. However, as long as the bond's *yield* changes promptly in response to new information, the manager may nevertheless be able to rely on paying a fair price for a bond purchased at any time, even if its rating is stale. As always, the passive manager relies on the efficiency of the market.

Active Default-Risk Management

Active strategies to manage default risk involve either security selection or market timing. In one relatively simple security-selection strategy the manager compares the yields on bonds in the same rating category and after adjusting for different maturities, call provisions, and so on, chooses the bonds that offer the highest adjusted yield premiums. This strategy is designed to uncover bonds that will provide the highest return for a given level of risk. However, one flaw in this strategy is suggested in the discussion above; that is, if bond ratings tend to be stale but market yields tend to reflect current information, this strategy tends merely to the selection of bonds whose ratings are likely to be downgraded in the near future. Therefore, the strategy may not provide superior risk-adjusted performance. If this is the case, then a modified version of the strategy in which the manager personally conducts a credit analysis of bonds may be more fruitful. Among the variables that should be included in credit analysis are those discussed in Chapter 14 that have been found empirically to explain Moody's and S&Ps bond ratings quite well. Developing credit analysis techniques can also be useful in the private placement market, where bond ratings are generally unavailable.

One well-known timing strategy for default-risky bonds involves *sector spread* analysis. First, bonds are separated into sectors, such as industrial and utility or investment and speculative grade. Then the yields on bonds in each sector are analyzed over time to establish average spreads, correlations, and so on. The analysis is used to identify periods when the yields on bonds in one sector are unusually high relative to their historical relationship to yields on bonds in other sectors, and the bonds in that sector are targeted for purchase. Such a strategy may be used to take advantage of (1) changes in the market's sensitivity to default risk, (2) changes in general supply and demand conditions, and (3) changes in the pricing of other characteristics of bonds that are more prevalent in one sector versus another (e.g., call provisions). Sector spread analysis often includes default-free bonds as well as default-risky bonds.

BOND MARKET INNOVATIONS AND BOND MANAGEMENT

A myriad of new debt instruments have been developed in the financial markets in the past twenty years or so. These innovations have emerged through a process known as *financial engineering*. Basically, financial engineering involves the creation of new financial securities, markets, or strategies that help issuers or investors or both to reduce costs, to manage risk, or to pursue profit opportunities. For example, a problem that led to substantial innovations in the debt market was the unprecedented volatility of interest rates in the late 1970s and throughout the 1980s. Also, the development of the junk bond and mortgage-backed securities markets in the 1970s and 1980s has allowed smaller individual borrowers to tap the capital markets and have provided capital market investors a much broader range of investment opportunities. We conclude this chapter with a brief discussion of several bond market innovations, with emphasis on the role they can play in debt management.

Variable-Rate Notes

Variable-rate notes provide coupon interest at a rate that varies with a specific short-term interest rate, such as the rate on three-month U.S. Treasury bills or the LIBOR. The first variable rate security was issued in 1979, and today corporations regularly issue variable-rate notes with maturities generally in the range of five to ten years. Variable-rate notes were developed in response to investors' concerns about the interest rate risk of long-term fixed-coupon bonds. Because the variable-rate bond essentially always pays the going short-term rate (possibly subject to caps or floors), its price is much more stable than those of fixed-coupon bonds in the face of changing interest rates (i.e., they have a very short duration relative to their maturity). Furthermore, to the extent that short-term interest rates reflect current inflation rates, variable-rate bonds provide a hedge against inflation. For these reasons variable-rate notes can serve effectively as tools to manage interest rate risk and to tailor future cash flows.

Inverse Floaters

Inverse floaters, also known as yield curve notes, pay interest at a rate that varies inversely with short-term interest rates. That is, they pay high coupon rates when interest rates are low and low coupon rates when interest rates are high. Consequently, the price of an inverse floater is much more sensitive to changes in interest rates than a fixed-coupon bond with the same maturity (i.e., they have a very long duration relative to their maturity). To date the principal issuers of inverse floaters have been banks, although inverse floaters also have been issued as a part of a CMO package of securities. The principal motivation for the issuance of inverse floaters is to reduce the issuer's exposure to interest rate risk (Ogden 1987a). However, active bond managers often purchase inverse floaters when they are bullish on the outlook for short-term rates (i.e., when they expect interest rates to fall).

Zero-Coupon Bonds

Zero-coupon debt comes in a variety of forms. Occasionally industrial firms and even some municipalities issue zero-coupon bonds with maturities ranging from twenty to thirty years. In addition, zero-coupon debt is occasionally issued as part of a package of securities associated with CMOs. And of course Treasury strips are zero-coupon bonds with a wide variety of maturities from under one year to thirty years. As noted earlier, zero-coupon bonds are useful in passive dedication strategies, since they provide a single cash payment on a specific date. In addition, active portfolio managers often purchase zero-coupon bonds when they are bullish on the bond market. Because they have a longer duration, zero-coupon bonds provide greater returns than coupon bonds with the same maturity when interest rates fall. Active managers also can target specific segments of the maturity spectrum better with zeros than with coupon bonds.

Putable Bonds

Putable bonds, also known as extendable or retractable bonds, have been issued occasionally by industrial firms and some financial institutions. As noted in Chapter 14, such bonds can be viewed as a portfolio consisting of a relatively long-term bond plus a put option allowing the investor to redeem the bond at its par value prior to maturity. The putable bond provides the investor with insurance that the value of the bond will not fall below its par value because of a rise either in the general level of interest rates or in the default risk premium required on the bond. Since most putable bonds are also variable-rate bonds, the protection against interest rate increases is of negligible value. However, protection against increases in default risk can be quite valuable. For this protection the investor accepts a lower promised yield. Active managers often monitor the yields on putable bonds to determine whether and when the yield discount is a bargain for the protection provided by the put option.

Reset Notes and Rating-Sensitive Notes

Coincident with the development of the junk bond market, a number of high-risk corporate borrowers have issued reset notes or rating-sensitive notes. Reset notes pay coupon interest at a rate that is updated periodically so that the new coupon rate is sufficient to render the market value of the note equal to its par value. Thus the coupon rate adjusts for changes in the general level of interest rates (like a variable-rate note) and for changes in the issuer's risk of default. The coupon rate on rating-sensitive notes also adjusts for changes in the issuer's default risk, as measured by Moody or S&P's bond ratings. The unique aspect of both of these notes is that they protect the investor from losses due to increases in the issuer's risk of default. The development of these notes has provided many high-risk firms easier access to the corporate bond market and at the same time has allowed investors to have greater opportunities to invest in such companies while limiting their exposure to default risk.

Bond Funds

The number and variety of bond funds has increased dramatically in recent years. The typical bond fund invests in a specific type of debt security. Investors purchase shares in the mutual fund, receiving principal and interest payments on a pro rata basis. Bond funds are managed by major brokerage firms such as Merrill Lynch and Dean Witter as well as by independent firms that specialize in bond fund management. Money market mutual funds, among the most popular bond funds, invest in short-term debt obligations such as Treasury bills and commercial paper. Other funds specialize in intermediate- and long-term government or corporate bonds (both investment grade and speculative grade), as well as municipal bonds, mortgage securities, and foreign bonds. Bond funds offer two principal advantages. First, they reduce the transaction costs required to develop and maintain specialized portfolios and thereby enhance the liquidity of investments in bonds. Second, for funds that are actively managed, the expertise that the fund manager develops by specializing in a particular segment of the bond market may lead to enhanced profits over time.

Swaps and Interest Rate Futures and Options

In recent years markets for a variety of debt-related derivative securities have grown tremendously. Among the most successful derivative securities are interest rate swaps, interest rate futures, and interest rate options. These derivative securities have greatly enhanced the tools available to bond portfolio managers to manage interest rate risk and to engage in active strategies. Since these securities are discussed in detail in later chapters, we provide only a brief discussion of them here.

A typical interest rate swap is between two parties exposed to opposite types of interest rate risk. For example, a savings and loan institution may have short-term liabilities (i.e., deposits) and assets primarily consisting of long-term fixed-rate mortgages, while a corporation may have issued long-term fixed-rate bonds and invested in short-term money-market securities such as Treasury bills. The S&L faces losses if interest rates rise, and the corporation faces losses if interest rates fall. In a swap contract the

S&L agrees to pay the corporation a fixed interest rate and the corporation agrees to pay the S&L a variable interest rate, both based on an agreed-upon principal amount known as the *notional principal.* The swap agreement thus reduces or eliminates both parties' exposure to the risk of changing interest rates.

A futures contract is a commitment to purchase (long position) or sell (short position) a specific asset at a specific price on a specified date. Futures contracts are traded on U.S. Treasury bills, notes, and bonds as well as on municipal bonds and other debt securities. Since futures contracts require no initial investment except margin balances, they provide a highly leveraged means of either hedging interest rate risk or speculating in the bond market. For example, a pension fund manager may be concerned because the fund is temporarily heavily invested in long-term fixed-rate bonds. The manager can reduce this risk by engaging a short position in Treasury bond futures. In another example the manager of a bond mutual fund who is bullish on the intermediate-term bond market may engage a long position in Treasury note futures. If indeed intermediate-term interest rates fall, the long futures position will provide a profit.

A call option gives the holder the right, but not an obligation, to purchase an asset at a specified date and price, and a put option gives the holder the right, but not an obligation, to sell an asset at a specified date and price. Like interest rate futures, interest rate options are traded on Treasury bills, notes, and bonds as well as on municipal bonds and other debt securities. Options also provide a highly leveraged means of either hedging or speculating on the bond market. Continuing with the above examples, the pension fund manager concerned that long-term interest rates may rise can hedge that risk by either selling Treasury bond call options or buying Treasury bond put options, while the bullish money fund manager can speculate by buying Treasury note call options or selling Treasury note put options.

SUMMARY

The management of bond portfolios is a complex task, since bonds have many important differentiating characteristics, including maturity, default risk, and premature retirement provisions. This chapter discusses various passive and active strategies for managing both default-free and default-risky bond portfolios. Although these strategies share many common threads with management strategies for common stock portfolios, the complex nature of bonds requires at the least a modification of these strategies and in some respects completely different strategies for the effective management of bond portfolios. Various innovations in the bond market in recent years provide enhanced opportunities for both managing bond portfolio risk and exploiting profit opportunities.

Questions and Problems

1. Calculate the duration of a five-year, 10 percent coupon bond. The yield is 6 percent.

2. Given a yield of 10 percent, the price of a ten-year, 10 percent coupon bond is equal to its par value, and its duration is 6.76 years. Using duration, estimate the percentage change in the bond's price if its yield falls to 6 percent. Assuming a par value of $100, the actual new price of the bond is $129.44, and thus the percentage change in its price is $(129.44/100) - 1 = .2944$, or 29.44 percent. How do you explain the discrepancy?

3. Your pension fund is expected to pay out $2 million per year for the next twenty years. To immunize the fund's portfolio, what must be the duration of the fund's assets? Assume that the interest rate is 8 percent.

4. Describe each of the following interest rate risk management strategies:
   1. Buy-and-hold (with indexing)
   2. Dedication
   3. Duration-based immunization
   4. Contingent immunization
   5. Riding the yield curve

5. Distinguish fundamental from technical interest rate forecasting techniques. What are the two basic concerns of an active manager who trades on the basis of interest rate forecasts?

6. Discuss the implementation of each of the following default-risk management strategies:
   1. Buy-and-hold (passive)
   2. Security selection (active)
   3. Market timing (active)

7. Discuss the usefulness of each of the following bond market innovations in bond management:
   1. Variable-rate notes
   2. Inverse floaters
   3. Zero-coupon bonds
   4. Putable bonds
   5. Reset notes and rating sensitive notes
   6. Bond funds
   7. Swaps
   8. Interest rate futures and options

REFERENCES

Bierwag, G. O., and G. G. Kaufman. 1983. Immunization strategies for funding multiple liabilities. *Journal of Financial and Quantitative Analysis* 17:113–124.

Cox, J. C., J. E. Ingersoll, and S. A. Ross. 1979. Duration and the measurement of basis risk. *Journal of Business* 52:51–61.

Fisher, L., and R. L. Weil. 1971. Coping with the risk of interest-rate fluctuations. Returns of bondholders from naive and optimal strategies. *Journal of Business*. October, 408–431.

Fong, H. G., and F. J. Fabozzi. 1989. Interest rate anticipation strategies. In *The institutional investor focus on investment management*. F. J. Fabozzi, ed. Cambridge, MA: Ballinger.

Leibowitz, M. L., and A. Weinberger. 1981. The uses of contingent immunization. *Journal of Portfolio Management* 8:51–55.

Macaulay, F. R. 1938. *Some theoretical problems suggested by the movements of interest rates, bond yields, and stock prices in the United States since 1856*. New York: National Bureau of Economic Research.

Ogden, J. P. 1987a. An analysis of yield curve notes. *Journal of Finance* 42:99–110.

Ogden, J. P. 1987b. Determinants of the relative interest rate sensitivities of corporate bonds. *Financial Management* 16:22–30.

Pinches, G. E., and K. A. Mingo. 1973. A multivariate analysis of industrial bond ratings. *Journal of Finance* 28:1–32.

Smith, C., and J. Warner. 1979. On financial contracting. An analysis of bond covenants. *Journal of Financial Economics* 7:115–161.

Sullivan, K. H., and T. B. Kiggins. 1989. Convexity. The name is new but you always knew what it was. In *The Institutional Investor Focus on Investment Management*. F. J. Fabozzi, ed. Cambridge, MA: Ballinger.

Van Horne, J. C. 1990. *Financial market rates and flows*, ed 3. Englewood Cliffs, NJ: Prentice Hall.

Weinstein, M. I. 1986–87. A curmudgeon's view of junk bonds. *Journal of Portfolio Management*, 13, 76–80.

Yawitz, J. B. 1989. Convexity. An introduction. In *The institutional investor focus on investment management*. F. J. Fabozzi, ed. Cambridge, MA: Ballinger.

PART FOUR

Risk Management and Financial Engineering

PORTFOLIO MANAGEMENT OFTEN ENTAILS THE IMMUNIZATION OF THE portfolio's value against unanticipated changes in interest rates, exchange rates, and equity prices, at least temporarily. For instance, a fixed-income fund manager who is uncertain about the direction of future interest rates and who fears the wealth consequences of potential interest rate increases may wish to hedge the portfolio against the adverse effects of such increases over the period of heightened uncertainty. Doing so protects the fund's investors and maximizes expected utility.

The past two decades have witnessed the development of securities and trading strategies that allow portfolio managers to engage in such hedging efficiently. Especially noteworthy are futures and option contracts, which are known as derivative securities because they are written on, or derived from, some underlying asset like a stock or bond. Other popular hedging strategies are swap transactions and various forms of portfolio insurance. These securities and strategies are said to be *financially engineered*, since they are created with the express purpose of helping individual investors and institutional portfolio managers immunize against the potential wealth losses associated with adverse changes in the above variables. In addition, these securities and strategies are employed in more proactive asset allocation strategies.

The purpose of Part 4 is to familiarize you with these important securities and strategies. The emphasis is on the use of futures, options, swaps, and portfolio insurance for hedging preexisting portfolio positions and for efficient asset reallocation. Thus applications are stressed. Ancillary issues, such as the valuation of these securities and their institutional subtleties, are addressed in accompanying appendices.

In Chapter 16 we introduce stock index, interest rate, and currency futures contracts and demonstrate how these contracts can be employed to hedge equity, interest rate, and exchange rate risk, respectively. In addition, we describe applications of futures contracts for portfolio recomposition.

Chapter 17 provides an analogous discussion related to option contracts. An analysis of swaps and swap options is provided in Chapter 18, and Chapter 19 concludes Part 4 with a detailed description of various portfolio insurance techniques, especially dynamic hedging. The modern portfolio manager who wishes to be successful and competitive within the portfolio management field must be cognizant of these securities and strategies. ∎

CHAPTER *16*

Futures Contracts

Introduction

Part 1 of this book illustrates two important concepts. First, rational investors are expected-utility maximizers who understand the disutility of risk; second, risk is reduced by forming portfolios of less closely correlated assets. Futures contracts were engineered to offer negative correlation not commonly found in securities markets. Therefore, by properly combining futures contracts with security portfolios, an investor or portfolio manager can reduce the risk of the preexisting portfolio position. The other derivative securities and hedging strategies described in subsequent chapters—options, swaps, and portfolio insurance—can also be employed to reduce risk and its disutility by introducing negative correlation with the preexisting security portfolio. They also can be employed in more proactive asset allocation strategies.

A *futures contract* is an agreement to purchase or sell a specified asset in the future for a specified price that is determined today. Thus, by engaging in a short futures position—agreeing to sell an asset in the future for a prespecified price—an investor can hedge a preexisting long position in the contract's underlying cash asset. If the underlying asset's value declines over the life of the futures contract, then the losses on the cash asset are offset, at least in part, by the gains from the short futures position because the long cash asset and short futures position are negatively correlated. A combination of a short asset and a long futures contract also represents a type of negatively correlated two-asset portfolio.

The purpose of this chapter is to demonstrate how a manager can employ futures contracts to affect the composition of security portfolios. We will examine three types of futures contracts: (1) stock index futures, which can be used to alter the beta of an existing equity portfolio; (2) interest rate futures, which can be used to alter the interest rate exposure (duration) of an existing bond portfolio; and (3) currency futures, which can be used to alter the exchange rate exposure of an internationally diversified security portfolio. An important advantage of futures trading is that it entails lower transaction costs than other available methods of altering portfolio composition and exposure, such as selling securities and purchasing Treasury bills.

We begin the chapter with a description of the specifications and institutional features of each of the contracts examined. Next we briefly discuss the three uses of futures contracts. Besides hedging, futures can be used for speculative trading and for price discovery. Following that we provide explicit examples of hedging applications. We conclude the chapter with a discussion of alpha funds and commodity funds, which employ futures contracts in more proactive asset allocation strategies. We also describe how futures are used to alter the market and interest rate exposures of portfolios and how they are used to facilitate the management of index funds and reduce tracking error. Finally, please keep in mind that the issue of futures pricing is inextricably linked to the concepts of futures hedging and trading. However, pricing issues have been relegated to Appendix 16A.

COMMON INSTITUTIONAL FEATURES

The three types of futures contracts examined in this chapter share a number of common institutional features. For example, each is traded on an organized exchange, which is a physical place or trading floor where listed contracts are traded face-to-face on a competitive auction basis. The oldest and largest organized futures exchange is the Chicago Board of Trade (CBOT), established in 1848. This not-for-profit association of members (those holding seats on the exchange) has been used as a model for the development of other organized futures exchanges, such as the Chicago Mercantile Exchange (1919), the New York Commodity Exchange (1933), the London International Financial Futures Exchange (1982), and the Singapore International Monetary Exchange (1984). Other common institutional features are presented next.

Clearinghouses

Every organized futures exchange has a clearinghouse that guarantees contract performance to all market participants. It does so by breaking down each futures trade into two distinct contracts: one between the buyer (the long position trader) and the clearinghouse acting as the seller, and one contract between the seller (the short position trader) and the clearinghouse acting as the buyer. Hence each trader has obligations to the clearinghouse, and needs to be concerned with the integrity of the clearinghouse only. Clearinghouses do not default on contracts; to do so would damage market confidence. Since the clearinghouse matches its long and short positions exactly, it is perfectly hedged; that is, its net futures position is zero.

The clearinghouse is organized as an independent corporation. Its stockholders are its member clearing firms. These member clearing firms facilitate the mechanics of futures trading, which are discussed later. All futures traders must maintain an account with a member clearing firm, either directly or through a brokerage firm.

Margin Requirements

Each futures trader represents a source of credit risk to the clearinghouse. For instance, the long futures trader may have insufficient capital to purchase the underlying asset at the specified futures price. Because of this credit risk each trader is required to post margin, usually with a member clearing firm. A *margin*, often a cash deposit, exists to insure the clearinghouse against credit risk and thus represents a type of performance bond.

Besides cash, the margin deposit may be met at least in part with liquid securities or a bank letter of credit. For example, U.S. Treasury bills may be posted. The initial margin varies somewhat across markets and contracts but is often set equal to the contract's maximum daily price limit. Such maximum limits are instituted to help ensure market safety and are related to a procedure known as daily resettlement (discussed below). Exhibit 16.1 displays daily limits and other information for some of the contracts that we review in this chapter. Margins also vary by the type of trading strategy involved. Hedging trades and futures spreads typically require lower margins than purely speculative trades. The margin is returned upon completion of the futures contract. If securities were posted, then the interest earned is paid to the trader. In addition, interest is accumulated on any cash portion of the margin.

Daily Resettlement

The initial margin is always a small fraction of the underlying asset's value. For instance, at the CBOT an initial margin of about $1,350 is adequate security for a contract on $100,000 of face value of U.S. Treasury

EXHIBIT 16.1

Contract Information for Selected Futures

Commodity	Delivery Months	Contract Size	Minimum Price Fluctuation	Daily Limit
CHICAGO BOARD OF TRADE				
U.S. Treasury Bonds	Mar/Jne	$100,000	1.32 pt.	3 pts.
	Spt/Dec	8% coupon	= $31.25	= $3,000
U.S. Treasury Notes	Mar/Jne	$100,000	1/32 pt.	3 pts.
	Spt/Dec	8% coupon	= $31.25	= $3,000
CHICAGO MERCANTILE EXCHANGE INTERNATIONAL MONETARY MARKET DIVISION				
British Pound	Jan/Mar	BP25,000	$.00005/BP1	None
	Apl/Jne		= $12.50	
	Jly/Spt			
	Oct/Dec			
Swiss Franc	–"–	SF125,000	$.0001/SF1	None
			= $12.50	
CHICAGO MERCANTILE EXCHANGE INDEX AND OPTION MARKET DIVISION				
SP500	Next four months and	500 × SP500	5 pts. = $25	Varies (contact
	Mar/Jne/Spt/Dec			exchange)

notes. An initial margin can be small because of a procedure known as *daily resettlement*. Daily resettlement, or *marking to the market*, is a futures market requirement that traders realize losses (and gains) daily.

For illustration, assume that you have a long position in a Swiss franc futures contract traded on the International Monetary Market (IMM) division of the Chicago Mercantile Exchange (CME). Assume that the futures price is $0.70/SF1 and that the contract entails SF125,000. Also assume that the initial margin is $2,000. If the contract (i.e., futures price) closes today at $0.694, down $0.006/SF1, then you suffer a one-day loss of $750 ($0.006 × 125,000). As the long trader, you lose because you contracted at a futures price of $0.70 and the futures price has depreciated to $0.694. At the end of the trading day the $750 is deducted from your margin deposited with the broker or member clearing firm. Then there is a margin call; you must replenish the margin to resume trading the next day. This procedure is daily resettlement; you have realized your loss at the end of the trading day, and presuming you replenished your margin (i.e., met your margin call), the contract is now said to be marked to the market, that is, the value of the contract reverts to zero. Here the $750 is credited to the short trader's margin account.

The $750 deposit is known as the variation margin and must be met with cash. In general, a cash deposit is required any time the margin account drops below what is called a maintenance margin, which is often equal to about 75 percent of the initial margin. Thus if you suffer a small one-day loss, no variation margin deposit is required. If the loss is large enough to make the margin level drop below the maintenance margin, however, then a cash variation margin deposit is required.

A broker or clearing firm normally has permission from the trader to withdraw the required deposit monies from the trader's established account; this facilitates the daily resettlement process, especially if a margin call should occur during the trading session. Such a call may be issued if the futures price changes dramatically and no maximum daily price limit is applied to the contract. Exhibit 16.2 provides another self-contained illustration of the daily resettlement procedure.

Daily Resettlement, Margins, and Leverage. Given the above discussion of the daily resettlement process, it is now appropriate to discuss the relation between this process, margins, and leverage. First, it should be obvious why the initial margin is so small. The margin only has to be sufficient to cover one-day price changes, since contracts are marked to the market each trading day. One-day price changes are typically quite small, representing only a fraction of the futures price. Second, you should now understand why initial margins are often set equal to the contract's daily price limit. This limit bounds the daily price change, thus limiting the trader's one-day loss. Finally, it is now easy to understand why futures are highly leveraged instruments. In the above illustration a futures price change of less than 1 percent ($0.006/$0.700) resulted in a margin loss of more than 37 percent ($750/$2,000).

EXHIBIT 16.2

A Self-Contained Illustration of Daily Resettlement

Assume that on Monday, March 1, you enter a futures contract to buy one CBOT March Treasury bond futures contract at the futures price of $98,156.25 (98 5/32). The initial margin is $2,500 and the maintenance margin is $2,000. For simplicity, you do not withdraw excess monies from your margin balance. Also, all margin requirements are met with cash and no interest is earned. You hold your long position through Friday, March 5. Then you sell the contract (a reversing trade) at the opening price on Monday, March 8. Below is a schedule of assumed prices and the associated margin requirements. Your gross profit on the entire transaction is −$1,062.50

Trading Date	Settlement Price	Marked-to-the-Market	Other Entries	Account Balance
3/1	$98,250.00 (98 8/32)	+$ 93.75	+2,500.00[a]	$ 2,593.75
3/2	96,687.50 (96 22/32)	−1,562.50	1,468.75[b]	2,500.00
3/3	97,000.00 (97 9/32)	+312.50		−2,812.50
3/4	97,593.75 (97 19/32)	+593.75		3,406.25
3/5	96,937.50 (96 30/32)	−656.25		2,750.00
3/8	97,093.75 (97 3/32)[c]	+156.25	−2,906.25[d]	0.00
			+1,062.50[e]	

[a]$2,500 initial margin deposit.

[b]$1,468.75 deposit to meet $2,500 margin, since you have dropped below the maintenance margin. This deposit is the variation margin.

[c]$97,093.75 opening futures price on March 8.

[d]Entire account balance withdrawn after reversing trade.

[e]Deposits less withdrawals. A positive amount indicates a loss. Also note that $1,062.50 = $98,156.25 − $97,093.75.

Daily Price Limits and Position Limits

As noted above, exchanges impose daily price limits on some contracts to help ensure market safety. If the price of a futures contract hits a limit during a trading session, there is a limit move. Limit moves can be limit up or limit down. The exchange usually does not permit trading at prices above the limit up or below the limit down. However, the exchange's officials may elect to alter these limits if trading has ceased for a long period. In addition, exchange regulators often alter price limits as policy dictates. Also to ensure contract performance and market safety, exchanges often impose position limits, which limit the number of contracts a trader can hold at any one time.

Delivery Terms

How a futures contract is delivered varies among contracts. Some contracts may be delivered on any business day of the delivery month. Others permit delivery after the last trading day, which also varies across contracts. Most contracts call for the physical exchange of the underlying asset; others, such as stock index futures contracts, call for a cash settlement. Since it is difficult to deliver an entire stock index, delivery entails a cash transfer that is a function of the contract's futures price and multiplier. Also, many futures contracts permit more than one deliverable asset. For instance, a short wheat trader may be allowed to deliver different qualities of wheat. Here the contract specifies a price adjustment reflecting the quality of the delivered asset.

However, most underlying assets are never actually delivered because the vast majority of all futures traders make reversing trades prior to contract delivery. A reversing trade effectively makes a trader's net futures position equal to zero, thus absolving the trader from further trading requirements. For example, if you were long an SP500 futures contract with a March delivery month, you could enter a reversing trade by shorting one SP500 March futures contract. Since your net position is now zero, the clearinghouse absolves you from any further trading obligations. In most futures markets, over 90 percent of all futures positions are closed out via a reversing trade.

Finally, while the vast majority of all futures are closed out (offset) via reversing trades, it is important to note that the method of delivery still influences the futures price. This point is addressed in Appendix 16A.

Executing Trades

Futures trades are executed in a similar manner across markets. For illustration, assume that you (the client or principal) want to assume a long position in a June British pound futures contract. This contract trades on the IMM division of the CME. You are willing to assume the position at market, meaning that you are seeking the best available price.

The process begins with a phone call to your agent (account executive or broker), who must trade through an exchange member. Exchange members are individuals who hold seats in the exchange and trade on the floor. A member may be a commission broker (more formally called a futures commission merchant) or a local. A commission broker's seat is usually financed by a trading firm such as Shearson Lehman. Thus, calling an account executive or broker of a trading firm with which you have an established account effectively gives you access to a commission broker. Over the past decade seat prices at the CME have ranged between $200,000 and $400,000.

Your agent next places the order through to the commission broker, who in turn executes the trade and earns a commission. Thus commission brokers are exchange members who execute trades for public clients for a fee.

The actual trading is conducted in a designated floor area, called a pit, for the particular futures contract involved. In these pits trades are executed through sophisticated hand signals. Once the trade is executed, the commission broker confirms the trade with your agent, who notifies you of your completed transaction and the futures price. You must then deposit your initial margin with a member firm of the clearinghouse. Typically your broker or account executive handles this process by withdrawing funds from your established account.

The commission broker may have dealt with another commission broker who represented another public client. Alternatively, he or she may have transacted with a local. Locals are exchange members who trade for their own accounts. They earn a living by buying at one price, the bid price, and selling at a higher price, the ask price. Locals are sometimes called scalpers, day traders, or position traders, depending on their trading behavior. Scalpers trade actively, holding their positions for no more than a few minutes. Thus they attempt to profit from volume trading. Day traders hold their positions for a longer period but less than a full trading session. They attempt to profit on price movement but do not wish to assume the risk of holding longer positions. Position traders assume longer-term positions. Traders on the floors of U.S. futures exchanges are allowed to trade both for themselves as locals and for public clients as commission brokers. This is known as dual trading.

Types of Orders

Besides placing a market order, a public futures trader can place any of the following order types:

- A limit order. This stipulates a specific price at which you will contract. A limit order may be good only for a trading session (a day order) or until canceled (an open order).

- A fill-or-kill order. This order instructs the commission broker to fill an order immediately at a specified price. The order is canceled if it cannot be transacted quickly.
- An all-or-none order. This order allows the commission broker to fill part of the order at one specified price and the remainder at another price.
- An on-the-open or on-the-close order, which is an order to trade within a few minutes of opening or closing, respectively.
- A stop order. This order triggers a reversing trade when prices hit a prescribed limit. Stop orders are used to protect against losses on existing positions.

Transaction Costs

Transaction costs in futures markets are very small, especially for exchange members. At present it costs locals about 24¢ per round-trip trade, that is, to get into the contract and to get out later via a reversing trade. Of course public traders incur other costs. The following transaction costs are realized from futures trading:

- Floor trading and clearing fees. These are the small fees charged by the exchange and its associated clearinghouse. If a trade is executed through a commission broker, these fees are built into the broker's commission. Locals pay the fees directly.
- Commissions. A commission broker charges a commission to transact a public order. This commission is paid at the order's inception and covers both the opening and reversing trades.
- Bid-ask spreads. Locals simultaneously quote bid and ask prices. The bid-ask spread represents a transaction cost when effecting a trade with a local. The spread represents the cost of obtaining trading immediacy, since locals offer the public trading liquidity. A bid-ask spread is typically equal to the value of the contract's minimum price fluctuation, called a tick.
- Delivery costs. A trader who holds a position until delivery is subject to delivery costs. However, as noted above, the overwhelming majority of futures contracts never entail actual delivery of the underlying asset.

Taxes

Determining the tax consequences of futures trading can be complex, especially when spreads are involved. Below are presented a few generally applicable tax guides:

- Marking to the market. At the end of the calendar year a futures contract is marked to the market so that any unrealized gains or losses are treated for tax purposes as though they were actually realized during the tax year. This rule applies to speculative transactions only.

- Gains. The realized and unrealized gains from speculative futures trading are considered to be 60 percent capital gains and 40 percent ordinary income. All profits from hedges are taxed at the ordinary income tax rate.
- Losses. The realized and unrealized losses are deductible by offsetting them against any other investment gains. Losses exceeding gains by up to $3,000 can be deducted against ordinary income.
- Commissions. In general, brokerage commissions are tax deductible.

Market Growth and Globalization

Futures trading has exhibited tremendous growth since the 1970s. Figure 16.1 portrays the growth in all U.S. futures trading for the period 1972 through 1991. During this period annual trading volume grew more than tenfold to nearly 325 million contracts entailing over $63 trillion in underlying commodities and financial securities. In addition, eight new futures exchanges have developed in the free world since 1982.

The advent of these overseas markets has given rise to cooperative linkages that facilitate international futures trading. For example, Japanese yen futures may be traded on the CME and the position closed on the Singapore International Monetary Exchange (SIMEX). Also, the CME recently instituted an after-hours electronic futures trading system called Globex, which is designed to recapture business from Japanese and other Far East futures traders.

Market Regulation

Organized futures markets are regulated to ensure contract performance and to prevent insider trading and price manipulation such as frontrunning. Frontrunning occurs when dual traders give priority to their own trading at the expense of outside clients. For instance, if a dual trader knows that a client will soon enter a large order, then the trader can profit by assuming a position prior to executing the client's order.

Futures exchanges are regulated by a number of bodies, including the Commodity Futures Trading Commission (CFTC) and National Futures Association (NFA). The CFTC was created by Congress in 1974, and the NFA was established in 1982. The NFA is a private self-regulatory agency funded by transaction fees assessed on futures trading. Together these two bodies are empowered to approve new contracts, set maximum daily price limits, ensure the competency of brokers, and the like. Each futures exchange also regulates trading through the imposition of trading rules and conducting market surveillance designed to ensure orderly trading and the prevention of price manipulation. Overall, the effectiveness of these regulatory practices in preventing trading abuses has been mixed.

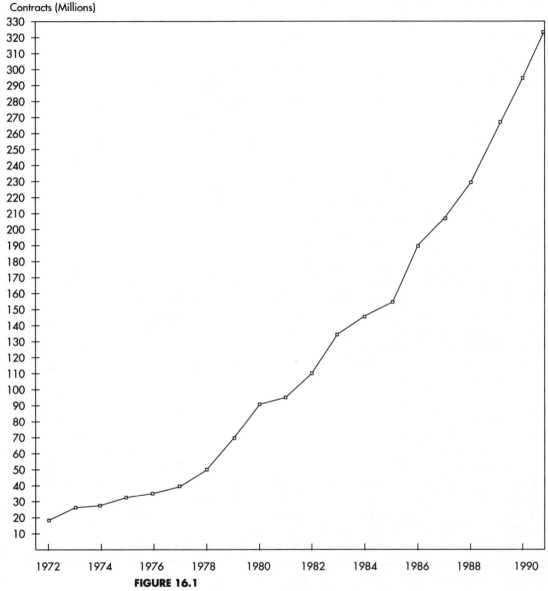

FIGURE 16.1

Annual Volume for all U.S. Futures Trading

CONTRACT SPECIFICATIONS

The three types of futures contracts examined in this chapter share the common institutional features described in the previous section. But they also exhibit unique contract specifications, which are described next.

Stock Index Futures

Stock index futures are cash-settled futures contracts written on indices of stock combinations. The first stock index futures contract was introduced on February 16, 1982, when the Kansas City Board of Trade began trading its Value Line composite index futures. In April of 1982 the CME began futures trading on the SP500 stock index, which is the most active index futures contract (accounting for 70 percent of index futures trading volume) and represents the fourth most active futures contract worldwide (1990). In May of 1982 the New York Futures Exchange also introduced the trading of NYSE composite index futures, another highly successful contract.

A fourth actively traded index futures contract is written on the MMI and is traded on the CBOT. In its first year of trading, volume in all stock index futures was nearly 5 million contracts. Since that time annual trading volume has grown more than sixfold to over 30 million contracts. In fact, the dollar volume of underlying stocks traded in the index futures contracts actually exceeds the dollar volume of the U.S. stock market itself. The popularity of stock index futures stems from the ability of traders to use these contracts to hedge stock positions, to speculate on general market swings, and to arbitrage the contracts against highly correlated stock portfolios.

Exhibit 16.3 provides contract specifications for these four stock index futures contracts. The size of each contract is some multiple of the underlying index. For the MMI the contract multiple is $250. For the other three indices the contract multiple is $500. Thus if you engage in, say, a long SP500 futures contract with futures price 300 and the day's settlement price is 302, then your margin account is credited by $1,000 upon marking to the market.

Exhibit 16.3 also shows that the MMI contract exhibits monthly settlement dates and the other contracts have a March-June-September-December delivery cycle. Of course, actual delivery of the underlying index never occurs; instead each contract is cash-settled. The final settlement payment at contract expiration is determined uniquely with each contract. For instance, for the NYSE composite futures contract the final settlement value is determined by the difference between the daily settlement price on the last day of trading and the final value of the spot

EXHIBIT 16.3

Contract Specifications for Stock Index Futures Contracts

Index	Contract Multiplier	Delivery Months	Initial Margin
MMI	$250	Monthly	$21,000
VLCI	$500	Mar/Jne/Spt/Dec	$21,000
SP500	$500	–"–	$22,000
NYSE	$500	–"–	$10,000

index on the last business day of the month. Like other futures contracts, positions in stock index futures are typically closed out via reversing trades rather than held to expiration.

Interest Rate Futures

The four most popular interest rate futures contracts are the Treasury bond and Treasury note contracts traded on the CBOT and the Eurodollar and Treasury bill contracts traded on the IMM division of the CME. Exhibit 16.4 presents the specifications for these four contracts. Contract sizes, daily price limits, margin requirements and other specifications are identified. In addition, you should be aware of the following features: The Treasury bill futures contract calls for the delivery of ninety-, ninety-one-, or ninety-two-day Treasury bills; the Eurodollar futures contract calls for the delivery of a ninety-day Eurodollar and is cash settled; the Treasury note futures contract calls for the delivery of a Treasury note with a maturity of six to ten years; and the Treasury bond futures contract calls for the delivery of a Treasury bond with at least fifteen years to maturity or first call date, whichever comes first. Also, both the Treasury note and Treasury bond futures contracts exhibit wild card and delivery options, which stem from unique settlement practices in these markets. The wild card option is the opportunity of a short trader to exploit information about bond prices after the futures market has closed. The delivery option is the opportunity of the short trader to deliver the cheapest eligible note or bond.[1] Finally, volume in the Treasury bond and Eurodollar contracts is vast. The CBOT's Treasury bond futures is the most liquid futures contract worldwide, with more than 75 million contracts traded annually. With a face value of $100,000, trading entails an annual dollar volume of $7.5 trillion. The Eurodollar futures is now the second most liquid contract worldwide, with nearly 35 million annual contracts encompassing $35 trillion.

Currency Futures

The IMM is the largest trader of listed currency futures contracts. Exhibit 16.5 on page 412 shows contract sizes and other details for these contracts. Futures trading is conducted on seven foreign currencies and the European currency unit (ECU). The ECU is a weighted-average index of the exchange rates of the nations comprising the European Economic Community. Contract sizes vary by underlying currency, as do margin requirements and minimum price fluctuations. There are no daily price limits on IMM currency futures.

  IMM currency futures trading has grown substantially during the past decade. Over the period 1977 through 1991 annual volume has grown

---

[1] For more detail on these options see Tucker (1991), Chapter 10.

EXHIBIT 16.4

Interest Rate Futures Contract Specifications

90-DAY U.S. TREASURY BILLS (IMM)

Contract Size	$1 Million
Minimum Price Change	One Basis Point ($25)
Daily Price Limit	None
Delivery Months	March, June, September, December
Trading Hours	7:20 a.m.–2:00 p.m. Central
Last Trading Day	Varies
First Delivery Day	Business Day after Last Trading Day
Margin	$810 Initial; $600 Maintenance

EURODOLLARS (IMM)

Contract Size	$1 million
Minimum Price Change	One Basis Point ($25)
Daily Price Limit	None
Delivery Months	March, June, September, December
Trading Hours	7:20 a.m.–2:00 p.m. Central
Last Trading Day	Second London Business Day before Third Wednesday of the Month
First Delivery Day	Not Applicable (Cash Settled)
Margin	$810 Initial; $600 Maintenance

PANEL C: U.S. TREASURY NOTES (CBOT)

Contract Size	$100,000
Minimum Price Change	1/32 Points ($31.25)
Daily Price Limit	96/32 Points ($3,000)
Delivery Months	March, June, September, December
Trading Hours	7:20 a.m.–2:00 p.m. Central
Last Trading Day	Business Day prior to Last Seven Days
First Delivery Day	First Business Day of the Month
Margin	$1,350 Initial; $1,000 Maintenance

PANEL D: U.S. TREASURY BONDS (CBOT)

Contract Size	$100,000
Minimum Price Change	1/32 Points ($31.25)
Daily Price Limit	96/32 Points ($3,000)
Delivery Months	March, June, September, December
Trading Hours	7:20 a.m.–2:00 p.m. Central
Last Trading Day	Business Day prior to Last Seven Days
First Delivery Day	First Business Day of the Month
Margin	$2,700 Initial; $2,000 Maintenance

from 586,428 contracts to more than 27 million contracts. The Deutsche mark leads all other currencies, with the British pound, yen, and Swiss franc also exhibiting active volume. Futures on the French franc, Australian dollar, and ECU are relatively inactive.

Currency futures are traded on a number of organized exchanges besides the IMM. These include the Philadelphia Stock Exchange, the SIMEX, the Sydney Futures Exchange, the London International Financial

EXHIBIT 16.5

Contract Specifications for IMM Currency Futures

Currency	Delivery Months	Contract Size	Minimum Price Fluctuation	Initial Margin	Maintenance Margin
Australian Dollar	Jan/Mar/Apr June/July/Sept/Oct/Dec/Spot	AD100,000	$0.001/AD1	$2,000	$1,500
British Pound	"	BP62,500	$0.005/BP1	$2,000	$1,500
Canadian Dollar	"	CD100,000	$0.001/CD1	$ 900	$ 700
Deutsche Mark	"	DM125,000	$0.0001/DM1	$2,000	$1,500
French Franc	"	FF250,000	$0.00005/FF1	$2,000	$1,500
Japanese Yen	"	JY12,500,000	$0.000001/JY1	$1,500	$1,000
Swiss Franc	"	SF125,000	$0.0001/SF1	$2,000	$1,500
ECU	Mar/June/Sept/Dec	ECU125,000	$0.001/ECU1	See	IMM

Notes: There are no daily price limits. The IMM removed daily price limits on currency futures in February 1985. Trading hours are approximately 7:20 A.M. to 1:20 P.M. Central time. Delivery takes place on the third Wednesday of the contract month. The last trading day is the second business day before delivery. The margin on spreads is zero. Hedge margins are usually less than the speculative margins shown here.

Futures Exchange (LIFFE), and others. The LIFFE is the second largest trader of listed currency futures contracts.

A Word on Forward Contracts

Like futures contracts, forward contracts entail the trading of an asset in the future for a prescribed price that is determined today. While forward contracts are available for several assets, the only liquid forward market entails foreign exchange trading. Estimates place the size of this interbank market at twenty times that of the currency futures market when measured in terms of the dollar amount of underlying foreign exchange traded. Because of the similarities between currency futures and forward contracts, our subsequent currency future hedging applications generally hold for currency forward contracts as well. Yet while both contracts exhibit many similarities, important differences remain:

- Qualified public speculation is encouraged for futures but not for forwards.
- Currency forward contracts are accessible only to large creditworthy customers that deal in foreign trade.
- Contract sizes and delivery dates are standardized for currency futures but are not tailored for forward contracts.
- The majority of forward contracts are settled by delivery of the underlying currency, but the majority of futures contracts are settled through reversing trades.
- Currency futures trading entails posting margin and requires daily resettlement; forward trading does not require a margin deposit and entails no cash flows until contract expiration. In general, credit or counterparty risk is far less serious for forward contract trading.

USES FOR FUTURES CONTRACTS

There are three principal uses for futures contracts: hedging, speculating, and price discovery. We will now briefly address the latter two uses, then discuss hedging shortly thereafter.

Investors can employ futures to speculate on spot asset price changes. For instance, a speculator who believes that a spot price and hence a futures price will increase can assume a long position in the futures contract. Such a position offers greater leverage than assuming a long position in the spot asset itself. To profit, the speculator must be correct on two accounts: the spot price must increase, and it must do so prior to the expiration of the futures contract. For a forecast of price decline, the speculator can assume a short futures position. More elaborate speculative strategies can be constructed by combining futures contracts. For example, for a forecast of price increase, the speculator can also assume a long position in a deferred (longer-term) futures contract and contemporaneously assume a short position in a nearby (shorter-term) futures contract. This speculative trade is known as an *intracommodity futures spread*. If the forecast is correct, the profits from the deferred long contract will be greater (in absolute value) than the losses on the nearby short contract. If the forecast proves to be incorrect, however, the profits on the nearby short contract will offset at least some of the losses on the deferred long position. Other elaborate speculative strategies can also be constructed. The principal point to remember is that the contracts are being employed in a speculative manner, since no preexisting spot asset position exists.

It can be argued that the futures price largely reflects what traders expect the actual spot price to be at contract expiration. In fact, under certain restrictive assumptions (namely risk-neutrality and no daily resettlement), the futures price is an unbiased estimator of the subsequent spot asset price. This result, known as the unbiased forward rate hypothesis, is demonstrated in Appendix 16A. Thus the observed futures price may be used to obtain a forecast of a subsequent spot price. In other words, futures contracts can be employed for price discovery. Empirical studies have shown that futures prices are not perfect predictors of subsequent spot prices. In fact, pricing errors can be 20 percent or more, even for nearby contracts. Yet these same studies tend to support the view that alternative forecasting methods, which are much more costly, are no better predictors on average than the simple futures price (Levich 1983).

Hedging with Futures Contracts

While futures contracts can be used for speculation and price discovery, their principal function is to hedge preexisting spot positions. There are four questions that an investor must address when utilizing futures contracts for hedging: (1) Should a short or long position be undertaken? (2) Which futures commodity should be employed? (3) Should a nearby or more deferred futures contract be assumed? (4) Most important, how many futures contracts should be traded?

The answers to these questions share a common origin, namely the minimizing of basis risk. Consider what happens when an investor uses a futures contract to hedge. In particular, consider a short hedge in which the futures contract is shorted at a price of $_Tf_0$. At time t the hedge is lifted by selling the spot asset and longing a futures contract at the new price of $_T\tilde{f}_t$ (a reversing trade). The profit from the short hedge is

(16.1)
$$Profit_t = (\tilde{S}_t - S_0) - (_T\tilde{f}_t - _Tf_0)$$
$$= (\tilde{S}_t - _T\tilde{f}_t) - (S_0 - _Tf_0),$$

where S_0 and $\tilde{S}_t$ refer to the spot asset's price at time 0 (the hedge inception) and time t, respectively. The *basis* is the difference between the spot and futures prices.[2] Thus we can rewrite equation 16.1 as follows:

(16.2)
$$Profit_t = \tilde{b}_t - b_0,$$

where $\tilde{b}_t$ and b_0 refer to the basis at time t and at time 0, respectively. Hence the profit from the hedge is merely the change in the basis. In other words, when an investor uses a futures contract to hedge, the profit realized depends on how the *basis* changes. Without the hedge the profit depends on how the *spot price* changes. Because spot and futures prices tend to be highly correlated, however, the variability of the basis is much lower than that of the spot price. This simple result ultimately represents why futures hedging tends to be effective in reducing risk.

The uncertainty regarding how the basis will change over the life of the hedge ($\tilde{b}_t$ is a random variable) is known as basis risk. Hedging applications are generally designed to minimize it. With this in mind, let's return to our four questions.

First, should a short or long futures position be undertaken? The answer is whichever minimizes basis risk. If a long position in the spot asset is held, the futures contract should be shorted. In this way the high (positive) correlation between the spot and futures prices is effectively made negative, reducing portfolio risk. If a short spot position exists, the investor should assume a long futures position to introduce negative correlation and thereby reduce basis risk.

Second, which futures commodity should be selected? Again, the answer is whichever commodity minimizes basis risk. In general, you seek a futures contract whose underlying commodity is the most highly

---

[2] See Appendix 16A for more discussion of the basis.

correlated with your spot asset. This stratagem will serve to maximize the correlation between the spot and futures prices, thereby minimizing basis risk. If a futures contract is written on a commodity or asset that is identical to your spot asset, then you can engage in a direct hedge. For instance, if you want to hedge a long position in British pounds, then you short a BP futures contract traded on the IMM. If no futures contract is traded on your spot asset, however, then you are forced to engage in a cross-hedge. For instance, there are no futures contracts traded on corporate bonds, so corporate bond fund managers often employ U.S. Treasury bond futures to cross-hedge their interest rate exposure. This strategy is effective in reducing basis risk, since the prices of long-term high-quality corporate bonds and Treasury bonds are very strongly correlated.

Third, should a nearby or more deferred futures contract be used? In general, a futures contract with delivery occurring beyond the hedger's planning horizon should be selected. In this way the hedge does not have to be lifted prematurely. Also, to obtain the greatest reduction in basis risk the hedger should hold the futures position until as close to expiration as possible. Thus the futures contract selected will be the one whose maturity occurs nearest to (but after) the hedger's horizon. Finally, if the horizon is so long that a sufficient futures maturity is unavailable, then the hedger should engage in a process called *rolling the hedge forward*. Here a more liquid nearby futures contract is selected, and when it approaches its maturity, the futures position is closed out via a reversing trade and a new position is established in the next-deferred contract. The process is repeated until the hedge is ultimately lifted.

Fourth, how many futures contracts should be traded? This is the most important question faced by the hedger because it is the most difficult to answer. In general, there is no exact method of determining the optimal number of futures contracts—the *hedge ratio* in the lingo of the futures market—for minimizing basis risk before the hedge is lifted. However, there are several ratios and several methods to estimate the hedge ratio. In the applications in the next section we will make use of three different hedge ratios. The first is the naive hedge ratio, wherein each unit of the asset held in the spot market is hedged with a unit in the futures market. For instance, if you wish to hedge £125,000 and employ a naive hedge ratio, then you will trade five BP futures contracts (each entailing £25,000) listed on the IMM. The naive hedge ratio is effective in minimizing basis risk when a direct hedge can be employed, or put another way, when the spot and futures prices are highly positively correlated. The other two ratios that we'll employ are (1) the minimum variance hedge ratio, which is used in conjunction with stock index futures trading, and (2) the price sensitivity hedge ratio, which is used in conjunction with interest rate futures trading. These ratios are derived in Appendix 16B.

HEDGING APPLICATIONS

Armed with a familiarity of the institutional features of futures trading and the theory underlying futures hedging, you are now prepared to examine some specific hedging applications. We will review three applications. One entails stock index futures to eliminate the systematic market risk of an equity portfolio. The second entails interest rate futures to eliminate the interest rate risk of a corporate bond portfolio. The third involves currency futures to reduce the exchange exposure of a country fund.

Hedging an Equity Portfolio[3]

Suppose that a portfolio manager who oversees a $10 million stock portfolio considers the outlook for the market very uncertain. The manager decides to insulate the portfolio from adverse market swings by hedging with stock index futures over a one-year horizon. Assume that the CAPM holds:

(16.3) $$E[\tilde{R}(S)] = r + \beta_S\{E[\tilde{R}(M)] - r\},$$

where $E[\tilde{R}(M)]$ is the expected return on the market portfolio and β_S is the stock portfolio's beta. Also assume that the characteristics of the portfolio and the market environment are as given in the top portion of Exhibit 16.6.

Part A of Exhibit 16.6 displays the transactions the manager must undertake to achieve the minimum-risk hedged position. The stock portfolio represents 40,000 index units ($10,000,000/250); since its beta is .7, representing the minimum variance hedge ratio (see Appendix 16B), the manager will short 28,000 units (40,000 × .7) in the futures market. Of course traded futures contracts will be written for quantities of more than one index unit. For example, if the standard contract entails a multiplier of $500, the manager will short fifty-six contracts (28,000/500).

Part B of Exhibit 16.6 demonstrates the overall return achieved by the manager if consensus expectations are fulfilled and the market rises to 280 by year-end. If the portfolio behaves as expected, its value increases by $960,000 in capital gains and $400,000 in dividend income. But covering the short futures position will result in a loss of $560,000 and an overall return of 8 percent, the riskless rate.

Instead, suppose that the market index drops 10 percent, meaning that the market's realized return including dividends is –6 percent for the year. The return on the portfolio, using the CAPM, is –1.8 percent, or .08 + .70(–.06 – .08); this return consists of a 4 percent dividend yield and a capital loss of 5.8 percent. However, part C of Exhibit 9.6 reveals that the futures hedge will produce a profit of $980,000. Hence the overall return is still 8 percent, the riskless rate. The long position in

---

[3] This hedging example is based largely on one presented by Figlewski and Kon (1982).

EXHIBIT 16.6

Portfolio and Market Environment

Portfolio	Market
Value = $10 million	Riskless rate r = 8%
Beta = 0.70	E [R (M)] = 16%
E [R (S)] = 13.6%	Dividend = δ = 4%
Dividend = 4%	Expected Capital Gain = 12%
Expected Capital Gain = 9.6%	I (0) = 250
	E [$\bar{I}$(1)] = 280
	$_1f_0$ = 260 = I (0) [1 + r − δ]

(a) INITIAL POSITION, INDEX = 300

Stock	Futures
Total Expected Return = 13.6%	Write 28,000 units at 260
Dividend = 4.0	
Capital Gain = 9.6	

(b) ONE YEAR LATER, INDEX = 280

Stock	Futures
Total Realized Return = 13.6%	Cover Short Position at 280
Dividend = 4.0	Loss = $560,000
Capital Gain = 9.6	
Portfolio Value = $11,360,000	
Overall Return = $10,800,000 (8%) = r	

(c) ONE YEAR LATER, INDEX = 225

Stock	Futures
Total Realized Return = 1.8%	Cover Short Position at 225
Dividend = 4.0	Profit = $980,000
Capital Gain = −5.8	
Portfolio Value = $9,820,000	
Overall Return = $10,800,000 (8%) = r	

the stock portfolio and the short stock index futures position are clearly negatively correlated.

This analysis demonstrates that the manager was assured a risk-free return of 8 percent whether the index climbed by 12 percent or fell by 10 percent over the one-year period. By taking other possible market changes, we can show that the overall return is *always* 8 percent. Thus we can conclude that through index futures trading the manager eliminated all systematic risk, effectively reducing the preexisting equity portfolio's beta from .7 to 0. After all, only a zero-beta asset should earn the riskless rate of interest. The use of stock index futures in conjunction with the minimum variance hedge ratio allowed the manager to immunize the stock portfolio fully. By artificially introducing negative correlation, the derivative security provided the manager with an effective and relatively low-cost way of altering risk-return outcomes, thereby enhancing expected utility.

A More Realistic Equity Hedging Example

In the prior example the stock portfolio and stock index futures were perfectly positively correlated. Also, dividends were known and constant and the portfolio's beta remained unchanged over the one-year period. So too did the risk-free rate of interest. Finally, the manager was able to write exactly 28,000 index units in the futures market; problems associated with imperfect security divisibility were ignored. Certainly these assumptions are somewhat unrealistic. They were invoked to simplify the demonstration that the employment of stock index futures can dramatically alter the risk associated with holding a stock portfolio. Below we again demonstrate this concept using real price data for traded stocks and futures contracts. The example illustrates that while not completely eliminating risk and wealth loss, the use of stock index futures serves to offset losses in the spot portfolio.

Exhibit 16.7 reports closing prices for eight actively traded stocks on March 1 of a recent year. Also reported is the settlement June SP500 futures price, 291.85. Individual stock betas, obtained from an investment advisory firm, are also reported. Suppose that an investor owns a portfolio of these stocks as shown in the exhibit. Since a portfolio's beta is simply a weighted average of the betas of the component stocks, the portfolio beta is .95.

The investor, concerned about a possible market decline over the next several weeks, intends to liquidate the stock portfolio on May 31 to transact a real estate deal and wants to employ the June SP500 futures contract to safeguard the wealth over the period. Since the current value of the portfolio is $216,200, the investor holds about 740.79 index units ($216,200/291.85). Given a portfolio beta of 0.95, the investor should short 703.75 (740.79 × 0.95) index units in the futures market to hedge fully. Given a contract multiple of $500, the investor should short 1.41 (703.75/500) June SP500 futures contracts. Of course shorting 1.41 contracts is impossible; not being too risk averse, the investor decides to short just one contract.

The results of the investor's strategy are displayed in the lower half of Exhibit 16.7. Given the general market decline over the period, the investor's loss on the stock portfolio was $3,569 after incorporating all dividend income earned over the period. However, the June SP500 settlement futures price on May 31 was 287.50, yielding a profit of $2,175 on the short futures position. Thus the net profit on the hedge was −$1,394. The cross-hedge was successful in offsetting part of the loss on the stock portfolio.

There are several reasons why the loss was not completely offset and why the investor was not assured a risk-free rate of return. Foremost, the investor was not fully hedged because he could not short 1.41 contracts. The indivisibility of futures contracts frustrated the hedging strategy. Other possible causes include nonstationary betas and an underdiversi-

EXHIBIT 16.7

Hedging a Stock Portfolio

MARCH 1

Stock	Price	Shares	Value	Weight	Beta
DuPont	$94.375	800	$75,500	.349	0.85
Enron	37.250	200	7,450	.034	0.70
Jamesway	11.125	200	2,225	.010	0.70
Motorola	42.125	600	25,275	.117	1.15
Navistar	6.125	400	2,450	.011	1.25
Penzoil	80.875	600	48,525	.224	1.05
Polaroid	42.000	300	12,600	.058	1.10
Xerox	60.250	700	42,175	.195	0.90
			Total Value $216,200		

Portfolio Beta = (.349) (0.85) + (.034) (0.70)+ . . . + (.195) (0.90)
        = 0.95

June SP500 futures price = 291.85

Futures price per contract = $145,925

Write 1 contract

MAY 31

Stock	Price	Value	Dividends
DuPont	$91.125	$ 72,900	$224
Enron	35.750	7,150	36
Jamesway	11.000	2,200	0
Motorola	39.875	23,925	180
Navistar	6.250	2,500	0
Penzoil	80.875	48,525	210
Polaroid	41.250	12,375	0
Xerox	60.250	42,127	231
	Total Value $211,750	Total Dividends $881	

June SP500 futures price = 287.50

Futures price per contract = $143,750

Profit on stock portfolio = −$3,569

Profit on futures position = $2,175

Net profit = −$1,394

fied stock portfolio. Yet the important point to recognize is that because of the introduction of negative correlation the hedge was largely successful in protecting the investor's wealth. Without hedging, the investor's dollar loss would have been nearly three times as great.

Resolving Stock Selection and Market Timing Conflicts

A portfolio manager can earn excess returns by two means: superior stock selection and superior market timing. Stock index futures allow the manager to separate these activities, thereby resolving any conflicts between the two. For instance, suppose that a manager thinks the market will generally decline in the near future. However, the manager has also identified a number of undervalued high-beta stocks. Holding such stocks presents a problem: any abnormal returns attributable to the stocks' undervaluation may be more than offset by their systematic price movements as the market declines. However, the manager can still buy the stocks while hedging against market risk via shorting stock index futures. For instance, suppose the portfolio manager identifies an equity portfolio that will earn 2 percent above its equilibrium return but reduces market exposure by being one-half in Treasury bills. The return on the portfolio will be only 1 percent above equilibrium value. Shorting index futures, however, will earn the full 2 percent on the portfolio.

Similarly, a manager can buy undervalued low-beta stocks when the forecast calls for a market rise by assuming a long position in the futures market. Here it is not necessary to forgo riding bull swings by purchasing low-beta stocks. In addition, therefore, the returns earned on the futures contracts represent a proxy for measuring the market timing abilities of the manager.

Hedging a Bond Portfolio

Just as stock index futures contracts can be used to alter the beta of an equity portfolio, interest rate futures can be employed to alter the duration of a bond portfolio. Suppose that it is March 1 and a pension fund manager holds AAA-rated corporate bonds with $5 million of face value, a coupon rate of 12 percent, and a maturity of nearly twenty years. The bond is priced at 117 per $100 par value and its yield is 10 percent. The bond's duration is 9.09 years.

Assume that the bonds must be sold on June 1 to meet scheduled pension payments. The manager is concerned about an unexpected increase in market interest rates during this period, since such an increase will reduce the market value of the bonds and thus may cause the fund to fail to meets its liability. Consequently the manager seeks to employ the June Treasury bond futures contract to cross-hedge against the possibly adverse effects of interest rate changes. The current June futures price is 87-22 (read eighty-seven and twenty-two thirty-seconds of a dollar of face value), or $87,687.50 per contract (a $100,000–face value contract).

Because of the delivery option in the Treasury bond futures market, the Treasury bond futures price tends to track the cheapest-to-deliver bond. Hence the pension fund manager must identify this unique bond to determine the duration and implied yield on the June futures contract. This information is needed to compute the price sensitivity hedge ratio described in Appendix 16B. Suppose that the manager identifies the cheapest to deliver as the Treasury bond with coupon 10⅜ and maturity of about twenty-five years. If the futures contract expired on the first day of the delivery month, June 1, and the futures price was 87-22, then the

deliverable bond has a duration of 8.96 years and a yield of .1194.
With these figures the price sensitivity hedge ratio is –68.87:

$$N_f = -\left[\left(\frac{9.09}{8.96}\right)\left(\frac{5,850,000}{87,687.50}\right)\left(\frac{1.1194}{1.1100}\right)\right] = -68.87.$$

Thus the fund manager will short sixty-nine Treasury bond futures contracts to immunize the current bond value of $5,850,000.[4] If interest rates rise unexpectedly, this short position will offset most, if not all, of the loss incurred on the long corporate bond position. In other words, shorting 69 Treasury bond futures contracts should drive the bond portfolio's duration from 9.09 years down to 0.

Exhibit 16.8 illustrates this concept. In this exhibit it is assumed that on June 1 the bond price is down to 110-20 and the June futures price is down to 82-31. The pension manager sells the bonds for $5,531,250, sustaining a loss of $318,750. However, the profit on the short futures position is $4,718.75 per contract, or $325,593.75. Thus the short hedge was sufficient to overcome all of the loss sustained in the spot position. This type of strategy is suitable for many investors who hold fixed-income securities, including banks, mutual funds, insurance companies, and the like.

EXHIBIT 16.8

Hedging a Long Corporate Bond Position

MARCH 1

Spot market
  Current bond price is 117–20
  Current value of bonds held is $5,850,000
Futures Market
  June Treasury bond futures price is 87–22
  Price per contract is $87,687.50
  Short 69 contracts

JUNE 1

Spot market
  Sell AAA-rated bonds at 110–20
  Price per bond is $1,106.26
  Value of bond position is $5,531,250
Futures market
  Reverse short position at 82–31
  Price per contract is $82,968.75
  Profit on short position:
    $325,593.75 = (82,968.75 – 87,687.50) (–69)
  Overall portfolio value:
    $5,856,843.75 = 5,531,250 + 325,593.75
  Overall profit = $6,843.75

---

[4] Accrued interest is ignored, since it is not subject to any uncertainty; the coupon rate on the bonds held is fixed at 12 percent.

Hedging a Country Fund against Exchange Rate Risk

Currency futures contracts can be employed to reduce the exchange exposure of an internationally diversified security portfolio. For instance, consider a country fund such as the Fidelity United Kingdom Fund or the Fidelity Canada Fund. The dividends and capital gains earned by these funds have to be periodically repatriated into U.S. dollars, exposing the fund's investors to exchange rate risk. By shorting currency futures contracts, however, the funds' management can insulate investors against adverse currency movements. Management must estimate the number of units of foreign currency to be converted to dollars and then contract to sell this number in futures at the prespecified rate of exchange (the futures price). A naive hedge ratio is usually a judicious choice, since currency spot and futures prices are very highly correlated.

The potential benefits of currency hedging are depicted graphically in Figure 16.2. The top curve shows the risk-reducing benefits of purely domestic diversification, and the middle curve shows the added benefits of overseas diversification (discussed in Chapter 8). The bottom curve in Figure 16.2 depicts the additional effect of hedging currency risk through futures trading.

Several empirical studies have documented that hedged international portfolios exhibit less risk than their unhedged counterparts. For instance, Madura and Reiff (1985) estimated the returns of country stock indices with and without hedging (from a U.S. perspective), to determine the degree of risk reduction achievable from currency hedging. They

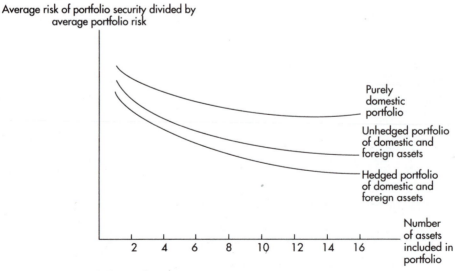

FIGURE 16.2
Risk Reduction from Currency Hedging

THE CORRELATION OF CURRENCY SPOT AND FUTURES PRICES

The correlation structure between spot exchange rates and currency futures prices is assessed by regressing spot currency returns onto contemporaneous returns on nearby futures contracts. The regression estimation uses settlement prices for the first trading day of each week for IMM-traded contracts on the British pound, Deutsche mark, and Japanese yen. Spot exchange rates are obtained from the *Wall Street Journal.* The sample period is January 1981 through December 1990. The sample is divided into two subsets: (1) January 1981 through May 1985, reflecting a strong U.S. dollar; and (2) June 1985 through December 1990, reflecting a weak U.S. dollar.

The correlation coefficients for each currency for both periods are reported below. In each case the correlation between currency spot and futures returns is over 90 percent, suggesting a strong and direct relationship. This evidence implies that the naive hedge ratio should be effective when engaging in direct currency futures hedging.

| | Correlation Coefficients | |
Currency	Strong Dollar	Weak Dollar
British pound	.94	.97
Deutsche mark	.96	.98
Japanese yen	.98	.92

---

developed an *ex post* efficient frontier of unhedged portfolios and compared it with an efficient frontier of hedge portfolios. The hedged portfolios exhibited about half the variance for a given return level. These results are due to higher variances of unhedged stock index returns and higher covariances between the unhedged stock index returns. Eun and Resnick (1988) documented similar benefits on an *ex ante* basis.

ALPHA FUNDS

As noted in the chapter introduction, futures contracts are also employed in more proactive asset allocation strategies. The remainder of this chapter is devoted to this subject, beginning here with alpha funds.

An alpha fund is a relatively new type of mutual fund that involves the trading of stock index futures contracts. Specifically, an alpha fund is created by continually engaging in a short index futures position such that the preexisting equity portfolio's beta is maintained at zero. An alpha fund therefore exhibits no systematic risk and has an *expected* return equal to the riskless rate of interest. Our previous hedging strategy entailing stock index futures effectively created an alpha fund. An interesting aspect of these funds is that they allow participants to assess the stock selection performance of the funds' managers. The *actual* return earned on the fund will be equal to the riskless rate plus a (nonsystematic) gain or loss attributable to stock selection. This additional return component is called the alpha, hence the name alpha fund. A positive alpha indicates superior stock selection, and a negative alpha indicates the opposite. Unfortunately, we are not aware of any empirical evidence regarding the performance of alpha funds.

COMMODITY FUNDS

A publicly traded commodity fund (also called a futures fund) is similar to any mutual fund in that investors buy shares and the proceeds are pooled and managed by a professional manager known as a commodity pool operator.[5] What is unique about these funds is that they invest about 20 percent to 30 percent of their capital in financial, metallurgical, and agricultural futures contracts, both long and short. The remaining capital is typically held as cash and in money market instruments to accommodate drawdowns. These funds allow small public traders to participate in futures markets with reduced risk due to diversification, lower susceptibility to margin calls, and lower transaction costs.

Commodity funds began in the late 1970s, and over eight hundred exist today. The funds are actively managed and are speculative in nature. Most operators have taken a technical approach to managing their funds.

Two empirical studies, Elton, Gruber, and Rentzler (1987) and Irwin and Brorsen (1985), have focused on the performance of commodity funds. Both reported rather dismal findings. Elton, Gruber, and Rentzler found that for the period 1980–1988 commodity funds averaged a 2.3 percent annual return and a 10.4 percent standard deviation of monthly returns. During this same period the SP500 had an average annual return of nearly 15 percent and a 4.9 percent monthly standard deviation. The Shearson bond index had an average annual return of 11.4 percent and a monthly standard deviation of 2.4 percent. Irwin and Brorsen attributed much of this poor performance to high management fees and commissions. The average commodity fund's operating costs were over 19 percent!

CHANGING MARKET AND INTEREST RATE EXPOSURES

Earlier we examined how managers could utilize stock index and interest rate futures contracts to hedge their preexisting asset positions fully. Of course managers of mixed funds composed of stocks and bonds could similarly hedge. However, managers often seek to alter their market and interest rates exposures less dramatically, and so they employ futures contracts to fine-tune their exposures. An equity fund manager may

---

[5] Commodity pools are often organized as limited partnerships.

trade index futures to affect the fund's beta without driving it to zero. Analogously, bond fund managers can make small changes in their fund's duration through trading interest rate futures. Indeed, this method may be the only one available to alter duration if the portfolio consists of thinly traded government or corporate bonds.

A principal advantage of trading futures to fine-tune exposures is the relatively low transaction costs. For instance, it is substantially less costly to trade index futures than, say, to trade stocks and Treasury bills to change the portfolio beta. It is also less costly to trade index futures than to engage in stock swaps.

Managers who engage in market timing activities often use futures to exploit their forecasts of market turns. For example, bond fund managers are typically timers, trading interest rate futures to alter their portfolio duration. Thus the profits earned on their futures trading activities can often be a useful barometer of managers' timing abilities.

FUTURES IN INDEX FUND MANAGEMENT

Index fund managers truly have a difficult time exactly matching the performance of the target index, which results in tracking error. There are several causes of tracking error, including changes in the composition of the target index itself, dividend payments, and transaction costs. In addition, a frustrating problem is that a cash position must be maintained by the fund to accommodate investors who liquidate their positions (redemptions). Indeed, some index funds have even begun to impose penalties on investors who do not stay with the fund for a prescribed period of time.

The major consequence of holding a cash position is that the fund's beta will be slightly below 1 (with respect to the target index). As a result the fund's management will commonly maintain a long position in index futures to raise the beta to 1 and consequently to reduce tracking error. This practice is important from the manager's perspective, since compensation is typically partly determined by how closely he or she replicates the index's return performance.

We should also note that a few managers may synthetically replicate the index through trading Treasury bills and index futures, if the futures contracts are deemed to be mispriced. This synthetic strategy is identified in Chapter 19. Clearly, however, such an approach to index fund management cannot be regarded as passive.

Finally, index futures are now being blended with traditional index funds to create new classes of mutual funds that may appeal to younger investors. For example, Vanguard is now considering the creation and offering of a "1.2" fund, a combination of an ordinary index fund and a sustained long index futures position with a resulting beta of 1.2. Such a fund would offer low expenses like a typical passive index fund but would provide greater returns in appreciating markets.

FUTURES IN PENSION FUND MANAGEMENT

Pension funds have liability streams that in turn have durations determined by actuarial factors like the life expectancies of the participants, disability rates, and the like. To hedge against interest rate exposure, pension fund managers can match the durations of the asset (bonds) and liability streams, a practice commonly called immunization. Of course this practice implies massaging the asset duration, since the liability duration cannot be altered (save killing off a pensioner or two). Pension fund managers therefore commonly employ interest rate futures contracts to affect asset duration and thus interest rate exposure. Other institutions engage in a similar practice.

This practice is particularly evident when interest rates are so high that even long-term bonds have short durations. Here pension fund managers simply cannot find bonds with sufficient durations to match those of their liabilities streams. Consequently, long positions in interest rate futures contracts are required for immunization.

SUMMARY

A futures contract represents an agreement to trade an underlying asset in the future for a prescribed price that is determined today. Although futures contracts can be used for speculation and for price discovery, their principal purpose is to help investors hedge the risk of a preexisting spot asset position. By combining an appropriate futures position with a preexisting spot asset position, a trader effectively creates a negatively correlated two-asset portfolio. The hedged portfolio's return depends on changes in the basis—the difference between spot and futures prices—and its volatility is determined by the variance of the basis—known as basis risk. Since basis risk is substantially lower than the risk associated with merely holding the preexisting spot asset—an unhedged position—investor utility can be enhanced through futures trading. Such trading can also be more cost effective than alternative means of altering portfolio composition, such as liquidating risky assets and purchasing short-term Treasury bills or engaging in stock swaps. Futures are popular derivative securities and are regularly employed by portfolio managers to immunize against adverse changes in equity prices, interest rates, and foreign exchange rates. In addition, they are used in more proactive asset allocation strategies by alpha funds and commodity funds, and they represent a relatively inexpensive means of altering a portfolio's market and interest rate exposure. They are also used by index funds to reduce tracking error.

Questions and Problems

1. Describe the roles played by clearinghouses and margin deposits in assuring contract performance.

2. Describe an initial margin, a maintenance margin, and a variation margin.

3. Describe how the vast majority of futures contracts are closed out.

4. Assume that on Monday, March 1, you enter a futures contract to buy one CBOT March Treasury bond futures contract at $98,156.25 (98⁵⁄32). The initial margin is $2,500, and the maintenance margin is $2,000. For simplicity, you do not withdraw excess monies from your margin balance. All margin requirements are met with cash and no interest is earned. You hold your long position through Friday, March 5. Then you sell the contract (a reversing trade) at the opening price of $98,125.00 (98⁴⁄32) on Monday, March 8. Presented below is a schedule of assumed prices. Using Exhibit 16.2 as a guide, fill in the following information cells. Also, be sure to determine your gross profit on the entire transaction.

TRADING DATE	SETTLEMENT PRICE	MARKED TO THE MARKET	OTHER ENTRIES	ACCOUNT BALANCE
3/1	$98,000.00 (98⁰⁄32)			
3/2	96,250.00 (96⁸⁄32)			
3/3	96,750.00 (96²⁴⁄32)			
3/4	98,093.75 (98³⁄32)			
3/5	98,937.50 (98³⁰⁄32)			
3/8	98,125.00 (98⁴⁄32)			

5. Describe an alpha fund and a commodity fund.

6. What are the major differences between forward and futures contracts?

7. Describe basis risk. Why is basis risk less than the risk associated with an unhedged position?

8. What factors must the futures hedger consider when choosing a hedging strategy? Explain how each decision is consistent with minimizing basis risk.

9. Explain the difference between a short hedge and a long hedge, and provide an example of each.

10. Define a cross-hedge. When would a trader engage in one?

11. Define the hedge ratio. What three hedge ratios were employed in this chapter?

12. Using equation 16.2, explain why a growing (i.e., strengthening) basis benefits a short hedge and impairs a long hedge.

13. Describe how stock index futures can be employed to resolve conflicts between stock selection and market timing.

14. Assume you forecast that the yield curve will flatten; i.e., the spread between long and short interest rates will narrow. Discuss a futures trading strategy that you may employ to exploit your forecast.

15. Assume you are managing the six-stock portfolio described below. It is April 18, and you intend to sell your stock holdings on June 1. Anticipating a possible market decline over the next six weeks, you decide to employ June SP500 futures contracts to hedge fully. The futures price is 300, and none of the stocks go ex-dividend prior to June 1. Determine the profit outcome of the hedge if the resulting futures price on June 1 is 294 and the resulting stock prices are as given below.

| | | | PRICES | |
STOCK	SHARES	BETA	APRIL 18	JUNE 1
A	1,000	1.25	$20.125	$20.250
B	2,500	1.09	34.500	31.875
C	1,900	1.35	9.125	8.875
D	3,100	0.80	51.750	50.000
E	1,400	0.63	14.875	14.125
F	800	1.16	29.125	27.250

Questions 16 and 17 refer to the following information: Suppose that on August 27 a portfolio manager holds $2 million face-value Treasury bonds with a coupon of 11⅞ maturing in nearly nineteen years. The bonds sell at 101 per $100 par value, and the yield is 11.75 percent. The duration of the bonds is 7.83 years. The bonds must be sold on October 1, and concerned about the prospect of rising interest rates, the manager decides to hedge using the December Treasury bond futures contract. The futures price is 70-16. The cheapest-to-deliver bond, which this price is tracking, has a coupon of 10⅜ and matures in twenty-five years. Its duration is therefore 7.2 years, and its yield is 14.91 percent.

16. How many December Treasury bond futures contracts will the manager write? In other words, what is the price sensitivity hedge ratio?

17. Suppose that on October 1 the Treasury bond price is 97-12 and the December futures price is 67-28. What is the profit on the bond position? What is the profit on the futures position? What is the overall profit?

18. Suppose that a U.S.-based country fund that specializes in U.K. stocks needs to transfer £2 million from a bank account in London to an account in New York. The transfer will be made early next June. How many June BP futures contracts should the fund's management short? Assume that a naive hedge ratio is used. Also, what are the net profits from the hedge assuming the following price information?

	SPOT EXCHANGE RATE	JUNE FUTURES PRICE
Today:	$1.7225/£1	$1.7076/£1
Early June:	$1.6720/£1	$1.6640/£1

19. Describe how index futures are employed to facilitate the management of index funds.

20. Suppose that U.S. interest rates are extremely high, around 30 percent. What problems does this condition present for pension fund managers, and how can they use futures contracts to resolve these problems?

Self-Test Problems

Self-test problems 1 through 6 refer to the following information:

STOCK	SHARES	BETA	SHARE PRICES AUG. 1	SEPT. 1	SEPT. SP500 FUTURES AUG. 1	SEPT. 1
A	900	1.25	8.750	9.250	225.15	232.50
B	700	0.80	21.250	22.000		
C	1,400	0.75	14.750	14.500		
D	2,000	0.95	33.500	36.250		
E	1,600	1.05	68.250	71.125		
F	300	1.45	19.750	20.000		
G	300	0.55	28.750	28.250		
H	1,100	1.80	26.250	26.750		
I	600	1.05	41.500	44.125		
J	800	0.95	38.000	40.500		

ST-1. Assume that you hold the above portfolio and that it is August 1. What is each stock's portfolio weight?

ST-2. What is the portfolio's beta?

ST-3. Assume that you want to hedge the portfolio fully. How many September SP500 futures contracts should you write?

ST-4. Assume that you liquidated your portfolio on September 1 at the given prices. Assume no dividends were paid over the period. What was the stock portfolio's profit?

ST-5. What was the profit on the futures position, given that the September SP500 futures price was 232.50 on September 1?

ST-6. What was the net profit from the hedge?

Solutions to Self-Test Problems
ST-1.

STOCK	VALUE	WEIGHT
A	$ 7,875[a]	0.0244[b]
B	14,875	0.0461
C	20,650	0.0641
D	71,000	0.2203
E	109,200	0.3388
F	5,925	0.0184
G	8,625	0.0267
H	28,875	0.0896
I	24,900	0.0772
J	30,400	0.0943
Total Value	$322,325	

[a]E.g., $900 \times 8.750 = \$7,875$.
[b]E.g., $\$7,875 / 322,325 = .0244$.

ST-2. $\beta_S = 0.0244(1.25) + 0.0461(0.80) + \ldots = 1.0537$.

ST-3. $[\$322,325 / (500 \times 225.15)] \times 1.0537 = 3.017$. Therefore short three contracts.

ST-4. $(\$9,250 - 8,750)(900) + (22.00 - 21.250)(700) + \ldots + (\$40,500 - 38,000)(800) = \$10,775$.

ST-5. $(232.50 - 225.15) \times (-3) \times (\$500) = -\$11,025$.

ST-6. $\$10,775 - 11,025 = -\$250$.

APPENDIX

16A

Futures Pricing

This appendix concerns the determination of futures prices. Two related approaches are presented. The first focuses on the costs of carrying assets forward in time. This approach represents the *carrying charge theory* of futures prices. The second focuses on expectations about future spot prices. We shall refer to it as the *expectations approach*. Before turning to our two approaches, however, it is useful to distinguish between price and value.

Price Versus Value

It is important to distinguish between price and value when dealing with forward and futures contracts. The forward or futures price is the price at which the contract parties agree to exchange the underlying asset in the future. As such, it simply represents an observable figure on a contract. It is not the contract's value. In general, the contract's value is determined by unanticipated changes in the asset's spot price, which in turn "cause" subsequent changes in forward and futures prices.

In this appendix we are vitally concerned with the determination of *prices*, that is, we are concerned with how market participants go about determining the prices at which they agree to trade assets in the future. Still, some statements about contract value are appropriate at this time.

Contract Value at Inception

The value of a forward or futures contract is zero at the contract's inception. This follows from the fact that neither party to the contract sells or receives anything of monetary value. The long position (the buyer) does not pay for the contract and the short position (the seller) does not receive any money for the contract. Indeed, with a forward contract no cash flow occurs until contract expiration, and the futures margin is only a security deposit, not a contract payment. Provided that the forward or futures price does not change, neither party can profit. Thus the contract generates value only when prices subsequently change and has no value when the contract is initially transacted.

Forward Contract Value at Expiration

At expiration the forward contract calls for immediate delivery of the underlying asset. Thus the forward price at contract expiration must be equal to the asset's prevailing spot price, ignoring delivery costs and multiple qualities of the deliverable asset. Since no cash flow has occurred prior to expiration, the value of the forward contract at expiration must equal the spot price at expiration minus the original forward price.

Forward Contract Value Prior to Expiration

Assuming that no default risk exists, the value of a forward contract prior to expiration is the difference between the new forward price and the original forward price discounted at the risk-free rate of interest over the remaining time to contract expiration. For example, assume that you buy a forward contract today with a forward price of $1. This contract expires in six months. Now suppose that in four months there exist new forward contracts expiring at the same time (in two months), transacted at a forward price of $1.05. Assuming that the risk-free rate is 8 percent, the value of your forward contract is $0.04934:

$$\$0.04934 = (\$1.05 - \$1)e^{(2/12)(-.08)}.$$

This value follows from simple arbitrage restrictions. When both forward contracts expire in two months, you can buy the underlying asset for $1 with the first contract and sell the asset for $1.05 with the second contract. Your proceeds are $.05. Since no default risk is assumed to exist and the forward prices are known, these proceeds are discounted at the risk-free rate to yield a present value of $0.04934. Any other contract value would result in riskless profit opportunities, ignoring market imperfections.

Futures Contract Value

As noted before, the value of a futures contract is zero at the contract's inception. However, the contract's value is also zero each time the contract is marked to the market. Suppose that you long a futures contract. Its current value is zero. By later in the trading session, however, the futures price has increased. At this point you can profit by conducting a reversing trade. The contract has value. Once the trading session is over, however, the contract is marked to the market, and any proceeds are credited to your margin account. Thus the contract's value reverts to zero.

THE CARRYING CHARGE THEORY OF FUTURES PRICES

The carrying charge theory of determining futures prices evolves from arbitrage restrictions related to the costs of carrying an asset forward in time. Before we turn to this approach, it is important to discuss the concepts of carrying charges, the basis, and spreads.

Carrying Charges

The three costs of carrying an asset forward in time are storage, transportation, and financing. Define SC, TC, and FC as the storage, transportation, and financing costs, respectively, of carrying a particular asset forward to contract delivery. Also, let SC, TC, and FC be expressed as a percentage of the underlying asset's spot price. Therefore the total cost of carrying an asset to contract delivery, expressed in percentage form, is

(16A.1) $$CC = SC + TC + FC,$$

where CC is the total percentage cost. CC represents the total carrying charges particular to the underlying asset. For instance, suppose that the asset in question exhibits storage costs equal to −1.5 percent of the spot price and transportation costs of .5 percent of the spot price. An asset can exhibit a negative cost of storage if it pays dividends or interest over the carrying period. Also let the current repo rate be 10 percent. The repo rate is the interest rate on repurchase agreements and often represents the cost of financing an asset faced by a futures trader, especially if the asset in question is a financial security. A repurchase agreement (or *repo*) is an arrangement in which a security owner sells the security to a financial institution with the agreement to repurchase it, often just one day later (an overnight repo). The repo rate is relatively low, typically exceeding the rate on U.S. Treasury bills by a small amount, because anyone wanting to finance the security purchase can offer the security itself as collateral for the loan. Given $SC = -.015$, $TC = .005$, and $FC = .100$, the percentage carrying charges for the asset total to 9 percent:

$$CC = -.015 + .005 + .100 = .09.$$

Thus if the spot price is $100 and contract delivery occurs in one year, then assuming continuous compounding, the futures price will be approximately $109.42:

$$\$109.42 = \$100e^{(.09)(1)}.$$

This futures price reflects the cost of carrying the asset to delivery.

The Basis

The basis is defined as the difference between the spot price and the futures price:

(16A.2) $$Basis = spot\ price - futures\ price.$$

Under the carrying charge theory of futures prices the basis represents the dollar cost of carrying an asset forward in time. For instance, in the above illustration the basis is −$9.42. This represents the dollar cost of carrying the asset to delivery in one year.

There are a few important points to remember concerning the basis. First, the basis depends on the spot price of a commodity at a specific location. By the law of one price an asset should not sell for different prices in two markets. However, because of frictions such as search and transportation costs, the price of, say, corn may be different in Nebraska than in Pennsylvania. This difference likely arises because of the added transportation costs of shipping corn to Pennsylvania. Since the spot price of corn differs between these two locations, the basis will also differ according to delivery location.

Second, the basis should approach zero as the delivery date approaches. This is evident from the fact that the futures and spot prices must be equal at delivery, ignoring transaction and transportation costs as well as different qualities of the deliverable asset.

Third, the basis typically is the difference between the spot price and the nearby futures price. However, there is a basis for each delivery date. When measured in absolute value, the basis should be greater for more deferred contracts, reflecting the added dollar charges of carrying an asset forward over a progressively longer time period.

Spreads

The difference between two futures prices is often called a spread. A spread may entail two futures contracts written on the same underlying asset but with different delivery dates. This combination produces an *intracommodity spread*. An *intercommodity spread* is the difference between the prices of futures contracts exhibiting the same maturity but different underlying assets.

Intracommodity spreads (also called *time spreads*) are important for determining futures prices. The prices of nearby and more deferred futures contracts should be intimately related. Arbitrage restrictions ensure such relationships. Under the carrying charge theory the time spread should reflect the different dollar costs of carrying an asset forward to different delivery dates. For instance, if the maturity of our futures contract is six months instead of one year, then the futures price will be $104.60, not $109.42.

Carrying Charges and Futures Prices

Armed with the above terminology and concepts, we are now ready to demonstrate how futures prices are determined by arbitrage restrictions. To begin, suppose that a trader observes a spot asset price of $100, $CC = .09$, but a one-year futures price of $115. Recall that the futures price should be $109.42 to reflect carrying costs accurately. To exploit this situation the trader can undertake the following transactions:

Today: Buy one unit of the asset for $100 in the spot market

Arrange to carry the asset forward for one year at a cost of $9.42

Short the one-year futures contract, contracting to sell the asset in one year for $115

In one year: Remove the asset from storage and deliver it against the futures contract, collecting $115

These transactions represent a winning arbitrage strategy, assuring proceeds of $5.48 per unit of the underlying asset in one year. The original transactions assured the trader of the positive proceeds while requiring no investment. There is no investment because no cash outflow occurs at inception of the trading strategy. The trader borrowed the money required to purchase the asset and to carry it forward through time. The cost of borrowing the capital is already reflected in CC vis-à-vis the financing cost component, FC.

The above transactions are an example of *cash and carry arbitrage*. Cash and carry arbitrage is a theoretically riskless transaction involving a long position in the spot asset and a short position in the futures contract that is held until contract delivery. As the trader executes the cash and carry arbitrage, the spot and futures prices, and perhaps the carrying charges, should change in such a way that arbitrage is no longer profitable. Exactly how prices and carrying charges will change is difficult to determine. In general, however, they should change to reflect the following condition:

(16A.3)
$$_Tf_o = S_o e^{CC(T)},$$

where $_Tf_o$ is the futures price today for a contract with delivery in T years and S_o is the current spot price of the asset. For instance, if S_o remains unchanged at $100 and CC remains unchanged at 9 percent, then the one-year futures price, $_1f_o$, should converge to $109.48:

$$\$109.48 = \$100e^{(.09)(1)}.$$

If the observed futures price was below $109.48, then an analogous strategy known as reverse cash and carry arbitrage would lead to riskless profits.

Equation 16A.3 expresses the carrying charge theory of futures prices under perfect market conditions. Equation 16A.3 states that the current futures price must equal the asset's spot price plus the cost of carrying the asset forward to contract delivery. Equation 16A.3 follows from arbitrage restrictions. Also notice from equation 16A.3 that the basis is given by $S_o[e^{CC(T)} - 1]$:

$$\$9.42 = \$100[e^{(.09)(1)} - 1].$$

Implicit Assumptions Underlying the Carrying Charge Theory

The carrying charge theory invokes two important assumptions: (1) no default risk exists; and (2) carrying charges are constant over the life of the futures contract. For example, consider the strategy employed when $S_o = \$100$, $CC = .09$, and $_1f_o = \$115$. Ignoring transaction costs, a profit of $5.58 could be attained by buying the asset, storing it for one year, and shorting the one-year futures contract. However, this profit is certain only if (1) the long futures trader does not default on the contract, and (2) the carrying charges ($9.42) do not vary over the year.

It is reasonable to assume that the long futures trader does not default, since daily resettlement substantially reduces default risk and the clearinghouse guarantees both sides of the contract. However, the assumption that carrying charges are constant is suspect. Although transportation costs are likely to be small and inflexible, both storage costs and financing costs are likely to vary somewhat over time. Storage costs can vary if the underlying asset is a financial security that pays dividends or interest. Such payments can vary intertemporally, causing the storage cost component of CC to be nonconstant. Financing costs can also change over time because market rates of interest are time-varying. For instance, the overnight repo rate changes on a nearly continuous basis. Still, term financing can reduce most uncertainties significantly.

THE EXPECTATIONS APPROACH TO DETERMINING FUTURES PRICES

The costs of carrying an asset forward in time greatly influence the relationships (1) between the futures price and the current spot price and (2) among the asset's nearby and deferred futures prices. However, because futures contracts entail the delivery of an asset at a future date, we should anticipate that futures prices are largely determined by the expectations of market players concerning the asset's spot price at delivery. The expectations approach of determining futures prices stresses the role of market expectations in generating futures prices. We investigate this approach below under the assumptions that investors are risk neutral and that no daily resettlement occurs.

The Forward/Futures Price under Risk Neutrality and No Daily Resettlement

Suppose that we are considering buying an asset in T years. Also suppose that the current yield to maturity on risk-free bonds is $_TY_o$, if these bonds exhibit a maturity of T years. Further, suppose that we purchase $(1 + {}_TY_o)^T$ forward or futures contracts today and that each contract obligates us to buy one unit of the underlying asset at the forward or futures price. Since we assume no daily resettlement, the forward and futures contracts and their prices are identical. Additionally, we buy $\$_Tf_o$ worth of the risk-free bonds with T years to maturity, where $_Tf_o$ is the forward or futures price. Since this price is established so that the initial value of the forward or futures contract is zero, our total initial investment must be $\$_Tf_o$.

In T years the forward or futures contracts expire and their value is given by

(16A.4)
$$\$(1 + {}_TY_o)^T(\tilde{S}_T - {}_Tf_0),$$

where $\tilde{S}_T$ is the asset's spot price at contract maturity. Of course this price is currently unknown. The payoff from the bond investment is

(16A.5)
$$\$_Tf_o(1 - {}_TY_o)^T.$$

Therefore, combining 16A.4 and 16A.5 gives our total proceeds from the investment:

(16A.6) $\$(1 + {}_TY_o)^T(\tilde{S}_T - {}_Tf_o) + {}_Tf_o(1 + {}_TY_o)^T = \$(1 + {}_TY_o)^T\tilde{S}_T$

Thus, we invest $\$_Tf_o$ and receive $\$(1 + {}_TY_o)^T\tilde{S}_T$. By arbitrage it must therefore be true that the current forward or futures price is equal to the present value of $\$(1 + {}_TY_o)^T\tilde{S}_T$. Ignoring market imperfections, any other price would give rise to arbitrage opportunities.

To determine this present value we discount the expected proceeds of the investment: $E[(1 + {}_TY_o)^T\tilde{S}_T] = (1 + {}_TY_o)^T E(\tilde{S}_T)$. We can discount at the risk-free rate if investors are risk neutral. Thus the present value is

(16A.7) $${}_Tf_o = \frac{(1 + {}_TY_o)^T E(\tilde{S}_T)}{(1 + {}_TY_o)^T} = E(\tilde{S}_T).$$

Hence the current forward or futures price, ${}_Tf_o$, is equal to the asset's expected spot price at contract expiration, $E(\tilde{S}_T)$, if investors are risk neutral and we ignore daily resettlement.

Equation 16A.7 is a very powerful result. It states that under risk neutrality and no daily resettlement (and ignoring market frictions such as transaction costs), the observed forward or futures price represents the marketplace's expected spot price at contract expiration. Hence if you wish to obtain a market-determined forecast of the subsequent spot price and are willing to live with the assumptions of risk neutrality, no daily resettlement, and perfect markets, then you need only observe the current forward or futures price. This price is said to be an unbiased predictor of the future spot price under these assumptions.[6] Equation 16A.7 is commonly called the unbiased forward rate (price) hypothesis.

Of course if any of the above assumptions are violated, then the price is no longer an unbiased predictor. There have been several theoretical and empirical investigations regarding this issue. For a summary see Tucker (1991, Chapter 6).

---

[6] An unbiased predictor/estimator occurs if and only if the expected value of the estimator equals the actual value of the parameter being estimated.

16B

Hedge Ratio Derivations

This appendix provides derivations of (1) the minimum variance hedge ratio, used in hedging applications involving stock index futures, and (2) the price sensitivity hedge ratio, used in hedging applications entailing interest rate futures. We also show that the naive hedge ratio is merely a special case of the minimum variance hedge ratio.

THE MINIMUM VARIANCE HEDGE RATIO

The one-period rate of return on a long position in a stock index futures contract, denoted $\tilde{R}(f)$, is given by:

(16B.1)
$$\tilde{R}(f) = [\tilde{I}(1) - {}_1f_0]/I(0),$$

where ${}_1f_0$ is the one-period futures price, $I(0)$ is the spot value of the index underlying the futures contract (e.g., SP500), and $\tilde{I}(f)$ is the end-of-period value of the underlying stock index, which is unknown.

Now consider a hedged portfolio constructed by shorting one index unit of the futures contract for each spot index unit held. For instance, if you hold an index fund (tied to the SP500) whose capital value is equal to 1,000 units of the SP500, then you short 1,000 units of the SP500 futures (or two SP500 futures contracts, since the contract multiplier is $500). The rate of return on the hedged portfolio, denoted $R(H)$, is

(16B.2)
$$R(H) = \tilde{R}(I) - \tilde{R}(f) = \frac{\tilde{I}(1) - I(0)}{I(0)} + \delta - \frac{\tilde{I}(1) - {}_1f_0}{I(0)} = \frac{{}_1f_0 - I(0)}{I(0)} + \delta,$$

where δ is the index's dividend yield. Notice that the hedged portfolio's return exhibits no uncertainty, since ${}_1f_0$, $I(0)$, and δ are all observable and known today. Hence, by arbitrage and the law of one price the hedged portfolio's return must equal the riskless rate: $R(H) = r$. This result implies a necessary equilibrium relationship between $\tilde{R}(I)$, r, and $\tilde{R}(f)$. Specifically, substituting r for $R(H)$ gives us

(16B.3)
$$r = \tilde{R}(I) - \tilde{R}(f),$$

or

(16B.4)
$$r = \frac{{}_1f_0 - I(0)}{I(0)} + \delta.$$

Also notice that rearranging equation 16B.4 yields

(16B.5)
$$_1f_0 = I(0)[1 + r - \delta].$$

Equation 16B.5 is nothing more than the one-period version of the carrying charge model for index futures prices.

Most portfolios are not index funds designed to replicate a broad market index. Suppose that an equity portfolio manager holds an arbitrary stock portfolio whose current value is $V(0)$. Define N_S as the number of index units of value in the spot portfolio and N_f as the number of index units sold short in the futures market. Thus $N_S = V(0)/I(0)$ and the hedge ratio, h, equals N_f/N_S. By varying h, the manager can obtain an entire set of portfolio risk-return combinations yielding a wide range of choice for a given stock portfolio.

The expected rate of return on the hedged portfolio, $E[\tilde{R}(H)]$, is given by

(16B.6)
$$E[\tilde{R}(H)] = E[\tilde{R}(S)] - hE[\tilde{R}(f)],$$

where $E[\tilde{R}(S)]$ is the expected return on the stock portfolio. The negative sign in equation 16B.6 denotes that a short futures position has been undertaken. Using the concepts related to portfolio return variance learned in Chapter 2, the variance of return for the hedged portfolio is

(16B.7)
$$VAR[\tilde{R}(H)] = VAR[\tilde{R}(S)] + h^2 VAR[\tilde{R}(f)] - 2hCOV[\tilde{R}(S), \tilde{R}(f)].$$

Figure 16B.1 portrays the portfolio risk-return possibilities achieved for different values of h. The point where $h = 0$ corresponds to an unhedged position, and here, $E[\tilde{R}(H)] = E[\tilde{R}(S)]$ and $VAR[\tilde{R}(H)] = VAR[\tilde{R}(S)]$. Differentiating equation 16B.7 and solving for the minimum risk portfolio yields[1]

(16B.8)
$$h = COV[\tilde{R}(S), \tilde{R}(f)]/VAR[\tilde{R}(f)].$$

Substituting $R(I) - r$ for $R(f)$ (see equation 16B.3) in equation 16B.8 gives

(16B.9)
$$h = COV[\tilde{R}(S), \tilde{R}(I)]/VAR[\tilde{R}(I)] = \beta_S.$$

Equation 16B.9 states that the minimum variance hedge ratio is the stock portfolio's beta.[2] By selling β_S index units of futures against each unit

---

[1] $dVAR[\tilde{R}(H)]/dh = 2hVAR[\tilde{R}(f)] - 2COV[\tilde{R}(S),\tilde{R}(f)]$. Setting this equal to zero (to determine an optimum) and solving for h gives equation 16B.8. A check of the second-order condition ensures a minimum.

[2] Actually, the minimum variance hedge ratio is only the stock portfolio's beta if the index underlying the futures contract represents the market portfolio. However, since the indices underlying the traded futures contracts are broadly diversified, equation 16B.9 likely yields an accurate estimate of the portfolio's beta.

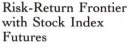
Risk-Return Frontier
with Stock Index
Futures

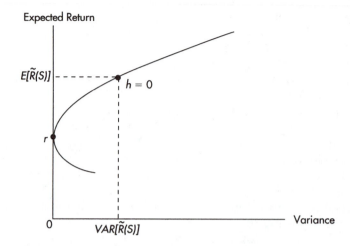

in the portfolio the investor hedges all market (i.e., systematic) risk. In other words, the manager effectively drives the equity portfolio's beta down to zero. This alters the market risk of the portfolio without changing its stock composition. Of course unsystematic risk is diversified away via holding adequate numbers of stocks. Hence the expected return on the fully hedged (zero beta) portfolio must be the risk-free rate, labeled r in Figure 16B.1.

The Naive Hedge Ratio: A Special Case

Suppose that the manager did not oversee an arbitrary equity portfolio but instead managed an index fund designed to replicate the futures contract's underlying index. Recognizing that $\tilde{R}(S) = \tilde{R}(I)$, we can rewrite equation 16B.9 as follows:

(16B.10) $h = COV[\tilde{R}(I), \tilde{R}(I)] / VAR[\tilde{R}(I)] = 1.$

In other words, the hedge ratio that minimizes risk is 1, that is, short one index unit in the futures market for each index unit held in the spot index fund. Such a one-to-one correspondence is known as a naive hedge. The naive hedge ratio equals one. Thus we can conclude that the naive hedge ratio is merely a special case of the minimum variance hedge ratio; the naive hedge ratio obtains when the preexisting equity portfolio's beta is one. In more general terms we can state that the naive hedge ratio holds whenever the spot asset being hedged is perfectly positively correlated with the asset underlying the futures contract. Thus if you hold an index fund, the appropriate hedge ratio is one. However, if the equity portfolio's beta is, say, .5, then you need to short only half the number of index futures contracts.

The Price Sensitivity Hedge Ratio

The basic idea underlying the price sensitivity hedge ratio is this: determine a position in the interest rate futures contract such that wealth is insulated from changes in interest rates. To obtain this ratio, assume that interest rate changes on all bonds result from a change in a single interest rate, r, which is the risk-free government bond rate. In other words, when r changes, so too do all other bond yields (a one-factor model).

For the next point it is necessary to define the following variables:

S is the price of the bond held in the spot market.
f is the price of the interest rate futures contract.
Y_S is the yield on the spot bond held.
Y_f is the yield on the futures contract implied by f.

A hedged portfolio can be constructed by assuming a position in the futures contract along with the spot bond position held:

(16B.11)
$$V = S + V_f N_f,$$

where V is the value of the hedged portfolio, V_f is the value of the futures contract, and N_f is the price sensitivity hedge ratio. It is N_f that we wish to determine.

The change in V with respect to a change in r is determined by taking the total derivative, dV/dr. Since $dV_f/dr = df/dr$, we have

(16B.12)
$$dV/dr = dS/dr + (df/dr)N_f.$$

To ensure that the hedge portfolio's value is insulated from changes in interest rates, we set the total derivative equal to zero. Since we do not know the derivatives dS/dr and df/dr, we employ the chain rule for differentiation:

(16B.13)
$$dV/dr = \frac{dS}{dY_s} \times \frac{dY_s}{sr} + \frac{df}{dY_f} \times \frac{dY_f}{dr} \times N_f = 0.$$

Notice that this procedure introduces the yield changes dY_S/dr and dY_f/dr into the analysis. It is usually assumed that these yield changes are equal. Thus, substituting and solving for N_f gives us

(16B.14)
$$N_f = -[(dS/dY_S)/(df/dY_f)].$$

The discrete version of equation 16B.14 is approximated by

(16B.15)
$$N_f = -[(\Delta S/\Delta Y_S)/(\Delta f/\Delta Y_f)].$$

Equation 16B.15 represents one form of the price sensitivity hedge ratio. However, it is useful to express N_f in terms of the durations of the bond and futures contract. The duration of the spot bond, D_S, can be approximated as follows:

(16B.16)
$$D_S \approx -[(\Delta S/S)(1 + Y_S)]/\Delta Y_S.$$

Similarly, for the futures contract, duration is approximated by[3]

(16B.17)
$$D_f \approx -[(\Delta f/f)(1 + Y_f)]/\Delta Y_f.$$

Letting $\Delta Y_f = \Delta Y_S$ and substituting in equation 16B.15 gives

(16B.18)
$$N_f = -[D_S S(1 + Y_f)]/[D_f f(1 + Y_S)].$$

Equation 16B.18 is the price sensitivity hedge ratio.

REFERENCES

Arak, M., and L. Goodman. 1987. Treasury bond futures. Valuing the delivery option. *Journal of Futures Markets* 7:269–286.

Breeder, D. 1980. Consumption risk in futures markets. *Journal of Finance* 35:503–520.

Chang, E. 1985. Returns to speculators and the theory of normal backwardation. *Journal of Finance* 40:193–208.

Chiang, R., G. Gay, and R. Kolb. 1983. Interest rate hedging. An empirical test of alternative strategies. *Journal of Financial Research* 6:187–197.

Cornell, B. and M. Reinganum. 1981. Forward and futures prices: Evidence from the foreign exchange markets. *Journal of Finance* 36:1035–1046.

Cox, C., J. Ingersoll, and S. Ross. 1981. The relation between forward and futures prices. *Journal of Financial Economics* 10:321–346.

Dusak, K. 1973. Futures trading and investor returns: An investigation of commodity risk premiums. *Journal of Political Economy* 81:1387–1406.

Ederington, L. 1979. The hedging performance of the new futures markets. *Journal of Finance* 34:157–170.

Elton, E., M. Gruber, and J. Rentzler. 1984. Intra-day tests of the efficiency of the Treasury bill futures market. *Review of Economics and Statistics* 66:129–137.

Elton, E., M. Gruber, and J. Rentzler. 1987. Professionally managed publicly traded commodity funds. *Journal of Business* 61:175–199.

Eun, C., and B. Resnick. 1988. Exchange rate uncertainty, forward contracts, and international portfolio selection. *Journal of Finance* 43:197–215.

Fama, E. 1976. Forward rates as predictors of future spot rates. *Journal of Financial Economics* 3:217–239.

Fama, E. 1984. Forward and spot exchange rates. *Journal of Monetary Economics* 319–388.

---

[3]Actually, the duration of a futures contract, D_f, refers to the duration of the bond underlying the contract as of the date of the contract's expiration.

Figlewski, S. 1984. Hedging performance and basis risk in stock index futures. *Journal of Finance* 39:657–669.

Figlewski, S., and S. Kon. 1982. Portfolio management with stock index futures. *Financial Analysts Journal* 38:52–60.

French, K. 1983. A comparison of future and forward prices. *Journal of Financial Economics* 12:311–342.

Gay, G., and R. Kolb. 1982. Immunizing bond portfolios with interest rate futures. *Financial Management* 11:81–89.

Gay, G., and R. Kolb. 1984. The quality option implicit in futures contracts. *Journal of Financial Economics* 13:353–370.

Hicks, J. 1939. *Value and capital*, ed 2. Oxford: Clarendon Press.

Houthakker, H. 1957. Can speculators forecast prices? *Review of Economics and Statistics* 39:143–151.

Johnson, L. 1960. The theory of hedging and speculating in commodity futures markets. *Review of Economic Studies* 27:139–151.

Kane, A., and A. Marcus. 1986. Valuation and optimal exercise of the wild card option in the treasury bond futures market. *Journal of Finance* 41:195–207.

Keynes, J. 1930. *A treatise on money*. London: Macmillan.

Irwin, S., and B. Brorsen. 1985. Public futures funds. *Journal of Futures Markets* 5:463–485.

Jarrow, R., and G. Oldfield. 1981. Forward contracts and futures contracts. *Journal of Financial Economics* 9:373–382.

Levich, R. 1983. Currency forecasters lose their way. *Euromoney* 140–147.

Madura, J., and W. Reiff. 1985. A hedge strategy for international portfolios. *Journal of Portfolio Management* 70–74.

Park, H. and A. Chen. 1985. Differences between futures and forward prices: A further examination of the marking-to-the-market effects. *Journal of Futures Markets* 5:77–88.

Richard, S., and M. Sundaresan. 1981. A continuous time equilibrium model of forward prices and futures prices in a multigood economy. *Journal of Financial Economics* 10:347–372.

Roll, R. 1985. Orange juice and weather. *American Economic Review* 861–881.

Treus, A., and D. Jacob. 1986. Futures and alternative hedge methodologies. *Journal of Portfolio Management* 12:60–70.

Tucker, A. 1991. *Financial futures, options, and swaps*. St. Paul: West.

Weiner, N. 1981. The hedging rationale for a stock index futures contract. *Journal of Futures Markets* 1:59–76.

Williams, J. 1987. Futures markets: A consequence of risk-aversion or transactions costs. *Journal of Political Economy* 95:1000–1023.

Option Contracts

Introduction

Like futures contracts, options are derivative securities that can be employed to alter the risk and expected return of a security portfolio. In this chapter we examine how stock index options, interest rate options, and currency options can be used by portfolio managers to change their exposure to systematic market risk, interest risk, and exchange rate risk, respectively.[1] Thus, consistent with our treatment of futures contracts in Chapter 16, we will stress hedging applications and proactive asset allocation strategies and will relegate option pricing issues to Appendix 17A.

This chapter also proceeds like Chapter 16. First we define an option and discuss related terminology. We also describe common institutional features and individual contract specifications. Next we discuss the various uses of options, focusing on hedging techniques. Following that we illustrate some specific hedging and asset allocation strategies. We conclude the chapter with a brief description of option funds.

---

[1] We principally analyze spot, or cash, options in this chapter. Appendix 17B discusses options on futures contracts.

OPTIONS: DEFINITION AND TERMS

An option contract conveys the right but not the obligation to purchase or sell an underlying asset at a specified price on or before a specified date. The underlying asset may be common stock, gold, foreign exchange, a stock market index, or other asset. An option contract specifies the amount of this underlying asset. For instance, a standard stock option contract involves a hundred shares of stock. The specified price is determined at contract inception and is known as the option's exercise price, or strike price. Most trading involves an option whose underlying asset price is close to its exercise price; this is known as an *at-the-money* option. The specified date is the option's expiration, or expiry, date. Often these dates are three, six, or nine months from the option's inception, although shorter and longer maturity options exist. For instance, long-term equity options, called LEAPs, have recently begun trading on the Chicago Board Options Exchange. LEAPs have maturities out to about three years.

If the option buyer has the right to purchase the underlying asset, the buyer owns a call option. For instance, the buyer may own an option to purchase (call) 100 shares of Ford stock in three months at an exercise price of $90 per share. Of course, whether the call option buyer exercises that right is contingent on the price of Ford stock at the option's expiration. He will exercise it only if Ford stock is selling above $90 per share at that time. For this reason options are often called contingent claims. Alternatively, if the option buyer has the right to sell the underlying asset, then the buyer is said to own a put option. For example, a put option buyer may have the right to sell (put) 100 shares of IBM in three months at an exercise price of $70 per share. Whether this right (option) is exercised or not is contingent on IBM's stock price in three months.

An option contract also involves a seller, or option writer. In the example of Ford stock the call option writer agrees to sell the hundred shares at $90 each should the buyer exercise the call option. For the IBM put option, the writer agrees to buy the shares at $70 each. Of course the option writer charges a price for selling the option. The price should reflect the present value of the buyer's right. Its determination is the subject of Appendix 17A.

Option contracts can be either European or American. With a European option the buyer may exercise only at expiration. With an American option, however, the buyer may exercise prior to the option's maturity. It may be in the buyer's interest to exercise an option prematurely. Hence an American option typically commands a greater price than an otherwise equivalent European option; the buyer pays a premium to be able to exercise prematurely. Quantifying this early exercise premium can be difficult. This issue is also addressed in Appendix 17A. Most trading involves American-style options.

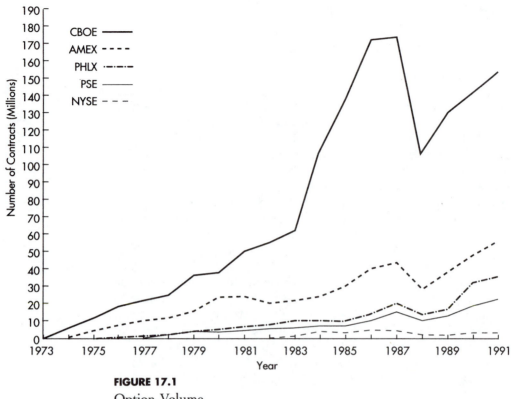

FIGURE 17.1

Option Volume

The volume of options trading has grown rapidly over the past two decades. Figure 17.1 portrays option volume for a recent period for the five major U.S. option exchanges: the Chicago Board Options Exchange (CBOE), the American Stock Exchange (AMEX), the Philadelphia Stock Exchange (PHLX), the Pacific Stock Exchange (PSE), and the New York Stock Exchange (NYSE). The CBOE accounts for about 56 percent of all trading volume and will likely command a greater share of the total market due to the recent deregulation of stock options trading. Historically an exchange was awarded the exclusive right to trade options on listed stocks through a lottery system established by the SEC. Beginning January 1991, however, options can be traded on any of these five exchanges. The CBOE also retains a large market share because of its popular SP100 stock index option. This contract, which began trading on March 11, 1983, and is called OEX, its ticker symbol, was the first stock index option ever traded. Contract volume is over 120 million annually. Later we will examine how the OEX can be used to alter the market risk of equity portfolios and index funds.

COMMON INSTITUTIONAL FEATURES

Each of the three types of option contracts that we'll examine in this chapter exhibit some common institutional features. For instance, they may be traded on organized exchanges (such as CBOE) or on an over-the-counter (OTC) market. Organized option exchanges evolved in response to the illiquidity of OTC options. Today the majority of options are listed. Yet there is an active OTC stock option market as well as a growing interbank market for European currency options. Here banks write tailored options on foreign exchange for their commercial customers. There is also a growing OTC market for exotic options that exhibit unique features such as extendable lives, floating exercise prices, and payoffs that depend on the greater of two or more asset prices.

Option Players

Ignoring transaction costs, options trading (like futures trading) is a zero-sum game. In other words any profits (losses) experienced by option buyers are offset by the losses (profits) experienced by option writers. Once transaction costs are included, however, total options trading must sum to less than zero. Yet options trading may result in utility gains through the transfer of risk between the market players. These players are option hedgers and speculators.

Hedgers. An option buyer or writer who employs the option to reduce risk is a hedger. As we saw in the previous chapter, hedgers can employ futures contracts to reduce risk. Unlike futures hedging, however, option hedging generally eliminates downside risk while allowing the hedger to capture any potential upside gain. Examples of option hedging are provided later in this chapter. For now, suffice it to say that options can facilitate the transfer of price uncertainty (risk), thus enhancing the expected utility of risk-averse hedgers.

Speculators. An option buyer or writer who uses options primarily to profit is a speculator. In principle a speculator accepts the hedger's unwanted risk in order to generate profits. Since speculators are by definition less risk averse than hedgers—that is, the cost of risk to the speculator is less—the transfer of risk from hedgers to speculators can result in net utility gains. Such potential gains underlie the very existence of options.

With futures contracts we saw that arbitrage plays an important role in determining prices. As shown in Appendix 17A, arbitrage activities also determine option values. An option player who engages in arbitrage should be regarded as a speculator. The arbitrageur trades to exploit profit opportunities that are rarely risk free.

The Clearing Corporation

An essential part of any organized options market is its clearing corporation. For all U.S. option markets except those trading futures options, the Options Clearing Corporation (OCC) standardizes contracts and facilitates trading and option exercise. The OCC was formed in 1975 from the option clearinghouse of the CBOE. When an option trade is initiated, the OCC acts as a dealer creating two separate contracts: one option between the buyer and the OCC acting as the writer and one between the writer and the OCC acting as the buyer. The OCC guarantees both sides of the contract. This procedure facilitates trading and promotes liquidity. For instance, the buyer can close a position by simply selling offsetting contracts (an *offset*), and the writer can buy into a previous position. Also, should the buyer decide to exercise the option, the OCC randomly selects a writer to accept exercise. This writer is said to be *assigned*.

Margins

An option writer is a source of credit risk to the OCC. For example, an uncovered call option writer (one who does not own the underlying asset) may have insufficient funds to purchase the underlying asset should the call buyer exercise. To insure itself the OCC requires the writer to post margin, usually in cash. For covered options writing, this cash margin is often set equal to the market price of the option plus a percentage of the underlying asset's value. This percentage varies as the option's price changes through time. Margins for uncovered options writing are greater because of the added risk involved. Margin requirements are more complicated when writing option combinations. Finally, the option buyer has no margin requirement; the most the buyer can lose is the original purchase price of the option, so the buyer is not a credit risk to the OCC.

Position and Exercise Limits

Further to ensure contract performance, option exchanges impose limits on the number of contracts that a trader can hold. For example, the Philadelphia Exchange imposes a position limit of 50,000 contracts for its listed currency options. Position limits are applied to one side of the market. Purchased calls and written puts are considered one side of the market because each contract's value increases (decreases) as the underlying asset's price increases (decreases). In other words, purchased calls and written puts are positively correlated positions. Written calls and purchased puts also constitute one side of the market. Thus a currency option trader who both writes calls and purchases puts on the same underlying currency is limited to a position of 50,000 contracts. Of course different exchanges impose different position limits on their option contracts.

Exchanges sometimes impose exercise limits as well. An exercise limit is the total number of option contracts that may be exercised within some specified time. The imposition of exercise limits also serves to ensure contract performance.

Executing Trades

Option trades are executed in a similar manner across markets. Assume you (the client or principal) want to purchase an IBM call contract, with $65 exercise price and December expiration, at market. The option trades on the CBOE. *At market* means that you are willing to buy at the best current price.

The process begins with a phone call to your agent (account executive or broker), who must trade through an exchange member. A member may be a market maker or floor broker. Typically a floor broker's seat is financed by a trading firm such as Prudential-Bache. Thus calling an account executive or broker of a trading firm effectively gives you access to a floor broker. The price of an exchange seat varies directly with the level of trading volume. Recently an exchange seat at the CBOE sold for over $400,000.

Your agent places the order by booking and clocking it and relaying it electronically to the firm's floor broker on the exchange. A floor broker executes trades for public clients and earns a commission on each trade. Trading is conducted in a designated pit for the particular option involved. The floor broker then shouts a bid of, say, $3. This bid is countered by offers to sell from other traders on the exchange floor. The floor broker accepts the lowest counteroffer, say $3.125, implying a contract price of $312.50 ($3.125 × 100 shares per stock option contract). The two traders match tickets, confirming the trade in pencil on slips of paper. The buying trader hands these slips of paper to an exchange official, who quickly checks them and passes them to an exchange employee. The employee enters the trade information into the CBOE's computerized reporting system. This information is flashed on the trading floor screens and private wire service screens. Traders monitor these screens throughout the day. The time of the price agreement (trade) to the time the information is flashed is usually less than two minutes. The floor broker wires confirmation of the trade back to the agent, who notifies you of your completed trade and its price. The entire execution process typically takes place in a few minutes, and the agent later forwards a written confirmation of the trade. You pay a commission charge to buy the option (and pay another should you later sell or exercise the option).

You must deposit the $312.50 with an OCC member clearing firm by the next business morning. Typically your broker or account executive handles this process by withdrawing funds from your established account.

This money is credited to the option writer, who must post the appropriate initial margin by the same morning. When all of this occurs the trade is cleared through the OCC member clearing firm.

The counteroffer of $3.125 may have come from another floor broker serving as an agent for another client. Alternatively the counteroffer may have been made by a market maker at the CBOE. Market makers are entrepreneurs who trade for themselves. They are also charged with the duty of satisfying a public order. That is, they must be willing to buy or sell an option when no other public trader (acting through a floor broker) is willing to transact. Thus, as the title suggests, the market maker ensures that a public order can be filled. However, their performance in fulfilling this duty has often been called into question.

A market maker earns a living by buying at one price and selling at another, higher price. This process is accomplished by continuously quoting a bid price and an ask price on a particular option. The bid price is the maximum price that the market maker is willing to pay, and the ask price is the minimum price at which he will sell the option. The ask price is higher, of course, resulting in a bid-ask spread. Exchange regulation and market competition prevent this spread from being too large. Still, the bid-ask spread is an important cost for those who must transact with a market maker. Presently an average spread at the CBOE is about one-eighth of a point (e.g., bid $3, ask $3.125). Individuals and institutional option traders can have immediate and continuous access to bid and ask prices via on-line private wire service screens.

Market makers are sometimes called scalpers or position traders, depending on their trading behavior. Scalpers trade actively in short-term positions on both sides of the market, and position traders take longer-term positions, perhaps for a few hours or entire trading session.

Types of Orders

Besides placing a market order (an order to trade at the best available price), you may have placed any of the following order types, many of which were discussed in Chapter 16:

- Limit order. Stipulates a specific price at which you are willing to trade; a limit order can be a day order, which is good only for the trading day on which it is placed, or an open order, which is good until canceled. At the CBOE the order book official (an exchange employee) tracks and transacts all limit orders.
- Fill-or-kill order. Instructs the floor broker to fill the order immediately at a specified price; if the order cannot be filled quickly at this price, then it is canceled.
- All-or-none order. Allows the floor broker to fill part of the order at one specified price and part at another specified price.
- On-the-open or on-the-close order. Orders to trade only within a few minutes of opening or closing, respectively.

- Stop order. Triggers a transaction when prices hit a certain level. Unlike limit orders they are used to protect against losses on existing positions.

Other Systems of Executing Trades

The CBOE trading system just described is called a market maker system. Some exchanges, namely the American and Philadelphia, use a slightly different system known as a specialist system. Here a specialist must make the market and transact limit orders. Thus the specialist handles the tasks of both the market maker and order book official. Also at the American and Philadelphia exchanges are registered option traders (ROTs) who can both trade for themselves and act as floor brokers. This is known as dual trading. At the CBOE an individual can be both a market maker and floor broker, but not during the same trading session.

Transaction Costs

The following transaction costs are realized from options trading:
- Floor trading and clearing fees. These are the small fees charged by the OCC, a clearing firm member, and the exchange itself. If the trade is executed through a broker, these fees are built into the broker's commission. Market makers pay these fees directly, so they are implicit in the bid-ask spread.
- Commissions on options. A broker charges a commission to handle an order. Full-service brokers charge higher commissions than discount brokers. Currently the commission on an option trade, one way, is about $30 for one contract at a discount brokerage.
- Commissions on spot assets. Exercising an option implies the trading of the underlying spot asset. Thus commissions may also have to be paid on the underlying asset.
- Bid-ask spreads. A bid-ask spread is incurred when transacting via a market maker or specialist. This spread imposes a sizable transaction cost paid for obtaining trading immediacy. Studies have shown that the spread can be greater than 4 percent of the option's value.

Taxation

Determining the tax consequences of options trading can be complex. Below we provide a few generally applicable tax guides:
- Gains. The realized gains from options trading are taxed at the ordinary personal income tax rate.
- Losses. The realized losses are deductible by offsetting them against any other investment gains. If losses exceed gains, the excess up to $3,000 is deductible against ordinary income.

- Nonequity options. Options on indices, foreign exchange, and other nonequity options exhibit the following special tax consideration: all unrealized gains are taxed at the ordinary income rate and all unrealized losses are deductible as described above.
- Commissions. In general, brokerage commissions are tax deductible.

Market Regulation

The SEC is the primary regulator of options trading, including the trading of options on individual common stocks, stock indices, and foreign exchange. CFTC is the primary regulator of all futures options. The regulatory process also consists of self-regulation by the exchanges and OCC as well as regulation by the National Association of Securities Dealers (NASD), state authorities, and other agencies.

These regulatory agencies interact to ensure contract performance and to prevent illegal and manipulative practices that might erode the integrity of the market and the confidence of the trading public. For instance, regulation seeks to ensure the competency of brokers and prevent abusive trading practices. These agencies are also empowered to review new contract proposals, listing requirements, position limits, and the like. Overall the U.S. options industry has a good record of performance since the inception of listed options trading in 1973.

CONTRACT SPECIFICATIONS

In this section we describe the contract specifications particular to stock index options, interest rate options, and currency options.

Stock Index Options

The tremendous success of the OEX quickly led to the development and trading of stock index options on the other organized exchanges. Highly successful contracts include the major market index (first traded on the AMEX less than two months after the inception of the SP100 option) and the NYSE composite index (traded on the NYSE). Taken together, annual trading volume in all stock index options is about three-fourths of the combined annual trading volume of all listed stock options.

Exhibit 17.1 describes the various index options now offered on organized exchanges. The contracts can be categorized as belonging to one of two groups, broad market indices or more specialized industry indices. Options on broad market indices are those written on the SP100, SP500, MMI, Value Line index, national OTC index, and the NYSE composite index. Options on industry indices include those written on the computer technology index, the gold/silver index, the utilities index, and others.

EXHIBIT 17.1

Currently Traded Index Options

Index	Exchange	Description
A: BROAD MARKET INDICES		
SP100	CBOE	100 stocks weighted by market value
SP500	CBOE	500 stocks weighted by market value; European
Major Market Index	AMEX	20 blue-chip stocks weighted by price; highly correlated with SP100 and SP500
Value Line Index	PHLX	1700 stocks equally weighted and geometrically averaged
National OTC Index	PHLX	100 OTC stocks weighted by market value
NYSE Composite	NYSE	All NYSE stocks weighted by market value
B: INDUSTRY INDICES		
Computer Technology Index	AMEX	30 computer stocks weighted by market value
Oil Index	AMEX	15 oil stocks weighted by market value
Institutional Index	AMEX	75 stocks held widely by institutions and weighted by market value; European
Gold/Silver index	PHLX	7 mining stocks weighted by market value
Utilities Index	PHLX	20 electric utility stocks weighted by market value
Financial News Composite Index	PSE	30 blue-chip stocks weighted by price; European

These specialized index options were developed to attract traders who analyzed specific industries. However, volume in these contracts has been insignificant, disappointingly so for exchange officials. For this reason we will concentrate on the broader market options such as the OEX.

Index options exhibit some unique features that differentiate their trading from that of individual stock options:

- A contract multiple. The size of an index option contract is defined as some multiple of the underlying index. For instance, the OEX has a multiple of 100, meaning that the option contract buyer actually purchases 100 options.
- Cash settlement. When an index option is exercised, the writer pays the buyer cash equal to the contract multiple times the difference between the index level and exercise price. For example, if a put index option is exercised and the contract multiple is 100, the index level is 300, and the exercise price is 310, then the assigned writer pays the put buyer $1,000: $100 \times (310 - 300)$. We cannot determine whether the put buyer made a profit here, since we do not know the price paid for the option.
- End-of-day exercise. When an index option is exercised, the index value occurring at market closing is used to determine the cash settlement. Therefore traders find it optimal to wait until the end of the trading session to exercise; it is possible to order the exercise of an in-the-money index option during the day only to find at the close that it is out of the money.

- Expiration cycle. Some of the most liquid index options have frequent expiration cycles. For instance, the OEX has a cycle consisting of the current month plus the next three consecutive months, reflecting its popularity among traders.
- Taxation. Stock index options have a different tax status than ordinary stock options. Specifically, at the end of the calendar year all realized and unrealized gains are taxed as ordinary income. Also, all losses (both realized and unrealized) can be offset against other investment gains.

Interest Rate Options

A number of different securities can be safely described as being an interest rate option or containing an embedded interest rate option. The ability to refinance a home mortgage is a type of interest rate option. The call provision exhibited by most long-term bonds is an interest rate option. Caps, floors, and collars on variable-rate loans and interest rate swaps are forms of interest rate options.[2]

Concerning exchange-traded interest rate options, there are two types: (1) those traded on bonds, such as the AMEX's Treasury note options and the CBOE's Treasury bond options; and (2) those traded on interest rate futures, such as the Treasury note and Treasury bond futures options traded on the CBOT and the Eurodollar futures options traded on the CME. The former are traded on fixed-income securities, and the latter are traded on futures contracts written on fixed-income securities.[3]

We will concentrate on interest rate futures options because these are the more liquid type of exchange-traded interest rate option. They are more popular for two important reasons. First, a trader can readily obtain an interest rate futures quote to price a futures option, but obtaining a real-time bond quote can be very difficult. The futures contracts are actively traded on an organized market, but bond trading is principally OTC, and bond quotes are often stale. Second, it is easier to deliver a futures contract against the futures option than to deliver a bond against the spot option. Exhibit 17.2 provides contract specifications for the three interest rate futures options mentioned above.

EXHIBIT 17.2

Specifications for Interest Rate Futures Options

Underlying Futures Contract	Contract Size	Exercise-Price Interval	Minimum Price Fluctuation	Exchange
U.S. Treasury Bond	$ 100,000	2 points	1/64 pt.	CBOT
U.S. Treasury Note	$ 100,000	2 points	1/64 pt.	CBOT
Eurodollar	$1,000,000	25 basis points	1/64 pt.	CME

[2] We examine interest rate swaps and their caps, floors, and collars in Chapter 18.

[3] Again, see Appendix 17B for a general discussion of futures options.

EXHIBIT 17.3

Contract Specifications for PHLX-Traded Currency Options

Currency	Symbols[a]	Exercise-Price Intervals	Underlying Units	Premium Quotations
Australian Dollar	CAD XAD	$0.0100	50,000	Cents per unit
British Pound	CBP XBP	$0.0250	31,250	Cents per unit
Canadian Dollar	CCD XCD	$0.0100	50,000	Cents per unit
Deutsche Mark	CDM XDM	$0.0100	62,500	Cents per unit
French Franc	CFF XFF	$0.0050	125,000	Tenths of a cent per unit
Japanese Yen	CJY XJY	$0.0001	6,250,000	Hundredths of a cent per unit
Swiss Franc	CSF XSF	$0.0100	62,500	Cents per unit
ECU	ECU	$0.0200	62,500	Cents per unit

Note: For all contracts: (1) expiration months are March, June, September, and December, plus two additional near-term items; (2) the expiration date is the Saturday before the third Wednesday of the expiration month; (3) the expiration settlement date is the third Wednesday of the month; (4) the margin for an uncovered writer is the option premium plus 4 percent of the underlying contract value less the out-of-the-money amount if any, to a minimum of the option premium plus .75 percent of the underlying contract value, which equals the spot price times the number of units per contract; (5) the position limit is 50,000 contracts; (6) the delivery method requires the call buyer (seller) to deliver dollars (foreign currency) to an OCC domestic (foreign) bank account; the opposite is the case for puts.

[a]C = European options, X = American options. Only America ECU options are traded.

Currency Options

Beginning in December 1982 the Philadelphia Stock Exchange began trading American-style options on the British pound. The PHLX now offers American options trading on seven foreign currencies: the Australian dollar (AD), the British pound (BP), the Canadian dollar (CD), the Deutsche mark (DM), the French franc (FF), the Japanese yen (JY), and the Swiss franc (SF). The PHLX also provides side-by-side trading of European-style options on these seven currencies. The PHLX also trades options on the ECU, a weighted-average index of exchange rates for the member nations that make up the European Economic Community. However, trading volume has been very low for ECU options.

Exhibit 17.3 presents the contract specifications for the seven individual currency options now traded on the PHLX. All currency options are cleared and guaranteed by the OCC. In addition, if an option is exercised, then traders must deposit currency to OCC-approved bank accounts.

The volume of listed currency options trading has grown tremendously since the inception of trading. For the period 1983 to 1992, annual volume increased more than 25-fold to over 10 million contracts. The most popular contracts are those on the DM and JY, accounting for approximately 60 percent of all trading volume. Growth in currency options trading is also exemplified by the recent advent of evening and early morning trading sessions. The PHLX now trades currency options for 20.5 hours of each trading day.

USING OPTION CONTRACTS

Options can be used to speculate on forecasts of subsequent spot asset price changes. To profit from a forecast of appreciation the investor can purchase a call option or write a put option. Reciprocally an investor who anticipates a depreciation of the underlying asset's value should write a call or purchase a put. Such transactions offer greater leverage than simply trading the spot asset itself. Of course to profit the speculator must be correct on two accounts: that the spot price moves in the direction forecast and that it does so prior to option expiration. In addition, traders can employ option combinations to profit from a given forecast. Popular combinations include bull money spreads, bear money spreads, straddles, strips, and straps. These combinations are simply portfolios of options that exhibit particular payoff patterns and thus can be used to exploit predicted spot price changes. In addition, options and option spreads allow speculators to wager on forecasts of changing security volatility; as described in Appendix 17A, the volatility of the returns on the underlying security is an important determinant of option value.

While options are often used for speculative purposes, the principal reason for their existence and popularity is their ability to alter the risk of a preexisting spot position. For instance, buying a put option ensures a minimum price (the exercise price) at which the underlying asset can be sold in the future. Buying a call option ensures a maximum price at which an asset has to be bought in the future. Below we present some popular and powerful strategies that employ option contracts to alter the exposures of preexisting spot asset positions. After this presentation we illustrate some specific applications.

Call Writing

Call writing entails writing call options against an asset already held. By writing a call on the asset, the investor can reduce or eliminate downside risk because any loss incurred on the asset due to a price decline will be offset, at least in part, by the premium received on the written call option. The two positions—long the underlying risky asset and short the call option—are negatively correlated.

Consider a combination of one call option and h units of the underlying asset. The value of this portfolio, V, is given by

(17.1)
$$V = hS + C,$$

where S and C represent the current prices of the spot asset and call option, respectively. To hedge fully, determine the value of the hedge ratio, h, that will immunize V against any changes in the asset's value, S. Taking the total derivative of V with respect to S gives

(17.2)
$$dV/dS = h + dC/dS.$$

To make the portfolio's value V unaffected by changes in S, set dV/dS equal to zero. Solving for h yields

(17.3) $h = -dC/dS.$

Thus the hedge ratio is the negative of the derivative of the call price with respect to the underlying asset's price. This particular derivative is called the option's delta. Its value lies between 0 and 1, implying that the number of units of the asset owned for each written call is between 0 and 1. Thus the hedged portfolio will entail more calls than units of the underlying asset. Intuitively, this result obtains because the (dollar) change in a call option's price will be less than a given (dollar) change in S.

A Numerical Example. Suppose that a call option currently exhibits a delta of .60. In other words, the derivative of the call's price with respect to S is .60. To hedge fully the owner of the underlying asset would write 100 calls for every 60 units of the asset held. For each $1 change in S the call's price should change by about $.60. Thus if the asset's price declines immediately by $1, the $60 loss on the long spot asset position (60 units) will be fully offset by the $60 gain on the short call option position (0.60×100). The investor could buy 100 call options at the new lower price, thereby reversing his short option position and gaining $60 on the option trades. He is now net zero in options. Because of the offsetting nature of the two positions under the call writing strategy, the strategy is often called *delta-neutral hedging*.

Covered Call Writing

In the above illustration the change in asset price will cause the hedge ratio to change.[4] Furthermore, the hedge ratio will change with time as the option contract unwinds. This result implies that in order to remain fully hedged the investor must (in theory) continually rebalance the asset and option portfolio. However, as a practical matter and in light of transaction costs, continual rebalancing is undesirable.

There exists an alternative and simpler strategy known as *covered call writing*. In this static strategy a hedger simply writes one call option for each unit of the asset held. Thus if the number of asset units remains unchanged over the option's life, rebalancing will not occur. Covered call writing may be considered a more realistic and practical hedging strategy than call writing that necessitates continuous rebalancing. Of course the covered call strategy will not fully protect the investor. Instead, the payoffs to the hedged portfolio will vary according to the resulting spot asset price.

A third possibility is discrete-time rebalancing, a hedging strategy that lies on a continuuum between continual rebalancing (delta-neutral

---

[4] Recall that derivatives are local measures only.

hedging) and no balancing (the static covered call writing strategy). Here the investor must determine the optimal rebalancing interval. This decision often depends on the rate of change of delta; in other words, it depends on the second derivative of the option's price with respect to the spot price, *S*. This second derivative is called the option's gamma. A small gamma implies that the hedge ratio, delta, is changing slowly, so rebalancing can occur less frequently and the hedge will remain nearly risk free. The opposite is true for a large gamma.

Selecting an Exercise Price.   The premium received from covered call writing serves to moderate the potential for loss on a long asset position. Because of its easy implementation covered call writing is popular among professional option traders and institutional investors. When writing calls, these traders must select an exercise price. Implementing a covered call strategy at a lower exercise price tends to reduce loss potential but also diminishes the gain potential. On the other hand, implementing a covered call strategy at a higher exercise price will offer more upside potential but less downside protection. Ultimately the choice of exercise price will depend on the writer's degree of risk aversion and forecast of the future spot price.

Synthetic Puts

Covered call writing entails writing one call for each unit of the asset held. But what if you seek to hedge a short position in the underlying asset? Obviously you could lower risk by contracting to buy call options. If the asset price should rise, the loss on the short position would be offset, at least in part, by the gain on the long option position. The two positions are negatively correlated.

Buying one call option for each unit of an asset sold short is known as a *synthetic put*. The name derives from the fact that the payoff to such a strategy resembles the payoff to a put option.

Protective Put Buying

Another popular way that an investor can alter the exposure of a long asset position is through purchasing put options on the asset. This strategy is known as *protective put buying*. With protective put buying the risk associated with a price decline is tempered by the long put position, which increases in value as the spot asset price falls. The two positions—long the asset and long the put option—are negatively correlated.

By fully exploiting this negative correlation through continual rebalancing, you can completely hedge via protective put buying. However, the transaction costs and persistent monitoring costs associated with continual rebalancing are so large that they render such a strategy very impractical. Instead, traders implementing the strategy often purchase one put option for every unit of the underlying asset held. The payoff associated with such a one-to-one strategy resembles the payoff to a call option. For this reason the protective put is also called a *synthetic call*.

Selecting an Exercise Price.   Although all options and other derivative securities can be employed to offer insurance-like protection, the protective put strategy may illustrate this concept best. This strategy provides insurance against downside price risk. If the spot price declines, the put option (i.e., insurance claim) is exercised. If the spot price does not decline, the put is allowed to expire (i.e., no claim is filed) and the cost of the put (i.e., the insurance premium) is sunk.

Choosing an exercise price for the protective put strategy is analogous to choosing a deductible on any insurance contract. By purchasing a higher exercise price put, the investor obtains more protection against downside price risk. However, with each consecutively higher exercise price, the trader pays more for the put options. In other words, the greater the insurance (the lower the deductible), the greater is the insurance premium. Ultimately the choice of an exercise price for the protective put strategy depends on the investor's willingness to trade off risk reduction for the cost of the coverage. This choice underlies virtually any decision regarding insurance; different individuals will contract for different deductibles and levels of coverage given the accompanying costs.

Combining Short Assets and Written Puts

To alter the exposure of the preexisting position we have considered combining long asset positions with written calls and purchased puts and combining short asset positions with purchased calls. The remaining strategy entails combining a short asset position with written puts. Should the spot asset appreciate, the loss on the short asset position will be somewhat offset from the premium realized by writing the put options. Thus the two positions are negatively correlated. And as before, altering the exercise price on the written puts will change the potential for profit.

The payoff to a combination of a short asset position and a short put option resembles the payoff to a written call option. For this reason the combination strategy is sometimes called a *synthetic short call*.

Creating Synthetic Futures Contracts

In Chapter 16 we demonstrated how futures contracts could be used both to hedge and to engage in more proactive asset allocation strategies. Ignoring the effects of daily resettlement, options can be combined to create synthetic futures contracts. Thus certain option combinations can be employed to achieve the same results portrayed throughout Chapter 16.[5]

Options can be held in combination to create a synthetic futures contract. A combination that consists of a written European call and a purchased European put, with the same exercise price (X) and expiration, is identical to a short position in a futures contract with futures price X. A long position in a synthetic futures contract with futures price X is created by purchasing European calls and writing corresponding puts.

As an example, suppose that a U.S.-based international mutual fund that will receive DM625,000 in September purchases ten September DM put option contracts with exercise price $.56/DM and simultaneously writes ten corresponding call option contracts. Each European option contract entails DM62,500. The result is that the multinational corporation can always sell its Deutsche marks at $.56/DM, regardless of how the dollar-DM exchange rate moves between now and September contract expiration. Thus the IMF has created a short position in synthetic DM futures with futures price $.56/DM.

Because synthetic futures can be created by option combinations, close pricing relations should be observed between options and actual futures. Arbitrage restrictions should ensure that the payoffs obtained from actual and synthetic futures strategies are nearly identical. Small differences may arise due to market imperfections.

Hedging Applications

Given our review of hedging strategies and our earlier discussion of the features of option markets and contract specifications, we are now prepared to examine some specific hedging applications. We will examine three, one involving an index fund that employs OEX options to hedge systematic market risk, one involving a long-term bond fund that employs Treasury bond futures options to hedge interest rate risk, and one entailing a country fund that uses currency options to immunize against an unexpected appreciation in the dollar's value.

Hedging with Stock Index Options

Assume that it is March 1 and that an index fund that mimics the SP100 writes SP100 (OEX) April 275 calls. The unit price of each call option is $6.25 and the spot SP100 is 272.29. The fund's market value is $25 million, or about 91,800 units of the SP100 ($25 million divided by 272.29). Since the option contract multiple is 100, the fund's management decides to write 918 contracts. The proceeds from writing these option contracts are $573,750 ($6.25 × 100 × 918).

---

[5] Understanding how futures contracts can be created through option combinations will also help the reader understand the hedging strategy known as portfolio insurance that is presented in Chapter 19.

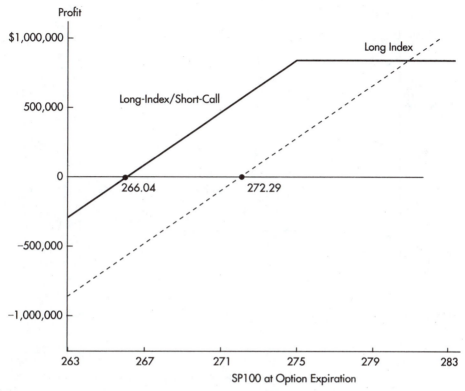

FIGURE 17.2
Profit Graph for Covered Call Writing

Figure 17.2 presents the profit graph for this covered call writing strategy at option expiration (solid line). Also presented is the profit graph for the long index (i.e. unhedged) position (broken line). As the figure demonstrates, the covered call position is less risky. The losses on the stock portfolio are offset in part by the option premium should the index level fall. For the covered call strategy the break-even expiration index level is 266.04 (272.29 − 6.25), whereas it is 272.29 for the unhedged long index position.

Figure 17.3 is another profit graph for our index fund purporting to mimic the SP100. Here the fund's management purchased SP100 April 275 puts for $6.875 per unit. Assuming 918 put contracts were purchased, the figure demonstrates that the protective put strategy is much less risky than an unhedged position. In the event of a market decline the protective put strategy assures the fund of a loss of no more than $382,309.[6]

---

[6]−$382,309 = [(275 − 272.29/272.29)($25,000,000)] − ($6⅞ × 100 × 918). For simplicity we assume that the purchase of the puts does not reduce the investment in the stock portfolio. Index funds typically are not fully funded, holding some cash reserves.

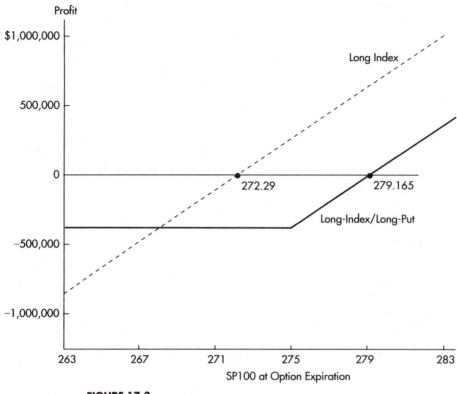

FIGURE 17.3

Profit Graph for Protective Put

HOW A MUTUAL FUND USED STOCK INDEX OPTIONS TO ENDURE THE OCTOBER 1987 CRASH

The U.S. stock market as measured by the SP500 declined in value by 21.6 percent during October 1987. Most of this market crash occurred on Black Monday, October 19, 1987, when the Dow Jones industrial average (DJIA) fell more than 500 points.

Milton Berg, founder and manager of the mutual fund Oppenheimer Ninety-Ten, which is sold by Oppenheimer Management of New York, used stock index options to survive and even profit from the crash.

Mr. Berg invested 90 percent of the fund's assets in money market instruments, stocks, and other financial securities and 10 percent in stock index options. Anticipating the October market decline, Mr. Berg purchased stock index put options in September. As a result the return on Oppenheimer Ninety-Ten was nearly 89 percent for the period 1 January 1987 through 19 November 1987. Contrastingly, the return on the SP500 for this same period was just 1.8 percent.

Of course, the fund's management did not have to trade a full 918 index option contracts. The point is that options can be used efficiently to alter the expected return distribution to meet management objectives, whatever they may be.

Hedging with Interest Rate Futures Options

Assume that it is July 17 and that you manage a long-term corporate bond portfolio with a current value of $10 million and a duration of approximately 15 years. You forecast a rise in long-term interest rates over the next six months, so you wish to hedge your portfolio by reducing its duration. You could sell some bonds and purchase shorter-maturity bonds, but such an approach to reducing duration is costly and unduly restrictive. Instead you decide to alter your interest rate exposure by purchasing Treasury bond futures put options traded on the CBOT. You decide to buy the December puts with exercise price 94 points (94 percent of face value), which are selling for $4,281.25 per contract (or 4 ^{18}⁄₆₄ points per $100 face value, where the contract size is $100,000).[7] Since the bond fund's value is $10 million, you purchase 100 contracts ($10 million divided by $100,000), resulting in an insurance premium of $428,125.[8] Exercising your puts allows you to assume a short position in December Treasury bond futures contracts with a futures price of 94 points (the options' exercise price). Thus if long-term interest rates rise as forecast, the loss on your bond position will be offset, at least in part, by the gains on your put contracts, since the interest rate rise will lower Treasury bond futures prices.[9]

For example, suppose that long-term rates do rise and that at option expiration you sustain a loss of $200,000 on your bond portfolio. However, the new prevailing Treasury bond futures price is 88-12, or $88,187.50. The put options are in the money (88-12 < 94), so you exercise them, assuming a short position in December Treasury bond futures at a futures price of 94. The futures contracts are immediately marked to the market, so the option seller (who is assigned the long futures position) must pay you $5,812.50 per option contract ($94,000 − $88,187.50). Your 100 put contracts are therefore worth $581,250. Since your initial insurance premium was $428,125, your option profit was $153,125. This profit offset part of your $200,000 loss on the corporate bonds. Thus the protective put strategy

---

[7] The CBOT's Treasury bond futures contract calls for the delivery of an 8 percent coupon Treasury bond. Thus if coupon rates on newly-auctioned Treasury bonds are greater than 8 percent, the futures price should be less than 100 points. In turn, the exercise price is often less than 100 points.

[8] Assume that the purchase of the put options does not reduce your investment in the long-term corporate bonds.

[9] Again, see Appendix 17B for a general discussion of futures option contracts. Especially note that the December Treasury bond futures contract expires after the December Treasury bond futures option.

allowed you to insure part of your long-term bond portfolio from adverse interest rate changes. Similar hedging examples can be illustrated with other interest rate option positions. For instance, a money market fund manager can immunize against short-term interest rate changes by trading Eurodollar futures options. Or a pension fund manager can use interest rate options to help maintain a fully funded plan. In general, managers can use these contracts to alter their interest rate exposures or even to profit on interest rate timing activities.

Hedging with Currency Options

Options on foreign exchange can be used to hedge exchange rate risk in a variety of settings. For instance, Feiger and Jacquillat (1979) provide an elegant example of how currency put options can protect foreign earnings that are contingent on the resolution of an overseas project bid.

International security managers can also use currency options to alter their exchange rate exposure. For example, consider the manager of a country fund such as Fidelity's Canada fund. The manager must repatriate foreign currency into U.S. dollars in order to pay the domestic shareholders a scheduled dividend. The manager can purchase CD put options traded on the PHLX or the interbank market, thereby ensuring a minimum U.S. dollar price (the put's exercise price) that the manager will receive for each Canadian dollar to be exchanged. In other words the CD puts protect the fund's shareholders against an unanticipated appreciation (depreciation) of the U.S. (Canadian) dollar, while still allowing the fund to capture any value from an unexpected depreciation (appreciation) of the U.S. (Canadian) dollar.

The manager who anticipates only a modest fall in the U.S. dollar's value may purchase a bounded-payoff put from, say, Citibank or Chase Manhattan. This is a currency put option whose payoff is limited. If at maturity the U.S. dollar–Canadian dollar spot rate (S) lies between the exercise price (X) and the limit (L), the payoff is that of a regular put ($X - S$). If the spot rate is below L, however, the payoff is bounded at $X - L$. Clearly this option should command a lower price than a corresponding ordinary CD put option. Other unique currency options offered by banks and brokerages include currency cylinder options, proportional coverage puts, range forwards, average rate options, and the like. Each of these unique options may be regarded as financially engineered, replicable by combinations of listed currency options or other financial assets.

OPTION FUNDS

Option funds are merely equity mutual funds that specialize in writing index call options or call options against the component stocks. Thus option funds are mutual funds that frequently engage in covered call writing. The performance of these funds should be comparatively good during market downturns or sideways-moving markets. A few of the largest are Dean Witter option income fund, Kemper option income fund, Putnam Options income trust II, and Shearson Lehman option income fund. Unfortunately, there has been no rigorous empirical investigation of the historic performance of these funds.

SUMMARY

An option is a derivative security that gives its owner the right to trade an underlying asset at a prespecified exercise price over the option's life, or, if European, at option expiration. The price of an option should reflect the present value of this right.

While options can be used to speculate on subsequent underlying asset price or volatility changes, they principally are used to hedge preexisting asset positions or alter various exposures. Equity fund managers can use stock index options such as the popular OEX to alter systematic market risk; trading index options efficiently changes the equity portfolio's beta. Interest rate options can be used by bond fund managers to alter the fund's duration, thereby protecting the fund from adverse interest rate changes or generating profits from interest rate forecasts. And foreign exchange put options can be used to establish a minimum price at which foreign currency can be repatriated into domestic currency, thus offering international security managers a device for hedging currency risk.

Questions and Problems

1. Distinguish between calls and puts and between American and European options.
2. Why is an option contract often called a contingent claim?
3. Why doesn't an option buyer have to post margin with an OCC member clearing firm?
4. How do index options differ from ordinary stock options? Be sure to discuss concepts such as cash settlement.
5. Why are interest rate futures options more liquidly traded than interest rate spot options?
6. Explain how a short spot-asset position can be hedged with options.
7. Explain how a long spot-asset position can be hedged with options.
8. What are the shortcomings associated with delta-neutral hedging?
9. Discuss how a protective put buying strategy is analogous to purchasing insurance on the underlying asset.
10. How is the choice of exercise price on a protective put buying strategy akin to a deductible decision on any insurance policy?

11. How can you create a synthetic short futures position with futures price X through combining option contracts? How is a synthetic long futures position engineered?

12. Suppose that you make a bet with a foreigner, and if you win, you will be paid in the foreign currency. How can you use currency options to immunize against your exchange exposure? Why wouldn't you use currency futures?

13. Assume that you manage a $50 million index fund that mimics the SP100, which is currently 306.27. Also assume that you engage in covered call writing, employing a three-month OEX call with exercise price 305. The option's price is $3.25. How many option contracts do you write? What are your proceeds? What is the break-even expiration index level under this strategy?

14. Now assume that you hedge the index fund by purchasing corresponding three-month OEX puts at $1.75. What is your insurance premium? Provide an expiration profit graph for this strategy and for an unhedged position. Assume that the purchase of the put options does not reduce your investment in the equities.

15. Assume that you manage a $40 million long-term corporate bond fund and decide to hedge it through purchasing December 90 Treasury bond put futures options traded on the CBOT. Each put's price is $1,625.50. How many put option contracts do you buy, and what is your insurance premium? If at option expiration the prevailing December Treasury bond futures price is 87-20, what is the value of your put options? If the bond portfolio's value declines by $250,000, what is your overall profit from the hedge?

16. Suppose that you are the manager of Fidelity's United Kingdom fund and are considering a covered call writing strategy. Describe the trade-offs associated with writing FT-SE100 call options traded on the London Futures and Options Exchange. Also, would it be judicious to write BP call options traded on the PHLX?

Self-Test Problems

ST-1. Assume that you hedge a $75 million index fund by purchasing six-month OEX puts with exercise price 300. The SP100 is 297.16 and the put price is $5.75. You are not fully funded, so the purchase of the puts does not reduce your investment in equities. Provide a profit graph (at option expiration) for this strategy and for an unhedged position.

ST-2. Assume that you hedge a $100 million long-term government bond fund by purchasing June Treasury bond put futures options with exercise price 92 points. The put price is $3,250. At option expiration what is your overall profit from the hedge if (a) the prevailing June Treasury bond futures price is 87-10, (b) the value of your bond position declined by $1,420,000, and (c) the purchase of the put futures options did not reduce your bond investment?

Self-Test Solutions

ST-1. You hold approximately 252,400 index units ($75 million divided by 297.16), so you purchase 2,524 OEX puts for an insurance premium of $1,451,300 (2,524 × 100 × $5.75). The break-even expiration index level is therefore 302.91 (297.16 + 5.75). The profit graph is:

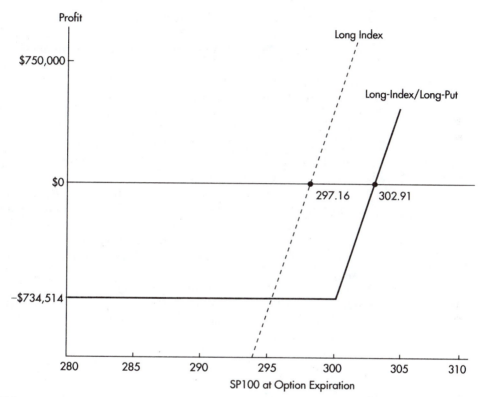

FIGURE 17.4

Self-Test Solution 1

ST-2. You purchase 1,000 Treasury bond put futures options ($100 million divided by $100,000), for an insurance premium of $3,250,000 (1,000 × $3,250). The puts expire in the money (87 − 10 < 92), so the put writer pays you $4,843,750: ($92,000 − $89,156.25) × 1,000. Subtracting the original premium of $3,250,000 and the bond loss of $1,420,000 yields an overall profit of $173,750 from the hedge.

17A

Options Pricing

This appendix provides two models to price option contracts: (1) the binomial option pricing model (BOPM), developed independently by J. Cox, S. Ross, and M. Rubinstein (1979) and R. Rendleman and B. Bartter (1979), and (2) the Black-Scholes (B-S) option pricing model, developed by F. Black and M. Scholes (1973).

We begin with the BOPM for three reasons. First, this model clearly illustrates how option prices result from arbitrage restrictions and the law of one price. Second, the BOPM clearly identifies the underlying determinants of an option's price. And third, the BOPM provides substantial insights into the B-S model, which is a more forbidding model whose derivation is quite complex.

Next we present the B-S model. A shortcoming of this model is that it is applicable only to European options, which cannot be exercised prematurely. Hence we discuss the conditions under which it may be optimal to exercise an option contract prematurely and show how the BOPM can be used to price American options. Examples are provided.

Finally, the better to demonstrate how the two models are intimately related, we show how the B-S model can be derived from the BOPM. In fact, the B-S model is the continuous-time analogue of the BOPM, which is a discrete-time model.

THE BINOMIAL OPTION PRICING MODEL

The BOPM assumes that the option's underlying asset has a price that obeys a binomial generating process. This assumption means that in any single period the asset price can go either up or down, possibly at different rates. The BOPM is often called a two-state model, reflecting the two possible states of the asset's end-of-period price. In reality an asset's price can assume more than two possible outcomes. However, the BOPM is useful as a pedagogical tool, since it demonstrates the process by which option prices are generated. Also, it can be shown that in a multiperiod world the model will converge to the B-S model, the preeminent options pricing model. Understanding the BOPM will therefore help you to comprehend the B-S model. And despite its limitations, the BOPM can be used to price American options, discussed later in this appendix.

The One-Period BOPM

Let us begin our examination of the BOPM by assuming a one-period world in which the option's maturity represents one time period. If the option expires in three months, then the one period is three months. If the option matures in nine months, then nine months is the period, and so on. Suppose that an asset currently worth $10 can increase in value by 20 percent over the one period or can decrease by 15 percent over the period. Let the probability of an increase be 50 percent and assume that the risk-free rate of interest is 10 percent. Hence the asset price follows a binomial generating process as shown in Panel A of Figure 17A.1, where S is $10.00, the asset's current price; p is .50, the probability of an increase in asset price; $(1 + r)$ is 1.1, one plus the risk-free rate of interest; u is 1.2, the multiplicative upward movement in the asset price; and d is 0.85, the multiplicative downward movement in the asset price.[10]

Now suppose that you want to determine the value of a call option written on this asset. Let the option's exercise price be $10.50. Given the above generating process, the option has a 50 percent chance of exhibiting a value of $1.50 at expiration and a 50 percent chance of having no value at expiration. These two payoffs are illustrated in Panel B of Figure 17A.1. To determine the option's value, construct a riskless hedged portfolio consisting of one unit of the asset and h units of the call option written against the asset. The variable h represents the hedge ratio. Panel A of

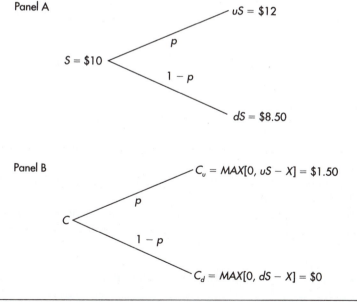

Panel A

$uS = \$12$

p

$S = \$10$

$1 - p$

$dS = \$8.50$

Panel B

$C_u = MAX[0, uS - X] = \$1.50$

p

C

$1 - p$

$C_d = MAX[0, dS - X] = \$0$

FIGURE 17A.1

One-Period Binomial Generating Process

[10] For the derivation of the BOPM to hold, it is required that $d < (1 + r) < u$. Also, d must be less than 1 to preclude a negative asset price in a multiperiod world.

FIGURE 17A.2

Payoffs to the
Hedged Portfolio

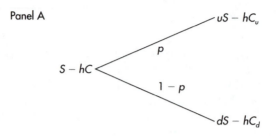

Panel A

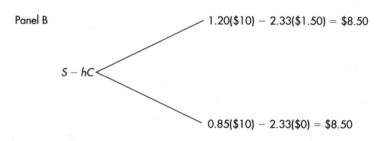

Panel B

Figure 17A.2 presents the two possible payoffs to the hedged portfolio. If you equate these two, then the end-of-period payoff will be certain and the hedged portfolio will be risk free. Equating the payoffs in Figure 17A.2 gives

(17A.1)
$$uS - hC_u = dS - hC_d.$$

Solving 17A.1 for h gives

(17A.2)
$$h = [S(u - d)]/(C_u - C_d).$$

In our problem, $h = 2.33$:

$$h = [\$10(1.20 - .85)]/(\$1.50 - 0).$$

Thus the riskless hedged portfolio will consist of one long unit of the underlying asset and 2.33 written call options. Such a combination will ensure an end-of-period payoff of $8.50 whether S goes up or down. See Panel B of Figure 17A.2.

Since the hedged portfolio is riskless, the initial portfolio investment must earn the risk-free rate of return over the period in order to prevent arbitrage:[11]

(17A.3a)
$$(1 + r)(S - hC) = uS - hC_u,$$

---

[11] Since the value of the hedged portfolio is the same whether S goes up or down, we can equate $(1 + r)(S - hC)$ to $uS - hC_u$ or to $dS - hC_d$ and obtain the same result.

or

(17A.3b) $C = [S[(1 + r) - u] + hC_u]/[h(1 + r)].$

Substituting 17A.2 for h and rearranging algebraically gives

(17A.4) $C = [qC_u + (1 - q)C_d]/(1 + r),$

where

$q = [(1 + r) - d]/(u - d)$ and $(1 - q) = [u - (1 + r)]/(u - d).$

Equation 17A.4 is the one-period BOPM for calls. The formula gives the call price as determined by the parameters C_u, C_d, q, and r. C_u and C_d are in turn determined by the parameters S, X, u, and d, and q is determined by r, u, and d. Thus the parameters that affect a call option's price are the spot asset price (S), the option's exercise price (X), the risk-free rate of interest (r), and u and d, which define the spot asset prices possible at option expiration.[12]

Returning to the numerical example, the price of the call option is $0.974:

$$\$0.974 = \frac{\left[\left(\dfrac{1.10 - .85}{1.20 - .85} \right) \$1.50 + \left(\dfrac{1.20 - 1.10}{1.20 - .85} \right) \$0 \right]}{(1.10)}.$$

You can confirm that this is the correct call price by ensuring that the initial investment in the hedged portfolio earns the riskless rate. If $C = \$0.974$, the initial investment is $7.73:

$$\$7.73 = S - hC = \$10 - (2.33)(\$0.974).$$

Since you are guaranteed an end-of-period payoff of $8.50, the return is 10 percent, the risk-free rate of interest: $(\$8.50 - \$7.73)/(\$7.73) = .10$.

Using a similar derivation, the one-period BOPM for puts is shown to be

(17A.5) $P = [qP_u + (1 - q)P_d]/(1 + r).$

---

[12] Besides understanding the parameters that affect the call option price, it is useful to note the parameters that do not. Specifically, notice that p and $(1 - p)$ do not enter equation 17A.4. Thus the equation contains no parameters that are affected by the risk preferences of investors. This result leads to so-called risk-neutral options pricing. All that is required for determining the option's price is that investors prefer more wealth to less such that arbitrage opportunities are eliminated. Also for this reason the terms q and $(1 - q)$ are often called risk-neutralized probabilities.

In this example, S is \$10, X is \$10.50, u is 1.20, d is 0.85, and $r = .10$, so that P_u is \$0 and $P_d = \$2.00$, so that $P = \$0.519$.

An Example of Arbitrage.   Suppose that the above call option was priced at \$1.25; that is, it was overpriced. You should be able to exploit this mispricing opportunity. To do so you buy one unit of the underlying asset at \$10 and write 2.33 calls. The initial investment is \$7.09. If the asset price goes up or down, you invariably receive \$8.50 at the end of the period. The return is therefore 20 percent, which is twice the risk-free rate. Obviously, a riskless portfolio that earns twice the risk-free rate will lure hungry arbitrageurs. Their trading should bid up S and/or bid down C until equilibrium is restored. For instance, if the asset price remains at \$10, C should be bid down to \$0.974. Similar arbitrage strategies work for underpriced calls and mispriced puts.

The *n*-Period BOPM

The assumption that an asset price can have only two possible end-of-period outcomes may be realistic for some lotteries, but not for most assets. The prices of stocks, bonds, and foreign currency represent continuous random variables, but a binomial generating process is applicable to discrete random variables. Thus, initially it appears that the BOPM is quite limited in application. However, consider a world in which there are two states but many time periods. That is, the option's maturity consists of thousands and thousands of short periods. Here the underlying asset price can take on thousands of different values at option maturity. Even if this maturity is just one day or one hour or one minute, the potential price outcomes are in the thousands or millions or billions. In short, the resulting distribution of price outcomes begins to appear continuous, as a tree diagram eventually appears to be continuous. Hence the BOPM should be very accurate when applied to continuous random variables if you allow the number of periods to be very large. Therefore the model can be applied in an iterative fashion to value options on assets such as stocks and foreign exchange.

Let us begin by extending the model to two time periods. The two-period binomial generating process is shown in Figure 17A.3. Assume that one plus the two-period risk-free rate is $(1 + r)^2$. To solve for C_u and C_d, which are the values of the one-period options initially traded at the end of the first period, we simply apply equation 17A.4, the one-period call BOPM:

(17A.6a) $C_u = [qC_{uu} + (1 - q)C_{ud}]/(1 + r),$

(17A.6b) $C_d = [qC_{du} + (1 - q)C_{dd}]/(1 + r),$

A. Spot Price Dynamics

FIGURE 17A.3

Two-Period Binomial
Generating Process

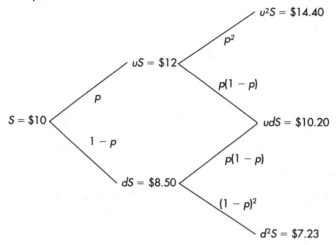

B. Call Price Dynamics

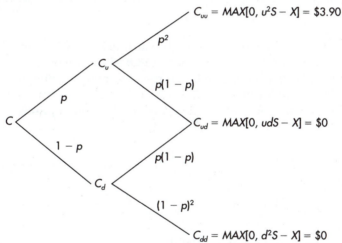

where C_{uu}, C_{du}, and C_{dd} are the three possible call prices at the end of two periods:

$$C_{uu} = MAX[0, u^2S - X];$$
$$C_{ud} = MAX[0, udS - X];$$
$$C_{dd} = MAX[0, d^2S - X].$$

As before, we can now construct a riskless hedged portfolio and determine the current value of the two-period call option:

(17A.7a) $C = [qC_u + (1 - q)C_d]/(1 + r).$

Substituting 17A.6a and 17A.6b into 17A.7a gives

(17A.7b) $C = [q^2C_{uu} + 2q(1 - q)C_{ud} + (1 - q)^2C_{dd}]/(1 + r)^2.$

The call option's value is $1.644:[13]

$$1.644 = \frac{\left[\left(\frac{1.10 - .85}{1.20 - .85}\right)^2 \$3.90 + \$0 + \$0\right]}{(1.10)^2}.$$

Equation 17A.7b results from applying the one-period BOPM twice. Reapplying the process in an iterative way produces this n-period generalization:

(17A.8) $$C = \sum_{j=0}^{n} \left\{ \frac{\frac{n!}{(n-j)!j!}q^j(1 - q)^{n-j}MAX[0, u^jd^{n-j}S - X]}{(1 + r)^n} \right\},$$

where j is the number of upward price movements $(j = 0,1, \ldots ,n)$. Equation 17A.8 is the generalized BOPM for call options. It states that the value of a call is the sum of the risk-neutral probabilities of each final call outcome multiplied by the value of that outcome and discounted at the risk-free rate for all n time periods. For put options the generalized BOPM is

(17A.9) $$P = \sum_{j=0}^{n} \left\{ \frac{\frac{n!}{(n-j)!j!}q^j(1 - q)^{n-j}MAX[0, X - u^jd^{n-j}S]}{(1 + r)^n} \right\}.$$

A Numerical Example. Recall that our one-period put was valued at $0.519. Now apply Equation 17A.9, the generalized BOPM for puts, to confirm this value:
For $j = 0$:

$$\frac{\frac{1!}{1!0!}\left(\frac{1.10 - .85}{1.20 - .85}\right)^0 \left(\frac{1.20 - 1.10}{1.20 - .85}\right)^1 MAX[0, 10.50 - (1.2)^0(.85)^1 10]}{(1.10)} = \$0.519.$$

---

[13] Increasing the option's maturity to two periods raised the option's value from $0.974 to $1.644, indicating that option value is directly related to maturity. Maturity is a determinant of option value.

For $j = 1$:

$$\frac{\frac{1!}{0!1!}\left(\frac{1.10 - .85}{1.20-.85}\right)^1 \left(\frac{1.20 - 1.10}{1.20 - .85}\right)^0 MAX[0, 10.50 - (1.2)^1(.85)^010]}{(1.10)} = \$0.$$

Summing gives $.519.

Although the application of the generalized BOPM seems tedious, the model is easily programmable and can be run on any microcomputer, and for small n, on many hand-held programmable calculators.

THE BLACK-SCHOLES (B-S) MODEL

In 1973 F. Black and M. Scholes developed a formula to value European options written on non-dividend-paying common stocks. Other assumptions included perfect markets, constant interest rates, and subsequent asset prices that are lognormally distributed with constant mean and variance. Numerous researchers have extended the model's basic framework in order to price options written on assets exhibiting leakages, to price American options, and to price more complex contingent claims.

The derivation of the B-S model entails the construction of a riskless hedged portfolio consisting of non-dividend-paying common stock and European call options. By continually rebalancing the hedged portfolio so that it remained risk-free, Black and Scholes were able to solve for the option's value using continuous-time mathematics. Later we show how the B-S model can be derived by extending the BOPM to a continuous-time setting. First, however, we inspect how the model is applied.

The Black-Scholes option pricing model is

(17A.10)
$$C^E = SN(d_1) - e^{-rT}XN(d_1 - \sigma\sqrt{T}),$$

where d_1 is $\dfrac{ln(S/X) + [r + (\sigma^2/2)]T}{\sigma\sqrt{T}}$; S is the underlying asset's price; X is the option's exercise price; r is the domestic short-term riskless rate of interest; σ is the annualized standard deviation of returns of the underlying asset; T is the option's maturity expressed as a fraction of a year; and $N(.)$ is the cumulative standard normal probability distribution function.

A Numerical Example.   Although equation 17A.10 appears rather forbidding, its application is really quite simple. It can even be programmed on many hand-held calculators. Suppose that you want to value a European call option where $S = \$17.50$, $X = \$17.00$, $r = .08$, $T = .25$, and $\sigma^2 = .10$. The first step is to compute the probabilities $N(d_1)$ and $N(d_1 - \sigma\sqrt{T})$. These are probability terms and therefore must lie between 0 and 1. The terms d_1 and $d_1 - \sigma\sqrt{T}$ represent the upper limits of integration of the standard normal probability distribution function. They are given by

$$d_1 = \frac{ln\ (\$17.50/\$17.00) + [.08 + (.10/2)](.25)}{\sqrt{.10}\ \sqrt{.25}} = 0.3889$$

$$d_1 - \sigma\sqrt{T} = 0.3889 - \sqrt{.10}\ \sqrt{.25} = 0.2308.$$

Thus we are looking for the areas under the standard normal curve from $-\infty$ to .3889 and from $-\infty$ to .2308. These are illustrated by the shaded areas in Figure 17A.4.

We obtain $N(.3889)$ and $N(.2308)$ by employing Exhibit 17A.1 on page 478 and interpolating: $N(.3889) = .6513$, and $N(.2308) = .5913$. Notice that the probability .5913 is fairly high. It can be demonstrated that $N(d_1 - \sigma\sqrt{T})$ is the probability that the call option will expire in the money. Hence this option's probability of being exercised at expiration is over 59 percent. We expect a high probability here, since this option is currently in the money $(S > X)$.

Given that we have computed $N(d_1)$ and $N(d_1 - \sigma\sqrt{T})$, the next step to obtain this option's price is to employ equation 17A.10:

$$C^E = \$17.50(0.6513) - \$17.00e^{-.08(.25)}(0.5913)$$
$$= \$11.40 - \$9.85 = \$1.55.$$

The call option's price is $1.55 per unit of the underlying asset.

Value of a Corresponding Put

Suppose that you want to price a corresponding put option, that is, a European put written on the same asset and exhibiting the same exercise price and maturity. One method is to invoke *put-call parity*, a condition relating corresponding European call and put prices that is based on an elegant arbitrage trading strategy developed by H. Stoll (1969). For non-dividend-paying common stocks, put-call parity is given by

(17A.11) $P^E = C^E - S + Xe^{-rT}.$

Here we have

$$P^E = \$1.55 - \$17.50 + \$17.00e^{-.08(.25)} = \$0.71.$$

Alternatively, we could obtain P^E directly through an application of the B-S model for puts:

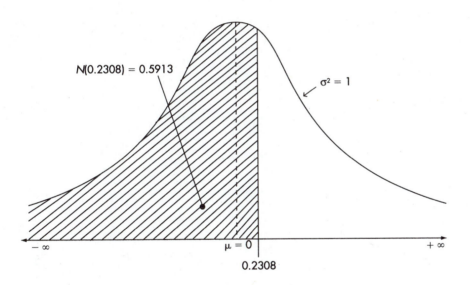

FIGURE 17A.4
Standard Normal
Probability
Distribution

(17A.12) $P^E = e^{-rT}X[1 - N(d_1 - \sigma\sqrt{T})] - S[1 - N(d_1)].$

We have

$$P^E = e^{-.08(.25)}\$17.00[1 - 0.5913] - \$17.50[1 - 0.6513]$$
$$= \$0.71.$$

Here [1 − .5913], or .4087, represents the probability that the put will expire in the money. The probability is low, reflecting the fact that $X < S$.

EXHIBIT 17A.1

Standard Normal Probabilities

		Values for *d* and *N(d)*			
d	**N(d)**	**d**	**N(d)**	**d**	**N(d)**
		−1.00	.1587	1.00	.8413
−2.95	.0016	−.95	.1711	1.05	.8531
−2.90	.0019	−.90	.1841	1.10	.8643
−2.85	.0022	−.85	.1977	1.15	.8749
−2.80	.0026	−.80	.2119	1.20	.8849
−2.75	.0030	−.75	.2266	1.25	.8944
−2.70	.0035	−.70	.2420	1.30	.9032
−2.65	.0040	−.65	.2578	1.35	.9115
−2.60	.0047	−.60	.2743	1.40	.9192
−2.55	.0054	−.55	.2912	1.45	.9265
−2.50	.0062	−.50	.0385	1.50	.9332
−2.45	.0071	−.45	.3264	1.55	.9394
−2.40	.0082	−.40	.3446	1.60	.9452
−2.35	.0094	−.35	.3632	1.65	.9505
−2.30	.0107	−.30	.3821	1.70	.9554
−2.25	.0122	−.25	.4013	1.75	.9599
−2.20	.0139	−.20	.4207	1.80	.9641
−2.15	.0158	−.15	.4404	1.85	.9678
−2.10	.0179	−.10	.4602	1.90	.9713
−2.05	.0202	−.05	.4801	1.95	.9744
−2.00	.0228	.00	.5000	2.00	.9773
−1.95	.0256	.05	.5199	2.05	.9798
−1.90	.0287	.10	.5398	2.10	.9821
−1.85	.0322	.15	.5596	2.15	.9842
−1.80	.0359	.20	.5793	2.20	.9861
−1.75	.0401	.25	.5987	2.25	.9878
−1.70	.0446	.30	.6179	2.30	.9893
−1.65	.0495	.35	.6368	2.35	.9906
−1.60	.0548	.40	.6554	2.40	.9918
−1.55	.0606	.45	.6736	2.45	.9929
−1.50	.0668	.50	.6915	2.50	.9938
−1.45	.0735	.55	.7088	2.55	.9946
−1.40	.0808	.60	.7257	2.60	.9953
−1.35	.0885	.65	.7422	2.65	.9960
−1.30	.0968	.70	.7580	2.70	.9965
−1.25	.1057	.75	.7734	2.75	.9970
−1.20	.1151	.80	.7881	2.80	.9974
−1.15	.1251	.85	.8023	2.85	.9978
−1.10	.1357	.90	.8159	2.90	.9981
−1.05	.1469	.95	.8289	2.95	.9984

Adjusting the B-S Model for Leakages

Any leakage (i.e., dividend payment or interest/coupon payment) exhibited by an underlying asset should result in a reduction in asset price. In the Black-Scholes world the reduction should equal the amount of the leakage per asset unit. For example, a stock that sells for $50 just prior to the ex-dividend instant should sell for $49 just afterward if the dividend per share is $1. Since the asset's price is affected by the leakage, so too should the option's price, provided the option is not leakage protected. Some OTC stock options are dividend protected because the exercise price is reduced by the amount of any dividend per share paid on the underlying stock. However, listed options offer no such protection. Hence the original Black-Scholes model requires some modification.

The modification required is really quite simple. Specifically, just replace S with S_D everywhere in the original *B-S* model, where S_D is equal to S capitalized by the present value of the leakage. For instance, if the underlying asset is a stock with ex-dividend date t, $t < T$, then $S_D = S - D_t e^{-rT}$, where D_t is the dividend per share. If the option's underlying asset exhibits a continuous leakage, then $S_D = S e^{-\delta T}$ where δ is the leakage rate. For example, δ is the index's dividend yield when valuing a stock index option, δ is the foreign risk-free rate of interest when valuing a currency option, and δ is the domestic risk-free interest rate when valuing all futures options.[14] Similarly, put-call parity (equation 17A.11) is adjusted for leakages by simply substituting S_D for S.

AMERICAN OPTIONS PRICING

The B-S model is applicable to European options. Yet most listed options are American. Often it is in the interest of an option owner to exercise an option prematurely. For instance, consider a put option whose underlying stock's price falls to zero (firm bankruptcy). Clearly the put option cannot become more in the money, so the put owner should exercise the option, thereby obtaining interest income on the exercisable proceeds (X). In general, it may be optimal to exercise any put option prior to its maturity and it may be optimal to exercise early if call options are written on assets exhibiting discrete or continuous leakages. Thus most American options command an early exercise premium; their prices are greater than those of corresponding European options. Below we provide an illustration of the early exercise premium followed by examples of how the BOPM can be used to price American options.

An Illustration of the Early Exercise Premium

We use a two-period BOPM and a zero leakage put to illustrate the early exercise premium. To provide a concrete example we employ the following parameters: $u = 1.25, d = .5, r = .1, X = \$40$, and $S = \$40$. Figure

---

[14] Futures contracts do not pay dividends or interest per se. However, the daily resettlement process may be regarded as representing a continuous leakage at the rate r. For a proof see Hull (1989, Appendix 6B).

FIGURE 17A.5

Two-Period Binomial
Generating Process

A. Spot Price Dynamics

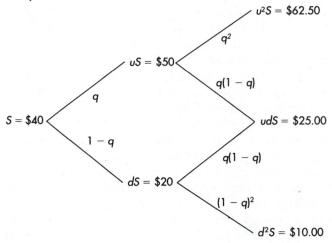

B. Put Price Dynamics

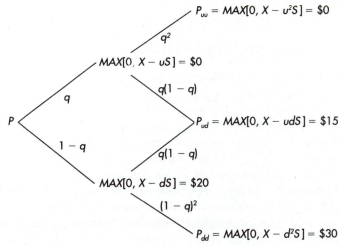

17A.5 provides the two-period binomial generating process. At the end of the second period the asset price may be $62.50, $25, or $10. The corresponding values of the put are $0, $15, and $30, respectively.

If the option in question is European, then it must be held until expiration and its value is given by a straightforward application of equation 17A.9. The European put's value, P^E, is $4.96:

For $j = 0$:

$$\frac{\dfrac{2!}{2!0!}\left(\dfrac{1.10 - .50}{1.25 - .50}\right)^0 \left(\dfrac{1.25 - 1.10}{1.25 - .50}\right)^2 MAX[0,40 - (1.25)^0(.50)^2 40]}{(1.10)^2} = \$0.99$$

For $j = 1$:

$$\frac{\frac{2!}{1!1!}\left(\frac{1.10 - .50}{1.25 - .50}\right)^1 \left(\frac{1.25 - 1.10}{1.25 - .50}\right)^1 MAX[0,40 - (1.25)^1(.50)^1 40]}{(1.10)^2} = \$3.97$$

For $j = 2$:

$$\frac{\frac{2!}{0!2!}\left(\frac{1.10 - .50}{1.25 - .50}\right)^2 \left(\frac{1.25 - 1.10}{1.25 - .50}\right)^0 MAX[0,40 - (1.25)^2(.50)^0 40]}{(1.10)^2} = \$0.00$$

$$\text{Total} \quad \overline{\$4.96}$$

For an American put, however, the problem is complicated by the fact that the option holder can exercise at the end of the first period. To determine whether exercise will occur, first compute the put values at the end of the first period, P_u and P_d. Applying the one-period BOPM, you have

$$P_u = \frac{[qP_{uu} + (1 - q)P_{ud}]}{(1 + r)} = \frac{\left[\frac{(1.10 - .50)}{(1.25 - .50)}(\$0) + \frac{(1.25 - .50)}{(1.25 - .50)}(\$15)\right]}{(1.10)} = 2.73;$$

$$P_d = \frac{[qP_{ud} + (1 - q)P_{dd}]}{(1 + r)} = \frac{\left[\frac{(1.10 - .50)}{(1.25 - .50)}(\$15) + \frac{(1.25 - 1.10)}{(1.25 - .50)}(\$30)\right]}{(1.10)} = 16.36.$$

We now compare these values with the option's exercisable proceeds. If the asset price falls to $20 at the end of the first period, the put holder will exercise prematurely. The option's market price is $16.36, but its exercisable proceeds are $X - dS$, or $20. Thus there is a good chance that the option will be exercised at the end of the first period.

The opportunity offered by an American put option to exercise early should in this case raise its price substantially above that of its counterpart European option. Indeed, in our illustration the American option should command a price of $5.62:

$$P^A = [qP_u + (1 - q)(X - dS)] \div (1 + r)$$

$$= \left[\left(\frac{1.10 - .50}{1.25 - .50}\right)(\$2.73) + \left(\frac{1.25 - 1.10}{1.25 - .50}\right)(\$20)\right] \div (1.10)$$

$$= \$5.62.$$

This pricing result is portrayed in Figure 17A.6.

FIGURE 17A.6

American Put
Option's Value

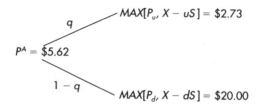

$$
P^A = \$5.62
$$

with branches labeled:

- q to $MAX[P_u, X - uS] = \$2.73$
- $1 - q$ to $MAX[P_d, X - dS] = \$20.00$

The American put price, $5.62, exceeds the counterpart European put price, $4.96, by more than 13 percent. In actual option markets the early exercise premium is typically much lower. Yet evidence suggests that the early exercise premium is significant and that incorporating it enhances the accuracy of the Black-Scholes model.

Valuing American Zero-Leakage Puts

As implied by the previous illustration, the BOPM is capable of valuing American options. The trick is to start at option expiration (time T) and work backward through the tree diagram to detect early-exercise opportunities. This procedure was followed in our previous illustration; for the two-period put we had to check whether early exercise was optimal at the end of the first period. This procedure, which is just an application of dynamic programming, is now further illustrated with two examples: a zero-leakage American put and a continuous-leakage American call.

Consider a four-month American put option written on a non-dividend-paying stock, where $S = \$25$, $X = \$25$, $r = 10\%$, and $\sigma = 16$. Suppose that you divide the option's life into four one-month intervals (.0833 years) in order to construct a binomial tree. To value the option properly you must choose values of $u, d,$ and q that give correct values for the mean and variance of the change in the stock price over the interval $\Delta t = .0833$. Cox, Ross, and Rubinstein (1979) prove that for zero leakage assets:

$$
q = (a - d)/(u - d) \qquad d = e^{-\sigma\sqrt{\Delta t}} = 1/u
$$

$$
u = e^{\sigma\sqrt{\Delta t}} \qquad a = e^{r\Delta t}.
$$

Thus in our example $u = 1.1224$, $d = .8909$, $a = 1.0084$, and $q = .5076$.

Figure 17A.7 shows the binomial tree. There are two numbers at each node. The top number shows the stock price at the node and the bottom number shows the value of the option at the node. Computations are illustrated using the nodes labeled A and B. At A, if the option is exercised immediately it is worth $25 - 22.27 = \$2.73$. If the put is not exercised, it is worth $2.52:

$$
(\$0 \times 0.5076 + \$5.16 \times 0.4924)e^{-.10(0.0833)} = \$2.52.
$$

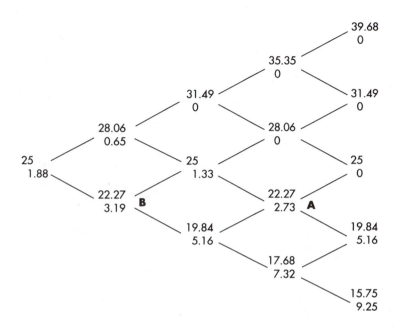

FIGURE 17A.7
Binomial Tree
Diagram for Zero-
Leakage Put

We discount at the risk-free rate, since investor risk preferences do not affect option value. Thus we are free to assume risk neutrality.

Since at node *A* the option's exercisable proceeds, $2.73, are greater than $2.52, the option should be exercised. Thus the value of the option at node *A* is $2.73. At node *B* the exercisable proceeds are $25 − $22.27 = $2.73. This amount is less than the option's market value, or $3.19:

$$(\$1.33 \times 0.5076 + \$5.16 \times 0.4924)e^{-.10(.0833)} = \$3.19.$$

Hence the put should not be exercised at node *B*.

By working backward through the entire tree we eventually obtain a time-0 option price of $1.88. This price reflects the premium associated with the privilege to exercise the American option at nodes such as *A*. We can obtain a more accurate American option value by allowing for a much smaller value of Δ*t*. Indeed, one should divide the option's life into 200 or more periods in order to obtain accurate option prices when using the BOPM.

Valuing an American Continuous Leakage Call

The BOPM can also readily price American options written on continuous-leakage assets, such as foreign exchange. The procedure used is the same as earlier, except that now $a = e^{(r - \delta)\Delta t}$, where δ is the continuous leakage rate. For currency, $\delta = r_f$, the foreign riskless rate of interest. For index options, δ is the index's dividend yield, and $\delta = r$ for all futures options.

FIGURE 17A.8

Binomial Tree
Diagram for
Continuous-Leakage
Call

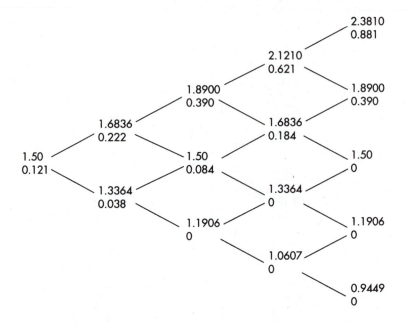

Consider a four-month American call on a British pound where $S = \$1.50/\pounds1$, $X = \$1.50/\pounds1$, $r = .08$, $r_f = .12$, and $\sigma^2 = .16$. Again dividing the option's maturity into four one-month intervals, we have $u = 1.1224$, $d = .8909$, $a = .9967$, and $q = .4569$. The resulting binomial tree is presented in Figure 17A.8. Working backward through the tree as before provides an American currency call option price of $\$0.115/\pounds1$.

DERIVING THE B-S MODEL BY EXTENSION OF THE BOPM

We conclude our discussion of option pricing by demonstrating that the B-S model is the continuous-time limit of the BOPM.

To begin, rewrite the generalized BOPM for calls, which is equation 17A.8:

(17A.13)
$$C^E = \sum_{j=0}^{n} \frac{\left\{ \frac{n!}{(n-j)!j!} q^j (1-q)^{n-j} MAX[0, u^j d^{n-j} S - X] \right\}}{(1+r)^n}.$$

Define x as a positive integer that bounds the states of nature in which $S > X$ at expiration. Thus we can rewrite 17A.13 as follows:

(17A.14)
$$C^E = \sum_{j=x}^{n} \frac{\left\{ \frac{n!}{(n-j)!j!} q^j (1-q)^{n-j} MAX[0, u^j d^{n-j} S - X] \right\}}{(1+r)^n}.$$

Next rewrite 17A.14 as follows, separating it into two parts:

(17A.15)
$$C^E = S\left[\sum_{j=x}^{n}\left(\frac{n!}{(n-j)!j!}\right)q^j(1-q)^{n-j}\left(\frac{u^jd^{n-j}}{(1+r)^n}\right)\right]$$
$$- (1+r)^{-n}X\left[\sum_{j=x}^{n}\left(\frac{n!}{(n-j)!j!}\right)q^j(1-q)^{n-j}\right].$$

The complementary binomial distribution function is

(17A.16)
$$B(j \geq x \mid n,q) = \sum_{j=x}^{n}\left(\frac{n!}{(n-j)!j!}\right)q^j(1-q)^{n-j}.$$

It provides the probability that the sum of j random variables, each of which can take the value 1 with probability q and the value 0 with probability $(1-q)$, will be greater than or equal to x. Substituting 17A.16 into 17A.15 gives

(17A.17)
$$C^E = S\left[\sum_{j=x}^{n}\left(\frac{n!}{(n-j)!j!}\right)q^j(1-q)^{n-j}\frac{(u^jd^{n-j})}{(1+r)^n}\right] - (1+r)^{-n}XB(j \geq x \mid n,q).$$

Next define q' and $1-q'$ as follows:

(17A.18)
$$q' = [uq/(1+r)], \quad 1-q' = [d(1-q)/(1+r)].$$

Therefore

$$q^j(1-q)^{n-j}[(u^jd^{n-j})/(1+r)^n]$$
$$= [uq/(1+r)]^j[d(1-q)/(1+r)]^{n-j}$$
$$= (q')^j(1-q')^{n-j},$$

and the bracketed expression in equation 17A.17 becomes $B(j \geq x \mid n,q')$. Thus equation 17A.17 becomes

(17A.19)
$$C^E = SB(j \geq x \mid n,q') - (1+r)^{-n}XB(j \geq x \mid n,q).$$

In the limit as n approaches infinity, Cox, Ross, and Rubinstein (1979) have proven that

$$B(j \geq x \mid n,q') \to N(d_1), \quad B(j \geq x \mid n,q) \to N(d_1 - \sigma\sqrt{T}).$$

Also, a well-known result from financial math is that $(1 + r)^{-n} \rightarrow e^{-rT}$ when n approaches infinity. Therefore, as n approaches infinity, equation 17A.19 becomes

(17A.20) $$C^E = SN(d_1) - e^{-rT}XN(d_1 - \sigma\sqrt{T}),$$

which is the Black-Scholes model. Hence the two-state binomial option pricing model converges to the Black-Scholes model when n becomes very large.

A PPENDIX

17B

Futures Options

In 1982 the Commodity Futures Trading Commission approved the experimental trading of options written on futures contracts. Each futures exchange was allowed to offer one futures option contract. This experiment proved successful, and futures options were authorized for permanent trading in early 1987. Futures options trading has grown substantially, with options on financial futures leading the way. In this appendix we describe futures options and explain how they differ from regular spot or cash options.

OPTIONS ON FUTURES VERSUS OPTIONS ON SPOTS

To illustrate the differences between spot and futures options, focus on a particular spot asset, namely the British pound. With a spot option the owner has the right to trade British pounds in the future for a prespecified exercise price. Exercise of a spot call or put option entails the actual transfer of pounds. However, with a futures option the underlying asset is a *futures contract* written on British pounds. The owner of a BP futures call option who exercises assumes a long position in the futures market with a futures price equal to the exercise price. With a BP futures put option the exerciser assumes a short BP futures position. Immediately upon exercise, the futures contract, which typically expires after the futures option, is marked to the market. Additionally, the exerciser and new holder of the futures contract must post the regular futures margin.

To illustrate this process, suppose that a BP call futures option with exercise price \$1.70/BP is exercised at option expiration. At this time the futures price is \$1.75/BP. Thus the option is in the money, a condition for rational exercise. If there are BP62,500 per futures contract, then the call option writer owes the exerciser \$3,125: (\$1.75 − 1.70) × 62,500. A payment of this amount is made immediately from the writer to the option buyer, and thus the newly created futures contract is immediately marked to the market. The exerciser assumes a long position in the yet-to-mature BP futures contract, and the option writer is assigned the short side of the BP futures contract. Both parties must post the normal futures margin requirements. From this point forward the two parties engage in a regular futures contract. Each is free to continue to hold his or her position or to relinquish it via a reversing trade.

Hence the major difference between a spot option and a futures option is that with the former, exercise entails the trading of the actual spot asset, while with the latter, exercise entails assuming a position in a futures contract written on the spot asset. In the above example we cannot determine if the BP futures call option buyer profited overall, since we do not know the original premium paid for the option contract.

REFERENCES

Arditti, F., and K. John. 1980. Spanning the state space with options. *Journal of Financial and Quantitative Analysis* 15:1–18.

Ball, C., and W. Torous. 1983. Bond price dynamics and options. *Journal of Financial and Quantitative Analysis* 18:517–532.

Bhattacharya, M. 1980. Empirical properties of the Black-Scholes formula under ideal conditions. *Journal of Financial and Quantitative Analysis* 15:1081–1106.

Black F. 1975. Fact and fantasy in the use of options. *Financial Analysts Journal* 31:36–41, 61–72.

Black, F. 1976. The pricing of commodity contracts. *Journal of Financial Economics* 4:167–179.

Black, F., and M. Scholes. 1973. The pricing of options and corporate liabilities. *Journal of Political Economy* 81:637–659.

Brenner, M., G. Courtadon, and M. Subrahmanyam. 1985. Options on the spot and options on futures. *Journal of Finance* 40:1303–1317.

Briys, E., and M. Crouhy. 1988. Creating and pricing hybrid foreign currency options. *Financial Management* 17:59–65.

Cox, J., S. Ross, and M. Rubinstein. 1979. Option pricing. A simplified approach. *Journal of Financial Economics* 7:299–264.

Dawson, F. 1979. Risks and returns on continuous option writing. *Journal of Portfolio Management* 5:58–63.

Evnine, J., and A. Rudd. 1985. Index options. The early evidence. *Journal of Finance* 40:743–756.

Feiger, G., and B. Jacquillat. 1979. Currency option bonds, puts and calls on spot exchange, and the hedging of contingent foreign earnings. *Journal of Finance* 5:1129–1139.

Grube, R., D. Panton, and J. Terrell. 1979. Risks and rewards in covered call positions. *Journal of Portfolio Management* 5:64–68.

Hull, J. 1989. *Options, futures and other derivative securities,* Englewood Cliffs, NJ: Prentice Hall.

Latane H., and R. Rendleman. 1976. Standard deviations of stock price ratios implied in option prices. *Journal of Finance* 31:369–382.

Merton, R. 1973. Theory of rational option pricing. *Bell Journal of Economics* 141–183.

Merton, R., M. Scholes, and M. Gladstein. 1978. The returns and risk of alternative call option portfolio investment strategies. *Journal of Business* 51:183–242.

Mueller, P. 1981. Covered call options. An alternative investment strategy. *Financial Management* 10:64–71.

Ogden, J., and A. Tucker. 1988. The relative valuation of American currency spot and futures options. Theory and empirical tests. *Journal of Financial and Quantitative Analysis* 23:351–368.

Phillips, S., and C. Smith. 1980. Trading costs for listed options. The implications for market efficiency. *Journal of Financial Economics* 8:179–189.

Pounds H. 1978. Covered call option writing. Strategies and results. *Journal of Portfolio Management* 4:31–42.

Pozen, R. 1978. The purchase of protective puts by financial institutions. *Financial Analysts Journal* 34:47–60.

Ramaswamy, K., and S. Sundaresan. 1985. The valuation of options on futures contracts. *Journal of Finance* 40:1319–1340.

Rendleman, R., and B. Bartter. 1979. Two-state option pricing. *Journal of Finance* 34:1093–1110.

Smith, C. 1976. Option pricing. A review. *Journal of Financial Economics* 3:3–51.

Stoll, H. 1969. The relationship between put and call option prices. *Journal of Finance* 24:810–824.

Welch, W. 1982. *Strategies for put and call option trading.* Cambridge, MA: Winthrop.

Wolf, A. 1982. Fundamentals of commodity options on futures. *Journal of Futures Markets* 2:391–408.

CHAPTER *18*

Swap Contracts

Introduction

In general terms, a *swap* is an agreement to exchange prescribed cash flows at periodic future intervals. The particular swaps that we investigate in this chapter—equity, interest rate, and currency swaps—all can be described as such an agreement.[1] Like futures and option contracts, swaps can be employed to immunize security portfolios against unanticipated changes in interest rates, exchange rates, and equity prices. In addition, swaps can be used in more proactive asset allocation strategies, especially for international fund managers. The purpose of this chapter is to introduce swaps and their role in portfolio management.

As with many financial engineering innovations, swaps began as low-volume, high-margin custom designs structured by leading investment and commercial bankers for their clients. Currency and interest rate swaps were introduced in the early 1980s, and equity swaps were introduced in 1989 by Bankers Trust. Swaps proved to be very popular and were quickly transformed into high-volume low-margin products. This "productizing" of financial innovations, as it is called by financial engineers, occurs whenever a structured deal has a significant market potential beyond the end user for whom it was first designed. Today swaps

---

[1]Commodity swaps also exist but are not emphasized here since they are not particular to the management of security portfolios.

are regularly employed by thrift institutions, central governments, and multinational corporations as well as institutional portfolio managers. Still, keep in mind that unlike futures and option contracts, swaps are negotiated deals and are not listed for trading. They are negotiated between two parties, one of whom is commonly a swap dealer operating under the auspices of an investment or commercial bank, such as Security Pacific, Morgan Stanley, First Boston Corporation, Salomon Brothers, or Bear Sterns & Co. The largest intermediaries in the swap market are major U.S. money-center banks, major U.S. and U.K. investment and merchant banks, and major Japanese securities companies. Commercial banks in Canada, France, Japan, Sweden, Switzerland, and the United Kingdom are also active swap dealers. The structure of a swap will become more apparent as we progress through the chapter. In addition, Appendix 18A elaborates on the role of swap dealers and on the movement toward standardizing swap agreements under the direction of the International Swap Dealers Association (ISDA).

This chapter proceeds as follows. First we provide a tutorial on the basic swap structure, including common swap terms and notation. We then discuss equity, interest rate, and currency swaps, providing examples of hedging applications. After that we offer a discussion of swap options, which are often called *swaptions*. We then offer a brief discussion of nonconventional swap forms. We conclude the chapter with an analysis of the role of swaps in international asset allocation. Our purpose here is to illustrate some of the profound advantages swaps may offer portfolio managers of all types.

The Basic Swap Structure

All swaps, irrespective of type, are founded on the same basic structure. First, there is some notional amount at the time the swap is written. This notional amount may be principal (as it is in the case of equity, interest rate, and currency swaps), or commodities (as it is in the case of commodity swaps). Except for commodity swaps and (occasionally) currency swaps, these notionals are typically not exchanged. The counterparties to a swap do exchange *usage* payments, however, which are made at designated intervals over the life of the swap. The life of the swap is called its *tenor*. Typically, one swap party pays a fixed price and the other pays a floating price determined by some index to which the floating price is pegged. Except for commodity swaps, these prices take the form of rates. The two sides of the swap are called the fixed and floating *legs* of the swap, and the fixed rate is typically called the *swap coupon*.

The vast majority of swaps are effected between an end user and a swap dealer, as opposed to directly between two end users. Swap dealers such as Bankers Trust, Swiss Bank, and Hong Kong Bank add liquidity to the market by eliminating the need to match precisely all of the provisions of

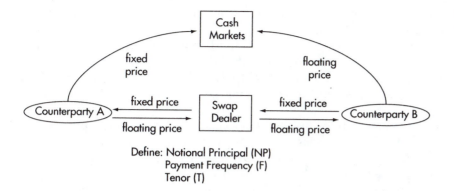

FIGURE 18.1
The Basic Swap Structure

swaps between end users. Also, end users need only be concerned with the creditworthiness of the swap dealer rather than with that of the other end user. For their services swap dealers earn a bid-ask spread and sometimes collect front-end fees when complex financial engineering is involved. Appendix 18A expands on the role of swap dealers.

Ignoring the initial and terminal exchange of notionals, which again are optional in the sense that most swaps do not require them, the basic swap structure is easily described using a boxed cash flow form of illustration. The two legs of a simple (sometimes called plain vanilla) swap with a dealer standing between the end users are illustrated in Figure 18.1, together with the accompanying cash market transactions. As the figure demonstrates, the swap converts counterparty A's fixed-price obligation to a floating-price obligation and converts counterparty B's floating-price obligation to a fixed-price obligation.[2] We will employ this cash flow framework to represent and analyze the various swap types that follow, beginning with equity swaps.

EQUITY SWAPS

Like most swaps, an equity swap involves a notional principal, a specified tenor, prespecified payment intervals, a fixed rate (swap coupon), and a floating rate pegged to some variable or index. For an equity swap the floating rate is pegged to the return on a stock index, typically including both dividend and capital appreciation. The index can be a broadly based stock index such as the SP500, DAX, London Financial Times index (FT-SE100), or the NIKKEI 225. Alternatively, the swap can be pegged to a narrower index (i.e., sector fund), such as that for a specific industry group: an oil industry index, gold mining index, electric utility index, or the like. One advantage of an equity swap is that it allows an equity

---

[2] If the cash markets of the two end users are the same, the swap can fix the price for both end users. This is typically the objective of commodity swaps.

portfolio manager to immunize against equity price declines over the swap's tenor. An example follows.

Assume that an equity index fund manager (an end user), whose portfolio is highly correlated with the SP500 return, wants to pay the SP500 return and in turn receive a fixed rate, thereby hedging the preexisting equity position against downside market risk. The manager may want to engage in this floating-for-fixed swap because it is less costly than, say, shorting stock index futures contracts or buying index put options. Alternatively, the manager may be employing the swap as a means to speculate on return spreads between equity and fixed-income markets. Here the usage payments are assumed to be made quarterly (qu) on a notional principal of $100 million, the approximate index fund size. The tenor is two years. The swap dealer prices the swap at 9.95 percent (a periodic rate of 2.4875 percent).[3] The cash flows of the swap together with the cash flows of the preexisting equity (cash) position are depicted in Figure 18.2.

This figure illustrates how a properly structured equity swap can be used to convert a variable equity return into a stable fixed-income return. Hence equity swaps can be said to bridge the debt and equity markets.[4] Also, it is important to observe that because an equity return can be positive or negative, the cash flow on the equity-pegged leg of the swap can go in either direction. From Figure 18.2, if the SP500 return is negative for a quarter, the swap dealer pays the end user the negative sum in addition to the regular swap coupon on the fixed leg.

Exhibit 18.1 provides the periodic cash flows for our equity swap based on the eight quarterly SP500 returns shown in column 2. These assumed returns suggest that the equity market was rather depressed over the tenor

FIGURE 18.2

Equity Swap

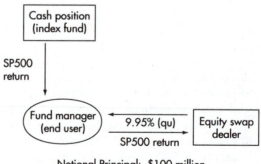

Notional Principal: $100 million
Tenor: 2 years

---

[3] Appendix 18C discusses how swaps are traditionally priced (i.e., how the coupon rate is determined). In general, the coupon rate for an at-market swap is set such that the expected present values of the fixed and floating payments are equal at swap inception.

[4] Besides revolutionizing modern risk management, swaps are serving to integrate formerly segregated capital markets. For more on this issue see Appendix 18B.

EXHIBIT 18.1

Periodic Cash Flows for an Equity Swap

(1) Quarter	(2) SP500 Return	(3) Swap Dealer Pays	(4) End User Pays	(5) Net Flow to End User
1	0.0271	$2,487,500	$2,710,000	-$ 222,500
2	0.0025	2,487,500	250,000	2,237,500
3	-0.0132	3,807,500	0	3,807,500
4	-0.0279	5,277,500	0	5,277,500
5	-0.0035	2,837,500	0	2,837,500
6	0.0129	2,487,500	1,290,000	1,197,500
7	0.0240	2,487,500	2,400,000	87,500
8	0.0316	2,487,500	3,160,000	- 672,500
				Total: $14,550,000

Note: The SP500 return includes both dividend and capital appreciation. The notional principal is $100 million. The swap coupon is 9.95 percent (2.4875 percent quarterly).

of the swap. Only in quarters 1 and 8 were the SP500 returns greater than the periodic swap coupon of 2.4875 percent. Consequently, the fund manager (end user) clearly benefited, *ex post*, from the swap arrangement. The overall net cash flow to the index fund was $14.55 million. This inflow surely helped the fund to offset some or all of its losses on its preexisting equity position due to the depressed equity market. Equivalently, the swap served to enhance the return on the preexisting equity portfolio vis-à-vis unhedged equity funds. Like engaging in a short stock index futures position or writing (buying) stock index call (put) options, the swap position of the manager is negatively correlated with the preexisting equity portfolio and thereby serves to immunize the portfolio against downside market risk.[5]

INTEREST RATE SWAPS

Although principally used by debt issuers and financial intermediaries (e.g., thrifts) to hedge interest rate risk, interest rate swaps can also be employed by fixed-income fund managers to immunize their portfolio

[5] As depicted in Exhibit 18.1, our equity swap assumes that cash flows occur instantaneously, i.e., as soon as the quarterly SP500 return is known. In practice, however, most swaps are settled up in arrears. That is, the first payment (usage) date is based on the SP500 return prevailing three months earlier, so the first payment date occurs three months after the inception of the swap, and the first payment is known at inception. The second payment is known three months after inception, and so on. We will return to this point later in the chapter. Also, the usage payments are typically netted. One party simply sends a check covering the difference between the fixed and floating payments to the other. In addition, the variable equity return in an equity swap does not have to be swapped for a fixed coupon rate. Many equity swaps are designed to swap the equity return for a variable interest rate. In addition, equity swaps can be designed to exchange the equity return on one index for that on another (discussed later).

values against unanticipated interest rate increases or to speculate on changing conditions in the debt market. For instance, a manager can engage in a swap to pay the swap dealer a fixed rate of interest in return for a floating rate on the notional principal. In this way the manager converts a cash stream from the cash market/bond fund from a fixed to a floating interest rate. Figure 18.3 illustrates the strategy. Should interest rates rise, the losses on the cash position (fixed-income portfolio) would be offset, at least in part, by the gains from the floating leg of the swap transaction. Of course if rates fall, the swap will serve to offset the *gains* on the cash position. But of course this possible offset represents the implicit cost of any hedging application. Presumably the hedge maximizes expected utility, perhaps because the fund manager forecasts a rise in interest rates over the swap's tenor.

The fixed and floating interest rates of the swap agreement depend on prevailing market conditions. Swap dealers regularly quote swap prices through the use of *indication pricing schedules*. Exhibit 18.2 provides a recent schedule, obtained from a leading swap dealer, for interest rate swaps. It assumes semiannual (sa) rates. Notice that there is a spread between the dealer paying a fixed rate and receiving a fixed rate. The dealer's revenue derives mainly from this spread. Also notice that no floating rates appear in the schedule, implying that the floating side is the six-month LIBOR

FIGURE 18.3

Interest Rate Swap

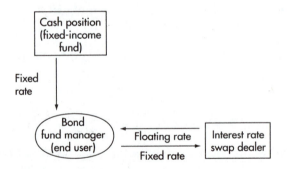

EXHIBIT 18.2

Indication Pricing Schedule for Interest Rate Swap Transactions

Maturity	Intermediary Pays Fixed Rate	Intermediary Receives Fixed Rate	U.S. Treasury Note Rate
2 years	2 yr TN sa + 19 bps	2 yr TN sa + 41 bps	8.50%
3 years	3 yr TN sa + 23 bps	3 yr TN sa + 49 bps	8.67
4 years	4 yr TN sa + 26 bps	4 yr TN sa + 54 bps	8.79
5 years	5 yr TN sa + 31 bps	5 yr TN sa + 56 bps	8.86
6 years	6 yr TN sa + 35 bps	6 yr TN sa + 63 bps	8.91
7 years	7 yr TN sa + 40 bps	7 yr TN sa + 69 bps	8.95

TN, Treasury note rate; sa, semiannual; bps, basis points.

flat.[6] Thus for the interest rate swap illustrated in Figure 18.3, the fixed (coupon) rate may be, say, the five-year Treasury note rate semiannually plus 56 basis points, and the floating rate is LIBOR flat on the prescribed notional principal.

The market for interest rate swaps has grown tremendously over the past decade. The first interest rate swaps appeared in 1982, and the volume of U.S. dollar interest rate swaps is estimated at over $1 trillion in 1990 alone. By year-end 1992 the outstanding notional principal of all outstanding interest rate swaps was about $3 trillion. The popularity and growth of these transactions are partly attributable to their usefulness in managing interest rate exposure (as the preceding example illustrated). As another example of such exposure management, consider a savings and loan or other thrift institution that employs an interest rate swap to manage the gap between its asset and liability maturities. As an alternative to offering adjustable-rate mortgages or selling mortgages and reinvesting the proceeds in shorter-term assets, the thrift may engage in swaps to reduce its interest rate exposure. By properly constructing an interest rate swap, the thrift can convert its fixed-rate assets to floating-rate assets, convert its floating-rate liabilities to fixed-rate liabilities, or both. Thrifts and insurance companies are active participants in the interest rate swap market.

In addition, these swaps are popular because they can be used to create synthetic instruments.[7] For instance, consider the combination of a fixed-rate loan and interest rate swap where the borrower pays fixed. This combination produces a reverse floating-rate loan. If interest rates rise, then the interest payments on the loan actually fall.

CURRENCY SWAPS

The benefits of international diversification were identified in Chapter 8. Based on such benefits the volume of cross-border security transactions has grown substantially over the past decade. Exhibit 18.3 displays the recent growth in gross purchases and sales of domestic stocks by nonresidents for four industrialized nations. Such diversification arises from direct investment in foreign securities or more often from the investment activities of international mutual funds such as the

---

[6] LIBOR, the London interbank offer rate, is a variable interest rate earned on Eurodollar deposits, which are dollar-denominated deposits in European banks or a European branch of a U.S. bank. The LIBOR is often used to establish coupon payments on floating-rate Eurobonds, which are bonds underwritten by international syndicates and sold outside the country of the currency that denominates the bonds. The term *flat* simply means the current six-month LIBOR with no markup or markdown, as opposed to, say, LIBOR plus 50 basis points.

[7] Thus like futures and options, swaps also serve to complete markets (in the Arrow-Debreu sense).

EXHIBIT 18.3

Cross-Border Stock Transactions

	Gross Purchases and Sales of Domestic Stocks by Nonresidents (in Billions of U.S. Dollars)			
Year	United States[a]	Japan[b]	Germany[c]	Canada[d]
1980	75.2	26.2	6.8	12.4
1981	75.5	43.7	6.9	9.2
1982	79.9	34.6	6.3	5.2
1983	134.1	71.5	13.4	8.4
1984	122.6	78.3	12.4	8.8
1985	159.0	81.9	36.9	11.9
1986	277.5	201.6	77.9	20.2
1987	481.9	374.7	76.8	45.7
1988	618.4	503.7	71.2	51.9
1989	746.9	516.4	68.6	63.1
1990	881.0	498.2	61.4	69.7
1991	1,036.3	387.0	88.0	82.5

Source: *FRBNY Quarter Review*, Summer 1992, p. 23.

[a]U.S. Treasury International Capital Data

[b]Japanese Ministry of Finance

[c]Deutsche Bundesbank

[d]Statistics Canada

Fidelity overseas fund or the Fidelity international growth and income fund.

Of course international diversification entails exchange rate risk, that is, the risk that a foreign currency will depreciate substantially so that the returns from foreign investment are tempered when repatriated to the domestic currency. Analogous to equity and interest rate swaps, currency swaps can be employed to hedge exchange exposure. By engaging in a swap in which the international portfolio manager pays a variable price based on exchange rate changes and in return receives a fixed-exchange-rate flow from the swap dealer, the former hedges the cash position against exchange rate risk. For this reason, currency swaps are popular, with year-end 1991 outstanding notional principal of about $807 billion.

Figure 18.4 illustrates the hedging concept. The value of the underlying cash position is determined in part by the applicable rate of exchange. By transacting with a swap dealer who receives the floating exchange rate in return for paying a fixed exchange rate, the end user uncouples the foreign security–return performance of the portfolio from its foreign exchange–return performance. In the case of a single country fund, such as Fidelity's Canada fund, a single exchange rate is required to set the floating leg; for a multicountry fund, such as Fidelity's Europe fund, an exchange rate index is required (e.g. the ECU).

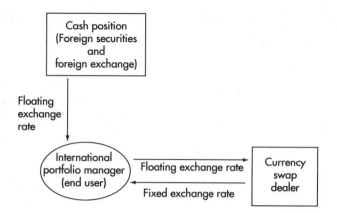

FIGURE 18.4
Currency Swap

FUTURES CONTRACTS, DEFAULT-FREE BONDS, AND SWAPS

Plain vanilla swaps may be created with combinations of other securities. To demonstrate this concept, we now describe how our equity swap can be expressed as a portfolio of stock index futures contracts or default-free bonds. Similarly, interest rate and currency swaps can be replicated by such portfolios. With an understanding of this concept portfolio managers can engineer their own swap transactions, thereby avoiding the spreads and front-end fees charged by swap dealers. Indeed, some contend that swaps are essentially redundant instruments; the cash flows associated with a swap may be replicated by combinations of extant securities.

As in Figure 18.2, one party to the equity swap simply sends a check covering the difference between the fixed and floating payments to the other. However, with most swaps the floating rate that is used on the payment (usage) dates is (here) the quarterly SP500 return that prevailed three months earlier. Therefore, from Figure 18.2 and assuming quarterly compounding, the fund manager (end user) would be required to pay the equity swap dealer the following amount on a given payment date:

(18.1)
$$(NP/4)(R - .0995),$$

where NP is the notional principal (here $100 million) and R is the SP500 return on the *previous* payment (or inception) date.

Equation 18.1 represents a futures contract (ignoring daily resettlement) on the quarterly SP500 that is settled up three months in arrears. This swap has a two-year tenor, so there are eight of these in-arrears stock index futures contracts. Thus the equity swap may be represented as a portfolio of futures contracts in arrears. A portfolio manager can engineer a synthetic equity swap with a series (sometimes called a *strip*) of stock

---

A Currency Swap Between IBM and the World Bank

I nternational Business Machines and the World Bank engaged in the first currency swap, engineered in August 1981. IBM had outstanding debt in both German marks and Swiss francs. The debt was fixed rate. The dollar had greatly appreciated against both foreign currencies earlier in the year. The management of IBM wanted to swap its foreign obligations for dollar obligations to reap the gain on its liabilities due to the dollar's appreciation. To do so, IBM engaged in a swap with the World Bank. The swap was arranged by Salomon Brothers. The World Bank issued two dollar Eurobonds, one with the same maturity as IBM's mark debt and one with the same maturity as IBM's franc debt. The World Bank paid all principal and periodic interest obligations on IBM's debt, and in return IBM paid the World Bank's dollar obligations. This transaction introduced an entirely new financial innovation, the currency swap.

---

index futures contracts. Likewise, synthetic interest rate and currency swaps can be created with strips of futures contracts. For example, a popular way to replicate an interest rate swap where the floating leg is tied to the LIBOR is to employ a strip of Eurodollar futures traded at the Chicago Mercantile Exchange.[8]

Our equity swap may also be expressed as a portfolio of default-free bonds, assuming that no default risk exists. Define B_1 as the value of a fixed-rate, default-free bond that pays 9.95 percent. Also define B_2 as the value of a default-free bond paying the SP500 return. In other words, B_2 is the value of an index-linked bond, an instrument often used by managers who seek an equity participation but are constrained by regulation to hold bond instruments. The value of the swap to the dealer is therefore $B_2 - B_1$. In other words, the swap can be expressed as a portfolio of paired default-free bonds.

SWAPTIONS

Swap options, or *swaptions*, are multiperiod options that are issued by a swap dealer in conjunction with a swap agreement or are issued independently by another swap dealer.[9] When the swaption is issued in

---

[8] Eurodollar futures are listed for up to four years out, implying that interest rate swaps with tenors of four years or less can be created synthetically with these futures contracts. Longer-term interest rate swaps can be replicated with a new futures contract introduced by the CBOT in June of 1991. It is a futures on a five-year swap coupon rate.

[9] Sometimes the term *swaption* is used to refer to an option to enter or exit an existing swap. In the present context we employ the term to represent a multiperiod option issued in conjunction with the swap, or issued independently.

conjunction with the swap, its cost is usually embedded in the swap spread or up-front fee. Otherwise, the swaption premium is charged directly to the client. There are three common types of swaptions: caps, floors, and collars, the last a combination of a cap and a floor. Portfolio managers (end users) can employ swaptions to limit their liability on the floating leg of a swap.

Consider a cap on the floating (SP500) leg of the equity swap illustrated in Figure 18.2. Suppose that the cap rate is 3 percent (qu). Thus in any quarter in which the SP500 return is above 3 percent, the swap dealer pays the end user the excess. From Exhibit 18.1, the cap implies that the end user only pays \$3 million in quarter 8, assuming that the swap dealer wrote the cap. Thus the cap imposes an upper limit on the end user's payout. For this reason it can be viewed as a call option (held by the end user) with an exercise price of 3 percent. Since the cap applies for each quarter over the two-year tenor of the equity swap, the cap therefore represents a type of multiperiod option contract.

A floor works in the opposite manner and thus can be regarded as a type of multiperiod put option held by the swaption dealer. For example, the floor rate (exercise price) may be zero, implying that in any quarter in which the SP500 return is negative the equity swap dealer pays only 2.4875 percent. This floor limits the dealer's liabilities in quarters 3 through 5 of Exhibit 18.1. A collared equity swap would be established by combining the cap and floor. Indeed, a judicious choice of exercise prices will cancel the values of the cap and floor, yielding a net zero initial value for the collar. Swaptions are also used in conjunction with interest rate and currency swaps and variable-rate loans. A discussion of swaption pricing is provided in Appendix 18C.

OTHER SWAP FORMS

The swaps presented thus far may be called straight or plain vanilla swaps because of their simple design. There are a number of variants of these swaps, commonly engineered by affixing addenda to the plain vanilla swap agreement. This agreement, which establishes the basic structure of any swap, is known as a *master agreement* and is described in greater detail in Appendix 18A. We now briefly describe a few of the more elaborate swap arrangements that represent extensions of a master agreement:

- *Amortized swaps.* Here the notional principal reduces over time, much as a home mortgage is amortized.
- *Deferred swaps.* Here usage payments do not begin until a deferred future date.

- *Circus swaps.* These are combinations of currency and interest rate swaps. The parties exchange fixed-rate debt denominated in one currency for floating-rate debt denominated in another currency.
- *Extendable swaps.* Here one of the parties has the option to extend the swap's life beyond the originally prescribed period.
- *Putable swaps.* Here one party has the option to terminate the swap before its originally prescribed period.
- *Delayed-reset swaps.* Here the usage payment at time $t + i$ is determined by the floating rate prevailing at time $t + i$ rather than the floating rate at time t. The equity swap depicted in Figure 18.2 and Exhibit 18.1 is a type of delayed-reset swap.

ASSET ALLOCATION WITH SWAPS

As demonstrated earlier, swaps can be used to hedge preexisting security portfolios. As mentioned in the chapter's introduction, however, swaps can also be used in more proactive asset allocation strategies. In this section we demonstrate the latter use by focusing on how equity swaps allow international money managers to create synthetic foreign equity. Because of market imperfections, including withholding taxes and custodial fees, synthetic equity may be superior to actual equity ownership.

Suppose that you are a portfolio manager of a newly created NIKKEI 225 index mutual fund. Your fund may be created through the actual purchase of the Japanese stocks that make up the index or may be created by assuming the floating-receive equity leg of a NIKKEI 225 swap. Indeed, at the time of this writing, swap dealers are offering the NIKKEI 225 return plus up to 100 basis points in exchange for LIBOR flat (floating equity for floating interest rate). These are several reasons why the latter stratagem may be superior. First, as the manager, you may be drawn to the swap partly because the swap structure guarantees 100 percent correlation with the index—a strong argument for fund managers whose compensation is based on how closely the fund tracks the targeted index.[10] Second, there are savings from circumventing market imperfections. Probably the dominant source of savings is the elimination of costs associated with acquiring and maintaining the cash portfolio, because cash market investing entails several out-of-pocket expenses: withholding taxes, custodial fees, portfolio rebalancings, bid-ask spreads, and stamp taxes. For instance, in Japan, bid-ask spreads are kept large through monopoly control. In addition, there is a turnover

---

[10] A similar advantage may accrue to purely domestic index fund managers who employ equity swaps. Indeed, many of the advantages discussed in this illustration may also accrue to domestic managers.

tax on transactions in securities. And stocks are held through custodial banks, as is the case with ADRs in the United States. The result is the required payment of custodial fees. There is also a transactions cost to rebalancing the cash equity portfolio each time there is a change in the composition of the NIKKEI 225.[11]

A NIKKEI 225 equity swap in which you are the floating-equity receiver can reduce or eliminate these costs, with the benefits accruing to your fund's shareholders. Current estimates of these (annual) costs are about 75 basis points in Japan and up to 175 basis points in the United Kingdom. As a consequence, the costs associated with acquiring and maintaining a cash portfolio may be substantially greater than the costs associated with entering and servicing a swap, that is, creating synthetic Japanese equity. In addition, if the direct investment in Japanese equity exposes your shareholders to currency risk (requiring hedging and imposing hedging costs), you may employ a *hedged swap*, in which the swap is written to pay the foreign index return in your domestic currency. Of course to some degree the implied hedging costs will be reflected in the pricing of the hedged swap. Finally, the swap helps to eliminate the accompanying problems of different settlement, accounting, and reporting procedures among the two countries under the cash portfolio alternative.

Swaps also provide advantages for other international asset allocation strategies. For example, suppose that an internationally diversified fund's manager wants to allocate more wealth to, say, Japan, reducing holdings in German stocks. This type of strategy, which may be called *nation rotating*, is analogous to the strategy of sector rotation among active domestic fund managers.[12] Rather than incurring the large transactions costs associated with trading the German and Japanese equities, the manager may choose to engage in an *equity call swap*. Here a counterparty pays the total return on one national stock index (DAX) in return for the total return on another (NIKKEI). In fact, the manager may have constructed the original fund itself through the use of a *rainbow*, a variant of an equity swap where a blended index is used. For instance, the equity leg of the swap can be 40 percent SP500, 30 percent NIKKEI 225, and 30 percent DAX.

---

[11] Countries other than Japan also impose custodial fees and the like. For instance, Germany and the Netherlands attach a withholding tax to dividends paid to foreign investors. If a foreign investor is subject to, say, a 15 percent withholdings tax and the dividend yield on the foreign index is, say, 3 percent, then the swap alternative translates to an immediate pickup of 45 basis points. The swap effectively allows the foreign investor to engage in tax and regulatory arbitrage.

[12] Recall that with sector rotation a manager identifies one or two economic sectors (e.g., autos) that are anticipated to perform well, and then, given the identified sector opportunity set, engages in optimal portfolio formulation using the procedures described in Part 1.

Ramesh Menon, Equity Swaps Dealer, Bear Sterns & Co.

Bear Sterns & Co. is one of the leading swap dealers in the United States. The investment bank's head of equity swap trading is Ramesh Menon (Bear Sterns & Co., 245 Park Avenue, New York, NY 10167; 212-272-4805). A typical swap constructed by Menon consists of a notional principal of $100 million, has a tenor of 1 year, and has quarterly resets. The bank pays the total return (capital gain plus dividends) on the SP500 in return for the three-month LIBOR minus 10 basis points. The equity swap is not a delayed-reset swap, so usage payments are made in arrears. The usage payments are netted. The notional principal of the swap is also adjusted quarterly, depending on the performance of the SP500. For example, if the index's total return is 10 percent for the first quarter, the notional principal will be increased to $110 million on the first reset date, and so on. Depending on the credit quality of the client, the swap may have to be collateralized. Menon has said that it is not uncommon to transact twenty or more of these swaps in a single day.

On the equity-receive side of the swap are institutional money managers, hedge funds, and indexers, such as Wells Fargo Nikkei and the like. For instance, if Wells Fargo Nikkei was long the NIKKEI 225, which only recently began to gain (September 2, 1992), then the client may look to sell the Japanese equity and convert to U.S. equity. Still, the client seeks to avoid the large commissions and stamp taxes associated with selling Japanese equity. Menon contends that in this case Wells Fargo Nikkei will likely engage in two separate equity swaps, one in which the client pays the NIKKEI 225 and another in which it receives the SP500, as in the swap described above.

According to the carrying charge model (Appendix 16A), the client's cost of purchasing and holding the SP500 should be represented by a short-term interest rate, provided that the equity swap pays the total SP500 return, *including* dividends. For institutional investors, this interest rate is commonly represented by the LIBOR flat. Wells Fargo Nikkei will therefore enter the equity swap with Bear Sterns, since the swap is offered at 10 basis points below the LIBOR flat. In other words, the client can buy the SP500 more cheaply through the swap. Presumably, Bear Sterns was able to offer the total index below LIBOR flat because the prevailing SP500 index futures contracts were relatively cheap. If the futures were appropriately priced, according to the carrying charge model, then the at-market price of the swap should have been LIBOR flat. Bear Sterns can create the equity swap synthetically through a strip of SP500 futures contracts and manage to offer the equity swap below LIBOR flat. Managers at Wells Fargo Nikkei did not create the synthetic swap directly, either because they did not have the expertise, or more likely, because they were restricted from trading index futures contracts.

SUMMARY

A swap can be defined as an agreement to exchange prescribed cash flows at periodic future intervals. Unlike futures and option contracts, swaps are not standardized contracts traded on organized markets. Instead, swaps are negotiated directly between two parties, commonly an end user and a swap dealer operating under the auspices of an investment or commercial bank. Equity swaps can be used by equity portfolio managers to protect against systematic market risk; interest rate swaps can be used by fixed-income fund managers to protect against interest rate risk; and currency swaps can be used by international security managers to protect against exchange rate risk. The manager simply swaps the floating (fixed) rate obtained from the cash position for a fixed (floating) rate paid by the swap dealer. In addition, swaps can be used by managers in tactical asset allocation strategies. For instance, an equity call swap may be used by an international mutual fund manager to engage in nation rotating. The manager should be careful to contract with a dealer who is financially healthy (e.g., Crédit Suisse) in order to ensure future contract performance, especially in these troubled times for investment and commercial banks. Recently, *Euromoney* magazine presented its excellence award for swaps to Chase Manhattan Bank (1992), a leading swaps dealer, especially of interest rate swaps. Finally, it is possible for a portfolio manager to engineer his or her own synthetic swap arrangement, principally through the use of a strip of futures contracts. Indeed, leading futures traders like Refco (Chicago) are beginning to compete for swaps volume with more traditional swaps dealers.

Questions and Problems

1. Define a swap and describe in general terms how a swap can be employed to hedge a preexisting cash position.

2. Identify the major source of difference between equity, interest rate, and currency swaps. (Hint: focus on the floating leg of a swap transaction.)

3. What is the ISDA? Describe its role in standardizing swap transactions. (See Appendix 18A.)

4. Some contend that the consequences of a swap default are far less severe than the consequences of a straight loan default for a commercial bank. Why? (Hint: focus on the concept of notional principal.)

5. Define the following terms as they relate to swaps: tenor, usage payments, notional principal, legs, matched counterparty, and coupon.

6. Ideally, how does a swap dealer hedge the swap book?

7. If a matched swap counterparty is unavailable, how will a swap dealer likely hedge exposure?

8. As an end user, why should you be concerned with the credit risk of a swap dealer?

9. Suppose that in an equity swap the end user paid the minimum of the periodic return of three indices, say the SP500, NIKKEI 225, and FT-SE100. What would likely be the coupon rate or front-end fee for such a swap, relative to a single-index equity swap? Why?

10. Describe how swaps can be synthetically engineered through the trading of listed futures contracts.

11. Why are swaptions types of multiperiod options? Also, describe a cap, a floor, and a collar.

12. Describe the difference between a typical swap and a delayed-reset swap.

13. Using Exhibit 18.1 as a guide, provide the total net flow to the end user under the following new SP500 quarterly returns:

QUARTER	SP500 RETURN	QUARTER	SP500 RETURN
1	0.0191	5	0.0135
2	0.0328	6	0.0028
3	0.0304	7	−0.0050
4	0.0216	8	−0.0185

14. Using the quarterly returns from Problem 13, provide the total net flow to the end user, given a cap of 2.8 percent (qu).

15. Using the quarterly returns from Problem 13, provide the total net flow to the end user, given a collar with floor 0 percent and cap 2.8 percent (qu).

16. Discuss how equity swaps can be used to circumvent market imperfections such as withholding and stamp taxes.

17. Describe a hedged swap, a rainbow, and an equity call swap. Discuss how the last can be employed by an international money manager to engage in nation rotating.

Self-Test Problems

ST-1.   Assume that you manage a $250 million index (SP500) fund and employ an equity swap to immunize the fund for the next four quarters. The swap has a coupon rate of 12 percent per annum; usage payments occur quarterly; it is a delayed-reset swap; and a cap with exercise price 3.25 percent qu accompanies the swap. Compute your quarterly net cash flows given the following SP500 returns:

QUARTER	SP500 RETURNS
1	0.0350
2	0.0125
3	−0.0230
4	0.0245

ST-2.   Assume that you manage a $1 billion bond fund and employ an interest rate swap to hedge the fund for the next four semiannual periods. The swap has a floating rate of LIBOR plus 200 basis points; usage payments occur every six months; it is a delayed-reset swap; and a cap of 9.5 percent sa accompanies the swap. Compute your semiannual net cash flows given the following six-month LIBORs:

SA PERIOD	SIX-MONTH LIBOR
1	0.0625
2	0.0675
3	0.0725
4	0.0775

Solutions to Self-Test Problems

ST-1.

(1) QUARTER	(2) SP500 RETURN	(3) DEALER PAYS	(4) MANAGER PAYS	(5) = (3) − (4) NET FLOW TO MANAGER
1	0.0350	$ 7,500,000[a]	$8,125,000[b]	$ −625,000
2	0.0125	7,500,000[a]	3,125,000[c]	4,375,000
3	−0.0230	13,250,000[d]	0	13,250,000
4	0.0245	7,500,000[a]	6,124,000[e]	1,375,000
			Total	$18,375,000

[a]$250 million NP × .12 pa (.03 qu).
[b]$250 million NP × cap rate of 0.325 qu.
[c]$250 million NP × .0125.
[d]$250 million NP × (.03 + .0230).
[e]$250 million NP × .0245.

ST-2.

(1) SA PERIOD	(2) 6-MONTH LIBOR	(3) DEALER PAYS	(4) MANAGER PAYS	(5) = (3) − (4) NET FLOW TO MANAGER
1	0.0625	$82,500,000[a]	$90,000,000[b]	$−7,500,000
2	0.0675	87,500,000[c]	90,000,000[b]	−2,500,000
3	0.0725	92,500,000[d]	90,000,000[b]	2,500,000
4	0.0775	95,000,000[e]	90,000,000[b]	5,000,000
			Total	$−2,500,000

[a]$1 billion NP × (.0625 + 200 bps).
[b]$1 billion NP × .09 sa.
[c]$1 billion NP × (.0675 + 200 bps).
[d]$1 billion NP × (.0725 + 200 bps).
[e]$1 billion NP × cap rate of .095 sa.

18A

The Roles of Swap Dealers and the International Swap Dealers Association

Investment banks, commercial banks, and independent brokers and dealers facilitate swap transactions. In the early days of the swap market these intermediaries served as brokers who simply matched the swap parties. For this service the intermediary would charge a commission. The intermediary, serving only as a broker, took no credit risk.

Today most intermediaries in the swap market act as dealers, thus serving as a counterparty to the swap. Consequently the dealer is subject to default risk on the part of the end user (and vice versa), as well as interest rate, exchange rate, and systematic market risk. As an example of the extent of these risks, Chemical Bank had a notional principal outstanding for interest rate swaps of $148.5 billion as of September 30, 1988. Chemical Bank's total assets as of that date were $69.8 billion. To limit these sources of risk, the dealer typically engages in an offsetting swap (also known as a *matched swap*), thereby laying off its nondefault swap risk. For instance, with the equity swap depicted in Figure 18.2 the dealer would seek a swap counterparty who desired to *receive* the floating SP500 return in exchange for *paying* a fixed coupon rate. Here the dealer would most likely profit from a basis point spread between the fixed coupon rate received from this counterparty and the fixed coupon rate paid to the end user illustrated in Figure 18.2. The dealer may also structure a spread between the floating legs of the matched swaps or charge each client a front-end fee.

If the dealer cannot find a counterparty who will fully engage in a matched swap, which occurs often, then the dealer typically tries to offset the residual nondefault swap risk by trading existing securities, particularly derivative securities. For instance, consider Figure 18A.1, which extends our earlier equity swap treatment. Here the swap dealer has found a counterparty who receives the floating SP500 in return for paying a fixed coupon rate of 10.05 percent. Thus the dealer earns 10 basis points per annum from the coupon spread. However, the counterparty only assumed the SP500 return on a notional principal (*NP*) of $60 million, $40 million less than the original *NP* of $100 million. The dealer must hedge the residual $40 million position, and as depicted in Figure 18A.1 does so through shorting a series (strip) of SP500 futures contracts. Dealers often use listed derivative securities, such as SP500 futures, to hedge their swap books.

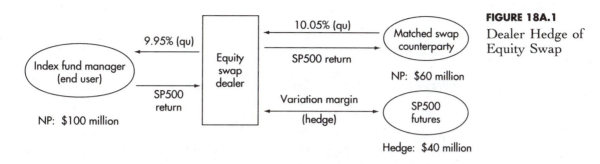

Nevertheless, default risk remains a sticky and sensitive issue for swap banks and their regulators. Given the present competitive nature of the swap market, the smaller spreads being earned by dealers, the off–balance sheet nature of swap arrangements, and the fact that commercial banks are becoming bigger players in swap intermediation, regulators of these banks (e.g., the Fed) are becoming more and more concerned with default risk as it relates to swaps. The Fed is considering a number of methods to control swap default risk, especially the implementation of a risk-weighting scheme now used widely in the United Kingdom. There, a bank's capital adequacy requirement is determined by assigning to each balance sheet and off–balance sheet item, including swaps, a weight reflecting the item's riskiness. The major determinants of this weight for asset items are the credit risk of the other party and the asset's maturity.

Another major player in the swap market is the International Swap Dealers Association (ISDA), an organization of leading swap intermediaries founded in 1985. During 1985 the ISDA published *The Code of Standard Wording, Assumptions, and Provisions for Swaps,* a document that has been revised and expanded annually since 1985. The purpose of the code is to establish master agreements from which every swap transaction could be created as a supplement to these agreements. In other words, master agreements provide a set of terms applicable to any swap transaction; the parties can tailor the transaction by appending specific terms to the master agreement.

Today two master agreements exist: the interest rate swap agreement and the interest rate and currency exchange agreement. The former agreement relates to U.S. dollar–denominated interest rate swaps, and the second relates to currency and circus swap transactions. The actual swap contract that is negotiated between the parties typically represents some extension of these basic agreements. In this way the costs of negotiation are limited to these extensions.

A P P E N D I X

18B

Integrating World Markets with Swaps

It is difficult to overstate the impact of swaps on financial markets: equity swaps bridge the debt and equity subsets of the capital market; currency swaps speed the integration of the world's formerly segregated capital markets; interest rate swaps nullify the traditional distinction between the money and capital markets; and commodity swaps make it possible to achieve long-term fixed pricing in a volatile real asset market. In short, swaps have expanded the investment environment. We demonstrate this important concept by combining the equity, interest rate, and circus swaps described in Chapter 18. Specifically, we show how you can combine a dollar-based equity swap with a dollar-based interest rate swap and a dollar–Deutsche mark circus swap to create a fixed-rate Deutsche mark return from holding a U.S. stock portfolio. Thus we show, for purposes of illustrating how swaps can integrate world markets, how the U.S. equity market and German bond market are linked.[13]

Figure 18B.1 presents the three swap transactions. Notice that the SP500 dollar-based return from the cash position is cancelled by the floating leg

FIGURE 18B.1

Combining Swap
Transactions

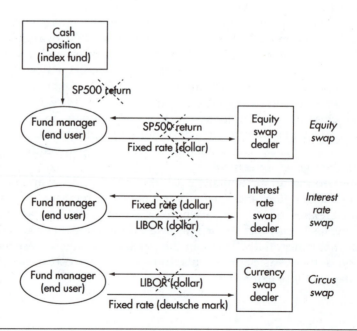

---

[13] This illustration is based on one provided by Marshall, Sorensen, and Tucker (1992).

of the equity swap. The dollar coupon of the equity swap is in turn canceled by the dollar coupon of the interest rate swap. Finally, the floating leg of the interest rate swap is canceled by the floating leg of the circus swap. The end result, remarkably, is a fixed cash flow in Deutsche marks from holding a U.S. equity portfolio.

Swap and Swaption Pricing

In Chapter 18 we demonstrated that a swap can be decomposed into a portfolio of paired default-free bonds or into a portfolio of futures contracts. It follows, therefore, that a swap price (i.e., the fixed coupon rate) can be determined using the mechanics of pricing bonds or futures contracts. In other words, a person who knows how to price bonds or futures contracts should be able to price swaps. In this appendix we demonstrate swap pricing via the first approach, namely the mechanics of bond pricing. The demonstration entails an interest rate swap, but we could easily have chosen an equity or currency swap. Also, the swap is at market, meaning that the net present value of the fixed and floating cash flows of the interest rate swap is zero at swap inception. Later we discuss the pricing of off-market swaps.[14]

Suppose that firm X enters into an interest rate swap with a swap dealer. X makes floating payments based on LIBOR flat, and the dealer makes fixed coupon payments. The terms of the swap are

Notional principal	$1 million
Tenor	1 year
Payment frequency	Semiannual
Floating index	Six-month LIBOR flat
Fixed coupon rate	?

---

[14] In the bond approach to pricing swaps, the actual or expected floating-rate payments at time periods $1, 2, \ldots, T$ are first determined by spot and forward interest rates obtained from the prevailing term structure. Then the fixed coupon rate is revealed by setting the net present value of the fixed and floating payments equal to zero. The alternative futures approach simply relies on observed futures prices rather than the term structure to obtain forward interest rates and then proceeds in an analogous manner to determine the fixed coupon payment. An important limitation of this approach, however, is that it cannot be used to price long-tenor swaps, since long-dated futures contracts are usually unavailable. This limitation is analogous to having only a short term structure when trying to price long-tenor swaps via the bond approach.

FIGURE 18C.1

LIBOR Term
Structure at Swap
Inception

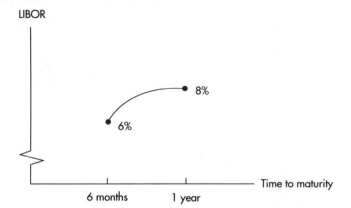

What is the appropriate fixed coupon rate such that the swap has a zero net present value at its inception (an at-market swap)?

Given the above terms, firm X will make two floating payments: at the six-month settlement, a payment based on the six-month LIBOR in effect at contract inception ($\tilde{R}_1$), and at the twelve-month settlement, a payment based on the six-month LIBOR prevailing at month 6 ($\tilde{R}_2$). To determine these two payments the LIBOR term structure (also called the spot term structure) prevailing at swap inception is required. Suppose that it is given by Figure 18C.1. Thus the current (also called the spot or zero) six-month LIBOR is 6 percent and the current twelve-month LIBOR is 8 percent. Therefore the first floating payment ($\tilde{R}_1$), will be $30,000, or

$$(\tilde{R}_1) = \$1,000,000 \times .50(.06) = \$30,000.$$

To obtain the second floating payment ($\tilde{R}_2$), we need the six-month LIBOR prevailing at month 6. It is just the forward interest (LIBOR) rate. A simple arbitrage argument ensures that

(18C.1) $$(1 + {}_0r_{12}) = [1 + .50({}_0r_6)][1 + .50({}_6r_{12})],$$

where ${}_0r_{12}$ and ${}_0r_6$ are the current twelve-month and six-month rates, respectively, and ${}_6r_{12}$ is the forward rate of interest. In our example, ${}_6r_{12}$ is 9.71 percent:

$$(1 + .08) = [1 + .50(.06)][1 + .50({}_6r_{12})].$$

Therefore, the second floating payment is expected to be $48,550, or

$$\tilde{R}_2 = \$1,000,000 \times .50(.0971) = \$48,550.^{[15]}$$

---

[15] If this were a longer-tenor swap, then subsequent expected floating payments ($\tilde{R}_3, \tilde{R}_4, \ldots$) would be obtained from subsequent forward rates implied by the current term structure.

Now that the floating payments have been determined, the appropriate fixed coupon rate can be identified. It must assume a value that forces the swap to exhibit a zero NPV at contract inception, or

$$\frac{\$30{,}000 - \overline{R}_1}{1 + .50(.06)} + \frac{\$48{,}550 - \overline{R}_2}{1.08} = \$0,$$

where $\overline{R}_1 = \overline{R}_2$, or the fixed dollar payments made by the swap dealer. Solving this equation gives $\overline{R}_1 = \overline{R}_2 = \$39{,}055$. Thus the appropriate fixed coupon rate is 7.81 percent, or[16,17]

$$(\$39{,}055/\$1{,}000{,}000)(2) = .0781.$$

To conclude our discussion of swap pricing, next consider an off-market swap. An arbitrary coupon rate is selected at swap inception, the consequence being that the swap will not have a zero NPV at inception. To mark the contract to the market, therefore, an up-front payment will have to be made from one party to the other. For example, if the fixed coupon rate in the previous illustration were set at 8 percent rather than 7.81 percent, the swap would have a NPV (to the swap dealer) of –$1,792:

$$\frac{\$30{,}000 - \$40{,}000}{1 + .50(.06)} + \frac{\$48{,}550 - \$40{,}000}{1.08} = -\$1{,}792$$

Hence firm X would have to pay the swap dealer $1,792 in order to engage in this off-market interest rate swap.

To illustrate the concept of pricing a swaption, suppose that we have an instantaneous interest rate cap on a floating-rate loan whose principal amount is L, whose floating rate is reset every three months to equal the three-month LIBOR, and whose cap is 10 percent per annum. If interest

---

[16] This rate is the fixed coupon rate that makes the swap have a zero NPV at inception. After inception the term structure will change, meaning that forward interest rates and thus expected future floating payments will also change. Consequently, since the coupon rate on the swap is fixed, the swap will take on some nonzero NPV. If the LIBOR increases at each maturity (an upward shift in the term structure), then the swap will have a positive (negative) NPV for the fixed (floating) leg of the swap, and vice versa. Swap dealers continually track the present values of their swaps (i.e., mark them to the market) for hedging purposes. Also notice that interest rate movements therefore have consequences for the probability of swap default, since the floating leg (firm X) will surely not choose to default on a swap that exhibits a positive NPV (from firm X's viewpoint).

[17] It is instructive to note that our solution, 7.81 percent, is also the par rate, that is, the coupon rate $(\overline{r})$ that would make a one-year semiannual-coupon-bearing bond trade at par/face value:

$$100 = [(.50\overline{r} \times 100)/(1 + .50(.06))] + [(.50\overline{r} \times 100)/1.08] + [100/1.08],$$

and solving for $\overline{r}$ gives .0781.

rates are expressed using quarterly compounding and interest is paid at the end of each quarter, then the party making the loan must pay the borrower the following amount at the end of each quarter:

$$0.25L[MAX(R - 0.1,0)],$$

where R is the three-month LIBOR in effect at the beginning of the quarter and $MAX(R - 0.1,0)$ represents the payoff from a call option on R. Hence the cap is a portfolio of call options on R where payoffs occur three months in arrears.

More generally, if the cap rate is X and interest payments on the loan are made at times $t, 2t, \ldots, nt$, the cap writer must make the following payments:

$$tL[MAX(R_{k-1} - X,0)]$$

where R_{k-1} is the LIBOR in effect at time $(k-1)t$. Almost equivalently, we have

$$\frac{tL}{1 + \tilde{R}_t} MAX(R_{k-1} - X,0)$$

where $\tilde{R}_t$ is an estimate of the rate of interest between times $(k-1)t$ and kt. Thus, as an approximation, the cap can be viewed on a portfolio of European call options on the ninety-day interest rate with payoff occurring at the maturities of the options, rather than ninety days later. The principal amount for each option is $tL(1 + \tilde{R}_t)$. Floors and collars can be valued using similar arguments.

REFERENCES

Abken, P. 1991. Beyond plain vanilla. A taxonomy of swaps. *Economic Review*, Federal Reserve Bank of Atlanta. March/April, 12–29.

Arak, M., A. Estrella, L. Goodman, and A. Silver. 1988. Interest rate swaps. An alternative explanation. *Financial Management*. Summer, 12–18.

Arnold, T. 1984. How to do interest rate swaps. *Harvard Business Review*. September-October, 96–101.

Aspel, D., J. Cogen, and M. Rabin. 1989. Hedging long term commodity swaps with futures. *Global Finance Journal* Fall, 77–93.

Beckstrom, R. 1986. The development of the swap market. In *Swap finance*, vol 1. Boris Antl, ed. London: Euromoney Publications.

Beidleman, C. 1985. *Financial swaps*. Homewood, IL: Dow Jones-Irwin.

Bicksler, J., and A. Chen. 1986. An economic analysis of interest rate swaps. *Journal of Finance* July, 645–655.

Briys, E., M. Crouhy, and R. Schöbel. 1991. The pricing of default-free interest rate cap, floor, and collar agreements. *Journal of Finance* December, 1879–1892.

Campbell, T., and W. Kracaw. 1991. Intermediation and the market for interest rate swaps. *Journal of Financial Intermediation* March, 362–384.

Cooper, I., and A. Mello. 1991. The default risk of swaps. *Journal of Finance* June, 597–620.

Felgran, S. 1987. Interest rate swaps. Use, risk, and prices. *New England Economic Review* (Federal Reserve Bank of Boston). November, 22–32.

Gary, R., W. Kruz, and C. Strupp. 1983. Interest rate swaps. In *Swap Financing Techniques*. B. Antl, ed. London: Euromoney Publications.

Hull, J. 1993. *Options, futures, and other derivative securities*. Englewood Cliffs, NJ: Prentice Hall.

Kapner, K., and J. Marshall. 1991. *The swaps handbook*. New York: New York Institute of Finance.

Kidwell, D., W. Marr, and R. Thompson. 1985. Eurodollar bonds. Alternative financing for U.S. companies. *Financial Management*. Winter, 18–27.

Lipsky, J., and S. Elhalaski. 1986. *Swap-driven primary insurance in the international bond market*. Salomon Brothers.

Litzenberger, R. 1992. Presidential address: Swaps: plain and fanciful. *Journal of Finance*. July, 831–850.

Marshall, J., V. Bansal, A. Herbst, and A. Tucker. 1992. Hedging business cycle risk with macro swaps and macro options. *Journal of Applied Corporate Finance*. Winter, 103–108.

Marshall, J., V. Bansal, and A. Tucker. 1991. Interest rate swaps as a cash management tool. *Corporate Risk Management*. April, 20–22.

Marshall, J., and K. Kapner. 1990. *Understanding swap finance*. Cincinnati: South-Western Publishing.

Marshall, J., E. Sorensen, and A. Tucker. 1992. Equity derivatives: The plain vanilla equity swap and its variants. *Journal of Financial Engineering*. September, 219–241.

McNulty, J. 1992. Pricing of interest rate swaps. *Journal of Financial Services Research*. March 53–63.

Melnik, A. and S. Plaut. 1992. Currency swaps, hedging, and the exchange of collateral. *Journal of International Money and Finance*. October, 446–461.

Park, Y. 1984. Currency swaps as a long-term international financing technique. *Journal of International Business Studies*. Winter, 15:3, 47–54.

Powers, J. 1986. The vortex of finance. *Intermarket Magazine*. February, 3:2, 27–38.

Price, J., J. Keller, and M. Nelson. 1983. The delicate art of swaps. *Euromoney*. April, 118–125.

Shirreff, D. 1985. The fearsome growth of swaps. *Euromoney*. October, 247–261.

Smith, C., C. Smithson, and L. Wakeman. 1986. The evolving market for swaps. *Midland Corporate Finance Journal*. Winter, 20–32.

Smith, C., C. Smithson, and L. Wakeman. 1988. The market for interest rate swaps. *Financial Management*. Winter, 34–44.

Smith, C., C. Smithson, and D. Wilford. 1990. *Managing financial risk*. New York: Harper Business.

Tucker, A. 1991. *Financial futures, options, and swaps*. St. Paul, MN: West Publishing.

Turnball, S. 1987. Swaps: A zero sum game. *Financial Management*. Spring, 15–22.

Wall, L. 1989. Interest rate swaps in an agency theoretic model with uncertain interest rates. *Journal of Banking and Finance*. May, 261–270.

Wall, L., and J. Pringle. 1989. Alternative explanations of interest rate swaps: A theoretical and empirical analysis. *Financial Management*. Summer, 59–73.

Whittaker, J. 1987. Interest rate swaps. Risk and regulation. *Economic Review* (Federal Reserve Bank of Kansas City) March, 3–13.

Yaksick, R. 1992. Swaps, caps, and floors: Some parity and price identities. *Journal of Financial Engineering*. June, 105–115.

CHAPTER *19*

Portfolio Insurance

Introduction

In Chapters 16 and 17 we examined how futures and options contracts could be employed to hedge preexisting portfolio positions. In this chapter we analyze a popular but somewhat more complex hedging strategy known as portfolio insurance. In general, *portfolio insurance* is the hedging of security portfolios to ensure that the portfolio's value does not fall below some prescribed minimum level.

The idea of portfolio insurance was introduced in part in Chapter 17. There we examined how stock index put options could be combined with equity portfolios to ensure a minimum future portfolio value. If the stock market climbs, the index put option is not exercised, and thus the purchased insurance is not used (i.e., no "claim" is filed). On the other hand, the put is exercised if the market declines, providing a portfolio value equal to the option's exercise price.

The use of stock index put options to insure equity portfolios is the earliest form of portfolio insurance (Pozen 1978). However, this strategy has not been popular among institutional portfolio managers for four reasons. First, adequate contracts, corresponding to the horizons of institutional managers, have not been introduced. The maturities of listed index options are typically much shorter than the planned holding horizons of institutional portfolio managers, although recently, long-dated index options, called LEAPs, have been introduced at the CBOE and other exchanges. These institutional portfolios are typically pension fund portfolios, although portfolio insurance often is used by mutual fund and insurance company portfolio managers. Second, typically the traded options are American, and as argued in Chapter 17, their prices reflect an early exercise premium. Portfolio insurers with fixed horizon dates are unwilling to pay this cost. They prefer European index options. Third, there are position limits for listed options that may prevent large institutional portfolio managers from obtaining all of the insurance desired. It is fairly common for a pension fund to have assets in excess of $1 billion. Fourth, the fixed exercise prices of traded index options may not appeal to managers who seek more refined insurance floors.

Recognizing these shortcomings, Leland and Rubinstein[1] sought to provide alternative paths to portfolio insurance. They showed how portfolios could be insured with calls, U.S. Treasury bills, and stock index futures. More specifically, Leland and Rubinstein demonstrated how managers could replicate an option-insured portfolio through a process of continually revising, in a prescribed manner, the proportions of a hedged portfolio consisting of the underlying asset and (originally) the risk-free asset. Thus, they created a synthetically insured portfolio put option through dynamic trading. Using this technique, they developed a highly successful and nationally recognized portfolio insurance consulting firm, Leland, O'Brien, Rubinstein Associates, Inc. Many large pension funds, including those of General Motors, Daiichi Mutual, Delta Airlines, and the Idaho Public Employees Retirement Association, have their portfolio insurance operations handled by this California-based partnership. Several leading investment banks, such as Chase Manhattan Corporation (United States), Midland Montagu and County NatWest (both United Kingdom) and Wells Fargo Nikkei (United States), also provide portfolio insurance services.

The purpose of this chapter is to review the portfolio insurance techniques developed by Pozen and by Leland and Rubinstein. Specifically, we will analyze four techniques commonly known as (1) stock-put insurance, (2) stock–Treasury bill insurance, (3) call–Treasury bill insurance, and (4) dynamic hedging. The first three techniques entail options trading, at least indirectly, and the fourth involves the trading of stock index futures. Also, the first technique may be regarded as static, but the last three are dynamic, since they entail frequent trading and portfolio reallocation.

We will first analyze each of the four techniques separately and under the simplifying assumption of a one-period horizon. Then we will provide a unified analysis entailing several periods and based on the binomial framework presented in Appendix 17A. In general our analysis will follow

---

[1] See Leland (1980, 1985), Rubinstein (1985), and Rubinstein and Leland (1981).

that of O'Brien (1988). While our emphasis in this chapter concerns insurance for equity portfolios, the techniques and concepts presented are also applicable to fixed-income portfolios and portfolios influenced by currency movements. For instance, Chase Manhattan Corporation recently began providing $2 billion of currency-related portfolio insurance for its clients, and BEA of New York provides dynamic currency risk management services for Unisys. In addition, currency risk management boutiques, such as FX Concepts and Pareto Partners, offer dynamic currency management.

PORTFOLIO INSURANCE TECHNIQUES
Stock-Put Insurance

By combining an equity portfolio with index put options, a portfolio manager can ensure that the portfolio's value does not fall below some minimum level. As an illustration, suppose a manager oversees a diversified portfolio that replicates the SP500.[2] The SP500 is 280 and the portfolio is worth $560,000, or 2,000 units of the index. Assume that it is mid-November and that the December 280 SP500 put contract, which sells for $1,250, expires in one month. Further assume that the option is European and that the one-month risk-free rate of interest is .0085. Finally, assume that the annualized return variance of the SP500 is .015.

The manager seeks to insure the portfolio by purchasing the December puts. Purchasing four contracts would reduce the investment in the stock portfolio by $5,000. Thus the stock portfolio now contains approximately 1,982 units of the SP500 index, and the manager holds four put contracts entailing 2,000 index units. Of course, if the stocks and put contracts were perfectly divisible, the manager could assume a one-to-one correspondence between the portfolio index units held and the number of index units underlying the put contracts.

If the resulting SP500 index level is at or above the exercise price of 280 at contract expiration, the options expire worthless. For instance, if the expiration SP500 is 310, the puts are not exercised and the resulting portfolio value is $614,463.40 (1,982.14 units × 310). Here the opportunity cost of undertaking the insurance is $5,536.60, since a 100 percent investment in the stock portfolio would have yielded a portfolio value of $620,000 (2,000 units × 310). This $5,536.60 cost represents about 1 percent of the portfolio's original value, implying that the upside capture was about 99 percent. The *upside capture* is the percentage of the uninsured appreciation in an up market that is captured by the insured portfolio.

On the other hand, if the expiration SP500 is below 280, the put contracts are exercised and the proceeds are used to offset losses in the

---

[2] This assumption eliminates problems associated with basis risk.

equity portfolio. For example, if the SP500 is 250 at option expiration, the resulting insured portfolio value is $555,535:

$$(1.982.14 \times 250) + (280 - 250)(2,000).$$

Of course, an uninsured portfolio's value would have been just $500,000 (2,000 units × 250). In general, the minimum insured level of the portfolio is $555,000, occurring when the expiration SP500 level is exactly 280 (1,982.14 × 280 = $555,000).[3,4]

The above illustration of portfolio insurance employing index put options should be familiar. It is analogous to the hedging strategy illustrated in Figure 17.3. The simple idea driving the strategy is that the purchase of put options introduces negative correlation with the preexisting equity position and as a result guarantees a certain minimum future value for the portfolio. The cost of the strategy is the accompanying reduction in upside capture.

Stock–Treasury Bill Insurance

The stock-put insurance technique described above appears to be simple to implement and effective in insuring investor wealth. As discussed in the introduction to this chapter, however, the technique is not widely used in practice because put options with the appropriate terms are not traded on organized exchanges. Recognizing this, Leland (1980) sought to obtain portfolio insurance through trading other securities. The initial technique he proposed involved the use of Treasury bills and is described next.

Define TB as the current price of a $10,000 Treasury bill that expires in one month. Since the one-month risk-free rate is .0085, TB should be $9,915.72:

$$\$9,915.72 = \$10,000(1.0085)^{-1}.$$

To ensure that the portfolio attains the same minimum value that can be achieved with the put options, $555,000, the manager must purchase 55.5 Treasury bills ($555,000 divided by 10,000). Given the inability to purchase fractional amounts of the security, the manager chooses to buy 56 Treasury bills. Thus the investment in the equity portfolio is reduced by $555,280.32 (56 × $9,915.72), leaving just $4,719.68 in equities (or 16.856 index units).

---

[3] If stocks and put contracts were perfectly divisible so that a one-to-one correspondence was attainable, then the minimum insured level of the portfolio, V_{MIN}, would be given by the following expression: $V_{MIN} = XV/(S + P)$, where X is the option's exercise price, V is the original value of the portfolio, S is the original level of the stock index, and P is the per index unit price of the put option.

[4] Assuming perfect markets, the guaranteed *percentage* return on the insured portfolio must be less than the risk-free rate to prevent arbitrage. One cannot insure a minimum return on a risky portfolio that is greater than the riskless rate of interest in an efficient marketplace.

As before, suppose that the resulting SP500 index level is either 310 or 250 in one month. The resulting insured portfolio values are \$565,225.36 and \$564,214.00, respectively:

$$\$565,255.36 = (16.856 \times 310) + (56 \times 10,000);$$
$$\$564,214.00 = (16.856 \times 250) + (56 \times 10,000).$$

Each of these values exceeds \$555,000. Indeed, the stock–Treasury bill insurance technique must provide a minimum value of \$560,000, since the SP500 index has a floor value of zero.[5] Thus, the stock–Treasury bill insurance technique provides the same coverage as the stock-put insurance technique.

Figure 19.1 portrays the resulting portfolio values for various levels of the SP500 at the end of the one-month holding period. For SP500 levels above 280, the stock–Treasury bill portfolio's value increases at a slower rate than the stock-put portfolio's value. This is because the former has less upside capture. The upside capture for the stock-put portfolio was about 99 percent, but it is about 90 percent for the stock–Treasury bill portfolio:

$$1 - [(\$620,000 - 565,225.36)/(\$560,000)].$$

FIGURE 19.1

Stock-Treasury Bill Insured Portfolio Values

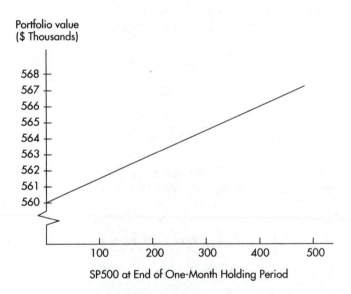

<hr>

[5] Do not be fooled into believing that the stock–Treasury bill insurance technique is superior because its guaranteed minimum portfolio value (\$560,000) is greater than that provided by the stock-put insurance technique (\$555,000). This difference only arises because of the rounding assumed when undertaking contract positions. Indeed, each insurance technique examined can be demonstrated to provide the exact same minimum insured value if all securities are assumed to be perfectly divisible.

Call–Treasury Bill Insurance

The third technique, call–Treasury bill insurance, replicates the previous two insurance techniques by assuming positions in Treasury bills and stock index call options. In our example, call–Treasury bill insurance is obtained by purchasing the same number of Treasury bills, 56, and employing the remaining $4,719.68 in portfolio wealth to purchase index call options. By arbitrage and the law of one price, the price of a corresponding December 280 SP500 call option is $4.86 per index unit.[6] Thus the manager is able to purchase 971.13 call index units ($4,719.68/ 4.86), which at a multiplier of 500 represents 1.942 call contracts. To simplify the analysis, we allow the manager to purchase fractional amounts of index call option contracts.

As before, we assume that the expiration SP500 index level is either 310 or 250. The resulting call–Treasury bill portfolio values are $589,130 and $560,000, respectively:

$$\$589{,}130 = (310 - 280)(1.942)(\$500) + 56(\$10{,}000);$$
$$\$560{,}000 = 56(\$10{,}000).$$

Further, the minimum insured portfolio value is $560,000, since the call options are not exercised for expiration index levels below the 280 exercise price. This insurance technique therefore provides results similar to those obtained by the stock-put and stock–Treasury bill techniques.

Figure 19.2 portrays the values of the call–Treasury bill portfolio for different expiration index levels. Notice that the graph is similar to that of a protective put strategy. (For instance, compare Figure 19.2 with Figure 17.3, which portrays profits from a protective put involving SP100 index options.) For the call–Treasury bill strategy, the upside capture is about 95 percent:[7]

$$1 - [(\$620{,}000 - 589{,}130)/(\$560{,}000)].$$

---

[6] Recall that the options are assumed to be European. Furthermore, an implicit assumption here is that no dividends are paid on the index's underlying stocks over the one-month holding period. Given these assumptions, an application of put-call parity—a well-known formula relating the prices of corresponding European put and call options—yields a call option price of $4.86. See Equation 17A.21 of Appendix 17A.

[7] It is instructive to note that the upside capture on the call–Treasury bill insurance technique would be exactly the same as that on the stock-put technique if all securities were perfectly divisible. Specifically, under the former technique 55.5 Treasury bills would be purchased, leaving $7,677.54 in portfolio wealth to purchase 1,991.26 call index units. At an expiration index value of 310, the call–Treasury bill portfolio would be worth $614,737.80, implying an upside capture of 99 percent. This is the same upside capture as that exhibited by the stock-put insurance technique. This result confirms the fact that the stock-put insurance technique can be replicated by a combination of index call options and Treasury bills.

FIGURE 19.2

Call–Treasury Bill
Insured Portfolio
Values

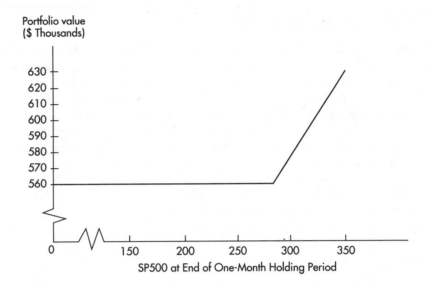

Dynamic Hedging

As discussed earlier, the stock-put insurance technique suffers from the inability to obtain traded index put options exhibiting the desired terms. Tailored portfolio insurance may be acquired by contracting with investment banks to purchase customized index options, but such contracts are likely to be expensive. The alternative insurance techniques that involve Treasury bills also have shortcomings. Most importantly, these techniques require portfolio managers to trade tremendous numbers of individual stocks, entailing prohibitive transaction costs. Furthermore, not all institutional managers can use these techniques, as someone must hold the stocks.

Because of these problems, Rubinstein (1985) sought to provide an alternative insurance technique that both replicated the desirable properties of stock-put insurance and reduced stock trading and the associated transaction costs of the stock–Treasury bill and call–Treasury bill techniques. The method he developed entails the trading of stock index futures contracts and is usually called dynamic hedging. *Dynamic hedging* replicates the behavior of a stock-put-insured portfolio by continually rebalancing a portfolio of stocks and index futures contracts. Because this technique achieves such replication with comparatively low transaction costs, dynamic hedging has become a popular form of portfolio insurance among institutional managers. Leland, O'Brien, Rubinstein Associates, Inc., among others, has been successful in marketing this type of portfolio insurance to pension fund managers. In this subsection we examine this popular portfolio insurance technique.

Dynamic hedging with stock index futures entails writing a number of futures contracts so that the portfolio achieves the same price action as a stock-put-insured portfolio. Appendix 19.A describes a procedure for determining the number of index futures contracts required. Defining this number by N_f, we have

(19.1) $N_f = [(V/(S + P))(1 + (dP/dS)) - (V/S)] \times e^{-rT}$.

The term N_f is called the *dynamic hedge ratio*. Notice that the portfolio manager must continually adjust this ratio, since the variables in equation 19.1 will change over time as the index varies and as the futures contract unwinds.

Getting back to our example, the dynamic hedge ratio is[8]

$$N_f = \left[\frac{560,000}{280 + 2.50}(1 - .394) - \frac{560,000}{280}\right] \times (.9915) = -791.94.$$

Since the index futures multiple is 500, the manager requires −1.584 contracts (−791.94/500). The cost of a futures contract is zero at contract inception. Thus, the dynamic hedging technique entails holding $560,000 in stock (2,000 index units) and *shorting* 1.584 index futures contracts with a one-month maturity. The futures price should be 282.38.[9]

To illustrate how this stock-futures portfolio achieves the same price action as a stock-put-insured portfolio, assume that the derivatives dP/dS and df/dS accurately reflect the changes in the option and futures prices, respectively, for a discrete one-point change in the SP500. In other words, a one-point decline in the index will change the put option price by 39.4¢ and the index futures price by −$1.0085. For our earlier stock-put-insured portfolio, whose manager held 1,982.14 index units in stock and four index put option contracts, the resulting value change is −$1,184.14 for a one-point decline in the index;:

Stock	4,982.14 unis × −$1 =	−$1,982.14
Options	4 contracts × 500 × (−$1) × (−.394) =	788.00
	Total:	−$1,194.14

---

[8] The derivative dP/dS is −.394 for the put option. Since no dividends are assumed to be paid over the one-month holding period, $dP/dS = N(d_1) - 1$. Recall that this is the put option's delta. See equation 17A.22 of Appendix 17A.

[9] The index futures price of 282.38 obtains because there is one-month period and no dividends occur over the period. By the cost-of-carry model (Appendix 16A), we have

$$f = S(1 + r) = 280(1.0085) = 282.38.$$

Notice that $df/dS = (1 + r)$, or 1.0085.

For the stock-futures portfolio, the resulting value change is −$1,201.27:

Stock	2,000 units × −$1 =	−$2,000.00
Futures	−1.584 contracts × 500× (−$1) × (1.0085) =	798.73
	Total:	−$1,201.27

The difference between the two outcomes is nominal and attributable to rounding error. Hence the two techniques appear to achieve the same price action. Had the index increased by one point, then both insured portfolios would have risen by about $1,200 in value. We can conclude that dynamic hedging effectively replicates the protection offered by the stock-put insurance technique.

Some Issues Regarding Dynamic Hedging

There are a few issues regarding dynamic hedging that deserve further inspection at this time. First it appears that this insurance technique is nearly cost free, since the cost of a futures contract at contract inception is zero and the transaction costs of futures trading are lower than those of trading stocks, options, and Treasury bills. Indeed, such low (direct) transaction costs are in part what attract portfolio managers to insure with this technique rather than with, say, the stock–Treasury bill technique described earlier. However, dynamic hedging still entails the important opportunity cost associated with appreciating equity markets. From the portfolio manager's perspective, this opportunity cost is the most important drawback of dynamic hedging. The portfolio gains less when the short index futures position is assumed and the market rises than when no futures position is assumed and the market rises. Shorting the futures contract introduces negative correlation, which helps to insure a minimum future value for the portfolio, but along with this insured value comes the potential for losing some gains in a rising market. Hence the apparent low cost of the technique is misleading. Like the other techniques described above, dynamic hedging has an upside capture that is less than 100 percent.

Another important issue concerns rebalancing. Dynamic hedging requires continual trading to adjust the hedge ratio and thereby guarantee a specific future portfolio value. This issue will become more evident when we explore a multiperiod setting later in this chapter. However, continual trading clearly is impossible. Frequent rebalancing entails large monitoring and trading costs, but less frequent rebalancing can jeopardize the future insured value of the portfolio. The portfolio manager must decide how often to rebalance in light of this trade-off. Since the put option's delta appears in equation 19.1, as discussed in Chapter 17 the put option's gamma may serve as a useful rebalancing indicator.

A closely related issue concerns the sensitivity of the portfolio's value to changes in the market index (here the SP500). The derivatives dP/dS and *df/dS* provide only approximate changes for the option and futures prices as the market varies. When large market movements occur, these approximations can be poor.[10] This result implies that dynamic hedging may be ineffective in fast-moving markets. Indeed, the technique proved to be quite ineffective during the crash of October 1987, resulting in a postcrash decline in its use; however, the popularity of the technique is now reemerging.

Finally, to ensure the target portfolio value the manager must short fewer futures contracts to achieve the insured value when stock prices climb and similarly must short more and more futures contracts as stock prices fall. Hence, it is often said that with dynamic hedging one longs index futures when stocks are high and shorts them when stocks are low. In other words, one buys high and sells low. This strategy would be an unfortunate one to earn profits but is sensible when insuring a position against losses in case of a market downturn. Some have argued that such a strategy can exacerbate downturns in the market. Indeed, a Presidential commission reported that dynamic hedging in conjunction with index arbitrage activities may have fueled the stock market crash of October 19, 1987. For more on this see the box "Portfolio Insurance and Its Role in the October 1987 and October 1989 Market Crashes."

A Unified Analysis of Portfolio Insurance

In this section we provide a unified analysis of portfolio insurance. The analysis is based on the binomial generating process and permits us to extend the discussion of portfolio insurance to a multiperiod setting. This extension provides more insight and detail, especially with respect to the dynamic nature of the insurance techniques. We begin below with a presentation of the underlying equity portfolio dynamics and the resulting option prices and dynamics. We then compare the stock-put insurance technique with dynamic hedging, which again entails the frequent trading of index futures contracts.

The Underlying Portfolio Dynamics

The assumed prices of the underlying portfolio in the insurance program are presented in Figure 19.3 on page 525. The figure, known as a tree diagram or lattice, depicts a three-period, two-state process in which the multiplicative upward movement is 1.2 times the current portfolio value and the multiplicative downward movement is 1/1.2. The original portfolio value is assumed to be $100. Thus after one period its value may be $120 or $83.33, and so on. This is the same binomial generating process found in both Cox, Ross, and Rubinstein (1979) and Rendleman and

---

[10] Recall that partial derivatives are local measures only.

Bartter (1979). Recall from Appendix 17A that these authors developed a discrete-time version of the Black-Scholes model known as the binomial option pricing model. The price dynamics shown in Figure 19.3 will be used here to demonstrate the stock-put and dynamic hedging portfolio insurance techniques in a multiperiod world.

PORTFOLIO INSURANCE AND ITS ROLE IN THE OCTOBER 1987 AND OCTOBER 1989 MARKET CRASHES

The Brady Commission, appointed by President Ronald Reagan to study the causes of the October 1987 stock market crash, concluded that dynamic hedging in conjunction with stock index arbitrage exacerbated the precipitous decline in equity values on October 19. Specifically, the commission reported that the initial market decline was a result of changes in a number of fundamental macroeconomic indicators, including domestic and international trade deficits and other factors such as proposed legislation to make corporate takeovers more difficult and costly. This initial market decline in turn triggered a wave of index futures selling by institutional portfolio insurers. The commission reported that portfolio managers sold over $4 billion worth of index futures contracts on October 19 alone.

The commission suggested that the selling of vast amounts of index futures caused a disparity between futures and stock prices that resulted in more than $1.7 billion worth of index arbitrage trading. Program traders, through the designated order turnaround (DOT) system of the NYSE, sold the stocks and bought the futures. Such stock selling was concluded to have fueled the market's decline.

Presumably the activities of portfolio insurers and index arbitragers tend to counteract and not exacerbate the initial market decline. However, recall that portfolio insurance can be ineffective during fast-moving markets. Trading delays due to unprecedented volume also drove a wedge between the activities of portfolio insurers and program traders. Further complicating matters was the fact that NYSE officials stopped members from using the DOT system to engage in index arbitrage on October 20. The commission concluded that this action effectively segmented the trading activities of portfolio insurers and program traders. In turn, the equilibrating effect of index arbitrage was frustrated, and the commission found that the technical trading systems actually served to depress the market.

More recently, technical trading systems appeared to have fueled the 190-point drop in the DJIA occurring on October 13, 1989. On this day the DJIA lost 6.91 percent, and investors lost nearly $190 billion in the equities market. The initial market decline was attributed to a U.S. Labor Department announcement concerning higher wholesale prices and to a failed attempt to take over UAL Corp., the parent company of United Airlines. The pilot-management group seeking to take UAL private failed to obtain the necessary financing, and selling pressure was exerted by speculators who feared further financing problems with other takeover deals—a type of contagion effect.

However, over 80 percent of the 190-point decline occurred in the last hour of the trading session. Furthermore, trading was (then) unusually heavy, with more than 251 million shares changing hands at the NYSE. Such rapid market swings and heavy volume are clear indicators of intense program trading.

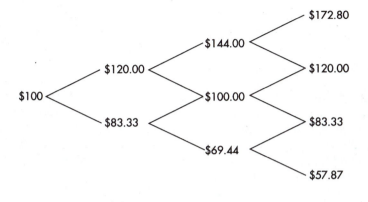

FIGURE 19.3
Underlying Portfolio
Price Dynamics

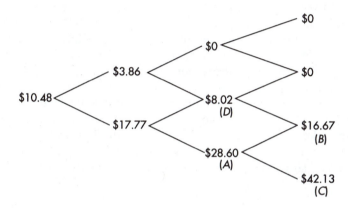

FIGURE 19.4
Index Put Option
Price Dynamics

The Option Prices and Dynamics

Assuming a one-period risk-free rate of 2 percent and an exercise price of $100, Figure 19.4 depicts the index put option price dynamics corresponding to the equity portfolio price dynamics presented in Figure 19.3. These European put option prices are produced by the BOPM, where the risk-neutralized probability of an upward movement in the portfolio's value, q, is assumed to be .5093.

As an example of how these option prices are computed, consider the price of $28.60 identified by node A in Figure 19.4. The associated option prices at nodes B and C are known, since at option expiration the put's value must be $MAX[0, X - S_T]$. For node B the put's price is $MAX[0, \$100 - 83.33]$, or $16.67, while for node C the put's price is $MAX[0, \$100 - 57.87]$, or $42.13. The price at node A is determined as a weighted average of the known prices, discounted for one period at the risk-free rate:

$$\$28.60 = [(.5093)(\$16.67) + (.4907)(\$42.13)] \times (1.02)^{-1}.$$

By using this valuation procedure in a recursive manner, the current put option price is eventually obtained. In our example the price is $10.48.

Stock-Put Portfolio Insurance

We begin by demonstrating the stock-put insurance technique under the assumption that such a technique is feasible. Specifically, suppose that the above three-period European index put option was available with exercise price $100. The option is assumed to correspond to the portfolio insurer's horizon and target insured value. Thus, the manager can simply purchase the option for $10.48 and be fully insured.[11]

Figure 19.5 depicts the dynamics of the stock-put-insured portfolio. The values presented are simply the sums of the underlying portfolio values (Figure 19.3) and the put values (Figure 19.4) for each corresponding node. For example, at node A the insured portfolio's value is $69.44 + $28.60, or $98.04. As the figure demonstrates, the expiration portfolio value is always at least $100. Thus, *if an index put option with the appropriate terms is available*, the manager can ensure a future portfolio value of at least $100.

Before considering dynamic hedging with index futures contracts, it is instructive to mention that a combination of a $100 face value, pure discount riskless asset and an index call option with exercise price $100 will achieve the same price action as depicted in Figure 19.5. The current prices of the riskless asset and call option are $94.23 and $16.25, respectively.[12] Thus, $110.48 again is required to ensure a future portfolio

FIGURE 19.5

Stock-Put Insured
Portfolio Price
Dynamics

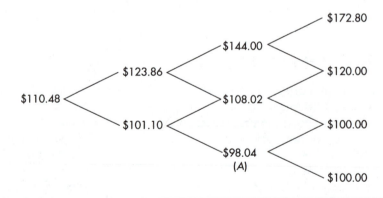

---

[11] For simplicity, assume that the manager has $110.48 and wishes to insure for $100. Later we show how the manager can insure at the same level of initial capital with associated reductions in upside capture.

[12] The current price of the pure discount, risk-free asset is given by

$$\$94.23 = \$100(1.02)^{-3}.$$

The current price of the European index call option is obtained from put-call parity:

$$\$16.25 = \$10.48 - \$100(1.02)^{-3} + 100.$$

See equation 17A.21 of Appendix 17A.

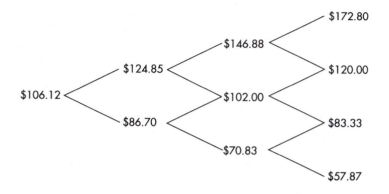

FIGURE 19.6

Index Futures Price
Dynamics

value of $100, the face value of the riskless asset. Therefore, the call–Treasury bill insurance technique can be used to replicate the stock-put technique. Similarly, it is easy to demonstrate how the stock–Treasury bill technique achieves the same price action. In this case, the manager initially purchases .5138 $100 face value Treasury bills maturing in three periods and invests the remaining $62.06 in the stock portfolio. Through reallocating the stock and Treasury bills each period in the prescribed manner, the manager can attain the same terminal portfolio values as those appearing in Figure 19.5.

Dynamic Hedging

We are now ready to demonstrate the mechanics of the dynamic hedging insurance strategy under our three-period setting. Given the assumptions of constant interest rates and no intervening stock dividends, Figure 19.6 portrays the index futures prices as determined by the cost-of-carry model (see Appendix 16A). For example, the current (time 0) index futures price is $106.12, or $100(1.02)^3$. Note that the expiration futures prices are the same as the expiration index values depicted in Figure 19.3. As always, the spot and futures prices converge at contract expiration.

In the dynamic hedging technique, the portfolio insurer must determine the number of index futures contracts to write at the beginning of each period. For the index put option employed here, $dP/dS = -.389$ at time 0. Thus the initial dynamic hedge ratio, obtained from equation 19.1, is $-.4654$:

$$N_f = [((110.48/(100 + 10.48))(1 - .389)) - (110.48/100)] \times (1.02)^{-3} = -.4654.$$

The portfolio insurer should initially *short* .4654 index futures contracts exhibiting a three-period maturity.

Figure 19.7 presents the initial stock-futures-insured portfolio and its values at the end of the first period (time 1). The initial portfolio contains $110.48 in stock, since the value of the futures contract is zero at time 0. At the end of the period the insured portfolio's value is either $123.86 or

FIGURE 19.7

Stock-Futures Price
Dynamics

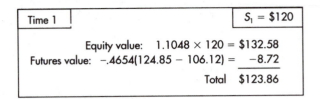

Time 1		$S_1 = \$120$
	Equity value: $1.1048 \times 120 = \$132.58$	
	Futures value: $-.4654(124.85 - 106.12) =$ -8.72	
	Total $\$123.86$	

Time 0		$S_0 = \$100$
Buy 1.1048 Shares $\$100.00$		
Write .4654 Futures 0.00		
Total $\$110.48$		

Time 1		$S_1 = \$83.33$
	Equity value: $1.1048 \times 83.33 = \$\ 92.06$	
	Futures value: $-.4654(86.70 - 106.12) =$ 9.04	
	Total $\$101.10$	

$101.10, depending on the resulting index value. Notice that the portfolio values, $123.86 and $101.10, are exactly the same as the values for the stock-put-insured portfolio appearing in Figure 19.5. Thus the initial stock-futures position, based on the dynamic hedge ratio given by equation 19.1, was successful in replicating the price action of the stock-put-insured portfolio over the first period. Of course now the manager must adjust the stock-futures portfolio based on the new dynamic hedge ratio calculated at the beginning of period 2. Clearly the ratio will change, since the variables S and T have changed, as has the put's delta. However, by computing the new hedge ratios at the start of each period and dynamically hedging, the manager can ensure a payoff profile at expiration that is equivalent to that in Figure 19.5. You are encouraged to engage in this exercise.

Dynamic Hedging with Longer-Term Horizons

When a portfolio manager's holding horizon is longer than the maturity of a liquid index futures contract, the manager can employ a series (i.e., strip) of shorter-term futures contracts to hedge. For example, suppose that the above three-period setting represents three six-month intervals, implying a horizon of 1.5 years. Here the manager can insure the portfolio while using three consecutive six-month index futures and the very same procedure described earlier. It is perfectly accurate to employ the same dynamic hedging procedure when using a strip of futures contracts to satisfy longer-term holding horizons.

Dynamic Hedging with a Fixed Capital Constraint

In the preceding analysis we conveniently assumed that the manager had initial capital of $110.48 to insure for $100. But what if the manager had less than $110.48 or desired to insure for more than $100? In this section we describe how the manager must alter his or her actions when insurance of $100 is desired but a capital constraint of $100 is imposed. The ultimate result is that the insurance costs more in the sense that the upside capture is reduced. Although we limit the analysis to the stock-put insurance technique, the resulting price dynamics can be replicated through dynamic hedging as well.

Time 0 index put option prices for various exercise prices are reported in Exhibit 19.1. These prices are computed using the procedure portrayed in Figure 19.4. The exhibit also provides the corresponding value of n, defined as the target insurance floor ($100) divided by the option's exercise price. In the last column of Exhibit 19.1, the total costs of buying n shares and n puts are provided. The portfolio insurer must select the corresponding option so that the total cost figure is $100, the initial capital constraint. This occurs when the exercise price lies somewhere between $119 and $120. To simplify the analysis, assume that the manager employs the $120 exercise price puts. Thus, the manager holds .8333 shares ($83.33) and .8333 puts ($16.37), yielding an approximate expenditure of $100.[13]

The stock-put-insured price dynamics are illustrated in Figure 19.8 for the above portfolio. Again, these dynamics could be replicated by trading index futures contracts. Figure 19.8 shows that the portfolio will attain a value of at least $100 at option expiration; the insurance strategy is

EXHIBIT 19.1

Index Put Option Prices for Various Exercise Price Levels

Exercise Price	Put Price	n^a	Total Cost^b
$100	$10.48	1.0000	$110.48
105	12.80	0.9524	107.43
110	16.38	0.9090	105.79
119	19.41	0.8403	100.34
120	19.64	0.8333	99.70

$^a n$ is $100 ÷ exercise price.

^{b}Total cost is n($100 + put price).

[13] This example illustrates why index options with fixed exercise prices may be undesirable even if they are long term and European. The portfolio insurer may still prefer dynamic hedging because of the ability to refine the target insurance floor (i.e., exercise price).

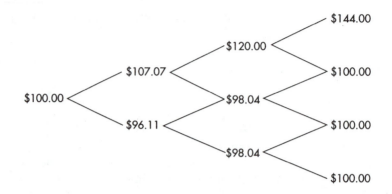

successful. However, the upside capture has been reduced, since higher exercise price puts had to be employed. From Figure 19.5, recall that the stock-put-insured portfolio value was $172.80, for a resulting index value of 172.80, when the $100 exercise price puts were used and the amount of original capital was $110.48. In Figure 19.8, however, the corresponding stock-put-insured portfolio value is just $144. The upside capture has been reduced to .8333 ($144.00/$172.80). This loss in upside capture is attributable to employing $120 exercise price puts due to the $100 capital constraint imposed. Once again, the loss in upside capture represents an important cost of any portfolio insurance technique.

SUMMARY

Portfolio insurance is another method of hedging security portfolios. This chapter examined the mechanics of portfolio insurance so that as a future portfolio manager, you can institute the strategy directly or in conjunction with investment banks offering this type of insurance. The most straightforward form of portfolio insurance entails the purchase of long-term European index put options. Since such options are not liquid, however, alternative paths to portfolio insurance have been developed.

The most popular of these alternatives is dynamic hedging, which involves the continual trading of stock index futures such that a synthetic stock-put-insured portfolio is maintained. In this chapter we demonstrated how a stock-futures-insured portfolio could achieve the same price action as a stock-put-insured portfolio. Other strategies entailing the trading of index call options and Treasury bills were also shown to replicate the payoffs of a stock-put-insured portfolio.

Portfolio insurance may be regarded as a form of hedging for investors holding well-diversified equity portfolios. Users of portfolio insurance tend to be institutional managers, including pension and insurance fund managers. Because of the somewhat complex nature of this special hedging strategy, we devoted an entire chapter to it. However, for the purpose of understanding how portfolio insurance fits into the broader realm of contemporary portfolio theory and risk management, it is best to think of portfolio insurance as simply another hedging application. Finally, portfolio insurance may be applied to portfolios composed of securities other than stock.

Questions and Problems

1. Why has the use of index put options to insure equity portfolios not been a popular technique among institutional portfolio managers?

2. What constitutes the major cost of any portfolio insurance technique?

3. The guaranteed percentage return on an insured portfolio must be bounded above by what rate of return?

4. What are some of the shortcomings of the stock–Treasury bill and call–Treasury bill insurance techniques?

5. What are some of the advantages offered by the dynamic hedging insurance technique? Describe this technique and why it is dynamic.

6. What factors are likely to be considered by portfolio managers when deciding how often to rebalance under the dynamic hedging technique? Describe the role played by the put option's delta and gamma in this decision process.

7. Why might dynamic hedging be ineffective in a fast-moving market environment?

8. In Figure 19.4, describe how the price of $8.02 appearing in node *D* is determined.

9. From Exhibit 19.1, use a lattice to show how the price of $12.80 was determined for the $105-exercise price put option.

Problems 10 through 19 refer to the following information: You are a portfolio manager who oversees a small index fund designed to mirror the SP100. The SP100 is 215, and the portfolio is worth $15,050,000. Thus, assuming the portfolio is fully funded, you are managing 70,000 index units. Assume that it is mid-November and that the December 215 SP100 put contract, which expires in one month, sells for $1,125 (or $2.25 per underlying index unit). This option is European, and the one-month risk-free rate of interest is .0085. Finally, assume that all securities are perfectly divisible and that the annualized return variance of the SP100 is .015.

10. In the stock-put insurance technique, how many units of the index and put contracts will you hold to ensure an expiration portfolio value of $15,050,000?

11. What is the resulting insured portfolio value if the expiration SP100 level is 200?

12. What is the resulting insured portfolio value if the expiration SP100 level is 240? What is the portfolio's upside capture?

13. Under a stock–Treasury bill insurance technique, how many one-month $10,000-face value Treasury bills must you purchase to ensure the same minimum value as in the above stock-put insurance technique? What is the current price of the Treasury bill, and how many index units will you hold in your equity portfolio?

14. Assuming that the SP100 is 240 in one month, what is the upside capture for the stock–Treasury bill insurance strategy?

15. Assuming no dividends occur on the underlying stocks during the one-month period, what is the current price of a corresponding index call option?

16. Under the call–Treasury bill technique, how many call option contracts will be purchased?

17. Employing a contingency graph, illustrate the resulting call–Treasury bill insured portfolio values at option expiration. At an expiration index level of 240, what is this strategy's upside capture?

18. Under the dynamic hedging technique, what is the initial dynamic hedge ratio, N_f? What is the initial futures price?

19. Given a one-point decline in the SP100, how does the stock-futures insured portfolio value change? How does this change compare with the change in the stock-put-insured portfolio?

Self-Test Problems

ST-1.   Given a starting stock price of $50, a multiplicative upward jump of 1.20, and a multiplicative downward jump of .85, use a lattice to show the stock price dynamics over a three-period horizon.

ST-2.   The one-period interest rate is .01 and the European put option's exercise price is $50. Use a lattice to demonstrate the index put option's price dynamics. Assume the option expires in three periods and that the risk-neutralized probability of an upward jump, q, is .52.

ST-3.   Assuming a capital constraint of $54.391, use a lattice to demonstrate the dynamics of a stock-put-insured portfolio designed to ensure an expiration value of $50.

Solutions to Self-Test Problems

ST-1.

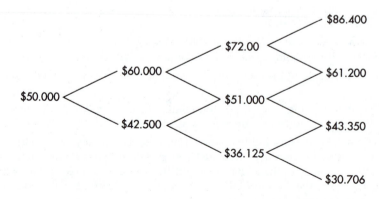

ST-2.

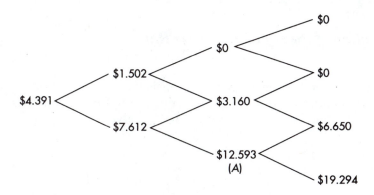

Example:
(A) $12.593 = [(6.650)(.52) + (19.294)(.49)] \times (1.01)^{-1}$.

ST-3.

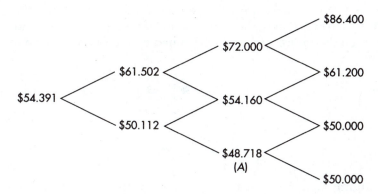

Example:
(A) $36.125 + $12.593= $48.718.

19A

Derivation of the Dynamic Hedge Ratio

Assume that you construct a portfolio consisting of N_S shares of stock and N_f futures contracts. Since the initial value of the futures contracts must be zero, the initial value of the portfolio, V, is given by the investment in stock:

(19A.1)
$$V = N_S S.$$

The change in the value of the portfolio for a small change in S is given by

(19A.2)
$$dV/dS = N_S + N_f(df/dS),$$

where df/dS represents the change in the futures price for the given small change in S, that is, the futures delta. If no dividends are paid on the stock, then the futures price is determined by the following cost-of-carry model:

(19A.3)
$$f = Se^{rT}.$$

Thus

(19A.4)
$$df/dS = e^{rT}.$$

Substituting equation 19A.4 into equation 19A.2 and recognizing that $N_S = V/S$ gives

(19A.5)
$$dV/dS = V/S + N_f e^{rT}.$$

Equation 19A.5 expresses the change in portfolio value with respect to a small change in S in terms of N_f, the number of futures contracts.

Now consider a stock-put-insured portfolio all of whose securities are perfectly divisible. Thus there is an equal number of stocks and puts, and by definition the portfolio's value is

(19A.6)
$$V = N(S + P),$$

where N is the number of stocks and puts and P is the put price per share of stock. The change in the portfolio's value with respect to a small change in S is given by

(19A.7) $dV/dS = N + N(dP/dS) = N(1 + (dP/dS))$.

Using equation 19A.6, equation 19A.7 can be rewritten as follows:

(19A.8) $dV/dS = [(V/(S + P))(1 + (dP/dS))]$.

In the dynamic hedging strategy the objective is to maintain a specified number of futures contracts, N_f, such that the stock-futures-insured portfolio achieves the same price action as a stock-put insured portfolio. This objective is accomplished by setting the two derivatives, equations 19A.5 and 19A.8, equal to one another. By doing so we equate the changes in the two portfolios' values for a given small change in S. Equating 19A.5 and 19A.8 gives us the following expression:

(19A.9) $V/S + N_f e^{rT} = (V/(S + P))(1 + (dP/dS))$.

Solving for N_f gives

(19A.10) $N_f = [(V/(S + P))(1 + (dP/dS)) - (V/S)] \times e^{-rT}$.

This is equation 19.1.

A P P E N D I X

19B

Primes and Scores

A recent development in the derivative securities market is the introduction of *primes* and *scores*. These securities are created through the establishment of a trust that purchases common stock and in turn issues a unit of the trust. Each unit contains a prime and a score. The prime component receives all dividend payments and any stock appreciation up to a termination value. The score component receives any stock appreciation beyond the termination value. The termination value is therefore akin to an option's exercise price. Thus the trust effectively separates each stock's cash flow into a dividend-based component (the prime) and an option-based component (the score).

The trust typically exhibits a maturity of five years, after which the units are reconnected to form the underlying stock. The prime, score, and unit for each trust are traded separately on the American Stock Exchange. The termination price, which is established at trust inception, is commonly 20 percent to 25 percent above the original stock price. It is called a termination price because the trust cannot accept more investors if the stock price exceeds the termination price.

Since the trust has a five-year life, the creation of the score component represents a long-term European option on the underlying stock.[14] Thus the score component may offer the kind of long-term portfolio insurance attainable through dynamic hedging. Indeed, since the score component can provide long-term insurance while avoiding the transaction costs of dynamic hedging, the joint value of the prime and score can actually exceed the value of the underlying common stock.

In fact, the joint value was found to be greater in an empirical study of primes and scores conducted by Jarrow and O'Hara (1989). Analyzing five trusts created before June 1987, Jarrow and O'Hara report that the combined prime and score prices exceed the price of the underlying stock, often by a considerable amount and beyond the required transaction costs of arbitrage. Presumably, if the combined prime and score price is greater, then arbitrageurs will buy the stock and sell (short) the prime and score. Jarrow and O'Hara conclude that the apparent overpricing of primes and scores is attributable to the unique ability of the score component to avoid the transaction costs of dynamic hedging. Jarrow and O'Hara's results are intriguing, since they suggest that it may be possible to create value simply by splitting a security into different parts. (Do you recognize an analogy to particle physics here?)

Whether the prime and score market will grow remains to be seen. At the time of this writing only about twenty-five trusts exist. Furthermore, a recent tax ruling has apparently hurt this market. Specifically, a March 1986 amendment to Treasury Regulation Section 301.7701-4(c) classifies such a trust as an association taxable as a corporation. This ruling effectively subjects holders in the trust to the triple taxation of dividend income at the personal level.

REFERENCES

Asay, M., and C. Edelsburg. 1986. Can a dynamic strategy replicate the returns of an option? *Journal of Futures Markets* 6:63–70.

Becker, K., J. Madura, and A. Tucker. 1990. Dynamically hedging exchange rate risk. Working paper, Temple University, Philadelphia.

Benninga, A., and M. Blume. 1985. On the optimality of portfolio insurance. *Journal of Finance* 40:1341–1352.

Brooks, R., J. Madura, and A. Tucker. 1991. Portfolio insurance for foreign exchange risk management. *Global Finance Journal* 2:55–69.

---

[14] To demonstrate this more formally, define the following variables: T, the maturity of the trust; X, the termination price; S_t, the current stock price; P_t, the current prime price; and K_t, the current score price. Since the prime receives all dividends, the score may be viewed as a long-term European call option on the stock with exercise price X and maturity T. At maturity the score price is $K_T = MAX[S_T - X, 0]$, and the prime price is $P_T = MIN[S_T, X]$.

Cox, J., S. Ross, and M. Rubinstein. 1979. Option pricing. A simplified approach. *Journal of Financial Economics* 7:229–263.

Etzioni, E. 1986. Rebalance disciplines for portfolio insurance. *Journal of Portfolio Management* 13:59–62.

Gatto, M., R. Geske, R. Litzenberger, and H. Sosin. 1980. Mutual fund insurance. *Journal of Financial Economics* 8:283–317.

Hill, J., A. Jain, and R. Wood. 1988. Portfolio insurance. Volatility risk and futures mispricing. *Journal of Portfolio Management.* Winter, 23–29.

Jarrow, R., and M. O'Hara. 1989. Primes and scores. An essay on market imperfection. *Journal of Finance* 44:1263–1288.

Leland, H. 1980. Who should buy portfolio insurance? *Journal of Finance* 35:581–594.

Leland, H. 1985. Option pricing and replication with transaction costs. *Journal of Finance* 40:1283–1301.

O'Brien, T. 1988. The mechanics of portfolio insurance. *Journal of Portfolio Management* Spring, 40–47.

Pozen, R. 1978. The purchase of protective puts by financial institutions. *Financial Analysts Journal* 34:47–60.

Rendleman, R., and B. Bartter. 1979. Two-state option pricing. *Journal of Finance* 34:1093–1110.

Rendleman, R., and R. McEnally. 1987. Assessing the costs of portfolio insurance. *Financial Analysts Journal* 43:27–37.

Rubinstein, M. 1985. Alternative paths to portfolio insurance. *Financial Analysts Journal* 41:42–52.

Rubinstein, M., and H. Leland. 1981. Replicating options with positions in stock and cash. *Financial Analysts Journal* 37:63–71.

Singleton, C., and R. Grieves. 1984. Synthetic puts and portfolio insurance strategies. *Journal of Portfolio Management* 10:63–69.

Wallace, A. 1982. Marketing a 'miracle' model. *Institutional Investor* 16:101–106.

Assessing Performance

WE CONCLUDE THIS BOOK WITH PART 5, ON THE PERFORMANCE EVALUATION of professional money managers. An integral part of any investment process entails the evaluation of investment performance, so it is important for investors to assess how managers have performed relative to both the market as a whole and other managers. For instance, IBM currently allocates its pension funds to more than fifty managers. Clearly, the company is concerned with the performance of these managers. As a company known widely for being family oriented, IBM wants to protect the interests of its vested employees and retirees. In addition, studies suggest that stock prices reflect the degree of overfunding or underfunding of a firm's pension plan. Money managers themselves are also vitally concerned with performance evaluation because their compensation is tied to performance, either directly through compensation schedules or indirectly through their long-run management reputations.

There are several performance evaluation services and measures, and a large body of empirical evidence assesses performance, especially that of mutual funds. We describe these services and measures and provide a summary of this body of empirical evidence in Part 5. ■

Portfolio Management Performance Evaluation

Introduction

There are presently over 3,800 mutual funds in the United States collectively managing over $1.6 trillion, and recent average growth in these funds has been about 16 percent per annum. While some of this growth stems from capital appreciation of the funds' existing assets, most has been achieved through *de novo* investment. The pension fund universe in the U.S. is over $3 trillion. The larger pension funds, such as those of AT&T and TIAA-CREF, often employ dozens of managers to oversee the funds' assets. Indeed, more than 80 percent of all U.S. corporate pension plans with assets greater than $2 billion have more than ten managers. Growth has also occurred in college endowments, trusts, and discretionary accounts, among others. With such vast markets, it is no wonder that professional money management has become an intensely competitive business and that performance evaluation is such a vital aspect of the industry.

The performance evaluation of professional money managers has evolved dramatically during the past twenty years, principally because of the development of modern portfolio theory and associated asset pricing models such as the CAPM and APM. In this chapter we both discuss the current state of performance evaluation and offer a summary of extant empirical evidence on the performance of mutual funds.

The chapter is divided into five major sections. In the first section we detail some of the pitfalls commonly witnessed in performance evaluation. One is that the relative performance of different funds and their management is often assessed without regard to the funds' risk. While it may seem obvious that performance should be evaluated on a risk-adjusted basis, the major fund evaluation services, such as S.E.I., Morningstar, Lipper, CDA, Wilshire, Russell, and Barra, still commonly ignore risk adjustment or otherwise only employ very crude risk-adjustment procedures. In the second section we detail ways in which comparisons can be made in a more judicious manner, so that differential risks are accommodated. In the third section we discuss methods whereby performance can be decomposed into security selection and market timing elements. In the fourth section we briefly address some problems with applying the evaluation techniques introduced, such as the inability to borrow and lend at the same rate of interest and the complexities associated with changing risk levels over time. We conclude the chapter with a summary of empirical evidence regarding the performance of mutual funds. Most studies of investment performance focus on mutual funds because of their abundance of publicly available information. Overall, the risk-adjusted return performance of the U.S. mutual fund industry has been rather unimpressive. Still, these funds remain popular because they offer substantial diversification at a very low cost.

PITFALLS OF PERFORMANCE EVALUATION

Several common pitfalls lie in assessing portfolio performance. We address four in this section: (1) mismeasurement of portfolio returns; (2) ignoring constraints imposed on the fund's investment activities and policies; (3) the use of inappropriate risk proxies; and especially (4) the direct comparison of funds with different risk levels. Accurate performance evaluation must avoid these commonly observed problems.

Mismeasurement of Portfolio Returns

The measurement of portfolio returns is complicated by the many cash inflows and outflows of a fund as well as by the fact that different amounts of capital are invested at different points in time. As an example, consider Exhibit 20.1, which portrays two different cash flow patterns, one

EXHIBIT 20.1

Cash Flow Patterns, Funds 1 and 2

	Period			
	0	**1**	**2**	**3**
FUND 1				
Value prior to Inflow/Outflow	$200	$300	$385	$435
Inflow/Outflow	50	50	50	
Amount Invested	250	350	435	
Ending Value	300	385	435	
FUND 2				
Value prior to Inflow/Outflow	$200	$420	$462	$462
Inflow/Outflow	150	0	0	
Amount Invested	350	420	462	
Ending Value	420	462	462	
Rate of Return for Each Fund	20%	10%	0%	

corresponding to each of two funds. For each fund the net inflow (inflows less outflows) is $150 over the entire period. Also, the rate of return earned by each fund is identical in each period. However, the resulting dollar value of fund 2 is greater simply because its manager had the fortune of having more available funds in the highly profitable period (period 0). By merely examining ending values compared with beginning values over the entire period, we would erroneously conclude that fund 2's manager was superior. That manager would be unduly rewarded, and reciprocally, fund 1's manager would be unduly penalized. In reality, however, the managers' performances were identical.[1]

To control for the timing and size of cash flows we must compute the rate of return in each time period and then compute the overall (compounded) return. The returns in each time period for each fund are 20 percent, 10 percent, and 0 percent, respectively. Thus the overall return for each fund is 32 percent: $(1.20)(1.10)(1.00) - 1$. Thus the two funds' performances appear identical, as they should, in light of the overall return. This return, often called the *time-weighted rate of return*, therefore appropriately accounts for the timing and size of inflows and outflows.

In practice the time-weighted rate of return is obtained by examining the unit value of a fund. Funds are commonly sold in units. Cash inflows and outflows affect the number of units making up the fund but do not affect the value of the unit. In other words, buying any one unit reflects the same initial investment; therefore, tracing the performance of one unit is tantamount to computing the time-weighted rate of return.

---

[1] This conclusion assumes that cash flows are not under the control of the managers, which is typically the case, and ignores differences in risk.

Ignoring Constraints Imposed on the Fund's Activities

An inappropriate assessment of the relative performance of managers results when an assessor compares funds that must operate under different constraints or policy initiatives. For instance, it is not appropriate to compare the performance of a bond fund that must invest in bonds rated AA or better directly with that of another bond fund that is unconstrained in its investment activities. While such a static/univariate comparison may lend insight into the value of the constraint itself, it does not offer an appropriate indication of relative management performance. In addition, it is often difficult to compare management performance when different investment policies are pursued, such as high growth versus stable income. The fact is that the investment *policy* dictates the majority of the investment plan's return and variation in that return. Indeed, using ten years of quarterly data for ninety-one pension plans in the S.E.I. Large Plan Universe, Brinson, Hood, and Beebower (1986) found that investment policy (normal asset class weights and the passive asset classes under the policy directive) accounted for nearly 94 percent of the total variation in actual plan returns. Return variation due to timing and security selection activities accounted for very little of the return variation.

Inappropriate Risk Proxies

When assessing performance, you must decide the appropriate measure of risk, either systematic risk (beta) or overall risk (standard deviation). For instance, if an investment in a fund represents the vast majority of an investor's overall wealth, then the standard deviation is the appropriate risk measure, at least from the investor's perspective. As another example, the performance of bank security portfolios is often undertaken with the standard deviation serving as the risk proxy, since banks are required by law to invest in high-grade securities that are too highly correlated to provide any meaningful diversification of nonsystematic risk. On the other hand, systematic risk should be employed when assessing the performance of most fund managers; since a fund is commonly broadly diversified, only systematic risk should be priced. It is necessary to utilize the appropriate risk measure when assessing performance.

Comparing Funds While Ignoring Differential Risk Levels

Perhaps the most egregious error committed during assessment of performance is comparing fund returns without consideration of differential fund risk levels. Competent academic studies of fund performance are very careful to account for differential risk, often by using risk-adjusted return measures (discussed later) or by constructing benchmark portfolios of the same risk class. For instance, the latter procedure was followed by Friend, Blume, and Crockett (1970), who compared the mean returns earned by a group of mutual funds with those of randomly generated portfolios exhibiting the same approximate risk.[2]

While financial economists have been aware of the need to account for differential risk for more than twenty years now, industry practitioners and others still often persist in ignoring this critical issue. For instance, many investment professors are quite critical of the popular AT&T Investment Challenge Game because it simply rewards the student-manager who earns the greatest return while not accounting for the risk undertaken by that student. Typically the game's winner is someone who underdiversified and just happened to, say, overinvest in a stock that became a takeover target. Or perhaps the winner undertook a substantial short position in naked call options written on a stock of a firm that eventually went bankrupt and used the proceeds to speculate in grain futures. The fact is that if such a naked position was actually assumed and the stock had appreciated, the manager could be sued for breach of fiduciary duty to shareholders.[3]

Business magazines and other periodicals (e.g., *Consumer Reports*) also ignore this critical issue. They commonly rank mutual funds on the basis of their rates of return earned over a recent time period, without regard to risk. The fact is that the ranking is much more likely to depend on the target risk level of the fund (i.e., the fund's policy directive) and the performance of the market than the skill level of the manager.

Most professional evaluation services are also guilty of ignoring differential risk levels. Instead of using a benchmark like that employed by Friend, Blume, and Crockett, these services select as a benchmark the performance of funds administered by other professional managers. The problem is that the other funds may not be in the same risk class, so the comparisons and information provided are tenuous at best.

Exhibit 20.2 provides part of a recent report provided by a large evaluation service regarding a pension fund that we'll call PF. It shows the returns earned by the manager over a recent period, compared with the

EXHIBIT 20.2

Balanced Funds, Returns for Years Ending June 30

	1985	1986	1987	1988	1989
5th Percentile	35.7%	38.0%	20.2%	6.0%	18.8%
25th Percentile	30.1	30.9	15.3	3.0	16.0
Median	27.3	26.1	12.5	0.6	14.5
75th Percentile	24.5	22.5	10.3	−1.7	12.8
95th Percentile	20.1	16.6	5.9	−6.9	10.8
Fund PF	28.4	22.7	11.7	−0.4	14.9
Percent Rank	35	74	61	62	40

[2] The results of Friend, Blume, and Crockett are described in detail later in the chapter.

[3] The manager may be found to have violated the prudent man rule, as originally enumerated in Harvard v. Amory [26 Mass. (9 Pick.) 446, 461, (1830)].

EXHIBIT 20.3

Balanced Funds, Quarterly Return Variability[a]

	1981–85	1982–86	1983–87	1984–88	1985–89
5th Percentile	14.9%	15.5%	14.8%	16.3%	15.7%
25th Percentile	11.6	12.9	13.1	13.7	12.6
Median	10.3	11.4	11.1	12.1	10.8
75th Percentile	9.1	9.6	9.6	10.1	9.2
95th Percentile	7.6	7.5	7.4	7.6	7.0
Fund PF	10.4	11.1	9.7	13.6	12.2
Percent Rank	48	59	73	26	31

[a]For moving five-year periods ending June 30.

returns of other (balanced fund) managers. Exhibit 20.3 provides analogous information about PF's risk.[4] Note that while both return and risk measures are provided, it is difficult at best to draw a general inference about PF's performance. Commonly there is no consistent pattern of return or risk over time. The use of a benchmark portfolio of the same risk class would provide a better indication of PF's performance.

As noted above, another way to compare funds of different risk is to employ a risk-adjusted performance measure. In the next section we describe four available measures. Later in this chapter we discuss a number of empirical studies that utilize these measures to investigate the historic performance of the U.S. mutual fund industry. Using one of these measures should greatly reduce the propensity for portfolios with unusually high or low risk levels to earn unusually high or low marks, irrespective of the performance of the market.

RISK-ADJUSTED PERFORMANCE MEASURES

Below we investigate four performance measures that accommodate different fund risk levels. The first two employ the standard deviation as the risk measure, and the other two utilize beta.

Sharpe's Performance Index

In Chapter 3 we saw that all combinations of a riskless asset and a risky portfolio lie along a straight line (or ray) connecting the riskless asset and risky portfolio (provided that we operate in return–standard deviation space). Figure 20.1 on page 548 portrays a number of such lines connecting the riskless asset to portfolios *A* through *D*. Provided that a riskless asset exists, rational investors prefer *A* to *B*, *B* to *C*, and so on. The preferred

---

[4]Here risk is measured by the standard deviation. Typical reports also include information about fund betas. In addition, most reports include a corresponding graphical presentation of the return and risk information.

portfolio, A, lies on the most counterclockwise ray emanating from the riskless asset.

Equivalently, the preferred portfolio, A, lies on the ray having the greatest slope. In Chapter 4 we demonstrated that the slope of the line was

(20.1)
$$(\overline{R}_P - \overline{R}_F)/\sigma_P.$$

Equation 20.1 is known as the *Sharpe index* (developed by William Sharpe in 1966). It is also called the excess return to variability measure. This name derives from the fact that the measure is a ratio of the fund's return above

---

CHAOS IN PERFORMANCE EVALUATION SERVICES

In 1993 there were 3,848 mutual funds in the United States—more funds than the number of stocks listed on the NYSE and AMEX combined and nearly four times as many as existed ten years earlier. The vast growth of this industry has given rise to another, spin-off industry, namely one that evaluates the performance of money managers. Professional fund performance evaluation services include Lipper Analytical Services of New York, Morningstar Inc. of Chicago, and CDA Investment Technologies Inc. of Rockville, Maryland, among others. In addition, business periodicals including the *Wall Street Journal* (WSJ) also provide regular reports on fund performance. Using data supplied by Lipper, the WSJ assigns letter grades to funds based on their total returns compared with those of their peers, and on a time frame that changes Tuesday through Friday. On Tuesdays, for example, funds are ranked on their one-year performance; Wednesdays through Fridays show three-, four-, and five-year results.

There are plenty of other ranking systems and variables: *Money* magazine and *Business Week* adjust five-year numbers to account for risk factors. *USA Today* excludes funds whose management changed hands recently. Some others account for commissions and loads; others do not. Some discard funds that have not been through both an up and a down market. *Financial World* recently began a ranking system that attempts to forecast the *future* performance of stock funds by evaluating the prospects of their current holdings.

The consequence of all of these evaluation services and their different techniques is often a state of confusion by individuals looking to evaluate funds for potential investment. For instance, Baltimore-based Legg Mason's U.S. Government intermediate bond fund was recently ranked as a D by the WSJ and yet contemporaneously received four out of five stars from Morningstar. Fidelity's limited term municipals fund recently received letter ratings of A, C, and E from three different evaluation services.

Perhaps even more disturbing is how funds can select from the ratings of different services to bolster advertisement of their performance. For instance, the Neuberger & Berman guardian fund, which in its defense has been a strongly performing fund, recently touted itself as "No. 1." The ad's small print explains that this ranking stems from Lipper's comparison of just eight growth and income funds—those between $500 million and $1 billion in assets—for the twelve months that ended September 30, 1992.

the riskless rate to its standard deviation of returns. Thus it represents a performance measure that calculates risk by the portfolio's standard deviation.

In one of the earliest studies of the performance of mutual funds, Sharpe used his index to compare thirty-four funds with one another and with the DJIA for the period 1954–1963. Exhibit 20.4 and Figure 20.2 replicate Sharpe's results. In the figure a ray is drawn connecting the riskless rate of interest (assumed to be 3 percent by Sharpe) and the DJIA (designated *M*). As the figure indicates, the minority of mutual funds had greater excess return to variability measures than the DJIA. The implication of course is that most of these funds' managers would have improved their

FIGURE 20.1

Combinations of a Riskless Asset and Risky Portfolios

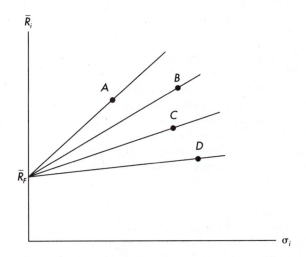

FIGURE 20.2

Fund Returns and Standard Deviations, 1954–1963

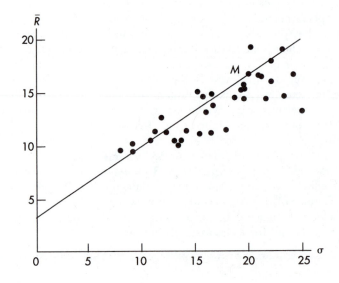

EXHIBIT 20.4

Mutual Fund Performance, 1954–1963

Mutual Fund	Average Annual Excess Return (%)	Standard Deviation of Annual Return (%)	Sharpe Index
Affiliated Fund	11.6	15.3	0.75896
American Business Shares	7.0	9.2	0.75876
Axe-Houghton, Fund A	7.5	13.5	0.55551
Axe-Houghton, Fund B	9.0	16.3	0.55183
Axe-Houghton, Stock Fund	8.9	15.6	0.56991
Boston Fund	9.4	12.1	0.77842
Broad Street Investing	11.8	16.8	0.70329
Bullock Fund	12.7	19.3	0.65845
Commonwealth Investment Company	7.9	13.7	0.57841
Delaware Fund	11.4	21.4	0.58253
Dividend Shares	11.4	15.9	0.71807
Eaton and Howard, Balanced Fund	8.0	11.9	0.67399
Eaton and Howard, Stock Fund	12.2	19.2	0.63486
Equity Fund	11.6	18.7	0.61902
Fidelity Fund	13.4	23.5	0.57020
Financial Industrial Fund	11.5	23.0	0.49971
Fundamental Investors	13.0	21.7	0.59894
Group Securities, Common Stock Fund	12.1	19.1	0.63316
Group Securities, Fully Administered Fund	8.4	14.1	0.59490
Incorporated Investors	11.0	25.5	0.43116
Investment Company of America	14.4	21.8	0.66169
Investors Mutual	8.3	12.5	0.66451
Loomis-Sales Mutual Fund	7.0	10.4	0.67358
Massachusetts Investors Trust	13.2	20.8	0.63398
Massachusetts Investors—Growth Stock	15.6	22.7	0.63687
National Investors Corporation	15.3	19.9	0.76798
National Securities—Income Series	9.4	17.8	0.52950
New England Fund	7.4	10.2	0.72703
Putnam Fund of Boston	10.1	16.0	0.63222
Scudder, Stevens & Clark Balanced Fund	7.7	13.3	0.57893
Selected American Shares	11.4	19.4	0.58788
United Funds—Income Fund	13.1	20.8	0.62698
Wellington Fund	8.3	12.0	0.69057
Wisconsin Fund	10.8	16.9	0.64091

Source: W. Sharpe, "Mutual Fund Performance," *Journal of Business* 39 (1966), 119–138. Reprinted with permission of The University of Chicago Press.

performance by simply investing in the DJIA and lending or borrowing at the riskless rate to achieve their target risk level.

Sharpe's Performance Index: A Variant

The naive or passive strategy just described, wherein a manager invests in a market index (DJIA) and lends or borrows to achieve the target risk level, suggests the existence of another risk-adjusted performance

FIGURE 20.3

Differential Return
in Return-Standard
Deviation Space

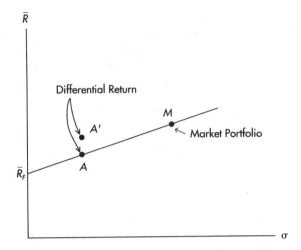

measure that represents a slight variant of the original Sharpe index. To develop this idea, consider Figure 20.3, which displays the return and standard deviation of Fund A'. If the manager of A' had engaged in the naive strategy, then he or she would have earned the same return as the portfolio labeled A in the figure. Portfolios A' and A exhibit the same standard deviations. The differential return earned by the manager of Fund A' is therefore given by the distance $A'A$; it represents a measure of how much better (or worse) the manager did relative to the benchmark passive strategy.

The slope of the line connecting $\overline{R}_F$ and M in Figure 20.3 is $(\overline{R}_M - \overline{R}_F)/\sigma_M$, and the intercept is $\overline{R}_F$, so the equation of the line is

(20.2)
$$\overline{R}_i = \overline{R}_F + \sigma_i[(\overline{R}_M - \overline{R}_F)/\sigma_M],$$

where i denotes any particular portfolio. Thus, the return to portfolio A is determined by substituting the standard deviation of A' in equation 20.2. For instance, if $\overline{R}_F = .03, \overline{R}_M = .10, \sigma_M = .25, \sigma_i = \sigma_{A'} = .12,$ and $\overline{R}_{A'} = .08$, then

$$\overline{R}_A = .03 + .12[(.10 - .03)/.25] = .0636.$$

Thus, the differential return (the distance $A'A$) is

$$\overline{R}_{A'} - \overline{R}_A = .08 - .0636 = .0164, \text{ or } 1.64\%.$$

Figure 20.4 illustrates the differential return measures of the funds studied by Sharpe (1966). The vertical lines indicate the differential returns for each fund. Exhibit 20.5 on page 552 provides the differential returns in tabular form. Notice that Figure 20.4 is identical to Figure 20.2. That is,

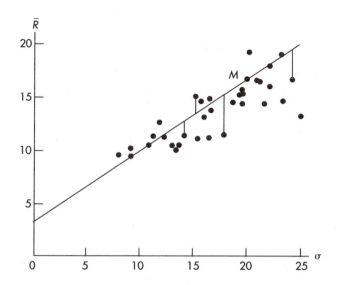

FIGURE 20.4

Fund Differential Returns, Graphical Form

both the Sharpe index and its variant, the differential return measure, identify the same funds as performing better or worse than the market portfolio, *M*. To this extent the two measures are redundant.

However, the two measures can provide different information about the *relative* performance of the funds. This result can be seen by comparing Exhibits 20.4 and 20.5 and recognizing that the rank order of the funds differs somewhat under the two measures. For example, Scudder, Stevens & Clark balanced fund has a lower Sharpe index (.57893) than Selected American Shares (.58788), yet the former has a higher differential return (−1.17 percent) than the latter (−1.54 percent). The reason that this difference can occur is illustrated in Figure 20.5 on page 553. Here the Sharpe index would rank Fund *A'* as superior to Fund *B'* (*A'* lies on the ray exhibiting the greater slope), but the differential return measure would rank *B'* higher than *A'* (the distance *B'B* is greater than *A'A*).

Treynor's Performance Index

Sharpe's index has an analogue that uses beta as the risk measure. It is called the Treynor index (Treynor 1965). Consider a line or ray that connects the riskless asset and a risky portfolio *P* in return-beta space. The line has an intercept of $\overline{R}_F$ and a slope of $(\overline{R}_P - \overline{R}_F)/\beta_P$.[5] This slope represents Treynor's index. The greater the slope, the more counterclockwise lies the associated portfolio in return-beta space. For instance, in

---

[5]Suppose that a portfolio, *i*, consists of a position of w_P in a risky portfolio *P* and a position of w_{R_F} in the riskless asset R_F. Thus, $\beta_i = w_P\beta_P + w_{R_F}\beta_{R_F}$, where β_P and β_{R_F} are the betas of *P* and R_F, respectively. Since a riskless asset has a zero beta, however, we have $\beta_i = w_P\beta_P$, or $w_P = \beta_i/\beta_P$. The expected return to portfolio *i*, $\overline{R}_i$, is $\overline{R}_i = w_P\overline{R}_P + w_{R_F}\overline{R}_F = w_P\overline{R}_P + (1 - w_P)\overline{R}_F$. Substituting β_i/β_P for w_P gives $\overline{R}_i = (\beta_i/\beta_P)\overline{R}_P + [1 - (\beta_i/\beta_P)]\overline{R}_F$ or $\overline{R}_i = \overline{R}_F + \beta_i[(\overline{R}_P - \overline{R}_F)/\beta_P]$.

EXHIBIT 20.5

Fund Differential Returns, Tabular Form

Mutual Fund	Average Annual Return (%)	Return on Equal Risk Portfolio (%)	Differential Return
Affiliated Fund	14.6	13.20	1.40
American Business Shares	10.0	9.14	0.86
Axe-Houghton, Fund A	10.5	12.00	−1.50
Axe-Houghton, Fund B	12.0	13.87	−1.87
Axe-Houghton, Stock Fund	11.9	13.40	−1.50
Boston Fund	12.4	11.07	1.33
Broad Street Investing	14.8	14.21	0.59
Bullock Fund	15.7	15.87	−0.17
Commonwealth Investment Company	10.9	12.14	−1.24
Delaware Fund	14.4	17.27	−2.87
Dividend Shares	14.4	13.61	−0.79
Eaton and Howard, Balanced Fund	11.0	10.94	0.06
Eaton and Howard, Stock Fund	15.2	15.81	−0.61
Equity Fund	15.6	15.47	−0.87
Fidelity Fund	16.4	18.67	−2.27
Financial Industrial Fund	14.5	18.34	−3.80
Fundamental Investors	16.0	17.47	−1.47
Group Securities, Common Stock Fund	15.1	15.74	−3.64
Group Securities, Fully Administered Fund	11.4	12.40	−1.00
Incorporated Investors	14.0	20.01	−6.01
Investment Company of America	17.4	17.54	−0.14
Investors Mutual	11.3	11.34	−0.04
Loomis-Sales Mutual Fund	10.0	9.94	0.06
Massachusetts Investors Trust	16.2	16.87	−0.67
Massachusetts Investors—Growth Stock	18.6	18.14	0.46
National Investors Corporation	18.3	16.27	2.03
National Securities—Income Series	12.4	14.87	−2.47
New England Fund	10.4	9.80	−0.60
Putnam Fund of Boston	13.1	13.67	0.57
Scudder, Stevens & Clark Balanced Fund	10.7	11.87	−1.17
Selected American Shares	14.4	15.94	−1.54
United Funds—Income Fund	16.1	16.94	−0.84
Wellington Fund	11.3	11.00	0.30
Wisconsin Fund	13.8	14.27	−0.47

Source: W. Sharpe, "Mutual Fund Performance," *Journal of Business* 39 (1966), 119–138. Reprinted with permission of The University of Chicago Press.

Figure 20.6 portfolio *A* has the greatest Treynor index and thus is the preferred portfolio. Please note that Treynor's index is identical to Sharpe's index (equation 20.1), except that β_P replaces σ_P.

Jensen's Performance Index

The differential return measure (Sharpe index variant) described earlier also has an analogue when risk is measured by beta. It is known as the Jensen index (Jensen 1969). Thus, the Jensen index is to the Treynor index as the differential return measure is to the Sharpe index.

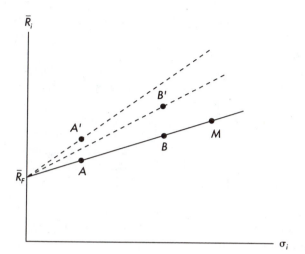

FIGURE 20.5

Sharpe's Index versus Differential Performance Measure

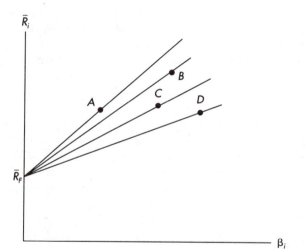

FIGURE 20.6

Portfolios in Return-Beta Space

Consider a line connecting the riskless asset to the market portfolio in return-beta space. A manager could hold any portfolio on this line by simply investing in both the riskless asset and the market portfolio (a naive or passive strategy). Thus if a manager willingly engages in a more active strategy, the performance can be measured by the difference in returns between the actively managed fund and the corresponding benchmark passive fund exhibiting the same risk (beta).

The equation of the line connecting the riskless asset and market index in return-beta space is

(20.3)
$$\overline{R}_P = \overline{R}_F + \beta_P(\overline{R}_M - \overline{R}_F).$$

The differential return (Jensen index) is simply the actual fund return less the return of a portfolio with identical beta that lies on this line. The latter return is calculated by using equation 20.3 along with the beta of the fund being evaluated. For instance, if $\overline{R}_M = .12$, $\overline{R}_F = .06$ and the fund beta is .75, then a passively managed benchmark fund with equal beta has an expected return of 10.5 percent: $.105 = .06 + .75(.12 - .06)$. If the actual fund return is 9 percent, then the differential return (Jensen index) is -1.5 percent (inferior performance).

Exhibit 20.6 presents part of a report published by the SEC in 1971, the result of a thorough study of the performance of 125 mutual funds for the period 1960–1969. Based on the Jensen index, the evidence indicates that fund managers in general slightly outperformed the passive asset allocation strategy for the period. The average differential return was about +.05 percent per annum.

Many of you will recognize that equation 20.3 is merely the CAPM in its basic form. Thus the Jensen index is simply the difference between the actual fund return and that predicted by the CAPM. Also, since there are several variations of the CAPM (Chapter 10), several different versions of the Jensen index exist. For example, you could compute the index using the zero-beta version of the CAPM. More generally and more importantly, we can conclude that a differential return measure is merely the difference between the realized return and the return predicted by an equilibrium asset pricing model, whether it be the CAPM or some alternative paradigm, such as the APM or a multifactor model specification.

For instance, Fama and French (1992) provided compelling evidence that a firm's size and excess returns (returns above the riskless rate of interest) are inversely related and that a firm's *BE/ME* ratio (i.e., book-equity to market-equity ratio) and excess returns are inversely related. Prior research suggests that the *E/P* ratio (i.e., earnings-to-price ratio) may also explain a large proportion of the cross-sectional variation in stock returns, but Fama and French find that the relationship between *E/P* and average return seems to be absorbed by the combi-

EXHIBIT 20.6

Mutual Fund Performance, 1960–1969

Beta Range	No. Funds	No. of Observations (months)	Monthly Fund Return (%/month)	Average Beta	Monthly Market Return (%/month)	Jensen Index
0–0.4	3	120	0.43	0.23	0.77	0.007
0.4–0.8	35	120	0.63	0.68	0.77	0.004
0.8–1.0	44	120	0.79	0.91	0.77	0.066
1.0–1.2	30	120	0.86	1.07	0.77	0.056
1.2+	13	120	1.05	1.33	0.77	0.130
TOTAL	125	120	0.78	0.91	0.77	0.051

Source: SEC, *Institutional Investor Study*, Part 2 (Washington: U.S. Government Printing Office, 1971).

nation of size and book-to-market equity. The implication is that the following three-factor model may be superior to a univariate model using beta as the independent variable when explaining cross-sectional variation:

(20.4) $$R_j = \hat{\lambda}_0 + \hat{\lambda}_1\beta_j + \hat{\lambda}_2 ln(BE/ME_j) + \hat{\lambda}_3 ln(ME_j) + \mu_j$$

where R_j is the actual excess return of firm j's stock, $\hat{\lambda}_1$ to $\hat{\lambda}_3$ represent regression coefficients, and μ_j, the error term, represents an abnormal return for firm j. Thus, with equation 20.4 as a representative model of predicted or so-called normal returns, the error terms of the model represent the abnormal returns upon which performance evaluation would be assessed. Presumably, a firm would be identified as exhibiting superior performance should its error term be positive for the sample period. The model can be generalized to assess equity fund performance as well as individual stock performance. In a similar spirit, Sharpe (1992) offers an alternative (twelve-factor!) model that can be employed to assess a fund's deviation from the performance of a benchmark portfolio and thus to assess the performance of the fund's management subject to its policy directive.

Finally, viewing the Jensen index as above, that is, as a residual from a fitted CAPM, has important implications for the mutual fund performance described in Exhibit 20.6 and elsewhere. Specifically, recall from Part 2 of this book that empirical estimates of the CAPM have a higher intercept and lower slope than the basic CAPM suggests (Black, Jensen, and Scholes 1972). Thus, employing the empirical line rather than the theoretical line connecting R_F and M in return-beta space tends to result in portfolios with betas less than one having lower differential returns, and vice versa. As Exhibit 20.6 indicates, most mutual funds have betas that are less than one. (This is still true today.) Therefore, using the empirical CAPM may result in an overall negative Jensen index for the 125 funds studied.[6]

DECOMPOSING PERFORMANCE

Recall that any abnormal fund performance is attributable to one of two sources: market timing or security selection. In this section we describe various techniques that can be used to decompose management performance into market timing and security selection elements. The analysis generally follows the work of Henriksson and Merton (1981) and Henriksson (1984).

---

[6]Other performance measures not addressed in this chapter include those of Ang and Chua (1979), Prakash and Bear (1986), and Grinblatt and Titman (1989), among others.

Market Timing

Managers must change their fund betas to enhance performance through market timing. Changing fund betas can be accomplished via security trading (e.g., altering the bond-stock mix) or transacting in derivatives (e.g. shorting stock index futures contracts). One way to examine the timing ability of management, therefore, is to compare market movements and the fund's beta over time. Figure 20.7 provides an example. For this fund there is no convincing evidence of successful market timing; there is no apparent correlation between beta and market returns. If the fund has a target beta due to its risk policy, then one can examine the relationship between target-beta deviations and market returns over time. Figure 20.8 portrays an example of this form of timing analysis. Again, there is no indication of timing ability; the plot does not suggest a significant correlation between market returns and deviations from the target beta.

Another way to assess timing performance is to compare the fund return and the market return directly. If the fund's manager does not engage in market timing, then the portfolio beta should be sticky over

FIGURE 20.7

Relationship of Fund Beta and Market Returns

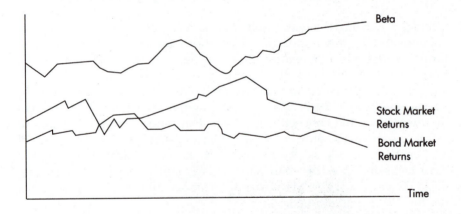

FIGURE 20.8

Relationship of Fund Beta Deviations and Market Returns

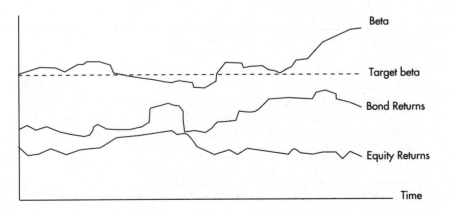

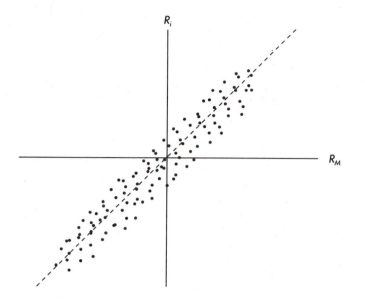

FIGURE 20.9
No Evidence of
Market Timing

time. Thus, the portfolio should earn a fairly constant fraction of the market return over time (presuming the fund is well diversified). Visually, the market returns and fund returns should plot on a straight line or if there is random noise should plot as a scatter of points about a straight line. An example is given in Figure 20.9. On the other hand, if the manager exhibited superior market timing, then the points would plot above the "normal" line given in Figure 20.9. An example is provided in Figure 20.10. Here there is a curvature to the scatter of points, indicating market timing ability.

Treynor and Mazuy (1966) examined the timing ability of mutual fund managers by testing for such curvature. Specifically, they fit the following quadratic to the data:

(20.5) $$(R_{it} - R_{Ft}) = a_i + b_i(R_{Mt} - R_{Ft}) + c_i(R_{Mt} - R_{Ft})^2 + u_i$$

where R_{it} is the return to fund i in period t, R_{Mt} is the return to the market index in period t, R_{Ft} is the t period riskless rate, u_i is the residual return, and a_i, b_i, and c_i are constants. If there is no market timing ability, there should be a linear relationship between R_i and R_M (as shown in Figure 20.9), so the coefficient c_i should be statistically insignificant. If there is superior market timing, however, Figure 20.10 will apply, so c_i will be positive (and vice versa). The addition of the squared term in equation 20.5 will improve the empirical fit between R_i and R_M. Hence, c_i can be regarded as an indicator of the manager's market timing ability. Treynor and Mazuy report that only one of thirty-seven mutual funds studied exhibited a significantly positive c_i coefficient—fewer than the number expected to occur by random chance.

FIGURE 20.10

Evidence of Superior
Market Timing

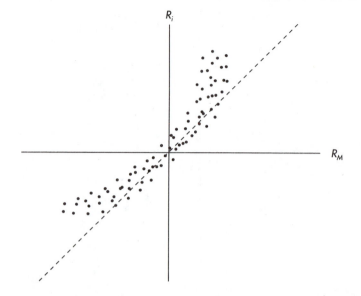

An alternative specification to that of Treynor and Mazuy involves
fitting two separate lines, one using observations when the market return
is above the riskless rate (an up market) and one using observations when
the market return is below the riskless rate (a down market). A manager
who possesses superior market timing should have a high beta in an up
market and a low beta in a down market. Consider the following
regression specification:

(20.6) $(R_{it} - R_{Ft}) = a_i + b_i(R_{Mt} - R_{Ft}) - c_i D(R_{Mt} - R_{Ft}) + u_i$

where D is a dummy variable whose value is zero in an up market and
$R_{Mt} - R_{Ft}$ in a down market. Thus b_i is the up-market beta, $b_i - c_i$ is the
down-market beta, and consequently c_i is their difference, or an indicator
of market-timing ability. If c_i is insignificantly different from zero, then the
up- and down-market betas are the same and we can conclude that no
market timing was exhibited.

There are still other methods that can be employed to detect timing
ability. In all of them the principal idea is to construct an appropriate
testing procedure. For example, some fund managers engage in a practice
known as *sector rotating*, in which they move in and out of certain
economic sectors (e.g., durable goods, energy, transportation, and financial services), depending on their forecasts of each sector's performance.
Thus sector rotating may be considered a type of sector timing strategy. To
assess the ability of a manager to time sectors, plot each sector's periodic
return against the proportion of fund wealth invested in each sector for
each period. If the manager can indeed time sectors, then a discernible
pattern should emerge. A procedure similar to this was used by Brinson,

Hood and Beebower (1986) to assess the timing abilities of the managers of ninety-one large pension funds. Overall, they report that the average fund lost 66 basis points per annum from market timing activities, relative to the returns earned on passive benchmark portfolios. A somewhat comparable result was reported by Sharpe (1992, Figure 18).

Security Selection

There are also many ways to investigate the ability of fund managers to select securities with abnormally high returns. One consequence of a manager actively engaging in security selection is that the construction of the fund deviates from that of the market index. This result implies that the fund will exhibit some degree of diversifiable risk. The degree of a fund's nonmarket risk is therefore a proxy of sorts for the degree of security selection exhibited by its manager.

The degree of a fund's diversification is usually measured by the percentage of its total risk that is accounted for by market movements— the R^2 of a regression relating fund and market returns. Figure 20.11 presents the R^2 of fifty-nine mutual funds for a recent time period. The

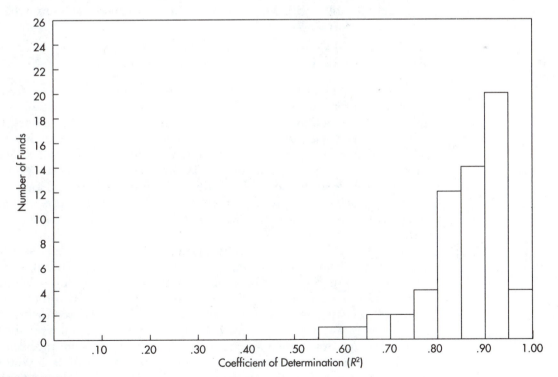

FIGURE 20.11

Degree of Diversification for Fifty-nine Mutual Funds

market index is given by the SP500. While most of the funds are clearly well diversified, a number bear substantial diversifiable risk, as indicated by their low R^2. To justify this added risk the fund must be able to produce additional returns. However, the evidence that we will soon review strongly indicates that most funds do not earn sufficiently high abnormal returns to justify incurring nonmarket risk. In addition, there is no convincing evidence to indicate that any superior performance is linked to a lack of diversification. Indeed, using the same ninety-one pension funds, Brinson, Hood, and Beebower (1986) report that the average plan lost 36 basis points per annum from the security selection activities of their managers, relative to the returns earned on passive benchmark portfolios. Overall, we can conclude that mutual fund managers have not in general done well in detecting mispriced securities.

PERFORMANCE MEASURES: SOME IMPORTANT PROBLEMS

The risk-adjusted performance measures introduced earlier (e.g., Sharpe's index) present some problems upon practical implementation. Three problems are briefly addressed in this section: (1) the inability both to borrow and to lend at the riskless rate; (2) changes in portfolio risk over time; and (3) Roll's critique. These problems may cause ambiguity when assessing performance.

Borrowing and Lending at Different Rates

The risk-adjusted performance measures described earlier all stem from the standard form of the CAPM. Thus, when using these measures, you implicitly assume that securities are priced in accord with this model. If this assumption is incorrect, then biased performance rankings can result.

As an illustration, suppose that the standard CAPM fails because investors must borrow at a higher rate. While individual and institutional investors can lend at the riskless rate of interest (investing in riskless securities), they commonly cannot borrow at this low rate. This asymmetry results in a nonlinear CAPM and in turn can produce ambiguous performance valuation. For instance, consider the Sharpe index in conjunction with Figure 20.12. In the figure, borrowing at the riskless rate is required to move out beyond portfolio A on the ray R_FA. If such borrowing were possible, we could unambiguously conclude that A dominates B; an investor who wishes to hold a portfolio with the same standard deviation as B would be better off holding A and borrowing at the riskless rate to move to A'. However, if such borrowing is not feasible, then A may not dominate B. For instance, if borrowing is accomplished at the rate $R_F + \epsilon$, where ϵ represents a credit risk premium, then the investor must follow the broken line to move beyond A. Here A dominates B for

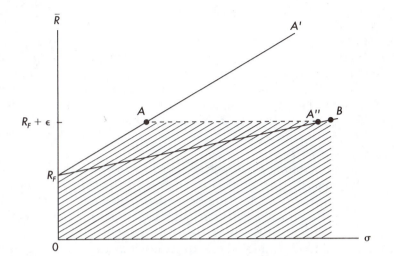

FIGURE 20.12
Efficient Frontier
with Unequal
Borrowing and
Lending Rates

risk levels up to A'', but beyond A'' portfolio B dominates A. In general the portfolios that A would dominate are given by the shaded region below $R_F A A''$ in Figure 20.12.

Ultimately, whether portfolio A dominates B or any other portfolio depends on ϵ, the credit risk premium that drives a wedge between borrowing and lending rates for investors, and the risk level assumed. Thus differences in ϵ and the target risk level among various investors can result in different performance assessments according to the Sharpe index as well as most other performance measures described earlier. Therefore, different rates at which investors can lend and borrow may introduce a degree of uncertainty into the performance evaluation procedure. One must be careful to identify the credit risk premium (ϵ) applicable and to rank the funds assessed in light of ϵ and the target level of risk appropriately. Ultimately, we can conclude that measurement is simplified if a linear benchmark can be employed.

Changes in Portfolio Risk over Time

Changes in portfolio risk occur over time as the manager alters the portfolio's composition and as changes occur in market expectations about the performance of each component security. Consequently, estimating risk from a historical series of portfolio returns can produce a risk measure that is unreflective of the portfolio's risk at any point in time. In addition, it may be difficult to ascertain whether the fund's manager closely followed the stated risk policy of the portfolio. To address these problems, performance evaluation should be conducted on a regular basis with little calendar time between evaluations. Most fund performance is assessed quarterly.

Roll's Critique

Roll (1978) observes that beta can change with the market proxy used in the estimation procedure. For instance, a different beta may arise if you use the SP500 rather than the DJIA. In turn, the ranking of portfolios based on a measure such as Treynor's or Jensen's index can change. Thus, the use of different market proxies can lead to ambiguity in assessments of fund performance. This ambiguity is the subject of Roll's critique. It is exactly the same problem researchers face when trying to test the CAPM, as addressed in Part 2.

Roll's critique implies that performance should be investigated under several different market proxies. If the investigation's results are consistent, then the user can be confident about the inferences drawn on performance. Empirically, Peterson and Rice (1980) have found that Roll's critique may not be far-reaching, since the relative performances of the fifteen mutual funds tested were statistically indistinguishable under the different market indices employed. Exhibit 20.7 replicates the results of Peterson and Rice. The funds showed similar rankings, based on both the Jensen and Sharpe performance measures, under each of the four market proxies used and for each of the two time periods studied.

MUTUAL FUND PERFORMANCE: EMPIRICAL EVIDENCE

In this section we summarize a large body of empirical evidence regarding the performance of both domestic mutual funds and U.S.-based international mutual funds.[7]

Domestic Fund Performance

One of the earliest and most comprehensive studies of domestic mutual fund performance was conducted by Friend, Blume, and Crockett (1970). They examined eighty-six funds over the period January 1960 to June 1968. Exhibit 20.8 on page 564 provides some of their results. Variance was used as the risk measure. The eighty-six funds were divided into high-, medium-, and low-risk categories, and random portfolios with similar approximate risks were generated. The columns under mean variance show how similar the mutual funds and randomly generated portfolios are in terms of risk. The last two columns show the returns on each group of funds and random portfolios. Based on this matching procedure, it

---

[7]Mutual funds incur transaction costs when they trade securities. Also, they often charge a yearly management fee, typically about .5 percent of net asset value. In addition, load funds charge an initial fee to the purchaser of fund shares, often about 8 percent of the purchase made. No-load funds do not charge a load fee. All of the exhibits in this chapter were prepared by deducting transaction costs and management fees, but not loads, from returns. This somewhat distorts the performance of no-load funds relative to load funds.

EXHIBIT 20.7

Mutual Fund Performance Rankings under Different Market Proxies

	1967-1971					1972-1976				
	Dow Jones Industrials	SP500	Equally Weighted CRSP	Value Weighted CRSP	Standard Deviation	Dow Jones Industrials	SP500	Equally Weighted CRSP	Value Weighted CRSP	Standard Deviation
Bulloch	4*	4*	4*	4*	4*	6*	6*	6*	5*	6*
Delaware	10	10	10	10	9	8	8	7	8	8
Dreyfus	13	13	12	13	12	9	9	9	9	9
First Investors Growth	8	9	8	9	10	15	15	15	15	15
Fundamental Investors	14	14	14	14	13	13	13	13	13	13
National Security Income	6	6	6	6	6	5*	7	5*	7*	5*
New Horizon	1*	1*	1*	1*	1*	14	12	14	12	14
Pioneer	3*	3*	3*	3*	3*	2*	2*	2*	2*	2*
Putnam Growth	5	5	5	5	5*	7*	5*	8	6*	7
Putnam Income	12	12	11	11	11*	12*	14	10	14	10
Templeton Growth	2*	2*	2*	2*	2	1*	1*	1*	1*	1*
United Income	7	7	7	7	7	10	10	12	10	12
Value Line Income	9	8	9	8	8	4*	4*	4*	4*	4*
Value Line Special Situations	11	11	13	12	15	3*	3*	3*	3*	3*
Wellington	15	15	15	15	14	11	11	11	11	11

*The fund outperformed the market index on a risk-adjusted basis.

Source: D. Peterson and M. Rice, "A Note on Ambiguity in Portfolio Performance Measures," *Journal of Finance* 35 (1980), 1251–1256.

EXHIBIT 20.8

Mutual Fund Performance, 1960–June 1968 (Variance Criterion for Risk)

Risk Class	Number in Sample		Mean Variance		Mean Return	
	Mutual Funds	Equally Weighted Random Portfolios[a]	Mutual Funds	Equally Weighted Random Portfolios[a]	Mutual Funds	Equally Weighted Random Portfolios[a]
Low risk	43	62	0.00120	0.00118	0.102	0.128
Medium risk	25	51	0.00182	0.00184	0.118	0.142
High risk	18	50	0.00280	0.00279	0.138	0.162

[a]Equal beginning-of-period investment in each stock included; NYSE-listed stocks only.

Source: I. Friend, M. Blume, and J. Crockett, *Mutual Funds and Other Institutional Investors* (New York: McGraw-Hill, 1970). Reprinted with permission from the Twentieth Century Fund, New York.

EXHIBIT 20.9

Mutual Fund Performance, 1960–June 1968 (Beta Criterion for Risk)

Risk Class	Number in Sample		Mean Beta Coefficient		Mean Return			
	Mutual Funds	Equally Weighted Random Portfolios	Mutual Funds	Equally Weighted Random Portfolios	Mutual Funds	Equally Weighted Random Portfolios	Proportionally Weighted Random Portfolios, Variant 1	Proportionally Weighted Random Portfolios, Variant 2
Low risk ($\beta = 0.5$–0.7)	28	17	0.614	0.642	0.091	0.128	0.116	0.101
Medium risk ($\beta = 0.7$–0.9)	53	59	0.786	0.800	0.106	0.131	0.097	0.084
High risk ($\beta = 0.9$–1.1)	22	60	0.992	0.992	0.135	0.137	0.103	0.092

Source: I. Friend, M. Blume, and J. Crockett, *Mutual Funds and Other Institutional Investors* (New York: McGraw-Hill, 1970). Reprinted with permission from the Twentieth Century Fund, New York.

appears that the mutual funds performed worse than the random benchmark portfolios for the sample period.

Friend, Blume, and Crockett repeated their analysis, using beta as the risk measure. Their results are reported in Exhibit 20.9. Here three different methods were used to construct the random portfolios: (1) equally weighted, as in Exhibit 20.8; (2) proportionally weighted so that the odds of selecting any stock are proportional to the dollar amount of that stock outstanding but equal dollar investments occur; and (3) proportionally weighted so that the odds of selecting any stock are equal but the dollar amount invested in any stock is proportional to the dollar amount of that stock outstanding. Overall, the performance of the mutual funds was mixed compared with those of the benchmark portfolios, with the method used to construct these portfolios affecting the performance tests. The underlying reason is that small-firm stocks performed better during the period, so equally weighted random portfolios with greater representation of these small firms performed best.

Another important study of mutual fund performance was conducted by Jensen (1968). He analyzed 115 funds for the period 1945–1964 and drew some damaging conclusions about the timing and security selection expertise of fund managers. Specifically, he found that on average the funds did not outperform a passive investment strategy and further that only five managers earned extra returns sufficient to cover their management fees. Note that five should be detected in a sample of 115 due to random chance. Figure 20.13 is taken from Jensen's study. It shows the expected returns and betas of the funds studied. The scatter about the estimated security market line is uniform, indicating that the fund managers, on average, did not possess superior selection ability relative to other groups of investors operating under limited information. This evidence can be construed as supporting the strong form of the efficient markets hypothesis, since fund managers were unable to demonstrate superior performance regardless of the information and selection proce-

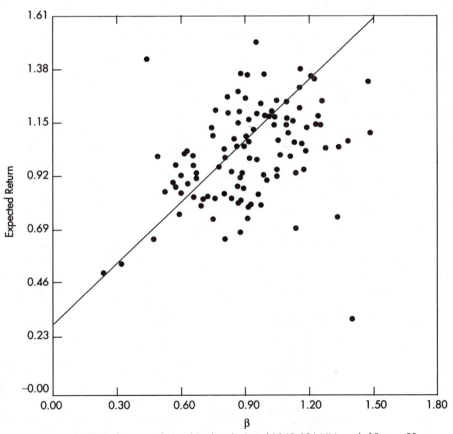

FIGURE 20.13

Mutual Fund Expected Returns and Betas, 1945–1964

Source: M. Jensen, "The Performance of Mutual Funds in the Period 1945–1964," *Journal of Finance* 23 (1968), 402.

dures they employed. Still, these managers may have largely fulfilled the policy initiatives of their funds (e.g., high growth or growth plus income), so their overall returns may have been consistent with returns of corresponding benchmark portfolios (e.g., for high growth, the BARRA growth stock index). Again, the fund policy is likely to be the greatest determinant of returns and return variation. Jensen's results focus on management expertise beyond fund policy, strongly suggesting that on average managers demonstrate no ability to time the market or to select securities after accounting for return performance due to policy directives.

While the studies of Friend, Blume, and Crockett and of Jensen are now somewhat dated, their general finding that fund managers cannot on average outperform the market continues to be supported by more recent evidence. Other studies of mutual fund performance that we have not reviewed here include McDonald (1974), Williamson (1972), Crenshaw (1977), Chang and Lewellen (1984), Henriksson (1984), and Ippolito (1989), among others.[8,9]

International Fund Performance

Eun, Kolodny, and Resnick (1991, EKR) examined thirteen U.S.-based international funds over 1977–1986. Using the Sharpe, Treynor, and Jensen measures, they found that most of the funds performed better than SP500 but most did not outperform the Morgan Stanley capital international world index. Though the three performance measures gave conflicting results in certain cases, the authors determined that investors could have obtained diversification benefits from investing in a majority of the funds examined, compared with investing in the U.S. stock market alone. Rao and Aggarwal (1987) examined the performance of nine of these same thirteen international funds for the period 1979–1983. They also found that the funds provided substantial diversification in relation to the systematic risk of the U.S. stock market (SP500). However, the returns earned by the funds on average were determined to be commensurate with the risks of their portfolios. Finally, Cumby and Glen (1990) used the Jensen index and Grinblatt and Titman's (1989) performance measure to analyze fifteen funds, eight of which were also in EKR's sample. Over the 1982–1988 period, the funds outperformed the Morgan Stanley U.S. equity index but

---

[8] Of these, only Ippolito (1989) concludes that managers outperform the market on average. Examining 143 funds for the period 1965–1984, Ippolito reports that fund returns, before load fees but after other expenses, are on average .83 percent per year above the Sharpe market line (from the one-year Treasury bill rate through the SP500 portfolio). However, Elton, Gruber, Das and Hklarka (1991), using a three-factor model, do not confirm Ippolito's results.

[9] Pension plans and endowment funds also do not appear to outperform the market index on a risk-adjusted basis. For evidence, see Beebower and Bergstrom (1977), Berkowitz, Finney, and Logue (1988), Brinson, Hood, and Beebower (1986), Ippolito and Turner (1987), and Munnell (1983).

not the world index, either collectively or individually. They attributed the funds' superior performance (compared with the U.S. stock index) to the benefits of international diversification rather than to the superior ability of fund managers. Overall, it appears that international mutual fund managers are not able to outperform a naive benchmark strategy of investing in a world market index.[10]

Benefits of Diversification

Despite the fact that mutual funds cannot in general outperform a passive investment strategy, they remain extremely popular with investors. As mentioned in this chapter's introduction, mutual funds are growing at about 16 percent per annum (Baumol, Goldfield, Gordon, and Kohen 1990). The results of a survey conducted by Lewellen, Lease, and Schlarbaum (1977) found that the sustained attraction of mutual funds is due to the extensive diversification that they provide. Figure 20.11 corroborates this feature, indicating that mutual funds reduce all but about 13 percent of nonmarket risk, on average. Elton and Gruber (1977) have shown that for an individual investor to construct a random portfolio that is similarly diversified, nearly fifty securities must be held. Thus it appears that mutual funds can provide diversification at a relatively low cost. This result is justification enough for their existence but not for their active management activities.

In light of this evidence an interesting question is whether there are any characteristics of mutual funds that can be used to predict *relatively* superior performance. If there are such characteristics, then investors who wish to purchase shares in mutual funds to diversify should select funds exhibiting these same characteristics.

Very little research has been done to identify characteristics associated with mutual funds that earn higher returns than other mutual funds. The few attempts made have focused on the investment performance of the mutual fund industry as a whole and have all been univariate studies. One of the earliest studies, the Wharton School *Study of Mutual Funds* (1962), examined the relationship between fund performance and portfolio turnover, sales charges, management fees, and brokerage affiliations. Each characteristic was examined in turn, and no consistent relationship was found in any case. Friend, Blume, and Crockett (1970) also found no clear, consistent relationship between performance and size, once risk was held constant. However, they did observe a positive relationship between performance and portfolio turnover and between performance and expense ratio as well as a slight negative relationship between performance and sales charge. Their results seemed to indicate that mutual fund

---

[10] For an examination of the performance of European-based international mutual funds, see McDonald (1973) and Farber (1975).

managers were successful in taking advantage of investment opportunities through higher trading activity and in channeling the benefits of research to the investor. Lakonishok (1981) studied the relationship between the performance of mutual funds and various resources expended by them in terms of brokerage commissions, operating expenses, and management fees. However, his results indicated that there was no significant relationship between fund performance and the resources expended. Instead some evidence suggested that low levels of expenses achieved better results on a net return basis. Sharpe (1966) has also found that good performance is associated with low expense ratios but is unrelated to fund size as measured by net asset value.

SUMMARY

The vast size and competitive nature of the money management industry underlie the importance of assessing the performance of professional money managers. While evaluation services do exist, they provide poor information, since they commonly assess a fund's performance relative to other funds that undertake different risks. Based on the tenets of modern portfolio theory, several risk-adjusted performance measures have been developed. These measures, including Sharpe's, Treynor's, and Jensen's indices, can be used judiciously to compare the performance of any fund against that of other funds and the market index. Dozens of empirical studies have employed these measures to assess the overall performance of the U.S. mutual fund industry. The majority of the evidence strongly suggests that on average fund managers cannot outperform a passive strategy of investing in the market index and using the risk-free asset to achieve the target risk level. Analogously, recent studies indicate that U.S.-based international mutual funds are unable on average to outperform a world market index. These funds do outperform a purely domestic market index, but only because of the added diversification offered by overseas investment and not because of any superior market timing or security selection ability of their managers. Despite this evidence, mutual funds are popular and the industry is experiencing solid growth because the funds offer diversification at a relatively low cost. On average, mutual funds exhibit less than 15 percent of nonmarket risk, and there are now mutual funds that specialize in investing in other mutual funds.

Questions and Problems

1. Business periodicals often rank mutual funds on the basis of return performance only. Discuss the problems associated with this approach to performance evaluation.

2. How can you control for the timing and size of cash flows when computing fund returns for the purpose of performance evaluation?

3. Describe a procedure for evaluating the effects of a constraint imposed on a fund's activities.

4. Describe how Friend, Blume, and Crockett (1970) controlled for differential risk levels when evaluating fund performance. Summarize their principal findings.

5. Discuss how Sharpe's index and its variant, the differential return measure, can lead to different fund rankings. Is this likely to occur frequently? (Hint: Compare Exhibits 20.4 and 20.5.)

6. Describe how the Jensen index would appear if the APM was the asset pricing model chosen to represent expected returns.

7. Discuss the ramifications of using the empirical security market line, in conjunction with Jensen's index, for performance evaluation. Be sure to assess the impact on funds having different betas.

8. Describe some common techniques for decomposing management performance into market timing and security selection elements. Is there substantial empirical evidence that suggests that fund managers exhibit timing or selection expertise? Discuss.

9. Discuss why performance evaluation can be complicated by the use of a nonlinear benchmark.

10. Describe Roll's critique in the context of portfolio performance evaluation. What do the results of Peterson and Rice (1980) imply about this issue?

11. Summarize the empirical evidence regarding the performance of U.S.-based international mutual funds.

12. Why do mutual funds remain so popular in light of evidence that their managers are unable to outperform the market index?

Questions 13 through 17 refer to the following data on six mutual funds:

FUND	RETURN	STANDARD DEVIATION	BETA
A	.16	.06	0.90
B	.15	.07	0.85
C	.11	.06	1.05
D	.19	.08	1.20
E	.22	.09	1.15
F	.14	.05	0.90

13. What are the Sharpe indices and performance rankings of the six funds if the risk-free rate is 4 percent?

14. What are the differential return and ranking of each fund if $R_M = .15$ and $\sigma_M = .05$?

15. What is each fund's Treynor index?

16. What is each fund's Jensen index?

17. What is Fund A's Jensen index if the zero-beta CAPM applies and $R_Z = .03$?

REFERENCES

Ang, J., and J. Chua. 1979. Composition measures for the evaluation of investment performance. *Journal of Financial and Quantitative Analysis.* June, 361–364.

Arditti, F. 1971. Another look at mutual fund performance. *Journal of Financial and Quantitative Analysis.* June, 909–912.

Baumol, W., M. Goldfeld, A. Gordon, and M. Kohen. 1990. *The economics of mutual fund markets. Competition versus regulation.* Boston: Kluwee Academic Publishers.

Barineau, J. 1969. Does "good portfolio management" exist? *Management Science.* February, B322–B324.

Beebower, G., and G. Bergstrom. 1977. A performance analysis of pension and profit-sharing portfolios 1966–1975. *Financial Analysts Journal.* May/June, 31–42.

Berkowitz, S., L. Finney, and D. Logue. 1988. *The investment performance of corporate pension plans.* New York: Quorum Books.

Black, F., M. Jensen, and M. Scholes. 1972. The capital asset pricing model. Some empirical tests. In *Studies in the Theory of Capital Markets,* M. Jensen, ed. New York: Praeger.

Brinson, G., L. Hood, and G. Beebower. 1986. Determinants of portfolio performance. *Financial Analysts Journal.* July/August, 39–44.

Carlson, R. 1970. Aggregate performance of mutual funds 1948–1967. *Journal of Financial and Quantitative Analysis.* March, 1–32.

Chang, E., and W. Lewellen. 1984. Market timing and mutual fund investment performance. *Journal of Business* 52:57–72.

Crenshaw, T. 1977. The evaluation of investment performance. *Journal of Business.* October, 462–485.

Cumby, R., and J. Glen. 1990. Evaluating the performance of international mutual funds. *Journal of Finance* 45:497–522.

Elton, E., and M. Gruber. 1977. Risk reduction and portfolio size: An analytical solution. *Journal of Business.* October, 415–437.

Elton, E., M. Gruber, S. Das, and M. Hklarka. 1991. Efficiency with costly information. A reinterpretation of evidence from managed portfolios. Working paper, New York University.

Eun, C., R. Kolodny, and B. Resnick. 1991. U.S.-based international mutual funds. A performance evaluation. *Journal of Portfolio Management.* Spring, 88–94.

Fama, E. 1972. Components of investment performance. *Journal of Finance.* June, 551–567.

Fama, E., and K. French. 1992. The cross-section of expected stock returns. *Journal of Finance.* June, 427–465.

Farber, A. 1975. Performance of internationally diversified mutual funds. In *International Capital Markets,* Elton and Gruber, eds. North Holland.

Friend, I., and M. Blume. 1970. Measurement of portfolio performance under uncertainty. *American Economic Review.* September, 561–575.

Friend, I., M. Blume, and J. Crockett. 1970. *Mutual Funds and Other Institutional Investors.* McGraw-Hill, New York.

Gibb, W. 1968. Critical evaluation of pension funds. *Journal of Finance.* May, 337–343.

Grant, D. 1977. Portfolio performance and the "cost" of timing decisions. *Journal of Finance.* June, 837–838.

Grinblatt, M., and S. Titman. 1989. Portfolio performance evaluation. Old issues and new insights. *Review of Financial Studies* 2:393–421.

Henriksson, R. 1984. Market timing and mutual fund performance: An empirical investigation. *Journal of Business* 52:73–96.

Henriksson, R., and R. Merton. 1981. On market timing and investment performance. II. Statistical procedures for evaluating forecast skills. *Journal of Business* 513–533.

Ippolito, R. 1989. Efficiency with costly information: A study of mutual fund performance, 1965–1984. *Quarterly Journal of Economics* 104:1–23.

Ippolito, R., and J. Turner. 1987. Turnover , fees, and pension plan performance. *Financial Analysts Journal.* November/December, 16–26.

Jensen, M. 1986. The performance of mutual funds in the period 1945–1964. *Journal of Finance.* May, 389–415.

Jensen, M. 1969. Risk, the pricing of capital assets, and the evaluation of investment portfolios. *Journal of Business.* April, 167–247.

Jobson, J., and B. Korkie. 1982. Potential performance and tests of portfolio efficiency. *Journal of Financial Economics.* December, 443–466.

Joy, M., and B. Porter. 1974. Stochastic dominance and mutual fund performance. *Journal of Financial and Quantitative Analysis.* January, 25–31.

Lakonishok, J. 1981. Performance of mutual funds versus their expenses. *Journal of Bank Research* 12:110–113.

Kon, S., and F. Jen. 1979. The investment performance of mutual funds: An empirical investigation of timing, selectivity, and market efficiency. *Journal of Business.*

Lee, C., and F. Jen. 1978. Effects of measurement errors on systematic risk and performance measure of a portfolio. *Journal of Financial and Quantitative Analysis.* June, 299–312.

Lewellen, W., R. Lease, and G. Schlarbaum. 1977. Some evidence on the patterns of mutual fund ownership. *Journal of Economics and Business* 57–67.

Malkiel, B. 1977. The valuation of closed end investment company shares. *Journal of Finance.* June, 847–886.

McDonald, J. 1973. French mutual fund performance: Evaluation of internationally diversified portfolios. *Journal of Finance* 28:1161–1180.

McDonald, J. 1974. Objectives and performance of mutual funds 1960–1969. *Journal of Financial and Quantitative Analysis.* June, 311–333.

Monroe, R., and J. Trieschmann. 1972. Portfolio performance of property-liability insurance companies. *Journal of Financial and Quantitative Analysis.* March, 1595–1611.

Munnell, A. 1983. Who should manage the assets of collectively bargained pension plans? *New England Economic Review.* July/August, 18–30.

Peterson, D., and M. Rice. 1980. A note on ambiguity in portfolio performance measures. *Journal of Finance* 35:1251–1256.

Prakash, A., and R. Bear. 1986. A simplifying performance measure recognizing skewness. *Financial Review.* February, 135–144.

Rao, R., and R. Aggarwal. 1987. Performance of U.S.-based international mutual funds. *Akron Business and Economic Review* 18:98–107.

Roll, R. 1978. Ambiguity when performance is measured by the security market line. *Journal of Finance* 33:1051–1069.

Smith, K. 1978. Is fund growth related to fund performance? *Journal of Portfolio Management.* 4 Spring, 49–55.

Securities and Exchange Commission. 1971. *Institutional Investor Study*, part 2. Washington: U.S. Government Printing Office.

Sharpe, W. 1966. Mutual fund performance. *Journal of Business*. January, 119–138.

Sharpe, W. 1992. Asset allocation: Management style and performance measurement. *Journal of Portfolio Management*. Winter, 7–19.

Treynor, J. 1965. How to rate management of investment funds. *Harvard Business Review*. Jan./Feb., 63–75.

Treynor, J., and M. Mazuy. 1966. Can mutual funds outguess the market? *Harvard Business Review*. July/Aug., 131–136.

Wharton School of Finance and Commerce, University of Pennsylvania. 1962. *Study of Mutual Funds*. House Report 2274, 87th Congress, 2nd Session, Washington.

Williamson, P. 1972. Measurement and forecasting of mutual fund performance. Choosing an investment strategy. *Financial Analysts Journal*. Nov./Dec., 78–84.

Afterword

Portfolio management is an exceedingly difficult field to master through textbooks. There is simply no substitute for experience when it comes to the complexities of real economies and markets. Yet the student needs to be exposed to this field in such a way that a balance is struck between theory and practice. As noted in the Preface, the student who is solely introduced to one-period equilibrium models with homogeneous investor expectations and perfect markets surely will not be prepared for employment in a world that only approximates these assumptions and in a field searching for inefficiencies that yield a few extra basis points of return. On the other hand, an approach that lacks any systematic nature would be purely ad hoc and would leave the student confused and devoid of an analytic understanding, hence equally unprepared for the demands of real-world portfolio and risk management.

In this book we have tried to present the existing theory while being forthright about its shortcomings. We have also delved into the micro-mechanics of everyday practice without claim that such mechanics are necessarily widely adopted or even well founded. Armed solely with such material, the student would have little more than a bag of anecdotal stories whose lessons can become stale as quickly as a new exotic derivative can become plain vanilla.

We could use this space to reiterate the many formulas, concepts, and heuristic practices that have been detailed in the previous twenty chapters. However, such an exercise would consume nearly as much space and effort. Instead, we would like to take this time to remind our readers of the goals of this book, with the hope that they consider that the goals have been met and furthermore that they have laid the foundation for a more confident entry into the field of portfolio management. Specifically, the purpose of this book is to provide an analytic framework for constructing and managing optimal security portfolios and to introduce the concepts, problems, and applications of contemporary portfolio theory and risk management.

The future of portfolio management is unclear at best. Little can be predicted other than that the field will become more complex as technological advances continue to facilitate ever more trading practices, rapid access to markets including overseas markets, and empirical research of valuation models and investment stratagems. New products will likely be engineered to facilitate risk management and the efficient implementation of tactical asset allocation. Competition probably will also intensify, and money management firms that operate at the margin will die off while a few profitable firms come to dominate the industry. In short, the industry should exhibit the classical patterns of growth, competition, and retrenchment that characterize other service industries.

The good news of all this uncertainty is that a well educated, well trained, technology-proficient individual who exhibits a strong work ethic can make a mark in the field and contribute to the welfare of society as a whole. Some of the leading social scientists of our time and contributors to the welfare of our society have been the men and women identified within the pages of this book.

Software Description

Software designed for an IBM or IBM compatible personal computer is provided on a single 3.5-inch disk. To load the software, put the disk in drive A (or B) and type 'cd\FM' followed by 'FM'. After an introductory menu, which is eliminated by hitting the Enter key, a menu providing ten modules should appear. With this software, efficient portfolios and the minimum variance portfolio can be computed using the Markowitz model, which is discussed in Chapters 2 through 4 (Module 1), or the single index model, discussed in Chapters 5 and 6 (Module 2). Variables such as the expected return and correlations can be input or computed from historical data provided by the software.

Fixed income analysis (material covered in Chapters 14 and 15) is contained in Modules 3 through 5. Software Module 3 computes the yield to maturity of a bond while Module 4 estimates the duration of a bond or bond portfolio. Module 5 constructs future interest rates from the yield curve.

Modules 6 through 9 relate to the pricing of options, which is covered in Chapter 16. Module 6 computes European call and put option prices using the Black-Scholes option pricing model. The current stock price, exercise price, time to maturity of the option, risk-free interest rate, and volatility of the returns of the underlying asset are necessary inputs along with dividend information. Module 7 computes option prices using the binomial option pricing model. Module 8 computes implied volatility; the current asset price, exercise price, interest rate, time to maturity, and market price of the option is provided and the corresponding volatility is computed.

Module 9 supplies delta, gamma, and theta values for option portfolios. These values provide information on how the option portfolio value changes with respect to changes in the underlying asset price and time to maturity. Lastly, Module 10 computes stock prices using the net present value model.

To illustrate, Module 1 (Markowitz Mean Variance) provides efficient portfolios given expected returns, standard deviations, and correlations for assets under consideration. To access this option, type '1' at the main menu. A blank screen should appear with available options at the bottom of the screen. Type the F2 key. The software can compute efficient portfolios with inputs you provide or it can compute expected returns, standard deviations, and correlations from raw returns that you provide. Type '1' if you already have these inputs. Then type in the expected returns, standard deviations, and correlations of the assets under consideration followed by the F10 key. The output is a set of efficient portfolios along with the minimum variance portfolio. Hit the escape key to obtain the main menu and another module may be selected.

GLOSSARY

Abnormal return The difference between a stock's return for a given period and the stock's expected return, where the latter is generally defined by a market model regression.

Absolute risk aversion A measure of an individual's propensity to undertake risky alternatives as total wealth changes.

Active approach Any investment approach that deviates from a passive approach. It is characterized by high security turnover and large management fees.

Aggressive security A security with a market beta greater than one.

Alpha A measure of the extent to which a security is mispriced, i.e., plots off the Security Market Line (SML), in the context of equilibrium pricing according to the Capital Asset Pricing Model (CAPM).

American option An option contract that allows for premature exercise.

Anomalies, stock return Observed and generally unexplained patterns or seasonalities in stock returns, particularly patterns that seem inconsistent with market efficiency and/or equilibrium pricing models such as the CAPM or APT.

Arbitrage Simultaneous purchase and sale of the same security that results in a profit with no risk and at no cost.

Arithmetic return The sum of the holding period returns divided by the number of returns.

Ask price The price at which a market maker offers to sell a primary or derivative security.

At-the-money An option where the underlying asset price is equal to the option's exercise price.

Autocorrelation (of returns) The tendency for future returns to be correlated with past returns. First-order autocorrelation is the correlation of returns for period t with returns for period t-1; k-order autocorrelation is the correlation of period t returns with returns for period t-k.

Balanced fund A blend of income and growth funds.

Basis The difference between the spot and futures prices.

Basis risk The risk associated with variation in the basis over time.

Bear market A market in which prices are generally declining.

Beta, adjusted An adjusted value of beta based on evidence that estimated betas tend to regress toward a value of 1.0.

Beta (or factor) coefficient A measure of the systematic (nondiversifiable) risk of a security or portfolio, i.e., the sensitivity (degree of covariance) of a security's return to an underlying factor. (See also *Market beta*.)

Bid-ask spread The difference between the bid and ask prices.

Bid price The price at which a market maker offers to buy a primary or derivative security.

Binomial option-pricing model (BOPM) A model for valuing options in which the underlying asset price can take on two possible values at the end of any one period of time.

Black-Scholes model A model for pricing European option contracts.

Bounded-payoff put A currency put option where the payoff is limited to less than the exercise price.

Brady Commission A commission appointed by President Reagan to study the causes of the October 1987 stock market crash.

Bull market A market in which prices are generally rising.

Call option An option giving the buyer the right to purchase the underlying asset at the prescribed exercise price.

Call provision An option held by the issuer of a debt security allowing the issuer to retire part or all of the issue prior to the stated maturity at prespecified prices defined over time.

Capital market line (CML) A line that plots the different possible combinations (efficient set) of the risk-free asset and all risky assets which provide the best risk-return investment opportunities.

Capital markets The markets for long-term securities.

Carrying-charge model A model used to determine futures or forward prices. It holds that such prices are given by the asset's spot price plus the costs of carrying the asset forward to delivery.

Carrying charges The total costs of carrying an asset forward in time, including storage, transportation, and financing costs.

Cash-and-carry arbitrage A theoretically riskless arbitrage trading strategy that underlies the carrying-charge model of futures prices.

Cash settlement A procedure applicable to certain futures and options contracts wherein a cash transfer is employed at contract settlement rather than the actual delivery of the asset in question.

Certainty equivalent The maximum amount an individual will pay for a risky gamble.

Cheapest to deliver That unique Treasury note or Treasury bond that the short trader will deliver against the Chicago Board of Trade's Treasury note or Treasury bond futures contract.

Circus swap A combination of a currency swap and an interest rate swap.

Clearing firm A firm that is a member of a futures or options clearinghouse.

Clearinghouse A firm that is associated with an options or futures exchange that guarantees contract performance and otherwise facilitates trading.

Closed-end fund An investment company that has a fixed number of shares outstanding, and these shares cannot be redeemed but must be traded like ordinary common stock.

Collateralized mortgage obligations (CMOs) Mortgage-backed securities generally backed by a previously-issued, pass-through security, CMOs are a collection of securities broken into classes, called tranches, each of which has a distinct claim on the cash flows of the pass-through.

Commission broker A futures floor trader who executes public orders.

Commodity Futures Trading Commission (CFTC) A federal agency empowered to regulate futures trading.

Commodity pool See *Futures fund.*

Comparative statics A procedure for examining the effects of a marginal change in one particular variable while holding all other determinants constant.

Commodity swap A swap typically designed to fix the price of a particular commodity for both counterparties.

Contingent claim A financial asset that will provide payoff only under certain conditions, or contingencies.

Contingent immunization A quasi-active bond management strategy that combines forecast-based bets on the course of interest rates with a passive immunization strategy. The passive strategy is invoked if and when forecasts prove wrong and lead to losses.

Continuous random variable A random variable that can take on any value in an interval.

Conversion price Pertaining to a convertible bond, the dollar amount of principal value of debt that must be tendered upon conversion to receive one unit of the new security (usually one share of the borrowing firm's common stock).

Conversion ratio Pertaining to a convertible bond, the number of units of a new security (usually common stock of the borrowing firm) that will be received for each $1,000 of principal value of debt tendered upon conversion.

Convertible bond A debt security that includes an option which allows the investor to convert the bond into specified units of another security, usually shares of the borrowing firm.

Convexity A measure of the rate of change of a bond's duration as the level of the bond's yield changes.

Correlation coefficient The covariance between two random variables divided by the product their standard deviations. The resulting measure ranges from −1 to 1.

Country fund A particular type of international mutual fund that invests in one particularly foreign securities market.

Covariance The expected value of the product of the deviations from the mean for two random variables. The covariance is an unbounded measure of association between two random variables.

Covered call writing A strategy in which a call option is written on an underlying asset that is already held.

Critical line The locus of portfolios that exhibit minimum variance for given levels of expected return.

Cross hedge A futures hedge in which the asset underlying the futures contract differs from the asset being hedged.

Cross rate An exchange rate between two currencies that is implied from the exchange rates entailing a third currency.

Currency swap An arrangement in which two parties agree to exchange currencies at recurrent intervals, typically stemming from debt issues.

Daily resettlement A futures market requirement that traders realize losses each trading day.

Dedication An immunization strategy in which exact matching of inflows and outflows over time is achieved.

Defensive securities A security with a market beta of less than one.

Delivery option The option that the short trader has to deliver the cheapest-to-deliver Treasury note or Treasury bond against the Chicago Board of Trade's Treasury note or Treasury bond futures contract.

Delta An elasticity measure of the sensitivity of an option's price to changes in the price of the underlying asset.

Designated Order Turnaround (DOT) A system at the New York Stock Exchange that expedites the trading of large amounts of stocks, such as amounts associated with program trading.

Deterministic Outcomes are said to be deterministic when outcomes of the alternatives are known.

Diminishing marginal utility A property of rational economic agents in which the additional utility from consumption or wealth decreases as consumption increases.

Discrete random variable A random variable that can take on a countable number of values.

Diversifiable (or Unsystematic) risk Risk that is specific to an asset or a portfolio which can be diversified away through portfolio diversification.

Diversification The process of adding securities that are not perfectly correlated to a portfolio to reduce portfolio risk.

Dollar returns The gain or loss in the value of the initial investment. This dollar amount must consider cash payments from holding the instrument (interest or dividends) and capital gains or losses.

Dual trading A futures trading practice in which a floor trader can trade both for his or her own account and for the public during the same trading session.

Duration A measure of the price elasticity of a bond with respect to changes in the bond's yield. Also a measure of effective maturity.

Dynamic-hedge ratio The ratio that determines the number of index futures contracts such that the equity portfolio is continually hedged.

Dynamic hedging A strategy in which an

equity portfolio is insured through the continual trading of stock index futures contracts.

Early-exercise premium The premium that an American option commands over an otherwise identical European option because of the ability of traders to exercise American options prior to their maturity.

Economic choice problem The fundamental problem underlying all investment and consumption decisions. It is solved using a two-step procedure: defining an opportunity set and selecting from that set the investment or consumption combination that provides the greatest expected utility.

Efficient frontier The set of portfolios that maximize expected portfolio return for a given level of risk.

Efficient market A market in which new information is instantaneously reflected in asset prices.

Efficient market hypothesis The set of arguments leading to the assertion that market prices fully reflect available information. Such information may consist of past prices (weak form), all publicly available information (semi-strong form), or all information, both public and private (strong form).

Efficient portfolio A portfolio that is located on the efficient frontier.

Equity swaps A swap involving the payment of a floating rate determined by movements in a national stock market index, in return for fixed or variable interest payments or variable payments determined by a second national stock market index.

Eurodollar A dollar-denominated deposit in an overseas bank.

European currency unit An index that measures the value of the dollar against a basket of currencies of the members of the European Community (EC).

European option An option that can be exercised only at expiration.

Event study Research focusing on the market's reaction to new information of a given type (e.g., an earnings announcement), measured as the abnormal return on the firm's stock.

Ex Ante **return** The rate of return that an investment is expected to provide in the future.

Exchange rate risk The risk accompanying non-domestic investment in which returns can be reduced by adverse changes in currency values.

Exercise price The price at which an option owner may buy or sell the underlying asset if the option is exercised.

Expectations model An approach for determining futures prices that stresses the role of market expectations.

Expectations theory A theory of the term structure of interest rates in which forward rates of interest represent the market's unbiased expectation of future interest rates.

Expected return The rate of return expected from an investment. Statistically measured as the average of all possible returns weighted by their respective probabilities.

Expected utility The expected utility of a risky alternative is a weighted average of the possible units of utility from the gamble and the associated probabilities.

Expected value A measure of central tendency, which is a measure of the center of a return distribution.

Ex Post **return** Rate of return already realized on an investment.

Factor analysis A statistical technique used to extract, from the covariance matrix of a set of securities, one or more series of values ('factors') that explain the collective variability of those securities. Such factors may be priced in the market via the APT.

Factor coefficient See *Beta coefficient*.

Factor model A model which relates a security's return to changes in one or more common systematic factors.

Financial engineering The process of designing new financial instruments, especially derivative securities.

Forward contract An agreement between two parties to trade foreign currency at a future date and at a prescribed exchange rate which is determined today.

Forward (interest) rate The marginal rate of interest received for extending the term of a bond by one period.

Frontrunning An illegal trading scheme in which brokers place orders in front of public market orders that are large enough to likely change prices.

Fundamental betas Beta coefficients computed with the use of fundamental accounting information and previous security prices.

Futures commission merchant A firm that executes futures trades for public clients.

Futures contract A contract between two parties to trade a specified asset in the future for a prescribed price determined at contract inception.

Futures fund A mutual fund that specializes in the trading of futures contracts.

Futures option An option that is written on a futures contract.

Geometric return The nth root of the product of one plus the individual returns. The geometric return is the growth rate needed for the initial amount to grow to the ending value.

Growth fund A relatively risky equity mutual fund that seeks strong capital appreciation by investing in more speculative stocks.

Hedge A transaction in which a trader tries to protect a preexisting position in the spot asset market through the trading of derivative securities.

Hedged portfolio A combination of an asset and its derivative security such that the return is ensured to be risk-free.

Hedge ratio A ratio that determines the number of derivative securities to trade such that a hedged portfolio is attained.

Holiday effect The observed tendency for all stocks to provide higher returns on the last trading day before a holiday.

IMM index The method of quoting Treasury bill and Eurodollar futures prices at the International Monetary Market division of the Chicago Mercantile Exchange.

Immunization A portfolio management strategy in which the maturities of assets and liabilities are selected so as to eliminate interest rate sensitivity of the difference (i.e., the equity).

Implied volatility The variance of the returns of an asset that is derived by equating an observed option price with a theoretical model price.

Income fund A relatively safe equity mutual fund designed to provide high dividend income by investing in high-yield stocks.

Index fund A portfolio or mutual fund designed to replicate a target index, such as the SP500. An index fund commonly serves as a proxy for a passive investment approach.

Indication pricing schedule A schedule used by swap intermediaries to quote swap prices.

Indifference curve A curve providing combinations of goods that provide the same level of total utility.

Industry risk The risk associated with positive correlations between firms in the same industry.

Inflation The rate of change in the general level of prices of goods in an economy.

Initial margin The amount that must be posted in order to originally engage in a futures transaction.

Insatiability An individual will prefer more of a commodity to less.

Interbank market An informal network of banks that execute transactions in currency, currency forwards, and currency options.

Intercommodity spread A futures combination entailing long and short positions in contracts written on two different assets but having the same delivery dates.

Interest rate swaps An arrangement in which two parties agree to swap periodic interest payments on outstanding debt.

International mutual fund A mutual fund providing diversification into non-domestic securities.

International Swap Dealers Association An informal association of large swap intermediaries that seeks to provide greater standardization of swap transactions.

In-the-money A call (put) option where the underlying asset price is greater (less) than the option's exercise price.

Intracommodity spread A futures combination entailing long and short positions in contracts written on the same asset but having different delivery dates.

Inverse floaters Also known as yield curve notes, debt securities that pay coupon interest at a rate that varies inversely with short-term interest rates.

Investment-grade bond A bond that has a rating of at least Baa (BBB) by Moody's (Standard and Poors) rating agency, reflecting relatively low default risk.

Investment opportunity set The set of assets eligible for trade for a particular investor.

Iso-mean lines The set of portfolios that deliver a given portfolio expected return.

Iso-variance curves The locus of portfolios that provide the same portfolio variance.

January effect The tendency for stock returns, particularly those of small firms, to be higher in January.

Jensen index A risk-adjusted measure of portfolio performance where abnormal returns are measured with respect to some equilibrium asset pricing model. Jensen's index is often called a security's or portfolio's "alpha".

Lagrangian multiplier A method utilized to solve constrained optimization problems.

Law of one price An economic law stating that two identical assets cannot sell for different prices.

Least squares analysis Methodology used to quantify the relation between independent variable(s) and a dependent variable.

Limit down Occurs when the futures price moves down to its daily lower limit.

Liquidity preference theory A theory of the term structure of interest rates in which longer-term bonds provide higher expected returns than shorter-term bonds, for a given investment horizon.

Load fund A mutual fund that charges an up-front fee, typically 6.5 to 8 percent.

Local A trader on the floor of a futures exchange who trades for his own account.

London interbank offer rate The variable interest rate earned on Eurodollar deposits.

Long position Denotes the position of one who buys a primary or derivative security.

Maintenance margin The margin that must be maintained after the initial day of trading in the futures contract; it is typically about 75 percent of the initial margin.

Margin Collateral that must be posted to transact in a futures or options contract in order to insure the clearinghouse against credit risk.

Margin, equity A position consisting of an asset with a positive weight and a short position in a debt instrument. Capital is borrowed to finance additional purchases of the risky asset.

Marginal utility The additional utility derived an additional unit of consumption or wealth.

Margin call Indicates that a futures trader must post additional margin in order to continue trading in the contract.

Market beta A measure of the sensitivity (degree of covariance) of a security's return to the return on the market portfolio (in the context of the CAPM) or a market index (the single index or market model).

Market efficiency The tendency for market prices of assets to immediately and rationally reflect available information.

Market maker A trader on an exchange who is charged with the duty of filling public market orders.

Market model A regression equation in which the dependent variable is the return on a given security and the independent variable is the return on a market-wide portfolio (the 'market').

Market portfolio, proxy A well-diversified portfolio of securities (generally including only stocks but may include other securities or assets) used as a proxy for the unobservable market portfolio.

Market return The return on the market portfolio.

Market risk *Systematic risk.* ("Market" reflects

that systematic risk influences all securities in the market.)

Market risk premium The excess or additional return expected from the market portfolio or a market index over the risk-free rate of return.

Market segmentation theory A theory of the term structure of interest rates which posits that the maturity spectrum is segmented, such that in effect separate markets exist for short-term, medium-term and long-term debt, and the equilibrium interest rates in each market are not integrated on the basis of factors such as expectations of future interest rates.

Market timing One of two means by which a manager can earn abnormally high returns. It refers to an ability to predict turns in the market.

Marking-to-the-market See *Daily resettlement.*

Markowitz model Model used to compute the expected portfolio return and risk. Developed by Harry Markowitz.

Master agreements Standardized forms that provide the basic makeup of currency and interest rate swap arrangements.

Mean-variance efficient portfolio A portfolio that provides the highest possible expected return for its level of risk (measured by the standard deviation or variance) or the lowest risk for its expected return.

Mean-variance rule (E-V Rule) Two rules designed to eliminate inefficient portfolios. Specifically, investors will (1) minimize portfolio risk for a given portfolio return, and (2) maximize portfolio return for a given level of risk.

Minimum-variance hedge ratio A hedge ratio commonly used in conjunction with stock index futures contracts that indicates the number of futures contracts to trade in order to immunize the portfolio against systematic market risk.

Minimum variance portfolio The portfolio that minimizes the portfolio risk for given set of securities and their expected returns, variances and levels of association.

Mispriced security A security whose price is different from its equilibrium price (See *Overpriced Security* and *Underpriced Security*).

Money market fund A very safe, low return fund that invests in various money market instruments like U.S. treasury bills.

Monthly effect (or Turn-of-the-month effect) The observed tendency for all stocks to provide relatively high returns on several consecutive trading days beginning with the last trading day of each month.

Mortgage-backed securities Debt securities of various types that are secured by portfolios or 'pools' of mortgages, usually home mortgages.

Morgan Stanley world index A comprehensive index of the world's leading equity markets. This index may be regarded as a benchmark for passive international investment.

Municipal bond A bond issued by a state or local government. Interest on municipal bonds are exempt from federal taxation, and are generally exempt from state income taxes for in-state investors.

Mutual fund An investment company (usually open-end) that pools, invests, and manages investors' monies according to the fund's policy directive.

Naive hedge ratio A simple hedge ratio in which one unit in the futures market is matched with each unit of spot asset held; it is commonly used in conjunction with currency futures hedging applications.

National Futures Association An organization of firms involved in futures trading that self-regulates the industry.

Nation rotating Analogous to sector rotating, it refers to the shifting of funds from one national economy to another as dictated by management forecasts.

Nominal interest rate The interest rate actually observed on a debt security such as a CD, bond, etc.

Nonsynchronous trading effect The tendency for some of the prices used to develop the value of a stock index at a point in time to reflect trading from an earlier point in time, due to lack of continuous trading among some stocks.

Normal distribution Bell shaped and symmetric around the mean, the normal distribution is a family of distributions with different specifications of the mean and standard deviation.

Notional principal The principal underlying an interest rate swap; it is notional in the sense that it is never exchanged.

Open-end fund An investment company/mutual fund that permits new participants.

Option A derivative security that gives the buyer the right to trade an underlying asset at a prescribed exercise price on or before a specified maturity date.

Option fund A mutual fund that specializes in writing covered calls.

Options Clearing Corporation The corporation that serves as the clearinghouse for all options traded on U.S. markets except futures options.

Order book official An employee of the Chicago Board Options Exchange who manages public limit orders.

Out-of-the-money A call (put) option where the underlying asset price is below (above) the option's exercise price.

Overpriced (or overvalued) security A *mispriced* security which provides a lower return than it should for its level of risk.

Overreaction hypothesis A hypothesis, grounded in empirical evidence, stating that stocks performing poorly in the past have a propensity to outperform stocks that performed well in the past.

Passive approach An investment approach designed to mimic some broadly diversified market portfolio. It is characterized by low security turnover and management expenses.

Pass-through securities A type of mortgage-backed security in which all payments to the pool of mortgages are passed through to the investor on a pro-rate basis.

Percentage return The dollar return relative to the initial investment. This return must consider cash payments from holding the instrument (interest or dividends) and capital gains or losses.

Pit An area on the trading floor of a futures or options exchange where contracts are traded.

Political risk A risk that accompanies non-domestic investment. The term is usually employed to describe such possibilities as wealth expropriation by foreign governments and the like.

Portfolio beta Weighted average of the beta coefficients of a portfolio's component securities.

Portfolio insurance A strategy using combinations of options, futures, and/or other securities designed to ensure a minimum future value of an equity portfolio.

Portfolio theory Theory regarding the construction of optimal portfolios given the properties of each of the assets contained in the investment opportunity set.

Precious metals fund A mutual fund specializing in the stocks of gold and silver producers and other precious metals.

Preferred habitat theory A theory of the term structure of interest rates in which lenders and borrowers have preferred maturity 'habitats' because a given maturity matches the timing of their planned expenditures or receipts, respectively. Lenders (borrowers) may deviate from their maturity habitat of the expected additional return (expected reduction in borrowing costs) outweighs the additional transaction costs and risk involved.

Price discovery A function of the futures market wherein future price information can be gleaned from current futures prices.

Price-sensitivity hedge ratio A hedge ratio commonly used in applications entailing interest rate futures contracts; it determines the number of futures contracts to trade such that a fixed-income security is immunized from unanticipated changes in interest rates.

Prime A security created through the establishment of a trust that receives all dividend payments on a stock as well as any stock appreciation up to a termination value.

Probability distribution A graphical representation of the probabilities of all possible outcomes of a random variable.

Program trading The use of computers to assimilate real-time data in order to detect arbitrage opportunities.

Protective put An investment strategy in which put options are purchased to provide a minimum future value for a spot asset held.

Pure discount bond A bond that provides one payment at maturity with no interim payments such as coupon interest.

Pure expectations theory A theory of the term structure of interest rates in which the expected returns on bonds of all maturities are equal for a given investment horizon.

Pure factor (or factor mimicking) portfolio A portfolio that has unit systematic risk (a beta of 1) on one factor and zero systematic on all other factors in a factor model.

Put A derivative security giving the buyer the right to sell an underlying asset at a prescribed exercise price on or before a specified maturity date.

Put-call parity A pricing relation between puts and calls that follows from arbitrage restrictions.

Put-call-futures parity A pricing relation between calls, puts, and futures that follows from arbitrage restrictions.

Put provision (on a bond) An option which allows the purchaser of a debt security to tender the security to the issuer for payment of principal prior to the stated maturity.

Q ratio The ratio of the firm's market value to its book value.

Quadratic utility function A specific utility function in which return provides utility and risk is a source of disutility.

Random variable A rule that assigns a number to possible outcomes of a random experiment.

Random walk (in stock returns) Stock returns are said to follow a random walk if the expected return is constant and deviations of the return from the mean are not predictable.

Rational expectation The market's expectation of a random variable, such as a future stock price, is said to be rational if the market's assessment of the distribution of the random variable (e.g., expressed in terms of mean and variance) is the true distribution of the random variable.

Real interest rate Approximately, the difference between the nominal interest rate and the inflation rate.

Redemption fee A fee charged by some mutual funds (particularly index funds) for redeeming shares before a prescribed date.

Registered option trader An options floor trader at the American Stock Exchange who trades for his or her own account.

Relative risk aversion A measure of how the percentage of total wealth invested in risky assets by an individual changes as wealth changes.

Repo rate The interest rate applicable to repurchase agreements.

Repurchase agreement A transaction in which an investor sells a security with the obligation to repurchase it at a specified later date, often the next day.

Residual The difference between an observed value for a random variable and its regression predicted value.

Residual variance A measure of the tendency of an asset to deviate from predicted values from a least-squares line.

Return dispersion A measure of the asset's risk or propensity to deviate from its expected value. See standard deviation and variance.

Reversing trade A trade that unwinds an existing position; the vast majority of all futures positions are closed out via reversing trades.

Riding the yield curve A quasi-active bond management strategy designed to capture return premiums associated with particular maturities. The strategy involves purchasing bonds with a given initial maturity and yield and holding them until their maturity shortens to a designated point.

Risk aversion A characteristic exhibited by rational investors in which higher levels of disutility are associated with increasing levels of risk.

Risk-free or riskless rate of return The return provided or expected from a virtually riskless asset such as the short-term U.S. Treasury bill.

Risk management The use of derivative securities and other products and techniques to control financial risk.

Risk neutrality A situation in which agents are indifferent toward risk.

Risk premium The dollar amount that a risk averse individual will command for assuming risky alternatives.

R-square A measure providing the percentage of the fluctuations of the dependent variable explained by the independent variable(s).

Score An instrument created through the establishment of a trust that receives all stock appreciation beyond a termination value; it is akin to a long-term European option written on the stock.

Seat A membership of a securities exchange.

Securities and Exchange Commission (SEC) A federal agency charged with the regulation of all U.S. security and option markets.

Security Market Line (SML) The line that depicts the equilibrium relation between expected return and systematic (market) risk in the Capital Asset Pricing Model.

Security selection One of two means by which a manager can earn abnormal returns. It refers to an ability to systematically identify mispriced securities.

Sector fund A mutual fund that invests exclusively in a particular economic sector like defense, autos, or utilities. It is also called a special purpose fund.

Sector rotating A money management practice in which funds are rotated from one economic sector to another, depending upon the manager's forecast of the performance of these sectors.

Separation theorem Selection of the optimal risky portfolio is independent of the individual's attitude toward risk.

Settlement price The futures price established at the end of each trading day upon which daily resettlement is based.

Sharpe index A risk-adjusted measure of portfolio performance wherein risk is measured by the standard deviation of returns.

Short position A transaction in which a security is borrowed and sold, with the obligation to return the borrowed security at a later date.

Single index model An approach that utilizes simplifying assumptions to approximate the Markowitz model portfolio variance.

Sinking fund provision Requires the issuer of a debt security to retire a specified portion of the issue each year prior to the stated maturity.

Size effect An empirical anomaly showing that smaller firms' share prices generally outperform larger firms' share prices on a risk-adjusted basis.

Specialist A floor trader charged with the duty of making a market in certain securities or options.

Speculative-grade bond Also called a 'junk bond,' a speculative-grade bond is any bond whose rating by Moody's (Standard and Poors) is Ba (BB) or below, reflecting relatively high default risk.

Speculation Investment strategies characterized by large risks that usually do not entail the trading of a spot asset.

Speculator One who engages in speculation.

Spot market The market for assets that entail immediate delivery.

Spot price The current price of an asset traded in the spot market.

Standard deviation The square root of the variance. The standard deviation is a measure of the dispersion of a probability distribution.

Swaps A negotiated agreement between two parties to exchange cash flows at specified future dates according to a prescribed manner.

Systematic risk Risk that is due to a pervasive factor which cannot be diversified away through portfolio diversification. See also *Market risk.*

Tactical asset allocation A phrase employed to describe any investment strategy underlying an active management approach.

Tax exempt fund A mutual whose returns and dividend distributions are exempt from federal and state taxes. The fund commonly consists of municipal securities.

Tax-loss selling hypothesis An explanation for the January effect, positing that investors tend to sell, in December, small firm stocks that have lost value over the preceding period, for tax purposes, which tends to depress their values. When the values of these stocks return to equilibrium in January, the result is observed high January returns.

Term structure of interest rates The current relationship between the interest rate and maturity of a given type of debt instrument, particularly default-free debt securities.

Tracking error The difference between an index fund's return and the return of the index the fund is designed to replicate.

Treynor index A risk-adjusted measure of portfolio performance wherein risk is measured by beta.

Underpriced (or undervalued) security A *mispriced* security which provides a higher return than it should for its level of risk.

Unique risk or unsystematic risk Firm specific risk that can be diversified away.

Unsystematic risk See *Diversifiable risk.*

Upside capture The percentage of the uninsured appreciation in an up market that is captured by the insured portfolio.

U.S. Treasury strips Pure discount bonds created by stripping each of the coupon and principal payments of a U.S. Treasury note or bond and selling them separately.

Utility A measure of satisfaction derived from consumption or wealth.

Utility function The relation between an agent's utility and total consumption of a good.

Utility theory Study of rational economic behavior.

Variable rate note A debt security that pays interest at a rate that varies with short-term interest rates, such as Treasury bill rates or LIBOR.

Variance Expected value of the squared deviations from the mean. The variance is a measure of the dispersion of a probability distribution.

Variation margin The cash deposit required to satisfy a futures margin call.

Wash sale A stock sale and subsequent repurchase deemed to be executed to realize a tax loss only; tax law disallows the loss deduction.

Weekend effect The observed tendency for all stocks to provide low or negative average returns on Monday, particularly in the first few minutes of trading.

Wild-card option An option enjoyed by the short trader of a Treasury note or Treasury bond futures contract on the Chicago Board of Trade; it arises because of the contract's unique delivery system, and presumably the value of this option confounds the futures price.

Yield curve A graphical depiction of the term structure of interest rates.

Zero-beta portfolio A portfolio whose return is uncorrelated with the return on the market portfolio but may have individual variance of return.

Zero-sum game Refers to securities trading where the gains (losses) exhibited by long-position holders are equal to the losses (gains) exhibited by short-position holders.

I N D E X